[THE]

COMPLETE DICTIONARY

OF SYMBOLS

[THE]

COMPLETE DICTIONARY
OF SYMBOLS

Jack Tresidder, General Editor

CHRONICLE BOOKS

SAN FRANCISCO

The Complete Dictionary of Symbols

First published in the United States in 2005 by Chronicle Books, LLC.

Conceived, created, and designed by Duncan Baird Publishers.

Library of Congress Cataloging-in-Publication Data available.

ISBN 0-8118-4767-5

Manufactured in Thailand

Managing Editor: Christopher Westhorp
Editor: Peter Bently
Editorial assistance: Kelly Bishop and Hanne Bewernicke
Managing Designer: Manisha Patel
Designer: Clare Thorpe
Design assistance: Justin Ford

Typeset in Times NRMT

Distributed in Canada by Raincoast Books
9050 Shaughnessy Street
Vancouver, British Columbia V6P 6E5

10 9 8 7 6 5 4 3 2 1

Chronicle Books LLC
85 Second Street
San Francisco, California 94105

www.chroniclebooks.com

Notes
The abbreviations CE and BCE are used throughout this book:
CE Common Era (the equivalent of AD)
BCE Before the Common Era (the equivalent of BC)

Contents

Foreword

A basic symbol is the image of an object or living thing made to stand for a concept or quality. For example, Egyptian artists made the lion a forceful symbol of power and majesty – a personification of the divine sun. In the ancient world, symbolism of this sort endowed some of the most familiar and ordinary things with a larger dimension, often a spiritual, magical, moral or ethical one. Carved, painted or worked into effigies, clothing or ornaments, images that became familiar symbols through repetition were used to ward off harm, to entreat or placate gods – and also to unify and control societies.

This book explains the many and varied meanings of a vast range of these traditional symbols, which became a kind of visual shorthand for fundamental ideas but often seem mysterious now. It combines this with extended articles on other great sources of symbolic imagery – mythology and religion, philosophy and literature – which have enriched art for several thousand years. The book presents an interwoven cultural tapestry of these sources in A–Z form. Although many of the symbolic themes, figures, subjects, and attributes it deals with in detail are drawn from Classical and Christian traditions, its general scope is worldwide.

Like all good stories, myths often spread far beyond their place of origin. So did the individual symbols based on features of the earth or the visible universe – stars, planets, mountains, caves, rocks, plants, animals, birds, fish or insects, many of which were seen as embodying concepts and qualities thought to be worth celebrating. The bull of potency, the light of divinity, the snake of fertility,

the swastika of cosmic dynamism were all powerful symbols in many cultures. Some other symbols read differently according to their context. For example, the dragon became a symbol of evil and disorder in the West but in the East represents the fertilizing power of thunder and rain. However, far distant cultures surprisingly often chose the same object to symbolize the same thing.

Knowing the meaning of symbols or symbolic stories not only allows us to read the art and literature of the past with more understanding. It also helps to put us in touch with the mind-set of societies that developed the language of symbolism over thousands of years. For them, the realm of space and time was penetrated by a higher consciousness. Today's scientific concept of a universe governed purely by physical laws indifferent to human life and the way it is lived would have struck pre-modern cultures as bleak, even terrifying. The structures of mythology and symbolism grew out of societies that believed the individual was not alone and that life had a spiritual dimension. For them, symbols based on apt metaphors, analogies or psychic intuitions provided reassurance, group solidarity and moral or ethical inspiration. Throughout the ancient world, traditional symbols more often stood for positive than negative aspects of existence. A coherent system of symbols could make people feel in harmony with themselves, their community and the cosmos.

Myths were themselves extended symbol systems, encapsulating religious, philosophical or psychological "truths", often based on tribal memories. These traditional tales, written or oral, handed down for centuries and dealing mainly with supernatural beings, prehistorical events, religious and social customs and the origin of the cosmos, differ from folk tales and sagas in having more sacral or cultic significance – in short, myths are more charged with symbolism. Their subtext is that they describe a common heritage, explaining mysteries, filling in a shadowy past, conveying lessons about life, and often fostering virtues such as courage or loyalty that tended to support and strengthen the culture out of which they grew.

The belief underlying both traditional symbols and mythology that life had a spiritual or mystical dimension is made more specific in organized religion, which is also full of emblematic rituals, objects and figures. Christianity in particular has left a remarkable heritage of narrative art in which symbols are used to portray moral allegories or to identify figures in paintings by showing them with attributes conventionally associated with them. Understanding this heritage is becoming increasingly difficult without a guide to the symbolic figures, personifications, attributes and biblical themes that appear in hundreds of the greatest representational paintings and sculptures ever created. One important aim of this book is to provide a clear reference guide to the stories they tell.

Jack Tresidder

How this Book is Organized
This book combines A–Z entries of four main kinds. Articles on traditional symbols such as objects, animals, gemstones, plants, elements, graphic shapes and so on immediately define their most important symbolic meaning and then discuss any subsidiary meanings in a variety of cultures.

Mythological entries on deities, heroes and heroines, nymphs, satyrs, legendary places or themes, describe characters or tell complete myths in summary form, often with references to works of art based on these stories. These entries range from Classical or Nordic myths to those of Africa, Asia, America and Polynesia.

Articles on Christian figures, stories and themes are based on biblical accounts (canonical or apocryphal), legends of saints and other medieval writings. They are designed particularly to show how these figures or themes influenced Western art and usually include references to paintings and sculptures.

A fourth strand deals with literature, philosophy, moral allegories, or historical figures, concentrating especially on the Classical age and its legacy in Western art.

Feature panels cover themes of particular interest and generic categories of symbols, such as those used to personify abstract concepts.

Cross references in the margin alert the reader to entries elsewhere in the dictionary that expand on subjects mentioned in the text.

Finally, a useful Index of Supplementary Words covers those symbols, mythological, biblical or historical characters and works of art or literature that are discussed in the text but are not themselves the subject of a main entry in the dictionary.

Aaron

In the Bible, Aaron was the eloquent elder brother of Moses. He represented the Israelites' need for a single, powerful priesthood, and often appears with this symbolism in Christian art. Returning from Mount Sinai, Moses had to reprove Aaron when he found he had given in to the people's wish for a graven image to worship in Moses' absence. Poussin's painting *The Adoration of the Golden Calf* shows Aaron condoning this breach of God's commandment. But God confirmed his position as high priest dramatically after it had been contested by a rival, Korah the Levite.[1] When Korah brought his followers and offered incense to God, a rite reserved for priests, the earth "swallowed them up".[2] In *The Punishment of Korah* Botticelli depicts Aaron with papal tiara, swinging a censer – a warning to anyone challenging papal authority.

Aaron's primacy was undisputed after leaders of the 12 tribes of Israel were each ordered to place a rod on the tabernacle. The next day, Aaron's rod was found to have miraculously flowered and yielded almonds. Aaron appears in paintings or cycles of the life of Moses, as either a priest or a patriarchal figure with a long beard. He may carry a rod or a censer.

Abnoba

A Romano-Celtic goddess of the hunt. Abnoba's cult was centred around the Black Forest.

Abraham

First Hebrew patriarch, a symbol of God's blessings on the faithful. In the Bible he is told to leave his birthplace with Sarah, his wife, and Lot, his nephew.[1] Abraham settled in Canaan, while Lot settled in Sodom and had all his possessions seized. Abraham pursued the raiders, recovered the loot and on his triumphal return to Canaan was blessed and given bread and wine by Melchizedek, king of Salem. This scene appears in Christian art as prefiguring the Eucharist.

Sarah bore no children and offered her handmaid Hagar to Abraham so

Aaron: *see* Almond; Moses; Pig
[1] *Exodus 28*
[2] *Numbers 16:32*

Abraham: *see* Lot
[1] *Genesis 12:1–5*

that he might have a son; thus Ishmael was conceived. But Hagar began to despise Sarah, and as a result, Hagar was driven into the wilderness. An angel instructed her to return to her mistress, and predicted that Ishmael would be "a wild man; his hand will be against every man, and every man's hand against him;"[2] yet God promised that he would beget twelve princes and rule a great nation (the Arabs regard Ishmael as their ancestor).

Despite their old age a son, Isaac, was born to Sarah and Abraham. The baby's arrival had been prophesied by three angels to whom Abraham had shown hospitality. Jealous of Isaac, Ishmael and his mother were banished. As they began to die of thirst, an angel led them to water.

To test his faith, God demanded that Abraham sacrifice Isaac but just as Abraham was about to slay his son on an altar, an angel intervened and substituted a ram for the sacrifice.[3]

Artists have represented many episodes from the life of Abraham, such as Giambattista Tiepolo's *The Angel Appearing to Sarah* and Claude Lorrain's picturesque landscapes with Hagar and the Angel. However, the sacrifice of Isaac was the most common scene, since Abraham was seen as the paragon of unquestioning faith in God, and Isaac as prefiguring Christ: God sacrificed his son as Abraham was prepared to, the wood of the fire representing the Cross. In 1401 this was the subject of a competition to decorate the doors of the Baptistery in Florence (both Brunelleschi's and Ghiberti's panels still exist). Caravaggio's *Sacrifice of Isaac* shows the scene with customary violence, while Ferdinand Olivier's *Abraham and Isaac* has the two on their way to the sacrifice.

Absinthe

A green liqueur flavoured with wormwood, first used medicinally by French troops in the 19th century. It is both addictive and poisonous; Zola describes the bitterness and sorrow it causes in his novel *L'Assommoir* and Degas painted the frank and poignant image of *The Absinthe Drinker*.

Abstinence

Sexual continence is usually illustrated in art by figures from antiquity famous for their self-restraint. Seleucus, king of Syria, gave his young wife to her stepson, who was dying of love for her; Alexander the Great did not take sexual advantage of the defeated family of Darius; the Roman general Scipio refused a young girl betrothed to another. In allegory, an adolescent Cupid (Eros) may be taken from the arms of a naked woman by wise Minerva (Athene), as in Pietro da Cortona's fresco in the Room of Venus (Pitti Palace, Florence).

Abuk

The first woman, in the mythology of the Dinka people of southern Sudan. Abuk was responsible for the arrival of death and illness on earth. In the beginning, according to Dinka myth, the High God allowed Garang, the first man, and Abuk, his wife, to plant one grain of millet a day, which satisfied all their needs. But one day Abuk greedily decided to plant more. In doing so she struck the High God on the toe, making him so angry that he withdrew to a great distance from humanity and severed the rope which linked heaven and earth. Since then humans have had to work hard to procure food and have suffered sickness and death.

Abundance

The female figure of Abundance represents the prosperity brought about by peace and justice. Her attribute is a cornucopia, or horn of plenty, brimming with fruit and jewels. She may be shown near a sheaf of corn or surrounded by children and once-wild animals that have clearly been tamed.

Acacia

A symbol of immortality, especially in Judeo-Christian thought. Hardwood of an acacia species, the *shittah*, was used to build the Tabernacle and, by tradition, acacia spines formed Christ's crown of thorns. The red and white flowers suggest life–death duality. Freemasonry uses an acacia bough as an initiation symbol and funerary tribute – a reference to the branch supposedly laid on the grave of King Solomon's master builder, Hiram, by fellow workers who killed him when they could not make him reveal the mysteries of his craft.

Academy

Named after the garden near Athens where Plato (*c.*427–347BCE) taught philosophy, the term was loosely applied to any scholarly circle in the Renaissance. The first Academy of Art was founded in Florence in 1562 by Giorgio Vasari under Duke Cosimo I. An academy was established in Rome in 1593, in France in 1648, and in England in 1768, and by the end of the 18th century there were over 100 in Europe. Zoffany painted *The Academicians of the Royal Academy* in 1770, showing intellectuals discussing the merits of numerous masterpieces.

Academies promoted "history painting", which derived in both style and subject matter from Classical antiquity. Monumental, didactic, narrative painting was considered the highest form of art, since it contained universal moral truths and provided inspiration to noble ideals. The rigidity of the French academic system led the Impressionists to find alternative means of exhibiting their works from 1874. Since then respect for academic art has declined.

Acanthus

A Greco-Roman triumphal image of life's trials surmounted, a symbolism suggested by the plant's thorns and its vigorous growth. Stylized acanthus leaves on the Corinthian capital may refer to a Greek myth of an acanthus springing up on the grave of a hero.

Acheron

The "River of Woe" in northern Greece, which, because it flows partly underground, was believed to be one of five rivers linking this world to the underworld realm of the dead. The name Acheron was sometimes used to refer to the underworld itself.

Achilles

A celebrated hero of Greek mythology and the central character of the *Iliad*, Homer's great epic of the Trojan War. The son of a mortal king, Peleus, and the Nereid (sea nymph) Thetis, Achilles was born in Thessaly. Thetis dipped him in the Styx, a river of the underworld, to render his body both immortal and invulnerable[1] – except for the heel by which she held him. Achilles was educated by Chiron, a wise Centaur.[2] Regnault's *The Education of Achilles* shows Achilles learning how to draw a bow.

The Fates offered the young Achilles the choice between a long life of ease

Abundance: *see* Cornucopia

Acacia: *see* Branch, Bough; Crown; Red; Thorn; Trees

Acanthus: *see* Thorn

Acheron: *see* Charon; Cocytus; Hades; Styx; UNDERWORLDS

Achilles: *see* Agamemnon; Amazon; Centaur; Fates, The; Hector; *Iliad, The*; Nereid; Odysseus; Paris; Peleus; Polyxena; Styx; Thetis; Trojan War, The; TROJAN WAR, THE HEROES OF THE

[1] Statius, *Achilleid 1:269* and Hyginus, *Fabulae CVII*
[2] Philostratus the Elder, II:2
[3] Hyginus, *Fabulae XCVI*

Acorn: *see* Oak; TRUTH

Actaeon: *see* Artemis;
Cadmus; Stag
[1] Ovid, *Met III: 138–252*

Achilles kills Penthesilea; from a jar painting by Exekias, c.540 BCE.

or early death and immortal glory in the Trojan War: he chose the latter. In one account, however, in order to prevent Achilles from joining the Trojan War, his mother disguised him as a girl and hid him at the court of King Lycomedes. Here he fell in love with Deidamia, the king's daughter, by whom he had a son, Neoptolemus. Achilles was unmasked by Ulysses (Odysseus), who, laying gifts before the court, noticed his disregard for feminine luxuries and fondness for weapons.[3] In the 1630s Rubens made *The Achilles Tapestries* of these scenes, together with others from the Trojan War, now hanging at the Boymans-Van Beuningen Museum, Rotterdam, and in Detroit.

In another account, Achilles was reluctant to join the campaign and disguised himself as a woman. He was unmasked by his comrades when a war trumpet sounded and he alone reached for a weapon.

During the siege of Troy, Achilles angrily withdrew from the fighting after the Greek commander, Agamemnon, claimed Achilles' war booty, the Trojan woman Briseis, for

himself. With Achilles, the most feared Greek warrior, no longer fighting, the Trojans under Hector pushed the Greeks back to their ships. Patroclus, Achilles' best friend, persuaded the hero to lend him his armour so that the Trojans would think Achilles had returned to the fray. But Hector killed Patroclus and Achilles returned to the battle to avenge his death, pursuing Hector three times around the walls of Troy before killing him in single combat. Achilles refused to give up the corpse for burial until the gods forced him to accept a ransom from Hector's father, King Priam.

During the final battle for Troy, Achilles killed the Amazon queen, Penthesilea, falling in love with her as she died. Achilles himself was killed by Hector's brother, Paris (or in other accounts, Apollo), who shot him in the heel, his vulnerable spot, with an arrow. The Greeks awarded Achilles' armour to Odysseus.

Acorn

A symbol of fecundity, prosperity and the power of spiritual growth from the kernel of truth – a symbolism that accounts for the "acorn" on the red cord of a cardinal's hat. Acorns were sacred to the Norse god Thor as part of the cult of the oak. They may have phallic significance in Celtic carvings.

Actaeon

In Greek mythology, Actaeon[1] was the grandson of Cadmus, the founder of Thebes. One day while out hunting he strayed deep into some woods, where he spied Artemis, goddess of hunting and chastity (in Roman myth, Diana), bathing with her nymphs. In punishment for having seen her naked, Artemis turned him into a stag. He

ADAM AND EVE

In the Bible, God created Adam in his own likeness to "have dominion over the fish of the sea, and over the birds of the air, and over the cattle, and over all the earth, and over every creeping thing that creeps upon the earth".[1] Having formed Adam from the dust of the earth, God breathed life into him; God then placed him in Eden and forbade him to eat the fruit of the tree of knowledge.

Adam named the animals and God created Eve from Adam's rib to be his companion.[2] The cunning serpent tempted Eve to know good and evil by eating the forbidden fruit, and she in turn persuaded Adam to taste it. At once their eyes were opened and, ashamed, they took fig leaves to hide their nakedness. In punishment, God commanded the snake to go on its belly and eat dust, and, for their disobedience, expelled Adam and Eve from Eden. Eve was to bear children in sorrow and Adam to toil in thorny ground.[3]

The Creation, Temptation and Fall of Adam and Eve were popular themes in medieval and Renaissance art as depictions of the sinfulness of humankind from its very beginning (this was to become the Catholic doctrine of Original Sin). Only through the sacrifice of Christ could human sinfulness be redeemed. These themes were illustrated alone or as a cycle. The Temptation and Expulsion from Paradise introduce the fresco cycle *The Life of St Peter* by Masolino and Masaccio (Brancacci Chapel, Florence). The Fall may also form part of the background of paintings of the Annunciation, referring to Christ's mission to redeem humankind; similarly, Adam's skull may appear at the foot of the Crucifixion.

ADAM AND EVE: *see*
Apple; Creation; Fig Leaf;
NUDE; True Cross, The
[1] *Genesis 1:26*
[2] *Genesis 2:7–22*
[3] *Genesis 3*

fled, but his own hounds caught him and tore him to pieces. Titian, in *Diana and Actaeon*, shows Actaeon astounded by Diana's beauty, while *The Death of Actaeon* shows the fleeing hero in the process of transformation.

ADAM AND EVE *see panel above*

Adapa

In Babylonian (Akkadian) myth, a priest of the god Ea (known as Enki to the Sumerians) and one of the Seven Sages of prehistory.

Aditi

"The Limitless", a primordial Indian goddess seen as the personification of infinity and sustainer of all things. Vedic hymns refer to her as the mother of the major gods, who were called the Adityas after her. They include Varuna, Indra and Daksha.

Admetus

In Greek myth, a king of Pherae in Thessaly. After the god Apollo had killed the Cyclopes, Zeus ordered him to serve Admetus for a year as a shepherd in penance. Apollo later helped him to win the hand of Alcestis.

Adonis

In Greek myth, a young hunter and the lover of the goddess Aphrodite (the Roman Venus). He is possibly of

Adapa: *see* Anu (1); Ea

Aditi: *see* Daksha; Indra;
Varuna; Vishnu

Admetus: *see* Alcestis;
Apollo; Cyclops

Adonis: *see* Aphrodite; Eros;
Dumuzi; Persephone; Zeus
[1] Ovid, *Met X:503–739*

Near Eastern origin and is sometimes identified with the
Mesopotamian god Dumuzi (Tammuz). Aphrodite caused a princess
called Myrrha to fall in love with her
own father, King Theias (or Cin-
ryas). Myrrha duped him into sleeping with her, as a result of which she
became pregnant. When the king discovered the deception he wanted to
kill his daughter, but the gods transformed her into the tree that bears
her name (myrrh). From this tree
Adonis was born.

Aphrodite handed the beautiful
child over to the fertility goddess
Persephone, queen of the underworld,
for safekeeping. Persephone later
refused to give him back, so the god
Zeus (Jupiter) decided that Adonis
would spend a third of the year with
Aphrodite, a third with Persephone,
and a third as he wished. In one
account, Adonis chose to spend his
free months with Aphrodite.

The goddess knew that Adonis was
destined to die while hunting and
tried to dissuade him from this pursuit. Titian's *Venus and Adonis* shows
a naked Venus clinging to Adonis as
he sets off to meet his fate. Adonis
was killed by a wild boar, said in one
account to be the goddess's jealous
lover Ares (Mars). When she found
the wounded and dying Adonis she
turned his blood into an anemone,
which became associated with sorrow
and death. In one account, the goddess fell passionately in love with
Adonis after being struck accidentally
by Cupid's arrow.

Adrasteia

According to the Orphics, followers of
an ancient Greek mystery religion,
Adrasteia ("Necessity") was one of

two primal deities present at the
beginning of creation, the other being
Chronos ("Time").

Aeëtes

A son of the Greek sun god Helios,
and the king of Colchis on the eastern
shore of the Black Sea. Aeëtes possessed the Golden Fleece sought by
the hero Jason.

Aegisthus

In Greek myth, a scion of the feuding
house of Pelops, the son of Thyestes
by Thyestes' own daughter, Pelopia.
Aegisthus seduced Clytemnestra, the
wife of his cousin Agamemnon, king
of Argos. With her connivance,
Aegisthus assassinated Agamemnon
on his return from the Trojan War
and became king. Aegisthus and
Clytemnestra were later killed by
Orestes, Agamemnon's son.

Aeneas

A Trojan prince, a minor character in
Greek mythology but a central figure
in Roman mythology (as related in
Virgil's epic poem *The Aeneid*) as the
forefather of the Romans, the founder
of the dynasty which established the
city of Rome. The subject was popular in Rome both in ancient times and
later (for example, it was sculpted by
Bernini) because it illustrated the
city's Trojan origins and the noble values of family respect and piety.

Aeneas, the son of King Anchises
and the goddess Aphrodite (the
Roman Venus), is portrayed in
Homer's *Iliad* as a valiant warrior.
According to *The Aeneid*, he escaped
the destruction of Troy, and carried
Anchises and his son Ascanius to
safety, together with the sacred relics
and images of their household gods.[1]

Aeneas's wife Creusa perished, but her shade told him to travel to the land of the Tiber.

Aeneas embarked on a long voyage during which he was variously aided and thwarted by the gods, especially the vengeful Juno (the Greek Hera), who had sided with the Greeks against the Trojans. The difficulties thrown in his way were often offset by the guidance of Jupiter (Zeus), which Virgil used as proof that the origins of Rome were divinely sanctioned.

Aeneas' quest for Italy led him over land and sea, through storms whipped up by Juno and calmed by Neptune (Poseidon), to the island of Delos. Here the king and priest, Anius,[2] showed Aeneas and his father, son and companions the holy site where Apollo was born. The scene is the subject of Claude Lorrain's *Coast View of Delos with Aeneas*. Aeneas and his company later landed at Carthage where Venus told him how Queen Dido founded the city.[3] Fearing an outbreak of war between Aeneas and Carthage, Venus engaged Cupid (Eros) to contrive a love affair between Dido and Aeneas.[4] In *Dido Receiving Aeneas and Cupid Disguised as Ascanius*, Francesco Solimena shows the stately Dido welcoming Aeneas and his son to a banquet in their honour. Cupid, disguised as Ascanius, kisses her hand to make her fall in love with Aeneas.

Turner's *Dido and Aeneas* shows them setting out to hunt with a magnificent re-creation of Carthage in the distance. Their affair began during a storm, and Giovanni Romanelli's *Dido and Aeneas* illustrates them hurrying to shelter in a cave where their love was consummated.[5] Forgetting their duties, they spent the winter

Aeneas hunting, from a mosaic.

together until Jupiter sent Mercury (Hermes) to rebuke Aeneas and remind him of his destiny. A distraught Dido pleaded with Aeneas to remain, but he was resolute.

Aided by her sister Anna, Dido constructed her own funeral pyre. After watching Aeneas and his fleet sail out of Carthage, she fell on the sword left by her heartless love. Juno took pity on her and sent Iris, goddess of the rainbow, to release her spirit. As she flew across the sky, Iris trailed a thousand colours, sparkling like dew in the light of the sun.[6] Aeneas looked back to see the city aglow with the flames of Dido's funeral pyre.

Aeneas landed on Sicily, where he held games in honour of his father, who had died one year previously.[7] Having reached the Italian mainland, Aeneas reached Cumae, where he visited the Cumaean Sibyl, a prophetess of Apollo, and requested to see Anchises once more.[8] Accompanied by the Sibyl and bearing a gift of a golden bough for Proserpina (Persephone), queen of the underworld, Aeneas descended into its shadows.

The Trojan prince passed disease, fear, hunger, evil, poverty, sin and war, and saw many, including his kinsmen, who had been denied burial. These

AFTERLIFE

A belief in continued existence after death is found in most mythologies. The dead are commonly said to inhabit underworlds, overworlds or regions which may be on the same plane as the earth but imprecisely located (like the Aztec paradise Tlalocan and the Slavic land of the dead). The afterworld abode of the dead may be directly linked to this world: the Greek and Roman underworld was accessible to any mortal (such as Orpheus, Herakles and Aeneas) prepared to venture into its deep caverns and underground rivers. In ancient Irish belief, the afterworld was accessible through the prehistoric barrows and mounds known as *sidh*, from which the dead and other denizens of the otherworld would emerge at night, especially at Samhain (Hallowe'en).

As one of his labours, the hero Herakles had to drag Cerberus, the guard-dog of the underworld, from the gate of Hades; from a detail on an Attic vase.

The afterworld often resembles this world. The Egyptian Duat (variously described as an underworld or an overworld) was a paradisial Egypt, with a great river flanked by eternally abundant fields, and the afterworld of the Native Americans of the Plains was a "Happy Hunting Ground", a world very like this one but with more game. The Chinese heaven and hell mirrored the Chinese empire on earth, each with an emperor and vast bureaucracy.

After death, sinners and evildoers are often dispatched to regions of judgment and punishment such as the Japanese Jigoku or Yomi, or the Christian hell. The symbolism of these regions is remarkably consistent: they are generally dark, desolate, putrid, smoky and pain-filled underworlds. In the Egyptian Hall of Judgment, the heart of the deceased, symbolizing the conscience, was weighed against the feather of the goddess Ma'at (Truth). The archangel St Michael may be shown similarly weighing the good and evil deeds of the dead.

The great and the good may have their own special place in death, such as the Elysian Fields or Islands of the Blessed of the Greeks and Romans, and the Scandinavian Valhalla for slain warriors.

The dead may roam among mortals, or may be invoked by prayer and ritual to intervene in the destiny of the living. Rebirth or reincarnation is a belief found in Hinduism and Buddhism. The nature of one's reincarnate form depends on *karma* – how one has acted in this life.

souls were destined to roam aimlessly for a hundred years before they could rest. Aeneas was rowed by the ferryman Charon across the River Styx, and in a myrtle wood he saw Dido, but she turned away from him to her former husband.

Finally, Aeneas reached the Land of the Blessed in the Fields of Elysium, where he found his father. Anchises foretold how Aeneas would marry Lavinia, who would bear him a son, Silvius, and how his destiny would be fulfilled through his descendant Romulus, the founder of Rome, and illustrious figures in Roman history, down to Virgil's own day.

Aeneas and the Trojans continued their journey to the mouth of the Tiber in Latium, where they were welcomed by King Latinus. However, Juno instigated hostilities between the Trojans and the Latins that began when Ascanius shot a stag tamed by Princess Silvia. This scene is depicted by Claude Lorrain in *Landscape with Aeneas Shooting the Stag of Silvia*.

Aeneas reluctantly engaged in a series of wars, and as Boucher shows in *Venus Requesting Arms for Aeneas from Vulcan*, Venus asked her husband Vulcan (Hephaistos), the god of fire and forge, to make Aeneas a set of weaponry. This included a shield embellished with the events that would shape the future of Rome.

Latinus and Aeneas later formed an alliance. Aeneas married Latinus's daughter Lavinia and founded the town of Lavinium in her honour. Ascanius established the town and ruling dynasty of Alba Longa. From this dynasty sprang Romulus and Remus, the founders of Rome. According to one tradition, Aeneas founded Rome himself.

Aeneid, The

A Latin epic poem, the unfinished masterpiece of the writer Virgil (Publius Vergilius Maro, 70BCE–19BCE). Begun *c.*30BCE, its twelve books recount the wanderings of Aeneas, the ancestor of the Roman nation, from Troy to Latium in Italy.

Aeolus

In Greek myth, the keeper of the winds. A son of the god Poseidon, Aeolus gave the hero Odysseus a sack in which all the winds that were unfavourable to his voyage were confined. When curious crewmen opened the bag, the winds escaped and blew Odysseus' ship off course. The abode of Aeolus, the Aeolian Islands off northern Sicily, were named after him.

Aesculapius *see* Asklepios

Aesir, The

The Norse sky deities, one of two divine races – the other being the Vanir – said to reside in Asgard, the realm of the gods. The Aesir include Odin (ruler of Asgard), Balder, Frigg, Tyr and Thor.

Aeson

In Greek myth, a king of Iolcus in Thessaly and the father of the hero Jason.

AFTERLIFE *see panel opposite*

Agamemnon

In Greek myth, a king of Argos or Mycenae and leader of the Greeks in the Trojan War. Perhaps the most famous of the feuding Pelopids, Agamemnon was the son of King Atreus of Argos and his wife Aerope. Atreus was murdered by his nephew

Aegisthus, whose father Thyestes seized the throne. Agamemnon and his brother Menelaus fled to safety in Sparta. The Spartan king Tyndareos helped Agamemnon to recover the throne of Argos, forcing his uncle Thyestes into exile.

With the blessing of Tyndareos, Agamemnon married Clytemnestra, daughter of Tyndareos and his queen, Leda, and was appointed commander of Menelaus' campaign against the Trojans. He assembled his forces at Aulis in Boeotia, but the goddess Artemis caused adverse sailing conditions and, in order to secure good winds, Agamemnon had to sacrifice his daughter, Iphigeneia. The Greeks finally left Aulis, and Agamemnon established camp outside Troy.

After ten years Troy fell and the victorious Agamemnon headed home with Cassandra, the prophetess daughter of King Priam, as his prize.

In his absence, Clytemnestra had grieved bitterly for Iphigeneia and become the lover of Agamemnon's cousin Aegisthus, with whom she connived to murder Agamemnon. When her husband arrived with his entourage, Clytemnestra greeted him and invited him to take a bath. As Agamemnon stepped out of the water she threw a fine mesh over his head, at which point Aegisthus appeared and cut down Agamemnon as he struggled in the net. He fell into the bath and Clytemnestra beheaded him. Cassandra was also killed, but Agamemnon's children, Orestes and Elektra, lived to avenge their father.

Agate
A lucky gemstone prized since antiquity. Its variously coloured bands are sometimes linked with the moon, sometimes with the planet Mercury. Qualities associated with agate include fortitude, happiness, prosperity and sexual success. Folklore claims that agate can deflect weapons.

Agatha, Saint
Legend¹ claims that in the 3rd century CE the Christian noblewoman Agatha was pursued by Quintianus, the lecherous Roman consular official in Sicily, but nothing would persuade her to give in to his demands. Infuriated, Quintianus threw her in prison, tortured her cruelly and cut off her breasts. St Peter appeared and restored her, but she was then rolled naked over live coals strewn on the ground and a tremendous earthquake shook the city of Catania. Agatha died in prison, and a year after her martyrdom Mount Etna erupted; the inhabitants of Catania brought her veil to the volcano, and it miraculously stopped the flow of molten lava and saved the city. Breasts are Agatha's attribute and in art she is often shown carrying them on a plate. Because of their shape, she was adopted as the patron saint of bell founders.

AGES OF MAN, THE *see panel, above right*

Ages of the World, The
In Classical mythology, the four Ages of the World were the Ages of Gold, Silver, Bronze (or Copper) and Iron.¹ The Golden Age was free of fear and conflict, an everlasting springtime; its rivers flowed with milk and nectar, and animals lived in harmony. Zeus (the Roman Jupiter) introduced the four seasons in the Age of Silver, forcing people to seek shelter. In the Age of Bronze men became fiercer and

AGES OF MAN, THE

Thinkers and artists have often viewed the span of human life as divided into several stages, and these "Ages of Man" were popular themes in Renaissance art. Sometimes there are four, corresponding to the seasons, and sometimes three. Children may play near a dead tree to represent the cycle of life; youth may be shown as a soldier or pair of lovers; and old age may be a man contemplating a skull. Where there is a fourth figure, it is usually that of the mature man, placed somewhere between youth and age. Usually it is the transience of life that is implied, but Titian's painting of the subject uses the three ages of man as an allegory of prudence. In this work, the faces of three different generations are placed above those of a dog, lion and wolf to suggest that the present should learn from the past in order that it might profit for the future.

AGES OF MAN, THE: *see* Ages of the World; SEASONS

inclined to conflict, but they were still free from wickedness. The Age of Iron introduced treachery, deceit, violence, greed and war.

Pietro da Cortona likened the Four Ages of the World to the Ages of Man in frescoes in the Sala della Stufa (Pitti Palace, Florence). Gold represents youth and bounty and Silver the agrarian life; Bronze reaps the rewards of middle age while Iron brings violence and death.

Aglaia *see* Graces, The

Agnes, Saint

An early Christian martyr who is said to have died in Rome in 304CE, aged thirteen. St Agnes[1] can often be identified in paintings by her attribute, a lamb, which she probably acquired because *agnus*, Latin for lamb, resembles her name. She is generally represented as a young girl with long hair.

The son of a Roman prefect fell in love with Agnes but she scorned his promise of wealth, declaring that she had become a bride of Christ. When she refused to worship the goddess Vesta, the prefect had her stripped naked and taken to a brothel, but her hair grew miraculously and covered her nakedness. An angel appeared in the brothel and provided her with a cloak of heavenly light which converted everyone inside to Christ and frightened away those who came to harm her. Her suitor was struck dead by a demon when he tried to ravish her and her executioners were burned by the flames intended for her. She finally died when a knife was plunged into her throat.

Agnes appears as an elegant figure holding her lamb, for example in Duccio's *Maestà*. Her half-sister Emerantiana was stoned to death and in art sometimes appears with her, often with stones in her lap.

Agrippina

The noble Agrippina, granddaughter of the emperor Augustus, symbolizes fidelity in marriage. She dearly loved her husband Germanicus, a wise and popular Roman general named after his successful conquests in Germany. He was poisoned by his political enemies in Syria, and the grieving Agrippina brought his ashes back to Italy.

Agnes, Saint: *see* Brothels, Martyrs
[1] *Golden Legend, St Agnes*

Agrippina:
[1] Tacitus. *Annals II:71–72* and *III:1*

Her intimate friends, together with several Roman officers and many others who had served under Germanicus, went to Brundisium (Brindisi) to meet her fleet. As Agrippina disembarked with her two children, clasping the funeral urn, her eyes were riveted to the earth and there was a universal sigh from the crowds of mourners.[1] The grieving widow may be seen descending from her ship with her husband's ashes, as in *Agrippina Landing at Brundisium with the Ashes of Germanicus* by the American painter Benjamin West.

Agung, Mount

A sacred volcano on the island of Bali, locally called Gunung Agung ("Great Mountain"). In Balinese Hindu myth, when neighbouring Java converted to Islam (*c*.1600), the gods moved to Bali and built high mountains to reflect their exalted rank. In the middle was Gunung Agung, the highest of them all and the centre of the world. Shrines to Mount Agung exist in all Balinese temples, the holiest of which, Pura Besakih, stands on the volcano itself.

Ah Mun

A Mayan god of corn (maize), who is typically depicted with a maize cob sprouting from his head.

Ahalya

In Hindu myth, the wife of Gautama, a powerful sage and ascetic. She was seduced by the god Indra, but when Indra left her she met Gautama, who knew at once what had happened. The sage cursed Indra to lose his testicles, while Ahalya was cursed to lie, invisible, on a bed of ashes for thousands of years with only air to live on. Her plight would be lifted only when the

god Rama visited her. On hearing this story, Rama went to Ahalya and freed her from the curse.

Ahat

The son of a patriarch called Daniel in ancient Canaanite myth. Daniel (who may be related to the biblical figure) was childless until, at the instigation of the storm god Baal, the supreme god El granted him a son, Ahat.

When Ahat grew up, a divine craftsman gave him a bow and arrows, but the goddess Anath coveted them. Anath sent her attendant, Yatpan, to kill Ahat and take his bow, but the weapon was broken in the assault and so the goddess's plan came to nothing. Furious at Ahat's murder, Baal withheld the rains from the land.

The end of the myth is lost, but it probably tells of the resurrection of Ahat and the end of the drought. The story may account for the summer drought and its eventual breaking, which is symbolized by the death and subsequent resurrection of Ahat.

Ahau Kin

"Lord of the Sun Face", the Mayan sun god. In his daytime manifestation Ahau Kin was often depicted with jaguar features. However, between sunset and dawn he actually became the Jaguar God, the lord of the underworld, as he travelled from west to east through the lower regions.

Ahriman

A later form of Angra Mainyu, the name of the ancient Persian god of dark forces.

Ahura Mazdah

"Wise Lord", the supreme god of ancient Persia, also known as

Ohrmazd. Ahura Mazdah represented the sky and embodied wisdom, fruitfulness and benevolence. His opponent (and also his creation) was Angra Mainyu, god of darkness and sterility. There were other deities, but life was essentially a struggle between the two gods of good and evil.

In the 7th or 6th century BCE the prophet Zoroaster, the founder of Zoroastrianism, declared Ahura Mazdah alone worthy of absolute worship. Ahura Mazdah was the essence of beneficent nature, creator of heaven and earth, the fount of law and morality and supreme judge of the universe. His offspring includes Gayomart, the archetypal man.

Air

A symbol of spiritual life, freedom and purity, air is the primal element in most cosmogonies, equated with the soul by Stoic philosophers (followers of the Greek Zeno, 2nd century BCE). Air shares much of the symbolism of breath and wind (both of which are somewhat easier for artists to depict).

Air Spirit, The

One of the three great spirit forces in Inuit belief, together with the Sea Spirit and the Moon Spirit. Known in far northern regions as Sila ("Weather", "Intelligence"), the Air Spirit lives far above the earth, controlling rain, snow, wind and sea. It is inherently benevolent but is perceived as threatening because of its sensitivity to human misdeeds, to which it responds by sending sickness, bad weather, and failure in hunting.

Aither

"Ether", the bright upper air, one of the elemental Greek deities which, according to Hesiod's *Theogony*, came into being in the first stages of creation. It features little in myth.

Ajax (1)

A Greek hero, son of the Argonaut Telamon, king of Salmacis, and known as the Greater Ajax to distinguish him from Ajax (2). Described in Homer's *Iliad* as a stubborn and taciturn man of huge physical stature, Ajax was, after the hero Achilles, the most distinguished Greek warrior in the Trojan War.

After the death of Achilles, Ajax rescued his corpse and armour while Odysseus fought off the enemy. Both men claimed the dead hero's armour as a prize, and when it was awarded to Odysseus, Ajax was so furious that he planned to kill his own commanders. To thwart the assault, the goddess Athene (the Roman Minerva) drove him mad, so that instead he slaughtered a flock of sheep. After the madness had passed, Ajax felt so deeply humiliated that he killed himself by thrusting his sword into his side. Hyacinths grew where his blood fell on the earth, although Poussin in *The Kingdom of Flora* shows a carnation.

Ajax and Achilles playing checkers; after a black-figure amphora of the 6th century BCE.

Air: *see* Breath, Breathing; Wind

Air Spirit, The: *see* Moon Spirit, The; Sea Spirit, The

Aither: *see* Erebos; Nyx

Ajax (1): *see* Achilles; Argonauts, The; Hector; Odysseus; Trojan War, The; TROJAN WAR, THE HEROES OF THE
[1] Ovid, *Met XIII:1–398*

Ajax (2)

A Greek hero, son of the Argonaut Oileus and known as the Lesser Ajax to distinguish him from Ajax (1). During the sack of Troy he raped King Priam's daughter Cassandra on the altar of Athene, a desecration for which the gods caused the victorious Greek fleet to be shipwrecked on its way home. Ajax swam to a rock but drowned after it was struck by a thunderbolt hurled by the god Poseidon.

Alalu

The first supreme deity, according to ancient Hittite mythology. In the beginning Alalu was king in heaven for nine years before he was deposed by his servant, the god Anu, and descended to the underworld.

Albatross

Emblem of a burden of guilt – a symbolism created by *The Rime of the Ancient Mariner*, a ballad by Samuel Taylor Coleridge (1772–1834) in which the shooting of an albatross broke a mariners' taboo. Traditionally, the bird was a good omen, its power and stamina so admired that in folklore it embodied the souls of dead sailors.

Alcestis

A Greek princess, the daughter of King Pelias of Iolcus and his wife Anaxibia. Alcestis was renowned for her beauty and had many princely suitors, but Pelias insisted that any man wanting to marry her must first yoke a lion and a boar to a chariot. King Admetus of Pherae achieved this feat, assisted by the god Apollo.

Alcestis believed that the sorceress Medea could rejuvenate her aged father, King Pelias of Iolcus; and so,

directly following the witch's instructions, she and her sisters cut up the body or drained the blood of the king (accounts vary). However, the scheme was just a ruse by Medea to bring about the death of Pelias.

According to one account, Apollo got the Fates drunk one day and extracted a promise that when the time came for Admetus' death he would live on if someone volunteered to die in his place. The Fates came for Admetus soon afterwards, but no one was prepared to die instead of him, so Alcestis offered to sacrifice herself on his behalf to appease the shade of her father.¹ In *The Death of Alcestis*, Pierre Peyton shows her on her deathbed as the epitome of a devoted wife. However, she was rescued from the underworld by the hero Herakles (Hercules). Touched by her virtue, he fought with death, brought her back to earth and restored her to Admetus.²

Alchemy

An ancient symbol for the perfectibility of the human soul, alchemy derives, via Greek writings, from the Egyptians and Babylonians. Its practice came to medieval Europe through the Arabs. Alchemists sought to dis-

An alchemist at his furnace, after a German woodcut of 1519.

cover a fabled medium known as the Philosopher's Stone that would transmute base metals to gold and silver, and also form the basis of an elixir of eternal life. This medium was made from the elements of earth, fire, air and water, together with a primal quintessence ("fifth essence"). The process was overlaid with symbolism taken from philosophy, astrology, mysticism and, in the medieval era, religion, and for its most serious practitioners became a mystical spiritual quest for closeness to the divine. Symbolic forms or terms were used for equipment, materials and processes, partly to borrow their force, partly to baffle the uninitiated. The colours black, white, red and gold symbolized a process leading from "reduction" to "distillation" (purity). Charlatans abounded, but many alchemists worked with a sincere sense of spiritual purpose, believing divine intervention would bring success.

The alchemist is usually seen at his furnace surrounded by flasks, crucibles and other objects of his craft, as in Vasari's and his associates' *The Alchemist's Laboratory*, Studiolo of Francesco I, *c.*1570. From the 17th century, when alchemy began to be misunderstood and discredited with the rise of modern scientific enquiry, the alchemist was depicted often as a symbol of foolish and fruitless labour.

Alcmena *see* Alkmene

Alcohol
A symbol of vital energy, uniting the contradictory elements of fire (masculine) and water (feminine), the *aqua vitae* ("water of life") of alchemy. Alcohol was also linked with creativity and wisdom.

Alexander the Great
King Alexander III of Macedonia (356–323BCE), or Alexander the Great, conquered the entire Near East and Egypt, and founded Alexandria.[1] As a young prince, he was taught by Aristotle and commanded cavalry at the age of 18. He is often depicted on his horse, Bucephalus, usually shown as a white charger, which only his gentle control was able to tame.

Alexander was told by the famous oracle of Delphi that he was invincible. His conquests began with Greece itself. After he sacked the Greek city of Thebes, his captain raped the noblewoman Timoclea and demanded her money. She led him to a well where she claimed she had thrown her valuables and, as he looked over, pushed him in. She was brought before Alexander, who in recognition of her spirit and dignity, released her and her children. Pietro della Vecchia's *Timoclea Brought Before Alexander* shows this scene.

Alexander went on to invade Asia Minor, where his conquests included Gordium, capital of Phrygia. Here there was a chariot fastened with a knot of fabulous intricacy. The Phrygians believed that the one who could undo this knot would rule the world. Some accounts report that Alexander was able to untie it easily, but in the more famous account Alexander simply hacked through it with his sword.

In 333BCE Alexander defeated the Persians, archenemies of the Greeks, in the narrow plain of Issus in Cilicia. In *The Battle of Issus*, Albrecht Altdorfer shows his mighty army as a mass of tiny figures. Fighting in the foremost ranks, Alexander wounded and put to flight Darius, the Persian king. Alexander's army pillaged the

Alcohol: *see* Alchemy; Fire. Flame; Intoxication; Soma; Water; Wine

Alexander the Great: *see* Abstinence; Apelles; Aristotle
[1] Plutarch, *Lives, Alexander*

Alkmene

Persian camp, but Darius's mother, wife and two daughters were treated with respect and consideration. Veronese's *The Family of Darius Before Alexander* shows Alexander and his friend Haephestion visiting Darius's family after the battle. At first Darius's mother mistook the taller Haephestion for her conqueror, but Alexander put her at ease, saying that Haephestion was another Alexander.

Alexander pursued Darius and found him on the point of death, fatally wounded by his own men. The dying Darius paid homage to his enemy, who covered him with his own cloak. According to tradition – the truth was often very different – Alexander showed restraint and clemency towards defeated peoples and cities, believing it was better to rule through goodwill than force.

He married Roxana, who in some accounts was the daughter of Darius and in others the daughter of a conquered Asian chieftain. It is said that this union greatly pleased the Persians, and Alexander exercised restraint before their marriage. Sodoma's frescoes of scenes of his life include *The Marriage of Alexander and Roxana* (Villa Farnesina, Rome), which accords with a description by Lucian of a Classical painting.[2]

Lysippus was Alexander's court sculptor and Apelles his court painter – considered the greatest in antiquity. Scenes of Alexander, often helmeted and in armour, may show his magnanimous and honourable behaviour.

Alkmene

In Greek myth, the queen of Tiryns and the mother of the hero Herakles. Alkmene married her uncle, King Amphitryon of Tiryns. When he left to fight cattle raiders, the god Zeus assumed his form to visit Alkmene. She was delighted to see her husband returned so soon and that night the couple made passionate love – Zeus lengthening the night to three times its normal duration in order to extend his pleasure.

The real Amphitryon returned home victorious the following day but was surprised at his wife's lack of sexual ardour. Alkmene in turn was surprised that her husband had forgotten the previous night's pleasures. The couple discovered the truth from the blind prophet Teiresias. Alkmene subsequently bore twins: the hero Herakles, the son of Zeus, and Iphikles, the son of Amphitryon. Alkmene and Herakles (usually given their Roman names, Alcmena and Hercules) may appear in depictions of the infant Herakles killing a pair of snakes.

Alligator *see* Crocodile

Almond

The almond may symbolize fertility, purity and virgin birth (an association with both pagan and biblical roots), divine grace, and hidden truth.

The juice of the pressed almond was equated in the ancient world with semen, leading to the story that Attis, consort of the Phrygian and Greco-Roman earth goddess Cybele, was conceived from an almond, the pure fruit of nature. In European folklore it is said that a virgin can wake pregnant if she sleeps under an almond tree and dreams of her love.

Almonds may also symbolize divine favour. They occur in the biblical story in which God chooses Aaron to be High Priest by way of a miracle: "the rod of Aaron for the house of

Levi had sprouted and put forth buds and produced blossoms, and it bore ripe almonds".[1]

As a convenient pictorial shape, heavenly light in the form of a mandorla (Italian for almond) may enclose the figure of Christ in various contexts.

The sweet nut within its casing suggested to Arab mystics a secret reality masked by appearances. The almond is a Chinese Yin symbol. The early-flowering tree is linked with rebirth, watchfulness, delicacy.

Alpha and Omega (A and Ω)

The first and last letters of the Greek alphabet represent the totality of God. "I am the Alpha and the Omega, the beginning and the ending, says the Lord God, who is and who was and who is to come, the Almighty."[1] They appear with the Chi Rho in early Christian art and in mosaics such as the image of Christ in San Miniato al Monte, Florence.

Ama-no-minakanushi-no-kami

"Lord of the Centre of Heaven", the oldest of the Japanese gods. He was the first of three invisible deities who came into existence when the earth was not yet fully formed, and was one of the five primordial "Separate Heavenly Deities".

Ama-no-uzume

A beautiful young goddess of Japanese myth. Possibly a deity of the dawn, she is important for her role in resolving the "Divine Crisis".

Amalthea

In Greek myth, a goat or goat-nymph that suckled the infant Zeus on Crete. According to one account, the grateful god broke off one of Amalthea's

horns, promising that it would produce a never-ending abundance of fruit, nectar and ambrosia. This horn was known as the Cornucopia ("Horn of Plenty"). Zeus then turned his nurse and the horn into stars.[1]

Amaranth

A long-lasting flowering plant, depicted on Greek tombs and sculptures as a symbol of immortality. Amaranth was linked with Artemis (Diana) and credited with healing properties. In China, its flowers were offered to the lunar hare at the Moon Festival as a token of immortality.

Amaterasu

The Japanese sun goddess, in full Amaterasu-no-mikoto ("August Person Who Makes The Heavens Shine"). Perhaps the greatest deity in the Shinto pantheon, Amaterasu is revered as an ancestor of the emperors of Japan. Her shrine at Ise on Honshu island is the most important of all Shinto shrines.

The goddess was born from the left eye of the primal creator Izanagi as he bathed in a stream on the island of Kyushu. Izanagi assigned her the realm of the heavens. Her brother, the moon god Tsuki-yomi, was entrusted with the realms of the night and another brother, Susano, was made ruler of the ocean.

Susano declared himself unhappy with his lot and Izanagi banished him for ingratitude. Before leaving, Susano went to bid farewell to Amaterasu in heaven. The goddess suspected, rightly, that her unruly brother wanted to usurp her domains. When he arrived, the storm god suggested that they prove which of them was the mightier by having a reproduction

The Greek letters Alpha (top) and Omega. In each case the capital letter is given on the left, the lower-case form on the right.

*Amaterasu emerging from her cave,
after a 19th-century triptych.*

contest: whoever bore male deities
would win. Amaterasu agreed and
broke Susano's sword in three, chewing the pieces and spitting them out as
three goddesses. Next, Susano chewed
Amaterasu's beads and spat them out
as five male gods. He declared himself
the winner, but Amaterasu pointed
out that the five gods had sprung
from her possessions. Her brother
refused to concede and began to celebrate his victory by causing havoc in
Amaterasu's realm.

Terrified, Amaterasu withdrew into
a cave, depriving the world of the sun
and causing various calamities during
what is known as the "Divine Crisis".
The other deities failed to draw her
out until the goddess Ama-no-uzume
performed an erotic dance, causing
the gods to laugh so loudly that
Amaterasu was overcome with curiosity and left her cave. The sunlight
returned. The deities fined Susano
and expelled him from heaven.

Amaunet

In Egyptian myth, one of the eight
primal deities or divine forces known
as the Ogdoad.

Amazon

In Greek myth, the Amazons were a
race of mounted women warriors
who lived near the Black Sea. Expert
riders and archers, they displayed
their fighting abilities in raiding expe-
ditions. They kept men as slaves for
procreation. It was said that any male
offspring of these unions were abandoned to die, while the girls were
brought up to be warriors like their
mothers. "Amazon" was said to mean
"without breast" in Greek, since they
were said to cut off their right breasts
in order to draw their bows more easily. In art, however, Amazons almost
invariably have two breasts .

The Amazons were eventually
defeated in a famous battle, known as
the Amazonomachy ("Battle of the
Amazons"), fought against the Athenians under Theseus.¹ The conflict
was depicted on the Parthenon and
Rubens' *The Battle of the Amazons*
shows the violent battle of the sexes in
which the women were overcome.

The term Amazon is also applied to
woman warriors of Slavic mythology.
An 11th-century Bohemian legend
tells of a group of Amazons who
fought like men and took the initiative
sexually. Led by their bravest warrior,
Vlasta, they lived in a castle on the
banks of the Vltava (Moldau) River.
In Russian folk epics, the Amazons
(*polenitsa*) are lone riders. In one
story a hero, Dobrynia, encountered

An Amazon fighting an Athenian, based on a frieze from the Parthenon, Athens, 5th century BCE.

an Amazon and attempted to overcome her. However, she wrenched him from his horse and dropped him in her pocket. She eventually agreed to release him on condition that he married her.

Amber

Amber is linked by its colour with solar energy. In ancient China, the word for amber literally meant "tiger soul" – resin supposedly formed from the remains of tigers, hence embodying courage. In mythology, many divinities shed tears of amber; the sisters of Phaeton were transformed into weeping pine trees as they grieved for their brother's death after he had rashly driven his father's (Helios's) sun chariot. Amber was long used as a talisman and cure for everything from rheumatism to headaches.

Ambrose, Saint

Ambrose (died 397CE) is one of the four Latin Fathers (or Doctors, meaning "teachers") of the Church, with SS. Augustine, Jerome and Gregory the Great. He studied law in Rome and was made prefect of Milan, the administrative centre of the Western Roman Empire. Disagreement broke out between the Arians, who did not believe in the divinity of Christ, and the orthodox Christians over the election of a new bishop. During the dispute a child is said to have cried out, "Ambrose shall be bishop." He was duly elected, though he had not even been baptized.

Ambrose was a great orator and resolute theologian. When, in 390CE, the Emperor Theodosius I ordered a savage massacre in punishment for the death of a Roman governor, Ambrose instructed him to do public penance, thereby asserting the superiority of the church over secular rulers. He introduced the Ambrosian chant, the first successful form of hymn, into the church service.

An early 6th-century mosaic in the cathedral of San Ambrogio (St Ambrose), Milan, shows him as a middle-aged man in Roman dress. However, he is more frequently seen as a bishop, often one of the four Doctors of the Church, as in the wings of a mid-15th-century triptych by Antonio Vivarini and Giovanni d'Alemagna. He may also be seen with the twin brothers, Saints Gervase and Protase, who according to legend[1] were martyred for their faith and revealed the site of their relics to Ambrose in a vision. In the early 16th century, Ambrogio Bergognone painted scenes from Ambrose's life, beginning with the saint as a baby in his cradle with bees buzzing around the window and over his face, without harming him, and his father predicting his illustrious future.[2] In other paintings he may have a bee hive, symbolizing his future eloquence, and a book with the words, "be nourished by food, but the food of angels not human". This alludes to his name, since ambrosia is the food of the

Amber: *see* Amulet; Sun; Tiger

Ambrose, Saint: *see* Augustine, St; Bee
[1] *Golden Legend, Saints Gervasius and Protasius*
[2] *Golden Legend, St Ambrose*

gods; however, it is also the name of the whip with which he drove the Arians out of Italy.

Amen

A biblical affirmation, a Hebrew word meaning "so be it", "truly". In Christianity it has something of the symbolic force of the sacred Hindu and Buddhist mantra *Om* (or *Aum*) as an embodiment in sound of the divine spirit, summoned to answer prayers.

Amethyst

A quartz gemstone symbolizing temperance, peace, humility and piety. Amethyst was worn by bishops because of the stone's modest violet or cool purple colour, and the Greek belief that it promoted sobriety (*amethustos*, "not intoxicated"). As talismans these stones were thought to promote wholesome dreams.

Amitabha

"Unending Light", a celestial Buddha who is said to rule a paradise in the west. In Mahayana Buddhist traditions, Amitabha is said to offer rebirth in his western paradise to anyone who invokes his name and shows true repentance for their sins. In this blissful realm, or Pure Land, his devotees will find the perfect conditions in which to pursue enlightenment. Amitabha became popular in Tibet and China, and he is of great importance in Japan, where he is known as Amida or Amida-butsu. He is the central figure in Jodo-shu and Jodo-shinsu, the Pure Land sects of Japanese Buddhism. These are founded on the belief that the faithful, simply by repeatedly invoking Amida's name with devotion, will attain rebirth into his Pure Land.

Amma

An egg which, according to the Dogon people of Mali, existed at the beginning of creation and was the seed of the cosmos.

Amphitrite

A sea nymph of Greek myth, the wife of the god Poseidon. When Poseidon made advances to the nymph Scylla, the jealous Amphitrite dropped magic plants into the water where Scylla bathed, turning her into a hideous monster. Amphitrite and Poseidon had two daughters, Rhode ("Rose"), from whom Rhodes was said to take its name, and Benthesicyme. Their son, Triton, was half man, half fish.

Amphitryon

In Greek myth, a king of Tiryns and the husband of Alkmene.

Amulet

A symbol or embodiment of beneficial power. Often used of an object worn to keep the wearer from harm or ill fortune, an amulet may be a natural object or specially made, such as an inscribed medallion or locket.

Amphitrite (left) with the god Poseidon, from a vase fragment.

Amun

In Egyptian belief Amun was originally one of the eight divine forces of chaos known as the Ogdoad. He was worshipped as a fertility god at Thebes in Upper Egypt and became a national deity in the 2nd millennium BCE when that city rose to prominence. He was combined with that of the supreme solar deity to give Amun-Ra, one of the four great creator deities (the others being Atum, Khnum and Ptah). Amun-Ra was the hidden power who made the gods. According to one account, the snake form of Amun was the earliest being to exist in the primeval waters.

Anahita

"The Immaculate", a Persian fertility goddess of Assyrian and Babylonian origin. She was believed to be the source of the cosmic sea and all the waters on earth, as well as that of human reproduction. Sometimes identified with the goddess Aphrodite (Venus) and the planet Venus, Anahita later became a popular goddess in many parts of the Near East and even farther west.

Ananta

"The Infinite", a giant serpent of Hindu myth. The god Vishnu rests on the serpent's coils in the cosmic waters during the intervals between the emanations of the cosmos. He is also referred to as Shesha ("Remainder"). Ananta is said to be the son of Kadru, a daughter of the god Daksha and the ancestor of all snakes.

Anat

An Egyptian warrior goddess derived from the Syrian (Canaanite) goddess Anath. In Egyptian myth Anat is the daughter of the solar deity Ra. She was usually depicted carrying a shield, spear and axe. Anat was also a cow goddess.

Anath

An Ugaritic (Canaanite) fertility goddess, warlike sister and chief helper of the storm god Baal. Anath descended to the underworld to try to persuade Mot, the god of death, to release Baal from his power. She also played an important role in the legend of Ahat.

ANCESTORS *see panel overleaf*

Anchises

In Greek and Roman myth, a king of Dardanus near Troy and father of the hero Aeneas. Anchises was a shepherd when Aphrodite (the Roman Venus), the goddess of love, seduced him in the form of a mortal young woman. Having become pregnant, Aphrodite prophesied that Anchises' child would be the ancestor of an everlasting dynasty. Anchises went on to become a king and his child, Aeneas, was the ancestor of the Romans.

Anchor

A symbol of hope, salvation, safety, firmness, fidelity, prudence. Its Christian symbolism was drawn from its form as well as its function in that the top bar could suggest a cross – its clandestine meaning in catacomb carvings. Hope of salvation is the New Testament "anchor of the soul" (Hebrews 6:19). A popular Renaissance motif combined an anchor (restraint) and dolphin (speed) with the Augustan motto *festina lente* ("hasten slowly"). As an emblem of St Nicholas, patron saint of sailors, the anchor signified safety. It appears

Amun: *see* CREATION; Ogdoad, The; Ra;

Anahita: *see* Aphrodite

Ananta: *see* Daksha; *Naga*; SNAKES AND SERPENTS; Vishnu

Anat: *see* Anath; Ra; Ugarit

Anath: *see* Ahat; Anat; Baal; Mot

Anchises: *see* Aeneas; *Aeneid, The*; Aphrodite; Zeus

Anchor: *see* CROSS; Dolphin; Phallus; Snake; VIRTUES

ANCESTORS

Many peoples believe that the invisible spirits of ancestors remain active in this world. For example, the Slavs used to leave food by graves for their ancestors to consume, and the Chinese honour their ancestors to this day in the annual festival of Qingming.

In many cultures, myths about ancestors often reinforce social distinctions, such as those between hereditary rulers and their subjects or between social classes or castes. Kingship tends to be validated by claims to divine ancestry: the pharaohs of Egypt claimed descent from the deities Isis and Osiris, and until 1945 Japanese emperors traced their lineage back to the sun goddess Amaterasu. The social hierarchy is frequently reflected in the order in which the ancestors first appeared on earth. For example, the Carabaulo people of Timor in Indonesia relate how their first ancestors came out of a huge vagina in the ground: the first to emerge were the landowning aristocrats, followed by commoners and tenants.

A representation of ancestral spirits, based on a Yoruba ceremonial mask from Nigeria.

also in Egyptian iconography as a creation image – the shape combining a boat (female) and phallic mast, snake entwined.

Andrew, Saint (Apostle, Disciple)

Andrew (died *c*.60CE) was a fisherman on Lake Galilee and the first of the followers of Christ, who summoned him with his brother, Simon Peter.[1] According to legend,[2] Andrew later travelled through Greece, Asia Minor and Russia, preaching, per-

forming miracles and converting. He converted a boy who was able to extinguish the flames of a burning house on fire with a few drops of water; cured a man of lust; caused lightning to strike dead a woman who had falsely accused her son of attempting to rape her; expelled from a city demons that appeared to him as dogs; and brought back to life forty men who had drowned on their way to receive his blessing.

Among those whom Andrew converted was the wife of the proconsul who, unable to make the saint worship false gods, had him crucified. According to a relatively late tradition, Andrew died on an X-shaped cross, which became his attribute. Even after his martyrdom, Andrew is said to have come back as a pilgrim to save a bishop from the Devil disguised as a beautiful woman.

Andrew is usually painted as an old bearded man, together with his characteristic cross, as in El Greco's *St Andrew and St Francis*. His statue was carved to Bernini's designs in the 17th century for St Peter's, Rome, which possessed the relic of his head. He may also be shown with a fish or fishing net. He is the patron saint of Greece, Russia and Scotland.

Andrians

In Greek mythology, the god Dionysos (Bacchus to the Romans) made a river of wine flow on the island of Andros.[1] The inhabitants, known as Andrians, danced and sang and their voices became thick with wine from the river, which "makes men rich, and powerful in the assembly, and helpful to their friends, and beautiful". At the mouth of the river, Tritons blew wine from sea shells, and Dionysos moored his ship in the harbour to lead Laughter and Revel, and reap the river's harvest.

Titian's painting *The Bacchanal of the Andrians* shows a merry crowd in which some people are becoming amorous in their revelry.

Androgyne

Divine wholeness – an ancient symbolism derived from widespread worship of primal gods who were simultaneously male and female. The Chinese yin-yang symbol epitomizes an androgynous perfection in which all opposites are complementary to one another. Platonic philosophy, Sufi mysticism, and Greek, Egyptian, Oriental, Aboriginal and Mesoamerican mythology all perceived the original state of being as androgynous. By implication, Adam himself contained male and female.

The androgyne was also an alchemical symbol, embodying the oneness with God, the mystic union that was the goal of Hermetic (alchemical and magical) science. Love and marriage have been seen as practical ways to attain oneness, symbolized in Greek mythology by the story of Hermaphroditus, a son of Hermes and Aphrodite who was loved so fervently by a nymph of Salmacis that she became absorbed into his body. From this stems the term hermaphrodite (strictly, in biology, one who has incomplete male and female organs).

Andromeda

In Greek myth, a princess of "Ethiopia" (probably Joppa in Palestine). Andromeda was the daughter of King Cepheus and Queen Cassiopeia. Cassiopeia made the sea god Poseidon angry by declaring herself to be lovelier than the Nereids, a race of beautiful sea nymphs. Poseidon flooded the kingdom and sent a hideous sea dragon to ravage the land. An oracle told Cepheus that he would save the kingdom if Andromeda was sacrificed to the dragon. At the insistence of his subjects, Cepheus had Andromeda chained to a rock and left to be eaten by the creature. As Andromeda lay naked on the rock, the hero Perseus flew past and fell in love with

Andrians: *see* Bacchus
Philostratus the Elder,
Imagines I: 25

Androgyne: *see* Alchemy;
Circumcision; Man;
Marriage; Woman;
Yin and Yang

Andromeda: *see* Nereid;
Perseus; Poseidon

The androgyne, an alchemical symbol of the unity of spirit and matter (17th century).

Anemone

her at once. He offered to kill the monster in return for her hand.

Cepheus accepted the offer and Perseus, who was wearing his cloak of invisibility and winged sandals (and, in some accounts, riding the winged horse Pegasus), cut off the beast's head with his curved sword. He freed Andromeda and married her. After death Andromeda became the constellation that bears her name.

Anemone

A symbol of the transience of life, fragility, grief, death, virginity – attributes based on the ephemeral nature of this wild flower, its scarlet petals, and its name (meaning "of the wind"). Anemones are identified with the biblical "flowers of the field" and sometimes appear in depictions of the Crucifixion. They were also linked with dying god symbolism from the Greek myth that the flower sprang up where Adonis fell dead.

Angelica

Angelica appears in *Orlando Furioso*, an epic poem by Ariosto (1474–1533), recounts the legend of Charlemagne and Orlando (Roland), the Saracen invasion of France, and the conflict between Christians and Muslims. The poem takes the form of a parody of medieval romances, with combative knights, damsels in distress, monsters and witchcraft.

Orlando was driven mad by his love for the beautiful but fickle Angelica. She was promised to whichever of Orlando or his cousin Rinaldo slaughtered more Saracens.[1] She fled from her suitors, and had many adventures. In *Angelica and the Hermit* Rubens depicts the episode when a lustful hermit put her to sleep with

a magic potion, but when he tried to satisfy his desire he found he was too old to perform.[2] Ingres' *Ruggiero Delivering Angelica* illustrates the Andromeda-like story of Angelica being chained to a rock to feed the orc, a huge sea-monster. She was spotted by Ruggiero (Roger), a Saracen champion, who flew down on a hippogriff (a creature with the hindquarters of a horse and the wings and head of an eagle) to slay the monster and save her.[3]

By Cupid's will, Angelica fell in love with Medoro, a young Moorish soldier who was wounded by a Scottish knight. She healed him with the juice of mountain herbs; they were married among herdsmen and proclaimed their love by carving their intertwined initials on the bark of trees.[4]

ANGELS *see panel opposite*

Angelus, The

The Angelus is the prayer devoted to and giving thanks for the Annunciation. Its name comes from the opening words: *Angelus Domini* ("The Angel of the Lord") and is said at morning, noon and sunset. Jean-François Millet's painting of peasants praying in the fields at the sound of the Angelus bell is an image of religious devotion. The picture became widely known through reproductions and was perversely re-interpreted by Salvador Dali.

Angra Mainyu

The Persian god of dark forces, the opponent of the supreme deity Ahura Mazdah (Ohrmazd). He is also known as Ahriman.

ANIMALS *see panel overleaf*

ANGELS

Angels are anthropomorphic winged forms personifying divine will. Possibly evolved from Semitic and Egyptian winged deities, they appear in a number of religions as intermediaries between material and spiritual planes, but their symbolism is most elaborate in the Islamic, Jewish and especially Christian faiths. Angels and archangels are said to be divine messengers (the word angel comes from the Greek *aggelos*, meaning "messenger") and appear frequently throughout the Bible, not only bringing God's word to humankind but also delivering his protection or punishment.

The 5th-century CE Christian theologian known as Pseudo-Dionysios the Areopagite grouped angels in three hierarchical orders, each order comprising three types of angel:[1] In the first hierarchy, Seraphim surround the throne of God and are often red in colour; Cherubim know and worship God, and are depicted as gold or blue; and Thrones, wearing judges' robes, support his seat and represent divine justice, which they confer on the second hierarchy.

The angels of the second hierarchy are called Dominions, Virtues and Powers. They govern the stars and the elements and light up the third hierarchy with the glory of God. Dominions have crowns, sceptres or orbs to represent the power of God; Virtues have white lilies or red roses, also symbols of the Passion of Christ; and Powers are militant figures, who are seen fighting devils.

The third hierarchy, consisting of Princedoms, Archangels and Angels, maintains contact between heaven and earth and executes God's will. Princedoms oversee territories. Archangels are the independent figures of Michael, Gabriel, Raphael and Uriel, who together with angels, transmit the word of God to humankind. The most commonly depicted archangels are Gabriel, who appears especially in representations of the Annunciation, and Michael, the *signifer* or standard-bearer of the heavenly host, who is often depicted as a warrior leading the host against Satan and his rebel angels or slaying a dragon (another symbol of the Devil). The rebel angels were those who fell from heaven with Satan, an episode mentioned in the New Testament[2] but dating back to much earlier nonbiblical scriptures. Domenico Beccafumi's *Archangel Michael and the Fall of the Rebel Angels* shows them vanquished by Michael and metamorphosing into demons as they tumble down to Hell. Fallen angels, led by Satan, symbolized the sin of pride – it is said that Satan refused God's instruction to worship Adam.

Botticini's *Assumption of the Virgin*, part of the Palmieri Altarpiece, shows the three orders of angels, each with its three ranks. Angelic attributes in art include trumpets, harps, swords, censers and sceptres or wands. Angels are commonly depicted as young men with wings and haloes, although in Christian art they were also often dematerialized, appearing as winged heads, or in the playfulness of baroque art, as *putti*, Cupid-like winged boys or infants.

Angels: *see* Archangels; Cherubim; Devils; Gabriel; Harp; Meteorite; Michael, Saint; Putto; Raphael; Sceptre; Seraphim; SEVEN DEADLY SINS, THE; Sword; Trumpet; Wand; Wings

[1] Pseudo-Dionysius, *Celestial Hierarchy*
[2] *Revelation 12:9*

ANIMALS

The symbolism and iconography derived from animals is uniquely rich and varied. Many cultures have perceived animals, with their often superior physical and sensory abilities, to be in touch with spirit forces, and they have often been adopted as shamanic or clan totems.

In myth, animals may take on cosmic dimensions. In North America, the huge Thunderbird wages a perpetual battle with water-dwelling serpents or dragons. A similar idea occurs in southern Africa, where the Lightning Bird rules the sky and the cosmic serpent governs the watery underworld. In some mythologies, animals are precursors or creators of humans. An Egyptian creation myth describes the world coming into being with the cry of a heron; for the Khoisan of southwest Africa the first living thing was a tiny mantis, which created humankind.

Myths commonly affirm a kinship between humans and animals. Native American myths refer to a primordial time when people and beasts were indistinguishable and would readily assume each other's shapes. Animal metamorphosis occurs in most cultures: the werewolf of European tradition is paralleled in parts of Africa,

A figure of a bear, a totem animal of the Haida of northwest Canada.

where some powerful people are said to turn into lions and hyenas. Central and South American shamans are said to be able to transform themselves into jaguars.

Another common theme is the animal consort. Southern African myth tells of the python god who takes a human wife, dragging her into his watery underworld. Many Scottish folktales tell of seals assuming female form to marry men.

In the Bible, God created the animals in Eden and Adam named them.[1] They were innocent of human sinfulness and so were saved from the Flood.[2] These stories represent a time when humans and animals lived in harmony, However, as the Bible also relates, humankind has sacrificed animals on a vast scale to appease its gods: the Parthenon in Athens was said to smell like a slaughterhouse.

Overcoming a wild or fabulous beast usually represents the triumph of good over evil. Medieval bestiaries catalogued the characteristics of real and imagined animals and accorded them extensive moral symbolism. Psychology has followed suit in attaching to animals the symbolism of the instinctual, the unconscious, the libido, and the emotions.

Ankh

The ancient Egyptian "key of life" or "cross of life", a symbol like a cross with a loop at the top, representing life, especially life after death. Its shape has been variously understood as the rising sun on the horizon, as the union of male and female, or other opposites, and also as a key to esoteric knowledge and to the afterworld of the spirit. The Coptic church of Egypt inherited the *ankh* as a form of the Christian cross, symbolizing eternal life through Christ.

Anna or Anne, Saint

Anna, or Anne, the legendary mother of the Virgin Mary, does not appear in the New Testament but became popular through *The Protevangelium of James* (2nd century CE) and other early Christian writings about the life of Mary. An early image of her (*c*.650CE) appears in Santa Maria Antiqua, Rome, where she is shown with the Virgin. By the 14th century she was a popular figure, partly because her conception of Mary at an advanced age confirmed the developing doctrine of the Immaculate Conception of the Virgin. The meeting of Anna and her husband Joachim, a similarly legendary figure, at Jerusalem's Golden Gate after he has learnt that that she will miraculously conceive, is a common scene in cycles of the life of the Virgin. However, Anne is most frequently portrayed as a maternal figure with her daughter, particularly in Renaissance Florence; the most graceful examples are Leonardo's *Virgin and Child with St Anne and St John the Baptist*, and his *Burlington House Cartoon*. She is also depicted with her extended family, the Holy Kinship, by artists such as

the Master of St Veronica. Legend[1] claims that Anna married three times and had three daughters.

Anointing

A rite of Near Eastern origin in which consecrated oil is used as a symbol of divine grace to sanctify rulers or those undergoing priestly ordination, conferring holy authority.

Ansanus, Saint

A nobleman of Siena, Ansanus (died *c*.304CE), was brought up as a Christian by his nurse, and was openly preaching the faith by the age of 19, in spite of persecutions under Emperor Diocletian. He was whipped, thrown into a pot of boiling oil and finally beheaded. A patron saint of Siena, he appears as a young man with a banner and a cross, primarily in the art of that school. With St Margaret, his image by Lippo Memmi flanks the altarpiece of Simone Martini's *Annunciation*, which was originally intended for his chapel in the cathedral of Siena, and is now in the Uffizi, Florence.

Ant

A symbol of diligence, patience, humility and foresight. In China, the ant symbolized order and the tireless servant. Its industry, seen in the Bible as a virtue, is considered somewhat excessive in Hindu and Buddhist thought; thus it became an image of the ceaseless, petty activity of those blind to the transience of human life. In Mali, ants were beneficent organizers, originators of the skills of building and weaving, and by sympathetic magic their nests could bring fecundity. Anteaters, conversely, symbolized harm.

Ankh: see CROSS; Key; Sun

Anna or Anne, Saint: *see* Joachim; Virgin. The *Golden Legend, The Birth of the Blessed Virgin*

Anointing: *see* Oil

An ankh *combined with the sun and the symbols for "eternity" (*djed, *the pillar or spine of Osiris) and "soul" (*ka, *the raised arms) in this 2nd-century* BCE *image.*

Antaboga

A great primordial serpent which, according to the Balinese account of creation, existed when there was neither heaven nor earth. Antaboga initiated creation by bringing into being, through meditation, the cosmic turtle Bedawang, which was the foundation of the earth.

Antaeus

A giant, the offspring of the Greek god Poseidon and the goddess Gaia. Antaeus lived in Libya and challenged travellers to wrestle to the death. The giant always won because he could renew his strength just by touching the earth with his feet. He was killed when Herakles lifted him off the ground for long enough to throttle him.

Antelope

A symbol of grace, speed, clarity of vision – a spiritual ideal and a fit mount for gods in African and Indian traditions. To the San of southern Africa the antelope was an embodiment of the supreme creator, and in Mali it was a culture hero who brought humankind the skills of agriculture. The gazelle is an attribute of Vayu, the Persian and Indian god of air and wind. For Islamic thinkers, its soulful eyes symbolize the contemplative life.

Anthony of Padua, Saint

Anthony (1195–1231) was born in Portugal, where he joined the Franciscan friars. He taught and preached in Morocco, France and Italy with remarkable learning and powers of oration. He is the patron of Padua, where he died, and many miracles are credited to him. For the high altar of Sant' Antonio, Padua, Donatello

cast scenes including *The Miracle of the Irascible Son*, in which the saint restored a boy's leg, cut off in remorse for having kicked his mother. Another tale tells how, at a miser's funeral, Anthony preached: "Where your treasure is, there will your heart be also."[1] The miser's heart was found in his treasure chest (consequently Anthony became the patron saint of lost property). He is shown as a young man in Franciscan robes, perhaps holding a lily or a flaming heart, or carrying the Christ Child, referring to a vision he had of the Virgin and Child.

Anthony the Great, Saint (or Abbot)

According to legend,[1] the 18-year-old Anthony (251–356CE) gave all his worldly goods to the poor in order to live with hermits in the desert near the Nile, where he suffered countless torments by demons. A popular theme in art was the saint tempted by lust, as in paintings by Veronese and Cézanne. In a dream Anthony was told of St Paul, thought to be one of the earliest Christian hermits (died 347CE), who had taken refuge from persecution in the Theban desert and lived in a cave until a great age. He was led to him by a centaur, a satyr and a wolf; Dürer shows them together in the forest. When Paul died, Anthony buried him with the help of two lions.

St Anthony was sought out for his wisdom and guidance. He advocated self-denial and is thought of as the founder of monasticism. As he was apparently over 100 when he died, he is depicted as a bearded old man with a crutch wearing a hooded robe. Pisanello shows him with a pig, probably symbolizing gluttony, and a bell with which he exorcized demons.

Antigone

In Greek myth, a princess of Thebes, the elder daughter of King Oedipus and his mother Queen Jocasta. After Oedipus had discovered his unwitting acts of parricide and incest, he blinded himself and eventually went into exile, accompanied only by his daughters Antigone and Ismene.

Antigone died tragically having been shut up in a cave by Creon (Jocasta's brother) for burying the body of her brother, Polyneices, against Creon's orders. The prophet Teiresias insisted that Creon set her free, but when the cave was opened they discovered that Antigone had already hanged herself.

Antiochus and Stratonice

The son of Seleucus, who ruled the Asian territories of Alexander the Great after his death, Antiochus fell desperately in love with his father's young wife, Stratonice. Seeing the hopelessness of his passion he resolved to die by refusing nourishment. The court physician, Erasistratus, realized the cause of his illness and informed the king, who immediately annulled his marriage and united Antiochus and Stratonice.[1] In *Erasistratus Discovering the Cause of Antiochus's Illness* Jacques-Louis David shows Antiochus lying ill as a dignified Stratonice is brought to him.

Antiope (1)

In Greek mythology, Zeus disguised himself as a satyr in order to ravish Antiope, daughter of the king of Thebes,[1] as depicted by Ingres in *Antiope and the Satyr*. She bore the twins Amphion and Zethus and fled to avoid her father's anger, but he killed himself in despair. Antiope was then imprisoned by her uncle and tor-mented by his wife, Dirce. When she finally managed to escape, her grown-up sons took revenge: they deposed her uncle and tore Dirce apart on the horns of a bull.

The twins ruled Thebes and built its walls. Amphion played the harp so beautifully that the stones fell into place on their own.[2] Giambattista Tiepolo painted *Amphion Building the Walls of Thebes with his Song* as part of an allegory of eloquence.

Antiope (2)

In Greek myth, Antiope was an Amazon warrior, the sister of the Amazon queen Hippolyte. Antiope became the wife of Theseus, king of Athens.

Antlers

A symbol of spring fertility, prosperity and fecundity. Celtic antlered gods such as Cernunnos symbolized crop growth. The ten-pointed antlers of the shaman were considered to be an emblem of his supernatural powers.

Anu (1)

A senior deity of ancient Mesopotamia, Anu (known as An to the Sumerians) was revered as lord of the heavens and father of the gods. In the Sumerian account of creation, the goddess Nammu, the primeval sea, was the mother of An and Ki, the goddess of the earth, who coupled to produce the great gods, such as Enlil. In the Akkadian creation epic, the union of Apsu (the sweet-water ocean) and Tiamat (the salt-water ocean) produced a succession of deities culminating in the great gods Anu and Ea. In Hittite mythology, Anu deposed Alalu, the first king in heaven. The god Kumarbi then waged war on Anu and bit off his penis in the struggle.

Antigone: *see* Oedipus; Seven Against Thebes, The; Teiresias

Antiochus and Stratonice: *see* Abstinence
[1] Plutarch, *Lives, Demetrius*

Antiope (1): *see* ZEUS, THE CONSORTS OF
[1] Hyginus, *Fabulae VIII* and Ovid, *Met VI:111*
[2] Philostratus the Elder, *Imagines I:10*

Antiope (2): *see* Amazon (1); Hippolyte; Theseus

Antlers: *see* Deer; Horn

Anu (1): *see* Alalu; Apsu; Ea; Enlil; Ki; Kumarbi; Marduk; Nammu; Teshub; Tiamat

Anu's sperm impregnated Kumarbi with the weather god Teshub, who eventually triumphed over Kumarbi.

One Akkadian myth tells of Adapa, a priest of Ea in the city of Eridu and one of the Seven Sages, powerful beings who were evoked during magical rites. One day, Adapa angrily stopped the south wind after it had overturned his fishing boat. In doing so he deprived the land of the moisture brought by the wind, so Anu summoned him to heaven to justify himself. Ea warned him not to accept Anu's food or drink, because it would cause his death. In fact, Anu offered Adapa the food and water of immortality. When Adapa refused the offering, Anu realized the mistaken advice Adapa had been given and, laughing, sent him back to earth. At this point the narrative breaks off, but it appears that Anu granted special privileges to Eridu and its priesthood.

Anu (2)

An ancient Irish earth and fertility goddess, described as the mother of the gods. She may be related to (or even identical with) the goddess Danu or Dana, the ancestor of the heroic race called the Tuatha Dé Danann ("People of Danu"). Anu has strong links with the province of Munster: in County Kerry there are twin hills known as "The Paps of Anu".

Anubis

The Egyptian jackal-headed god of embalming. He is sometimes said to be the son of the god Osiris, the first king on earth, and his sister Nephthys. After Osiris was killed by his brother Seth, Anubis embalmed the body and wrapped it in linen bandages, making Osiris the first mummy.

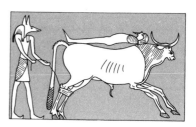

Anubis forcing Bata, the bull, to carry the mummy of Osiris. From an early Greco-Roman period papyrus.

Anubis later defended the corpse from the attacks of Seth. In death, Osiris became the ruler of the underworld, where Anubis guided the deceased through into the presence of Osiris and oversaw their judgment.

Apaosha

The demon of drought in Persian myth. Apaosha was overcome by Tishtrya, the rain god.

Ape

An animal of sharply diverging symbolism, respected in ancient Egypt, Africa, India and China, but deeply distrusted in Christian tradition where it was equated with vice, lust, idolatry and heresy. In Egyptian iconography the caped baboon represents Thoth, god of wisdom. The Hindu ape god Hanuman represents courage, strength and self-sacrifice.

In Western art, an ape may represent the base instincts of man. In Molenaer's *Lady World* a monkey slips his paw into a slipper, a representation of lust. An ape may also be used to satirize human affectation, folly and vanity. Artists were aware that they "aped" or imitated nature, as Chardin shows in *The Monkey Painter*; while 19th-century caricaturists mocked students as apes imitating their masters. Alternatively, apes or monkeys may appear as part of an exotic menagerie, as in Gentile da Fabriano's *Adoration of the Magi.*

Apelles

The court painter to King Philip of Macedonia and his son, Alexander the Great, in the 4th century BCE, and s considered the greatest of Classical painters. One story relates how his painting of a horse was so lifelike that it prompted a real horse to neigh. He possessed such courtly manners that Alexander frequently visited his studio. Apelles wrote treatises on art but neither these nor any of his paintings have survived. Apelles was allowed to paint Alexander's favourite courtesan, Campaspe, in the nude. He fell in love with her, whereupon Alexander did him the honour of presenting her to him.[1] Giambattista Tiepolo painted himself as Apelles and his wife as Campaspe in *Alexander and Campaspe in the Studio of Apelles.*

Apep

A great serpent or dragon of the Egyptian underworld, also known as Apophis. Apep, lord of darkness, was the arch-enemy of the sun god and attacked his barque every night as it travelled through the underworld. The barque was successfully defended by the hosts of the dead, led by Seth, the strongest of the gods.

Aphrodite

The Olympian goddess of love and sexuality, one of the most famous of the ancient Greek deities, best known in Western tradition by her Roman name, Venus. Before being wholly identified with Aphrodite, the Roman goddess was a goddess of gardens and springtime fruitfulness.

Aphrodite ("Born of Foam") sprang fully grown from the white foam which arose from the severed genitals of the castrated god Uranos, where they fell into the sea. After her birth the goddess came ashore either on the island of Cythera (by which name she is sometimes referred to) or on Cyprus. She was soon taken to the realm of the gods, where she was attended by the Graces and the Seasons. Botticelli's *Birth of Venus* shows her being blown by the winds on a scallop shell to Cyprus.

Aphrodite married Hephaistos (the Roman Vulcan), the craftsman god, but also took several lovers, most notably the war god Ares (Mars). The lovers were spotted in flagrante by Helios, the sun, who told Hephaistos. The god trapped the couple in a wonderful net and then summoned the other gods and goddesses to witness the outrage. To his annoyance they simply laughed. In the end Ares was freed when he agreed to pay Hephaistos a fine. Another famous lover of Aphrodite was the young hunter Adonis, who was killed by a wild boar.

Aphrodite bore numerous sons, the most famous of whom were Aeneas (by Anchises) and the winged god of love, Eros (the Roman Cupid), who often accompanies images of the goddess and is sometimes said to be the child of Aphrodite and Ares. Her other sons included Hermaphroditus (by Hermes) and Priapus (by Dionysos, Hermes, Pan or Zeus).

The goddess was frequently represented in art to show the ideal of female beauty, as in the most famous ancient depiction of her, the *Venus de Milo*. Later painters of the female

Apelles: *see* Alexander the Great; Calumny
[1] Pliny the Elder, *Natural History XXXV:85–89*

Apep: *see* DRAGON; Seth

Aphrodite: *see* Adonis; Aeneas; Anchises; Apollo; Apple; Ares; Dionysos; Eros; Hephaistos; Hermaphroditus; Hermes; OLYMPIANS, THE; Pan; Paris; Priapus; ZEUS, THE CONSORTS OF

Aphrodite, from a terracotta figurine of the 5th century BCE.

nude have traditionally depicted her
reclining provocatively, ever since
Giorgione's *Sleeping Venus*. She may
also be shown at her toilet, as part of
an allegory, or in scenes directly relating to her mythology. Many images of
nude women have probably been given
the title "Venus" simply to deflect any
inference of lewdness.

As well as Eros or Cupid, the goddess's attributes include roses and myrtle, which were sacred to her; swans
and doves, which may fly near her or
pull her chariot; and the golden apple
awarded to her by the Trojan prince
Paris. He was asked by the god Zeus to
present the apple, inscribed "To the
Fairest", to Aphrodite, Hera or
Athene. Paris chose Aphrodite and, in
consequence, Hera and Athene sided
against Troy in the city's ensuing war
with the Greeks.

Apocalypse

"Revelation" (Greek *apokalupsis*) of
the end of the world and the triumph
of good over evil, a genre of prophetic writing common to both ancient
Jewish and Christian literature. In the
Hebrew Scriptures, Ezekiel and
Daniel had apocalyptic visions and in
the New Testament the apocalyptic
genre is represented by *The Revelation
to St John the Divine*, or *The Book of
Revelation*. It was written at a time
when Christians were suffering persecution, toward the end of the 1st century CE, and many of its images and
references are no longer clearly understood. The famous "beast" is probably "Emperor Nero", which in Greek
(the language of *Revelation*) is made
up of letters that have the numerical
value of 666. He was a notorious persecutor of Christians and there was a
belief that he would return from the

dead to lead the forces of Satan at the
final battle. In *Revelation* angels
speak, mighty forces clash, and saints
are rewarded; God faces huge opposition but is triumphant.

Some passages from *Revelation* are
well known: God as the Alpha and
Omega; the four apocalyptic beasts
surrounding the throne of heaven,
resembling a lion, a calf, a man and a
flying eagle, which originated in the
visions of Ezekiel and were understood by Christians as symbols of the
four Evangelists; and the visions of
God, the Lamb and the Seven Seals.¹
Each seal opened to reveal a vision.
The first four seals disclosed the four
horsemen: the Conqueror with bow
and crown, on a white horse; War, the
destroyer with a sword, on a red
horse; Hunger, with a pair of scales,
on a black horse; and Death, the pale
horseman, with Hell on his heels.

The fifth seal revealed the souls of
those slain for preaching the word of
God, who were given white robes. The
sixth seal brought a great earthquake,
when the sun blackened, the moon
became blood red, the stars fell, heav-
en departed and men hid in the mountains from this day of wrath. An angel
anointed the "seal of the living God"
on the foreheads of his servants, while
four angels held back the four winds
of the earth. Silence filled heaven
when the seventh seal was opened,
until an angel threw a censer to earth
and caused thunder, lightning and
earthquakes. The call of seven trumpets released further revelations, of
the wonders of heaven, of the Devil
and his angels cast out of Heaven,
and of the "whore of Babylon", the
scarlet woman, mother of harlots and
of the earth's abominations (an allusion to Rome). The last decisive battle

was fought at Armageddon before the Day of Judgment.

In the Middle Ages, scenes from *Revelation* illustrated manuscripts and, and featured in stained glass windows, frescoes and carvings in churches. Dürer made a series of woodcuts, *The Apocalypse*, and El Greco painted *The Opening of the Fifth Seal*. The most popular subject, however, was St Michael vanquishing Satan and his rebel angels.

Apollo

The Greek god of light, music, prophecy and healing, the son of the Titan Leto and the god Zeus (Latona and Jupiter to the Romans) and the twin brother of Artemis (the Roman Diana). Abandoned by their mother, Apollo and Artemis were nourished on ambrosia and nectar, which gave them dazzling appearances. Apollo personified youth and male beauty.

Apollo was born on the island of Delos, the site of his most important festival. His other main place of worship was Delphi. In Greek myth, Delphi was the centre of the world, a place sacred to the goddess Gaia and originally guarded by her dragon, the Python. But Apollo chose Delphi for his own sanctuary and killed the dragon; Turner's *Apollo and the Python* shows him resting after the deed. For this, Zeus exiled him for many years. On his return, Apollo founded the Delphic oracle and the Pythian Games.

Apollo's oracles at Delphi were communicated through a priestess, the Pythia, who sat on a sacred tripod of gold over a chasm in the rock. The famous shrine at Delphi features frequently in Greek and Roman myth. In his *Coastal View of Delos* Claude Lorrain shows the picturesque landscape

where Aeneas went to consult the oracle, which told him that his descendants would rule the earth. Herakles (Hercules) once contested Apollo's possession of the oracle and tried to carry away the sacred tripod, but Apollo came to the Pythia's defence. Zeus settled the quarrel by throwing a thunderbolt between his two sons.[2]

As a god of light, Apollo came to be associated with the sun and acquired the epithet Phoebus ("Brilliant"). At his birth on Delos, a blaze of light shone over the island and sacred swans flew around it seven times. Apollo adopted many attributes and myths of the sun-god, Helios (Sol in Roman myth), drawing a four-horse sun chariot across the sky each day, often preceded by the figure of Eos (the Roman Aurora), goddess of the dawn. The subject lent itself to paintings on Baroque ceilings, such as Guido Reni's *Aurora* (Casino Rospigliosi, Rome) and Giambattista Tiepolo's *Course of the Chariot of the Sun* (Palazzo Clerici, Milan). He is also seen rising or setting, as in a pair of tapestries designed by Boucher, *The Rising and Setting of the Sun*, or with Phaëthon (originally the son of Helios), who foolishly asked to drive the sun chariot but could not control it and perished.

As the patron of music and the arts, Apollo was often depicted with a lyre, and among his retinue were the nine Muses, the goddesses of artistic inspiration, by whom he was worshipped on Mount Parnassus. Artists such as Poussin and Raffael Mengs were influenced by Raphael's painting *Parnassus* (Stanza della Segnatura, Vatican, Rome), where Apollo sits surrounded by the Muses and great poets. Along with Calliope, the Muse of epic poetry, Apollo inspired poets and bestowed on

Apollo: *see* Agamemnon;
Alcestis; Artemis; Asklepios;
Athene; Cassandra;
Cyclops; Daphne; Eos;
Gaia; Herakles; Hermes;
Hyacinthus; Marsyas;
Midas; Niobe; Phaëton;
Trojan War, The
[1] Ovid, *Met I:416–451*
[2] Apollodorus, *The Library*,
II vi 2
[3] Ovid, *Met XIV:130–153*

them the sacred crown of laurels in memory of his unrequited love for the nymph Daphne.

Apollo hated to see his prowess contested. The satyr Marsyas found a flute abandoned by the goddess Athene, which played wonderful music of its own accord. He declared that Apollo himself could not play more beautifully on his lyre and the god duly challenged him to a competition, with the winner permitted to do just as he chose with the loser. Both played beautifully, but finally Apollo turned his lyre upside down and carried on playing. Unable to do the same with the flute, Marsyas was defeated. Apollo had him flayed alive for his arrogance.

Apollo was also the patron of medicine, and the father of Asklepios, the demigod of healing. Zeus killed Asklepios for resurrecting a dead man and Apollo avenged his son's death by killing Zeus's servants, the Cyclopes. As penance for this, Zeus sent Apollo to Thessaly for one year as the humble herdsman of Admetus, king of Pherae.

Most of Apollo's many love affairs ended badly. He granted Cassandra, the daughter of King Priam of Troy, the gift of prophecy, but she rejected his affection and he cursed her never to be believed. The Cumaean Sibyl asked to live as many years as there were grains in a heap of dust, and Salvator Rosa's *River Scene with Apollo and the Sibyl* shows her holding the dust in her hand before the god. But she scorned his love, and as she had forgotten to ask for eternal youth, Apollo condemned her to the misery of a protracted old age.[3]

Apollo was also associated with the protection of flocks and herds. He is often portrayed as a shepherd with a crook, in the company of satyrs.

Apollo is the god of the civilized arts, but like his sister Artemis he could be cruel, as the fate of Marsyas shows. Also like Artemis, Apollo was a hunter and archer, and acted as the protector of athletes and young men in war. In the Trojan War he sided with Troy, raining death and disease on the Greeks with arrows and poison darts.

Apollo's attributes are various: a lyre, a bow and arrow, a golden chariot drawn by four horses or sunbeams, and a laurel wreath or crown.

Apollonia, Saint

A deaconess of the church, Apollonia was martyred at Alexandria, Egypt, during an anti-Christian revolt in 249CE. According to legend,[1] her persecutors pulled her teeth out, an episode shown in a 15th-century Umbrian School painting, and when they threatened to burn her alive, she walked into the flames herself. She was invoked against toothache and her attribute is a pair of forceps grasping a tooth, as shown by Francisco Zurbarán.

Apostles, The

After the Resurrection, eleven of Christ's twelve principal disciples became the apostles ("envoys", "messengers") of his gospel: Andrew, Bartholomew, James the Great, James the Less, John, Jude, Matthew, Peter, Philip, Simon and Thomas. The new twelfth apostle was Matthias, chosen by lot to replace Judas Iscariot. St Paul is also counted among the apostles, as sometimes is his missionary colleague Barnabas.

Apple

The apple was widely used as a symbol for love, marriage, springtime, youth, fertility, longevity and sexual

Apollo, after a frieze on the Parthenon, Athens; 5th century BCE.

happiness – and therefore suggested temptation in Christian tradition. Its fertility and sexually-related symbolism is perhaps linked with the seeds within the vulva-shaped (in long section) core. Greek, Celtic and Nordic mythology all describe it as the miraculously sustaining fruit of the gods. The Greek hero Herakles (in Roman myth, Hercules) wins the golden apples of immortality from the Hesperides. The golden apple, or Apple of Discord, is the attribute of Aphrodite (the Roman Venus). The goddess Eris (Discord or Strife) was not invited to the wedding of Thetis and Peleus, at which the gods of Olympus were present, and in her anger she sent a golden apple to the feast, which was inscribed "To the Fairest".[1] The goddesses Aphrodite, Hera (Juno) and Athene (Minerva) each argued that she should have the apple, but the Trojan prince Paris awarded it to Aphrodite, who fatefully rewarded him with the fairest mortal woman, Helen of Troy – thus both causing the Trojan War and earning Troy the enmity of Hera and Athene.

Although the fruit of the Tree of Knowledge that tempted Eve in the Garden of Eden is unnamed in Genesis (and is said to be a fig in some non-biblical writings), it was understood to be an apple, perhaps because *malus* is Latin for both "apple" and "evil". In Christian tradition, an apple therefore represents Original Sin and the Fall of Man. It may be the attribute of Eve the temptress and may be included in works of art to refer to sin. For example, Augustus Egg's *Past and Present* shows a mother cast out of her comfortable home for committing adultery, the apple in the painting creating a parallel with Eve's responsibility for the expulsion from Eden. An apple may be held by the Christ Child to signify salvation and redemption from Original Sin

For alchemists, who noted the five-fold shape of the core (in cross-section), the fruit symbolized the mystic "fifth essence" (quintessence) and hence complete knowledge. In China, the apple stands for peace and its blossom for beauty.

Apsu

A Babylonian (Sumerian-Akkadian) deity embodying the primordial sweet-water ocean. In Sumerian myth, Apsu is described as the home of Enki, the god of wisdom. According to the Akkadian creation epic, in the beginning Apsu and his female counterpart, Tiamat, the salt-water ocean, united to produce a succession of divinities culminating in the gods Anu, Ea (the Sumerian Enki) and Marduk. Ea killed Apsu in a struggle that eventually saw the emergence of Marduk as the greatest of the gods.

Ara and Irik

The two primordial creator spirits which, according to the Iban people of Borneo, were the first beings to exist. The Iban creation myth recounts how Ara and Irik floated above a vast expanse of water in the form of birds. They gathered from the water two great eggs, from one of which Ara formed the sky while Irik formed the earth from the other. Ara and Irik moulded the first humans from earth and brought them to life with their bird-spirit cries.

Arabesque

In Islamic art, the ultimate visual symbol of the difficult and complex journey toward sublime clarity. A decorative linear style based on intertwining flowers, leaves and stems, it brilliantly skirts the Islamic prohibition on figurative art, forming a kind of visual incantation, an infinitely varied aid to contemplation.

Arachne

In Greek myth,[1] Arachne was a young woman famous for her talent at spinning. Her movements were so graceful that the river nymphs would come to watch her at work, and she even gained the praise of her teacher and patron, Athene (the Roman Minerva). However, Arachne became filled with conceit and foolishly challenged the goddess to a weaving contest. Athene's tapestry showed the gods enthroned; Arachne's depicted them metamorphosing to consummate their love for mortals. Tintoretto's *Minerva and Arachne* depicts the goddess watching her rival at work.

Arachne's tapestry was flawless. Furious at her success and indelicate choice of subject, Athene tore it to pieces and beat Arachne until the girl attempted to hang herself. Athene took pity on her and turned her into a spider, so that she could spin eternally.

Arcadia

A mountainous area in the Peloponnese, Greece, where the god Zeus (the Roman Jupiter) was born in some accounts. It is said to take its name from Arcas, son of Zeus and Callisto.

Arcadia, or Arcady, was associated with an ideal of rustic life and with the Golden Age. As the home of the god Pan, nymphs, satyrs and shepherds, it inspired ancient Greek and Roman pastoral poetry. In Poussin's painting *Et in Arcadia Ego* (Latin, "And I too was once in Arcadia"), shepherds come across a tomb bearing this inscription. The theme of *Et in Arcadia Ego* has been variously interpreted as a reminder of mortality (death exists even in an earthly paradise) or as a nostalgic lament for the idylls of youth.

Arch

A ceremonial gateway, a triumphal feature of Roman architecture, recalling ancient Classical associations of the arch with the sky and its supreme god Zeus (in Roman myth, Jupiter). Initiates passing under an arch symbolically leave their former lives (hence the ceremonial arches formed for newlyweds).

Archangels

An order of angels with specific and personalized symbolism. Most prominent in art are Gabriel, the divine herald of the Annunciation, who holds a lily or a fleur-de-lys sceptre; Michael, warrior-guardian of the righteous and instrument of judgment, who holds a sword or scales; and Raphael, linked with healing and the protector of children, pilgrims and travellers, who holds a staff. A less well-known biblical archangel is Uriel, and there are a number of others found in non-biblical writings.

Archimedes

The Greek Archimedes (287–212BCE) was one of the greatest mathematicians of antiquity.[1] He was also an astronomer and physicist, and in mechanics discovered the principle of the lever. He is said to have shouted "Eureka!" ("I have found it!") when he realized how to test the purity of metal from observing the volume of bath water displaced by his body.

Archimedes died when the Roman general Marcellus captured his city, Syracuse in Sicily, during the Second Punic War (218–201BCE). His inventions had prevented the Roman invasion for two years. Archimedes did not notice that the city had fallen, so engrossed was he in a mathematical problem, and when commanded by a soldier to come before Marcellus he refused until the problem had been solved. The enraged soldier drew his sword and ran him through. Sebastiano Ricci depicted this scene in *Archimedes and the Hero of Syracuse*.

ARCHITECTURE *see panel overleaf*

Areop-Enap

The primordial spider, which, according to the mythology of Nauru in Micronesia, initiated the creation of the sea and sky. Areop-Enap found a clamshell and asked a shellfish to prise it open. The shellfish was only partly successful, so Areop-Enap turned to a caterpillar for assistance. The caterpillar opened the shell fully, but died of exhaustion. The top part of the shell became the sky and the sweat of the caterpillar became the salt sea. The caterpillar became the sun and the shellfish the moon.

Ares

The Greek god of war, known as Mars to the Romans, who regarded him more highly than did the Greeks and depicted him more frequently. One of the twelve Olympian gods, Ares was the son of Hera and Zeus (Juno and Jupiter to the Romans). He is generally depicted as a strong, even brutal warrior who relished the violence and carnage of battle.

During the Trojan War, Athene viewed Ares as a double-dealing villain and easily conquered him.[1] Apart from such appearances on the battlefield, the god figures in myth primarily as the lover of Aphrodite (Venus). The pair were trapped in bed by a net made by the god Hephaistos (Vulcan), Aphrodite's husband, and humiliated before the other Olympians.[2] This affair is shown in numerous paintings. Whenever Ares rested in the company of Aphrodite, he took off his armour and the world was at peace. Painters followed the Classical description of the couple together: "Mars potent in arms, rules the savage works of war, yet often casts himself back into your lap, vanquished by the ever-living wound of love."[3] The theme may be treated humorously, with *putti* disrespectfully playing with the god's discarded armour. Ares/Mars also appears in allegories illustrating the triumph of love (Aphrodite/Venus) or wisdom (Athene/Minerva) over war.

Ares is sometimes said to be the father of Aphrodite's son Eros. There is also a tradition that the boar which killed Adonis was the jealous Ares in transformed guise.

Arethusa

In Greek myth,[1] the nymph Arethusa was cooling herself in clear waters when her beauty attracted the river god Alpheus. He chased her and she fled, still naked, but could not outrun him. She was rescued by Artemis (the Roman Diana), who hid her in a cloud. However, the persistent Alpheus waited for her to appear, so Arethusa was turned into an underground stream.

Argonaut

One of the fifty members of the crew of the ship *Argo*, in which the Greek

Areop-Enap: *see*
CREATION

Ares: *see* Adonis; Aphrodite; Furies, The; Hephaistos; Hera; Trojan War, The; TROJAN WAR, THE HEROES OF THE
[1] Homer, *Iliad* V:814–909
[2] Homer, *Odyssey* VIII: 265–346 and Ovid, *Metam.* IV:167–189
[3] Lucretius, *De Rerum Natura* I:32–40

Arethusa:
[1] Ovid, *Met* V:572–641

Argonaut: *see*
ARGONAUTS, THE VOYAGE OF THE; Jason; *and individual names*

Argos

hero Jason voyaged in quest of the
Golden Fleece. Eminent Greeks often
claimed that they had an ancestor
among the Argonauts, who included
the following mythical figures:

ARGUS, builder of the *Argo*.
ATALANTA, huntress and the only
woman Argonaut.
CASTOR and POLYDEUCES (POLLUX),
heroic twin sons of Zeus and Leda.
HERAKLES, greatest of all heroes.
IDMON and MOPSUS, legendary seers.
LYNCEUS, famously sharp-sighted.
MELEAGER, Herakles' brother-in-law.
NAUPLIUS, father of Palamedes, a
noted trickster.
OILEUS, father of the hero Ajax (2).
ORPHEUS, great singer and lyre player.
PELEUS, father of the hero Achilles.
PERICLYMENUS, son of the sea-god
Poseidon.
TELAMON, father of the hero Ajax (1).
TIPHYS, helmsman of the *Argo*.
ZETES and CALAIS, winged sons of
Boreas, the north wind.

ARGONAUTS, THE VOYAGE OF THE *see panel overleaf.*

Argos

In Greek myth, An unsleeping giant
with eyes all over his body, only one
pair of which were ever closed. Argus
was set by the goddess Hera to guard
Io, the lover of her husband Zeus. Io
was freed by the god Hermes, who
lulled Argus to sleep with stories and
then cut off his head. Hera scattered
his eyes on the peacock's tail.

Argula

A trickster figure associated with sorcery in the Aboriginal mythology of
Australia's western Kimberley region.
In this area, antisocial behaviour may
be punished by painting a distorted

human figure om the walls of a rock
shelter and singing insulting songs at
it that are believed to inflict disability
or death upon the transgressor. Such
paintings are sometimes said to be the
work of Argula.

Ariadne

The daughter of King Minos of Crete
and lover of Theseus.[1] Before Theseus
entered the dark Labyrinth, the lair of
the monstrous Minotaur, Ariadne
gave him a ball of twine, by means of
which he was able to retrace his steps
after killing the monster.

Together they set sail back to Athens,
but on the island of Naxos, where
Dionysos (the Roman Bacchus) was
worshipped, Theseus cruelly abandoned Ariadne on the shore. Accounts
differ about her first meeting with
Dionysos. One describes her asleep
when he appeared; another recounts
that she was on the shore lamenting
her fate, when Dionysos, afire with
love, greeted her with his companions,
some brandishing garland-covered
points, some waving limbs torn from a
bullock, some entwined with serpents,
and some playing instruments or beating tambourines.[2] Dionysos turned
Ariadne's crown into a circle of stars
(the constellation Corona Borealis),
which brought her eternal glory, and in
some accounts they were wed.

In *Bacchus and Ariadne*, Titian has
the god leaping down from his chariot
to claim her, followed by his rowdy
throng; while in Sebastiano Ricci's
Bacchus and Ariadne, Hymen presides
over their marriage as Bacchus gently
takes Ariadne by the hand.

Arion

An ancient Greek poet, whose story is
mainly legendary.[1] Arion played the

ARCHITECTURE

The symbolic meaning of architecture in painting depends on both its context and style. In 15th-century Flemish painting, the nave of a church may be Romanesque with a Gothic east end, brightly lit through tall narrow windows, to represent the coming of the new Order with the birth of Christ. In Jan van Eyck's *Madonna with Chancellor Rolin* the town in the landscape behind the donor is early Gothic, while a corresponding one behind the Virgin and Child is in the then modern Gothic style. The capitals of pillars near Christ may be carved with scenes of the Fall of Man to illustrate that he has come to redeem humankind. In the Arena Chapel, Padua, Giotto painted the Virtues within Gothic canopies, while the Vices are framed by Romanesque arches. Buildings in ruin are often found in scenes of the Adoration of the Magi and the Nativity, and imply the delapidation of the old order and the establishment of the new with the advent of Christ.

Elaborately carved architectural elements in scenes of the Passion of Christ refer to the high social status of his tormentors, especially Pilate, in contrast to the poverty of Christ and his disciples.

Architecture may have a political as well as a religious meaning. The Florentine Renaissance rejected the Gothic style favoured north of the Alps and readopted Classical elements of architecture. In Rome, enthusiasm for the antique inspired reconstructions of the past, as shown in Raphael's cartoons of *St Paul at Athens* and *The Blinding of Elymas*. The cartoons also provided settings as affirmation of the noble heritage of Paul and Elymas.

The use of the orders on columns may be significant: the plain Doric signifies simplicity and restraint; Ionic scrolls suggest learning; and the highly carved Corinthian or Composite orders signify important figures or settings. In stage design, Classical architecture was used for tragedy; Gothic for comedy. Later inclusions of Classically-inspired buildings might signify nostalgia for the past or, in the 18th century, might advertise the fact that the learned patron had visited Classical sites on the Grand Tour.

lyre so beautifully that he would make birds and wild animals halt in their tracks. Artemis (in Roman myth, Diana) compared his playing to that of her brother, Apollo. Sailing from Italy, where he had amassed wealth, his ship was attacked. Arion begged to play a final melody and as soon as it was finished he jumped overboard. He rode ashore on the back of a dolphin which, with the ocean waves, had been charmed by his music. Dürer shows him in *Arion* with his harp on the back of curious-looking fish.

Aristotle

Aristotle (384–322BCE) was a Greek philosopher, scientist and pupil of Plato. He founded the Peripatetic School in Athens, named after his habit of walking up and down while teaching. He wrote on logic, physics,

ARGONAUTS, THE VOYAGE OF THE

The greatest exploits of the hero Jason, a prince of Iolcus in Thessaly, took place during his journey to the easternmost shore of the Black Sea to obtain the Golden Fleece of Colchis at the behest of his uncle, the usurper, King Pelias.

The fleece came from a magic flying ram. This ram had been sent by the god Hermes to help the children of King Athamas of Boeotia (another of Jason's uncles) when their step-mother had threatened their lives. One child, Helles, fell off the ram during their escape and drowned in the sea (since known as Hellespont, literally "Helle's Sea"). However, the other, Phrixus, managed to reach the shores of Colchis. Once there he sacrificed the ram to Zeus and donated its fleece to the king of Colchis, Aeëtes. The king kept the fleece under the watchful eye of an unsleeping dragon.

In order to attempt his voyage Jason ordered the construction of a ship, the *Argo*. Sometimes said to be the first ship ever built, the *Argo* was fashioned by the shipwright Argus with the help of either the goddess Hera or the goddess Athene. Its construction incorporated a bough from Zeus's prophetic oak tree at Dodona and it was fitted with fifty oars – one for each member of Jason's fifty crew.

Eventually, the *Argo* set sail and reached its first port of call, the island of Lemnos. Here the women had killed all their menfolk because they had taken concubines, claiming that their own women stank. The Argonauts were told that the Lemnian women had merely forced their men to flee, The visitors stayed for several months in order to repopulate the island. Jason was taken by the island's queen, Hypsipyle, who bore him twins. The Argonauts then sailed on to a land called

The Argonauts, with their protector, the goddess Athene (left), after a painted drinking vessel.

Cyzicus. They were well received by the king and Herakles cleared the land of marauding giants. However, the visit ended in tragedy because when the *Argo* put to sea again it was driven back to shore at night by a storm. The Cyzicans, believing they were under attack from pirates, assailed the ship and were unintentionally massacred by the Argonauts, who were also unaware of the identity of their attackers. When the truth was discovered Jason ordered funeral games in honour of his former hosts.

The land of the Bebryces was next on the *Argo*'s itinerary. It was ruled by a son of Poseidon, Amycus, who challenged strangers to box to the death, hurling any who refused over a cliff. Polydeuces accepted the challenge and killed Amycus.

The Argonauts sailed on. Near the Bosphorus they encountered Phineus, an old and blind king who was eternally plagued by Harpies, bird-like monsters with the faces of hags, which snatched his food and defecated on it. Calais and Zetes saw off the monstrous creatures and, in gratitude, Phineus gave Jason valuable guidance for the onward journey.

However, the route to Colchis was barred by the Symplegades, two huge moving rocks which crashed together like cymbals, allowing no vessel to pass safely. Phineus advised the Argonauts to send a dove on ahead: if it succeeded in passing through the rocks, so would they. The dove negotiated the Symplegades safely except for the loss of a tail feather. The *Argo* proceeded and, with the help of Athene and Hera, sailed through the rocks without danger, but lost its helmsman, Tiphys. Thereafter, the rocks became stationary for ever.

Eventually, the expedition reached Colchis, the land of the Golden Fleece. King Aeëtes said that

Map of the Voyage of the Argonauts

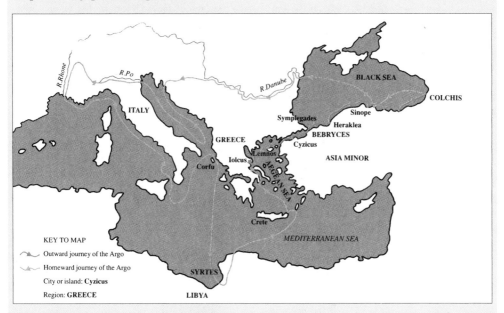

The map illustrates the voyage of the Argo and her crew, showing the most important stopping points, according to the most famous account of the epic journey, the Argonautica, which was written c.3rd century BCE by the poet Apollonius of Rhodes.

he would hand the fleece over if Jason would fulfil certain tasks: yoke the king's bronze-footed, fire-breathing bulls; use them to plough a field; sow the teeth of a dragon; and kill the giants who would spring from the planted teeth. The gods caused Medea, the sorceress daughter of Aeëtes, to fall in love with Jason. She gave him a magic potion so that he was able to succeed in the tasks.

However, Aeëtes refused to hand over the fleece, so Medea bewitched the dragon that guarded it and Jason seized his prize. The Argonauts and Medea fled from Colchis with Aeëtes and his entourage in pursuit. In order to delay their pursuers, Medea murdered her brother, Apsyrtus, and dismembered his corpse, hurling the pieces from the *Argo*. Aeëtes had to stop to retrieve the remains so that he could give his son a proper funeral. The Argonauts escaped.

In one of the many accounts of the *Argo*'s long journey home to Iolcus, a bronze giant, Talos, barred the Argonauts from landing on Crete. So

Medea charmed him to sleep and then killed him by pulling out a plug in his ankle, unstopping the only vein in his entire body. The *Argo* was also said to have sailed up the Danube and to have become stranded on the sandbanks of Libya, forcing the crew to carry the vessel overland on their backs for twelve days. Before they finally returned to Iolcus, Jason and Medea visited her aunt, the witch Circe (who also appears in *The Odyssey*), to be ritually purified for the murder of Apsyrtus.

The *Argo* ended up in Corinth. It is said that Jason was killed when he sat beneath its rotting hulk and a piece of the ship fell off and hit him. In some accounts the gods lifted the ship to the sky, where it became the constellation Argo Navis.

the soul, the heavens, animals, metaphysics, poetics, rhetoric, politics and ethics. He was the great sage of reason and Raphael gave him place of honour alongside Plato in his fresco *The School of Athens* (Stanza della Segnatura, Vatican, Rome).

The tutor of Alexander the Great, a medieval legend relates how he expounded that women were the downfall of men and tried to persuade Alexander to abandon his favourite courtesan, Campaspe (Phyllis in some accounts). In revenge, Campaspe charmed the old philosopher. To prove his love, she insisted that Aristotle allow her to ride on his back, and Alexander saw how a woman could undo the wisest of men. The subject was often painted on domestic furniture along with related themes, such as Samson and Delilah.

Ark

A symbol of salvation, redemption, conservation, sanctuary, regeneration. The story of a vessel preserving the continuity of life from floodwaters is found in the mythology of many peoples all around the world. Especially noteworthy is the Mesopotamian *Epic of Gilgamesh*, the world's most

A detail from a medieval fresco of Noah's Ark in the church of St.-Savin-sur-Gartempe, France.

ancient work of literature, which has a flood story strongly anticipating that of Noah in the Bible. Judeo-Christian ark symbolism is probably the richest. The ark can stand for the Church (carrying saints and sinners), for Mary bearing her son, or for Christ as Redeemer. The Israelite Ark of the Covenant, a chest of gilded acacia, symbolized the pledge of divine protection.

Arm

A symbol of instrumental, protective or judgmental force, representing sovereign power in Egyptian, Hindu and Buddhist iconography, and the power of God in the Christian Trinity. Omnipotent gods often have several arms each carrying a symbol of their various functions. To the Bambara of West Africa, the forearm is a symbol of the spirit, a link between humanity and God. The most universal symbolic gesture of the arm is the raising of both arms in submission, to a god or an earthly power. In the early church the gesture, known as *orans* (praying) was a common gesture of prayer. In Egypt, raised arms formed the hieroglyph for *ka* (soul).

Armour

Armour is used in art to identify warriors. The most notable warriors in Classical mythology are Ares (in Roman myth, Mars), god of war, his female counterpart Bellona (War), and Athene (Minerva). Armour and weapons litter the forge of Hephaistos (Vulcan). Personifications of Peace and Victory may be shown over a pile of armour, and the theme of love triumphant may be represented by a *putto* standing on armour and weapons or, with or without Aphrodite (Venus), near a sleeping warrior. Fortitude wears armour, as does Europe because of her skill in war.

Several Christian saints wear armour, among them the Archangel Michael and Saints George and Liberale. The Roman soldiers and sometimes Pilate tend to be clad in armour in scenes of the Passion.

Because of the nature of epic drama and poetry there have been numerous warrior heroes and anti-heroes from the Trojan War to Don Quixote. In 15th-century Italy a popular topic was the value of a career dedicated to arms or letters. The ideal was a combination of the two, hence Berruguete portrays Federigo da Montefeltro, Duke of Urbino, dressed in armour, sitting reading a book.

Arrow

In Greek mythology, Eros (the Roman Cupid) had two kinds of arrow. The one "that kindles love is golden and shining, sharp-tipped; but that which puts it to flight is blunt, its shaft tipped with lead".[1] He was sent by the gods to play havoc among their companions and among mortals.

A bow and arrow is also the attribute of Apollo and of Artemis (Diana). At the beginning of Homer's *Iliad*, Apollo's arrows rain down on the Greek camp bringing death and disease. The ancient belief that his arrows brought the plague may have had some influence on the legend of St Sebastian. In Christian iconography arrows killed the martyrs Christina and Ursula, but they failed to kill Sebastian, who recovered from his wounds. He was therefore a popular saint to invoke against the plague; in Renaissance Italy, Sebastian was frequently painted bristling with arrows.

An angel pierced the heart of St Theresa of Avila with an arrow of divine love that gave her both intense pain and ecstasy, famously represented by Bernini's sculpture *The Ecstasy of St Theresa* (1645–52).

In Islam, arrows can stand for the wrath of Allah. Bundled or broken (as in Native American symbolism), they represent peace. In shamanistic cultures, feathered arrows may be an ascension symbol.

Artemis

The Greek goddess of hunting and childbirth, called Diana by the Romans. One of the twelve Olympian deities, she was the beautiful daughter of Zeus and the Titan Leto (Jupiter and Latona) and twin sister of the god Apollo. Artemis was a virgin and fiercely protective of her chastity and that of her companions. Her wrath was notorious, and myths which illustrate her anger include those of Actaeon, Callisto, Iphigeneia, Niobe and Orion.

Artemis was usually depicted as an athletic young woman archer in hunting garb, sometimes accompanied by nymphs and animals, which may include a bear (an allusion to her nymph Callisto, who was turned into a bear). Although she hunted and killed animals, Artemis was also the divine protector of young creatures.

As the goddess of childbirth, Artemis protected women when they were in labour, but she also brought them death and sickness. Many of her numerous cults were connected with important female times of transition, such as birth, puberty, motherhood and death. She was linked with the moon goddess Selene, and a crescent moon is one of her attributes.

Arrow: *see* Bow; Feathers; Lightning; PEACE; Sun

Artemis: *see* Actaeon; Alcestis; Apollo; Callisto; Iphigeneia; Leto; Niobe; Orion; ZEUS, THE CONSORTS OF

The goddess Artemis.

Artemisia:
[1] Pliny the Elder, *Natural History XXXVI:30–32*

Arthur: *see* Finn; Grail, The; Merlin

As a symbol of chastity, Artemis or Diana may be paired with Aphrodite (Venus) or Eros (Cupid), who represent sensual love. She may also carry a shield to fend off Cupid's arrows. The many breasts of Artemis of Ephesus in Asia Minor (Efes, Turkey) emphasized her fertility.

Artemisia

Artemisia, queen of Caria in Asia Minor, built the Mausoleum, a large tomb for her husband Mausolus, at Halicarnassus *c*.353BCE. It was one of the Seven Wonders of the ancient world.[1] In *Artemisia Building the Mausoleum*, Simon Vouet shows her studying an architect's drawing.

Arthur

A king or military leader of the ancient Britons, a figure of myth, legend, folklore, literature and (most tenuously) history. Hard facts about any real Arthur are lacking. His name is probably derived from Artorius, a well-known Roman clan name recorded in Britain in the 2nd century CE. In one of the earliest extant references to him, in the *Historia Britonum (History of the Britons* (c.830CE) by the Welshman Nennius, Arthur is a British chieftain fighting Saxon invaders of post-Roman Britain. According to Nennius and later writers, Arthur fought at Mount Badon (*c*.500CE), the undiscovered site of a great British victory over the Saxons.

Most Arthurian tales place Arthur in a context of myth and folklore. In general he fights monstrous adversaries, giants or magic animals. Some 12th-century texts describe him as the ruler of a subterranean kingdom and later traditions present Arthur himself

as a giant. The familiar Arthurian characters and themes, such as the knights of the Round Table and the quest for the Holy Grail, are part of a European literary tradition that began with the account of Arthur in the *Historia Regum Britanniae (History of the Kings of Britain)* by the scholar Geoffrey of Monmouth (*c*.1150). French, English, Welsh and Breton romances extended the story, which soon acquired Europe-wide popularity. The Arthurian legends were collected and edited by many sources, including Thomas Malory (died 1471) in *Le Morte d'Arthur* and Chrétien de Troyes.

In the chivalric romances, Arthur became king of Britain by removing the invincible sword Excalibur from a stone. However, he later lost Excalibur, and it was returned to him by the Lady of the Lake. Arthur gathered the best knights in the land to his Round Table at his court in Camelot. His court included his nephew Gawain, his magician and counsellor Merlin, his half-sister the enchantress Morgan le Fay, and his wife Queen Guinevere. The quest of the Holy Grail dispersed the knights and proved the valour of Galahad and Percival. Arthur's downfall came as a result of the love between Guinevere and Lancelot. He died from a fatal wound inflicted by his enemy (and his son in some accounts), Mordred.

The Celtic story of Tristan and Iseult or Isolde is also connected with Arthur in that Tristan was included among the knights of the Round Table. Tristan was sent to Ireland by his uncle, King Mark of Cornwall, to escort his uncle's betrothed, Iseult, to Cornwall. Aboard ship the two unwittingly drank a magic potion intended

King Arthur, from a medieval illustration.

for Mark and Iseult and fell eternally in love, with tragic consequences.

The Arthurian legends embody the chivalric qualities that appealed to English medieval revivalist painters such as William Morris and Dante Gabriel Rossetti in the 19th century.

Ascanius

In Roman myth, as embodied in Virgil's *Aeneid*, Ascanius was the son of Aeneas and his first wife Creusa, and the grandson of Anchises and Venus (Aphrodite). Ascanius established the town of Alba Longa in Latium, and was the ancestor of Romulus and Remus, the founders of Rome.

Asgard

The realm of the gods in ancient Norse cosmology. Two races of deities, the Aesir (sky gods) and Vanir (earth gods, who also had their own realm, Vanaheim, beneath the earth) were said to dwell in Asgard, which was ruled by the god Odin.

Asgard was apparently located in the heavens. A bridge, Bifrost – said to be a rainbow or the Milky Way – connected it with the earth. Bifrost was guarded by the god Heimdall against the giants who were the gods' enemies. Their realm, Jotunheim, was beneath Asgard but could be reached from it by a long, dangerous route overland. A similar route linked Asgard with the realm of the dead ruled by Hel, the daughter of the trickster Loki.

Within the walls of Asgard the gods built fine halls, including Valhalla, the Hall of the Slain, to which Odin summoned kings and heroes who had fallen in battle. They spent their time feasting and fighting, always ready to defend Asgard

against attack. However, Asgard was destroyed at the apocalyptic battle of Ragnarok.

Ash

The cosmic tree Yggdrasil of Norse myth, linking earth, heaven and underworld and symbolizing fecundity, the union of opposites; invincibility; and the continuity of life. In Greek myth, the ash embodies strength (and is therefore sacred to Zeus), but in Baltic folklore the tree is an emblem of the simpleton, perhaps because its leaves appear late and are shed quickly.

Ashera

A Canaanite (Ugaritic) fertility goddess, consort of the supreme god El and mother of the Canaanite pantheon. Also called Astarte, she is said to be related to the Mesopotamian Ishtar or Inanna.

Ashes

A symbol of extinction, bereavement, renunciation, penitence and, in some cultures, rebirth (as in the myth of the Phoenix being reborn from the ashes of its predecessor). Smearing the body with ash in some African tribal rites of passage also has this meaning. In Jewish and Arab tradition, ashes are a mark of mourning. Indian *yogi*s daub themselves with ashes to signify their renunciation of earthly vanities.

Asklepios

The Greek demi-god of medicine, known to the Romans as Aesculapius. Asklepios was the son of the god Apollo and the princess Coronis. Informed by a raven of the infidelity of Coronis, Apollo flew into a jealous rage and shot her with his deadly arrow. As she died he learned that she

The asphodel flower,
which was associated
with the underworld
in Greek and Roman
mythology.

was about to bear his child. Apollo turned his anger on the raven, who became black for ever more, and snatched the child from his mother's womb as she lay on her funeral pyre.

The wise Centaur Chiron taught Asklepios the arts of healing.[1] He became so skilled that he was able to resurrect the dead. However, Hades, the ruler of the underworld, feared losing his subjects and complained to Zeus about the demi-god. Zeus killed Asklepios with a thunderbolt. Then, in revenge, Apollo slew the Cyclopes, makers of Zeus's thunderbolts.

In 293BCE, during a plague in Rome, Asklepios was adopted into the Roman pantheon on the instructions of an oracle. It is said that he arrived disguised as a snake and resumed his divine appearance on the Tiber Island. The plague ceased. The caduceus, a serpent twined around a staff, is his attribute.[2]

Asp *see* **Cobra**

Asphodel
A symbol of mourning, the asphodel is a lily of pallid hue that was associated with the Greek underworld, and with its queen, Persephone (the Roman Proserpina). Its roots were once believed to cure snakebite.

Ass
A well-entrenched symbol of foolishness, sloth, obstinacy and stupidity, but traditionally of more varying significance. In the Bible, asses carry wood for the burnt offering in the story of the Sacrifice of Isaac. The prophet Balaam, sent to curse the Israelites, was unable to see an angel of the Lord barring his way. However, his ass saw the angel and did not pro-

ceed, whereupon Balaam beat it furiously. The beast was given the power of speech, Balaam's eyes were opened and he was converted.[1] The traditional presence of the humble ox and ass in Nativity scenes derives not from the New Testament but but from a passage in Isaiah: "the ox knoweth his owner, and the ass his master's crib".[2] An ass bears the Virgin on the Flight into Egypt and was chosen by Christ for his entry into Jerusalem, both in fulfilment of a prophecy and to signify the virtue of meekness: in Christian thought it thus usually stands for humility, patience and poverty.

In contrast, asses are associated with lust or comical stupidity in Classical myth. On account of its hoarse braying, the ass was considered to be tone-deaf. Apollo gave Midas ass's ears in punishment for preferring Pan's music to his own. *The Golden Ass* or *Metamorphoses* of Apuleius (2nd century CE), tells the story of young Lucian, who is turned into an ass by the maid of a sorceress. He is ill-treated until he eats roses that transform him back into human form.

The drunken Silenus, follower of Dionysos (Bacchus), rides an ass, as does Sancho Panza, Don Quixote's squire. Ass's ears are part of the jester's cap, and in a satire of love Bottom in Shakespeare's *A Midsummer Night's Dream* (c.1595) finds his head transformed into that of an ass .

Asses are sinister beasts in Egyptian and Indian myth, but in China white asses are the mounts of the immortals.

Astarte (1)
An ancient Syrian deity, the counterpart of the Mesopotamian goddess called Inanna or Ishtar. Astarte was identified with Aphrodite (Venus).

Rossetti's *Astarte* represents the mysterious goddess of love whose realm lay between the sun and the moon.

Astarte (2)

An Egyptian warrior goddess derived from Astarte (1). She was said by the Egyptians to be the daughter of the sun god or of the creator god Ptah. Astarte was a wife of the god Seth.

Astraea

Astraea lived happily in the Age of Gold but later, in the Ages of Bronze and Iron, could not endure human wickedness and became the "Starry Maid", the constellation Virgo. She represents innocence and justice, and is depicted (as on the criminal courts of the Old Bailey, London) wielding a sword of truth and scales of justice.

Asura

An opponent of the great Hindu gods or Devas. In earlier (Vedic) mythology "Asura" appears to mean "mighty" or "lord" and could be applied interchangeably with Deva to refer to the same figure, such as the god Varuna. In later Hinduism "Asura" acquired the sense of anti-god or demon, as in the myth of the churning of the ocean, when the Devas and Asuras are clearly differentiated. In Buddhism the Asuras are "Jealous Gods", higher beings than humans but below the Devas, whom they envy.

Ataentsic

The first woman and the ancestor of the human race, according to Iroquois and Huron mythology. Ataentsic was born in the sky world. When she was older, she married a great chief and became pregnant. The chief convinced himself, wrongly, that the father was a dragon. When Ataentsic bore to a baby girl, "Breath of Wind", the chief hurled mother and daughter through a hole in the sky.

Ataentsic fell towards the landless waters which then covered this world. The animals who lived in the waters tried to form earth for her to land on. The muskrat succeeded in bringing up some mud from the depths. He placed it on the back of the turtle and it grew at once into the dry land. Supported by the water birds, Ataentsic came safely to earth.

Atalanta

A huntress of Greek myth, the daughter of Iasus or Schoenus and Clymene. When Atalanta was born her father was disappointed at not having a son and abandoned her to die. However, she was discovered by a band of hunters who raised her as their own child. Atalanta became renowned for her ability to hunt and run faster than any other mortal. An Aetolian prince, Meleager, recruited her to join the hunt for a monstrous boar which plagued his town, Calydon. After the boar was killed, Meleager (who had fallen in love with Atalanta) awarded the huntress its pelt because she had drawn first blood.

Atalanta's fame spread and she was reunited with her father, who decided that she should find a husband. Apollo warned her that her husband would be her downfall,[1] so Atalanta swore that she would marry only the man who could beat her in a race – and would kill anyone she defeated.

A prince named Milanion (or Hippomenes in some accounts) took up the challenge. The goddess Aphrodite gave him three golden apples, which he dropped during the race. As Guido

Astarte (2): *see* Astarte (1); Ennead, The; Horus; Ishtar; Ptah; Seth

Astraea: *see* Ages of the World

Asura: *see* Ahura Mazdah; Churning of the Ocean, The

Ataentsic: *see* Earth Diver

Atalanta: *see* Argonauts, The; Meleager
[1] Ovid, *Met X:560–707*

Atalanta hunting with bow and arrow; after a mosaic.

The Greek goddess Athene, based on a marble statue of the 4th century BCE.

Reni shows in *Atalanta and Hippomenes*, Atalanta could not resist stopping to pick up the apples, with the result that she lost the race and married Milanion. However, he failed to thank Aphrodite and her sympathy turned to anger. She induced the couple to defile a sacred spot and had them turned into lions that drew the chariot of the goddess Cybele.

Atalanta is usually the only woman listed among the Argonauts.

Aten

In ancient Egypt, the *aten* was the disc of the sun seen in the sky, through which the light of the sun god shone. In the 18th Dynasty, the *aten* came to be venerated as a god in its own right, and the pharaoh Akhenaten (*c.*1352– *c.*1336BCE) actively promoted Aten as the supreme deity. This religious revolution was shortlived; Amun and other traditional deities were restored to prominence after Akhenaten's death.

Athene

The Greek goddess of intellect, kings and heroes, one of the principal Olympian deities, known to the Romans as Minerva. Athene was the daughter of Zeus (Jupiter) and the Titan Metis ("Cunning Intelligence"). A prophecy had claimed that Metis would bear a goddess equal to Zeus in wisdom, so the god devoured his wife in an attempt to prevent the birth. However, one day Zeus had a raging headache and asked the craftsman god Hephaistos to split his head open with an axe. Hephaistos did so and Athene emerged, fully formed and armed, from her father's head. True to the prophecy, Athene indeed rivalled Zeus in wisdom and

often gave him counsel. Her symbol was the owl, believed to be the wisest of all birds. She was a patron of crafts and was credited with inventing the olive tree, the potter's wheel and the flute.

Athene was also a martial figure, the protector of heroes such as Odysseus, Herakles, Jason and Perseus. Perseus presented the goddess with the head of the Gorgon Medusa, which she wore on her *aegis* (breastplate).

Athene contended with the sea god Poseidon (Neptune) for the patronage of Athens, the city that bears her name and which was the centre of her cult. The Athenians offered the protectorship of the city as the prize for the best invention either deity could come up with. Poseidon produced only a saltwater spring (or in some accounts a horse), but Athene won the contest by producing the first olive tree, a source of oil for lighting, cooking and perfume, and a symbol of peace. Athene may be depicted with an olive tree or branch, which may also decorate her dress, as in Botticelli's *Minerva and the Centaur* (*c.*1480, Uffizi, Florence).

Like Artemis, Athene was an unmarried virgin goddess. Among her titles were Parthenos ("Virgin"), hence the name of her most famous temple, the Parthenon in Athens.

Atlantis

Greek myth told of a great island civilization beyond the Pillars of Herakles (Straits of Gibraltar) that had been suddenly and catastrophically submerged. The myth may ultimately derive from accounts of the destruction of the Mediterranean island of Santorini in a huge volcanic eruption *c.*1400BCE. Atlantis symbolizes an ideal civilization, a lost Utopia.

Atlas

One of the Titans of Greek myth, the son of Iapetus and the sea nymph Clymene and the brother of Prometheus. Following the defeat of the Titans by the Olympians, Atlas was banished by Zeus to the western edge of the world and condemned to hold up the heavens (or in some accounts the whole world) on his shoulders for ever.

Later, Atlas refused hospitality to the hero Perseus, who produced the Gorgon Medusa's head from his bag and turned the Titan to stone[1] as the Atlas mountains in northwest Africa (modern Morocco). The Atlantic Ocean is also said to be named after him. Atlas also features in Herakles' quest for the apples of the Hesperides.

A book of maps is called an "atlas" because a famous volume of maps by Gerard Mercator (published in 1595 by his son Rumold) had an engraving of Atlas as the frontispiece.

A detail from a bowl showing Atlas (left) bearing the heavens as an eagle torments his brother Prometheus.

Atrahasis

In Mesopotamian myth, a king of Shurupak on the Euphrates river. According to the epic of Atrahasis, the human race was created to serve the gods and relieve them of the necessity of labour. But within twelve hundred years the noise that the people made disturbed the gods. The god Enlil decided to reduce their numbers by sending a plague and then a series of droughts. But the wise god Enki always warned King Atrahasis beforehand and told him what precautions to take. Finally, Enlil told the gods to send a great flood to wipe out humanity, binding the other deities to an oath of secrecy. Enki got around the oath by warning not the king directly but the reed hut in which he lived. Atrahasis built a boat in which he, his family and several animals took refuge when the flood struck.

Every other human being perished in the inundation and the gods soon began to miss the benefits of their labour. After seven days the flood subsided and Atrahasis reappeared to offer a sacrifice to the gods. Enlil was furious that he had once again survived but finally accepted that the human race should continue. Atrahasis was granted eternal life and a place among the gods. He has been identified with Utnapishtim in the Akkadian version of the epic of Gilgamesh.

Atreus

A king of Argos or Mycenae in Greece and a son of Pelops and Hippodamia. Atreus seized the throne of Argos from his brother, Thyestes. He was the father of Agamemnon and Menelaus and the uncle of Aegisthus, who murdered him.

Attila the Hun

Attila (*c*.406–453CE), king of the Huns, at one time ruled most of the land between the Rhine and the Caspian Sea. When Rome failed to pay trib-

Atlas: *see* Giants;
HERAKLES, THE
LABOURS OF; Hesperides,
The; OLYMPIANS, THE;
Pleiades, The; Prometheus;
TITAN
[1] Ovid, *Met IV:621–663*

Atrahasis: *see* Enki; Enlil;
Utnapishtim; Ziusudra

Atreus: *see* Aegisthus;
Agamemnon; Menelaus;
PELOPS, THE CURSE OF
THE HOUSE OF; Thyestes

ute he invaded Gaul, but in 452CE abandoned his efforts to capture Rome itself. Raphael's *Repulse of Attila* (Stanza del Eliodoro, Vatican, Rome) shows Saints Peter and Paul appearing in the sky to halt the invasion.

Attis

In Greek mythology,[1] Attis was driven mad by love, so castrated himself and died; violets were thought to have sprung from the blood of his wound.

Atum

One of the four principal creator deities of Egypt (the others being Amun, Khnum and Ptah). Atum, whose cult centre was at Heliopolis, first emerged from the primeval chaos in the form of a serpent, but was usually represented in human form. Like other creator deities, the god represented a totality which contained both male and female. He caused the first division into male and female when he put his semen in his mouth and sneezed or spat it out, creating the first divine couple, Shu and Tefnut.

As Ra-Atum, the god represented the evening sun, which descended into the Duat, or underworld, every night. As the god passed through the underworld on his barque, he confronted hosts of demons, which were destroyed by Atum and his myriad followers, headed by the fierce Seth. In the depths of the Duat, Atum and Osiris, the ruler of the underworld, became fused as one mighty deity, before the sun was reborn at dawn in the earthly realm.

Augustine, Saint

Augustine (354–430CE) is one of the four Latin Fathers of the Church, along with Ambrose, Jerome and Gregory the Great. He studied law and taught rhetoric in Rome and Milan. His mother, St Monica, converted him to Christianity and St Ambrose, bishop of Milan, baptized him. He became bishop of Hippo in his native Numidia (Algeria), where he remained for the rest of his life and formed a loose monastic community, dying of fever during a siege by the Vandals.

Augustine advocated that Christianity could be served by using the best of Classical culture. He was a prolific writer, whose *Confessions* and *The City of God* were highly influential. In the church dedicated to him in San Gimignano, Italy, Benozzo Gozzoli frescoed scenes from his life, emphasizing his scholarly nature. A predella panel by Botticelli (Uffizi, Florence) illustrates the legend that Augustine was walking by the sea, meditating on the Trinity, when he came across a boy trying to fill a hole in the sand with water using a shell. When Augustine commented that it was impossible, the child replied, "No more than for the human mind to comprehend the mysteries on which you are meditating".

Augustine often appears as a scholar reading and teaching; as a bishop; or in the black habit of the Augustinian monastic order, founded in the 11th century and based on his teachings. He may have a flaming heart, sometimes pierced by an arrow.

Augustus

Gaius Julius Caesar Octavianus (Octavian, 63BCE–14CE) was the first emperor of Rome and adopted the title Augustus ("Venerable"), in 27BCE. He gave his name to the Augustan Age, one of outstanding literary achievement. According to legend, prior to the birth of Christ, the Tiburtine Sibyl told Augustus that a Son of God would be born.

Aureole *see* **Halo**

Aurochs
An extinct wild ox of Europe and the Near East. In Assyrian and Sumerian iconography it symbolizes the power of the great god Enlil.

Aurora *see* **Eos**

Avalokiteshvara
"The Lord Who Looks Down", the bodhisattva of supreme compassion. Avalokiteshvara is especially revered by Buddhists in Tibet, where he is known as Chenrezi and is believed to be incarnate as the Dalai Lama. Avalokiteshvara is sometimes said to have one thousand arms, symbolizing his endless capacity to dispense mercy. From his tears of compassion arose the goddess Tara, Tibet's most popular female bodhisattva.

Axe
A widespread symbol of power and authority, the axe is found in Minoan, Greek, Hindu, Roman, Celtic, Norse, African and Oceanic symbolism, often linked with ancient sun and storm gods, such as Zeus and Agni, the Indian god of fire. Its flashing, thudding, spark-striking fall explains much of its symbolic association with fire and the thunderbolt; it was used directly to invoke thunder and rain in West Africa. Axes were used to split the skulls of sacrificial oxen in the Near East, and they are an attribute of several martyred Christian saints, notably Matthew.

An axe is also the attribute of warriors, and represents the forceful solving of a problem. It symbolizes the union of two families in Chinese marriages; and cures the headache of Zeus in the Greek myth in which Athene springs from a cleft in his head.

The double-headed axe on Minoan artefacts may invoke divine protection. Its dual, half-moon curves may be a lunar symbol or may stand for the reconciliation of opposites.

Axis
A linear symbol of the cosmic centre in nearly all cosmologies of the ancient world – the *axis mundi* (world axis), the spine or spindle around which everything rotates. The world axis provided shamans and spirits with a means of moving between different worlds – underworld, earth and heavens. Symbols of the axis include trees (such as the Norse Yggdrasil), sacred mountains, rods and columns.

Aztlan
The mythic place of origin of the Aztecs, whose name means "People of Aztlan". According to Aztec myth, the god Huitzilopochtli led the Aztecs to a new homeland in central Mexico.

The departure from Aztlan, redrawn from a 16th-century Aztec flint.

Aurochs: *see* ANIMALS: Ox

Avalokiteshvara: *see* Bodhisattva; Buddha; Guanyin; Kannon

Axe: *see* Fire, Flame; Moon; Thunder

Axis: *see* Cave; Mountain; Omphalos; Pillar; Tree

Aztlan: *see* Huitzilopochtli

The ba, *after a wooden
statuette of* c.*330 BCE.*

Ba

An Egyptian symbol for the soul, usually depicted as a bird with the head of the deceased. The *ba*, it was believed, could flit between the world of the dead and the living.

Baal

"Lord", the Ugaritic (Canaanite) storm and fertility god, identified with the Babylonian weather god Hadad. The young Baal is the central figure of the most important cycle of myths, probably intended to mark the end of the agricultural year and the coming of the autumn rains. The primeval monster Yam ("Sea"), claimed royal power on earth. Baal killed Yam in battle and proclaimed himself king. In defeating Yam, who represented the forces of chaos, Baal showed that it was he who controlled the flow of water from the heavens. A great banquet was held in honour of Baal's victory. There then followed a great massacre of the god's worshippers by the warlike goddess Anath, Baal's sister. Baal sought to placate Anath by

revealing to her the secret of the lightning that heralded life-giving storms and the end of drought.

Baal built a palace and challenged the primeval earth monster, Mot, the lord of death, to resist his power. Their struggle was inconclusive, as death can never be vanquished, not even by a god.

Baba Iaga

A witch or ogress, the best known figure in Slav folk myth. The Baba Iaga is described as a scrawny crone who travels in a mortar, propelling herself along with a pestle and erasing her tracks with a broomstick. However, she is more often encountered in her hut, which stands on chicken legs in a dense forest often said to lie beyond a fiery river. The witch fills the entire hut, her legs straddling its single room from corner to corner and her long nose touching the ceiling. Around the hut is a fence of bones.

The Baba Iaga was said to possess power over birds and beasts. As well as creatures, day and night are said to obey her commands. It has been sug-

Baba Iaga waving a pestle and riding a pig, from an 18th-century woodcut.

gested that she may originally have been a powerful (but not necessarily malign) goddess of the Slav Other World, the land of the dead, which was reached after a journey across a fiery river and through a thick forest.

Babel, The Tower of
The Bible states that humanity originally shared a common language. But people tried to build a tower to reach the heavens and God stopped this presumptuous project by making them speak in many tongues so that they might not understand each other.[1] He then scattered the people abroad, so the tower was left unfinished, a symbol of human folly.

Baboon *see* **Ape; Thoth**

Bacab
One of four wind gods who, according to Mayan cosmology, supported the upper world of the heavens.

Bacchus *see* **Dionysos**

Badger
In Japan, an artful dodger with a streak of malice, the hero of many folk stories, sometimes shown outside restaurants selfishly pot-bellied. Its solitary, secretive habits have also suggested slyness in European folklore.

Baladeva *see* **Balarama**

Balar
A leader of the Fomorians, a monstrous race of brigands who, in Irish myth, were the descendants of Ham, the cursed son of Noah. Known as Balar of the Evil Eye, he possessed a single huge eye with a venomous glance that meant instant death. Balar was killed at the Second Battle of Magh Tuiredh (Moytirra) when his grandson Lugh cast a slingshot at the eye, striking it with such force that it was propelled through Balar's head and into the view of his own troops, who all fell dead at the sight of it.

Balarama
The elder brother of the god Krishna. In Hindu myth, Balarama grew up with his brother among cowherds, and helped in his adventures, such as killing the serpent Kaliya and the evil King Kamsa. In Jainism, Balarama is known as Baladeva, and is one of a series of divine heroes who play a prominent role in Jain cosmology.

Balder
The favourite son of the Norse god Odin and his wife Frigg. Frigg tried to protect Balder by asking every living thing and everything made of metal, wood and stone to swear never to harm her son. However, the mistletoe

Babel, The Tower of:
[1] *Genesis 11:1–9*

Badger: *see* ANIMALS

Balar: *see* Fomorian; Lugh; Magh Tuiredh, The Battles of; Tuatha Dé Danann, The

Balarama: *see* Krishna; Shalakapurusha

Balder: *see* Frigg; Hel; Loki; Odin; Ragnarok

Ball

had not sworn the oath. The trickster Loki made it into a dart and gave it to the blind god Hother, who threw it at Balder and killed him.

The deities mourned deeply for Balder, whose wife, Nanna, died of grief. At Frigg's request Balder's brother Hermod rode to the land of the dead to free Balder. Hel, the queen of the dead, said that only the weeping of every person and thing in the world would secure his release. Hermod returned to the gods and messengers were at once dispatched all over the world asking everything to show its love for Balder by weeping. However, a female giant – believed to be Loki in disguise – refused to weep and Balder was unable to return from Hel.

Ball

Mesoamerican temples had elaborate courts for a violent and ritualistic "ball game". This was sometimes played with the head of the loser or of a sacrificial victim.

Bamboo

An Oriental symbol of resilience, longevity, happiness and spiritual truth – one of the three auspicious plants of winter. Bamboo is an attribute of the Chinese bodhisattva Guanyin, goddess of mercy, and its ringed stem is associated with the steps to enlightenment – hence it can also symbolize the Buddha. In South America, where bamboo was important as a cutting tool, blowpipe and instrument of sacred music, some peoples revered tall species of bamboo as Trees of Life. Bamboo was used in Africa for ritual circumcision.

Banner

An emblem of a group or its leader. The multiple banners of Japanese warriors invoked victory, whereas Daoist banners symbolize the protective help of spirits or gods of the elements. A fluttering banner is the attribute of Vayu, the Hindu god of air and wind. A banner of a red cross on a white field features in Christian art as a symbol of the Resurrection.

Bannik

The "bath being", a malign spirit of Slav folk myth. It is said to inhabit bathhouses, traditionally places of divination and magic. Belief in the *bannik* is said to persist to this day in remoter parts of Russia.

Banyan

The sacred tree of India, a probable model for the symbolism of the inverted Cosmic Tree in that it has an aerial root. Temples were sometimes built into the main trunks.

Baptism

A rite of purification and regeneration involving water. Its sacred use is ancient and widespread, sometimes as a rite of initiation for the living or the dead. Originating in the practice of John the Baptist, Christian baptism symbolizes entry into the community of the Church. However, many Protestant churches, notably the Baptists, practice adult baptism, a rite symbolizing the reaffirmation of faith.

Barbara, Saint

According to legend,[1] the beautiful Barbara (dates unknown) was locked in a tower by her pagan father to keep her from her many suitors. However, she managed to admit a Christian priest disguised as a doctor, and was converted. On discovering her new faith, her father handed her over to the authorities, who ordered him to cut off her head, but he was struck dead by lightning before he could behead her. It became the custom to invoke Barbara against sudden death. She is depicted as a young, elegant maiden and her attribute is a tower, as in Memling's *Donne Triptych*.

Bare Feet

Christ and his disciples are often depicted barefoot, referring to his command to "carry neither purse, nor scrip, nor shoes".[1] Following his example, some religious orders are barefoot (although most wear sandals), notably the Discalced Carmelites founded in the 16th century by St Theresa. Pilgrims are often depicted barefoot as a sign of humility or poverty.

Barley

An ancient grain symbolizing fertility and life after death, especially in the Near East. Barley was associated in Egypt with the resurrection of the god Osiris, and in Greece with Demeter, the goddess of fecundity, and her abducted daughter Persephone.

Barnabas, Saint (Apostle)

The missionary companion of St Paul.[1] He was also a missionary in his native Cyprus, where he is considered Father of the Church and where he is said to have cured the sick. Tradition claims that Barnabas was either burned alive or stoned to death.

Barong *see* Rangda

Bartholomew, Saint (Apostle, Disciple)

Bartholomew is recorded as a disciple in the gospels but little is known of his life. Legend[1] claims that he preached, exorcized and baptized in India and in Armenia, where he refused to worship pagan gods and was flayed alive. His attribute of a flaying knife is shown, for example, by Giambattista Tiepolo (San Stae, Venice).

Basilisk or Cockatrice

A legendary terrifying monster with a cock's body and wings, a dragon's tail and a stare that could kill. Hatched by a toad from a serpent's egg laid by an aged cock on a dunghill, it became a personification of sins such as lust.

Basket

The biblical Moses and heroes of other cultures were found floating in baskets. A basket of flowers signifies hope and, in China, fruitful longevity. The Buddhist scriptures are divided into "Three Baskets" (*Tripitaka*) of discipline, basic teachings and higher doctrines. Three baskets of wisdom also appear in Maori mythology, brought from heaven by the god Tane.

Bastet

The cat-headed goddess of love, sex and fertility. Like the ferocious war goddess Sekhmet, Bastet was originally a lioness deity, but from *c.*900BCE she began to be represented as a cat, perhaps because of her gentler nature. She was sometimes depicted with kittens, which symbolized her role as a fertility deity.

Basuki

A great serpent of the underworld, according to Balinese cosmology.

Bat

Widely a symbol of fear and superstition, associated with death, night and, in Judeo-Christian tradition, idolatry or Satanism. Bats can also signify

The goddess Bastet, based on a bronze statuette.

madness, as in Goya's *The Sleep of Reason*. The bat is a powerful underworld divinity in Central American and Brazilian mythology. In China, "bat" is a homophone of "good luck".

Batara Guru

A creator god of Sumatran myth. One day Batara Guru sent a swallow down to the sea with a handful of soil to create dry land, upon which Batara Guru scattered many seeds. From these sprang all the different species of animals. Batara Guru then sent down a heroic incarnation of himself to defeat Naga Padoha, the serpent ruler of the underworld. The divine hero was rewarded with the hand of Batara's daughter. They became the parents of the first humans.

Batara Kala

The divine ruler of the underworld in Balinese cosmology. He rules jointly with the goddess Setesuyara. Batara Kala created light and Mother Earth.

Bathsheba

In the Bible, the beautiful Bathsheba was bathing when King David saw her as he walked on his roof. She was the wife of one of his officers, Uriah the Hittite, but David desired her and sent messengers to bring her to him. Consequently she conceived his child. David then instructed that Uriah be placed "in the forefront of the hottest battle", so that he was killed.[1] David married Bathsheba, but their child died in punishment for their sin. Their second child was Solomon. Painters usually depict Bathsheba bathing in various states of modesty. Jacopo Amigoni shows her responsive to the message brought to her by David's slave.

Bavo, Saint

A wealthy Netherlander, Bavo (*c*.589–654CE) led a dissolute life until middle age, when he gave all his goods to the poor, became a hermit, and lived in a hollow tree. The patron of Ghent, he may be shown as a hermit or nobleman, sometimes with a falcon.

Beads *see* Rosary

Bean

Fecundity, especially male, linked in Egyptian and Greco-Roman tradition with the souls of the dead and the promise of life to come. They were used as love charms in India, and were talismans in Japan where they were scattered in a house to ward off lightning and evil spirits. On Twelfth Night in Flanders a bean was hidden in a pie; the one who found it was proclaimed "bean king" or head of the table for the evening. This scene was painted by Jacob Jordaens in *The Bean King*.

Bear

A symbol of primitive brute force. The bear was an incarnation of the Norse god Odin, and the fierce Viking Berserker ("Bear-shirt") warriors wore bearskin tunics. In Greece, the cult followers of Artemis dressed as bears. The beast is linked with many other warlike divinities, including the Norse Thor and the Celtic Artio. To the Ainu of northern Japan, and to Native Americans, the bear is an ancestral figure, the closest relative of humans (bears can walk on two legs). It is also linked with resurrection symbolism, perhaps from its hibernation.

The bear is viewed as a dark power in Christian and Islamic traditions: cruel, lustful, vengeful, greedy – a representation of the sin of gluttony in Western art. The formless bear cub, "licked into shape" by its mother, became an image of the heathen needing the spiritual ministrations of the Church. Similarly, the bear is the alchemical symbol for the primary state of matter.

Beard

A symbol of dignity, sovereignty, virility, courage, wisdom – gods, kings, heroes and sages are often bearded. Egyptian rulers, including female ones, wore false beards as a mark of status.

BEASTS OF FABLE *see panel overleaf*

Beaver

The beaver's busy creativity has always made it a symbol of industry and, in Christianity, asceticism.

Bedawang

A cosmic turtle of Balinese cosmology, created through meditation by the cosmic serpent Antaboga. Upon Bedawang rested two coiled snakes, the foundations of the earth, and the Black Stone, the lid of the underworld.

Bee

Among the many qualities attributed to bee are diligence, organizational and technical skills, sociability, purity, chastity, cleanliness, spirituality, wisdom, courage, abstinence, sobriety, creativity, selflessness, eloquence ("honeyed" words) and illumination (from beeswax candles). The bee symbolized royalty in the ancient Near East and Greece, and in Egypt where, by tradition, it was born from the tears of the sun god Ra. In Hittite myth, a bee saved the world from drought by finding the lost son of the weather god. Honey is linked with ambrosia, the food of the gods.

The bee is an attribute of many gods. In Greek myth, Zeus was raised on milk and honey by the nymph Amalthea. Eros (Cupid) was stung by a bee while stealing a honeycomb, only to be told by an unsympathetic Aphrodite (Venus) that he inflicted far greater wounds himself. The bee is also associated with the mother goddess Cybele, Artemis (Diana), and the fertility goddess Demeter, whose priestesses at Eleusis were called "bees". Essene priests were also known as "bees", and Christian tradition describes a monastic community, and the Church itself, as a beehive.

Bees were linked with the sweet "honeyed" words of eloquence; the Athenian Bee and Attic Bee were titles conferred on Plato and Sophocles, and for the same reason a beehive is the attribute of Saints Ambrose and Bernard of Clairvaux.

The bee's honey and sting represented the sweetness and pains of Christ. The bee is a resurrection symbol on tombs, perhaps because of its winter dormancy. It also represented the Virgin Mary because it was thought to reproduce chastely.

A symbol of reincarnation, the bee is also an attribute of Hindu gods. A blue bee on the forehead represents Krishna; a bee on a lotus, Vishnu; a bee above a triangle, Shiva.

Beer

To the Celts, beer was a drink of rulers and warriors, and the beverage of the gods. In Egypt, it was the gift of Osiris. Maize beers in South America were used in rites of passage.

Beggar

An image of piety and otherworldliness in many Eastern traditions, espe-

Beard: *see* God; Hair; King; WISDOM

Beaver: *see* ANIMALS

Bedawang: *see* Antaboga; Basuki; Batara Kala

Bee: *see* Amalthea; Ambrose, Saint; Bernard, Saint; Blue; Candle; CHASTITY; Eros; Hive; Honey; Lotus; Soul; Triangle; Virginity; Woman

Beer: *see* Barley; Intoxication; Mead

Beggar: *see* Belisarius; Blind and Blindfold
Percy. *Reliques* 1.11.6

BEASTS OF FABLE

Imaginary beasts appear worldwide in myth and folklore, as symbols of supernatural power or simply as compelling projections of the human psyche. They have vividly provided us with images that would otherwise be hard to objectify.

Animal hybrids form the largest category of fabulous beasts. Among the most notable are the Basilisk, Chimera, Dragon, Griffin, Makara, Sphinx and Unicorn. In Egypt, the beast Amut, with a crocodile jaws, lion's mane and hippopotamus's body, devoured damned souls; like the Greek hellhound Cerberus, which had a mane of serpents and many heads, it personified the fearful uncertainties of death.

A Harpy, a foul-smelling hybrid of hag and vulture in Greek myth; after a woodcut.

In Greek myth the Hydra, a dragon-serpent with many heads, symbolizes the difficulty in conquering vices; each time one of its heads was chopped off, two grew back. Pegasus, the winged horse that carried the hero Bellerophon to victory over the Chimera, is an opposing image of spirit over matter.

The most famous animal-human hybrids, like the classical horse-man Centaur, the bull–man Minotaur and the satyrs, represent the animal-spiritual duality of human nature. The fish-tailed merman (the Triton is one of these) is a marine version of the Centaur, as is the mermaid who has a gentler, wishful image in the folklore of lonely sailors. The mermaids' more dangerous mytho-logical counterparts are the Sirens, who tempt men to destruction.

The Lamia is the snake-bodied devourer of other women's children, a Greek metaphor for jealousy. The Gorgons (with hair of snakes, boars' teeth, gold wings and bronze hands) are more straightforward embodiments of adversarial evil. The Manticore (human's head, lion's body and scorpion's tail) was a Hebrew symbol of destructiveness. Some hybrids are incarnations of divine omnipotence, such as the goat-fish Capricorn, which for the Sumerians depicted the god Ea.

The elemental powers of nature evoked symbolic beasts of awesome size. The biblical Leviathan had an earlier destructive counterpart in the Babylonian chaos goddess of the sea, Tiamat.

Less gigantic embodiments of the power of the sea are Scylla and Charybdis, roaring multi-jawed symbols of risky passage. The Behemoth, a hippopotamus-like land version of Leviathan, represents another image of humanity's insignificance. Giant storm birds include the Babylonian Zu and the Arabian Roc.

The Phoenix and Salamander belong to a further category of beasts close to natural forms but with supernatural powers. The Hindu Nagas are guardian serpent beings of instinctual powers that can be profitably mastered.

cially Buddhism. In Thailand it is still customary for young Buddhist monks to beg for their food for a period. Many beggars occur in the lives of Christ and saints and are blessed or given alms. In the parable of Dives ("the rich man") and the poor man Lazarus it is the poor man who finds his reward in Heaven. Lazarus (at a feast) and the ascetic St Alexis appear in art as beggars. A beggar holding a heavy stone represents Poverty.

Beli the Great

A powerful god said to be the ancestor of several ancient royal lines of Wales. Beli (whose name means "light") is probably derived from the ancient Belenus or Belinus, a popular Celtic deity of light and healing. He may be associated with Beltane (1 May), the Celtic festival of light.

Belisarius

Belisarius (c.505–565CE) was the greatest general of the Byzantine emperor Justinian I. However, he was subsequently accused of treason, imprisoned and later pardoned. A story from the 10th century tells how Belisarius had his eyes gouged out and was reduced to begging in the streets of Constantinople. Jacques-Louis David's *Belisarius Recognized by the Soldier* shows Belisarius being recognized by a soldier who had served under him.

Bell

In many religions, the divine voice that proclaims the truth, especially of the Buddhist, Hindu, Islamic and Christian messages. In China where the bell also stood for respect, obedience and (by homophony) the passing of tests. Small tinkling bells can repre-sent happiness and also sexual pleasure, as in Greek rites where they were associated with the phallic Priapus. The bell is usually a passive, feminine principle, its shape a link with the celestial vault, its clapper symbolizing the tongue of the preacher. It was widely regarded as protective, warding off or exorcising evil. More generally, it marks the passing of time, proclaims good news, warns of danger and tolls for death, and hence can symbolize human mortality.

Bell Bird Brothers, The

Ancestral heroes of the Dreamtime who are associated with Uluru (Ayer's Rock) in central Australia. According to a version of their story related in 1976, the brothers were stalking an emu at Antalanya, a rock pool near Uluru. Unknown to them, a young woman was searching for grubs at nearby Wangka Arkal. On her head she carried a collecting dish supported by a pad. The load slipped from her head and disturbed the emu, which ran north toward Uluru with the brothers in pursuit. At the foot of Uluru is an indentation, said to be the girl's head pad, lying where it fell. A little further on is the pool where the emu drank.

Bellerophon

Queen Anteia of Argos fell in love with the Greek hero Bellerophon, the son of King Glaucus and Queen Eurynome of Corinth, and begged him to satisfy her passion. When he refused, the Queen told her husband that he had tried to ravish her.[1] The king therefore sent Bellerophon to the court of Lycia, in Asia Minor (modern Turkey), with a message requesting that he be put to death. He was charged with the impossible task of

Beli the Great: *see* Brân the Blessed; *Mabinogion*, The; Manawydan

Belisarius: *see* Beggar

Bell: *see* Book; Candle; Virginity; Word

Bell Bird Brothers, The: *see* ANCESTORS; Dreamtime

Bellerophon: *see* Amazons; Chimera, The; Medusa; Pegasus
[1] Homer, *Iliad VI:160–211*

Bellerophon killing the Chimera; after a sculpture of the 5th century BCE.

destroying the monstrous Chimera which was devastating the country. Bellerophon, mounted on the winged horse Pegasus, which he had tamed, slew the beast. His subsequent tasks were to fight the fierce Solymi tribe and the Amazons, both of whom he defeated. Impressed, the king of Lycia offered Bellerophon his daughter's hand and gave him half his kingdom.

Later, Bellerophon angered the gods by trying to fly Pegasus to the top of Mount Olympus. Zeus was irritated by the hero's presumption and sent a gadfly to sting Pegasus, causing the creature to rear and throw off Bellerophon. He survived the fall to earth but was lamed for life, thereafter wandering the world in solitude.

Belshazzar

In the Bible,[1] King Belshazzar of Babylon held a great feast. As the guests drank from golden vessels looted from the Temple of Jerusalem, a hand appeared and on the palace wall wrote the mysterious words: MENE, MENE, TEKEL, UPHARSIN – a scene dramatically painted by Rembrandt in *Belshazzar's Feast*. The fearful king offered riches to anyone who could interpret "the writing on the wall", but all his sages and astrologers failed. Daniel was summoned, and he warned Belshazzar that his kingdom would fall because he had pillaged God's Temple. Belshazzar was slain that very night and his kingdom divided.

Belt *see* Girdle

Benedict, Saint

Benedict[1] of Nursia (*c*.480–547CE) was born in Umbria and was sent to Rome to study, but abandoned the city to become a hermit. In *c*.529CE he founded his monastic order, the first in Europe, at Monte Cassino. His reputation spread, and his advice was sought by the king of the Ostrogoths. He was buried in the same grave as his sister, St Scholastica.

Little more is recorded about his life, but there are numerous legends. Benedict's nurse borrowed a sieve; when it broke into pieces Benedict miraculously restored it. As a hermit, he was tempted by the image of a woman, but quelled his lust by rolling naked in thorns and brambles. When he asked a community to observe a stricter life, they tried to poison him, whereupon Benedict blessed the poisoned glass, which shattered at once. Maurus and Placidus were young men in his care. When Placidus fell into a fast-flowing river, Benedict enabled Maurus to rescue him by walking on the the water.

It was said that the Devil tried to hinder the building of Benedict's monastery by making the stones too heavy and by crushing a young monk; Benedict restored the monk to life. Benedict also performed exorcisms and healings. Usually shown as elderly with a white beard, he may wear the black habit of his original order or the white of the reformed order.

Benjamin

In the Bible,[1] Benjamin was the youngest of the twelve sons of Jacob. Benjamin and Joseph were the sons of Rachel, while their half-brothers were the sons of Leah and her servants. After Joseph had been sold into slavery by his half-brothers, Benjamin took his place as Jacob's favourite son. Unknown to his family, Joseph went to Egypt and eventually became Pharaoh's most important official. Years later there was a famine in Canaan and Jacob's sons went to Egypt to buy corn; Benjamin stayed behind as Jacob did not want to lose a favourite a second time. Joseph recognized his brothers but concealed his own identity. He asked them to bring Benjamin on their next journey to Egypt. Joseph placed his silver cup in Benjamin's sack so that his brother would be caught as a thief. Joseph declared that the thief should become his servant, but the other brothers protested, saying that if Benjamin did not return with them to their father, then Jacob would die of sorrow. At this point Joseph revealed his true identity to his brothers.

Beowulf

A warrior prince, the hero of the 8th-century Anglo-Saxon epic poem of the same name. The events in *Beowulf* are told within a Christian context, but have a strong flavour of pre-Christian myth. As a youth, Beowulf came to Denmark from the land of the Geats (Gotland in southern Sweden) with a small band of followers to help Hrothgar, the aged Danish king, against the man-eating monster Grendel. Beowulf killed Grendel and the monster's mother came to avenge his death. The hero tracked the mother

back to her lair and killed her too before returning home.

In time Beowulf succeeded Hygelac as king of the Geats. He reigned peacefully for fifty years until his kingdom was threatened by a ferocious dragon. Beowulf confronted the beast, but his sword could not pierce its horny skin. The king's companions fled except for one loyal young chieftain, Wiglaf. When the dragon seized Beowulf in its jaws, Wiglaf pierced its underbelly with his sword. Beowulf then drew his knife and together the warriors killed the beast. However, Beowulf died, poisoned by the dragon's toxic breath.

Bernard of Clairvaux, Saint

Bernard[1] (1090–1153) joined Cîteaux abbey, France, in 1113. From there he expanded and reformed the Cistercian monastic order. He established a successful house at Clairvaux in Champagne. He attacked the luxury of the clergy and the abuses of the Roman *curia*. He was a great spiritual leader and his words were heeded by kings of England and France. Filippino Lippi and Perugino painted his vision of the Virgin: he appears as a young tonsured monk in the white robes of his order. Bergognone shows him with a chained dragon representing his suppression of heresy (Certosa, Pavia).

Bernardino, Saint

Bernardino (1380–1444) took over the hospital of La Scala, Siena, after most of its staff had died of plague. In 1402 he joined the Franciscans and preached all over Italy, notably against usury, and tried to establish stricter rules in the order. He was tried for heresy but acquitted. Pinturicchio frescoed scenes from his life in Santa

Benjamin: *see* Jacob; Joseph
[1] *Genesis 35:18 and 42:4*

Beowulf: *see* DRAGON

Bernard of Clairvaux, Saint: *see* RELIGIOUS ORDERS
[1] *Golden Legend, St Bernard*

Bernardino, Saint: *see* IHS

Maria in Aracoeli, Rome, but he appears mostly in Sienese painting. Pietro di Giovanni d'Ambrogio shows him as a skinny, toothless figure in the brown habit of his order (Pinacoteca, Siena). He is sometimes depicted with Christ's monogram (IHS), which he used when preaching. To eliminate gambling, he is said to have persuaded the dice-makers of Siena to make ivory discs with the IHS monogram instead, which he is said to have held up at the end of his preaching.

Bes

An Egyptian protective deity, usually portrayed as a hideous but jovial dwarf. He was revered as the god of pleasure and entertainment and as a protector of the family, especially of children and women in childbirth.

The dwarf-like deity Bes.

Bintu

A divine antelope in the mythology of the western Sahara. The first blacksmith in heaven is said to have made a hoe from Bintu's skull and then descended with it to earth in order to

teach people the arts of agriculture. Heavenly antelopes are often associated with the invention of agriculture throughout Saharan Africa.

Birch

A beneficial, protective tree of northern Europe and Eurasia, sacred to the Germanic gods Donar (the Norse Thor) and Frea (Frejya), and central in shamanistic rites much farther east as the cosmic tree linking this world with the spirit world. In Russia it symbolized spring and young women, and was planted near houses to invoke protective spirits. Its ability to cast out evil may be why witches were birched to rid them of demons. It is the national emblem of Estonia.

BIRDS *see panel opposite*

Black

Black has almost inescapable traditional symbolism as the colour of darkness, negative forces and unhappy events. It stands for death, ignorance, despair, sorrow and evil (the Prince of Darkness is Satan), for the underworld and for ominous augury. Blackbirds are a Christian symbol of temptation. In superstition black is synonymous with disaster: black cats, black days, black marks, blackballing. As the colour of mourning, it dramatizes loss and absence. As the colour of clerical robes, it signals renunciation of life's vanities.

However, Egypt and other ancient traditions expressed a more positive symbolism. Egypt was Kemet, the Black Land, a reference to the rich black alluvial soil renewed every year by the Nile flood. Black was the colour of Osiris, the god of the underworld, who ensured the growth of

BIRDS

Embodiments of both the human and the divine spirit – a symbolism suggested by their lightness and rapidity, the soaring freedom of their flight, and their mediation between earth and sky.

Birds play important roles in many creation myths or, like the Native American Thunderbird and the Lightning Bird of southern Africa, control elemental powers. The Aztec snake-bird god Quetzalcoatl combines celestial and earthly powers often separated in other myths, where birds battling snakes depict the fundamental conflict of light and darkness, spirit and flesh.

The concept of birds as souls is as common as the belief that they represent goodness, joy and immortality. In Egypt, the soul or personality (*ba*) was shown as a human-headed bird leaving the body at death. In the Indian *Upanishads*, two birds sitting in the Cosmic Tree symbolize the individual and the universal soul. Some birds may be ill omens, especially carrion birds like ravens, crows and vultures; but most are lucky. In Hinduism, birds symbolize the love of the gods, bringing the elixir of immortality (*soma*) to humanity.

Another widespread idea is that birds communicate with divinities.

The Celts venerated them for this reason. Shamans equipped with feathers and bird masks "fly" to higher realms of knowledge. Birds thus traditionally stand for wisdom, intelligence and the swift power of thought. Roman divination by the flight or song of birds reflected their superior knowledge and link to the gods. They confide useful secrets to the heroes of fairy stories – the expression "a little bird told me," echoes this ancient idea. An Aboriginal view is that songbirds can also bear information to one's enemies.

In Western art , the infant Christ is sometimes shown with a bird, often (as in Raphael's *Madonna of the Goldfinch* and Michelangelo's *Taddei Tondo*) a goldfinch, once a favourite children's pet It was a symbol of the Passion – the bird was said to have acquired the red spot on its plumage when it plucked a thorn from Christ's brow and a drop of blood fell onto it.

Caged birds (which for Plato represented the mind) appear in allegories of spring. In China, a bird is a male symbol (a homophone of "penis"). In a similar vein, in 17th-century Holland "bird-catching" was a euphemism for copulation; hence the dead birds in paintings of men and women flirting.

plants, and of the powerful Hindus goddesses Kali and Durga. Suggesting the duality necessary to all existence is the Chinese *taiji*, the black and white Yin-Yang symbol. At a socio-political level, stressing the positive symbolism and associations of black plays a small but significant part today in the process of eradicating racism and racial stereotyping.

Black Misery

The black light which, together with its counterpart Radiance (white light), was the first thing to exist, according to pre-Buddhist Tibetan creation mythology. After Black Misery and Radiance came into existence, there arose out of chaos multi-coloured streams of light which separated like a rainbow. From their five colours arose five elements, these were: hardness, fluidity, heat, motion and space. These fused to form a huge egg, from which Black Misery produced the darkness of non-being, which he filled with the evils of the world.

Bladder Festival, The

A winter ceremony of the Alaskan Inuit at which the inflated bladders of all the sea mammals caught during the year are pushed through holes in the ice. This act returns the creatures' souls to the spirit world, where they rejoin the society of animals and can be sent out once more as quarry.

Blaise, Saint

Little historical evidence exists concerning St Blaise or Blasius (thought to have died *c*.316CE). His cult spread during the 8th century, and legend[1] has it that he was bishop of Cappodocia in Asia Minor (present-day Turkey). It is in this role that he is often depicted, but he led the life of a hermit: birds brought him food and wild animals sought his blessing. He is said to have cured sick animals, and is still invoked to do so. St Blaise also cured a boy with a fishbone stuck in his throat, and hence he is also a protector invoked against illness, especially sore throats.

Blaise apparently refused to worship false gods and was cruelly tortured, notably with the iron-carders' combs which became his attribute, before being beheaded.

Blindness and Blindfold

Symbols of ignorance, self-delusion, the heedlessness of "blind rage" or sensual love – the Classical god Eros (Cupid) is blindfolded. Alternatively, blindness symbolizes unprejudiced justice (unswayed by mere appearances) and the inner visions of seers and poets. In Greece, the goddess Ate represented blind evil, whereas the blind Teiresias had the gift of prophecy. Homer was, by tradition, blind.

In art blindness is a characteristic of Ignorance, Justice, Avarice and Fate or Fortune. Blinding was often a punishment, as of Teiresias who saw the naked Athene. The subject of Christ healing the blind was taken as an allegory of spiritual blindness before his advent. Hence in medieval art the blindfolded figure of a woman represented the Synagogue, blind to Christ's teaching. His parable, "And if the blind lead the blind, both shall fall into the ditch,"[1] was illustrated by Pieter Bruegel the Elder in a painting which warns of the perils of choosing an unfit leader. Tobit, Belisarius and Elymas all went blind.

Blodeuwedd

In Welsh legend, a beautiful woman conjured out of flowers by the magician Math, lord of Gwynedd, and his nephew Gwydion. Blodeuwedd ("Flower Aspect") was created as a wife for the hero Lleu Llaw Gyffes, whose mother had sworn that he would never have a human wife. Blodeuwedd was unfaithful and with her lover, Gronw Pebyr, plotted to kill Lleu. However, they only wounded him and he escaped in the form of an eagle. He was later found and restored to human form by Gwydion, who killed Gronw Pebyr and turned

Blodeuwedd into an owl. *Blodeuwedd* is the modern Welsh word for "owl".

Blood
A symbol of the life force, believed in many cultures to contain a share of divine energy or, more commonly, the spirit of an individual creature. Blood had rain-bearing or fertilizing power according to some ancient traditions, as in Near Eastern marriage ceremonies where the bride stepped over the sprinkled blood of a sheep. Bull's blood was used for its supposed magical power in the Roman rites of Mithras and Cybele. With the same symbolism of life force, blood is sometimes still drunk at Mexican bullfights. At the height of the Aztec empire, the blood of thousands of victims a year was spilled to reinvigorate the sun. The mingling of blood is a symbol of union in many traditions and can mark a seal or covenant. In Roman Catholic doctrine, Christ's blood is present in the transubstantiated wine of the Eucharist.

Blue
Infinity, eternity, truth, devotion, faith, purity, chastity, peace, spiritual and intellectual life – associations that appear in many ancient cultures and express a general feeling that blue, the colour of the sky, is the coolest, most detached and least "material" of all hues. The Virgin Mary and Christ are often shown wearing blue, and it is the attribute of many sky gods including Amun in Egypt; the Sumerian Great Mother; the Greek Zeus (Jupiter to the Romans) and Hera (Juno); the Hindu Indra and Vishnu, and Vishnu's blue-skinned incarnation, Krishna. Blue is linked to mercy in Hebrew tradition and to wisdom in Bud-dhism. In folk traditions, it stands in Europe for fidelity, in parts of China for scholarship and happy marriage. More recently, the term "the blues" means melancholy or sad.

Boann
The divine spirit of the Boyne river in Ireland. Boann was originally the wife of Nechtan, a river god, but slept with the Daghdha, the father god, to produce Oenghus, the god of love. When Boann broke a ban by visiting Nechtan's well, its waters rose and engulfed her and she became the Boyne.

Boar
A primordial image of strength, fearless aggression and resolute courage, particularly across northern Europe and the Celtic world where it was the leading symbol of warriors. It also had sacred meaning elsewhere: as a sun symbol in Iran and as a moon symbol in Japan, where the white boar was taboo to hunters. Respect for the boar extended into India where, as Varaha, Vishnu took on a boar's form to dive into the flood and root the earth up with his tusks after it had been captured by demons. Destructive brutality is the other side of boar symbolism: it was a monstrous adversary to the Greek hero Herakles and also to the Egyptian solar god Horus whose eye was torn out by Seth in the form of a black boar. The boar was a Judeo-Christian symbol for tyranny and lust.

Boat
For many river and coastal peoples, small craft were the means of transition from the material to the spirit world. Boats cross the perilous regions of the underworld (as in

Blood: *see* Bull; Night Sea Crossing; Ram; Sun; Water; Wine

Blue: *see* CHASTITY; FIDELITY; Sky; VIRTUES; WISDOM

Boann: *see* Daghdha, The; Nechtan; Oenghus

Boar: *see* ANIMALS; Black; Eye; Forest; Moon; Pig; Sun; White

Boat: *see* AFTERLIFE; Ark; Crescent; Ship; Woman

A chalice filled with Christ's blood; after a 16th-century depiction.

Egyptian mythology) or are cast adrift with the bodies of chiefs, as in the Amazon. In Greek myth, a boat steered by the ferryman Charon carried dead souls across the river Styx into the underworld.

Bodhbh

An Irish sorceress and war goddess. Bodhbh (or Badhbh) brings terror and confusion among warriors with her battle cries, and frequently takes the form of a crow or raven. Her appearance in this guise is often an omen of death.

Bodhi Tree, The

The pipal tree at Bodh Gaya, India, under which the Buddha meditated until he attained *bodhi* (awakening, enlightenment). Also called the Bo Tree, it is a Buddhist symbol of meditation, teaching and spiritual perfection.

Bodhisattva

A future Buddha, literally "one whose essence is awakening", from Sanskrit *bodhi* (awakening). A bodhisattva has all the attainments of a Buddha but remains active in the world in order to assist humankind. In the mythology of Mahayana Buddhism, bodhisattvas are aspects of celestial Buddhas such as Amitabha. Among the more popular bodhisattvas are Avalokiteshvara, Maitreya and Manjushri. The Buddha before his enlightenment may be referred to as the Bodhisattva.

Bonaventura, Saint

Bonaventura (1221–74) studied, taught and preached in Paris. He acquired his name when he fell ill as a child and his mother took him to St Francis who, upon his recovery, is said to have exclaimed "*O buona ventura!*" ("Oh good fortune!"). He

The Bodhisattva Avalokiteshvara, from a 10th-century relief. He is especially revered in Tibet.

joined the Franciscan order and in 1257 became its head or minister-general; he was considered its greatest friar after St Francis himself.

In 1273 Bonaventura was made cardinal-bishop of Albano, but maintained a simple way of life. He wrote extensively, including a biography of St Francis. Zurbarán shows him addressing the Council of Lyons in 1274, but he is usually seen reading or writing, dressed as a Franciscan or a bishop; he may have a cardinal's hat.

Bonds

Beyond their obvious meaning as physical restraints, bonds symbolize judicial power, especially of deities or rulers, and its acceptance by those bound by the law. Varuna, the Vedic god of cosmic order, is shown holding cords. In Egypt, the king's name was written in a cartouche, a stylized loop of knotted cord.

Bones

Images of mortality and death, but also of the basis for bodily resurrection: bones were carefully protected in many ancient cultures for the latter reason, often under megaliths. Northern European peoples from Finland to Siberia buried the skeletons of bears and other game to ensure their rebirth.

Book

A self-evident emblem of wisdom, science and scholarship, the book also appears widely as a symbol for divine revelation, especially in the Christian and Islamic faiths. In art, books are held by Christ, the Virgin of the Annunciation, prophets, apostles (John the Evangelist may literally swallow his Book of Revelation), , and the figures of History, Philosophy and the Muses. A book with a cross on it represents Faith.

Christ holding the book of Scripture, from an 11th-century Byzantine mosaic.

Bota Ili

A wild woman of the mountains, in the mythology of the Kédang people of eastern Indonesia. One day Wata Rian, a fisherman, went to the top of a mountain. He found a hearth and climbed a tree to await the return of whoever had made it. Eventually Bota Ili came back from hunting. After she had rested, she hit her backside on a rock to strike a light but was unable to make fire. She realized that the presence of a stranger was to blame and soon spotted Wata Rian hiding in the tree. Bota Ili was angry at first but later relented and Wata Rian came down. She lit the fire and together they cooked their food. Wata Rian poured Bota Ili plenty of wine and when she had fallen into a drunken sleep he shaved her all over. To his astonishment he discovered that the hairy creature was in fact a woman. Later, after Bota Ili had learned to wear clothes, they were married.

Botoque

A youth who brought fire and the bow and arrow to humanity, according to the Kayapo people of central Brazil. One day Botoque became stranded on top of a high cliff. A jaguar, who was carrying a bow and arrow and all kinds of game, found him and adopted him as a son and hunting companion. The jaguar took Botoque into his home, where he saw fire and ate cooked meat for the first time. Later the jaguar taught Botoque how to make a bow and arrows. One day, when the jaguar was hunting, his wife threatened Botoque. The boy killed her with the bow and, stealing an ember and some cooked meat, and taking his bow and arrows, he returned to his village.

Once they had seen Botoque's gifts the other men from the village went to the jaguar's house and plundered it. Because of his losses, the jaguar now has to hunt with his claws and must eat his food raw.

Bones: *see* Bear; DEATH; Goat; Soul

Book: *see* Grail; VIRTUES; WISDOM; Word

Botoque: *see* CULTURE HERO; JAGUAR

Bow

A symbol of stored energy, willpower, aspiration, divine or terrestial power, and dynamic tension, especially sexual. Humanity's most effective weapon for 50,000 years, the bow was an obvious emblem of war and hunting, but the control needed to master it gave it a deeper significance. In Oriental thought, it represented spiritual discipline, the combination of force and composure. A Homeric test of fitness to rule (exemplified by the bow that only the hero Odysseus could draw), the bow is also an attribute of the Greek god Apollo, "the Far Shooter". The shape of the bow was linked with the crescent moon and the goddesses Isis and Artemis (Diana). The bow of the Greek god Eros (Cupid), symbolizes the tension of desire.

Bowl *see* Beggar; Pilgrimage

Box

Beyond the Freudian feminine symbolism of any receptacle, boxes represent mystery and the hazardous drama of surprise, pleasant or unpleasant. In Greek myth the opening of Pandora's box (more accurately, a jar) released ills upon the world.

Brahma

A Hindu creator deity, the lord of humanity and of the gods, and one of the *trimurti*, the great divine triad of Brahma, Shiva and Vishnu. Brahma is a frequent figure in later Hindu myth, but usually in a subordinate role to the other two gods. During the early centuries CE, however, he appears to have been the focus of an important cult, presumably as the supreme creator deity. In the great Hindu epics, Brahma is credited with some of the creation myths associated in earlier texts with Prajapati. They include the story of how he produced a beautiful young daughter, Sarasvati or Savitri, from his own body. Brahma was smitten with her beauty and, as she walked around him in a gesture of respect, his desire to stare at her caused five faces to appear (one face was later destroyed by Shiva). The pair committed incest to produce Manu, the first man.

As Brahma meditates, he is said to emit both the material elements of the universe and the concepts through which humanity may understand them. The duration of the universe is counted in terms of Brahma's enormous lifespan of one hundred Brahma years (equal to 36,000,000 years of the gods, where one year of the gods is 360 human years). In each day of Brahma the universe is created and in each night it is dissolved.

Eventually Brahma's creative activity became trivialized in mythology into a readiness to grant boons or favours to anyone who performed acts of penance or asceticism. As a result

Brahma emerging from the lotus that sprang from the navel of Vishnu.

the Asuras (demons) often acquire inordinate power for persistent asceticism until Brahma calls upon one of the other gods to help restore order.

In much of the mythology surrounding Vishnu, Brahma tends to be presented as a demiurge carrying out the intentions of the superior god. According to this tradition, as Vishnu lay on the cosmic serpent Ananta in the primordial waters, a lotus emerged from his navel and opened to reveal Brahma seated within and preparing to send forth the world.

Brân the Blessed

A giant warrior of Welsh myth, the son of Llyr and brother of Manawydan and Branwen. Brân gave Branwen in marriage to Matholwch, king of Ireland, who ill-treated her. To avenge his sister, Brân, who was so huge that no building could contain him, led an army of Britons against the Irish, striding through the sea next to his fleet. The Britons won the battle but only seven of Brân's men survived and Brân himself was mortally wounded by a poisoned spear. He ordered the seven survivors to cut off his head and bury it on the White Mount in London to protect the kingdom from invaders. On the journey to London the warriors spent seven years feasting at Harlech and another eighty years in the blissful otherworld of Gwales. Throughout the journey, Brân's head continued to talk as if he were still alive.

Branch, Bough

Branches, used for example in spring fertility rites, took on the symbolism of the trees from which they were cut. Thus, branches of palm or olive were triumphal emblems in processions, and

mistletoe branches were widespread resurrection symbols, particularly in the Celtic world. In Virgil's *Aeneid*, Aeneas carries a mistletoe branch to ensure his safe passage through the underworld. J. G. Frazer named his great study of comparative religion, *The Golden Bough*, after the implement used in the ritual slaying of the priest of Diana at Lake Nemi by his successor. A flowering bough stands for Logic in medieval iconography.

Bread

The sustainer of life and symbol of Christ's sacrifice, a metaphor for the food of the spirit and for the body of Christ himself. Christ said, "I am the bread of life; he that cometh to me shall never hunger."[1] At the miraculous Feeding of the Five Thousand, and in legends of the lives of saints, many people are fed by small amounts of bread. At the Last Supper, Christ broke bread and, with reference to his coming sacrifice, said, "This is my body which is given for you; this do in remembrance of me."[2] Hence bread is used at the sacrament of the Eucharist (Communion, Lord's Supper), symbolizing (or in Catholicism, literally becoming) the body of Christ.

Unleavened bread eaten at the Jewish Passover is a symbol of purification and sacrifice.

Breasts

Breasts are generally linked with maternal love, nourishment, security, protection, gentleness, and Mother Nature. The many breasts of the Greek goddess Artemis (Diana) of Ephesus emphasized her fertility. The hero Herakles sucked so hard on the breast of the goddess Hera (Juno) that milk spurted across the heavens, creating the

The many-breasted fertility goddess Artemis (Diana) of Ephesus.

Milky Way. Images of the Virgin Mary suckling Christ, common in earlier art, were forbidden by the Council of Trent (1545–63) as displaying unnecessary nudity. A platter bearing two breasts is an attribute of St Agatha.

Breath, Breathing

The life principle, spiritual as well as physical. The link between breath and spirit is part of Western, Islamic and Eastern traditions. In the Bible,[1] God breathes life into Adam's nostrils. Insufflation was once used symbolically to blow the Holy Spirit into, and demons out of, troubled people. Controlled breathing, an aspect of Eastern meditation, is most developed in the Hindu system of yoga where correct breathing is intended to concentrate the spirit and align individual respiration with the rhythm of the cosmos. Underlying much of the symbolism of breath/spirit is the mystical idea that breath is a divine gift, returned to its giver at death.

Brer Rabbit

A trickster rabbit of North American folk myth. Brer ("Brother") Rabbit derives from the Hare trickster of West Africa, which was brought to the United States by slaves and adopted aspects of southeastern Native American hare and rabbit characters. Brer Rabbit generally outwits more powerful characters such as Brer Bear and Brer Fox.

Bride or Bridget, Saint *see Brighid*

Bridge

The bridge symbolizes transition and connection, and also neutral ground – a place of meetings and trysts but also, like the ford, sometimes a contested place. The rainbow was often seen as a celestial bridge, linking earth to heaven. Zoroastrianism has Chinvat Parvatu, the Bridge of the Separator, which only the righteous could negotiate to paradise, a concept also found in medieval Christian iconography of heaven and hell. The Roman high priest was the Pontifex Maximus ("Chief Bridgemaker") – a title borne by Roman emperors and inherited by the Pope. In Norse myth the ice-bridge Bifrost leads to Asgard, the home of the gods. The Milky Way is a celestial bridge in the mythology of China and other cultures.

Brighid (Brigid, Bridget, Brid, Bride)

An Irish goddess, the daughter of the Daghdha. Brighid may originally have been a goddess of sovereignty: her name is derived from the Celtic root *brig* ("exalted") and she may be related to the British tribal god Brigantia. She was the patron of poetry and arcane lore, especially divination and prophecy, and the protector of women in childbirth. Brighid was sometimes said to have two sisters of the same name who were associated with healing and crafts. However, following the common Celtic pattern of triplication, the three Brighids were often treated as aspects of a single deity.

In Christian times, St Bride or Bridget of Kildare, Ireland's most important female saint and the founder, according to tradition, of the first Irish nunnery at Kildare, assumed many functions and legends of the goddess Brighid. She even took over Brighid's feast day, 1 February, the old Celtic festival of Imbolc.

Bronze

An alloy used, in the period before iron, for weapons and tools and hence symbolizing force, power and hardness. Cult objects made of bronze possessed protective power. In Greek myth, bronze was sacred to the smithgod Hephaistos. The people of the Age of Bronze were said to have developed civilization, but ended up slaughtering each other and being consigned to the underworld.

Broom

A domestic implement invested with considerable magical power from ancient times. Essentially a symbol of cleansing, it had to be used with care or it could drive out friendly spirits as well as dust. This belief explains folk prohibitions on sweeping a house at night in Brittany and, in North Africa, on sweeping a house in which someone had just died. Sacred brooms were used in some rites to drive out malign spirits. The image of witches riding on broomsticks is linked to the idea that evil spirits may take possession of the magic implement used to drive them out.

Brown

Humility, renunciation, poverty – a symbolism probably deriving from the unbleached and undyed garments of the poor. Hence the brown habits of Christian mendicant orders. In China, though, brown was the colour of the magnificent Song dynasty. Culturally there is little evidence for Freud's view that excremental associations are the predominant symbolism of brown.

Bruno, Saint

St Bruno (c.1033–1101), the French founder of the Carthusian monastic order, studied and taught at Rheims, but left after a row with the archbishop and in 1084 established a small monastic community near Grenoble at Char-

treuse (whence the name Carthusian, or Charterhouse for the order) that lived in quiet solitude. Bruno refused an archbishopric from the Pope but was allowed to found a monastery in Calabria. He is usually seen at prayer in Carthusian habit.

Brutus, Lucius Junius

In Roman legend,[1] Brutus was the nephew of King Tarquinius Superbus, and led an uprising which ousted his uncle. He was one of the first two consuls of the Republic, along with Tarquinius Collatinus. Two of Brutus' sons plotted to kill them and restore the monarchy, but their plans were discovered. Brutus watched, unflinching, as they were flogged and beheaded. Jacques-Louis David's *Lictors Bringing Brutus the Bodies of his Sons* shows Brutus unmoved as the womenfolk weep profusely.

BUDDHA, THE *see panel overleaf*

Buffalo, Bison

A symbol of formidable power in Asia and North America. The high status of the buffalo in India and Southeast Asia made it a sacrificial animal. Yama, the Hindu and Buddhist god of death, rode a buffalo, and a buffalo head was a death symbol in Tibet. The Chinese associated the quiet power of the buffalo with the contemplative life: in legend, the sage Laozi left China on a green buffalo.

The North American buffalo or bison (a different species from the Asian buffalo) symbolized to the Plains Indians the strength of the whirlwind, prosperity and plenty – before their wanton wholesale slaughter by white hunters, bison swarmed over the Plains in vast thundering

Bull

herds of many millions – but the flesh and hide of just one beast could feed and clothe many people. The white buffalo was particularly sacred.

Bull

Power, potency, fecundity – a protean symbol of divinity, royalty and the elemental forces of nature, changing in significance between different epochs and cultures. In cave art the bull is second only to the horse as the most frequently painted image of vital energy.

As the incarnation of many supreme Near Eastern gods, the bull was one of the most important sacrificial animals. In ritual and iconography, it has represented both moon and sun, earth and sky, rain and heat, feminine procreation and male ardour, matriarch and patriarch, death and regeneration. As a symbol of death and resurrection, it was central to Mithraism, a Persian cult popular in the Roman empire. Mithraic sacrifices celebrated the sun-god Mithras's slaughter of a primordial bull, from whose blood and semen sprang new life.

Bulls appear from northern Europe to India as an emblem of divine power, especially linked with lunar, solar and sky or storm gods, including the Mesopotamian El (who is bull-horned) and Baal; the Egyptian Ra, Osiris, Ptah (incarnated as the sacred Apis bull) and Seth; the Greek Zeus, Dionysos, Poseidon and Cybele; the Norse Thor and Frejya; and the Hindu Indra, Aditi, Agni, Rudra and Shiva. Tibetan Buddhism has the bull-headed fierce protector deity Yama Dharmaraja.

The physical attributes of the bull underlie much of its symbolism. Its horns are linked with the crescent moon; its strength suggests a support for the world in Vedic and Islamic tra-

ditions; its prolific semen is stored by the moon in Persian myth; and its colossal, dangerous energy was widely venerated, notably in Minoan Crete, where a dangerous ritualistic sport involved somersaulting over a bull's horns. The orchestrated ritual of modern bull-fighting continues an ancient Mediterranean tradition of using the bull to flirt with death.

Crete is the setting of numerous later Greek bull myths, most famously of the monstrous bull-man, the Minotaur. Zeus transformed himself into a bull in order to abduct Europa, carrying her to Crete. A bull is thus one of the attributes of Zeus and may also symbolize the continent of Europe.

A formidable beast, the bull from ancient times became adversary as well as icon. Challenging its power was a task of legendary heroes such as Herakles (who captured another Cretan bull as his seventh labour, and fought Achelous in the guise of a bull) and Theseus, who slew the Minotaur.

Butterfly

An ancient symbol of immortality, its life cycle providing a perfect analogy: life (the crawling caterpillar), death (the chrysalis) and rebirth or resurrection (the butterfly fluttering free). Hence images of the Christ Child may show him with a butterfly in his hand or nearby. In Greek myth, Psyche (literally "Soul"), a mortal freed from death by Zeus, had butterfly wings.

Butterflies as emblems of souls are found as far apart as Congo, East Asia, Mexico and New Zealand. They appear with this meaning on Christian tombs. In Japan the creature stands for transient joy, female vanity and the geisha; a pair of butterflies represents conjugal bliss.

BUDDHA, THE

Buddha ("Awakened One") is the name given to Siddhartha Gautama, the founder of Buddhism. Gautama (who lived *c*.500BCE) was a prince of the Shakya clan in Oudh and parts of Nepal. The earliest Buddhist scriptures embellished the story of his search for *bodhi*, spiritual awakening, or "enlightenment", and release from the eternal cycle of birth, death and rebirth. Said to have been born miraculously from his mother's side as she grasped a tree, Gautama was received by Brahma and the other gods. In myth, the newborn child took seven steps and declared that this was his final birth. He was raised in luxury in the palace of his father, King Shuddhodhana,

married and had a son. One day Gautama rode outside the palace and discovered sickness and death. He decided to abandon his life of privilege and seek enlightenment.

After seven years, Gautama decided to sit under what was later called the Bodhi Tree at Bodhgaya until he had resolved the problem of human suffering. Mara, the god of death and desire, assailed Gautama with earthly distractions – but to no avail. After forty-nine days, Gautama attained awakening and became a Buddha.

Left *The Buddha teaching.*

Below *A map of the northward spread of Buddhism from India.*

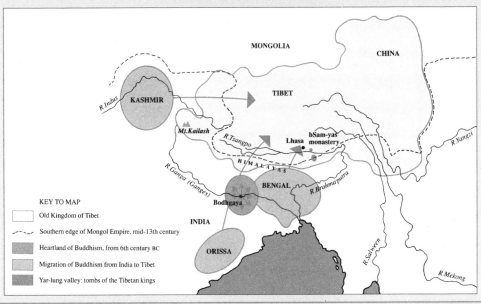

KEY TO MAP

	Old Kingdom of Tibet
‒ · ‒ · ‒ ·	Southern edge of Mongol Empire, mid-13th century
	Heartland of Buddhism, from 6th century BC
	Migration of Buddhism from India to Tibet
	Yar-lung valley: tombs of the Tibetan kings

*A winged caduceus is a
form associated with the
messenger-god Hermes
(the Roman Mercury).*

Cadmus

In Greek myth, the founder of the city of Thebes, son of King Agenor and Queen Telephassa of Phoenicia, and sister of Europa. When Zeus (in Roman myth, Jupiter) kidnapped Europa, Agenor sent his three sons to search for her. The Delphic oracle told Cadmus to abandon the hunt for Europa and found a city on the site to which a heifer with a moon-shaped mark on her flank would lead him.

The cow led Cadmus to a forest grove sacred to the god Ares (Mars). It was guarded by a fierce dragon, which devoured some of Cadmus's men, as depicted by Cornelis van Haarlem in *The Followers of Cadmus Devoured by a Dragon*. Cadmus fought the dragon and killed it after a furious battle.

Athene (in Roman myth, Minerva) then appeared and told Cadmus to sow half the dragon's teeth on the ground. From the teeth sprang armed men who fought each other until only five were left alive. With Cadmus, these warriors, the Spartoi ("Sown Men"), founded Thebes and were the

ancestors of its noble families. One warrior warned Cadmus, "Keep clear of family conflict." Cadmus married Harmonia, daughter of Ares (Mars) and Aphrodite (Venus). The couple had many offspring, including their ill-fated daughter, Semele. Their grandson, Actaeon, also met a grim fate. Cadmus and his wife left Thebes, bowed down with old age and sorrow. In reward for killing the dragon, they were turned into friendly snakes; with their bodies entwined, and disappeared into a grove.

Caduceus

A rod entwined by two serpents, sometimes capped by wings. It is now an emblem of medicine or commerce but has enjoyed a varied symbolism since ancient times. The Greek word from which caduceus is derived meant "herald's staff"; it was the staff of the god Hermes (the Roman Mercury), the messenger of the gods, and came to be used as a protective emblem by messengers on political or commercial business, hence perhaps it use in art as an attribute of Peace. A staff entwined with a snake was also associated with Asklepios (Aesculapius) the demi-god of healing. This symbolism derives from the link between the snake and rejuvenation.

A stick with entwined serpents combines several fundamental elements: an axial pole suggesting phallic power and the Tree of Life (a means of communication between earth and heavens); a double spiral formed by the snakes, suggesting cosmic energy, duality and the union of opposites. In alchemy it stood for the integration of opposites (mercury and sulphur). The serpents suggest the fertilizing forces of the earth and underworld. A similar emblem is a Hindu image of *kundalini* (awakening energy).

Caenis, Caeneus

In Greek myth, Caenis was famous for her beauty and had many suitors, but refused to marry. Wandering on a lonely shore, she was ravished by Poseidon (in Roman myth, Neptune), who then granted her any request. So that she would never have to endure such injury again, she asked to become a man and was changed into Caeneus. Later, Caeneus attended the wedding where the Centaurs tried to carry off the Lapith women; he fought valiantly, killing and wounding many Centaurs until the survivors hurled rocks and trees at him; overwhelmed, Caeneus turned into a bird and flew away into the sky.

Caesar, Julius

Gaius Julius Caesar (102BCE–44BCE)[1] was a celebrated Roman general (*imperator*), statesman and writer, conqueror of the Gauls (58BCE–50BCE), victor in the Roman civil war of 49BCE–46BCE and dictator of the Republic. In 49BCE Caesar crossed the Rubicon, a small river that separated Gaul from Italy, ruled by Pompey, against whom he launched a civil war. Caesar drove Pompey out of Italy and pursued him to Egypt, where Pompey was murdered. A string of victories against foreign powers followed, notably Egypt, and Caesar's dictatorship was secured. His triumphal march was depicted by Mantegna in *The Triumph of Caesar*. Caesar's ambition to remain sole ruler of Rome prompted a Republican plot, and on March 15th, 44BCE, he was stabbed to death by Marcus Junius Brutus and his collaborators in the Senate.

The family name of Caesar was used by his adopted son Octavian (Gaius Julius Caesar Octavianus), the first emperor – better known by his title Augustus (ruled 31BCE–14CE) – and by all subsequent Roman emperors. It is the origin of the German *Kaiser* and the Russian *tsar* (czar).

Cain and Abel

The sons of Adam and Eve, described in the Bible thus: "Abel was a keeper of sheep, but Cain was a tiller of the ground."[1] Both made offerings to God but Abel's sacrificial lamb was favoured above Cain's crops, and in a jealous rage Cain slew his brother. For his crime – the first murder – God cursed Cain and sent him to a land east of Eden. The conflict between the brothers may reflect ancient tensions between those who adopted a settled agrarian lifestyle and nomadic herders. Lorenzo Ghiberti used episodes from the story for a panel of the doors of the Baptistery in the cathedral of Florence. Titian's *Cain Slaying Abel* depicts the murder.

Caesar, Julius: *see* Augustus;
Brutus (Marcus Junius);
Cleopatra
[1] Plutarch, *Lives, Caesar, Pompey and Antony*

Cain and Abel:
[1] *Genesis 4:1–16*

Calais and Zetes

Calais and Zetes

Winged heroes of Greek myth, the twin sons of Boreas, the North Wind, and known as the Boreades, went on the voyage of the Argonauts and rescued their blind brother-in-law, King Phineus, from the Harpies by chasing them off. However, the Boreades then died, because at their birth it had been decreed that they must catch anything they pursued or perish.

Calchas

A prophet who accompanied the Greeks on their expedition to Troy and made many accurate prophecies about the Trojan War. He predicted that Achilles would cause the destruction of Troy and that it would fall only after nine years.

Calf

Purity in sacrifice – hence occasionally a symbol of Christ (more often depicted as a lamb). Calves also symbolized prosperity (killing the fatted calf). The biblical episode of the golden calf¹ is usually taken as an emblem of the worship of material rather than spiritual values.

Callisto

An attendant of the Greek goddess Artemis (Diana in Roman myth), Callisto was seduced by Zeus (Jupiter). Some time later, when Artemis and her nymphs were bathing, Callisto was reluctant to undress; when her companions undressed her it became apparent that she was pregnant. Palma Vecchio's *Diana Discovering Callisto* is a scene of beautiful nudes surrounding the chaste goddess as Callisto's condition is revealed. Artemis banished her, and Zeus's jealous wife, Hera (Juno), changed her into a bear. When Callisto's son Arcas was 15, he was hunting and chanced upon his mother. She approached him, and Arcas was about to spear her when Zeus swept them both up into the heavens to become the neighbouring constellations of the Great Bear and the Little Bear (Ursa Major and Ursa Minor).

Calumet

The sacred ceremonial "pipe of peace" of Native North Americans, usually with a reed stem carrying eagle feathers, symbolizes the union of nature and spirit, earth and sky, humans and the divine. The smoking of the pipe could signify peace (a white-feathered stem), and, once, also war (red); more generally it is a sign of hospitality. Pipes are often used in pairs, representing male and female, and are passed from east-to-west around a circle. The smoke, symbolizing vital breath, is ceremonially puffed toward the sky, the earth and the four cardinal points. Essentially, the calumet is a medium of prayer.

Calumny

A lost painting of *Calumny*, or Slander, by the Greek painter Apelles was known of throughout antiquity. It was described by Lucian¹ as showing a man with large ears receiving evil counsel from Ignorance and Suspicion, while the beautiful but crafty Calumny holds a lighted torch in one hand and with the other drags her victim by the hair.² Her guide is pale and filthy Hatred, and her handmaids are Envy and Fraud. Behind the group stand Penitence, followed by Truth. Several Renaissance artists, notably Botticelli, tried to reconstruct this famous picture.

Cambyses, The Judgment of

In the 6th century BCE, the Persian king Cambyses[1] found that one of his royal judges, Sisamnes, had taken a bribe. Cambyses had him executed and flayed, and the seat of judgment covered with his skin to demonstrate the fate of the corrupt. He then appointed Sisamnes' son to take his father's place. This severe example of justice was painted by Gérard David in *The Judgment of Cambyses*.

Camel

Sobriety and dignified obedience – associations that reflect Christian approval of the camel's ability to shoulder heavy loads without complaining (as noted by St Augustine) and plod long distances without drinking. In art, camels often appear in biblical scenes to give authenticity to the setting. They were also considered royal, and are seen with the three kings or Magi following the star. John the Baptist is often depicted wearing a tunic of camel hair. Christ used the camel in a famous analogy when he declared that it could pass through the eye of a needle more easily than a rich man could enter heaven.[1] On Roman coins and in Western art the camel personifies the continent of Asia.

Remarkably, considering its importance in North Africa, the Near East and India, the camel plays a minor role in the iconography and literature of these regions. Zoroastrianism, however, refers to a flying camel as a dragon-serpent image in paradise.

Camellia

In China, an image of health and beauty, and also of fortitude, perhaps because of the shrub's ability to bloom in autumn and winter. In Japan, the flower is associated with sudden death.

Camillus, Marcus Furius

Camillus[1] was a Roman general and statesman of the 4th century BCE, from whose story moral lessons were drawn. Episodes from his life were used to exemplify the modest, just and wise behaviour of a model citizen.

Camillus laid siege to the Etruscan town of Falerii, during which the beleaguered town's schoolmaster took the children to exercise outside the walls. Each day he led them further out toward the Roman camp, until he delivered them right into the enemy's hands. The schoolmaster declared to Camillus that by this act he had handed over the city. In *Camillus and the Schoolmaster of Falerii*, Poussin shows Camillus, astounded by such treachery, commanding his men to let the boys drive the master back to Falerii with rods and scourges. The Falerians acknowledged Camillus's act of justice and surrendered.

However, the general was accused of appropriating Etruscan spoils and went into exile. In 390BCE, he returned to drive the Gauls out of Italy. They had besieged Rome but failed to capture the Capitol because, in the dead of night, the Romans were alerted by the cackling of the sacred geese near the Temple of Juno. The Gaulish leader Brennus accepted a ransom of gold in exchange for Rome. As the gold was being weighed, Brennus threw his sword and belt on to the scales and cried, *Vae victis* ("Woe to the conquered"). Camillus halted the exchange of gold and told Brennus that it was Roman custom to deliver their country with iron, not gold.

Cambyses, The Judgment of:
[1] Herodotus, V.25

Camel: *see* ANIMALS; CONTINENTS; Dragon; Needle; Snake
[1] *Mark 10:25*

Camellia: *see* VIRTUES

Camillus, Marcus Furius:
[1] Plutarch, *Lives, Camillus*

Candle: *see* Breath,
Breathing; Candlestick;
Fire, Flame; Light; Soul;
VANITY; VIRTUES

Candlestick: *see*
AFTERWORLDS;
Almond; Candle; Gold;
Light; Oil; PLANETS;
Seven; TIME; Tree
[1] *Exodus 25: 31–40*

Cannibalism: *see* Giant;
Witchcraft

Canopy: *see* Baldachin;
Circle; Parasol; Sky, Square

Cao Guojiu: *see* Eight
Immortals, The; Lü
Dongbin

*The candelabrum
(Menorah) of the
Temple of Jerusalem,
after a 12th-century
Bible illustration.*

Can Nü

"Lady Silkworm", a girl responsible for the arrival of silk into the world, in Chinese myth. She missed her father greatly when he was away and declared that she would marry anyone who brought him home. Her stallion bolted and galloped away and fetched her father, who was relieved to find nothing amiss. Can Nü remembered her words but the father, furious that a horse should think of marrying his daughter, slaughtered the animal and skinned it. Later, the girl and her friends taunted the skin. It suddenly wrapped itself around her and flew into a tree. Later her father and his neighbours found her and saw that she had turned into a silkworm, a creature with a horse-like head that span a fine glossy thread.

Candle

As an image of spiritual illumination in the darkness of ignorance, the candle is an important symbol in Christian ritual, standing for Christ, the Church, joy, faith and witness. Eucharist candles represent Christ's presence at Holy Communion; the Paschal candle symbolizes the risen Christ at Easter. Candlemas Day, (February 2nd), was traditionally the day on which all the candles needed for the year are consecrated. In 17th-century Dutch still-lifes a candle may suggest the transience of life.

At a more personal level, the short-lived candle and its easily extinguished flame becoming a metaphor for the solitary, aspiring human soul. It appears with this meaning in devotional still-lifes and in the more widespread custom of placing candles around a coffin and lighting a candle in prayer. Blowing out candles on a birthday cake symbolizes life continuing beyond all the extinguished years.

Candlestick

The general symbolism of the candle is often extended by the form of the candlestick or candelabrum, most notably in the seven-branched Jewish Menorah. The original Menorah, described in the Bible[1] as made of gold with almond-shaped bowls for oil lamps (later, candles), alludes to the Cosmic Tree or Tree of Light, its seven branches representing the sun, moon and five ancient planets, the seven days of the week and the seven levels of heaven.

Cannibalism

In some cultures, cannibalism was a ritual custom symbolizing the absorption of the victim's vital power and forestalling any magical vengeance. Ancient fears of being consumed appear in many folk tales of giants and witches, and in a number of early myths, notably in the Greek story of the Titan Kronos, who swallowed his children at birth.

Canopy

In the Far East, a symbol of the sky, and thus of royalty and protective power. One of the Eight Auspicious Buddhist emblems, it is said to be linked with the royal parasol discarded by Prince Siddhartha. It also alludes to the Islamic paradise. In Hindu ritual the canopy is round for kings, square for priests.

Cao Guojiu

The brother of the empress Cao of the Song dynasty (960–1279CE) and one of the Eight Immortals of Daoist (Taoist) myth. Disillusioned with court life, Cao went into the mountains to seek the Dao. At a river he tried to impress the boatman with his golden tablet (his attribute in Chinese art) for admission to court. The boatman – the Immortal Lü Dongbin in disguise – asked him how any seeker of the Dao could show so little humility. Cao threw the tablet into the river and became Lü's disciple.

Cap

Caps of various kinds appear frequently in ancient iconography, and are often associated with high status, especially when tall or conical. The obvious attempt to make their wearers look more impressive may have been less significant than their solar and phallic symbolism of power. The pointed cap of the wizard symbolizes supernatural power and wisdom. The dunce's cap and the jester's cap with its flopping bells are mocking inversions of this tradition. Witches may also be shown wearing pointed caps, a reference to Satan's horns. The cap survives as a status symbol in the academic cap (mortarboard) and in the cap presented to sportspeople chosen to play for a national team.

CARDINAL POINTS, THE *see panel overleaf*

Cards

In art, Eros (in Roman myth, Cupid) may be shown holding a blank playing-card as a symbol of the hazards of love, or the ace of hearts as love triumphant. Cards became an allegory for the vice of idleness from the 17th century, when card games were a widespread form of gambling. Jan Steen's *Beware of Luxury* and *The Dissolute House-hold* both feature cards as a reminder of the expression, "Cards, women and drink have ruined many a man." A collapsing house of cards is an emblem of a disintegrating home in Augustus Leopold Egg's moralizing triptych *Past and Present*.

Cargo cults

In Oceania, contact with European civilization led to the creation and alteration of myths to account for the Europeans' place in the cosmos. Melanesians and others were staggered by the amount of material goods the newcomers brought in their ships and "cargo" became the pidgin word *kago*, which means "goods", "belongings" or "wealth". Melanesians believed that Europeans must have particularly effective magic to possess such wealth, and started "cargo cults" in an attempt to acquire this lore for themselves. Typically, it was thought that some ancestor, god or other revered figure would bring the *kago*. His arrival would herald a new age of plenty, justice and, some hoped, freedom from foreign control. Cargo cults persist to this day: for example, Prince Philip, the husband of Queen Elizabeth II, is the focus of a cult on Tanna Island in Vanuatu.

Carnation

Carnations can represent betrothal in 15th- and 16th-century Netherlandish art, and may be emblems of maternal love in Madonna and Child paintings.

Carnival

The period immediately preceding Lent, which is traditionally a time of frugality and abstinence. Carnival is marked in Catholic countries by feasting and revelry that culminates on Shrove Tuesday, the day before the start of Lent. The name is from Italian *carnevale*, derived from Late Latin

Cap: *see* Clown; Devils; Head; Horn; Phallus; Phrygian cap; Sun; WISDOM; Witchcraft

Cards: *see* Eros; Tarot; Vices

Cargo cults: *see* John Frum

Carnation: *see* Red

Carnival: *see* Solstice

*The castle as a
stronghold of evil (the
fire-breathing dragon
within its walls); after
a medieval illustration.*

carne levamen or *carne levarium*, literally "the taking away of meat". Carnival is an opportunity for amusement, licence and mild anarchy.

Carp
An emblem of courage and scholarship in China, and of samurai fortitude in Japan, possibly from the contrast between its leaping vigour in the water and its calmness when dying. Also admired for its longevity, the carp is a symbol of good luck. Images of carp were placed on ships' masts and on roofs to ward off fire

Carpenter *see* **Joseph, husband of the Virgin**

Carpet
An important medium for visual symbolism throughout the Islamic world. Animals, birds, plants and geometric motifs woven into Oriental carpets gave them mythic significance. In a similar way, the prayer mat took on the meaning of a sacred space. From the idea of a carpet that elevated the worshipper to a separate plane of existence, it was perhaps a simple step to the popular legends of flying carpets such as King Solomon's, which was made only of green silk but capable of supporting his throne and his entire retinue.

Cassandra
In Greek myth, the seeress daughter of King Priam and Queen Hecuba of Troy. The god Apollo gave her the gift of prophecy in the hope of winning her heart, but she did not return his love, so he condemned her never to be believed. When Troy fell, Ajax raped Cassandra near an image of Athene (the Roman Minerva), an outrage

depicted in *Ajax Abducting Cassandra* by Solomon Joseph Solomon. Taken to Greece as the concubine of the victorious King Agamemnon, she foretold bloodshed and refused to enter his palace. Agamemnon disbelieved her warnings and was violently assassinated. Cassandra herself was murdered shortly afterwards.

Castle
A shining goal or a fearful challenge. As such, castles appear in innumerable legends and folk tales, their symbolism usually varying with their colour. The dark castle, perhaps hidden in an almost impenetrable forest and often defended by a black knight, symbolizes evil forces, the underworld and fear of death. It contains a treasure or incarcerated maiden to be wrested by courage and ingenuity from these dark powers. The bright castle, which may appear and disappear like a mirage and is usually set on a height, symbolizes a spiritual quest or the City of God, difficult to attain. Castles in the air symbolize the never-accomplished goals of those who think that they can be achieved by wishing rather than through realistic effort. In art, the impregnable castle can signify chastity.

Castor and Polydeuces (Pollux) *see* **Dioscuri, The**

Castration
Loss of power – the symbolism of the savage judicial use of castration as part of the execution of traitors in Elizabethan England, and in the more widespread mutilation of slain enemies. Castration was sometimes used in ancient fertility sacrifices. In Greek myth, the supreme god, the Titan

CARDINAL POINTS, THE

The four cardinal points, East, West, North and South, graphically represented by a cross, formed an ancient symbol of the cosmos, with humankind at the centre (sometimes becoming the fifth point). Early rituals, especially in North and South America, suggest gods were thought to dwell at these points and control human life, thus explaining the importance of the number four in mythology and in daily and religious life. From these basic directions came the rain-bearing winds to fertilize or destroy crops, personified by gods to which veneration was paid, sacrifices offered, libations poured or smoke puffed. In Chinese thought, tigers symbolizing protective forces guarded the four points and the centre. Because the symbolism of individual directions was based largely on climate and the influence of sun, cross-cultural similarities are more marked for East and West than for North and South.

East almost invariably symbolized light, the source of life, the sun and solar gods, youth, resurrection and new life. There lay the biblical Eden, the Chinese celestial dragon and the Aztec crocodile of creation; it was the birthplace of heroes, the home of ancestors and, in many African traditions, where good souls went. Christ-ian prayer is directed eastward, and the Native American Dakota nations, among others, buried bodies with their heads facing East, the source of the wind of paradise.

West symbolized sleep, rest, the mystery of death, the Native American Happy Hunting Grounds, and the Indo-Iranian, Egyptian and Greek lands of the dead. In some cultures, this symbolism was tinged with fear. Westward lay the Nordic sea of destruction. St Jerome associated west with Satan. For some African tribes it was where bad souls went.

North symbolized belligerent power, darkness, hunger, cold, chaos and evil in most northern hemisphere traditions apart from those of Egypt and India, where it represented light and the masculine principle. Associated with furious winds, it was the seat of mighty gods including Ahriman (the Zoroastrian prince of darkness), Satan and Mictlanteculitli (the Aztec god of death). It is shown iconographically as the Aztec eagle of war, the Hebrew winged ox and the Chinese black tortoise.

In most parts of the world **South** symbolized fire, passion, masculinity, solar and lunar energy. Again, Egypt and India are the exceptions; South stood here for night, hell and the feminine principle.

Uranos, was overthrown by his youngest son, Kronos, who castrated him with a sickle (a frequent emblem of castration). The falling blood produced monsters; semen from the genitals formed the foam that bore the goddess Aphrodite (Venus).

Cat

Cleverness, stealth, the power of transformation and clairvoyance, agility, watchfulness, sensual beauty, and female malice. These almost universal associations had differing symbolic significance in ancient cultures.

Cat: *see* ANIMALS; Bastet; Black; Devils; LIBERTY; Lion; SEVEN DEADLY SINS, THE; Snake; Sun; Transformation; Witchcraft

In Egypt, notably in the worship of the feline goddess Bastet or Bast, cats were benign and sacred creatures. Bastet, originally shown as a lioness, was a tutelary lunar goddess, popularly linked with pleasure, fertility and protective forces. In her honour, cats were venerated and often mummified, along with mice for them to eat. In iconography, the cat appeared as an ally of the sun, severing the head of the underworld serpent.

Cats were also associated with other lunar goddesses, including the Greek Artemis (Diana to the Romans), and with the Nordic goddess Freyja whose chariot they drew. In Rome their self-sufficient freedom also made them emblems of Liberty. Elsewhere, their night wanderings and powers of transformation (pupil dilation, sheathing and unsheathing of claws, sudden switches from indolence to ferocity) were distrusted. Black cats in particular were linked with evil cunning in the Celtic world, with harmful *djinn* in Islam, and with bad luck in Japan where folk tales described how cats could take over the bodies of women. In India, where cats embody animal beauty, Buddhists seem to have held their aloofness against them: legend had it that, like the serpent, they failed to mourn the Buddha's death. The most negative view of all appears in the folklore of Western witchcraft, where cats appear as demonic familiars associated with satanic orgies – lustful and cruel incarnations of the Devil himself. In Western art, a cat may be shown as a peaceful domestic animal, but a stealthy cat about to pounce suggests trouble lurking. In Manet's *Olympia* a black cat, with arched back and bristling tail, announces an intruder into the courtesan's domain.

Caterpillar

Lowly and unformed, the caterpillar is an image of inadequacy in the Hindu doctrine of the transmigration of souls. In Native North American tradition, though, the caterpillar is a metaphor for sexual awakening, the first experience of sex.

Cathbhadh

A Druid who features prominently in the stories of the Ulster heroes Conchobar and Cú Chulainn as a great seer and a teacher of heroes.

Catherine of Alexandria, Saint

According to legend,[1] Catherine (4th century CE), was a beautiful, educated noblewoman. She argued with the emperor Maxentius that he should cease persecuting Christians and worshipping false gods. Overwhelmed by her eloquence and knowledge, he invited fifty masters of logic and rhetoric to challenge her in Alexandria. Catherine converted them all through her reasoning and faith in Christ.

The emperor, beside himself with rage, burned the learned men. Then, unable to persuade this bride of Christ to join him in his palace, he threw her into a dark cell without food for 12 days, but she emerged in full health, having been fed by a dove. The emperor then constructed a wheel with iron saws and sharp-pointed nails on which Catherine was to be tortured. However, she prayed to God and an angel shattered the wheel, killing 4,000 heathens. Catherine was finally beheaded and her body was taken to Mount Sinai.

Scenes from the life of St Catherine were illustrated by Masolino, the most popular being the episode of her mystical marriage to Christ. According to tradition, Catherine was converted by a hermit who gave her an image of the Virgin and Child. The image prompted a vision in which the Christ Child turned toward her and placed a ring on her finger. Veronese is one of several artists who depicted the betrothal of the richly dressed saint. Catherine's attribute is the wheel of torture.

Catherine of Siena, Saint

Catherine (c.1347–1380) resisted her parents' attempts to make her marry, and joined the Dominican order to tend the poor and sick. She had many mystical experiences: in one, Christ offered her a choice of two crowns, one of gold and one of thorns, and she took the latter; in another, she received the stigmata; and, like Catherine of Alexandria, she had a mystical marriage with Christ. She played an important role in returning the Papacy from Avignon to Rome. Catherine is now a patron saint of Italy and most highly revered in her native city of Siena, where Domenico Beccafumi painted her receiving the stigmata in a white habit, probably to reflect her purity. In other paintings she wears the black-and-white of her order and may have a lily or rosary, or show her stigmata.

Cato, Marcus Porcius, of Utica

For the Romans, the statesman Cato[1] (95–46BCE) symbolized total moral integrity. A firm supporter of the Republic, he opposed Julius Caesar and, after the death of Pompey, took his own life rather than live under tyranny. After reading Plato's dialogue on the soul twice, he plunged his sword into his breast, as depicted in Charles Le Brun's *The Death of Cato*.

Caul

The foetal membrane, sometimes partly covering the head of a baby at birth, was once considered a good omen. More particularly it was thought to be a charm against drowning. This superstition, dating at least from Roman times, led to some trafficking in cauls. In Slavic tradition, the caul was also held to be a sign of second sight and of metamorphosis, possibly into a werewolf.

Cauldron

Symbol of transformation, plenty, rebirth, rejuvenation, magical power. In art, several Christian saints are shown seated unhappily in cauldrons of boiling oil (which most survive), including St John the Evangelist, who is said to have emerged rejuvenated. False hope of their father's rejuvenation led the daughters of King Pelias of Iolcus in Thessaly to chop him up and throw the pieces into a cauldron on the treacherous advice of the sorceress Medea.

Also in Greek myth, Thetis, the mother of Achilles, lost several earlier children when she put them in a cauldron to find out if they had inherited their father. In Celtic myth, the most prized possession of the Irish father-god, the Daghda, was a life-giving cauldron that never emptied; another magic cauldron restored dead warriors to life. The Celtic ritual cauldron found at Gundestrup in Denmark is adorned with various sacred figures and symbols.

Cave

A primal image of shelter – hence a symbol of the womb, birth and rebirth, the origin, centre and heart of being. The cave can alternatively have dark meanings: the underworld, the Celtic entrance to hell or, in psychology, regressive wishes and the unconscious. More usually, as widely expressed in myths and initiation rites, it is a place where the germinating powers of the earth are concentrated, where oracles speak, where initiates are reborn in spiritual understanding, and where souls ascend to celestial light. Sacred caves and grottoes, usually on hills or mountains, formed earth-to-sky axial symbols, the focus of spiritual force often represented by a domed vault or pillar. Fertility symbolism associated with caves and dwarfish rain-gods appears in Mexico. [4] Prophets as well as gods and heroes were linked with caves or clefts, such as the famous oracle of Delphi, who sat over a deep chasm in the rock to deliver her cryptic utterances. The cave as a spiritual source also appears in Christianity: an apocryphal tradition, often represented in Orthodox paintings of the Nativity, claimed that Christ was born in a cave,[1] and it was said that John the Evangelist received his Revelation in a cave on Patmos.

Greek philosophy proposed the cave as a metaphor for the material world; hence Plato's image of humanity chained in a cave and seeing illusions – reflected light from a higher reality that only mind and spirit could attain. In folklore, caves often symbolize less ethical goals – the treasures of Aladdin, for example – protected by dragons or cunning gnomes.

Cecilia, Saint

Little is known of Cecilia[1] although it is certain that a lady of that name founded a church in Trastevere, Rome. She is said to have been a Roman noblewoman living in the 2nd or 3rd century CE, who was raised as a Christian and suffered martyrdom for refusing to worship pagan gods, Cecilia was put into a boiling bath for a night and a day but remained unharmed. Three blows of an axe failed to cut off her head; and, lingering on the point of death for three days, she gave all her possessions to the poor. Scenes from her life surround her image by the Master of St Cecilia, and Stefano Maderno carved her lifeless body. She is the patron of musicians either because she sang to God in her heart or because of the music at her wedding. Her attributes are instruments, particularly the organ, as in Raphael's famous image of her, and the lily of purity.

Cedar

The Tree of Life in Sumeria – a symbol of power and immortality. The fragrance, durability and awesome height (up to thirty metres) of this pine made the Lebanese species a biblical emblem of majesty and incorruptibility, its heartwood a later metaphor for Christ. Cedar was used to build the Temple of Solomon and for Greek and Roman busts of gods and ancestors. Its reputation for longevity may account for the use of cedar resin by Celtic embalmers.

Centaur

A symbol of man trapped by his baser impulses, especially lust, violence and drunkenness. First shown in Greek art as a man with the equine hindquarters, but later with both fore- and hindquarters of a horse, the Centaur may in origin derive from bands of mounted brigands in the hills of Thessaly. According to one myth, the mortal Ixion ravished a cloud, believing her to be the goddess Hera, wife of Zeus; the cloud duly gave birth to the monster Centauros, whose bestiality with mares in turn produced the Centaurs. With this sorry lineage, the Centaurs became wild, drunken rapists – Nessus, for example, tried to carry off the wife of Herakles. Piero di Cosimo depicts Centaurs in *Scenes of Primitive Man*: they are often shown in art with anguished faces and battling unsuccessfully against the forces of law and order. As such, they represent sensual passion, adultery and heresy in Christian iconography. The Centaur may also represent the base or animal aspect of humanity, as illustrated in Botticelli's *Pallas and the Centaur*, in which the lowly creature cowers beside wise Athene (Minerva).

An alternative, humanizing myth introduced a race of morally superior Centaurs. Chiron acquired his form because his father, Kronos (Saturn), hoping to conceal an illicit passion from his wife, transformed himself into a horse and made love to the nymph, Philyra. Chiron was a wise teacher, especially of music and medicine, and he educated many heroes including Achilles and Jason, and the demi-god Asklepios. He died accidentally when Herakles accidentally shot a poisoned arrow into Chiron's knee.[1] Chiron, with bow and arrow, became the constellation Sagittarius.

The renowned Battle of the Centaurs (the Centauromachy) occurred at the wedding of Pirithous to the lovely Hippodamia.[2] The Lapiths had invited the Centaurs, but at the sight of the beautiful bride, the fiercest Centaur, Eurytus, dragged her off by her hair and the others carried off whichever girl they could. The hero Theseus, a wedding guest, attacked

Centaurs beating a victim, after a Greek vase of the 5th century BCE.

them and a bloody fray ensued in which half the Centaurs were slain and the rest driven off. The celebrated Elgin Marbles from the Parthenon, Athens, illustrate the violent struggle.

Horse-man hybrids appear in Vedic myth as the Gandharvas – physical virility combined with intellect.

Centeotl

"Maize Cob Lord", an Aztec maize god and the male counterpart of the goddess Chicomecoatl, who represented sustenance in general. Both deities were closely associated with Chalchiuhtlicue, the water goddess and wife of the rain and fertility god Tlaloc. They were also said to be related to Xilonen, the goddess of the tender young shoots of corn.

Centre

The focal point of worship; the essence of the godhead; ultimate and eternal state of being; perfection. Most of the symbolism of centrality is self-evident thanks to the fact that the centre is the hub, pivot or axis, the point upon which lines of force converge or from which they radiate; it can symbolize not only divinity, the object of love or aspiration, but also rulership and administration. Less

Centeotl: *see* Chalchiuhtlicue; Tlaloc

Centre: *see* Axis; CARDINAL POINTS; Circle; Point

Cephalus and Procris: *see*
Aurora
¹ Ovid, *Met VII 661–865*

Cerberus: *see* Echidne;
Hades; HERAKLES, THE
LABOURS OF; Orpheus;
Sibyl; UNDERWORLDS
¹ Virgil, *Aeneid VI:417–424*

obviously, the centre is a symbol of totality in the metaphysical concept by which a central point concentrates and contains the energy and meaning of everything else.

Centurion

A Roman officer in charge of 100 men. Christ healed a centurion's servant, and a centurion was converted at the Crucifixion.

Centzon Totochtin

The "Four Hundred Rabbits", a group of little Aztec gods associated with the intoxicating beverage called *pulque* or *octli*, which was made from the maguey plant and widely used in public rituals and festivals. Aptly, the Centzon Totochtin include Tepoztecatl, the god of drunkenness. The rabbit is renowned for its fecundity and for its seemingly mischievous antics and this probably explains the creature's association with *pulque*. The liquor was also linked with fertility – sometimes depicted spurting from the breasts of a mother goddess.

Cephalus and Procris

In Greek mythology¹ Cephalus, just after his marriage to Procris, was abducted by the goddess Eos (the Roman Aurora) against his will. Poussin's *Cephalus and Aurora* shows how he rebuffed her and the goddess swore revenge. She planted suspicion in his mind and changed his appearance. The disguised Cephalus returned home to find Procris distraught at the loss of her husband. He resolved to test his wife's fidelity by offering her a bribe to become his mistress. At the moment she hesitated, he revealed his true identity, but Procris, overwhelmed with shame,

fled to the mountains. Here Cephalus found her and begged forgiveness, and for years they lived in harmony.

Artemis (in Roman myth, Diana) had given Procris a matchless hunting dog and a javelin as presents for her husband. While hunting, Cephalus spoke endearingly to the cool winds in the midday heat, but his words were overheard and he was mistakenly thought to be wooing a nymph. The rumour reached Procris, who refused to believe it unless she herself witnessed her husband's disloyalty. The next day Cephalus was again calling the winds when he heard a moan and rustling leaves. Thinking that a wild animal lurked in the bush, he hurled his javelin, only to spear Procris. In *Cephalus and Procris* Veronese painted her dying in the arms of her husband; as she begged Cephalus not to let the breeze take her place, he realized the dreadful misunderstanding.

Cepheus *see* **Andromeda**

Cerberus

A ferocious three-headed dog, one of the numerous monstrous offspring of Echidne and Typhon. Cerberus, who was sometimes said to have a serpent for a tail and dragon-heads sprouting from his back and necks, was given to the god Hades (Pluto in Roman myth) to guard the entrance to the underworld, the land of the dead, and to devour anyone who tried to leave. It was said that none could pass him, but Cerberus was so enchanted by the lyre of Orpheus that he allowed him to enter the underworld to look for Eurydice. In Virgil's *Aeneid* a Sibyl drugged the dog so that Aeneas could pass through. Cerberus returned to the world of the living on only one occasion, when Herakles forcibly dragged the beast before King Eurystheus as his twelfth and final labour.

Ceres

Originally a southern Italian deity of fertility, crops and the regenerative powers of nature (the word "cereal" derives from her name), who later became largely identified with the Greek goddess Demeter.

Cernunnos

"The Horned One", the Gaulish name – known from a single inscription – given to a male deity with horns or antlers whose image has been found in much of the ancient Celtic world, principally northern and central France (ancient Gaul) and Britain. Cernunnos appears to have been a deity of fertility and abundance, a dispenser of fruit, grain and wealth, and a lord of animals. He was sometimes depicted with serpents and the Celtic wheel symbol, which was an emblem of the sun.

Cernunnos had associations with the underworld of the dead: the ancient Celts placed small wheels in graves in order to provide the deceased with light underground. In one representation he was linked with the Roman gods Mercury, who conducted the souls of the dead to the underworld, and Apollo, who was the god of light.

Cerynean Hind, The *see* HERAKLES, THE LABOURS OF

Cessair

The woman who led the first group of people to settle in Ireland, according to the *Book of Invasions*. Cessair was the daughter of Bith, a son of the biblical Noah, and arrived in Ireland just forty days before the Flood. She and her followers all perished in the deluge, with the exception of her husband, Fintan mac Bóchra.

Chac

The Mayan god of water, rain and lightning. As guardian of the fertilizing rains, Chac presided over agriculture and opened the stone which concealed the first maize. The god is related to the Aztec rain deity Tlaloc, who, like him, is shown as an old man.

Chac, from the Dresden Codex *of the Post-classic period.*

Chain

Servitude, but also unity through bondage in friendship, communication or communal endeavour – a negative–positive symbolism nicely muddled in the famous Marxist rallying cry: "Workers of the world unite, you have nothing to lose but your chains!" As fetters, chains are emblems of slavery and, in Christian art, of Vice (humanity shackled to worldly desires) – they are associated particularly with Saints Leonard and Vincent. Broken chains signify freedom and salvation. As emblems of community linkage, chains are worn to show official status, or used in

Ceres: *see* Demeter; Hades; Persephone

Chac: *see* Cocijo; Tlaloc

Chain: *see* Bonds; Cord; Gold; Hephaistos; Leonard, St; LIBERTY; Marriage; Vincent, St

Christmas decorations as symbols of social or family cohesion. They can stand for marriage at the social level, and also for the marriage of spiritual and earthly powers, a symbolism dating back to the Greek poet Homer, who spoke of a golden chain hung from heaven to earth by the god Zeus. It was later interpreted as a metaphor for prayer.

In Greek myth, the gods were highly amused when Hephaistos (the Roman Vulcan) exposed the adultery of his wife Aphrodite (Venus) by catching her in a net of chains as she and Ares (Mars) embraced.

Chakra

The power of inner consciousness. In Hindu and Tantric doctrine the *chakras* ("wheels") are eight vital energy, situated at various points along the body, from the base of the spine to the crown of the head. Activated by reciting sacred words in meditation, they drive a flow of physiological and spiritual energy from the base *chakra* upward to open the "thousand-petalled lotus" at the crown of the head.

Chalchiuhtlicue

The Aztec goddess of rivers and lakes. Chalchiuhtlicue (which means "Jade Skirt") was the consort of Tlaloc, the rain god, and was regarded as the sister of his entourage the Tlaloque. She was said to possess the power to conjure up hurricanes and whirlwinds and to cause drownings. Some representations of the goddess portray her as a goddess of childbirth, an attribute derived from her association with the waters of birth. In the Aztec myth of the five "suns" or ages, Chalchiuhtlicue presided over the fourth age. It came to an end when the world was

The goddess Chalchiuhtlicue, after a 16th-century Aztec codex.

engulfed by cataclysmic floods. She has also been linked with the goddess Xochiquetzal, the Aztec goddess of flowers and craftsmen.

Chalice

A ritual goblet, associated particularly with the sacred wine (Christ's blood) of the Christian Eucharist and with the legend of the Holy Grail, said to be the chalice used by Christ at the Last Supper. It symbolizes the imbibing of spiritual illumination or knowledge; redemption; and, hence, immortality. The chalice appears in art as an emblem of Faith and is an attribute of several Christian saints. In China and Japan, and in marriage ceremonies worldwide, sharing a chalice signifies fidelity. Ceremonial goblets were used in the Celtic world to denote sovereignty.

Alternatively, the chalice can stand for a bitter destiny, as in the cup that Christ asked God to take from him, referring to his approaching crucifixion. The so-called "poisoned chalice" promises hope but delivers disaster.

Chameleon

Now simply a metaphor for changeability, this arboreal lizard has other remarkable characteristics (climbing ability, independently swivelling eyes, and a long, hunting tongue) that gave it sacred and ethical significance in many parts of Africa. Associated with thunder, lightning, rain and also with the sun, it appears widely as an intermediary between sky gods and humankind; and, in Pigmy folklore, as an agent in humanity's creation. In Western art it can personify Air.

Chaos (1)

In one Chinese creation myth, two emperors decided to repay Chaos (Hun Dun) for his hospitality by giving him the bodily orifices, which he lacked. So they bored holes in his body, but killed him in the process. However, as Chaos died the ordered world came into being.

Pan Gu, a creator god of Chinese myth, holding the cosmic egg of chaos; after a 19th-century lithograph.

Chaos (2)

According to the Greek account of creation in Hesiod's *Theogony*, Chaos ("Yawning Void") was the first thing to exist. However, it is unclear whether Chaos was conceived of as a divinity and so whether the next things to form (Gaia, Tartaros, Eros, Erebos and Nyx) were its progeny or unconnected phenomena. In the creation myth of the mystic Orphic sect, Chaos sprang from Chronos ("Time"), one of two primal deities said to have been present at the start of creation.

Chariot

A dynamic image of rulership, widely used in iconography to illustrate the mastery and mobility of gods and heroes, or the spiritual authority of religious and allegorical figures. Its triumphal symbolism probably owes much to the impact of the chariot on warfare when it was invented in the 2nd millennium BCE. Hindu mystics (later supported by psychologists such as Jung) saw charioteering as a symbol of the Self: the charioteer (thought) uses the reins (willpower and intelligence) to master the steeds (life force) tugging the chariot (the body). In moral allegory, the chariot thus became an image of the triumphant journey of the spirit, a symbolism used by the makers of the film *Chariots of Fire*.

A fiery chariot carried the prophet Elijah to heaven[1]. Wheel symbolism fitted aptly to the chariots of sun gods such as Apollo or moon goddesses such as Artemis. Equally, the sound of rumbling wheels suggested the chariots of Thor and other thunder gods. Gods or allegorical figures are more often identified by the specific symbolism of the creatures that draw their chariots. Thus Chastity is drawn by unicorns, Eternity by angels, Night by black horses, Death by black oxen and Fame by elephants.

[1] *2 Kings 2:11*

Charity

Charity: *see* Cimon and Pero; VIRTUES, THE
[1] *I Corinthians 12:13*
[2] *Matthew 25: 35–36*

Charles Borromeo, Saint: *see* Ambrose, St

Charon: *see* Hades
[1] Virgil, *Aeneid VI 300–305*

In Classical myth, Apollo's chariot may be drawn by white horses; that of Dionysos (Bacchus in Roman myth) by panthers, tigers or leopards; of Rhea (Cybele) by lions; of Artemis (Diana) by stags; of Hera (Juno) by peacocks; of Poseidon (Neptune) by sea-horses; of Hades (Pluto) by black horses; and of Aphrodite (Venus) by doves or swans. The colour of the chariot may be significant, too – Indra's is gold. The chariot card in Tarot symbolizes self-control.

Charity

Faith, Hope and Charity (or Love)[1] were sanctified by the medieval church as the three cardinal virtues. Charity was the "mother of the virtues" and may be personified as a woman giving alms. In many Renaissance and Baroque paintings, Charity is depicted as a loving mother with two or more children, perhaps nursing one of them, as in Lucas Cranach's *Charity* and Van Dyck's painting of the same title.

The theologian St Augustine saw charity as the love of God and the bond between God and humankind. It was also an example for ideal citizens to follow, living their lives according to the seven acts of mercy: "For I was an hungred, and ye gave me meat: I was thirsty, and ye gave me drink: I was a stranger, and ye took me in. Naked, and ye clothed me: I was sick, and ye visited me: I was in prison, and ye came unto me."[2] The seventh act of mercy is to bury the dead. Paintings representing these acts were commissioned in the 17th century, particularly by charitable confraternities.

Charles Borromeo, Saint

Charles Borromeo (1538–84) was made a cardinal by his uncle, Pope Pius IV, at the age of 22. In 1564 he became archbishop of Milan and he took an active part in the Council of Trent and the reform of the Catholic Church. He started Sunday schools, opened seminaries for training the clergy, and practised and preached that life should be charitable and that the sick and needy should be cared for. He was likened to St Ambrose, the patron saint of Milan, and may be shown with him in paintings. He appears wearing various forms of religious dress and in Baroque art he may be seen having a vision of Christ. Daniele Crespi depicted the saint fasting before a simple altar, weeping as he reads, his distinctively large, aquiline nose in evidence.

Charon

In Greek myth, the ferryman who rowed the dead across the rivers Acheron and Styx to the underworld, demanding a coin for his services. For this reason the Greeks would place a coin in a corpse's mouth before burial.

The offspring of Erebos ("Underworld Darkness") and Nyx ("Night"), Charon was described as "a ragged figure, filthy, repulsive, with white hair, copious and unkempt covering his chin, eyes which are stark points of flame, and a dirty garment knotted and hanging from his shoulders. Charon punts his boat with his pole or trims the sails, and so he ferries every soul on his dusky coracle, for though he is old, he is a god, and a god's old age is tough and green".[1] He can be seen in Christian art, such as Michelangelo's *Last Judgment*.

Charybdis *see* Scylla and Charybdis

CHASTITY *see panel opposite*

CHASTITY

Chastity, poverty and obedience are the vows of the monastic Orders, and personifications of chastity may have a veil or palm of the virgin martyrs, or stand in triumph on a symbol of lust, such as a pig. Chastity might be paired or locked in combat with the figure of Lust. The Greek goddess of chastity, Artemis (in Roman myth, Diana) might be juxtaposed with Aphrodite (Venus) and Eros (Cupid) representing sensual love. She may carry a shield on which Eros' golden arrows break, and the chain for binding love. Chastity may also be represented by the nymph Daphne, who became a laurel tree as she fled from the sun-god Apollo, or by virtuous Roman women such as Tuccia, or by biblical characters, notably the Virgin Mary,

the demure Susannah (in the biblical Apocrypha), or Joseph, who refused Potiphar's wife. Chastity is also famously personified by the unicorn.

In Christian art, St Anthony may be shown controlling erotic dreams through prayer; SS Benedict and Francis throw themselves into thorny bushes to quell their desires; and female saints who preserved their virginity may hold a lily.

Traditional symbols of chastity are numerous and include: the colours blue and white, bees, castles, chestnuts, crescents, crystals, diamonds, doves, elephants, enclosed gardens, ermine, girdles, hawthorns, irises, jade, laurel, lilies, mirrors, palms, pearls, the phoenix, the salamander, sapphires, sealed wells, sieves, silver, towers and violets.

Cherry

A samurai emblem, perhaps suggested by the hard kernel within the blood-coloured skin and flesh. In China, the cherry tree is considered lucky, a symbol of spring (from its early blossom) and virginity. The vulva is a "cherry spring". In Christian iconography the cherry is an alternative to the apple as the fruit of paradise, and is sometimes an attribute held by Christ.

Cherubim

The second order of angels, whose wings formed the throne of God in the Hebrew sanctuary that Moses was commanded to build (Exodus 37). Their protective symbolism derived from earlier Persian and Mesopotamian guardian spirits who flanked

temples. Cherubim, or cherubs, usually appear in art as blue-winged heads, sometimes with a book, symbolizing divine knowledge by reason of their proximity to God, whom they are sometimes shown supporting in flight. In Baroque art, cherubs are little distinguishable from cupids or *putti*.

Chess

Now an analogy for cold, tactical foresight, chess was an ancient metaphor for the wise handling of free will and fate in a dualistic universe – or, at a more practical level, for the responsible management of war and state affairs by the ruling class of India, where the game probably originated. Chess can be seen as a simple image of warfare safely removed to the plane of

*Chibinda Ilunga, based
on a wooden figure from
Congo-Kinshasa.*

an intellectual activity. However, richer accretions of symbolism, legend and allegory cling to the game, which dates back at least to the 6th century CE and probably earlier. Fate as well as logic intervened in ancient Indian chess, a four-handed affair in which dice were used to initiate moves.

A two-handed game with some similarities existed in Persia, where the Indian version of the game (*Chaturanga*) was taken over and developed into a more strictly intellectual contest (*Shatranj*) which entered Spain, and then became hugely popular in medieval Europe. Magic chessboards in Arthurian legend became allegories of the trials of love. Folk heroes played chess with the Devil. Craftsmen produced wondrously modelled chess pieces tailored to the dramatic intrigues of politics or to allegories of the struggle between the forces of good and evil, light and darkness, reason and passion, life and death, tyranny and good government.

The board's 64 squares derive from the fourfold (8 x 8) mandala of the Indian goddess Shiva, the field of action for the cosmic forces he controlled. Originally the key pieces were elephants (which also carried the kings), chariots, horses and foot soldiers. Their symbolism is complex, as their relative status, forms and patterns of movement changed over a long period before settling into the present values.

Chest

A Roman emblem of mystical religions. Greek and Hebrew chests were receptacles for mysteries revealed only to chosen initiates, as in the chests carried in the rites of the Greek Dionysos or Demeter, or the chest holding the Hebrew Tablets of the Law. In China, chests enshrined ancient traditions or ancestral spirits.

Chibinda Ilunga

A prince of the Luba-Lunda peoples of what are now southeastern Congo-Kinshasa and northeastern Angola. Chibinda Ilunga was the grandson of Mbidi Kiluwe, the forefather of the Luba kings. His face was said to be white and shining like the moon. He left the Luba kingdom after the king, who was jealous of his hunting prowess, insulted him by declaring that Chibinda Ilunga had never made war.

One day, Chibinda Ilunga encountered Lueji in the forest. Lueji was the Lunda queen and granddaughter of the primordial serpent Chinawezi. She invited the charming stranger to stay with her. In due course they were married and Lueji announced to the Lunda elders that she was standing down from her office and that Chibinda Ilunga would rule in her place. After handing her husband her bracelet of office, Lueji began an extraordinarily long menstruation. Her prolonged flow of blood meant that she was never able to bear children. In the end Lueji gave Chibinda Ilunga another wife, called Kamonga, who was fertile.

Chicomecoatl *see* Centeotl.

Child

Purity, potentiality, innocence, spontaneity – a symbol of the natural, paradisal state, free of anxiety. In iconography the child can also stand for mystic knowledge, openness to faith, as in the alchemist's image of a crowned child who represented the

Philosopher's Stone. Christ used child symbolism when he said that only those who humbled themselves as little children could enter the Kingdom of Heaven.[1]

Chimera

A monster of Greek myth, celebrated enough to become a general term for any figment of the imagination – hence the word "chimerical".– and for hybrid animals of all kinds in architecture. The Chimera had the mane and fire-breathing head of a lion, the body of a goat (it is often shown with a goat's head as well) and a snake-headed tail like a dragon's. The beast, which was sent by the gods to plague the region of Lycia in Asia Minor (modern Turkey), breathed terrible blasts of burning flame. It was slain by the hero Bellerophon, who rode on the winged horse Pegasus. His victory over the Chimera is an example of the common legend of confrontation between a heroic individual and a dragon-like creature which personifies profound human fears, evil and chaos.

In medieval art the Chimera represented satanic forces. Psychologists have seen it as an image of psychic deformations. Some mythologists interpret its threefold form as the embodiment of several destructive forces in nature, including volcanic eruptions and gas flares.

Chimney

The traditional focus not only of family life but of communication with supernatural forces, its axial symbolism dating back to ancient round dwellings in which the hearth was the central point (indeed, the word *focus* is the Latin for hearth or fireplace). Hence its importance in folklore as a

The Chimera, after an Etruscan bronze statue.

route out of the house for witches and into it for kindlier spirits such as Santa Claus.

Chinawezi

The name given in southern and central Africa to the primordial cosmic serpent which features widely in African mythology. In the beginning, Chinawezi (also known as Chinaweji), the mother of all things, divided up the world with her husband Nkuba, the Lightning. Nkuba set himself up in the sky with the heavenly bodies, and his urine became the beneficial rains. Chinawezi was governor of the earth and the waters: it was said that when the thunder rumbled she responded by causing the rivers to swell. Finally, after some time Chinawezi bore a daughter, Nawezi, and a son, Konde. These offspring married and had three children.

Chi-Rho

The name of the wheel-like monogram formed by the combined initial Greek letters (XP) of the Greek word *Khristos,* meaning Christ, intended to symbolize his protection and his triumph over death. For some centuries, the Chi-Rho was the leading emblem of Christianity apart from the fish. It displaced the eagle on the Roman

Chimera: *see* BEASTS OF FABLE; Bellerophon; Dragon; Echidne; Fire, Flame; Goat; Hero, Heroine; Lion; Pegasus; Snake; Triad; Volcano
[1] Homer, *The Iliad, VI 180–185*

Chimney: *see* Axis; Fire, Flame; Smoke; Witchcraft

Chinawezi: *see* Chibinda Ilunga; Lueji

Chi-Rho: *see* Alpha and Omega; Circle; CROSS; Eagle; IHS; INRI; Sun; Wheel

standard when Constantine the Great came to power by defeating Maxentius in 312CE. According to his biographer, Eusebius (*fl.* 4th century CE), Constantine's final conversion to Christianity was linked to an auspicious dream of the Chi-Rho sign superimposed on the sun – a clue to his probable identification of Christ as the incarnated sun.

The sign was not new, as the Greek word for "auspicious", *khrestos*, also began with X and P, and a similar spoked-wheel emblem within a circle was earlier a Chaldean solar symbol. Both XP (Christ) and IC (Jesus) appear as early Christian funerary monograms. The Chi-Rho may appear with the monogram of *alpha* and *omega* (AΩ), the first and last letters of the Greek alphabet.

Chiron

A Centaur who, untypically of these hybrid horse-man creatures, was famed for his wisdom, kindliness and civilized character. Chiron was said to be of nobler descent than most Centaurs and was educated by the gods Apollo and Artemis in the skills of hunting, medicine, music, poetry and warfare. He counselled the hero Peleus on how to win the hand of the sea nymph Thetis, and later became the tutor of their son, Achilles.

Jason was among the other heroes tutored by Chiron, who also taught the demi-god of healing, Asklepios, the son of Apollo. When Chiron died he was set among the stars as the constellation Sagittarius.

Chitimukulu

The first king of the Bemba people of Zambia. According to the Bemba origin myth, Chitimukulu and his two

brothers attempted to build a tall tower in their parents' royal village. But the tower collapsed, killing many people, and their father ordered the execution of his sons. However, the three brothers escaped to what is now Zambia. It was here that Chitimukulu founded the Bemba kingdom.

Christ, The Life of

The life and ministry of Christ, as recounted in by the four gospels, provided subjects for innumerable painted narrative series and separate devotional images. Most, but not all, of the episodes are found in all four gospels, although they are not always told in the same sequence. Christ is also be present in scenes from the lives of the Virgin and the apostles.

THE NATIVITY AND ADORATION

The Nativity, or birth of Christ, took place in Bethlehem in Judea. The Virgin Mary "brought forth her firstborn son, and wrapped him in swaddling clothes, and laid him in a manger; because there was no room for them in the inn".[1] The Infant is usually shown in a humble crib with an ox and an ass looking on, according to a prophecy of Isaiah.

An angel appeared to shepherds that night and told them of the birth of the Saviour. They are seen in the **Adoration of the Shepherds**. Three Magi (also known as the Wise Men or Kings) came from the East, following a star, and seeking "he that is born King of the Jews."[2] In depictions of the **Adoration of the Magi**, they worship the Infant and offer him gold, frankincense and myrrh; they are usually depicted as a young, a middle-aged and an elderly man. This scene was highly popular in 15th-century

Two forms of the Chi-Rho monogram; on the right, the X takes the form of the Latin cross.

Florence, where the most lucrative trades were textiles and banking. Unlike other scenes from the Life of Christ, the subject allowed the depiction of sumptuous costumes and, since the Church condemned usury (lending money at interest), the idea of the gift of gold might both ease a banker's conscience and encourage donations to the Church.

King Herod planned to destroy this newborn "King of the Jews", and an angel urged Joseph to escape. The **Flight into Egypt** shows Joseph leading the Virgin and the Infant out of danger. Meanwhile, Herod ordered all children under the age of two to be slaughtered in the **Massacre of the Innocents**.[3] Giotto painted these two scenes in the Arena Chapel, Padua, using a window to divide them in order to avoid the compositional problem that, in the sequence, if the Holy Family walked from left to right they would appear to be walking into the massacre. In Tintoretto's version, in the Scuola di San Rocco, Venice, the Holy Family walks forward as if to come out of the canvas.

After the death of Herod, an angel told Joseph to make the **Return to Israel** with his family; they were directed to Galilee and settled in Nazareth. When Christ was 12 years old the Holy Family went to Jerusalem for the Passover. Christ disappeared and was found engaged in a **Dispute with the Doctors** (teachers) in the Temple, his understanding astonishing those assembled here.[4] No other events of his childhood and youth are recorded in the gospels, but various apocryphal episodes occur in medieval art, such as the infant Jesus making sparrows from clay. John Everett Millais's *Christ in the House of his Parents*, or *The Carpenter's Shop* shows the boy Jesus holding up a wound on the palm of his hand; blood drips onto his feet and he is surrounded by many other symbols of his life and Passion.

THE BAPTISM OF CHRIST AND THE
CALLING OF THE DISCIPLES
At the age of about 30, Christ was baptized by John the Baptist. At his **Baptism** the Holy Ghost descended as a dove, and God the Father announced: "This is my beloved Son, in whom I am well pleased."[5] For 40 days and 40 nights, he fasted in the wilderness and suffered the **Temptation**, during which the Devil suggested that he turn stones to bread to ease his hunger. Christ's reply was, "Man shall not live by bread alone but by every word that proceedeth out of the mouth of God."[6]

Christ then went to the Sea of Galilee, where he preached and began to gather his disciples. The first were the fishermen Simon, called Peter, and his brother Andrew. At the **Calling of Simon and Andrew**, Christ said, "Follow me, and I will make you fishers of men."[7] They had been toiling all night but had caught nothing, yet when Christ asked them to cast their nets once more, they returned with so many fish that their boats began to sink. At this, known as the **Miraculous Draught of Fishes**, Peter realized Christ's identity.[8] Later, in **Christ's Charge to Peter**, he declared, "... upon this rock I will build my church ... And I will give unto thee the keys of the kingdom of heaven."[9] In the **Calling of Matthew** Christ summoned Levi, a publican (tax collector) as he sat in the customs house; he was subsequently known as Matthew. Christ also called James (known as the Great), his brother John, Bartholomew, James the Less, Jude, Philip, Simon, Thomas and Judas Iscariot.

COMPASSION AND FORGIVENESS

In the Sermon on the Mount,[10] Christ summarized his doctrine, including the eight Beatitudes, which begin: "Blessed are the poor in spirit; for theirs is the kingdom of heaven." He also taught the disciples the Lord's Prayer. Later, at the **Supper in the House of Matthew**, Christ was rebuked for eating with sinners, to which he replied, "They that be whole need not a physician, but they that are sick."[11] Christ's attitude to repentant sinners was exemplified in the **Woman Taken in Adultery**. The Pharisees brought her to Christ to gain his approval for stoning her to death; his reply was, "He that is without sin among you, let him first cast a stone at her."[12]

Another potent image of penitence and forgiveness was **Mary Magdalene Washing Christ's Feet**. This took place in the house of a Pharisee, who could not understand how Christ could allow Mary, a sinner, to approach him. Christ simply said to her, "Thy sins are forgiven."[13]

Mary Magdalene became one of Christ's most devoted followers, and was sometimes thought to be the sister of Martha, a busy housewife, with whom she is contrasted as a spiritual type. In the episode at the **House of Mary and Martha**, Martha was busy serving guests while Mary sat listening to Jesus, so Martha asked, "Lord dost thou not care that my sister hath left me to serve alone?" Christ replied that, of the two, Mary was concerned with

more important matters.[14] Another time, his disciples rebuked those who brought children to him, but Christ said, "Suffer little children, and forbid them not, to come unto me; for of such is the kingdom of heaven."[15] **Christ Blessing Little Children** occurs in northern European painting from the 16th century onward.

CHRIST'S TEACHINGS

Christ often taught through parables. The parable of **The Sower**[16] told how some seed (his teaching) fell on stony ground but some brought forth fruit. **The Good Samaritan** described an act of charity by a Gentile who stopped to tend a wounded man, who should have been his enemy; he took the man to an inn and paid for his care.[17] In the **Blind Leading the Blind**,[18] Christ warned that the Pharisees were misguided. The **Prodigal Son**[19] emphasized God's forgiveness of repentant sinners; while **Dives and Lazarus**[20] contrasted a rich man's sufferings in hell with a beggar's reward in heaven. **The Wise and Foolish Virgins**[21] warned always to be prepared for Christ's Second Coming.

Artists chose the particular moment in a parable that had the greatest emotional or artistic appeal. For example, Dürer's engraving of *The Prodigal Son* shows the repentant sinner surrounded by swine, kneeling in humility and wringing his hands as he gazes heavenward.

THE MIRACLES

Christ healed many sick people as he preached, in scenes such as the following: **Christ Healing a Leper**;[22] **Christ Healing the Centurion's Servant**,[23] an extraordinary expression of faith by a Gentile; **Christ Healing the Paralyt-**

ic;[24] **The Pool of Bethesda**,[25] where Christ cured a handicapped man; and **Christ Healing the Blind**.[26] He was admonished by the Pharisees for healing a man with a withered hand on the Sabbath; because he showed them that they were wrong, they began to plot his death.

Christ also brought the dead to life, in the **Raising of the Widow's Son of Nain**[27] and the **Raising of the Daughter of Jairus**.[28] Better known is his restoration of the brother of Martha and Mary in the **Raising of Lazarus**. Lazarus had been in the tomb for four days when Christ ordered the stone to be removed; at this, the young man came forth, bound in his shroud.[29] This was painted by Sebastiano del Piombo in *The Raising of Lazarus*. Christ also exorcised those possessed by the Devil – for example, the **Daughter of the Woman of Canaan**.[30] On another occasion, two men were possessed by devils which he cast out of them and into a herd of swine; in this miracle, known as **The Gadarene Swine**, the whole herd rushed headlong into the Sea of Galilee.[31]

Of the many other miracles in Christ's life, the most popular among painters were: the **Marriage at Cana**,[32] when he commanded six pots to be filled with water which turned into wine; the **Calming of the Waters**,[33] in which he was at sea with his disciples and stilled a great storm; the **Loaves and Fishes**,[34] in which he fed a multitude of 5,000 people with five loaves and two fishes; the **Walking on the Waters**,[35] in which he walked on the sea to reach his disciples who were being tossed about on a ship; the **Tribute Money**,[36] in which Christ told Peter to catch a fish, saying that he would find a coin in its mouth with which to pay the temple tax; and the **Transfiguration**, in which Christ took Peter, James and John up a high mountain, and shone as "white as the light:" the prophets Moses and Elijah appeared, and a voice from Heaven said, "This is my beloved Son, in whom I am well pleased." Meanwhile a man had brought his epileptic son to be cured by the disciples, but they failed; on his return, Christ chided them for having little faith and healed the boy himself. Unusually, Raphael painted the **Transfiguration** with the incident of the epileptic boy happening simultaneously (Vatican Rome).

BEGINNING OF THE PASSION

As Christ neared Jerusalem with his disciples, he prophesied that he would be betrayed and condemned to death.[37] In a sequence of paintings of the Life of Christ, the scene of Christ's **Entry into Jerusalem** usually marks the beginning of the **Passion of Christ** (*see separate entry* **Passion of Christ, The**).

Christina, Saint

There is no historical evidence for the existence of this saint, who is said to have been a Roman noblewoman. Legend[1] tells how, following a common pattern in martyr legends, she suffered multiple terrible ordeals because of her faith, including being thrown into a lake with a millstone around her neck. With Christ's blessing she survived until her martyrdom, when she was shot by arrows.

Christina is venerated at Bolsena in northern Italy, which claims to have her relics. Her attribute is a millstone depicted hanging from her neck, as seen in Signorelli's *Virgin and Child with Saints*.

Christina, Saint: *see* Martyrs
1 *Golden Legend,
St Christina*

Christmas tree

Christmas tree

Emblem of rebirth, especially the rebirth of light – a solar symbolism dating back at least to the Roman festival of Saturnalia, when evergreen decorations celebrated the death of the old year and birth of the new. Teutonic Yuletide rites in which fir trees were hung with lights and surrounded with sacrificial offerings are more direct antecedents of the modern decorated tree; Victorian ceremony took this Christmas tradition from Germany. Orbs, stars and crescents on the tree were once cosmic symbols. In the Christian era, the lights and candles came to symbolize souls.

Christopher, Saint

Christopher is Greek for "Christ bearer" and, according to legend,[1] the saint was a Canaanite of prodigious size and strength. He desired to serve the mightiest sovereign, and began by worshipping the Canaanite king. The king, however, was afraid of Satan, who therefore became Christopher's next figure of idolatry. However, then he realized that Satan was afraid of Christ so he chose to adopt the Christian faith.

A hermit told Christopher to go to help those who wished to cross a dangerous river, which he did, using a long pole to steady himself as he carried people across. One day a child begged to be taken over the river, so Christopher lifted him on to his shoulders and strode into the water. Little by little the water became more turbulent and the child became as heavy as lead, so that Christopher was in great distress until he reached the other bank. There the child revealed himself as Christ, who was carrying in his hand the weight of the whole world. He told Christopher to plant his staff, and the next morning it bore leaves and fruit.

Christopher recruited many converts and was cruelly tortured because his faith was steadfast. At one time 400 bowmen shot arrows at him but not a single one touched him; suddenly, one turned back and struck his persecutor, the king of Lycia, in the eye, blinding him. Christopher was beheaded the following day, but he had foretold that his blood would restore the tyrant's sight, and when this came true the king was converted to Christianity. As in the *Moreel Triptych* by Hans Memling, Christopher is usually shown striding through the river, balanced by his staff (which may be a branch or a whole tree which he pulled up with his enormous strength), and bearing the Christ Child on his shoulders.

Although his feast day has recently been removed from the Roman Catholic calendar as there is no proof of his existence, St Christopher has long been venerated as the patron saint of travellers.

Chronos

"Time", one of two primal deities (the other being Adrasteia, "Necessity") present at the beginning of creation, according to the Greek Orphic creation myth. Chronos represents an Orphic reinterpretation of the name of the Titan Cronos or Kronos, which is of uncertain origin.

Chrysanthemum

The imperial and solar flower of Japan, linked with longevity and joy. In China the chrysanthemum is an emblem of Daoist perfection, autumnal tranquillity and plenitude – perhaps because it continues to bloom into winter.

Churning of the Ocean, The

In Hindu myth, a great act of creation by the gods (known as Devas) and demons (known as Asuras). It focuses on winning the *amrita*, the elixir of immortality, and illustrates the universal concept of order emerging from upheaval. In this story the Devas and Asuras are clearly distinguished. This, however, is not always the case in earlier myths.

The Devas and Asuras assembled on Mount Meru and pondered how to win the *amrita*. Vishnu suggested that they should churn the ocean to produce the elixir, as well as all the herbs and jewels. The divinities agreed and uprooted Mount Mandara to use as a churning paddle, setting it on the back of a tortoise. They coiled the great serpent Vasuki around the mountain as a rope, with the Devas taking one end and the Asuras the other. They twirled Mandara about, causing its trees to topple and catch fire with the friction as they fell against each other. Indra put out the fire with water from the clouds, but the sap of all the plants flowed into the ocean, turning it to milk and then to butter. In one last great effort, the divinities produced the sun, the moon, the goddess of fortune and other treasures. Finally the physician Dhanvantari emerged from the ocean, bearing the *amrita*.

Vishnu tricked the Asuras into surrendering the elixir and gave it to the Devas to drink. The enraged Asuras offered battle but were defeated by the Devas, who then put Mount Mandara back in its proper place.

Cicada

Immortality – a symbolism probably derived from the creature's desiccated appearance and long lifespan. In Greece, where it was sacred to the sun-god Apollo, these aspects were combined in the myth of Tithonus, a mortal man loved by Eos (the dawn; in Roman myth, Aurora), whose ambrosia kept him alive but could not stop him from ageing. In pity, she turned him into a cicada. Chinese jade cicadas were used as amulets for the dead.

Cimon and Iphigenia

In Greek myth, Cimon,[1] meaning "brute", was the son of a nobleman of Cyprus, but was uneducated and uncouth. He was sent by his father to tend a farm where one day he spied the beautiful Iphigenia asleep in a meadow and became rapt in admiration. Cimon resolved to become a gentleman, to learn riding and the arts of music, and within four years he was the most perfect cavalier on the island. Iphigenia was betrothed to another, yet Cimon pursued her and the lovers were finally united.

Artists have painted the subject of Cimon finding Iphigenia asleep, as in *Cimon and Iphigenia* by Lord Leighton. Millais's work of the same title emphasizes the physical contrast between Cimon and Iphigenia.

Cimon and Pero

This story from antiquity[1] tells of filial duty and illustrates the virtue known as Roman Charity. The aged Cimon was condemned to death by starvation in prison but was saved by his daughter Pero, who visited him regularly and suckled him. The

Churning of the Ocean, The: *see* Asura; Indra; Vishnu

Cicada: *see* Amulet; Jade; LONGEVITY

Cimon and Iphigenia: [1] Boccaccio, *Decameron, 5th Day, 1st Story*

Cimon and Pero: *see* Charity [1] Valerius Maximus, *Book 5, Chapter IV*

*Three overlapping
circles, from a
representation of the
Christian Trinity.*

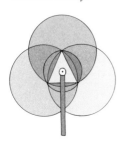

subject was popular with painters
including the 17th-century Dutch
artist Dirck van Baburen.

Circe

A sorceress of Greek myth, the
daughter of Helios, the sun god, and
the sea nymph Perse or Perseis. Circe,
who lived on the island of Aeaea near
Italy, was the aunt of the sorceress
Medea. When the hero Jason stole the
Golden Fleece from Aeëtes, Medea
assisted his escape by murdering her
half-brother Apsyrtus. Jason and
Medea went to Circe for purification.

Circe also features in the story of the
hero Odysseus (known as Ulysses to
the Romans). When some of his crew
visited Aeaea, the sorceress transformed them into pigs. One man,
Eurylochus, escaped to tell what had
happened. Odysseus rescued his crew
with the help of the god Hermes, who
gave him a special herb as an antidote
to Circe's magic. Circe persuaded the
hero to stay on her island, which they
did for more than a year, feasting on
meat and mellow wine. Odysseus
received valuable advice from Circe
for his onward journey, such as a
warning not to approach the Sirens.

The sorceress fascinated British Victorian painters such as J. W. Waterhouse, who in *Circe* showed her
enticingly offering Ulysses the poisoned cup with which she turned
sailors into swine. In his *Circe
Invidiosa*, the sorceress is shown consumed with jealousy at losing the hero,
and poisoning the sea in her anger.

Circle

Totality, perfection, unity, eternity – a
symbol of completeness that can
include ideas of both permanence and
dynamism. The correlation between

the discoveries of atomic physics and
mystical notions of the circle is striking. Apart from the point or centre,
with which it shares much of its symbolism, the circle is the only geometric
shape without divisions and alike at
all points. To the Neo-Platonists, the
circle embodied God, the uncircum-
scribed centre of the cosmos. Because
the circle, which can also represent a
sphere, is a form potentially without
beginning or end, it is the most
important and universal of all geometric symbols in mystical thought.
And because it is implicit in other
important symbols, including the
wheel, disc, ring, clock, sun, moon,
ouroboros and Zodiac, its general
symbolism is hardly less significant.

To the ancients, the observed cosmos presented itself inescapably as
circular – not only the planets themselves, including the presumed flat
disc of the earth circled by waters, but
also their cyclical movements and the
recurring cycles of the seasons. Symbolic meaning and function were
combined in the use of the circle to
calculate time (the sundial) and space
(directional, astrological or astronomical points of reference). Sky
symbolism and belief in celestial
power underlaid primitive rituals and
architecture throughout the world –
circular dancing or ceremonial walking around fires, altars or poles, the
circular passing of the calumet in
North America, the whirling of
shamans, the circular form of tents
and encampments, circular megalithic
markings, and fortifications or ringed
monuments of the Neolithic period.

Circles had protective as well as
celestial significance, notably in the
Celtic world – and they still have this
in the folklore of fairy rings and fly-

ing saucers. They also stand for inclusive harmony, as in the Arthurian Round Table or the "charmed circle" of acquaintanceship widely used in modern idiom. Interlocking circles (as in the modern Olympic emblem) are another symbol of union.

Dynamism is added to the circle in the many images of discs with rays, wings or flames found in religious iconography, notably Sumerian, Egyptian and Mexican. They symbolize solar power or creative and fertilizing cosmic forces.

During the Renaissance a circle was considered the perfect shape. According to the architect Vitruvius (1st century BCE): "If a man lies on his back with hands and feet outspread, and the centre of a circle is placed on his navel, his fingers and toes will be touched by the circumference." Leonardo da Vinci's "Vitruvian man" is perhaps the best known example of this human geometry. The Renaissance and later periods admired the few surviving ancient circular temples, such as the Pantheon in Rome. They inspired Bramante's Tempietto (San Pietro in Montorio, Rome). They were depicted frequently in paintings with Classical themes or settings.

Concentric circles can stand for celestial hierarchies (as in the choirs of angels symbolizing heaven in Renaissance art), levels in the afterworld or, in Buddhism, stages of spiritual development. Three circles can stand for the Christian Trinity but also for the divisions of time, the elements, the seasons or the movement of the sun and the phases of the moon. The circle can be masculine (as the sun) but also feminine (as the maternal womb). A circle (female) over a cross (male) is a symbol of union in Egypt, also known in northern Europe, the Middle East and China. The Chinese Yin-Yang symbol of male and female interdependence uses two colours within a circle, divided by an S-shaped curve, each including a smaller circle of the opposing colour. A dot within a circle is the astrological symbol for the sun and the alchemical symbol for gold.

The circle combined with the square is a Jungian archetypal symbol of the relationship between the psyche or self (circle) and the body or material reality (square). This interpretation is supported by Buddhist mandalas in which squares inside circles represent the passage from material to spiritual planes. In Western and Eastern thought, the circle enclosing a square stands for heaven enclosing earth. Circular domes, vaults or cupolas incorporate the celestial symbolism of the rounded decoration in Romanesque churches or pagan temples into architecture based on the square, cross or rectangle. "Squaring the circle" (the geometrically impossible task of forming a circle from a series of squares) was a Renaissance and alchemical allegory of the difficulty of constructing divine perfection with earthly materials. Conversely, the cabbalistic image of a circle within a square symbolizes the divine spark within a material body.

Circumambulation

The ritual of walking around a sacred object, or defining and sanctifying a space by making a circuit of it, imitates solar and astral cycles, and pays homage to celestial forces and the protective symbolism of the circle. In a celebrated example, at the holy city of Makkah (Mecca), Muslim pilgrims make seven circuits of the sacred Ka'aba stone.

Circumambulation: *see* Circle; Ka'aba; Wheel

Buddhist circumambulation of a temple or stupa places the worshipper in tune with cosmic rhythms and symbolizes progression toward self-knowledge and enlightenment or *nirvana*. The direction of the Hindu and Buddhist circumambulation is clockwise (following the apparent clockwise path of the sun in the Northern hemisphere).

Circumcision

An ancient ritual, widespread outside northern Europe, Mongolia and Hindu India, with both initiatory and sacrificial meanings in addition to any hygienic ones. The Hebrew commandment to circumcise males eight days after birth seems to have had both hygienic and symbolic importance, initiating children into a community chosen by God. In Christianity, the sacramental rite of baptism replaced this initiatory symbolism, and circumcision was not prescribed. Elsewhere, circumcision at puberty is a rite of passage to adulthood, often for females as well as males. An even earlier sacrificial symbolism has been suggested, with circumcision standing for a blood offering – a significant part of the body set aside in the hope of immortality. An alternative supposition is that circumcision, male and female, was an attempt to clarify sexual differences, the prepuce being seen as a feminine aspect of males, the clitoris as a masculine aspect of females.

Clare of Assisi, Saint

Clare (*c.*1194–1253) was strongly influenced by St Francis of her native town, Assisi. Rejecting her noble family and offers of marriage, she persuaded him to place her in the care of Benedictine nuns. Later she was joined by her sister and widowed mother, and in 1212 they founded their own community under the instruction of St Francis, which Clare led for 40 years.

The nuns followed his dictate of poverty and possessed no property of their own; they were therefore called the "Poor Ladies" or "Poor Clares". Clare's image, with scenes from her life, was painted 30 years after her death in the church of Santa Chiara, Assisi, where she appears in a grey tunic. Her attribute is the lily or a monstrance: legend claims that while besieged by the infidel she placed one or other of these things outside her convent, and the enemy fled.

Claudia

In Roman legend, a stone image of the earth goddess Cybele (in Greek myth, Rhea) was carried by boat to Rome from Pergamum in Asia Minor (modern Turkey), and its weight caused the boat to sink into the Tiber's muddy bed. Claudia, a Vestal Virgin, who had been falsely accused of breaking her vow of chastity, begged Cybele for a chance to prove her innocence. With only the slightest effort she pulled the boat upriver, so vindicating her virtue.

Clement, Saint

Clement (died *c.*101CE) is thought to have been a bishop of Rome (Pope Clement I), but little is known of his life. According to legend,[1] he had believed himself an orphan and received Christian instruction from the apostle St Barnabas in Rome and St Peter in Judea. Peter united him with his family and then went to Rome, where he appointed Clement as his successor as overseer of the faithful in Rome.

While preaching, converting and baptizing, Clement caused a riot among the pagans, and was sent to join prisoners condemned to hard labour in the Crimea; directed by a lamb, he struck the earth, whereupon a stream of water flowed out to quench the prisoners' thirst. He was thrown into the sea with an anchor tied around his neck, but the sea later receded to reveal a small temple containing the martyr's body. Scenes from his life were frescoed from the 6th century in San Clemente, Rome. Giambattista Tiepolo showed the saint as an elderly pope with tiara and triple-armed cross. Clement's attribute is sometimes an anchor.

Cleopatra
Queen Cleopatra VII[1] (68–30BCE) ruled Egypt jointly with her brother until he deposed her in 48BCE. However, she was reinstated by Julius Caesar, with whom she had a love affair; she bore his son, Caesarion. Egypt subsequently had to pay tribute to Caesar, a scene painted by Andrea del Sarto in *Egypt's Tribute to Caesar* (Villa Medici, Poggio a Caiano).

After Caesar's death civil war broke out in the Roman Empire, and the triumvir Mark Antony was assigned command of the eastern division. In 41BCE he summoned Cleopatra to meet him at Tarsus in Cilicia, and so began their famous relationship. She arrived in a barge with a gilded stern, its purple sails outspread while silver oars beat time to the music of flutes and harps. Under a canopy of cloth of gold she lay dressed as Venus, with boys painted like Cupids fanning her and attendant maids in the guise of sea nymphs and graces.

Giambattista Tiepolo's frescoes *The*

Meeting of Cleopatra and Antony and *The Banquet of Cleopatra* (both in the Palazzo Labia, Venice) shows the sumptuous banquet with which Antony welcomed her. She told her host, however, that she could produce a dish far more costly than he had provided, and, removing a pearl from her earring, she dissolved it in vinegar and drank it. The union of Antony and Cleopatra was opposed by Octavian (later the emperor Augustus), who destroyed their fleet at Actium in 31BCE. Realizing all was lost, they committed suicide, Antony by the sword and Cleopatra by the bite of an asp concealed in a basket of figs. Her death was the subject of many paintings, such as Guido Reni's *Cleopatra*.

Cloak
Power, protection, separation, metamorphosis, concealment – a diversity of symbolism related to the swiftness with which a cloak can change or hide the form. Magic cloaks appear often in Germanic and Celtic legends, particularly Irish; they are associated with special powers, including invisibility and forgetfulness. They were an emblem of royalty, brotherhood or separation from the materialistic world, as in some monastic orders. They could also be an emblem of divine protection. Alternatively, the cloak stands for intrigue – for example, the "cloak-and-dagger" world of espionage.

Clock
Moderation – an attribute of Temperance in art. In devotional still lifes, clocks appear as reminders of time passing, but some portraits included them instead to symbolize the even-tempered nature of the sitter.

Cleopatra: *see* Caesar; Snake
Plutarch, *Lives: Antony*

Cloak: *see* Transformation

Clock: *see* Circle; VIRTUES; wheel

Cloelia

Cloelia

During the wars between the Romans and Etruscans the noble woman Cloelia was taken hostage by the Etruscan king Porsenna. She escaped with companions and crossed the River Tiber on horseback, but when she reached Rome she was returned to Porsenna by the consuls. He was so impressed by her courage that he released her with the companions of her choice. Jacques Stella shows her on the bank of the Tiber about to transport her companions across.

Clotho *see* Fates, The

Clouds

Fecundity, elemental and spiritual. Apart from their obvious fertility symbolism as harbingers of rain, clouds also stood for revelation, the presence of God, a divinity almost made manifest. God guided the Israelites as a pillar of cloud, and Allah speaks from a cloud in the Qur'an. Clouds, especially pink ones, are symbols of happiness in China, and emblems of ascent to heaven. "Cloud Nine" is mystical bliss.

Clover

Trefoil in shape, the clover symbolizes the Christian Trinity. Ireland's use of the shamrock as its national emblem refers to a legend that St Patrick used the plant to illustrate and explain the doctrine of the Trinity.

Clown

The inheritor of a tradition that includes fools (simpletons or pretended simpletons), jesters (sharp-witted pranksters) and buffoons (knockabout comedians), categories often confused. The deepest and most sinister symbolism attaches to the fool, an ancient, inverted image of the king or ruler, used as a substitute for him in early sacrificial rituals. More generally the clown or fool represents, and acts as scapegoat for, human failure, the speed with which dignity and seriousness can collapse into farce, or wisdom turn into idiocy.

Club

An emblem of crushing power and physical strength, linked with gods and heroes. In Greek myth it is the attribute of Herakles and also of Theseus, who on his travels slew the robber Periphetes, the owner of a huge brazen club with which he battered passers-by to death.

A club is the Celtic symbol of divine force, an attribute of the Irish father-god the Daghda, whose club could take or restore life and was so heavy it needed wheels to shift it. This dual symbolism is analogous with the power of the thunderbolt both to fertilize or to destroy. In art, the club can represent either brutality or heroism. It appears as an attribute of Fortitude and is also an attribute of Saints James the Less and Jude.

Clytemnestra

In Greek myth, a queen of Argos (or Mycenae), the daughter of King Tyndareos and Queen Leda of Sparta. However, her father was often said to be the god Zeus, who assumed the form of a swan to have intercourse with Leda. In one account, Leda subsequently gave birth to two eggs, each containing a set of twins: Clytemnestra and Castor in one, and Helen (of Troy) and Polydeuces in the other.

Clytemnestra married Tantalus, a son of Thyestes, one of the feuding Pelopid dynasty. Agamemnon, the

Clytemnestra and Aegisthus, with Agamemnon trapped under a net.

king of Argos and the son of Atreus (Thyestes' brother and enemy), killed Tantalus and his son and claimed Clytemnestra for himself.

Tyndareos, who had earlier helped Agamemnon to win the throne of Argos from Thyestes, forgave him the murders and allowed him to marry Clytemnestra.

Before Agamemnon sailed at the head of the Greek expedition to fight the Trojans, he was obliged, according to one account, to sacrifice his daughter Iphigeneia to the goddess Artemis. Clytemnestra vowed to avenge her daughter's death and became the lover of Aegisthus, the brother of her murdered first husband, who had sworn to seize the Argive throne. Together they plotted the murder of Agamemnon on his return from Troy.

When her husband arrived with his entourage, Clytemnestra invited him to take a bath. However, as Agamemnon stepped out of the water, she moved towards him as if to offer him a towel, but instead threw a fine mesh over his head. Aegisthus stabbed the entangled Agamemnon, who collapsed, dying, into the bath. Clytemnestra decapitated the king with an

axe, and then struck down his concubine Cassandra. Aegisthus assumed the throne.

Orestes was able to escape but returned incognito with his sister Elektra after eight years to take revenge on his father's assassins. He murdered King Aegisthus before cutting off Clytemnestra's head with a single blow.

Clytie

In mythology[1] Clytie loved Apollo but he scorned her in favour of her rival, Leucothoe. In a fit of jealousy Clytie made the affair known to her rival's father, who buried his daughter alive. But still Apollo ignored Clytie, who pined away and became a sunflower (or marigold). In her transformed state, held fast by her roots, she turned her head to follow the course of the sun with steadfast adoration. Clytie may be shown with sunflowers; Frederic Leighton painted her stretching out her arms to the rising sun.

Coatlicue

An Aztec earth goddess, the mother of the god Huitzilopochtli. Coatlicue (which means "Snake Skirt") is said to have conceived Huitzilopochtli at Coatepec (Serpent Hill, near Tula, Mexico) when she was impregnated by a magic ball of down which descended from heaven.

Her existing offspring, the goddess Coyolxauhqui and her four hundred brothers, the Centzon Huitznahua, became angry at her pregnancy and murdered her, cutting off her head and hands. However, at the moment of death Coatlicue gave birth to the fully formed Huitzilopochtli, who immediately killed Coyolxauhqui and then hurled her dismembered

Clytie:
[1] Ovid, *Met IV 190–273*

Coatlicue: *see*
Huitzilopochtli

Coatlicue, the Aztec earth goddess.

corpse to the bottom of Coatepec, before setting out to rout his many brothers.

Cobra

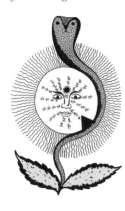

The cobra coiled around the sun, from an Indian folk drawing.

Apart from its general snake symbolism, the erect and hooded cobra has specific sacred significance in the iconography of India and Egypt. In Egypt, a female cobra with raised hood is the uraeus, the burning eye of the sun-god Ra, worn on the headdresses of kings and gods, and also carved on temples, to spit venom in the face of Pharaoh's enemies. Aaron's rod, which turned into a snake to impress the pharaoh in the *Book of Exodus* (7:8–12), may in fact have been the rigid body of a cobra. There is less doubt that Cleopatra's chosen instrument of suicide was the small asp cobra. The large Indian cobra is the magical Naga of Hindu mythology, guardian of treasure, corresponding also to Shesha or Ananta, the cosmic snake on which Vishnu rests between eras of creativity. In Buddhism the Naga cobra is the mastered power of instinct. In Cambodia the miraculous seven-headed Naga is a rainbow symbol, representing the passage from earth to heaven.

Cocijo

A Zapotec deity of lightning and rain, who is the equivalent of the great Aztec god Tlaloc.

Cock, Rooster

Watchfulness, courage, virility, prescience, reliability – and, as herald of the dawn, a symbol of solar and spiritual resurrection. These positive attributes are more widespread culturally than the pride, arrogance and lust also associated with the cock. It is linked with the dawn, the sun and illumination, almost everywhere except in Celtic and Nordic traditions. In China, where its red comb also suggested sunset and autumn, its name is a homonym of good fortune: a red cock wards off fire, a white one ghosts. The cock was sacrificed at initiations, but not eaten. It exemplified the five Chinese virtues of civil and military merit, courage, reliability and generosity (from its practice of offering food to its hens). It was also a funerary emblem, warding off evil.

Cocks were also sacred animals in Japan, hence the free run that they were given in Shinto temples. The cock calls Shinto worshippers to prayer as once, according to one account, it called the sun-goddess Amaterasu from the cave where she hid her light. In Buddhism, the cock, representing carnal desires, joins the pig and snake as one of the three emblematic animals that bind humanity to the round of birth and death.

The cock can also personify Lust in Western art. However, in Christianity its symbolism is generally positive. It represents light and rebirth, putting to flight the darkness of spiritual ignorance. Church weathervanes in the form of cocks are emblems of vigilance against evil. At cock crow, the ghostly apparitions of night vanish. This solar and protective symbolism is ancient throughout the Middle East. In ancient Greece, the cock was an attribute of many divinities including Zeus, Apollo, Attis and Persephone as gods and goddesses of rebirth, Ares and Athene as deities of pugnacity, Hermes as herald and Aesculapius as healer. The cock is also venerated in Islam: it was the giant bird seen by Muhammad in the First Heaven crowing, "There is no god but Allah."

The cock is a familiar messenger of the underworld in Celtic and Nordic traditions, leading souls, calling the dead to battle, or warning the gods of danger. Some African traditions associate its reputation for foresight with the idea of secret knowledge and hence witchcraft.

The cock's role as an emblem of France seems to derive from a Roman pun, the Latin *gallus* meaning both "cock" and "a Gaul". An odd link with time comes from the three cock crows that counted off the three denials of Christ by the disciple Peter. The cock has since become one of the attributes of St Peter, who is the patron saint of watchmakers. Fables in which animals arrogantly boast to each other are the origin of the expression "cock-and-bull".

Cockaigne, Land of

This was a fabled medieval land of idleness and luxury where "the houses were made of barley-sugar cakes, the streets were paved with pastry, and the shops supplied goods for nothing".[1] Peter Bruegel the Elder painted *The Land of Cockaigne*, showing a scene of gluttony and sloth with a scholar, a peasant and a soldier lying in idleness.

Cocytus

"River of Wailing", a river in northern Greece once believed to flow into the underworld. The unburied dead were said to wander its banks for 100 years.

Coffin

A protective womb, symbolizing the hope of rebirth. Hence the elaborate coffins and sarcophagi constructed for people of high rank and the reason that they are placed in sanctuaries, sepulchres or churches.

Coins

Coins or money often suggest avarice, bribery or corruption: "the love of money is the root of all evil".[1] In the gospels, the apostle Matthew was originally a tax-collector and may be seen in art counting money. Christ paid tribute money to the Pharisee, turned money-lenders out of the Temple, and was betrayed by Judas Iscariot for "thirty pieces of silver".

COLOURS *see panel overleaf*

Column

Drawing on the extensive symbolism of the pillar as an emblem of divine power, the emperors Trajan and Marcus Aurelius erected massive columns in Rome carved with scenes of their wars. At a height of 38 metres (125ft),

Cocytus: *see* Acheron; Hades; Styx; UNDERWORLDS

Coins: *see* Danaë; Judas Iscariot; Matthew, St
[1] *1 Timothy 6:10*

Column: *see* Passion of Christ, The; Samson; Solomon

COLOURS

Colours have a vast range of meanings. Generalizations about the specific symbolism of any one colour as if it had inherent and fixed significance psychologically or in nature are hard to sustain. Black and white (or light and dark colours) clearly stand for duality and antithesis. In some traditions black is the colour of death and mourning; in others it is white. Red, the colour of blood, is usually linked with the life principle, activity, fertility – but represented death in the Celtic world and was a menacing colour in Egypt. Experiments have shown that red is generally seen as strong, "heavy" and emotive. Blue is widely considered "good". People prefer lighter colours rather than darker ones. The colours that attract our attention most are red, yellow, green and blue (those preferred by children). The red-to-yellow end of the spectrum is "warm", the blue-indigo end "cool".

Most fundamental colour symbolism was drawn from nature. Thus green symbolized potency in arid regions and was a sacred colour in Islam. Gold was linked almost universally with the sun, suggesting illumination and rulership. Blue stood for the sky, therefore the spirit and truth. Religion often overlaid this with other significance. Thus yellow and saffron have a high value in Thailand not because they share the natural symbolism of light and flame, but because the Buddha chose these hues (traditionally worn by beggars and criminals) to symbolize renunciation of the material world. In Christianity, white – by natural observation the symbolic colour of death in many cultures – came to symbolize light, purity and joy in opposition to the black of evil and mourning. Many complex systems of colour symbolism, covering everything from the planets and the elements to the cardinal points, the metals and substances of alchemy, and the organs of the body, are hardly more than arbitrary forms of identification. What does seem true is that colours generally are life-affirming symbols of illumination, as reflected in the glories of ecclesiastical stained glass.

Colours have been used by artists in a variety of ways, not least as an important part of composition. Certain colours are more costly to produce than others. Ultramarine was made from expensive lapis lazuli, a semi-precious stone imported from Afghanistan, and therefore its use would reflect the wealth of the patron or the importance he attached to the work. Purple, also made from costly pigments, was associated with royalty and high status from Roman times.

The colour of a figure's dress may signify his or her identity. However, in Christian iconography, the colour of dress is by no means consistent. In Italian art the Virgin usually wears blue, while in Northern European art she may wear red. Figures may wear different colours to distinguish the stages of their life: for example, the red of Mary Magdalene's clothing may indicate her earlier life as a sinner, and green her chosen path as a penitent hermit.

and once topped with the emperor's head, Trajan's column displays a complete low-relief narrative of his military exploits – the most spectacular of its kind in history – intended to symbolize the emperor's own spiralling progression toward Heaven.

Comb
An ancient symbol of fertility and, in Japan, spiritual power – associations that probably derive from the long-toothed ornamental combs of wood, bone or horn used by women from antiquity, suggesting rays of the sun or falling rain.

In art, a woman combing her hair, often with a mirror and other worldly effects, may be an indication of vanity. Degas, however, painted women combing as part of their daily toilet. A wool-carder's comb is the attribute of the martyrs Blaise and Bartholomew, who were both flayed alive. The latter is depicted in Michelangelo's *Last Judgment*, holding both the instrument of his torture and his empty skin containing a self-portrait of the artist.

Comet
A portent of catastrophe. Early astrologers viewed any unusual celestial event with apprehension, and the appearance of a comet augured disasters such as war, plague, drought, famine, fire or the fall of kings. Thus Calpurnia in Shakespeare's *Julius Caesar* (2:2; *c.*1600) says: "When beggars die, there are no comets seen,/The heavens themselves blaze forth the death of princes."

Commedia dell'Arte
The Commedia dell'Arte was an Italian dramatic tradition, popular from the 16th to the 18th century, which influenced many European playwrights and modern pantomimes, and provided subjects for artists, especially Domenico Tiepolo and Watteau. The principal figures wore half-masks; their gesture, speech and costume identified their characters and became loosely standardized for easy recognition. The repertoire, however, relied upon improvisation, allowing for contemporary social satire; it also included acrobatics, mime and dance. Appealing to all levels of society, the plots concerned ill-fated lovers and mistaken identities.

Stock *commedia* characters include *zanni*, servants who are either witless or conniving and cause various misunderstandings (they give us the word "zany"); a Captain, who vainly boasts of his military success and thinks his queen is in love with him; a variant of the Captain, Scaramouche, who brags of his riches and success as a lover; an aged Doctor who believes he offers words of wisdom but only utters empty rhetoric; Pantalone who wears wide, loose trousers and is an earnest but comic figure; greedy, malicious and bad-tempered Pulcinello or Puncinello, who enjoys harming others and is the forerunner of Mr Punch; simple-minded Harlequin who is set curious tasks, tries his best but never fully succeeds; and lastly Columbine, Pantalone's daughter.

Compasses, Dividers
An emblem of geometry, architecture, astronomy and geography, and a symbol much used in medieval and Renaissance art as a visual shorthand for a reasoned and measured approach. A pair of compasses could also personify, by extension, associated virtues such as justice, prudence

Comb: *see* Rain; Rays

Comet: *see* Zodiac

Compasses, Dividers: *see* Circle; VIRTUES, THE
' *Proverbs :27*

and maturity. In China, it stood for rectitude. Because the compasses were used to draft circles (celestial in symbolism), they were often linked with the set square (signifying the earth) in images representing the relationship between spirit and matter.

God, as the architect of the universe, sometimes appears with compasses, setting the limits of earth or time as in William Blake's *The Ancient of Days*. With the same significance, the compasses are also an attribute of Saturn, leading to an unexpected link between the compasses and Saturnian melancholy. William Blake, in his famous painting *Newton*, gives a twist to compass symbolism by using them to attack the attempt of scientists to quantify creation. Compasses are also used to signify Melancholia.

Conán the Bald

An Irish warrior and follower of the hero Finn. In 12th-century Irish literature, Conán, the son of Morna and the brother of the great warrior Goll, is portrayed as an impulsive and malicious character, whereas later narratives present him as principally a comic figure who is boastful, cowardly and gluttonous. According to one such tale, the followers of Finn (who are collectively known as the Fian) found themselves stuck to the floor of the Rowan Tree Hostel, a dwelling in the Otherworld, through the sorcery of their enemies. Eventually, though, all of the warriors were released – except for Conán, who had to be torn from the floor, leaving the skin of his buttocks behind.

Conch

A horn-like shell, often used as a ceremonial musical instrument and symbolizing in many coastal traditions the primordial creative voice – notably in India and Polynesia. Indian mysticism links the conch to the sacred sound *Om* and to the breath of Vishnu that fills the universe. It is one of the eight Buddhist symbols of Good Augury. In Greece it is the attribute of each of the sea-god Poseidon's Tritons. Its spiral form could suggest hearing as well as sound, and in Islamic tradition it symbolized attention to the Word.

Conchobar

A king of Ulster, a key figure in the Irish epic *Táin Bó Cuailnge*. Conchobar was the illegitimate son of Nessa, queen of Ulster, and the druid Cathbhadh, who raised him. After the death of Nessa's husband, King Fachtna, Ferghus, his half-brother, succeeded him as king. Nessa agreed to become his lover on condition that Conchobar, then aged seven, be allowed to occupy the throne for one year. Ferghus consented but Conchobar acquired so much respect as king that the people would not allow Ferghus to return.

In fact King Conchobar was so popular among his people that whenever an Ulsterman married, he allowed the king to be the first to sleep with his new wife. However, he was less likeable when it came to his treatment of his foster-daughter, Deirdre, once she had eloped to Scotland with her lover Naiose. The couple agreed to return only when Conchobar had guaranteed Deirdre's safety and promised to send Ferghus to escort them. But when they arrived at Emhain Macha, Conchobar's capital, Naoise was put to death and Deirdre was brought before her foster-father with her hands bound. In disgust Ferghus defected to Conchobar's enemy, Queen Medhbh of Connacht, a war ensued and Conchobar was victorious against Medhbh, largely through the deeds of the hero Cú Chulainn, the Ulster king's foster-son.

Conchobar died after being hit by a brain-ball, a projectile made of solidified brains mixed with lime. It lodged in the king's head until, seven years later, he fell into a tremendous rage which caused the missile to split, killing him instantly.

Concord

Like Abundance, Concord – the harmony between people or nations – may be expressed by a cornucopia or a sheaf of corn, since peace is believed to bring fruitfulness. A bundle of fasces, or sticks, that symbolize justice, doves of peace or a branch of the olive tree of the wise goddess Athene (in Roman myth, Minerva) may be included in a scene to show that relations are amicable.

Cone

Fertility – a geometrical shape suggesting both male and female sexual symbolism, circle and triangle, tower and pyramid. It was an attribute of the Semitic goddess Astarte.

Confucius *see* **Kong Fuzi**

Conla

One of the Fian, the followers of the Irish hero Finn. One day a woman seen only by Conla appeared before him and bade him go with her to the Plain of Delight or Otherworld, an enchanted land of timeless content. On the orders of Conla's father, King Conn of the Hundred Battles, a druid drove the mysterious woman away, but as she disappeared she threw Conla an apple. The apple sustained him for a whole month without growing smaller. Conla began to long to see the woman again. Eventually she reappeared and told him that they could travel together in her ship of glass. The youth followed her to a crystal coracle, in which they sailed away, never to be seen again.

Constantine the Great

Constantine the Great (*c*.274–337CE) inherited his father's western forces and defeated the army of the emperor Maxentius just north of Rome at the Milvian Bridge. The River Tiber, swollen with autumn rains, caused the bridge of boats to collapse and swept Maxentius away to his death. Constantine thus became undisputed master of the West in 312CE.

According to Eusebius,[1] before the battle Constantine had had a vision of a flaming cross and heard a voice saying, "*In hoc signo vinces*" ("You will conquer with this sign"). Constantine bore the cross on a banner and was victorious, and so converted to Christianity, although historically it is uncertain whether he was ever baptised. Bernini carved him on a rearing horse in front of a flaming cross in *Constantine* (Scala Regia, Vatican, Rome). His vision may be shown occurring in a dream, as in fresco *The Dream of Constantine* by Piero della Francesca (San Francesco, Arezzo). Constantine's mother Helena, a Christian who brought relics of the True Cross to Rome, was thought to have influenced her son In 313CE, by the Edict of Milan, he granted tolerance to the religion. Giulio Romano frescoed scenes from the emperor's

Concord: *see* Fasces

Cone: *see* Circle; Phallus; Pyramid; Tower; Triangle

Conla: *see* Finn; Otherworld, The

Constantine the Great: *see* Helena; Sylvester, St

life (Sala di Constantino, Vatican);
and they were the subject of tapestries
designed by Rubens in 1622.

As the first Christian emperor, Constantine built huge basilicas in Rome
over the graves of the martyrs, the
most notable of which was St Peter's.
But conservative Romans opposed
the new faith and by 330CE Constantine left the West to found Constantinople, now Istanbul, as the "New
Rome", a new Christian capital in the
East. The emperors never again
resided in Rome. Before Constantine
left Rome, he was supposed to have
given his territories in the West to the
then Pope Sylvester; an act known as
the Donation of Constantine. However, in the 15th century, the document
recording this was proved to have
been forged during the early Middle
Ages in order to assert papal power
over the Holy Roman Emperor.

Continents, The

Subjects showing the four known continents were popular with Baroque
artists such as Giambattista Tiepolo,
who painted the sumptuous ceiling
fresco *Apollo and the Continents*.
Jesuits favoured the subject as it visu-
alized the Order's intention to spread
the Catholic faith worldwide. *The
Fountain of the Four Rivers* (Piazza
Navona, Rome), a sculpture by Bernini, shows the continents as personified
rivers.[1] Sometimes such personifications recline on urns from which water
flows; a veiled head indicates that the
river's source was unknown.

Certain indigenous animals associated with each continent may be
shown: Africa (the River Nile) may
wear coral, be shown with African
people or a sphinx, crocodile, snake,
lion or elephant; the Americas (the

River Plate) may wear a feathered
headpiece and be dressed as a hunter,
with coins representing rich natural
resources; Asia (the River Ganges) is
often shown with a camel, a rhinoceros, an elephant, palm trees, jewels or
exotic perfumes; Europe (the sea-
monster, or the River Danube) could
be represented by the bull of Europa
or a horse, surrounded by the arts and
civilized activities, and bearing a cornucopia and the crown of her
supremacy over the others.

Coral

Linked with healing power – an association based on tree, water and blood
symbolism. In Classical mythology,
the Mediterranean red coral grew
from the blood of the Gorgon
Medusa; after Perseus had rescued
Andromeda from Cetus, the sea-monster, it is said that he laid the Gorgon's
head down and immediately the sea-
weed turned into coral. Vasari illustrated this on a cabinet door of the
Studiolo of Francesco I (Palazzo Vecchio, Florence) to indicate the precious contents. Coral was also thought
to be a protection against evil. In
Roman times, amulets of coral were
thought to stem bleeding and protect
children from illness or the fury of the
elements, and coral necklaces were
also popular medieval talismans for
children. At one time, coral decorated
Celtic weapons and helmets. It was
prized in India where a jet-black coral
was used to make sceptres.

Cord

Cord symbolized the binding vows of
monks, and also union (the knotted
cords of Freemasonry). In mystical
thought, cords link the material and
spiritual worlds and can be ascended

by grace. The Silver Cord links body and spirit. Cords with fertilizing symbolism appear in Central American iconography, representing the fall of divine, fructifying seed or rain. In art, Fortune holds a cord representing mortal life, cut at whim. In Hinduism knots on cords are representative of devotional acts.

Coresus

A priest of Dionysos (in Roman myth, Bacchus), Coresus fell in love with the nymph Callirhoe, who scorned him. He complained to Bacchus, who sent a plague which would only come to an end when Callirhoe was sacrificed to him. In *The High Priest Coresus Sacrifices Himself to Save Callirhoe* Fragonard depicted how Coresus led his beloved to the sacrificial altar but, unable to kill her, stabbed himself instead. The nymph was then filled with remorse, and took her own life.

Corn

Fertility, growth, rebirth, the divine gift of life. In all regions where grain was a staple, corn seemed a miraculous and consoling image of the continuity of life through death, the grain (wheat, barley or maize) ripening in the earth and reappearing in spring. Thus Christ in the gospels: "Unless a grain of wheat falls in the earth and dies, it remains just a single grain; but if it dies it bears much fruit."[1]

In the Bible, Joseph dreamed that a single sheaf of corn in a field stayed upright while others bent toward it, and so prophesied that his brothers would bow down before him.

An attribute of the Greek fertility goddess Demeter, the ear of corn "reaped in silence" was the central symbol of the Eleusinian mysteries, promising new life, human and vegetable. Corn was a funerary emblem in China, Rome, the Near East and, as the attribute of the god Osiris, Egypt. In iconography, ears of grain appear as attributes of most earth gods and goddesses, and on the robe of the Virgin Mary in medieval and Renaissance art.

The Aztecs worshipped several corn gods, major and minor; while in Peru, fertility was represented as a woman made of maize stalks. Blue-painted maize icons in North America symbolized the fertilizing synthesis of red earth and blue sky.

There are many North American myths of the origin of corn (maize). That of the Mikasuki people of Florida tells of two brothers who lived with their grandmother, and one day, tired of meat, asked her for something new to eat. From then on, when they returned from hunting, she served them delicious corn. Their grandmother would not say where it came from, so the younger brother spied on her when she went to the storehouse. To his horror he saw her rub the corn from the sides of her own body. That night the brothers refused the corn, and the old woman could tell that they knew her secret. She announced that she would have to leave them forever, but that she would live on as corn, growing from her grave.

In art, the goddess Ceres (equivalent to Demeter) is crowned with ears of corn and holding a sheaf. A corn sheaf with ploughshare stands for the Age of Silver, a bound sheaf for Concord, corn and grapevines for the Christian Eucharist. Corn can also represent abundance and prosperity. It is food and seed – the cob, from which the nuggets grow, an image of ejaculation.

Corn: *see* Abundance; Barley; Blue; Ceres; Demeter; Earth; Joseph, Son of Jacob; Mother; Peace; Red; Sacraments; SEASONS; Silver

[1] *John 12:24*

Cornelia

Cornelia:
[1] Valerius Maximus, *Book 4 Ch V*

Cornucopia: *see* Amalthea;
CONTINENTS;
FLOWERS; FORTUNE;
FRUIT; Goat; Herakles;
PEACE; Wine
[1] Ovid, *Fasti V 111–129* and *Met IX 1–97*

Coronis:
[1] Ovid, *Met II 569-587*

Cosmas and Damian, Saints:
see Martyrs
[1] *Golden Legend, SS Cosmas and Damian*

Cornelia

Daughter of the Roman general Scipio Africanus, Cornelia[1] was renowned for her virtue. A lady once showed off her jewelry to Cornelia and asked to see hers in return. Cornelia thereupon produced her two sons and said, "These are the only jewels of which I can boast."

Cornucopia

The "Horn of Plenty", overflowing with fruits, flowers and grains, is a symbol not only of abundance, prosperity and good luck but also of divine generosity. Ancient associations between the horn and fertility lie behind the classical story that Zeus (the Roman Jupiter) accidentally broke off a horn of the goat that suckled him. He gave it to his nurse, Amalthea, whereupon it provided inexhaustible food and drink. In another version of the cornucopia's origin, Herakles (Hercules), as one of his 12 labours, fought Achelous as a bull and tore off a horn, but "the naiads filled it with fruits and fragrant flowers, and sanctified it".

A popular motif in art, the cornucopia appears as an attribute not only of vegetation or wine divinities such as the classical Demeter (Ceres), Dionysos (Bacchus), Priapus and Flora, but also of many positive allegorical figures including Earth, Autumn, Hospitality, Peace, Fortune and Concord. *Putti* were often painted spilling nourishment (for the spirit) from a cornucopia.

Coronis

In mythology Coronis,[1] the beautiful daughter of King Coroneus, was strolling on the sand when Neptune (in Greek myth, Poseidon) saw her and fell in love. As she did not reciprocate, he resolved to take her by force but she fled and prayed to the gods for help. Minerva took pity on her and turned her into a crow. In *Coronus and Neptune* Giulio Carpioni shows her with wings, flying away from Neptune's grasp.

Cosmas and Damian, Saints

Legend[1] relates how in Syria the Christian twin brothers Cosmas and Damian (thought to have died either *c*.287CE or *c*.303CE) learned the art of medicine and healed men, women and animals without payment. In one spectacular example of their cures the saints amputated the rotten leg of a man while he slept and replaced it with that of a Moor who had recently died. He woke joyfully to find he had two healthy legs, even though one was black and the other white. They refused to make sacrifice to pagan gods and were tortured, bound in chains and thrown into the sea, but an angel pulled them out and sat them before the judge who had condemned them. He thought them magicians and sought to know the secrets of their craft, but two demons appeared and struck him; the saints prayed and the demons disappeared. The twins were thrown into a huge fire, but they remained unharmed while the flames leaped out and burned the heathens. They were then sentenced to be stoned to death, but the stones turned back and wounded the throwers; they were shot at with bow and arrow, but the arrows turned around and shot the archers. They were finally beheaded, and a camel appeared to the Christians telling them to bury the saints in the same tomb.

Cosmas and Damian, the patron

saints of physicians and of the Medici family of Florence, feature in Renaissance Florentine painting, where they may be depicted as young martyrs in doctors' robes, perhaps with a phial or other medical instruments. Scenes from their lives were painted in the predella panels of the San Marco altarpiece by Fra Angelico.

COSMOLOGY *see panel overleaf*

Cow

An ancient symbol of maternal nourishment and, like the bull, an image of cosmic generative power. In cultures from Egypt to China the cow was a personification of Mother Earth. It was also lunar and astral, its crescent horns representing the moon, its abundant milk the countless stars of the Milky Way. Nut, the Egyptian sky goddess, sometimes appears with this symbolism in the form of a cow with stars on its belly, its legs the four quarters of the earth. Hathor, Great Mother goddess of joy and love and nourisher of living things, is also represented as a cow. As a protective emblem of royalty, she was often shown with the solar disc between her horns – a reference to the idea of a celestial, mothering cow nourishing the sinking sun with her warmth. A similar image of the cow as the nourisher of original life appears in the mythology of northern Europe where Adumla, wet nurse of the primordial giants, licks the ice to disclose the first man or, alternatively, the three creator gods. In Vedic literature, the cow is both sky and earth, its milk falling as abundant, fertilizing rain. The black cow played a part in funerary rites, the white was a symbol of illumination. To both Hindus and Buddhists,

the cow's quiet, patient rhythms of life presented an image of holiness so complete that it became India's most sacred animal. Its image is everywhere one of happiness – as in Greek rites where white heifers were garlanded and led in celebratory processions with dancing and music.

Cowrie

The vulva, source of life. Among primitive peoples, the beautiful, labia-like shell of this mollusc was the most widespread natural amulet against sterility and the evil eye.

The golden cowrie was an emblem of rank in Fiji and Tonga. Cowrie necklaces were used in trade throughout the Pacific, with ritual as well as commercial significance. Associations with fecundity, sexual pleasure and good luck also made cowries prized charms in Africa and elsewhere, often far from the shores where they were gathered. As funerary or decorative emblems they can also signify life and death, their power lasting after the death of the mollusc.

Coyote

A member of the dog family found from Alaska to Costa Rica, and one of the most popular of all Native American mythical characters. Coyote appears in the myths of the southwest, west and central plains of America in a wide range of roles, particularly as a cunning trickster. The Navajo, who feared to kill a coyote, said that Coyote accompanied the first man and first woman into the world, but had the foresight to bring with him seeds with which to provide food; the Shoshoni and other western tribes said that he was responsible for death, along with other natural ills

Cow: *see* Black; Bull; Crescent; Disc; Earth; Giant; Milk; Moon; Mother; Sky; Sun; White; Wreath, Garland

Cowrie: *see* Gold; Shell

Coyote: *see* ANIMALS; CULTURE HERO; Transformation; TRICKSTER

A coyote figure from a Native American plate, c.11th–13th centuries CE.

COSMOLOGY

According to most accounts of the structure of the universe, the visible world of everyday life is part of some larger whole. Above this world there is an overworld, or heaven, which is the abode of superior beings or divine ancestors, and below it an underworld, peopled by the dead and subterranean spirits.

This image is common to the Indo-European traditions, the cultures of the tribal peoples of Asia, Oceania and the Americas, and the peoples of the Arctic regions. Both overworld and underworld may be a mirror image of the middle world in which human beings live. More complicated versions of the three-world cosmos describe seven, eight or even nine levels of both upper and lower worlds.

Many mythologies also describe a central pillar or "World Tree" which is the axis uniting the three worlds. Yggdrasil, the World Ash of Norse tradition, is the best known of these, but the same idea is found in Indonesian Borneo, the Sahara and also among the aboriginal peoples of the Americas.

From a Norse memorial stone of c.500CE: whirling heavens (top); sun and moon (below); and the World Tree (centre). The ship carries the dead.

The lateral structure of the mythical universe is frequently described as being made up of four quarters, corresponding to north, south, east and west. A fifth "direction", the "centre", or "here", is found in the mythology of China, Ireland and North and Central America.

In many regions, dwellings are modelled on the cosmos. For example, to the island peoples of Southeast Asia, the left side of the house typically represents the underworld while the right is a representation of the world above, or heaven. The central pole of the dwelling house may represent the Tree of Life or cosmic axis, an idea also found in the Amazon and Siberia.

(winter, flood); the Sioux said that he invented the horse. The mythical Coyote is thus a resourceful animal whose blunders or successes explained life in an uncertain universe.

In one Navajo myth Coyote punished a giant that ate children. Under cover of darkness Coyote persuaded the giant that he could perform a miracle by breaking his own leg and mending it at once. Coyote pounded an unskinned leg of deer until it broke. The giant felt the broken leg and listened as Coyote spat on it and chanted: "Leg, become whole!". Coyote then presented his real leg to the giant, who was astonished that it was apparently restored. Coyote offered to repeat the "miracle" on the giant. He agreed and screamed in pain as Coyote smashed his leg with a rock.

Crab

A lunar symbol because, like the moon with its phases, it casts off its shell for a new one – an analogy linked with rebirth symbolism in Aboriginal tradition and sometimes so used also in Christianity.

Apart from its astrological significance as the zodiacal sign Cancer, the crab appears infrequently in iconography. Greek myth tells us that Hera placed the crab in the heavens for its courage in biting the heel of Herakles while he was struggling with the Hydra, a story that contrasts oddly with its reputation for timidity. It appears in Inca tradition as a devourer, connected with the waning moon, and in Thailand and elsewhere in rain ceremonies. Again at the level of analogy, its forward and backward movements sometimes symbolized dishonesty, as in China.

Crane

This bird with long legs and a long neck and bill represented vigilance because it was thought that, while the rest of the flock slept with their heads under their wings, their leader kept watch with his neck stretched out. He signalled a warning by his cry. The bird's role in art as the personification of Vigilance may also go back to a description in the works of Aristotle of the crane's holding a stone in its mouth so that it would wake if it dropped the stone in sleep.

A contrary symbolism appears in India (where the crane represents treachery) and some Celtic regions (as a bird of ill-omen). The ancients were impressed by the crane's beauty and stamina, its migrations and spring reappearances, its complex mating dance, its voice and its contemplative stance at rest.

The crane was linked in China with immortality, in Africa with the gift of speech, and widely with the ability to communicate with the gods. Its cyclic return also suggested regeneration, a resurrection symbolism sometimes used in Christianity.

In ancient Greece, the cries of migrating cranes announced spring sowings and autumn reapings. In China, where a crane flying toward the sun symbolized social aspirations, the bird's white body represented purity, its red head the fire of life. In Egypt, the double-headed crane represented prosperity.

Cranes appear in Raphael's *Miraculous Draught of Fishes*, on the alert for any fish that might slip out of the net.

CREATION *see panel overleaf*

Cremation

Purification, sublimation and ascension. Indo-Iranian peoples often preferred cremation to burial as a result of these associations, and it was also sometimes used in western Europe from the Bronze Age, later spreading through the Roman Empire, often as a mark of high status. Near-complete dissolution of the body in fire symbolizes the freeing of the soul from the flesh and its ascension in smoke. Burial was preferred where doctrines of bodily resurrection were popular (for example, in Egypt and Christian Europe), and by the Chinese who have always been wedded to their native soil.

Crab: *see* Moon; Rain; Zodiac

Crane: *see* Birds; Christ, The Life of; Doubles; Fish; LONGEVITY; Peter, St; Red; VIGILANCE; White
Pliny the Elder: *Natural Histories X:59*

Cremation: *see* AFTERLIFE; Fire, Flame; Smoke; Soul

Creation

CREATION

According to the Bible, in the beginning God created the heaven and the earth; on the first day he separated light from dark to make day and night; on the second he divided the waters; on the third he made the land grow plants and trees; on the fourth he made the sun, moon and planets and formed the seasons; on the fifth he brought forth the birds and fish and commanded them to multiply; and on the sixth he created the animals and made man in his own image and gave him control of every living thing that moved upon the earth. On the seventh day he rested and made it a holy day.¹ Michelangelo chose this story for the central section of the Sistine Chapel ceiling (Vatican, Rome) because it gave him the opportunity for dramatic narrative and potent images. These opening passages from Genesis were illustrated relatively rarely compared to the themes of the creation of Adam and Eve and the Fall

Usually in myth, creation is set in motion by some action which occurs either on its own by accident or as the deliberate act of a creator divinity. In ancient Egypt, the first act of creation was said to have been the rising of a mound of land out of the primordial watery abyss called Nun. The primal watery landscape which is envisaged by the Cheyenne people of North America was transformed when a humble watercoot brought up from the depths a beakful of mud which was then transformed into the first dry land by the great deity All-Spirit. Similar "earth diver" myths are found in other Native cultures.

In all mythologies creation signifies, initially, the appearance of duality in place of oneness. In Chinese myth, the cosmic giant and divine ancestor Pan Gu grew for 18,000 years inside the cosmic egg (which was thought to embrace all potentiality in many creation myths), until it split into two parts, a light half (the heavens) and a dark half (the earth).

In many traditions creation is the result of a death. In the Chinese account, Pan Gu, exhausted by the long labour of separating earth and heaven, lay down and died. The parts of his body then became transformed into the features of the heavens and the landscape. In Saharan Africa the world is traditionally said to have been made from the segments of the sacrificed cosmic serpent.

Some mythologies formalize the struggle between order and chaos in terms of a perpetual cycle in which worlds are eternally brought into being, destroyed and re-made. The Aztecs told of the successive creation and destruction of five worlds, but the most elaborate of all such cyclical schemes is probably that found in Hinduism. One version tells of how the great god Vishnu, resting on the coils of the cosmic serpent Ananta in the waters of chaos, sprouts a lotus from his navel which opens to reveal the creator god Brahma. Then from Brahma's meditation the universe comes into being. It lasts for an immense period of time before it dissolves back into chaos, from which a new cosmos emerges in exactly the same way.

Crescent

The emblem of Islam, signifying divine authority, increase, resurrection and, with a star, paradise. An ancient symbol of cosmic power in western Asia, the crescent (waxing) moon was taken as the barque of the great Babylonian moon-god Sin, as he navigated the vast reaches of space. The Latin etymology of "crescent" (increasing) indicates why the crescent image later developed as a symbol of Islamic expansion. It not only incorporated the idea of the constantly regenerating moon but could be read as two back-to-back horns, themselves symbols of increase. From the time of the Crusades, the crescent became a counter-emblem to the cross – and the Red Crescent is the Islamic version of the Red Cross today. Present-day countries that fly national flags bearing the crescent and one or more stars include Turkey, Libya, Tunisia and Malaysia.

Use of the crescent as an emblem long predated the Islamic empire. In Byzantium, coins were stamped with the crescent and star in 341 BCE when, according to one legend, the moon-goddess Hecate intervened to save the city from Macedonian forces (their attack revealed by the sudden appearance of a crescent moon). The image of the crescent moon as a cup holding the elixir of immortality appears in Hindu and Celtic as well as Muslim traditions. In Egypt, the crescent and disc symbolized divine unity. Greek and Roman lunar goddesses wearing a crescent in their hair symbolized chastity and birth. The Virgin Mary sometimes appears with a crescent at her feet imparting a similar chaste meaning in Christian iconography.

Crest

An emblem worn on a knight's helmet to symbolize his motivating thoughts, summarize the object of his quest or proclaim his personal allegiance.

Cricket

An emblem of happiness and good luck, especially in China, where singing crickets were often kept in boxes or ornate cages. They symbolized summertime, courage (they were encouraged to fight each other) and also resurrection, probably from their metamorphosis from the larval stage.

Crispin and Crispinian, Saints

The history of these Christian brothers is undocumented, but they were venerated in France by the 6th century. They apparently came from Rome to preach at Soissons where they made and mended shoes and were beaten, boiled in oil and flayed for their faith. In a fresco painting of the late 14th century in the Oratorio di San Stefano by Lentate sul Seveso they are seen as young laymen. They are the patron saints of leather workers and their attribute is a shoe or a shoemaker's model of a foot.

Crocodile

Destructive voracity an agent of divine retribution, and lord of water and earth, life and death. To Europeans, unfamiliar with this tropical and subtropical reptile, it was a subject of uninformed awe or moralizing hostility. The Greek author Plutarch (46–120 CE) thought that it was worshipped in Egypt because it had the divine qualities of silence and the ability to see all with its eyes covered by membrane tissue. In Egyptian

The crescent and star emblem of Islam.

Crocus:
¹Ovid, *Met IV: 283–284*

Crook, Crozier: *see* Sheep;
Shepherd; Staff

Crossroads: *see* Hekate;
Hermes; Jaguar; Pyramid;
Sacrifice; Sphinx (1); Triad

iconography, the dead often appear as crocodiles and the town of Crocodopolis was dedicated to the crocodile fecundity god, Sobek. In more monstrous imagery, Ammut, who devoured the hearts of wrongdoers, had crocodile jaws, and the god Seth took the form of a crocodile (in one account) to devour his brother Osiris.

Medieval bestiaries used the crocodile as an allegory of hypocrisy, its eyes streaming as it ate its prey (crocodile tears), its lower jaw mired in mud while the upper jaw was raised in a semblance of moral elevation. Where it was known, it was treated with fearful respect as a creature of primordial and occult power over water, earth and the underworld. In India it was the Makara, the fish-crocodile steed of Vishnu.

In Native American iconography, the crocodile, or alligator, appears with open jaws as the nocturnal sun-swallower. Some Central American myths say that the crocodile gave birth to the earth or supports it on its back. Rebirth symbolism appears in a Liberian initiation tradition to the effect that circumcision scars are the marks of a crocodile that swallows youths and returns them as adults. In the West, the crocodile is sometimes interpreted as a form of leviathan, as an image of chaos, or as the dragon that symbolically represents evil. It appears in art with this meaning, vanquished by the Roman St Theodore. Jungian psychology has seen it as an archetypal symbol of torpid ill-temper, an interpretation in conflict with its water and earth symbolism in many parts of Asia, including China where it appears as the inventor of the drum and song.

A crocodile, after a 17th-century plaque from Benin, West Africa, where its entrails were thought to have magical powers.

Crocus

In mythology¹ the beautiful youth Crocus was impatient for the nymph Smilax, and was turned into the crocus flower as punishment.

Crook, Crozier

A crook usually belongs to shepherds, and therefore may be shown as the attribute of Apollo or of Christ (the Good Shepherd) and his apostles. A bishop's crook-shaped staff or crozier likewise denotes him as the shepherd of his spiritual flock. With similar symbolism, the crook was an emblem of rulership in Egypt, Assyria and Babylonia, an attribute of Osiris and several of the Greek gods.

CROSS *see panel overleaf*

Crossroads

The unknown – hazard, choice, destiny, supernatural powers. The importance attached to intersecting ways in most ancient cultures is remarkable. The fact that they were natural stops for wayfarers only partly accounts for the number of shrines, altars, standing stones, chapels or Calvaries sited there. In Peru and elsewhere pyramids were sometimes built up over years by travellers adding votive stones as they passed through crossroads. Spirits were thought to haunt them, hence they were sites for divination and sacrifice – and, by extension, places of the execution or burial of people or things of which society wished to be rid. Many African tribes dumped rubbish there so that any residual harm might be absorbed. Roman crossroads in the time of Augustus were protected by two *lares campitales* (tutelary deities of place). Offerings were made to them or to the god Janus and other protective divinities, who could look in all directions, such as Hermes, to whom three-headed statues were placed at Greek crossroads. Hekate, as a death goddess, was a more sinister presence, as was the supreme Toltec god, Tezcatlipoca, who challenged warriors at crossroads. Some versions of the Oedipus myth place his fateful encounters with his unknown father, and with the Sphinx, at crossroads – an analogy for destiny. Jung saw the crossroads as a maternal symbol of the union of opposites. More often, they seem an image of human fears and hopes at a moment of choice.

Crow

The European carrion species, including crows and rooks, has been an emblem of war, death, solitude, evil and bad luck – a symbolism that appears in India also. The American species, which is gregarious and feeds mainly on grain and insects, has strikingly different symbolism – positive, even heroic, as in Tlingit myths where the crow appears as a solar, creative and civilizing bird, and in Navajo legends where it is the Black God, keeper of all game animals. Both American and Australian Aboriginal myths explain the crow's black plumage as a mishap and read no ill-omen into it.

More widely, the crow appears as a guide or prophetic voice – even in Greece, where it was sacred to the god Apollo and the goddess Athene, and in Rome, where its croak was said to sound like the Latin *cras* ("tomorrow"), linking it with hope.

In China, a three-legged crow on a sun disc was the imperial emblem. It also stood for filial or family love in China and Japan. Shintoism gives it the role of divine messenger. "Eating crow", the American phrase for humiliation, refers to an altercation behind British lines during a truce in the War of 1812 when a trespassing American soldier was made to eat a piece of a crow that he had just shot, but then, when his gun was returned to him, forced his British tormentor to eat a piece himself.

In mythology a crow tells her story to the raven before the birth of Aesculapius. She had been a king's daughter and Poseidon (in Roman myth, Neptune) had fallen for her charms. As he intended to take her by force she cried out to the gods for help and Athene (Minerva) transformed her into a crow, after which she became the goddess's attendant. St Paul the Hermit was fed by a crow.

Crow and Crab

Figures who showed humanity how to die, in the mythology of the Murinbata people of the northeastern Victoria River District. Crow and Crab argued over the best manner in which to die. Crab said that she knew a good way and went off to find a hole in the ground. She cast off her wrinkled old shell and waited in the hole while a new one formed.

She returned to their camp with a new shell but Crow declared that he knew a quicker way to die. He promptly rolled back his eyes and fell over backwards. Crab tried to revive Crow with water but could not, because he was dead. According to the Murinbata, people chose to die in Crow's way.

Crow: *see* Asklepios; BIRDS; Black; DEATH; Sun

Crow and Crab: *see* DEATH, THE ORIGIN OF

CROSS

In religion and art, the richest and most enduring of geometric symbols, taking many forms and meanings throughout history. It is both the emblem of the Christian faith and a more ancient and universal image of the cosmos reduced to its simplest terms – two intersecting lines making four points of direction. These stood for the four cardinal points and the four rain-bearing winds (notably in pre-Columbian America where the cross was often a fertility emblem of life and elemental energy), the four phases of the moon (Babylonia), and the four great gods of the elements (Syria).

The arms of the cross could be multiplied to six (as in Chaldea and Israel) or eight. In China, a cross within a square represented the earth and stability. In India, the cross was the Hindu emblem of the fire sticks of Agni; a cross within a circle, the Buddhist wheel of life; or, with arms extending beyond the circle, divine energy. The swastika – an ancient emblem of cosmic energy – was a cross given momentum by turning the ends of the arms.

The cross was also a summary of the Tree of Life, a widespread symbolism later often incorporated into Christian crucifixion iconography. The vertical axis has ascensional meaning while the horizontal axis stands for earthly life – in Hindu and Buddhist terms, an image of higher and lower states of being. In China the cross represented a heavenly ladder and also the number 10 (as a symbol of totality). Another symbol of totality is the cross formed by a man standing with arms outstretched – the image of Man as microcosm. More generally, the cross is associated with duality and union, conjunction and, in Jungian psychology, a kindling energy.

Widespread veneration of the cross by peoples who knew nothing of Christianity puzzled early missionaries, particularly in North and Central America; in Mexico the cross was an attribute of the wind and rain gods, Quetzalcoatl and Tlaloc. Aztec images of sacrificial crucifixions have also been found. The mark of the cross in Africa could signify protection, cosmic unity, destiny or (in a circle) sovereignty. In Scandinavia, runic crosses marking boundaries and important graves may have represented the fertilizing power of the god Thor's hammer. The form of the Celtic cross, incorporating a circle at the centre of the crossbar, appears to synthesize Christian and pagan cosmic symbolism. In Egypt, the *ankh* cross or key of life, symbolizing immortality, was adopted into Christianity by the Coptic Church.

In the Roman, Persian and Jewish world, the crucifixion cross was the brutal and humiliating instrument of execution for non-citizens such as slaves, pirates and foreign political agitators or other criminals. Thus, at the time of Christ's death, it hardly seemed an emblem likely to make many converts. Fear of ridicule as well as persecution probably influenced the various forms of *crux dissimulata* (anchor, axe, swastika or trident) used by early Christians as secret cross emblems. Even after the emperor Constantine's conversion, the cross remained for some centuries an emblem of faith secondary to Christ's Chi-Rho monogram. It became dominant as Christianity spread because it could inherit the older cross traditions and give them profound new meaning – redemption through Christ's self-sacrifice. In art, schematic representations of the crucifixion with an impassive Christ gradually gave way to powerful images of his agony, which culminate in Grünewald's Isenheim altarpiece (1515) that made the plain cross itself a consoling symbol of human suffering transcended.

The form of the cross has varied widely. The Latin *crux immissa* (its bar horizontal to and high up the upright) is traditionally the cross of Christ. Alternatively, this may have been the *crux commissa* (T-shaped, Tau or St Anthony cross). The transverse *crux decussata*, signifying martyrdom, is the cross of St Andrew, said to have felt himself unworthy of crucifixion on the cross of Christ. The Greek cross, *crux quadrata* (centrally positioned bar), is that of St George. Other Christian forms include the Y-shaped cross, strongly identified with the Tree of Life; the Calvary cross with three steps at the bottom; the Papal cross with three equal bars; the patriarchal cross with two bars, used for archbishops and cardinals, which also appears widely in Greece and became the Cross of Anjou and Lorraine, later the emblem of the Free French; the cross of St Peter, an upside-down form of the Latin cross; the axe-bladed cross of the Templars; the eight-pointed Maltese cross of the Hospitallers; and the triangle-armed cross of the Teutonic Knights. All are images with centripetal energy.

A cross tipped with arrows, was the emblem of the fascist Hungarian Nationalist Party. There are nearly 300 other forms of heraldic cross.

The cross is one of the most frequently misunderstood of all images. Crosses, particularly the transverse cross, are commonly woven into patterns with no symbolic meaning, or used simply as directional markers, signatures, or signs of dissent, assent and warning. The meanings of some ancient crosses scratched on stone or wood is therefore debatable. The symbolism of the Christian cross also created popular confusion. Superstitions that the Church found hard to eradicate included the idea that making the sign of the cross (as in benediction or prayer) could ward off bad luck. Crosses on bread, for example, were still commonplace in 17th-century England.

Four types of cross (clockwise from top): crux commissa or Tau-cross; crux decussata; crux immissa; and crux quadrata.

*The papal triple crown
or tiara, from a 17th-
century building in
Avignon, France.*

Crown

Victory, rank, merit or election – the supreme emblem of spiritual or temporal authority. Crowns acquired celestial, solar, spiritual or protective meaning in many cultures (through the symbolism of circularity, spoked rays, stars, thorns, turrets and so on) but are essentially forms of headdress designed to identify, glorify or consecrate chosen individuals. Crowns originated as simple wreaths, usually of woven laurel or olive leaves, herbs, reeds or other plants, used in wedding or funeral rites or conferred on victors at Greek games. Rulers awarded themselves more distinguished wreaths of gold or roses and diadems of cloth set with jewels, or ornate helmets with horns, jewels or feathers, and these various forms were gradually combined into metalled and jewelled crowns with increasingly elaborate significance.

In Christianity, Hinduism and Buddhism the crown represents spiritual illumination, the crown of everlasting life. Christ's mocking crown of thorns (which became the crown of martyrs) had ancient precedents in the crowning of sacrificial victims. Many gods wear crowns suited to their attributes (for example, the Greek Demeter was crowned with ears of corn, Dionysos or Bacchus with vine leaves, Apollo with laurel). At the ancient Olympic Games, victorious athletes were presented with a crown of olive leaves from a tree sacred to Zeus that grew in the sanctuary of the god at Olympia. Others who wear crowns in Christian art are poets, martyrs, saints, and allegorical figures including Faith, Hope, Wisdom, Fame, Truth and the Church. The Synagogue, in contrast to the Church, is shown as a woman with a toppling crown to indicate the supercession, and superiority, of Christianity.

Crucible

An alchemical symbol for transformation through dissolution, purification and union. The crucible could stand for the transmutation of materials or for the testing and blending of male and female in marriage.

Crucifix

An image of Christ on the Cross represents the Christian faith. Many saints are seen contemplating a crucifix, especially hermits and penitents, but it may appear in particular with Saints Francis, Jerome, John Gualbert, Nicholas of Tolentino and Scholastica, and between the antlers of a stag before St Eustace.

Crutch

A crutch supports the old or infirm and is the staff of hermits, beggars and pilgrims. It is the attribute of Saints Anthony Abbot and Romuald. Salvador Dalí, who had his own idiosyncratic symbolic vocabulary, often painted limp objects supported by a crutch – for example in *The Enigma of William Tell.*

Crystal

Clairvoyance, supernatural knowledge, spiritual perfection, chastity. The crystal, a solid that light can penetrate, struck the ancients as celestial and magical.

The crystal symbolized the notion of passing or looking beyond the material world, and was both emblem and tool of shamanistic powers. Hence the visionary crystal palaces and magical crystal (or glass) slippers of folklore. In Buddhism the crystal is the insight of the pure mind.

Cú Chulainn

An Ulster warrior and leading hero, Cú Chulainn was the son of Deichtine, the sister of King Conchobar of Ulster, and the warrior Sualtamh. However, he also had a divine father: Lugh, who appeared to Deichtine in a dream and announced that he would place in her womb a child named Sétanta. The newborn child had seven pupils in each eye, seven fingers on each hand and seven toes on each foot.

At the age of five, Sétanta went to Emhain Macha, the Ulster capital. When he was nearly seven, King Conchobar took him to a feast given by Culann the Smith, where he was attacked by the host's ferocious hound. Sétanta killed the animal but offered to act as Culann's watchdog until a new hound had been reared. The druid Cathbhadh gave him a new name: Cú Chulainn, "The Hound of Culann". He was trained in the arts of war by Scáthach, a woman with supernatural powers, who gave him his deadliest weapon, the *gae bolga*, a savagely barbed spear which penetrated every part of the body.

Cú Chulainn was the leading hero in the war between the Men of Ulster and the Men of Ireland (that is, Connacht) recounted in the epic *Táin Bó Cuailnge* (*the Cattle Raid of Cooley*), and demonstrated his prowess and apparent invincibility many times, notably in single combat against his foster-brother Fer Diadh. On the fourth day of gruelling fighting, Cú Chulainn fell into one of his characteristic "fury-spasms" – a fit of uncontrollable rage that caused his body to seethe and swell up – and killed Fer Diadh with the *gae bolga*. On another occasion he saved Conchobar from an assault by Ferghus, Medhbh's chief warrior. Shortly after, the hero defeated Medhbh, but spared her life because she was female.

Cú Chulainn's death was brought about by the children of Cailidín, a warrior slain by the hero in the war against Medhbh. After Cailidín's death, Medhbh sent his three daughters and three sons abroad to study sorcery. On their return they tracked Cú Chulainn down to the Valley of the Deaf, where Conchobar had ordered Cú Chulainn to remain under the protection of the princesses, noblewomen and druids of Ulster. Normally, no sound could penetrate the valley, but the war goddess Bodhbh conjured up a phantom army whose battle cries could be heard even in heaven, convincing Cú Chulainn that his enemies were plundering the land. He was lured into the open and killed by a magic javelin hurled by one of the sons of Cailidín. Three days later Bodhbh landed on Cú Chulainn's shoulder in the form of a crow, a sign that he was truly dead.

Cube

Perfect stability, firm ground – a symbol of the earth itself. The cube is the square in three dimensions, each face presenting the same view, hence an emblem of truth, used in art as the footrest of Faith and History.

The Mayan Tree of Life is said to grow from a cube. For both Judaism and Islam, the cube represents the centre of faith. Pilgrims in Makkah (Mecca) circumambulate a double cube, the Ka'aba, at the centre of Islam's most sacred mosque.

Cú Chulainn: *see* Bodhbh; Conchobar; Ferghus; Lugh; Medhbh; *Táin Bó Cuailnge*

Cube: *see* Centre; Circumambulation; Earth; Six; Square; VIRTUES

Cú Chulainn with the raven on his shoulder, after a 20th-century bronze sculpture.

Cuckoo

A parasitic bird that lays its eggs in other birds' nests – hence the word *cuckold* for a duped husband, and the bird's link in Europe with jealousy and opportunism. More generally, the cuckoo was traditionally a good omen – a herald of spring or summer, and of riches. Its repetitive call led to the superstition that it was lucky to rattle coins on hearing a cuckoo.

Cuichu

The Inca god of the rainbow, one of the attendants of Inti (the Sun) and Mama Kilya (the Moon).

CULTURE HERO *see panel opposite*

Cunegunda, Saint

The Holy Roman Emperor Henry II (973–1024) and his wife, the empress Cunegunda (died 1033), were dedicated supporters of the Benedictines; Henry founded the see of Bamberg and both he and Cunegunda are buried in its cathedral. As a widow, Cunegunda lived in the monastery that she had founded at Kaufungen in Hesse. In art, she is often depicted holding a model of Bamberg cathedral or with plough-shares. The latter relate to a legend that Henry suspected her of infidelity with a knight and made her walk barefoot over 15 feet of red-hot ploughshares. Cunegunda stepped over the glowing mass unharmed, thereby proving her innocence.

Cup

As the goblet, a cup is a symbol of the heart in Islamic, Egyptian and Celtic traditions – hence cups are the forerunners of the hearts suit in the Tarot. The cup also symbolizes love offered, or the blessings of revealed wisdom and everlasting life. Cups were used for making or exchanging vows, for divination (which survives in the reading of tea leaves) and for libations or offerings. In iconography, a cup on a pillar usually has the symbolism of both giving and receiving – for example, in Hinduism. The Buddhist begging bowl is a contrasting emblem that represents renunciation. An overturned cup in a still life symbolizes the emptiness of material values. Awarding cups of achievement is a more recent custom.

Cupid

Cupid (known to the Greeks as Eros) was the Roman god of love, and the son of Venus (Aphrodite); his father may have been Jupiter (Zeus), Vulcan (Hephaistos) or Mars (Ares). He is usually seen as a little winged archer or beautiful young boy who, according to Ovid, had two kinds of arrows, a golden one to kindle love and a lead one, which puts love to flight.[1] He is sometimes shown blindfolded, to imply that love is blind, or may be tying a knot, symbolically bonding a pair of lovers. He often has a mischievous role, perhaps teasing the many lovers of Jupiter (Zeus), and he may be chastised by Diana (Artemis), Minerva (Athene), or Venus who confiscated his arrows.

Cupid was thought to have been taught by Mercury (Hermes). Corregio's *Education of Cupid* shows Cupid engrossed in a book held out by Mercury, which suggests that, having discarded his bow and arrow, he has renounced sensual love in favour of learning. Cupid was once stung by a bee as he was pilfering honey from a hive. Cranach's *Cupid Complaining to*

CULTURE HERO

All mythological traditions feature heroic figures who carry out extraordinary acts in the course of laying the foundations of human society. Frequently, the "culture hero" is male and possesses supernatural or divine qualities. A typical story from Melanesia tells of one primordial culture hero known as Sida, Sido, Sosom or Souw, who journeyed through Papua New Guinea, shaping the landscape, teaching people to speak, stocking the seas and rivers with fish and providing vegetables for cultivation. Similar tales are widespread in Aboriginal Australia.

Culture heroes are frequently said to be responsible for the discovery or institution of important social rules, such as those governing the hunting of animals and the distribution of food. The origins of religious rites and ceremonies are also attributed to figures such as the mysterious White Buffalo Woman, bringer of the sacred pipe rituals to the Lakota people of North America. The theft of fire by a culture hero is widely seen as a key event in the development of society. In Greek myth, for example, the Titan Prometheus stole fire from the gods for the benefit of humanity.

An illustration based on a painted wooden mask from the Torres Strait Islands, Australasia, of a culture hero, thought to be Sida.

According to some tribal myths of South America, a young culture hero stole fire from the jaguar. In the Gilbert Islands of the western Pacific, the source of fire is the sun, which was snared by the culture hero Bue to obtain fire for the human race.

In North America the culture heroes, like the early creator divinities, are quite often represented as animals. For example, along the northwestern coast the local culture hero is Raven, who was made responsible for the discovery of fire, the tides, the alternation of night and day, and the positions of all the heavenly bodies in the sky. Like his counterparts in other areas of North America, such as the culture heroes Coyote and Glooskap, Raven also displays many attributes of the trickster.

Culture heroes of the Celtic world take on a more human form, and tend to be great warriors. Examples are Cú Chulainn, a figure of incredible strength whose exploits are found in the *Táin Bó Cuailnge*, and Finn, the central figure of a body of myths known as the Fenian Cycle. Finn was renowned not only as a warrior but also as a great hunter, and for his gift of prophecy.

CULTURE HERO: *see* Coyote; Cú Chulainn; Finn; HARES AND RABBITS; Prometheus; Raven; Sida; *Táin Bó Cuailgne*; TRICKSTER; White Buffalo Woman

Venus illustrates him asking Venus how such a tiny creature could cause such pain. Venus replied that he too was a tiny creature yet inflicted far worse wounds.

Curius Dentatus, Manius

In the 3rd century BCE, Curius was three times Roman consul, yet he lived a rustic life in a small cottage. Ambassadors from the enemy Samnites found him there, boiling turnips in the chimney corner, and offered him a bribe of gold. He replied that he had no need of gold and sent them away. He is usually depicted as an example of a virtuous Roman citizen.

Curtius, Marcus

In *c.*360BCE a chasm appeared in the Roman forum and an oracle explained that it would close only if Rome sacrificed its most precious possession. The soldier Marcus Curtius understood this to mean that the sacrifice of a young man was required so, fully armed and on horseback, he threw himself into the hole, which immediately closed over his head. Veronese used the subject in his ceiling decoration *Marcus Curtius*.

Cybele

In Greco-Roman mythology, Cybele was "the Great Mother", a goddess of fertility of eastern origin; she was identified with the Greek earth goddess Rhea (Ops in Roman myth). Cybele originated in Phrygia in western Asia Minor. She features relatively little in myth compared with other deities. In one account she turned the huntress Atalanta and her husband Hippomenes into lions which would draw her chariot. In 204BCE The Sybilline oracle advised the Romans

that if they wanted victory against Hannibal in the Punic Wars they must bring the Great Mother to Rome. Accordingly the goddess was brought from her sanctuary in Pergamon (Pergamum) in Asia Minor in the form of a block of block of stone and received, also in accordance with the oracle, by the Roman centurion Cornelius Scipio. Hannibal retreated and the goddess's cult became popular in Rome from that time.

In allegory Cybele represents the Earth, and is commonly shown with an abundance of fruit, as in Rubens' *The Union of Earth and Water*, which invokes peace and prosperity.

Cyclops

"Round-eye", one of a race of monsters or giants of Greek myth often described as possessing a single, round eye in their foreheads. The first three Cyclopes, the sons of the goddess Gaia and the god Uranos, were called Brontes ("Thunder"), Steropes ("Lightning") and Arges ("Bright").

When the Titan Kronos came to power in the heavens, he imprisoned the Cyclopes in Tartaros, the darkest depths of the underworld. They were freed by Zeus, whom they supported in his war against the Titans. As a reward for their assistance, Zeus made the Cyclopes his blacksmiths, responsible for forging his thunderbolts. When Zeus killed Asklepios, demi-god of healing, with a thunderbolt, to assist Hades, god of the underworld, the Cyclopes were slaughtered by Apollo, Asklepios' father.

Another tradition made the Cyclopes the assistants of the craftsman god Hephaistos, the Roman Vulcan. In Homer, the Cyclopes were a tribe of brutal, man-eating shepherds who lived in caves on an island, often identified with Sicily. The most notorious of these Cyclopes was Polyphemus, who captured the hero Odysseus and his crew, but was then blinded by Odysseus during his successful attempt to escape. Polyphemus also features in the story of Acis and Galatea as the unrequited lover of the nymph Galatea.

Cypress
An enigmatic Western symbol of death and mourning, an allusion made by the Swiss painter Arnold Böcklin in *Island of the Dead*. It is said that it was once used to make coffins, alluded in Shakespeare's song: "Come away, death, and in sad cypress let me be laid"[1]. Like other durable evergreens, in Asia and elsewhere it is an emblem of longevity, endurance and even immortality (it was the Phoenician Tree of Life). In Greece, its dual symbolism as the attribute of the gloomy god Hades as well as more cheerful deities such as Zeus, Apollo, Aphrodite and Hermes may mean no more than that its sombre form made it a suitable funerary image of life after death.

Cyrus the Great
According to legend, before his birth it was predicted that Cyrus,[1] the founder of the Persian Empire, would overthrow his grandfather Astyages, king of the Medes. In an attempt to defy fate, Astyages ordered his faithful servant, Harpagus, to kill the infant Cyrus. In *Harpagus Bringing Cyrus to the Shepherds*, Sebastiano Ricci illustrated Harpagus, unable to obey the king, giving Cyrus to a cowherd and his wife. When Astyages

by chance recognized his ten-year-old grandson, he punished his servant but was persuaded to let the boy live, despite his dream. When Cyrus reached manhood in Persia, he plotted revenge with Harpagus and together they succeeded in usurping the cruel Astyages, whose army deserted him and surrendered to Cyrus in 550BCE.

After inheriting the empire of the Medes, Cyrus had to consolidate his power over Persian tribes before expanding to the West. He gained control of Asia Minor, captured Babylon, and in 530BCE caused heavy losses to the Asian tribe ruled by Queen Tomyris. The queen then marched against Cyrus, slaughtered his army, and searched for his body among the dead. In *Queen Tomyris and the Head of Cyrus* Rubens shows how she placed his head in a bowl of blood saying, "Have your fill of the blood for which you thirsted!"

Cythera
In one account of the birth of the goddess Aphrodite (the Roman Venus), Cythera was the island where she is said to have come ashore after her birth from the sea (in another account it was Cyprus). Hence Cythera is also used as an alternative name of the goddess herself,[1] and by extension, the island was mythologized as an earthly paradise where sensual love prevailed and young girls found lovers or husbands.

Watteau, in *The Embarkation to Cythera*, seems in fact to represent a departure from the island, and gives the painting a melancholic air appropriate to lovers returning to the everyday world.

Cypress: *see* DEATH; Longevity; Tree
[1] *Twelfth Night, II.4*

Cyrus the Great:
[1] Herodotus, *I 108–129* and *214*

Cythera: *see* Venus
[1] Ovid, *Fasti IV 286*

*Daedalus making the
wings for Icarus, from
an antique bas relief.*

Daedalus

The greatest of mortal craftsmen, according to Greek myth. A member of the Athenian royal household, Daedalus became famous for his skill as an inventor, painter and sculptor. However, he fled to Crete after trying to kill his nephew Perdix, a rival craftsman, out of jealousy at his invention of the saw. He threw him over a cliff, but the gods changed him into a partridge (*perdix*) In Crete, Daedalus entered the service of King Minos. Pasiphaë, Minos's queen, ordered him to build a life-sized hollow model of a heifer in which she then hid to have sex with a bull. As a result of this coupling, Pasiphaë bore the Minotaur, a creature half-man and half-bull. A furious Minos ordered Daedalus to construct the Labyrinth as a prison for the monster.

Later, Daedalus gave Ariadne, the king's daughter, a ball of twine so that his fellow Athenian, the hero Theseus, could negotiate the Labyrinth to slay the Minotaur. Minos was so enraged that he locked Daedalus in the Labyrinth with his young son, Icarus. To escape, Daedalus made two pairs of wings from wax and feathers, warning Icarus not to fly too close to the sun, which would melt the wax. But Icarus failed to heed his father's warning and plummeted to his death. Daedalus reached Sicily (or mainland Italy in some accounts), where he lived the rest of his days.

Dagger *see* Knife

Daghdha, The

The "Good God", an Irish god of abundance, fertility, wisdom and magic. The Daghdha was the supreme tribal deity of the Tuatha Dé Danann, the fifth race of people to invade Ireland, and was also referred to as "Great Father" and "Mighty One of Great Knowledge". The Daghdha's offspring included Oenghus, the god of love, and the goddess Brighid.

The Daghdha possessed a massive club with one end that was lethal and one that brought the dead back to life, and a huge cauldron from which he

their families, to be thrown to the lions instead.[2] In *Daniel in the Lion's Den*, Rubens shows Daniel giving thanks to God for his survival. Another version of the story, in the Apocryphal additions to *The Book of Daniel*, relates how the Babylonians worshipped a dragon which Daniel claimed he could kill without a sword or staff. He fed the dragon cakes of pitch, fat and hair, which made it burst. Outraged, the Babylonians threw him into a den of seven lions for six days, but the lions did not harm him and he was fed by the prophet Habakkuk. On the seventh day he was released, and those who had imprisoned him were thrown into the den in his place.[3]

Among Daniel's visions was that of a ram fighting a one-horned goat. The angel Gabriel explained that the two animals represented warring kings and future oppression, and comforted Daniel as he sank to the ground in despair.[4] Rembrandt depicted this episode in *The Vision of Daniel*.

Dante

The Florentine poet Dante Alighieri (1265–1321) was one of the greatest writers of the Middle Ages and a creator of the modern Italian language. *La Vita Nuova* ("The New Life") of 1292 tells of his idealized love for a girl named Beatrice, who died prematurely. Inconsolable, Dante continued to contemplate her beauty and goodness, while his friends grew concerned by his grief. In Dante Gabriel Rossetti's *The First Anniversary of the Death of Beatrice*, Dante is seen drawing an angel, oblivious to the presence of others. Rossetti also painted scenes from *La Vita Nuova*.

Dante is best known for *La Divina Commedia* ("The Divine Comedy"), an epic poem concerning human destiny on earth and in the afterlife. The poem falls into three parts: the *Inferno* (Hell) and *Purgatorio* (Purgatory), in which the poet is led through these regions by Virgil, and the *Paradiso* (Paradise), in which the guide is Beatrice. The poem's journey leads the reader down through the twenty-four circles of Hell, up the two terraces and seven cornices of Mount Purgatory, and finally to Earthly Paradise and beyond the planets and stars to God. The poem contains much political and religious allegory, as well as personal experience. It has inspired many artists, including Raphael, who portrayed Dante alongside Virgil in *Parnassus* (Stanza della Segnatura, Vatican). Dante and Virgil are shown descending into the underworld in Delacroix's *The Barque of Dante*.

Danu

An Irish mother goddess. Little is known of her except that she was said to be the ancestor of the Tuatha Dé Danann ("People of Danu").

Dao De Jing

"The Classic of the Way and its Power", the central scripture of Daoism. The *Dao De Jing* is attributed to Laozi, Daoism's legendary founder.

Daphne

A naiad (river nymph) of Greek myth. Daphne[1] fled from the amorous advances of the god Apollo until she grew weary. She cried out for help, and was transformed into a laurel tree (*daphne*). Yet still Apollo loved her. He made a crown from her branches and entwined other branches and leaves around his quivers and lyre. Daphne symbolizes the triumph of

Dante: *see* Paolo and Francesca; Ugolino; Virgil
[1] Dante, *La Vita Nuova III 1–11*

Danu: *see* Anu (2); Dôn; Tuatha Dé Danann

Dao De Jing: *see* Eight Immortals, The; Laozi

Daphne: *see* Apollo; Laurel
[1] Ovid, *Met I 452–567*

Daphnis and Chloe

chastity and was popular in art; Bernini's sculpture *Apollo and Daphne* is a fine example.

Daphnis and Chloe

The son of the Greek god Hermes (the Roman Mercury) and a nymph, Daphnis was a cowherd on Sicily. A gifted musician, he pleased the goddess Artemis (Diana) with his shepherd's pipe, which Pan had taught him to play; he is also credited with inventing the bucolic or pastoral poem. In one story,[1] the nymph Chloe fell in love with him, and after several adventures they married. In *Daphnis and Chloe*, Paris Bordone shows the young couple with Eros (Cupid).

Darkness

Like the colour black, an ambivalent symbol of not only death, sin, ignorance and evil, but also of potential life – the dark of germination. In mystic thought, light and dark are equally necessary; darkness precedes light as death precedes resurrection. It symbolizes mystery (a "dark horse"), concealment (keeping someone "in the dark") and the unknown (a "leap in the dark").

Dasharatha

In Indian myth, a king of the holy city of Ayodhya and father of Rama, the seventh avatar of the god Vishnu.

Date

As an important food source in North Africa and the Near East, the date palm is linked with fertility and divine bounty. In the Bible, dates symbolize the just, who alone will receive riches in heaven. In the Qur'an, Mary bears Jesus beneath a date palm and is sustained by its fruit and by a rivulet that miraculously springs from its roots.

David

The biblical King David has multiple symbolism. As the slayer of the giant Goliath, he is a personification of physical prowess and courage, and the conqueror of evil. As the royal musician to his predecessor King Saul, he is depicted playing the harp in medieval manuscripts of the Psalms, which were ascribed to him. As the great king and saviour of Israel he is "anointed by God" (Hebrew *mashiah*, messiah)[1] and both a prefiguration and ancestor of Christ. Yet the story of Bathsheba also shows David, like his son Solomon, to be a symbol of flawed greatness.

The beautiful youngest son of Jesse, David was a shepherd boy chosen by the prophet Samuel to succeed Saul as king of the Israelites. Saul led the Israelite army into battle against the Philistines, whose champion was Goliath, an eight-foot giant clad in heavy armour. Goliath offered a challenge of single combat to the best of the Israelite warriors, and David volunteered for the contest. Refusing Saul's offer of armour, David confronted Goliath armed only with a sling. He killed the giant with the first stone, then took Goliath's sword and cut off his head.[2] The Philistines fled. The victorious youth featured in both Renaissance and Baroque sculpture. The statues by Donatello, Michelangelo and Bernini show different interpretations of the giant slayer. In *The Triumph of David*, Poussin shows David's triumphal entry into Jerusalem with Goliath's head.

David's success incurred the envy and wrath of Saul, and he fled for his life. In *The Cave of Adullam*, Claude Lorrain shows him hiding from Saul with three Israelites who broke through the Philistines' ranks to fetch water for him. But David would not drink, saying, "is this not the blood of the men that went in jeopardy of their lives?"[3]

David was thirty when Saul died and he became king of Judah. Seven and a half years of war ensued, after which he became established as ruler of the twelve tribes of Israel with Jerusalem as his capital. He brought the Ark of the Covenant to the city in triumph. David "danced before the Lord with all his might",[4] watched from a window by his wife, Michal.

David had seventeen sons. One son, Amnon, raped his half-sister Tamar, but the king would not punish him. Another son, Absalom, brooded for two years on Amnon's crime, before murdering him at a feast to avenge his sister. Mattia Preti depicted this incident in *The Feast of Absalom*. Absalom fled and David mourned the loss of his two sons. After many years David and Absolom were reconciled, until Absalom led a revolt against his father. During a battle Absalom's hair became entangled in the branches of an oak and David's general stabbed him through the heart.[5]

David sent men to greet the wealthy landowner Nabal to acquire food from him. But the men were rebuffed and David was planning retribution when Nabal's beautiful wife,[6] Abigail, came and threw herself at his feet and pacified him with food and drink. After Nabal died, David took Abigail as his second wife.

Dawn

A symbol of hope and youth – extensions of the self-evident symbolic associations surrounding dawn, illumination and new beginnings. In Buddhism, the clarity of the dawn light symbolizes enlightenment. The Greek dawn-goddess Eos (the Roman Aurora) is usually shown as a winged goddess driving a chariot, sometimes scattering flowers or preceding Helios, the sun. Dawn is generally linked with joy, but Eos may also appear mourning her son Memnon, slain by the hero Achilles, her tears falling as dew.

Dazhbog

"Giving God", the ancient Slav sun god. Dazhbog was the son of the supreme elemental deity Svarog and the brother of the fire god Svarozhich. He was often said to live in a celestial eastern land of never-ending light and bounty, from which he rode forth each morning in a chariot drawn by white horses. In some areas, Dazhbog was the consort of the moon. One tradition claims he was the ancestor of the Russians, the easternmost Slav people.

DEATH *see panel overleaf*

Decapitation

Among some societies, for example the ancient Celts, enemy heads were taken as trophies and preserved for the power they were thought to contain – a widespread symbolism linked with an ancient belief that the head was the seat of the soul. Respect for the head as the essence of a dead person may explain Paleolithic rituals in which it was buried separately from the body. It may also explain why in some traditions decapitation was regarded as an honourable means of execution – for example, in the Roman world and England, where it tended to be reserved for people of higher social rank.

Deceit

In Bronzino's *Allegory of Love*, Deceit or Fraud has the face of a beautiful

Dawn: *see* CARDINAL POINTS; Deer; Dew; Eos; Helios; Light; Obelisk; Orientation; Sun

Dazhbog: *see* Svarog; Svarozhich

Decapitation: *see* Head

DEATH

Most mythologies tell of the arrival of death to end humanity's original state of immortality. Death's origin is often ascribed to the rivalry between human beings and divinities. In Greek myth, for example, Prometheus defied Zeus by assuming the protectorship of humankind. As a punishment the gods sent the first woman, Pandora, with a "box" (in fact a jar) containing death and disease. As in this story, the arrival of death and misfortune is commonly linked with a woman: other examples are the Maori myth of Hine-titama and the story of Abuk told by the Dinka people of the Sudan.

The loss of immortality through a severing of contact with heaven is a common theme in African myth. According to the Luba people of the Congo, in the beginning humans and the High God lived in the same village. Tiring of their noisy quarrels, the god expelled his human neighbours to earth, where they encountered death and sickness for the first time.

A skeletal death image: a Native American shamanic statuette.

In Oceania mortality is widely linked with the sexual shaming of a culture hero. The Daribi of southern Papua relate how a young woman encountered the penis of the hero Souw. It tried to rape her, but she cried out and it withdrew. Humiliated, Souw visited death on humanity. In Polynesia, it is said that humans have been unable to achieve immortality since the hero Maui was killed as he tried to rape the goddess of death.

The ecological necessity of death is conveyed in a myth of the Shoshoni people of North America. Wolf and Coyote were discussing death. Wolf said that people could be revived after death, but Coyote argued that if that happened there would soon be no room on earth. Wolf reminded a grieving Coyote of his words when Coyote's own son became the first person to die.

Personifications of death are deliberately alarming. In the West, the most familiar representation of Death is the skeletal rider, cloaked and cowled, wielding a scythe, trident, sword or bow and arrows. He holds an hour glass to signify the measured span of life. Death or a skull might be included in a painting as a reminder that no one is spared; a skeleton may appear on or near a tomb as a *memento mori*.

Underworld gods who ruled the dead had grim auxiliaries to bring them souls, but were not themselves necessarily frightening. Other more gentle personifications of death are a veiled woman or an angel. The Druids taught that the god of death (Donn in Ireland) was the source of all life. Death could also appear as a drummer or dancer.

Plants linked with death include the poppy and asphodel flowers and the cypress and weeping willow trees. Many other death symbols have strong links with notions of the afterlife, including the wreath. Black is associated with death in Western tradition, white in Eastern.

DEATH: *see* AFTERLIFE *and individual names and terms*

Decius Mus:
[1] Livy, *The History of Rome*, X:xxviii

young girl, the body of a reptile and the feet of a lion. With one hand she offers a honeycomb, and in the other she holds the sting of her reptilian tail. Deceit may also be represented by a mask – for example, an old woman wearing the face of a young girl.

Decius Mus

The Roman consul Decius Mus devoted himself to the service of the state.[1] In 338BCE he threw himself into the thickest part of a battle against the Latins. Rubens depicted this episode in his designs for seven tapestries showing scenes from the consul's life, now in the princely gallery in Vaduz, Liechtenstein.

Deer

A universally benevolent symbol, associated with the East, dawn, light, purity, regeneration, creativity and spirituality. The stag or hart is a solar emblem of fertility, its branching antlers suggesting in Native American and other traditions the Tree of Life, the sun's rays and, through their annual shedding and regrowth, resurrection and rebirth. The stag is linked with virility and ardour, and in China with wealth and happiness – its name is a homophone of "abundance".

Swiftness is a more obvious attribute, also grace and beauty – hence, perhaps, the deer's link with poetry and music. Other symbolism, drawn from the habits of the red deer stag, includes solitude in European and Japanese traditions. The Celts believed that deer were the herds of fairies or divinities; the antlered "Horned God" Cernunnos was lord of the animals. Stags were the steeds of Hittite, Mesopotamian and Shinto divinities, and appear widely as supernatural messengers or guides who show heroes the path to their goals. Healing powers were also ascribed to deer, especially the ability to discover medicinal herbs. In art, a deer pierced by an arrow and carrying herbs in its mouth is an image of lovesickness. Prudence and Hearing are embodied by a deer.

In Christian iconography, deer may trample snakes underfoot – destroying evil – or maybe shown by at a stream, panting for water as the soul yearns for God.[1] Hence deer are shown on baptismal fonts or are drinking at the foot of the Cross.

The doe appears less often than a stag. It is an attribute of lunar hunting goddesses, notably the Greek Artemis (Diana). In Buddhism, two does flanking a Dharma wheel symbolize the occasion of the Buddha's first teaching, in a deer park at Sarnath. A doe was a popular ancestral figure in central Asia – hence the legend that Genghis Khan's forebears were a wolf and a doe. Both does and stags appear as symbols of transformation, as in the myth of Actaeon.

Deianeira

In Greek myth, the daughter of King Oenus and Queen Althaea of Aetolia and the second wife of Herakles.

Deirdre

In Irish myth, the daughter of Fedlimid, the bard of King Conchobar of Ulster. When Deirdre was a baby, the druid Cathbhadh prophesied that she would be very beautiful but would bring death and ruin to Ulster. Conchobar had Deirdre fostered in secret, intending to marry her when she came of age. But as a young woman she fell in love with Naoise son of Uisneach, with whom she eloped to Scotland.

Conchobar invited the couple to return, guaranteeing their safety by sending the great warrior Ferghus to escort them. But when they arrived at Emhain Macha, Conchobar's capital, the king instructed another warrior, Eoghan, to kill Naoise. Enraged at this treachery, Ferghus and his followers ravaged Ulster and switched their allegiance to Conchobar's enemy, Queen Medhbh of Connacht. The second part of the druid's prophecy was fulfilled in the ensuing bloody war between Ulster and Connacht. Deirdre did not smile or raise her head

Deer: *see* Actaeon; Antlers; Arrow; Artemis; Baptism; Cernunnos; CROSS; Dawn; Fairies; Horn; Light; LONGEVITY; Snake; Soul; Sun; Transformation; Tree; VIRTUES, THE; Water
[1] *Psalm 42:1*

Deianeira: *see* Herakles; Nessus

Deirdre: *see* Conchobar; Ferghus; Medhbh

The white hart was an emblem of England's Plantagenet dynasty; after the Wilton Diptych of c.1395.

from her knee for a year. Conchobar told her that she must live with Eoghan, and the next day the two men took her off in a chariot. As the vehicle approached a rock, Deirdre threw herself from the chariot and died.

Demeter

The Greek goddess of fertility, known to the Romans as Ceres. She was the daughter of the Titans Kronos and Rhea and sister of Hades, Hera, Hestia, Poseidon and Zeus. Demeter ("Mother Earth" or "Grain Mother") was the protector of crops, the bounty of the soil, and female fertility.

Demeter's daughter Persephone was abducted by Hades, the ruler of the underworld. Enraged and grief-stricken, Demeter left Mount Olympus and wandered the world disguised as an old woman. At Eleusis in Attica, King Celeus hired her as an attendant for his wife, Queen Metaneira, who asked Demeter to nurse her child, Demophöon. The goddess surreptitiously fed him on ambrosia, the food of the gods, and each night laid him on a fire to make him immortal. One night, Metaneira interrupted her and screamed in horror to see her child in the flames. Demeter hastily withdrew him and, revealing her identity, told Metaneira that Demophöon would now die like any other mortal. The goddess ordered the establishment of the Eleusinian Mysteries – the most famous mystery cult in the ancient Greek world – in her own honour, and then left her hosts.

Demeter withheld the grain from the earth, threatening to starve humanity unless she saw her daughter again. Zeus sent Hermes to bring Persephone back from the underworld. Demeter was delighted to see her, but warned that if she had eaten the food of the

Demeter with her sheaves of corn, based on a terracotta sculpture.

dead she must return to Hades for ever. In the underworld, Persephone had eaten some pomegranate seeds, but Zeus declared that she could spend two-thirds of the year with Demeter and the other third, the winter, with Hades. Mother and daughter rejoiced and fruitfulness returned to the land.

Before returning to Olympus, Demeter gave seeds, a plough and her dragon-drawn chariot to Celeus's son, Triptolemus, so that he could teach humankind the arts of agriculture.

Democritus and Heraclitus

The Greek Democritus (460–370BCE) wrote on philosophy, mathematics and music. He travelled extensively and retired to study in solitude. In *Democritus in Meditation*, Salvator Rosa depicts him among human and animal skeletons, meditating on the futility of life. Nicknamed the "laughing philosopher", he mocked human vanity and folly.[1] He was contrasted with the haughty and melancholic Heraclitus (*c.*500BCE). Raphael added Heraclitus to his fresco *The School of Athens* (Stanza della Segnatura, Vatican), giving him the likeness of Michelangelo.

Denys, Saint

St Denys (Denis, Dionysius) of Paris is a traditional patron saint of France. A 9th-century legend tells that he was a missionary, sent by Pope Clement I to Paris, where he was beheaded *c.*258CE on Montmartre (Martyrs' Hill). He is said to have carried his own severed head to his burial place, 2.5 miles (4km) away, the site of the future abbey of St Denys, which became the burial place of the kings of France. Henri Bellechose shows Denys as a young bishop receiving his last communion from Christ, and his decapitation. In altarpieces the saint may stand holding his severed head.

Descent into Hell, The

According to an apocryphal gospel,[1] after his Entombment Christ descended into Hell or Limbo, a region where souls since Adam had been consigned until Christ's coming. A great voice commanded that the gates be opened so that "the King of Glory shall come in". Beginning with Adam, the dead were released from their chains and the dark places were lit up. Christ bade Adam and the others to follow him to Paradise.

In paintings of the episode, also known as the Harrowing of Hell, Christ is usually depicted in white, holding the banner of the Resurrection at the entrance to a cave, where Adam and bearded prophets and patriarchs wait. Satan may be a small black figure recoiling at Christ's majesty or crushed by the gates on which Christ stands. In the Orthodox Church, a very similar scene forms part of traditional depictions of the *Anastasis* (Resurrection).

Desert

Commonly an image of sterility, the desert has deeper symbolism in both Islamic and Christian thought as a place of revelation that gave birth to both great religions. Christ was tested in the wilderness by Satan, and was also born in the desert, according to the Qur'an. The hermit exemplifies the man who seeks the desert's solitude and emptiness to confront the ultimate reality of God.

Deucalion and Pyrrha

In Greek myth,[1] the god Zeus was angered by the misdeeds of the Titan Prometheus and by humankind's transgressions, and prompted the sea-god Poseidon to send a great flood to cover the earth. However, Prometheus forewarned his son Deucalion and his son's mortal wife Pyrrha (Pronoia in some accounts). They built a vessel, in which they floated for nine days, until the flood had subsided.

Deucalion and Pyrrha went to Delphi to offer thanks to the Titan Themis, who in some accounts was the mother of Prometheus. Once there, Themis told them to throw over their shoulders the bones of the being from whom they were both descended. Bewildered at first, the couple soon realized that Themis was referring to Gaia, the earth, whose bones were the stones in the ground. Each stone thrown by Deucalion turned into a man and each thrown by Pyrrha became a woman; in this way the human race was recreated.

Devi

"The Goddess", the name under which the female divinities of the Hindu pantheon are often collectively grouped as different aspects of a single deity. Devi, also known as Mahadevi ("Great Goddess"), is frequently regarded as a major deity on a par with Vishnu and Shiva. In this case she is either linked with Parvati, the wife

Descent into Hell, The: see Passion of Christ
[1] *The Gospel of Nicodemus II: The Descent of Christ into the Underworld*

Desert: *see* Antony, Saint; Oven, Furnace; Sand

Deucalion and Pyrrha: *see* FLOOD MYTHS; Gaia; Prometheus; Themis; TITAN; Zeus
[1] Ovid, *Met I: 313–415*

Devi: *see* Durga; Kali; Krishna; Vishnu

*The devil, after an
engraving of 1492.*

of Shiva, and therefore benign, or
completely independent, in which case
her more fearsome aspects, such as
Durga and Kali, tend to predominate.

Devils

Adversaries of goodness personifying
darkness, temptation, deceit and evil,
especially within the great monotheistic religions. Evil and misfortune were
usually symbolized in the ancient
world either by monsters and goblins
or by the dual nature of divinities who
had cruel, capricious, or destructive
and demonic aspects. At the end of
the 7th century BCE, the Iranian prophet Zoroaster proposed a new explanation of creation's flaws – the
existence of Angra Mainyu (Ahriman), a dark creator spirit who had
chosen evil. This concept influenced
the development of Satan in Judaism
and Christianity. Iblis is his Islamic
counterpart. Alternative names for
the Devil are Lucifer (Satan before the
Fall), Beelzebub (a name based on
that of a Philistine god, whom the
Bible contemptuously calls "Lord of
the Flies") and Mephistopheles (who
in medieval German legend made a
pact with the sorcerer Dr Faust).

The most popular image of the
Devil, derived from the Classical god
Pan, shows him with horns, cloven
hooves, forked tail and sometimes bat
wings. Smaller devils follow him,
armed with pitchforks or spears.
A medieval obsession with the sin
of lust accounts for the addition of
a second face on the Devil's genitals
or buttocks.

Devils are linked with dragon and
serpent symbolism in Judeo-Christian
tradition. They stand for division, disintegration and the temptations of
disobedience and immorality.

Dew

Purity, spiritual illumination, rejuvenation – the nectar of the immortals.
Dew is a Buddhist emblem of evan-
escence, a symbolism found also in
Western art. More generally, links with
dawn and sky symbolism made dew
the purest of waters, a metaphor for
the divine word in Hinduism and for
the Holy Spirit in Christianity. The
Chinese "Tree of Sweet Dew" at the
centre of the world symbolized immortality. In the Classical world, dew was
linked with goddesses of fecundity.

Di Jun

"Lord of Heaven", the supreme sky
deity of early Chinese mythology.

Diadem *see* **Crown**

Diamond

A symbol of solar radiance, immutability and integrity. The diamond's
combination of brilliance and hardness give it a spiritual dimension, particularly in India, where the diamond
throne of Buddha is an image of the
unchanging Buddhist centre, and the
diamond thunderbolt a Tantric symbol of supreme wisdom. In Western
tradition, the diamond symbolizes
incorruptibility and hence moral
virtues such as sincerity and constancy
– the significance of its use in engagement rings. It is credited with healing
and protective properties.

Dian Cécht

An Irish deity of healing. In the *Book
of Invasions*, Nuadhu, king of the
Tuatha Dé Danann, lost his right arm
at the first battle of Magh Tuiredh
and renounced the kingship, because
the ruler had to be unblemished. But
Dian Cécht made Nuadhu a new arm

of silver, enabling him to resume his rule. After the second battle, Dian Cécht sang spells at the top of a well, bestowing upon its waters the power to heal mortally wounded warriors.

Diana see Artemis

Diarmaid

An Irish warrior, and companion of the hero Finn. Gráinne, the beautiful daughter of the warrior Cormac, reluctantly agreed to marry the ageing Finn. But at the wedding feast she fell in love with Diarmaid and bound him to her with a magic spell. The couple eloped, and when Finn and his men pursued them they were spirited to safety by Oenghus, the god of love.

Diarmaid and Gráinne wandered through Connacht and Ulster. After seven years Finn pardoned them, and some time later he invited Diarmaid to join a hunt for the magic boar of Beann Ghulbhan (Ben Bulben) in Sligo. This boar had once been Diarmaid's foster-brother, who, it was prophesied, would bring about Diarmaid's death. During the chase, Diarmaid was mortally wounded by the boar and his only chance of life was to receive a draught of water from the hands of Finn. Twice Finn came with water, but each time he remembered Gráinne and let the water trickle away. Diarmaid died and his body was taken by Oenghus to Brugh na Bóinne, the ancient burial grounds of Newgrange in Meath.

Dice, Die

Dice or a single die may represent fate, as in the saying "the die is cast". Dice may be the attribute of Fortune. At the Crucifixion, soldiers may be depicted dicing for Christ's cloak.[1]

Dido

The queen of Carthage and, according to Virgil's *Aeneid*, the lover of the hero Aeneas. Dido (or Elissa) was a princess of Tyre in Phoenicia. She was forced to flee after the murder of her husband and went with her sister Anna to North Africa, where she founded the city of Carthage (in modern Tunisia).

Carthage was nearing completion when the Trojan hero Aeneas and his companions were washed ashore. Dido and Aeneas fell in love. One day, on a hunting trip, they sheltered in a cave from a storm and consummated their love.[1] They lived as man and wife, and Aeneas behaved as if he were king of Carthage. Eventually,

Dido and Aeneas embracing, from a Roman floor mosaic.

Diarmaid: *see* Finn; Oenghus

Dice, Die:
  [1] *Matthew* 27:35; *Mark* 15:24; *Luke* 23:34; *John* 19:24; compare *Psalm* 22:18

Dido: *see* Aeneas; *Aeneid, The*
  [1] Virgil, *Aeneid*, 4:160–172
  Virgil, *Aeneid*, 4:642–705

Diogenes

however, the gods reminded him of his duty to found a new Troy in Italy. He left, despite Dido's accusations of treachery. In despair, she threw herself onto a pyre and stabbed herself with his sword.[2] Later, on his visit to the underworld, Aeneas encountered Dido's shade, but she would not speak to him and slunk off to join her husband, Sychaeus.

Diogenes
The Greek Diogenes of Sinope (*c*.412– 323BCE) was a Cynic philosopher and ascetic. In *Diogenes in the Market Place*, Jacob Jordaens illustrates the story of the philosopher's search for an honest man: Diogenes is shown in daylight, carrying a lantern, which represents his search for truth. He made his home in a large earthenware tub, casting off all worldly goods except his cloak and a drinking bowl. When he saw a young man drinking from the river with his hands, he even abandoned his bowl, as Poussin shows in *Landscape with Diogenes*. Alexander the Great, an admirer, visited Diogenes and asked if there was anything he required. Diogenes curtly replied: "Yes, step aside, you're blocking my sunlight."

Diomedes (1)
A hero of Argos and a leading Greek warrior of the Trojan War. At Troy, Diomedes drove the war god Ares from the battlefield and wounded the goddess Aphrodite with his spear. He came face to face with Glaucus, the leader of Troy's Lycian allies, who was an old friend. They refused to fight and exchanged armour as a sign of courtesy. Diomedes benefited from the exchange: his armour was of bronze, while that of Glaucus was of gold.

Diomedes was protected by the goddess Athene, who ensured that he, unlike many Greek warriors, returned home from Troy swiftly and safely. However, Aphrodite forced him to flee Argos and (according to Roman myth) he ended his days in Italy.

Diomedes (2)
In Greek myth, a king of the Bitones, a people of Thrace. Diomedes kept a herd of vicious mares, nourished on human flesh. As the eighth of his twelve labours, the hero Herakles killed Diomedes and fed him to the horses, which he tamed and led away.

Dionysius the Areopagite
Dionysius heard St Paul preaching at Athens[1] before the Areopagus, a council of judges that met on a hill of the same name (the "Hill of Ares"). Raphael shows Dionysius converted by the saint in *St Paul Preaching at Athens*. Tradition has connected him with St Denys and erroneously credited him with mystical writings.

Dionysos
The Greek god Dionysos (the Romans Bacchus) presided over all altered states, such as drunkenness, religious ecstasy and acting. Alone of the Olympians, he was of partly mortal parentage. In one account, Zeus and Persephone had a child, Zagreus, who, at the prompting of Zeus's jealous wife Hera, was devoured by the Titans. But Athene saved the baby's heart and Zeus's mortal lover Semele swallowed it and conceived Zagreus anew. On her death, Zeus stitched the unborn child into his thigh and it was born again as Dionysos.

Dionysos was above all the god of wine, which the Greeks revered as a

*Dionysos in a boat with dolphins
(transformed pirates); after a bowl.*

sacred drink. He was the focus of a great mystic cult involving ecstatic release through wine, music and dance. His mythical male followers, the satyrs, were devoted to wine, revelry and lust. His female followers were called Bacchants or maenads ("madwomen"). Two annual Athenian festivals were held in honour of Dionysos, as was the Roman Bacchanalia. From the Renaissance, the latter inspired images of revelry and intoxication. Whether with his rowdy throng or alone, the god is depicted as a beautiful youth, crowned with grapes and vine leaves or holding a cup or *thyrsus* (staff). Caravaggio's languid *Bacchus* provocatively offers the spectator a glass of wine.

Many myths about Dionysos depict him as a newcomer "from the east" travelling among human society, bringing gifts and establishing his cult, but punishing those, such as Pentheus, who did not accept him. He appeared in human (male or female) form or as an animal (usually a bull or lion). The god was once captured by pirates. He amazed them with a series of wonders:

wine flowed around the ship, vines and ivy grew over it and, finally, Dionysos turned himself into a lion. The pirates leapt into the sea in terror and were turned into dolphins.

Dioscuri, The

"Sons of Zeus" (Greek *Dios kouroi*), the semi-divine brothers Castor and Polydeuces (Pollux to the Romans). They were the offspring of Zeus and Queen Leda of Sparta, with whom Zeus had sex in the form of a swan. Leda subsequently laid two eggs: from one hatched Castor and Clytemnestra and from the other Polydeuces and Helen of Troy. In some accounts, Castor and Clytemnestra were the children of Tyndareos, Leda's husband, and therefore entirely mortal.

The Dioscuri were rarely separated. Castor gained renown as a horseman and Polydeuces as a boxer. They journeyed with Jason and in some sources took part in Meleager's boar hunt. They argued with their cousins Idas and Lynceus over the spoils of a cattle raid, and Lynceus killed Castor. In one account, Polydeuces begged Zeus to let Castor share his immortality, and Zeus let the twins divide their time between Hades and the heavens, where they appear as the constellation Gemini.

The patrons of mariners, the twins were said to cause Saint Elmo's fire. They were particularly honoured by the Romans, on whose behalf they were said to have intervened at the battle of Lake Regillus in 496BCE.

Dis Pater

"Wealthy Father", the Roman god of the dead. Dis Pater is a translation of the Greek Pluto ("Wealth Giver"), an alternative name for Hades, with whom he is identified.

Disc

A solar emblem, the disc appears in iconography throughout the Near East as the symbol of sun gods, for example as the *aten*, the visible manifestation of Ra, in Egypt; as Asshur in Assyria; and Ahura Mazda in Persia. Combining sun and eagle symbolism, the winged disc stands for the rising sun, itself an emblem of resurrection, and for cosmic energy. In Egypt, a disc with horns or a crescent is a symbol of solar and lunar unity. In India, a rayed disc is the weapon of Vishnu Surya, signifying his absolute power to destroy as well as to create. In China, a jade disc with a hole may be an image of spiritual perfection – the cosmic circle with the unknowable essence or void at its centre. Serpents or dragons encircling a disc represent the reconciliation of opposing forces.

A winged solar disc, from a Mesopotamian relief of the 9th century BCE.

Discord

In Greek myth, the goddess Eris (Discord or Strife) was not invited to the wedding feast of Thetis and Peleus, and angrily threw among the guests a golden apple inscribed "To the Fairest".¹ Paris gave it to the goddess Aphrodite, upsetting Athene and Hera and setting off the events leading to the Trojan War. Turner's

The Goddess of Discord shows Eris choosing the apple in the garden of the Hesperides.

Dismemberment

A form of sacrifice in which humans or animals were torn apart to symbolize disintegration leading to regeneration – to parallel the harvesting of crops. Osiris is one god whose death and dismemberment symbolizes this process in mythology. The magical restoration of the dismembered Osiris has parallels in other mythic episodes, such as the Greek story of Medea and the Mayan epic of the Hero Twins. Dismemberment is also imitated in some shamanic initiation rituals as a stage in spiritual rebirth.

Djunggun

A figure in an important Australian Aboriginal myth of the western Kimberleys that explains the origin of non-incestuous marriage. In early times, it is said, incest was common. But two men, Djunggun and Wodoy, married each other's daughters. Djunggun decided to keep his daughter for himself, so Wodoy knocked off his head with a stick. After that there were no incestuous marriages. Each man became a species of nightjar.

Doctor

A number of early Christian saints and theologians are known as "Doctors of the Church", the word "doctor" used in its original sense of "teacher". Saints Ambrose, Jerome, Augustine and Gregory the Great are known as the Four Doctors of the Latin Church; Saints Basil the Great, Gregory Nazianzen, John Chrysostom and Athanasius are the Four Doctors of the Greek Church.

Doctors of philosophy may be recognized by their gowns, loose-fitting caps, or lecturer's wands; they may carry a book or mark off the points of an argument on their fingers. Theologians may be absorbed in writing.

Rembrandt's *Anatomy Lesson of Dr Tulp* shows a public dissection of a corpse. A quack pedlar of potions appears in Gerard Dou's *The Quack*.

Dog

Loyalty, fidelity and protective vigilance are some of the many diverse qualities ascribed to dogs. They are depicted on medieval tombs lying at the feet of their masters, and in portraits they represent similar devotion. Their faithfulness was sentimentalized by the Victorians. Landseer, for example, in *The Old Shepherd's Chief Mourner* shows a sheepdog resting his head on his master's coffin.

In ancient times, the dog as guardian was associated almost universally with the underworld, in which it acted as both guide and gatekeeper – hence Cerberus, the terrifying three-headed dog of Greek myth which guarded the entrance to Hades. Hounds accompanied the Hekate, the sombre Greek goddess who haunted tombs and crossroads and to whom dogs were sacrificed. Other sinister dogs include the Scandinavian infernal dog Garm and the black dog of Satan.

Usually, the symbolism linking dogs with death is more positive. Their companionship in life and their supposed knowledge of the spirit world suggested them as suitable guides to the afterlife. They appear in this role as attributes of the Egyptian Anubis, and in Mayan myth they carried souls across the river of death. The dog-headed Aztec god Xolotl led the sun

through the nocturnal underworld and was reborn with it at dawn.

Dogs were often sacrificed as companions for the dead or as intercessors with the gods, as in Iroquois sacrifices of white dogs. Souls were passed to dogs more directly in the ancient Central Asian and Persian practice of feeding dead bodies to them.

Dogs are often symbols of uncouthness and base urges such as greed and lust. The followers of Diogenes were abusively called "Cynics" (Greek *kunikos,* "dog-like"), on account of their surliness and contempt for society – but they accepted the nickname as an apt description of their role as moral watchdogs. Dogs symbolize carnal desire in *Brothel Scene* by Frans van Mieris the Elder, in which a lady pours a man a glass of wine as two dogs copulate in the background. More positively, dogs are an emblem of the Christian clergy, watching the flock of the Good Shepherd, Christ. Dogs may symbolize the Dominican friars, punningly nicknamed *Domini Canes* ("Hounds of the Lord"). A dog is the attribute of St Roch.

The ancient Celts associated dogs with healing, hunters and with warriors such as the Irish Cú Chulainn (Hound of Culann). They are guardian symbols in Japan, and also in China, although there they often have demonic significance. The obedient dog is a symbol of adherence to the law, yet the Buddha said that those who lived like dogs would become them. In Buddhism and Hinduism dogs again appear as attributes of a death god, Yama.

The dog often appears with divinatory symbolism, especially in Africa. In Melanesian, North American and Siberian legends its intelligence made

Doctor: *see* Ambrose, St; Augustine, St; Gregory the Great, St; Jerome, St; Luke, St

Dog: *see* AFTERLIFE; BEASTS OF FABLE; DEATH; FIDELITY *and individual names and terms*

Dolphin

it a symbol of resourceful invention, the originator or stealer of fire.

Dolphin

An emblem of salvation, transformation, love, speed and the sea. Dolphin symbolism is drawn directly from the nature of this friendly, playful and intelligent marine mammal. Classical myth, in which the dolphin carries gods, saves heroes from drowning, or carries souls to the Islands of the Blessed, influenced its Christian symbolism. It was an attribute of the deities Poseidon (the Roman Neptune), Aphrodite (Venus), Eros (Cupid) and Demeter (Ceres). Dionysos (Bacchus) was said to have turned pirates into dolphins, and to have turned himself into a dolphin to carry his worshippers.

Like the fish an emblem of the sacrificial Christ, the dolphin can appear pierced by a trident or with the secret cross symbol of an anchor. Entwining an anchor, the dolphin is a symbol of prudence (speed restrained).

The heir to the French throne was called the Dauphin, a title inherited from the family name (Latin Delphinus, "Dolphin") of the Counts of Aubon, who wore a dolphin as a heraldic badge. They ceded their territory, the Dauphiné, to the French king in 1349 on condition that his eldest son retained the title Dauphin.

Dome

In sacred architecture, a symbol of the sky curving above the world. The Buddhist stupa extends the centre of the dome by means of a spire as an axial symbol of spiritual force.

Dominic, Saint

Dominic de Guzman (1170–1221) was

Hermes (Mercury) riding harnessed dolphins, after a mosaic of c.100BCE.

the founder of the Dominican Order, the "Preaching Friars". In 1206 he campaigned against the heretical Albigensians in the Languedooc area of southern France, and in 1215 he founded an order of preachers – the Dominicans – bound by vows of poverty. The order received papal approval in 1216 and founded friaries in Italy and throughout Europe.

St Dominic appears on altarpieces in chapels devoted to his order. He wears the black and white Dominican habit and may hold the rosary – he was said to have instigated its use – or a lily of purity. The presence of a black and white dog alludes to the nickname of his order, *Domini Canes* or "Hounds of the Lord" (a Latin pun on *Dominicanus*, "Dominican"), as in Andrea da Firenze's fresco (Spanish Chapel, Santa Maria Novella, Florence). St Dominic also appears with other illustrious founders of monastic orders, particularly St Francis.

Other scenes from Dominic's life that appear in art are mostly derived from legend.¹ For example, before he was born his mother dreamed that she carried a dog with a lit torch in its mouth, which set fire to the earth; and at Dominic's baptism, a brilliant star, which may appear in art as his attribute, appeared on his forehead to shed its light over the world. A heretic tried to burn Dominic's writings but they jumped out of the fire intact.

Domovoi and *Dvorovoi*

Domestic spirits of Slav myth. The *domovoi* ("house spirit") inhabited the homestead. He was usually invisible but those who claimed to have seen him described him as a hairy old man with a grey beard. He was active at night; families left food for him and avoided sleeping in his path, lest he smash crockery or torment their animals. Domestic prosperity relied upon keeping the *domovoi* happy. To ensure this, new farm animals were introduced to him. If a family moved home the *domovoi* went too, often enticed with coals from the old hearth.

The *dvorovoi* ("yard spirit") inhabited the farmyard, but in all else resembled the *domovoi*.

Dôn

A Welsh ancestral goddess, also known as "Mother of the Gods". Dôn was the sister of Math, the protagonist of the fourth branch of *The Mabinogion*. This part is dominated by the deeds of Dôn's family, particularly her offspring, including Arianrhod, Gilfaethwy and Gwydion. Dôn is probably related to the Irish Danu, divine matriarch of the Tuatha dé Danann.

Don Quixote

Miguel de Cervantes' *Don Quixote*, published in two parts in 1605 and 1615, is a satire on the ideal of chivalry. Cervantes' hero, a simple-minded, gaunt knight errant who rides an aged horse, Rosinante, believes that his destiny is to set the world to rights. Accordingly, he embarks on a series of adventures, each the bizarre product of his deluded imagination, fighting various inanimate and unharmful objects.

Quixote is accompanied by his rotund squire, Sancho Panza, on a donkey. Don Quixote was usually a figure of ridicule, therefore. However, 19th-century French artists often saw him as a tragic hero in pursuit of idealistic dreams.

Donar

The ancient Germanic god of the sky and thunder. Known as Thunor to the Anglo-Saxons, he was related to the later Scandinavian deity Thor.

Donkey *see* Ass

Donn

"The Dark One", the Irish god of the dead. Donn was the ancestral deity of the Sons of Míl – the Gaels – the last race to invade Ireland, according to *The Book of Invasions*. Donn arrived with his people in southwest Ireland on the feast of Beltane (1 May) and led them to victory against the Tuatha Dé Danann. But he insulted the earth goddess Ériu and was drowned in the sea in punishment. Near the supposed spot is the island of Tech nDuinn ("House of Donn"), where Donn resided as lord of the dead. It was here that the dead were said to embark for the Otherworld.

Dorje *see* Thunder

Dorothea, Saint

Legend[1] claims that Dorothea or Dorothy (died *c.*303CE) was persecuted with other Christians in Cappodocia in what is now Turkey. Two women who had abandoned Christianity were sent to make her renounce her faith, but instead she reconverted them. For this she was beheaded. On the way to her death a man asked her to send flowers and fruit from heaven. Miraculously, a child appeared with a basket of fruit and roses. In art Dorothea may appear before the Virgin and Child in a garden with the basket of flowers as her attribute – as in an early 15th-century painting of the School of Gentile da Fabriano in the Ducal Palace, Urbino.

Doubles

Animals are often duplicated in iconography to stress their totemic power, but doubles can also symbolize different, even opposing, characteristics. In some traditions, to encounter one's own double, or *doppelgänger*, is an omen of one's impending death – a superstition linked to the idea of body and soul as separate entities.

Dove

A symbol of peace, purity, love, tenderness and hope. The dove's universal importance as a peace symbol owes less to its true nature (often quarrelsome) than to its iconic beauty and the influence of the Bible. Noah sent out a dove to see if the waters had abated after the Flood, and it returned with an olive branch in its beak, signifying a new peace between God and man.¹ In the gospels, John the Baptist saw "the Spirit of God descending like a dove" upon Christ

Noah releasing a dove from the ark, after a Byzantine mosaic in St Mark's basilica, Venice.

after his baptism.² The dove is therefore a symbol of the Holy Spirit and it appears as such in depictions of the Annunciation and the Trinity.

By extension the dove represents the purified soul, and is often shown flying from the mouths of martyred saints. Doves could also represent souls in the Classical world and in India. They are associated with funerary cults, because a dove was believed to carry souls to the afterlife.

The dove also appears in Christian iconography as an emblem of chastity, despite more ancient and understandable links with concupiscence. A pair of doves have long symbolized sexual bliss, which may be why a dove came to personify an attentive and gentle wife. Winged phalluses shown with doves were found in Pompeii. Doves were the attribute of the Mesopotamian love goddess Ishtar or Astarte, and also of the Classical Adonis, Aphrodite (the Roman Venus) Dionysos (Bacchus) and Eros (Cupid). The moan of the dove was linked with both sex and childbirth. In China the dove is one of many symbols of longevity, as also in Japan, where a dove with a sword is an emblem of peace.

DRAGON *see panel opposite*

Dragonfly

A symbol of lightness, lightmindedness, elegance and speed. It sometimes shares the symbolism of the butterfly. The Japanese imperial ancestor-hero Jimmu-tenno is said to have given Honshu the name Dragonfly Island.

Draupnir

The magic golden ring of the Norse god Odin. Draupnir was forged by dwarfs in order to ensure that the gods

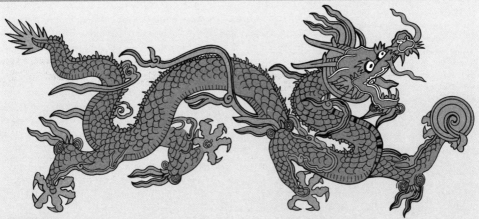

DRAGON

The dragon is probably the most universal of all mythical creatures. It is most often described as a great flying reptile, a ferocious and untamed (but not necessarily evil) beast that embodies the elemental forces of chaos and cosmic order. Dragons are generally beneficent symbols in the East, malevolent in the West, so their symbolism is complex.

In the West the dragon symbolized the four elements of earth, air, fire and water: it lived in the depths of earth or water, could fly and often breathed flame. In China, it was believed that the dragon's energy bound all the phenomena of nature, bringing benevolent rains but also cataclysmic typhoons. Chinese dragons had five or four claws; as a symbol, the five-clawed dragon was reserved solely for the emperor.

In myth and legend, the dragon and serpent are often synonymous – for example in China and also Greece, where large snakes were called *drakonates*, suggesting sharp-sightedness (from *derkomai*, "to perceive keenly"). The association with vigilance is seen in many tales of dragons as guardians of treasure or oracles. In Greek myth, dragons guarded the golden apples of the Hesperides and the Golden Fleece. The hero Cadmus killed a dragon to reach the spring of Ares, god of war, and Apollo slew the serpent Python that guarded the oracle of Delphi. The Norse hero Sigurd and the Anglo-Saxon Beowulf slew treasure-guarding dragons.

The fierce but beneficent five-clawed Chinese imperial dragon, clutching the Pearl of Wisdom.

Christianity was the primary influence behind the evolution of the dragon into a generalized symbol of adversarial evil. The New Testament identifies the dragon directly with Satan: "And the great dragon was cast out, that old serpent, called the Devil"[1] and goes on to link it with the sin of blasphemy. The dragons vanquished by saints, notably the archangel St Michael, symbolize Satan, disorder and heresy or unbelief. St George and the Dragon was a popular theme in 15th-century Italian art, where the monster may represent the Devil or the infidel. The medieval dragon may appear as a sea serpent, as in some paintings of St George, doubtless influenced by the Greek myth of Perseus, who slew a sea monster to save Andromeda. Elsewhere, water dragons are also generally negative in connotation. For example, eastern Native American myths tell of great horned dragons that live underwater and cause drownings.

As an image of power, the dragon was a popular emblem of warriors, appearing on Parthian and Roman standards, on the carved prows of Viking ships, on Anglo-Saxon banners. In the Celtic world it was a symbol of sovereign force. A red dragon, the legendary emblem of King Arthur, is the national emblem of Wales.

had a constant supply of gold. It was said that eight further rings dropped from Draupnir every nine nights.

Dreamtime

The primordial creation epoch, a central feature of Australian Aboriginal myth. The Dreamtime or Dreaming was the period in which ancestral beings traversed the continent, shaping the landscape, determining the form of society and depositing the spirits of unborn children as they went. Dreamtime is also a state of being that is briefly accessible to participants in ritual. They are believed to become the ancestors whose journeys are recreated, or whose power is released, by striking a sacred site with which the ancestors are associated.

Drum

A symbol of thunder, the voice of cosmic energy. Of all musical instruments, the drum is the most primeval means of communication, its percussive sound travelling to the heart and, by extension, suggesting the ability to communicate with supernatural forces. It symbolizes in Hinduism the creative–destructive power of Shiva, Kali and Indra; in Buddhism the voice of the Dharma; in China the voice of heaven. Its materials – wood and hide – themselves have protective symbolism, and its rhythms are widely used to achieve states of ecstasy in which spirits are invoked or shamans can move beyond the material plane. The ancient use of the drum to inspire warriors draws on the thunder symbolism of destructive force.

Duck

An Asian symbol of marital union and happiness – based on the syn-

chronized swiming of mandarin ducks. Sad tales of parted mandarin ducks are popular in both Japanese and Chinese folklore, and duck motifs as emblems of union decorate bridal chambers. Young lovers are "mandarin ducks in the dew".

The duck or other small waterfowl can appear as a creator in Native American myth.

Dumuzi

A Mesopotamian god of growth and fertility, also known by the Hebrew name of Tammuz and sometimes identified with the Greek god Adonis. The divine embodiment of vegetation and the creative forces of spring, Dumuzi spent the season of least growth, in the underworld. Although not one of the great gods, Dumuzi was held in high regard in popular religion and his cult was widespread. He often appear as consort to Inanna (Ishtar).

Durga

In Hinduism, a warrior aspect of Devi, the Goddess. Durga is said to be unapproachable by suitors (her name means "hard to approach") and invincible in battle. Sometimes Durga arises from Vishnu as the power of sleep or as his creative power; or she emerges from the goddess Parvati, Shiva's consort, when she becomes angry. At other times the male gods pool their attributes to form Durga as a champion against demons, her main role.

In one myth, the gods were subdued by the demons led by Mahisha ("Buffalo"). This made Vishnu and Shiva so angry that their wrath coalesced with the energy of the other gods to form a goddess, Durga, riding a lion. The demons attacked Durga, who

A depiction of dreamtime figures, based on an Aboriginal painting.

The Hindu goddess Durga, based on a statuette.

killed them with her club, noose, sword and trident. In the form of a buffalo, Mahisha terrorized Durga's troops and then attacked her lion. Durga, furious, noosed him and cut off his head. Mahisha became a man, sword in hand. Durga pierced the man and he became an elephant. She cut off its trunk and he became a buffalo again. Durga leaped onto the beast, pierced it with her trident, and finally beheaded Mahisha with her sword as he tried to struggle free.

Dvorovoi *see* Domovoi **and** Dvorovoi

Dwarf

A symbol of guardianship, both in mythology (the protective domestic god Bes of Egypt) and in folklore where dwarfs are almost universally credited with supernatural powers.

In Hindu and other iconography, dwarfs are sometimes demonic, suggesting a link between stunted growth and human ignorance or blind instinct. They can also be associated with the symbolism of the fool as an inversion of the king, a role sometimes played by dwarfs at court.

In folklore, dwarfs are often mischievous, miserly or malignant. They are jealous hoarders of treasures or secret knowledge, and are lovers of riddles and enigmas. In Nordic myth, the gods ruled that dwarfs should live underground because they were born from the corpse of the giant Ymir, whose body formed the earth.

Hence dwarfs are widely linked with subterranean life or, in South America, with rain, forests and caves. As a result, they were thought to be skilled workers with precious stones and metals, by nature suspicious and cunning, but easily tricked.

Dxui

The creator being of the San of the Kalahari. On the first and second days, Dxui was a flower at dawn and a man at sunset. At the third dawn he was a fruit tree and at sunset a man again. When he awoke he saw the sun for the first time and found that he was alone. He became a fruit tree again, but this time covered in thorns. The first woman appeared and tried to take the fruit, but the tree vanished. Weeping, the woman lay down and died. Dxui became a fly, then water, a flower, a bird, the snarer of the bird and the eater of the bird. He became a man again and other men hunted him, so he became a great bird and flew to his mother and father. His father recognized him and Dxui became a man. He died and became a lizard, the oldest creature of all.

Dwarf: *see* Cave; Clown; Earth; Giant; King; JEWELS; METALS; Rain; Scapegoat

Ea

The Babylonian (Akkadian) god of wisdom and the waters, equivalent to the Sumerian Enki. In the Akkadian creation myth, originally Apsu, the sweet-water ocean, and Tiamat, the salt-water ocean, coupled to produce a succession of deities culminating in the great gods known as Anu and Ea. Ea then produced Marduk and killed Apsu in a struggle for supremacy that eventually saw the emergence of Marduk as the greatest of the gods.

Ea (the figure on the left), from an Akkadian seal.

Ea features in myths dealing with death and immortality, such as the story of Adapa and Anu. The Akkadian version of the Mesopotamian flood myth (as told in the epic of the hero Gilgamesh), recounts how the god Enlil sent a flood to destroy humanity. But Ea spared one man, Utnapishtim, and his family, and persuaded Enlil not to destroy all humans but only to punish them when necessary.

Eagle

As the supreme master of the air, the eagle is one of the most unambiguous and universal of all symbols, embodying as it does the power, speed and perception of the animal world at its peak, together with majesty, domination, victory, valour, inspiration and spiritual aspiration. It is an attribute or personification of great gods; in the Greek myth of the beautiful youth Ganymede abducted by an eagle to be the cup-bearer of the gods, Zeus sends the eagle as his messenger or becomes himself the eagle, depending on the version. The wrath of Zeus is personified by the eagle that pecks at the liver of Prometheus.

Soaring toward the sun, the eagle seemed a creature capable of carrying souls to heaven – the origin of the Roman custom of releasing an eagle from the pyre of emperors. The biblical story of an eagle burning its wings near the sun and renewing them in the sea became a baptismal motif.

The eagle is one of the four creatures of the vision of Ezekiel, which were later said to represent the four Evangelists. The eagle was assigned to St John, on the grounds that his is the most mystical gospel. In medieval iconography the eagle is associated with Christ's ascension, the wings of prayer, the descent of grace and the conquest of evil (an eagle holding a snake in its mouth). In Egypt, western Asia, India and the Far East, the link between the eagle and sky gods is ancient and consistent. An eagle with human arms was a Syrian emblem of sun worship.

The eagle is often a storm and thunder symbol as well as a solar one, suggesting both light and fertilizing power. Garuda, the eagle–headed mount of the Hindu god Vishnu, is shown battling with the serpents of evil. In Native American myth the eagle has celestial and solar symbolism. The duality of sky and earth is represented in Central America by the eagle and jaguar. Among nomads, particularly in northern Asia, the eagle was a shamanic father symbol, its feathers used in initiation and ascension rites.

The eagle is one of the most ancient and popular emblems of victory, its flight taken as an augury of military success in ancient Persia and also in

An eagle overcoming a snake – a symbol of good overcoming evil; after a mosaic in Istanbul, Turkey.

Eaglehawk and Crow:
see Djunggun

Rome where, legend claimed, it had followed Aeneas from Troy to Italy, whereafter it was carried on Roman standards as "the bird of Jove". The late Roman and Byzantine empires used a double-headed eagle device, symbolizing the eastern and western halves of the empire; it was adopted by later empires that saw themselves as the successors of Rome or Byzantium: the Holy Roman, Habsburg and Russian empires. Heraldic use of the eagle was widespread throughout Europe. The American bald eagle with outstretched wings is the emblem of the United States. In art, the eagle can be an attribute of Pride.

Eaglehawk and Crow
The two men who, according to the Aboriginal mythology of southeast Australia, instituted marriage by specifying the degrees of kinship within which marriage was permissible. The two men appear as rivals in tales in which Crow (or Wagu) often tries to outwit or trick Eaglehawk (or Biljara). For example, in one story, Eaglehawk burned Crow black and turned him into the bird whose name he bears. Eaglehawk became a bird himself when Crow tricked him into soaring into the sky.

*Mother Earth and
her Bounty; after a
Renaissance engraving.*

Ear

A symbolic connection between hearing and insemination appears both in some African traditions where the ear has sexual connotations, and more curiously in the early Christian notion that Christ was conceived when the Holy Spirit entered the Virgin Mary's ear – hence the dove at Mary's ear in some Annunciation scenes. Long ear lobes signified wisdom or status in China, India and the Inca kingdom.

Earth

Universally a symbol of maternal protection, fecundity and sustenance. On the whole, earth is personified in mythology by mother goddesses such as the Greek Ge or Gaia – the Egyptian earth-god Geb is an exception. In many creation myths, the first humans are formed from mud, clay or, in Polynesia, sand. The sky couples with the earth – sometimes in an embrace so close that it must be broken by a hero-god to allow life to develop – an idea common to Polynesian and Egyptian myth. Earth fertility symbolism accounts for the use of soil in rites of passage. Couplings in furrows were a feature of European spring fertility festivities until fairly recent times.

There is a widespread ancient belief that destructive earthquakes emanated from the movements of creatures thought to support the earth – a giant fish (Japan), a tortoise (China) an elephant standing on a tortoise (India and southeast Asia) or a serpent (North America).

The earth is often represented graphically by a square, as in China.

Earth Diver, The

In Native American myth, the term given to the creature that goes to the bottom of the primeval ocean to retrieve mud from which the first land is formed. According to the Cheyenne, the supreme being Maheo ("All-Spirit") created the Great Water together with all the creatures of the water. The water birds soon grew tired of flying and took turns to dive to look for land. Finally the coot returned with a little ball of mud, which he dropped into Maheo's hand. As Maheo rolled the mud in his hand it expanded until only old Grandmother Turtle could carry it. The mud continued to grow on her back: in this way the first land was created.

East *see* CARDINAL POINTS, THE

Ebisu

The Japanese god of work. Perhaps once a deity of fishermen, he is usually shown with fishing line and a fish.

Echidne

In Greek myth, the offspring of the earth goddess Gaia and Tartarus, god of underworld darkness. Echidne had the upper body of a nymph and the lower body of a repulsive serpent. She lived in a cave and coupled with another monster, Typhon, to produce some of famous monsters of Greek myth: the Nemean Lion, Hydra, Chimera, and Cerberus. She was also sometimes said to be the mother of Orthus, Ladon and the Theban Sphinx.

Echo

A nymph of Mount Helicon in Greece. Her constant chatter distracted the goddess Hera from catching her husband, Zeus, in the act of infidelity. Hera punished Echo by cursing her to speak only the last words addressed to her. The nymph fell in love with the youth Narcissus, but Hera's curse frustrated all her efforts at conversation and Echo pined away until only her voice remained. She is often seen in paintings of Narcissus, wistfully gazing at her love. Before her death she cursed Narcissus to fall in love with his own reflection.

In another myth it was Pan, the god of woods and pastures, who cursed Echo after she had rebuffed his advances. Eventually the nymph's habit of repetition annoyed some shepherds so much that they tore her to pieces, leaving only her voice to reverberate around the mountains.

Eclipse

Almost universally an ill omen – symbolically the death of light, suggesting cosmic disorder. In China, solar eclipses were interpreted as the unwelcome dominance of the feminine Yin principle over the masculine Yang or, at the level of the imperial household, the empress over the emperor. Other interpretations of eclipses were that the sun was hiding its face in anger or that the sun, moon or stars had fallen victim to a devouring cosmic beast. In Peru an eclipse was said to have augured the Spanish destruction of the Inca empire.

Eel

Now a metaphor for slipperiness, the eel in Oceanic folklore sometimes appears as a trickster and more prominently as a phallic fertility symbol, replacing this aspect of snake symbolism in lands such as New Zealand where snakes were unknown.

Egg

Genesis, the perfect microcosm – a universal symbol for the mystery of original creation, life bursting from

the primordial silence. Few simple natural objects have such self-explanatory yet profound meaning, and the body of myth and folklore that surrounds the egg is huge. In many creation myths, ranging from Egypt and India to Asia and Oceania, a cosmic egg (sometimes fertilized by a serpent but more often laid in the primeval waters by a giant bird) gives form to chaos, and from it hatches the sun (the golden yolk), the division of earth and sky, and life in all its forms. Creation symbolism is strengthened by the egg shape of testicles and by the sexual duality of the egg's yolk and white – the yolk in the Congo standing for female warmth, the white for male sperm. In Hindu myth, the Cosmic Tree grows from the golden egg which bore Brahma.

Similarly, the egg is linked with resurrection: the phoenix, dying in fire, rose from its own egg; the god Dionysos was shown carrying an egg as a symbol of his rebirth. Associated in pre-Christian times with the promise and hope of spring, the egg took a ready-made place in Christian Easter ceremonies as a symbol of the Resurrection. The egg's white purity, the miracle of life contained within its blank shell, added other connotations, such as can be found in Piero della Francesca's altarpiece *Madonna and Child* (*c.*1450), in which an egg symbolizes the Immaculate Conception of Mary (and alludes also to the folklore notion that ostrich eggs hatch themselves).

In Jewish custom, at the Seder meal eaten at Passover, the egg is a symbol of promise, and traditionally eggs are the first food offered to Jewish mourners. In folklore throughout the world, the egg is a propitious symbol, suggesting luck, wealth and health. Magical eggs of gold or silver are guarded by dragons. From eggs are born gods and heroes. In one Greek myth, Helen of Troy came from an egg that had fallen from the moon. Alternatively, she was born from an egg laid by Leda, queen of Sparta, after she had coupled with a swan – the god Zeus in disguise. She laid two eggs; from one came Polydeuces (Pollux) and Helen and from the other Castor and Clytemnestra.

Ehecatl

The Aztec god of wind. Ehecatl, who was a manifestation of the great god Quetzalcoatl, was an important creator deity who assisted in the establishment of the present world order. In the myth of the Five Suns, the Aztec creation myth, the gods gathered at Teotihuacan after the destruction of the fourth sun. Nanahuatzin and Tecciztecatl jumped into a sacrificial fire and became respectively the fifth sun and the moon. However, they were motionless until Ehecatl blew upon them fiercely. At first only the sun rose into the heavens, but as the sun set then the moon rose also.

Eight

An emblem of cosmic equilibrium and of renewal, rebirth or beatitude. The octagon was perceived as a form mediating between the square and the circle, combining stability with totality. Adding to its symbolism of totality, the number eight represented the four cardinal points together with their four intermediate points.

Celtic, Hindu and other iconographic wheels were usually eight-armed – as is Vishnu in Hindu art. Octagonal baptismal fonts also incorporate the symbolism of renewal or new beginnings

derived from the fact that eight follows the symbolic "complete" number, seven, and begins a new cycle.

Eight and its multiples are traditionally lucky numbers in China, where there were eight Daoist Immortals, and also in Japan. In Hinduism and Buddhism, the lotus is often shown with eight petals – the number of *chakra*s, or energy centres of the body. The Buddhist path to awakening is the Noble Eightfold Path, and Buddhist iconography has eight Auspicious Emblems. In Islam, eight angels support the throne of Allah. The shape of the Arabic numeral 8 was equated with the caduceus, and eight is the number of the god Hermes (in Egyptian myth, Thoth) in Hermetic magic. The Star of Bethlehem is often shown with eight points. The octagram was an ancient symbol of the Roman goddess Venus, a Nordic protective symbol and a Gnostic sign for creation.

Eight Immortals, The

The central figures of Daoist (Taoist) mythology. Although the accounts of how each gained his or her immortality date from only the 15th century, some of their names are mentioned in

Two of the Eight Immortals: Zhang Guo (left) and Han Xiang.

earlier sources. The eight, in the order of their attainment of immortality, are: Li Xuan, Lü Dongbin, Han Zhongli, Han Xiang, Cao Guojiu, Zhang Guo, Lan Caihe and He Xiangu.

The most famous myth in which the Immortals appear together concerns a voyage to the undersea world. Instead of travelling on clouds, their usual means, they demonstrated their magical powers by using the objects which they carried as boats or rafts. During the journey the son of the Dragon King of the Eastern Sea stole Lan Caihe's musical instrument and took him prisoner. He was freed after a fierce battle in which the other Immortals defeated the Dragon King.

Eileithyia

The Greek goddess of childbirth, the offspring of the god Zeus and the goddess Hera. Eileithyia (also spelled Ilithyia), determined the duration of a mothers' labour pains and the precise moment of birth. Hera sometimes commanded her to stay away from the births of Zeus's numerous illegitimate offspring, in order to prolong the mothers' agonies. For example, after Zeus made the Titan Leto pregnant with the divine twins Artemis and Apollo, the jealous Hera forced her to wander the world to look for a place to give birth. But people were too afraid of Hera to take her in. However, the people of Ortygia (later called Delos) agreed to allow Leto to give birth on their island. Hera forbade Eileithyia to attend, but the other goddesses sent Iris ("Rainbow"), a divine messenger, to fetch her from Mount Olympus.

El

The supreme god of the Ugaritic (Canaanite) pantheon. Although a less active deity than, for example, Baal, El was the highest authority in all mortal and divine matters. He was a creator deity, described in Ugaritic texts as "the father of gods and men".

According to one myth, El had intercourse with two women (who probably represent the goddesses Ashera and Anath). They gave birth first to the divinities Shachar ("Dawn") and Shalim ("Dusk"), then to the remainder of the Ugaritic pantheon. The name El is related to the Hebrew *el* as in Gabriel and Raphael, and to the Arabic Allah ("God").

El Dorado

A mythical land or city of fantastic wealth which was believed by early European explorers to exist in the South American interior. El Dorado, Spanish for "The Gilded Man", once referred to the king of this fabulous land, who was said to possess so much gold that his body was powdered every day with gold dust. The myth derived from 16th-century eyewitness reports of Amerindian rites in the highlands of Colombia, where the body of the Muisca people's new king was smeared from head to foot in resin then covered with a fine layer of gold dust.

Elder

A magic tree in Northern Europe, especially in Denmark where it was unlucky to use its wood for furniture. It offered protection against witchcraft on Walpurgis Night, and people apologized when picking its flowers or berries. In some accounts, Judas Iscariot hanged himself on an elder.

Elegba

The name given in Benin to the trickster who is named Eshu in Yoruba.

El on his throne, after a Canaanite stela.

*The elephant-headed
Hindu god Ganesha,
after a wall painting.*

Elephant

Strength, sagacity, longevity, prosperity, happiness – a symbol of sovereign power in India, China and Africa. The elephant was the stately mount not only of Indian rulers but of the thunder and rain god, Indra. The elephant-headed Ganesha is the god of wisdom and the art of writing, and overcomes obstacles. By association, the elephant came to symbolize not only the qualities required for good government – dignity, intelligence, prudence – but also a whole range of general benefits including peace, bountiful harvests and rainfall. Fertility and rainfall symbolism were particularly attached to the white elephant in Burma, Thailand and Cambodia. In Buddhist legend, the impending birth of the Buddha was announced to his mother, Queen Maya, when she dreamed that a white elephant had entered her womb.

As an emblem of wisdom, the elephant was an attribute of Mercury in Roman myth. Its Roman association with victory (it personifies Fame in art) may account for its occasional use as a symbol of Christ's overcoming death or evil – as in depictions of an elephant trampling a snake. Elephants were used to pull chariots in Roman triumphal marches – and it was during the second Punic War in 218BCE that Hannibal famously crossed over the Alps with troops and elephants. The animals appear in Bible scenes to evoke the East. The medieval belief that the bull elephant refrained from sex during the long gestation period of his mate also made it a Western symbol of chastity, fidelity and love. The link with ponderous clumsiness appears to be modern, although there is a Hindu legend that elephants lost their powers of flight after being cursed by a hermit whose home in a banyan tree had been crushed by one when landing.

Eleven Associated by St Augustine with sin, because it suggested excess (being one more than the perfect 10), eleven was also linked with danger, conflict or rebellion. It was sometimes known in Europe as the "Devil's dozen". However, African shamans used 11 as a number propitious to fecundity.

Elf *see* **Fairies**

Eligius, Saint

Eligius, or Eloi (*c*.588–660CE), was trained at a mint in Limoges and became a talented engraver before founding a monastery at Solignac and a convent in Paris. In 641CE he became Bishop of Noyon and Tournai. He is the patron saint of metalworkers. His attributes are an anvil, or the tongs with which he is said to have held the Devil by the nose when he visited his workshop disguised as a woman. Nanni di Banco's sculpture and relief of *c*.1411 on the exterior of Orsanmichele in Florence shows Eligius as a bishop, and depicts the legend of how he sawed off, shod and miraculously restored the legs of a difficult horse.

Elijah

The biblical prophet Elijah spoke against Ahab, king of Israel, whose wife Jezebel had introduced the pagan cult of Baal. During a drought God sent Elijah east to live by a brook where ravens fed him. When the brook dried up he met a widow of the city of Zarephath whom he found gathering

ELEMENTS, THE

A complex system of symbolic correspondences was once attached to four – or sometimes five – substances thought to be primary constituents of the universe. In Western tradition, largely influenced by Greek philosophy, these were the elements of water, air, fire and earth, to which a fifth was sometimes added – ether, or the quintessence (fifth essence). Fire was the agent of transformation.

Because the elements were viewed as the basis of cosmic order and harmony, early medicine sought to balance the physical and temperamental characteristics assigned to each – phlegm, the brain and the phlegmatic temperament (water); blood, the heart and the sanguine temperament (air); yellow bile, the liver and the choleric temperament (fire); black bile, the spleen and the melancholic temperament (earth). Air and fire were seen as active and masculine, water and earth as passive and feminine. Increasingly arbitrary correspondences, including colours, seasons and stages of life, were added in an attempt to create a coherent symbolic system, which began to collapse only with the arrival of scientific method. In

Alchemical symbols used to represent the four elements (from top to bottom): earth, water, air and fire.

China, a corresponding system was based on the Five Elements of water, fire, wood, metal and earth, balanced by the duality of the active, masculine principles of Yang (air and fire) and Yin (water, metal, earth). The five-fold Indian symbolic system proposed as "cosmic states of vibration" the elements of *akasha* (ether), *apas* (water), *vayu* (air), *tejas* (fire) and *prithivi* (earth).

In Western art, **water** may be represented pouring from an upturned urn; or may be depicted by a seascape, or by a river scene with reeds and fish, or by a river-god, or by Neptune (the Greek Poseidon), or by the Birth of Venus from the sea. **Air** may be the peacock of Juno (in Greek myth, Hera), or birds flying, or Boreas, god of the North wind, and Zephyr, god of the West wind, or a woman with a chameleon. **Fire** can be the phoenix, or the god Vulcan (Hephaistos) at his forge, or a woman with a burning head and thunderbolt. **Earth** may be represented by the goddess Ceres (the Greek Demeter), who may have a globe or a cornucopia; other representations include Cybele, with her turreted crown and lion, and the bountiful Golden Age.

ELEMENTS, THE: *see* Air; Chameleon; Crown; Earth; Fire; Five; Four; METALS; Phoenix; Quintessence; Thunder; Water; Wood; Yin and Yang *and individual names*

sticks. She gave him food, and, in gratitude, Elijah cured her child of his sickness.[1] After three years of drought and famine, Elijah assembled 450 priests of Baal on Mount Carmel and built two sacrificial altars with King Ahab's blessing, for an offering of bullocks. Both Elijah and the priests of

Baal built fires, which were to be ignited by their respective gods. The priests' fire refused to catch alight, but Elijah's ignited immediately. The priests were put to death, thus appeasing the god of Israel, and the rains returned.[2] Fearing Jezebel's revenge, Elijah fled into the desert and prayed for his own death. He slept under a juniper tree and was fed by an angel.[3] On Mount Horeb Elijah encountered the voice of God, who told him to seek out his successor as a prophet. Elijah did so, finding Elisha ploughing a field. They travelled together until one day there appeared a chariot and horses of fire, and Elijah was taken up to heaven in a whirlwind.[4] As he ascended, Elijah's mantle fell from him, and Elisha took it up. In the New Testament, Elijah appeared with Moses to Christ at the Transfiguration. Because of his ascension he was seen as a forerunner of the Messiah, who would herald the Messiah's coming – hence the question put to John the Baptist: "Art thou Elijah?"[5]

Elijah appears in art as a bearded old man. Rubens shows him in his fiery chariot in *The Chariot of Elijah*. The prophet being fed in the desert by ravens or by the angel was also a favourite subject. Elijah was a popular subject for the Carmelite Order, who claim him as their founder.

Elisha

In the Bible, after Elijah's ascent to heaven, Elisha became his spiritual successor and it was his responsibility to anoint Hazel and Jehu, the kings of Syria and Israel, who would later kill Ahab and the followers of Baal. Elisha once miraculously filled a woman's empty vessels with oil; and a Shunammite woman, who gave Elisha a bed and food, was rewarded with a son, although her husband was old. Later, this child died, but was resuscitated by Elisha.[1] Naaman, a captain of Syria, suffered from leprosy and Elisha advised him to dip himself into the Jordan river seven times; Naaman did this and was cured[2] – a scene depicted by Lambert Jacobsz in *The Prophet Elisha and Naaman*.

Elizabeth of Hungary, Saint

Daughter of the king of Hungary, Elizabeth (1207–31) was happily married to Ludwig IV of Thuringia and had three children. In 1227 Ludwig joined the crusades and died suddenly. According to legend,[1] Elizabeth devoted herself to the seven works of mercy and, when her husband died, became a Franciscan to dedicate her life to the sick and needy. Particularly popular with northern European artists, she may be dressed either as a princess with a crown or as a Franciscan. She may have roses in her lap, from the tale that she was caught stealing food from her brother-in-law to give to the poor; when confronted, the food miraculously became flowers.

Elk *see* Deer

Elysium

In Greek myth, a paradise to which the great and virtuous went after death. According to earlier Greek myth, Elysium (also called the Elysian Fields or the Islands of the Blessed) lay beyond the great river Ocean that was believed to encircle the earth. Later, as the Greeks' geographical knowledge increased, a new tradition arose which located the lands of the dead in an underworld in the centre of the earth. In some accounts, the

Elysian dead could choose at any time to be reborn on earth: if they attained Elysium three times they won the right to live in the Islands of the Blessed, which were sometimes regarded as a separate, even greater paradise. It was occasionally said that the Titan Kronos governed Elysium after he was overthrown by Zeus.

Emerald

Regeneration and fertility – a symbolism probably based on the green colour of this beryl. It was an important stone in Aztec mythology, associated with the green-plumaged quetzal, harbinger of spring, and thus with the hero-god Quetzalcoatl. There and elsewhere it was associated with the moon, rain, water and the east. It is a Christian symbol of immortality, faith and hope, and the stone of the pope. Alchemists linked it with Hermes, astrologers with the planet Jupiter and the sign Virgo. Its extensive role in folklore as a healing amulet mingles fertility symbolism with a tradition of occult power which could be used for good or evil purposes, deriving from the story that it is an underworld stone, fallen from the crown of Lucifer. Hence it was among the most powerful talismans against illness (including epilepsy and dysentery). It was thought to speed childbirth and also to strengthen eyesight, perhaps because it was a stone used by wizards to see into the future.

Emituo-fo *see* **Amitabha**

Emma-ho

The ruler of Jigoku, the Japanese equivalent of hell. When male sinners descend to Jigoku they are brought to Emma-ho to be judged (his sister judges female sinners). Before Emma-ho and his court of demons, sinners face a huge mirror in which their misdeeds on earth are reflected. Depending on the transgression, the soul is condemned to one of sixteen regions of punishment – eight zones of ice and eight of flame.

Endymion

In Greek myth, the son of Zeus (Jupiter) and a nymph. Endymion was supremely beautiful, and the goddess Aphrodite (Venus) fell in love with him. His father granted him a wish, and he chose eternal sleep, remaining immortal and ageless.[1] The goddess may be depicted gazing at him as she visits him by night. Girodet's *The Sleep of Endymion* shows the idealized youth asleep, watched over by Cupid (Eros).

Enki

The Sumerian god of wisdom and the waters, the equivalent of the Akkadian Ea. Like the other "great gods" Enki was the offspring of the earth goddess Ki and the sky god An. His abode was said to be the subterranean sweetwater ocean, Apsu. Enki was important as the keeper of the *me*, the heavenly decrees which were the foundation of religion and society. To possess the *me* meant to hold supreme power and they were much coveted, for example by Inanna (the Akkadian Ishtar), the goddess of love and war, who travelled from her own city, Erech, to visit Enki. She was welcomed with a great feast at which the god got very drunk and, in his inebriated state gave her the *me*. Enki later tried to retrieve them but failed.

This story served to explain how both Erech and Inanna achieved dominant status among the ancient Sume-

Emerald: *see* Alchemy; Devils; Green; Hope; JEWELS; Moon; PLANETS; Rain; VIRTUES; Water; Zodiac

Emma-ho: *see* UNDERWORLDS

Endymion: *see* Diana
[1] Apollodorus, *The Library* I vii 5

Enki: *see* Anu (1); Atrahasis; Ea; Enlil; Ishtar; Ki; Utnapishtim; Ziusudra

rians. Enki (or Ea) often appears as the protector of humanity, for example, in the Mesopotamian flood myths.

Enkidu *see* **Gilgamesh**

Enkimdu

A farmer who appears in one Sumerian myth as suitor of the fertility goddess Inanna (the Akkadian Ishtar). When the goddess decided to marry, Enkimdu and Dumuzi, a shepherd, both sought her hand. Her brother, the sun god Utu, advised her to take Dumuzi, whose animals were the source of more valuable produce than that grown by Enkimdu. The two suitors argued but Enkimdu soon conceded defeat.

Enlil

The national god of the Sumerians and the greatest of their "great gods", who were the offspring of the earth goddess Ki and the sky god Anu. Enlil was the source of the ordered cosmos and of all plant life, cattle, farming tools and the skills of civilization. He lived on a great mountain. It was from this mountain that when angry, he would send storms, floods, famine or pestilence to enforce his will. The god played a crucial role in most versions of the Mesopotamian flood myth, in which he took the initial decision to destroy the human race. However, Enlil was eventually persuaded by Enki, his brother, that humanity should not be wiped out but simply punished when necessary.

Ennead, The

The collective name given to the great Egyptian deities otherwise known as the Nine Gods of Heliopolis, who feature in the fullest Egyptian account of

the creation of the world. The first of the Ennead (from the Greek *ennea*, nine) was the sun god Atum or Ra-Atum, who came into existence on the mound that rose from the Nun, the dark primordial waters. He planned all creation and then put his semen into his mouth, spitting (or sneezing) it out to produce the next two of the Ennead, Shu, the god of air, and Tefnut, the goddess of moisture. This was the first division into male and female. Shu and Tefnut went to explore the Nun, and Atum, fearing them lost, sent his Eye (personified as a fierce goddess) to find them. When the Eye returned with his children, the god wept tears of joy which became the first humans.

Shu and Tefnut had intercourse and produced the next two deities of the Ennead, the earth god Geb and the sky goddess Nut. Geb and Nut also had intercourse but embraced so tightly that their children could not be born until they were separated by their father, Shu. The air god supported Nut above the earth with the assistance of eight beings known as the Heh gods, thereby making room for living creatures and giving them air to breathe. Nut eventually gave birth to two sets of divine twins; Osiris and Isis, and Seth and Nephthys. Osiris, the eldest child, became the first ruler of Egypt.

Eochaidh mac Eirc

The ninth and last king of the Fir Bholg, the fourth race of people to rule Ireland, according to the *Book of Invasions*. Eochaidh was a model ruler, during whose reign there was no rain but only dew, and no year without harvest. Deceit was banished and Eochaidh was the first to establish the rule of justice in Ireland. He was killed at the first battle of Magh Tuiredh against the victorious Tuatha Dé Danann, the fifth race of invaders of Ireland. Eochaidh left the field to find water and was set upon by three invaders: all four men died in the fight.

Eos

The goddess of the dawn, daughter of the Titans Hyperion and Theia, and sister of the sun god Helios and the moon goddess Selene. In her chariot, Eos (the Roman Aurora) rode before Helios on his daily journey across the sky, announcing his coming in the east in the morning and his arrival in the west each evening.

Eos had several love affairs with mortals, notably Cephalus, and when infatuated she neglected her duty and the sun god's chariot lay idle. She was struck by the beauty of the youthful Tithonos, carried him off and secured his immortality. They married, but she had forgotten to ask for his eternal youth. Tithonos grew older and older until she could no longer bear his decrepit figure and locked him away. Their son, Memnon, was killed in the Trojan Wars: the tears she wept

Eos, shown here in her chariot.

for him became the dew.[1] The image of the goddess scattering petals from the sky perfectly suited the decoration of 17th-century ceilings, as in Guercino's *Aurora* (Casino Ludovisi, Rome).

Epimetheus

In Greek myth, one of the divine race of Titans, the son of Iapetus and the Oceanid Clymene, and the brother of Prometheus, Atlas and Menoetius. Epimetheus ("Afterthought", "Hindsight") was hasty and naïve, unlike his brother Prometheus ("Forethought"). The Olympian gods and goddesses sought to punish humankind for the favours Prometheus had shown them. Prometheus warned his brother not to accept any gift from the gods, but Epimetheus ignored this advice when they sent him the first woman, Pandora, as a wife. She came bearing a sealed jar ("Pandora's Box"), which she opened, releasing its contents – evils and sickness – into the world. The only thing to remain in the jar was hope.

Epona

The Gaulish name of the Celtic horse goddess, widely worshipped in the ancient Celtic world. She became known to the Romans, probably through Gauls in the Roman cavalry, and was the only Celtic deity granted the honour of a Roman festival, celebrated on December 18. Epona was also associated with water, fertility and death, suggesting a connection with Celtic earth mother goddesses.

Erasmus (Elmo, Ermo), Saint

Legend claims that Erasmus (died *c.*303CE) was a bishop in Syria. Poussin depicts his gruesome martyrdom by having his intestines wound

Eos: *see* Achilles; Cephalus and Procris; Helios; Hyperion; Orion; Selene; Theia; Tithonus; Trojan War, The
[1] Ovid, *Met XIII:576–622*

Epimetheus: *see* Atlas; Horse; Pandora; Prometheus; TITAN.

Erasmus, Saint: *see* Dioscuri, The; Martyrs

around a windlass (Vatican, Rome).
The windlass became his attribute,
and because windlasses are used on
ships, he became the patron of
sailors. The electrical atmospheric
phenomenon known as St Elmo's Fire
was seen as a sign of his protection.

Erebos

"Underworld Darkness", one of the
primal deities that, in Greek myth,
arose out of Chaos in the first stages
of creation, according to Hesiod's
Theogony. Erebos coupled with Nyx
("Night") to produce Aither ("Ether",
the bright upper air), Hemera ("Day")
and, in some accounts, Charon, the
boatman of the underworld.

Erichthonius

In Greek myth, a king of Athens, the
son of the god Hephaistos and the
goddess Gaia. Erichthonius was born
when Hephaistos (in Roman myth,
Vulcan) tried to rape the goddess
Athene (Minerva), but she fought him
off and he ejaculated on her thigh. She
wiped off his semen with a pad of wool
and hurled it in disgust onto the
ground, thereby impregnating Gaia,
the Earth. Erichthonius ("Born of the
Soil") arose from the spot where it fell.
Athene shut the baby in a chest, which
she put into the care of the three
daughters of Cecrops, a king who was
part human and part snake.[1]

Athene told the daughters not to
open the chest, but curiosity overcame
them. Rubens shows them untying the
knots of the casket in *The Daughters of
Cecrops Discovering Erichthonius*.
Inside, they found the child with
snakes coiled around him, or in other
sources, with legs that had turned into
snakes. The sisters went mad with horror and hurled themselves off a cliff.

Erichthonius became king of Athens
and instituted the Great Panathenaia,
the city's most important festival, in
honour of Athene. He is sometimes
associated with Erechtheus, another
mythical king of Athens.

Erinyes, The *see* **Furies, The**

Eris *see* **Discord**

Eros

Eros ("Desire") was the Greek god of
love. To Hesiod, he was a deity who
arose out of Chaos, and represented
the primal force of sexual desire.
Another tradition made Eros the offspring of the goddess Aphrodite and
her lover, the god Ares. He was known
to the Romans as Amor ("Love") or
Cupid ("Desire") and was often found
accompanying images of Aphrodite
(Venus). He was usually portrayed as
a handsome young man, but in
Roman times Eros/Cupid became the
cherub familiar to Latin poetry and
the *putto* of later Western art. The god
was often depicted blindfolded (to

*Eros, after a famous 19th century
statue by Alfred Gilbert.*

symbolize love's blindness) and bearing a bow, which he used to shoot the arrows of love and desire.

Erymanthian Boar, The *see* HERAKLES, THE LABOURS OF

Eshu

A West African divinity and the most celebrated trickster in African myth. Eshu (also known as Legba and Elegba) is renowned for his cunning and is portrayed as a restless being who inhabits thresholds, crossroads, market places and other places where people are likely to meet. Whenever transition, change and exchange occur, Eshu is said to be in attendance.

In popular myth Eshu is above all a bringer of chaos. He is blamed for all arguments and for quarrels between humans and gods. On one occasion Eshu played a trick on the High God himself, angering him so greatly that he withdrew from earth, where he had lived until then, to heaven. He ordered Eshu to come to him every evening and report the goings-on in the world.

Esther

A Jewish heroine of the Hebrew Bible (Old Testament) who saved the Israelites from persecution. Ahasuerus (Xerxes), king of Persia, had dismissed his queen for refusing to appear at a feast.[1] As a new wife he chose Esther from all the fair young virgins in his kingdom. Esther had been brought up by her cousin Mordecai, who told her to keep their Jewish faith secret.[2] He discovered that the royal favourite, Haman, had contrived the king's permission to kill all the Jews in the land. Mordecai tore his clothes, put on sackcloth and sat outside the palace to warn Esther.

Defying death – the penalty for anyone entering the king's inner court without permission – Esther went to the king, who lowered his sceptre over her as a sign of acceptance.[3] She invited the king and Haman to a banquet at which she made an impassioned speech on behalf of her people. As a result, Haman was hanged, Mordecai received high office and wealth, and the enemies of the Jews were put to death.[4] Esther may be portrayed as a richly dressed queen, as in Veronese's *Scenes from the Story of Esther*, and as an example of virtuous womanhood interceding for her people.

Etana

A historical Sumerian ruler of the city of Kish and, in one Babylonian myth, the first king. The deities chose Etana, a shepherd, to bring the blessing of kingship to humanity. However, his queen could bear him no heir and he had to ride an eagle to heaven to get the herb of birth from the goddess Ishtar. Overcome with giddiness, Etana panicked, causing the eagle to plummet to earth. The end of the story is lost, but Etana's mission was evidently an eventual success, since Sumerian records list both him and his son as historical kings of Kish.

Euphrosyne *see* Graces, The

Europa

In Greek myth, the princess Europa,[1] daughter of King Agenor and Queen Telephassa of Phoenicia, used to play with her companions on the shore. Zeus fell in love with her, and so, disguised as a snow-white bull, he joined the herd of oxen lowing nearby. The disguised Zeus frolicked and played until Europa lost her fear and hung

Eshu: *see* Ifa

Esther: *see* Judith
[1] *Esther 1:5–19*
[2] *Esther 2:2–10*
[3] *Esther 5:1–2*
[4] *Esther 7:1–10*

Europa: *see* Cadmus; CONTINENTS, THE; Minos; Sarpedon; ZEUS, THE CONSORTS OF; ZODIAC
[1] Ovid, *Met II:833–875*
[2] Fasti *V:603–621*

garlands on his horns (as in Veronese's painting in the Doge's Palace, Venice) and finally ventured to climb on his back. The bull suddenly ran into the waves and swam out to sea, taking Europa with it. They came ashore on Crete, where Zeus adopted the form of an eagle and had intercourse with the princess. Europa later gave birth to three sons: Rhadamanthus, Sarpedon and Minos.

Later, Europa married the Cretan king Asterios, who adopted her sons: Asterios was succeeded by Minos, famous for the Labyrinth and the Minotaur. Another version of the myth states that one of her children became the continent that bears her name, while she herself was turned into a bull, the constellation Taurus.

Eurydice *see* Orpheus

Eurynome *see* Graces, The

Eurystheus *see* Herakles.

Eustace, Saint
According to legend,[1] Eustace (said to have died 118CE) was a general in the Roman emperor Trajan's army. While he was out hunting deer, a stag of great size and beauty gave chase and, when it came to a halt, Eustace saw a crucifix between its antlers, shining brighter than the sun. The stag commanded Eustace to convert to Christianity. A similar story is told of St Hubert, with whom Eustace is sometimes confused. Pisanello shows Eustace dressed as a young nobleman, stopped in his tracks before the stag in the depths of a forest.

Eustace and his family were converted and baptized by the Pope. A series of misfortunes separated them: his wife was taken by pirates, and his sons by a wolf and lion. Miraculously, the family was later reunited, but the new emperor, Hadrian, observed that Eustace and his family would not worship idols, and so threw them into a pit of wild beasts. The family tamed the animals, so Hadrian finally had them roasted inside a huge brass bull.

Evangelists, The
The four writers to whom the gospels are attributed: Matthew, Mark, Luke and John. They may be depicted holding or writing their gospels in book or scroll form, or may appear in symbolic form as the four winged creatures seen in a vision by the biblical prophet Ezekiel: a man or angel (Matthew), a lion (Mark), a bull (Luke) and an eagle (John).[1] Similar beasts appear around God's throne in the Book of Revelation.[2] In the Middle Ages these attributes were explained thus: the man is Christ, whose ancestry forms the opening of Matthew; the lion alludes to John the Baptist, the "voice crying in the wilderness" at the beginning of Mark; the bull, a sacrificial animal, alludes to the sacrifice of Zecharias at the beginning of Luke; the eagle, soaring in the heavens, alludes to John's distinctly elevated and mystical tone.[3]

Eye
Visually the most compelling symbol based on the human body, often used to represent the omniscience of sun gods and, in early Christianity, God the Father (the omnipresent, all-seeing divinity: "For the eyes of the Lord are over the righteous"[1]) or the Holy Trinity (an eye within a triangle). A pair of eyes, often on a platter, is the attribute of St Lucy. The Egyptian *wedjat*, a painted hawk's eye, is the

emblem of the falcon sky god, Horus. Egyptian myth said that the moon eye of Horus had been restored after its destruction in a battle with Seth, a story that accounts for the popularity of the *wedjat* as a protective amulet. Eyes were also painted or carved on Egyptian tombs to assist the dead. Winged eyes in Egyptian iconography represent north and south.

In Western symbolism, the right eye is active and solar; the left passive and lunar, a system reversed in Eastern tradition. The hidden "third eye" symbolizes spiritual perception, associated with the power of Shiva and the synthesizing element of fire in Hinduism; with inner vision in Buddhism; and with superhuman clairvoyance in Islam. Its antithesis is the "evil eye" which, in Islamic thought, is a symbol of the destructive force of envy. The Gorgon Medusa, whose gaze could turn all who looked on it to stone, was a Greek symbol of the evil eye. Protective eyes for deflecting the evil eye are still painted on the prows of traditional Greek fishing vessels. In medieval Europe, the horseshoe was thought to be particularly effective against the evil eye of Satan, sometimes depicted with a displaced eye on his body. Eye talismans (still hung above doorways in Turkey) serve a similar deflecting function.

Multiple eyes could also have positive symbolism, representing vigilance and the stars in the sky. In Greek myth, the eyes of the unsleeping hundred-eyed giant Argos were scattered on the peacock's tail after Hermes lulled him to sleep and killed him. In Buddhism the peacock, attribute of the Buddha Amitabha, has similar symbolism. The eyes of some other animals had clairvoyant meaning.

The ancient Egyptians produced many amulets in the form of the wedjat, *or Eye of Horus, the solar and sky god.*

Hence the Parsee custom of bringing a dog to a deathbed so that the dying could see the afterworld in its eyes, and the belief of Aztec shamans that they could read the mysteries of the spirit world in the eyes of the jaguar.

Excrement

In Africa, particularly Mali, a symbol of fertilizing power, a residue of vital force which could be purified and put to use. Hence the burning and offering of excrement to creator beings such as the Nommo among the Dogon or Faro among the Bambara.

Ezekiel

One of the four "Greater Prophets" of the Hebrew Bible (Old Testament), together with Isaiah, Jeremiah and Daniel. Ezekiel had a vision of the throne of God surrounded by a winged lion, a winged man, a bull and an eagle.[1] The Christian Church interpreted these four beasts as symbols of the Evangelists. In *Ezekiel's Vision,* Raphael shows Ezekiel hovering above them. Another of his visions was of a valley of dry bones, which God covered in flesh and brought to life so that they stood like a great army. This was regarded as foretelling the resurrection of the dead at the Last Judgment.

Excrement: *see* Alchemy; Gold

Ezekiel: *see* Evangelists, The
[1] *Ezekiel 1:10*
[2] *Ezekiel 37:1–10*

Fabricius, Luscinus Gaius

In 280BCE the honest Roman Fabricius was sent as ambassador to Pyrrhus, king of Epirus, with whom Rome was at war. Fabricius refused bribes of gold offered to him by the king's soldiers. Thus, Pyrrhus, wishing to unnerve Fabricius, ordered that a huge elephant, an animal that Fabricius would never have seen before, be placed behind a hanging in the room where they talked. In *Pyrrhus and Fabricius* Ferdinand Bol shows the moment at which, with the hanging drawn aside, the elephant raised its trunk and trumpeted hideously. Unmoved, Fabricius said to Pyrrhus, "Neither your money yesterday, nor this beast today, makes any impression upon me."

Fafnir

A giant of Scandinavian myth. Fafnir killed his father Hreidmar to gain possession of a great horde of treasure and changed into a dragon to guard it. He was later killed by the young hero Sigurd the Volsung.

Fairies

Personifications of human wishes or frustrations in the form of little people with magical powers. They appear in most folk traditions under various names, usually as nature spirits enjoying their own lives at a supernatural level, sometimes meddling in human affairs. Their importance in symbolism is mainly oral and literary. As their name (derived from the Latin *fata*, "fate") suggests, they appear essentially to explain gently the workings of destiny with its unpredictable gifts or disappointments. Fairy tales are exceptionally rich in symbolism, psychological and social, portraying the challenges presented by the different stages in life.

Falcon, Hawk

Superiority, aspiration, spirit, light and liberty – like the eagle, a solar emblem of victory. As a hawk-like species (but with longer wings and a higher range) the falcon is hard to distinguish from the hawk in iconography, and their symbolism is therefore discussed together. In Peru, the falcon appears with solar significance as a companion or brother soul of the Incas, and also as a human ancestor. It was the king of birds in ancient Egypt, where many gods are shown with the body or head of a falcon, including Ra, who often has a disk in place of the crest, symbolizing the rising sun. Horus, god of the sky and of the day, is specifically a falcon god, his painted hawk-like eye a common emblem on Egyptian amulets signifying the sharpness of his protective vision. In Western tradition, the falcon is an emblem of the huntsman and is associated with the Germanic sky-gods Wodan and Frigg, as well as the Nordic trickster Loki. A hooded falcon represents hope (of light and freedom). Predatory symbolism appears more rarely. As the device of the family of Anne Boleyn (Henry VIII's second wife), a white falcon aptly symbolized her aspirations and her predatory behaviour in the view of those threatened by Henry's religious reforms. A hawk now symbolizes a warlike attitude.

Fame

In classical antiquity the female figure of Fame bore away on her wings the illustrious dead. By the Renaissance her image had acquired a trumpet with which to herald the famous. Bernardo Strozzi's *Fame* uses a winged young girl as the personification; she holds a gilded trumpet and a plain wooden recorder to represent the good and bad aspects of her proclamations.

Fame may also appear crowned or carrying a palm branch, seated on a globe or riding in a chariot drawn by

A falcon, after an Egyptian sculpture; a striking symbol of the rising sun.

elephants. Other symbols of fame include the winged horse Pegasus and the Roman god Mercury.

Fan

Large fans signify authority, especially in Asia and Africa, perhaps by association with the symbolism of wind, and with their power to kindle fire, as in the hand of the Hindu fire-god Agni. Ceremonial plumed fans, such as the *flabellum* carried in papal processions, certainly appear to have celestial symbolism. More prosaically, the use of fans to protect rulers or sacramental objects from heat and flies may have contributed to their association with status and dignity. A heart-shaped fan was used by the Daoist Immortal Chuang-li Chuan to restore life. Fan symbolism was highly developed in Japanese ritual as an analogy for the unfolding of life itself – or its closure in the case of condemned men who carried fans to their execution. The folding fan was also associated with the phases of the moon and, by extension, with the changing moods of women. Its use as an instrument of flirtation spread from Spain and Italy throughout the courts of Europe in the 18th century.

Fasces

Of Etruscan origin, the *fasces* was an axe with a bundle of birch or elm rods

FAME: *see* BEASTS OF FABLE; Crown; Elephant; Globe, Orb; Palm; Trumpet; Wings

Fan: *see* Feathers; Fire, Flame; Fly, Fly Whisk; Moon; Wind

Fasces: *see* Axe; Birch; Concord; Twelve; Whip, Flail

The Roman statesman Cicero holding the fasces *(without the axe); after a 15th-century fresco.*

signifying the power of Roman magistrates. The axe was removed from the *fasces* in Rome itself to acknowledge the citizen's right of appeal against capital punishment. *Fasces* were borne by lictors in front of magistrates, the number carried increasing to 12 for consuls and 24 for dictators. The *fasces* had a secondary meaning of unity, which is why it sometimes appears in art as the conjugal symbol of Cupid. *Fasces* is the origin of the word Fascism. For Mussolini, the *fasces* was a suitably symbol for the political aims of his Fascist party, which subordinated the interests of the individual to the direct action of a nationalist élite. In a show of communal idealism, Italian Fascism interpreted the bundled rods as different social classes, the axe as the supreme authority of the state.

Fasting

An ancient and almost worldwide tradition of self-denial which has been used in religion to symbolize penance, purification or worship, and socially to demonstrate protest or grief. Modern protest fasting is often more a political technique than a symbolic gesture, but in the Celtic world a fast was a symbol of personal dedication to righting an injustice or settling a grievance. Of the great religious fasts, the Islamic Ramadan, the Jewish Yom Kippur and the Christian Lent all have penitential meaning. In Hinduism, Jainism and Daoism, the relevance is purification and the creation of a physical state of spiritual visions.

Fates, The

The three Classical divinities of destiny. The Fates, known in Greek myth as Moirai, "The Apportioners" (in Latin, *Parcae*) determined a person's

birth, lifespan, portion of good and evil, and time of death. The length of a single human life was represented by a thread, which they spun together. Clotho held the distaff from which Lachesis pulled the thread, which Atropos, unmoved by the prayers of mortals, snipped. They are usually depicted as old and ugly but Rubens, in *The Destiny of Marie de' Medici*, shows them as three elegant youths, presided over by Zeus (in Roman myth, Jupiter) and Hera (Juno), spinning the thread of the yet unborn Marie d'Medici, queen of France.

Father

Dominion, solar and sky power, spiritual, moral and civil authority, reason and consciousness, law, the elements of air and fire, warlike spirit, and the thunderbolt – a range of symbolism that reflects the patriarchal nature of most traditional cultures. Most, although not all, supreme gods of myth and religion are personified as fathers.

Father Sky

A creator deity widespread in traditional Native American mythology. Father Sky (or Sky Father), with his female counterpart and consort Mother Earth (or Earth Mother), are usually described as the offspring of the remote supreme divinity or "Great Spirit". Once Father Sky and Mother Earth appeared, the supreme divinity withdrew from the world leaving them to continue creation.

Faunus and Fauns

Faunus was the ancient Roman deity of the woodlands and chief of the satyrs, worshipped by farmers and shepherds, and identified with the Greek god Pan. Fauns were rural gods with a human form and, like satyrs, had the legs, tails and ears of a goat. They were associated with lust.

Feast of the Gods

Two wedding feasts – of Eros (in Roman myth, Cupid) and Psyche, and that of Thetis and Peleus – attended by the gods are popular subjects in painting.

At the latter the gods sat on their 12 thrones, the Fates and Muses sang, Ganymede poured nectar, and fifty Nereids danced on the sands. The centaurs were also present. However, Eris, Discord, who stirs up war by spreading rumour, had not been invited. As Hera (the Roman Juno), Athene (Minerva) and Aphrodite (Venus) conversed happily together, Eris threw a golden apple at their feet dedicated "To the Fairest". The Trojan prince Paris judged that the fairest was Aphrodite, a decision that ultimately led to the Trojan War.

Feathers

Ascension – a symbolism derived both from the weightlessness of feathers and their association with the soaring power and spiritual qualities of birds. By extension, the feathers worn by shamans, priests or rulers symbolized magical communication with the spirit world or celestial authority and protection. The feathered cloak was an attribute not only of sky gods such as the Nordic Freyja but of Celtic Druids who sought by sympathetic magic to travel beyond the confines of the earth. A serpent covered by the bright green feathers of the quetzal bird was the emblem of the sky and earth power of the Aztec god Quetzalcoatl. In North America, eagle-feathered headdresses associated chiefs with the Great Spirit and

with the power of air, wind and thunder gods. The Feathered Sun (a disk with feathers pointing outward as well as inward) is a Plains Indian emblem of the cosmos and the centre. Feathers are widely an ascensional emblem of prayer; hence the symbolism of the feathered sticks used to invoke rain in Pueblo Indian solstice rituals. Feathers represent prayer and faith in Christianity, and were sometimes used as emblems of virtues, as in the Medici device of three feathers on a ring – signifying faith, hope and charity. In Egypt, feathers were the attributes of several sky gods but particularly of the goddess of justice, Ma'at, who had a single feather against which she weighed the hearts of the dead in the underworld. The association between white feathers and cowardice derives from cockfighting, in which white tail feathers were a sign that a bird lacked the aggression of a correctly bred gamecock.

Felicity, Saint

According to legend the Roman widow Felicity (died 165CE) and her seven sons refused to worship pagan idols. Felicity watched her children being put to death one by one before she was either beheaded or plunged in a vat of boiling oil. In *Saint Felicity* Neri di Bicci shows her as a matronly nun in a dark habit surrounded by her children, with the predella panel representing their martyrdom.

Fennel

A symbol of perception, sharp sight – apparently from Pliny's report that snakes improved their vision by eating it. Fennel wreaths were used in rites of the Phrygian and Thracian god Sabazius, whose attribute was the serpent.

Feasts of the Gods: *see* Paris;
Trojan War *and other
individual names*

Feathers: *see* Air; Arrow;
Birds; Eagle; Fan; Ostrich;
Rain; Sky; Snake; Sun;
Thunder; White; Wind;
VIRTUES, THE

Felicity, Saint: *see* Martyrs

Fennel: *see* Snake; Thyrsus;
Wreath, Garland

*A feather headdress
after an image in the
Aztec* Codex Mendoza.

Fenrir, the monstrous wolf of Norse myth; from a stone tablet.

Fenrir

A monstrous wolf of Norse myth, who was the offspring of the trickster god Loki. Fenrir was raised among the gods, of whom only Tyr, the god of battle, dared to go near him to feed him. No chain was strong enough to bind Fenrir, so Odin, who was the chief of the gods, commissioned the dwarfs to fashion a magic unbreakable leash. When the gods tried to place it around Fenrir's neck he insisted that one of them place his arm in his jaws as a guarantee of good faith. Tyr agreed to do this, and Fenrir bit off his hand. As a result, the wolf was bound to a rock with a sword clamped in his jaw as a gag. Fenrir remained tied to the rock until Ragnarok, the cataclysmic battle that saw the destruction of the old world order. As Loki led the assault against the gods, Fenrir broke his bonds and devoured Odin. Odin's son Vidar tore Fenrir to pieces.

Fer Diadh

An Irish warrior, the foster-brother of the great hero Cú Chulainn. Fer Diadh (also spelled Ferdia) and Cú Chulainn were raised together at the court of King Conchobar of Ulster and learned the arts of warfare from the warrior-sorceress Scáthach.

During the conflict between Ulster and Connacht, Fer Diadh fought on the side of Queen Medhbh of Connacht but avoided facing Cú Chulainn until persuaded to fight him by Medhbh. Their long duel ended when Cú Chulainn eventually killed Fer Diadh with a blow from the *gae bolga*, his barbed spear.

Ferghus

An Irish hero of superhuman size and strength. Ferghus, the king of Ulster before Conchobar, became renowned for his strength, martial prowess and huge sexual appetite.

One of the hero's lovers was Nessa, the mother of Conchobar, who agreed to have intercourse with Ferghus only if her son could become king of Ulster for one year. Ferghus consented, but Conchobar proved so popular that the people would not let Ferghus return. Ferghus accepted this, but following Conchobar's treacherous treatment of Deirdre he defected to the court of Connacht, where he became the lover of Queen Medhbh and fought against Conchobar in the war recounted in the epic *Táin Bó Cuailnge*. During the conflict Ferghus confronted Conchobar, and would have cut him down had not Conchobar's son Cormac persuaded him to spare his life.

The great Ulster hero Cú Chulainn then came to his sovereign's aid. Ferghus had vowed never to fight Cú Chulainn, to whom he had acted as foster-father, and at once withdrew from the fray. This led directly to the defeat of Medhbh.

Ferghus' love affair with Medhbh aroused the jealousy of her husband, King Ailill. The lovers were bathing in a pool one day when Ailill came upon them and killed Ferghus.

Fête Champêtre

Fête champêtre or *fête galante* scenes, showing members of the aristocratic classes pursuing romantic pleasures outdoors, were popular in early 18th-century France. They were painted most notably by Watteau. Typically, fashionably dressed *galant* couples are seen amusing themselves by dancing, making music or just conversing in an idealized pastoral landscape. There is often an air of gentle *ennui* and melancholy pervading the scene.

Fidelity

The secular counterpart of Faith, the personification of Fidelity may have a dog at her feet, and hold a key that signifies her absolute trustworthiness. Other attributes include: anchors; the colour blue; chalices; diamonds, emeralds, garnets, opals and topaz; cranes, ducks, geese and kingfishers; elephants; girdles; and ivy, hyacinths, pine and rosemary.

Fig

A symbol of abundance, maternal nourishment, procreation – the sacred tree of life in many regions (notably in Egypt, India, southeast Asia and parts of Oceania). Much of the fig's significance comes from its importance as a food source in the ancient world. The shape of the fig leaf (famous in art for covering the male genitals), and the milky juice extracted from larger varieties of fig trees as a form of rubber, added powerful sexual aspects to its symbolism.

In Genesis, Adam and Eve were the first to use fig leaves to protect their modesty after they ate the forbidden fruit of the tree of knowledge of good and evil in the garden of Eden and "knew that they were naked; and they sewed fig leaves together and made themselves aprons".[1]

The Greeks gave the fig phallic symbolism by making it an attribute of Priapus and of Dionysus. In Roman tradition, Rome's legendary founders Romulus and Remus were suckled under the protective shade of a fig, which became an augury of national prosperity – a symbolism found in Judaism, too. In the gospels, Jesus laid the curse of sterility upon a barren fig tree,[2] hence a withered fig in Christian art sometimes represents heresy.

Fecundity is the fig's more widespread meaning, notably in Egypt where the sycamore variety was the Tree of Life, associated with Nut and Hathor as nourishing sky goddesses; and in Chad where anyone pruning the fig was thought to risk sterility. The fig also has fecundity symbolism in India where it was linked with the procreative power of Vishnu and Shiva, and where the sacred variety *ficus religiosus* was the tree beneath which the Buddha achieved enlightenment (the Bo or Bodhi Tree). Hence the significance of the tree in Buddhism as an emblem of moral teaching and of immortality.

The fig, like the olive, appears in Islamic tradition as the forbidden fruit tree in paradise.

The fig or *fico* sign (a thumb thrust between the first two fingers) was a medieval sign against the evil eye as well as an obscene gesture (famously used by Michelangelo on the Sistine Chapel ceiling, where it is not visible from floor level).

Following biblical example, fig leaves were also used to cover the genitalia of Classical statues. Numerous Classical works of male nudes even had the genitalia amputated in later centuries so that fig leaves could fit more conveniently over the groin; many of these leaves have since been removed. The huge fig leaf that covered the genitalia of the replica of Michelangelo's *David* for the benefit of Queen Victoria and other visiting royal ladies can be seen behind the statue in the cast room of the Victoria and Albert Museum, London.

FIDELITY: *see individual names*

Fig: *see* ADAM AND EVE; Bo Tree; NUDE; Olive; Phallus; Tree
[1] *Genesis 3:7*
[2] *Matthew 21:19*

Adam with fig leaf; after a 12th-century Spanish manuscript illumination of the temptation of Adam and Eve.

Filial Piety, The Twenty-Four Examples of

The name given to a famous Chinese collection of tales compiled in the 14th century CE by the author Gui Jujing and designed to inculcate in the young the sacred virtue of reverence for their elders. Twenty-four examples are provided. One story tells of a boy who sliced some flesh from his thigh to make a broth for his sick mother and father. Another recounts how a son lay naked on a frozen body of water to melt the ice and catch a fish for his hungry parents.

Finger

Symbolism is attached to individual fingers by some African tribes, notably in Mali where the Dogon people associated the index finger with life, the middle finger with death (this finger was left exposed for the dead to use when their bodies were enshrouded). For the Bambara, the thumb had executive power while the little finger was used to cast spells.

The positive "thumbs up" gesture originally had phallic symbolism. In Christian benediction, three raised fingers are the sign of the Trinity. Superstitious belief in the apotropaic power of the Cross accounts for the custom of crossing fingers for luck. Symbolism shades into sign language in many finger gestures, famously in the Churchillian "V" for victory.

Finn

An Irish warrior hero, the central figure of the great body of myths, the Fenian Cycle. Finn and his followers, the Fian or Fianna ("Warriors"), were immensely popular in the Gaelic myth of Ireland and Scotland. "Fenian" derives from the Irish *féin-*

The thumb-sucking figure on this Celtic stone cross is probably the Irish hero Finn.

nidh ("member of the Fian"). Finn was a hunter, warrior and noble prophet of supernatural gifts. In one account, he was the son of Cumhall, the head of the house of Baoisgne and leader of the Fian, an élite band of hunter-warriors loyal to the High King of Ireland. Cumhall loved a woman, Muirne, but her father, a druid, forbade the union and sent the warrior Goll mac Morna to thwart it. Goll killed Cumhal and became leader of the Fian. Muirne was already pregnant by Cumhall and bore a son, Demhne (later Finn).

According to a popular tradition, Demhne acquired knowledge of supernatural lore and the gift of prophecy by scalding his thumb on the cooked Salmon of Knowledge. He sucked the thumb to ease his pain: this small taste was sufficient to receive the salmon's gift. His teacher, the poet Finnegas, renamed him Finn and thereafter, whenever Finn chewed his thumb, he learned whatever it was that he wanted to know.

When he had grown to manhood, Finn overthrew Goll and took over as leader of the Fian. The High King of Ireland acknowledged this change after Finn saved the royal seat, Tara, from an evil goblin. There are numerous accounts of Finn's death. According to one, Finn was deserted in his old age by many of the Fian and drowned when trying to leap the Boyne to prove his vigour. Another account relates that the hero still sleeps underground and will rise in Ireland's time of need.

Fir *see* **Christmas tree; Pine, Pine cone**

Fir Bholg

The name of the fourth race of people to invade Ireland, according to the *Book of Invasions*. After the third race of invaders had been defeated by the monstrous Fomorians, the survivors left Ireland. Some of them were forced into slavery in Greece, their ancestral home, where they acquired the name Fir Bholg ("Men of Sacks") because they were made to create cultivable land by covering rocks with soil carried in bags or sacks.

The Fir Bholg held Ireland for thirty-seven years, during which time their five leaders divided it into five provinces: this is the origin of Connacht, Ulster, Leinster, Munster and the former fifth province, Meath (Irish Midhe, "Centre"). They also established kingship. The Fir Bholg were defeated at the first battle of Magh Tuiredh by the Tuatha Dé Danann, the fifth race of invaders. Eochaidh mac Eirc, the last Fir Bholg king of Ireland, fell during the battle.

The Fir Bholg made peace with the victors and withdrew into Connacht.

Fire, Flame

Divine energy, purification, revelation, transformation, regeneration, spiritual ardour, trial, ambition, inspiration, sexual passion – a masculine and active element symbolizing both creative and destructive power. Graphically, fire was represented by a triangle in alchemy, where it was the unifying element. On a domestic scale (the hearth fire), its image is protective and comforting; as a consuming force of nature it is threatening.

A duality of praise and fear underlies the rituals of fire worship. In ancient or primitive cultures, fire appears to have been revered first as an actual god, later as a symbol of divine power. A seemingly living element, growing by what it fed on, dying and reappearing, it was sometimes interpreted as a terrestrial form of the sun, with which it shares much of its symbolism. Owing to the momentous repercussions of fire-making for human development, it is seen in nearly all myth as a godlike skill. Hence the legends of fire stolen from the sky gods by culture heroes such as Prometheus, or wheedled from an infernal deity, as by the hero Maui in Maori myth (where a volcanic origin of New Zealand was plausible).

In the myth and ritual of fire worship, the most enduring and the least ominous traditions have been those of Iran (from where the Vedic god Agni ultimately originates), and the classics with their beneficial gods such as Hephaistos (in Roman myth, Vulcan). Many fire cults were horrific, as in Aztec Mexico and also in the Canaanite worship of "Moloch" to whom

Fir Bholg: *see* Eochaidh mac Eirc; Fomorian; *Invasions,* The *Book of;* Tuatha Dé Danann

Fire, Flame: *see* Alchemy; Angels; Baptism; Candle; Chimney; Cremation; ELEMENTS; Fox; Heart; Phoenix; Pillar; Red; Sacrifice; Salamander; Smoke; Solstice; Sun; Sword; Transformation; Triangle; Virginity; Volcano

The Mayan god of fire, Huehueteotl, bearing a brazier on his head.

Fire, The Origin of

infants were sacrificed. Where fire was not worshipped directly, it was often a powerful symbol of divine revelation, as in the Book of Deuteronomy 12:11 when "the mountain burned with fire" and Jehovah spoke from the midst of it to the Hebrews. Again, in Christianity, fire is an incarnation of the Holy Spirit.

Fire is a manifestation of the Great Spirit in Native North American traditions, where the campfire was an image of happiness and prosperity, and the sun itself was called the Great Fire. In Buddhism, a pillar of fire is one symbol of the Buddha, and fire as illumination can be a metaphor for wisdom. In mystical thought, fire often symbolizes union with the god-head, transcendence of the human condition, the end of all things. Hence the concept of the spiritual fire that burns without consuming – the "sages standing in God's holy fire" of W. B. Yeats's poem *Sailing to Byzantium* (1927).

Fire in Christian art is the ultimate test of purity or faith, a flaming heart as the emblem of several saints including Saints Augustine and Antony of Padua. The linked concept of purging evil by fire led to the cruellest atrocities of the Christian Church. Judaism has also used flame as a punitive or defensive symbol – angels with flaming swords guard a lost Eden.

The resurrection symbolism of fire is personified by the phoenix and salamander – and also by the Paschal rituals of both Roman Catholicism and Eastern Orthodox Churches in which candles are extinguished and then lit from "a new fire". New Year bonfires have their origin in forms of sympathetic magic, linking the mak-

ing of new fires with the returning light and warmth of the sun. However, in Japan, Shinto fires at New Year are intended to forestall the risk of destructive fires in the year ahead. Foxes (also associated with fire) with torches tied to their tails used to be chased through grain fields in Europe with a similar objective. Apotropaic meaning is attached to Chinese firecrackers, thought to frighten demons.

The importance in primitive cultures of preserving domestic fires underlies the emblematic sacredness of an undying flame – as in the fire tended by the Vestal Virgins in Rome, or the modern Olympic tradition in which the flame carried to each new Games symbolizes the continuity of traditional sporting ideals. Similarly primal, the ancient friction technique of fire-making underlies the sexual symbolism of fire, which has often been used as a metaphor for desire.

Fire, The Origin of *see* **CULTURE HERO**

Fish *see panel opposite*

Five
The human number – often represented graphically by a man whose head and outstretched limbs form a five-pointed star, or geometrically by the pentagram, also called pentacle, drawn with lines crossing to the five points. Apart from its emblematic association with the human microcosm (and the hand itself), the number five was an important symbol of totality in Chinese, Japanese, Celtic and other traditions which included the centre as a fifth direction of space. Other associations are with love, health, sensuality, meditation, analy-

FISH

A positive symbol, widely linked with fecundity, sexual happiness and the phallus – but more famous as the earliest symbol of Christ. The letters of the Greek word for "fish", *ichthus*, form an acronym for "Jesus Christ, Son of God, Saviour" (*Iesous Christos Theou Huios Soter*). Seals and lamps in the catacombs of Rome bore this emblem as a secret sign. Gospel texts reinforced its symbolism – the miraculous draught of fishes and the analogy made by Christ between fishing and the conversion of the populace (hence the "fisherman's ring" worn by the pope); the feeding of the 5,000 with five loaves and two fishes; the baptism by water of converts. The baptismal font was in Latin called *piscina* ("the fishpond"), converts *pisciculi* ("little fishes"). Fish are shown in paintings of the Last Supper – the sacramental link with the Catholic custom of eating fish instead of other meat on Fridays. Three fishes intertwined or three fishes sharing a single head are symbols of the

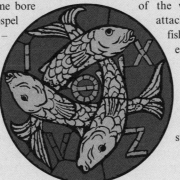

Three fishes, representing the Trinity, and the word "fish" in Greek; after a window in Wrexham Priory, Britain.

Trinity. Hebrew tradition prepared the way for this extensive symbolism. Fishes represented the faithful and were the food of the Sabbath and of paradise. A large fish may be a substitute for Jonah's whale; it also appears as the attribute of Tobias. Priests of the cult of Ea, the Mesopotamian god of the waters and of wisdom, also attached sacramental meaning to fish. As creatures of boundless liberty, not threatened by the Flood, they appear as saviours in Indian myth, avatars of Vishnu and Varuna. On the soles of the Buddha's feet, they symbolize freedom from the restraints of worldly desires. Buddha and the Greek Orpheus are called "fisher of men".

The sexual symbolism of fish is almost universal – linked with their prolific spawn, the fertility symbolism of water, and analogies of the fish with the penis. They are associated with lunar and mother goddesses and birth. In China they are emblems of plenty and good luck.

---

sis, criticism, strength, integration, organic growth and the heart. According to Pythagorean mysticism, five, like seven, was a holistic number, marrying three (heaven) with the terrestrial two, and was fundamental both in nature and in art. It was linked generally in the classical world with Aphrodite (in Roman myth, Venus), the goddess of love and hunting. The association with love and sex may be based on the combination of the male number three with the female number two. Or it may derive from a more ancient Mesopotamian tradition in which the five-pointed

star was an emblem of Ishtar whose planet was Venus, the primary morning and evening star. Ishtar was goddess not only of love but also of war, and the five-pointed star remains prominent in modern military insignia.

In Mexico, too, the Aztec god of the morning star, Quetzalcoatl, was associated with the number 5. He rose from the underworld (also linked with five) on the fifth day, traditionally the day the first corn shoots appeared after sowing. Extending the significance of this number, the Aztecs saw their own era as that of the "Fifth

Five Ages of Man, The

Sun". In India, the five-pointed star was an emblem of Shiva, who is sometimes shown with five faces. Five was a Japanese Buddhist emblem of perfection. In China, where five was a symbol of the centre, its significance was still greater: in addition to the five regions of space and five senses, there were said to be five elements, metals, colours, tones and tastes. In Christian iconography five refers to the number of Christ's wounds. It was a beneficial and protective number in Islam, the five fundamentals of religion being faith, prayer, pilgrimage, fasting and charity. Five was a symbol of strength in Judaism, and the number of the quintessence in alchemy. The number 500 also had symbolic weight – as in St Paul's assertion that the risen Christ revealed himself to more than 500 people (1 Corinthians 15:6).

Five Ages, The

The ancient Greeks accounted for the development (as well as the progressive degeneration) of the human race in the story of the Five Ages or Races. The people of the first age, the Age of Gold, arose (in some accounts) from Gaia, the earth, in the time of Kronos. They were free from old age, disease and labour and their lives were filled with revelry. They died as though falling into a gentle sleep and after death became benevolent spirits. The second race, in the Age of Silver, was created by Zeus and the Olympians. They lived for a hundred years but were violent, arrogant and in thrall to their mothers. They neglected the gods and were destroyed by Zeus: they too persist as spirits.

Zeus created next the race; the Age of Bronze, who discovered metal and established the beginnings of civiliza-

tion. But they were brutal and enjoyed making war with their bronze weapons. They all cut each other's throats and perished.

The fourth era, the Age of Heroes, appears in Hesiod. This race, born of divine fathers and mortal mothers, was noble, brave and of superhuman strength. After death the Heroic Race went to the Elysian Fields or Islands of the Blessed. Zeus then made a fifth race, the modern day Race of Iron, who had to labour and for whom good was always combined with evil.

Five Suns, The

The name given to the five world epochs, according to Aztec mythology. In the beginning the primordial being Ometecuhtli gave birth to four creator gods: Tezcatlipoca, the supreme deity, Xipe Totec, Huitzilopochtli and Quetzalcoatl (the Four Tezcatlipocas). These gods were joined by the rain god Tlaloc and his consort the water goddess Chalchiuhtlicue. The deities all took part in a great cosmic struggle which saw the successive creation and destruction of five "Suns" or world eras. Tezcatlipoca governed the first Sun, which lasted for 676 years. Quetzalcoatl overthrew Tezcatlipoca and jaguars devoured the world. A second Sun arose, ruled by Quetzalcoatl, who was ousted in turn by Tezcatlipoca and swept away in a mighty hurricane. Tlaloc governed the third Sun, which ended when Quetzalcoatl caused the earth to be consumed by a rain of fire. Chalchiuhtlicue presided over the fourth Sun. This era ended when a great flood destroyed the world.

The present era arose when the god Nanahuatzin jumped into a fire at the sacred city of Teotihuacan and was metamorphosed into the rising sun. However, the sun did not move until the other deities had made a sacrifice of their own blood, an event which underlay the Aztec belief that human sacrifice prolonged the existence of the universe. But such acts could only delay the inevitable end of this Sun, when earthquakes would destroy the world.

Flag

Originally an emblem of a god or a ruler borne into battle as a sacred symbol of supremacy. The flag therefore carries immense significance in terms of its triumphant advance, humiliating retreat or, worse still, capture. Outside the use of flags purely for identification or signalling, the ancient link with the status, honour and spiritual values of a clan or nation continues to underlie the individual symbolism of flags – an extensive but separate subject area.

Emperor Constantine had a vision of the Cross before he defeated Maxentius in 312CE. Henceforth, Constantine used it in his flag, designed as a red cross on a white background. This flag has come to represent Christian triumph. It may be carried by Christ in depictions of the Descent into Hell or at the Resurrection; or by St John the Baptist; or by the Lamb of God. It is also the attribute of St Ursula and the militant saints George and Liberalis.

Flagellation

When self-inflicted, a symbol of penance, purification, discipline or sacrificial worship. Known from ancient times in many cults and religions, flagellation became so popular among Christian sects between the 11th and 15th centuries that it was proscribed as heretical behaviour. It was believed not only to correct spiritual backsliding or exorcise personal temptations but also to drive away demons, plague, famine and sterility. Chastisement by flogging often had similar symbolism.

Fleur-de-lys

Better known as an emblem of French kings (and now of the Scouts) than as a symbol, it is nevertheless notable for the diversity of association attached to it, which ranges from purity to fecundity, prosperity and glory. The heraldic fleur-de-lys is a stylized lily with three flowers (it is actually more like a bearded iris).

The origin of the emblem is from the legend that a lily was given to Clovis, king of the Franks, on his baptism, symbolizing purity. The device was chosen as the emblem of the French king in the 12th century, and the plethora of lilies on the field was reduced to just three by Charles V in honour of the Trinity.

The lily also had ancient associations with fecundity, and versions of the fleur-de-lys appear in earlier Etruscan, Indian and Egyptian iconography, apparently with rebirth and solar symbolism. The central flower is often given an arrow or spear shape, suggesting military power, as well as masculine vigour.

FLOOD MYTHS *see panel overleaf*

Flora

The Roman goddess of flowers, Flora[1] was originally the Greek maiden Chloris, who was pursued and raped by Zephyr, who then made her his bride. Botticelli's *Primavera* shows

Flag: *see* Ansanus, Saint;Banner; Constantine the Great; George, Saint;John the Baptist, Saint;Liberalis, Saint;Star; Ursula, Saint

Flagellation: *see* Whip, Flail

Fleur-de-lys: *see* Arrow; Baptism; Iris; Lily; Phallus; Spear; Trinity

Flora: *see* Adonis; Ajax; Clytie; Flowers; Graces; Hyacinthus; Narcissus
[1] Ovid, *Fasti V:183–228*
[2] Ovid, *Met IV:283*

The fleur-de-lys. It has been an emblem of French royalty since the 12th century.

Flowers

*A footprint of the
Buddha, whose soles
were said to bear marks
that indicated a great
spiritual being.*

the metamorphosis of Chloris, who,
once caught in the embrace of
Zephyr, began to sprout flowers, and
was transformed into Flora. Flora
enjoyed perpetual spring in a garden
of countless flowers and fruit, where
the Graces twined garlands for their
hair, and Flora scattered seeds to
bring colour to the monochrome
earth. In Poussin's *Garden* or *Kingdom
of Flora*, she is seen with youths who,
in Classical myth, were turned into
flowers: Ajax, Hyacinthus, Narcissus,
Crocus[2] and Adonis.

FLOWERS *see panel overleaf*

Fly, Flywhisk
Flies generally symbolize evil and
pestilence, but in ancient Egypt they
were emblems of valour and persist-
ence – the king awarded gold "Flies
of Valour" to distinguished warriors.
They were such a problem in the
ancient world that deities were invoked to deal with them, including
Zeus under the title Apomyios ("fly-
preventer"). Flies were equated with
demons and became Christian symbols of moral and physical corruption. The flywhisk is a symbol of
authority in Africa (where it is possibly related to the ancient Egyptian
royal flail), China and India.

Fools and Folly
From the Middle Ages to the 17th
century jesters were the licensed fools
of royalty and aristocracy. Giotto's
Folly is a fat youth with a feathered
crown, tattered tunic and club. In
Bronzino's *Allegory of Love*, Folly is a
young boy about to throw petals over
Venus; he has bells around his ankles
and is grinning, unaware of a thorn
piercing his foot.

Foot, Footprint
Images of feet sometimes appear in
iconography as signs that indicate
contact between the earth and a divinity. In Buddhism, the spiritual superiority of the Buddha is depicted by the
soles of his feet, bearing seven symbols of his divine wisdom: conch,
crown, diamond sceptre, fish, flower
vase, swastika, and Wheel of the Law.
So-called "footprints" of gods, giants
or heroes (naturally formed in rock)
were superstitiously venerated.

At the level of fetishism, according
to Freud the foot is a phallic symbol.
The binding of women's feet in China
mingled fetishism with male posses-
siveness. In other contexts, kissing
someone's foot is a symbol of submission or abasement. Going barefoot, as
in some mendicant orders, signifies
humility. Christ's washing of his disciple's feet – a gesture that was imitated
by English sovereigns who washed the
feet of the poor to show their humility – had this meaning, although in the
ancient world the washing of feet was
also a gesture of hospitality or purification. Setting foot on territory is
often seen as an action invested with
particular significance, famously so in
recent history with Neil Armstrong's
first step onto the moon.

Ford
In Celtic myth, fords are a place of
challenge, especially in single combat.
Because fords were often difficult passages, such symbolism is fairly self-
evident, but Jung has drawn analogies
with the transition from one state of
being to another.

Forest
A Jungian symbol of the unconscious
and its threats, but in some traditions,

FLOOD MYTHS

Mythological traditions the world over describe how divine forces seek to punish human beings for their trans- gressions by destroying them with some form of cosmic disaster, which is most often envisaged as a flood. The best-known example of a flood legend is the biblical story of Noah, which itself is probably derived from a number of older Mesopotamian accounts of a

Noah's Ark on the waters of the biblical Flood; after an illustration in the Nuremberg Bible of 1483.

flood sent by the gods to punish humanity, which is wiped out save for one man (variously called Atra-hasis, Utnapishtim or Ziusudra) and his family. The "Noah's Ark" theme of these accounts is echoed in the Indian myth of Manu, the first man, who is forewarned by a great fish of a cataclysmic inundation and sur- vives by building a ship.

Similar themes occur in the south- ern Chinese myth of the Gourd Children, except that the universal flood which destroys humanity is seen as the arbitrary act of the Thunder God. Elsewhere in the world, the cosmic deluge may be prompted by the misdemeanour of a particular individual. For example, in the mythology of the Chewong peoples of Malaya, anyone who mocks an animal angers the pri- mal serpent of the underworld. In its rage, the serpent will release primeval waters as a great inundation.

The concept of a completely new world emerging from the deluge is common in Central America. For example, in the Aztec myth of the Five Suns, the present world (the fifth sun) is said to have arisen after the previous world was swept away by a flood.

Floods symbolize transformation through dissolution in water. Stories or depictions of a great flood, which appear in the earliest mythologies, have a recurring symbolic theme of cyclic regeneration. Human sin, folly or disorder is submerged, often in a judgmental cataclysm, leading to a new, reformed or wiser human society.

FLOOD MYTHS: *see* Ark;
Atrahasis; CREATION;
Deucalion; Five Suns, The;
Gourd Children, The;
Noah; Prometheus;
Transformation;
Utnapishtim; Water;
Ziusudra

particularly Buddhist, an image of sanctuary. In European folklore and fairy tales, the forest is a place of mys- teries, dangers, trials or initiation. Being lost in the forest or finding a way through it is a powerful metaphor for the terrors of inexperience and the achievement of knowledge – of the adult world or of the self. For settled communities, the forest is the unknown, the uncontrolled, the dwelling place of minor divinities and spirits, some of them terrifying, like the Slavic forest spirit, *leshii*.

The forest's moist, earthy, womb- like darkness was linked in the ancient

FLOWERS

Essentially, the flower is a concise symbol of nature at its summit, condensing into a brief span of time the cycle of birth, life, death and rebirth. In Eastern religions, flowers also represent the unfolding of spiritual life, symbolized specifically by the lotus. Flowers have spiritual significance in many religions. Thus Brahma and the Buddha are shown emerging from flowers. In the Middle Ages, many flowers took on a Christian significance: red flowers represented the blood of Christ's Passion; and white, especially the lily, iris and rose without thorns, the Virgin's purity. Cyclamen, jasmine, lily-of-the-valley and violets were also connected with the Virgin, and may be scattered across the ground in depictions of her walled garden. Flowers also had a numerical significance: five petals symbolized the wounds of Christ, and triple leaves the Trinity. The columbine may symbolize the Holy Ghost (Latin *columbus*, *columba* means "dove").

Flowers also appear in art as attributes of Hope and the dawn. In still life painting, flowers may represent the impermanence of life as a *memento mori*, but flower painters of the 17th and 18th centuries depict them more often as botanical jewels. Artists may show rare or unknown varieties from the New World or, by

including flowers from different seasons, illustrate what it was impossible to achieve in real life, as in *A Vase of Flowers* by Ambrosius Bosschaert.

The symbolism of individual flowers is varied, ranging from allegories of virtue (the lily of purity) or wisdom (the Daoist golden blossom flowering from the head) to associations with blood sacrifice (as in Aztec Mexico) and the death of gods or humans (red or red-spotted flowers, including the anemone, poppy and violet). Various flowers sprang from those who died of unrequited love: anemones from Adonis, violets from Attis, sunflowers from Clytie; narcissi from Narcissus; hyacinths from Hyacinthus. The colours, scents and qualities of flowers often determine their symbolism – the white lily of purity, for example; the heavily-perfumed frangipani of sexual invitation; the showy magnolia of ostentation or self-esteem.

The funerary use of more delicately scented flowers as emblems of continuing life or rebirth is known from the ancient Near East. Roses were scattered on Roman graves with this meaning.

The receptive cup-like form of the flower is symbolically passive and feminine, its triadic layers signifying cosmic harmony.

world with ideas of germination and the feminine principle. To the Druids it was the female partner of the sun. Understanding the forest, its plants and its animals was a mark of shamanistic gifts, notably in Central America. In Asian traditions, the forest can parallel the desert "wilderness" of Middle-Eastern hermits as a place of retreat from the world, where it is possible to enter into contemplation and spiritual development.

Forge *see* **Smith**

Fortune

The Roman goddess Fortuna, "Fortune", originally a deity of abundance, was depicted with a cornucopia, representing the favours she so unevenly meted out. She may also appear blindfolded with a wheel or a globe which spins in reference to her inconstancy. The goddess may also stand on gaming dice or have billowing "sails" of drapery, which refer to the variable winds of chance and the unpredictable moods of the oceans.

The idea that destiny is capricious is alternatively represented in medieval Western art by Dame Fortune, popular in Spanish iconography, who appears spinning a wheel on which some ascend while others are flung to the ground.

Forty

The number used ritually in Judeo-Christian and Islamic tradition to define significant periods of time – especially periods of spiritual preparation or testing, purification, penance, waiting, fasting or segregation. One explanation for the choice of the number forty is that Babylonian astronomers associated natural catastrophes, particularly storms and floods, with a forty-day period in spring when the Pleiades cluster of stars disappeared. Another is the ancient idea that the dead took forty days to entirely fade away. Roman funerary banquets were held after forty days. The idea that forty days was a suitable purification period led the port of Marseilles to impose a forty-day port ban (the *quarantine*) on ships from plague countries in the 14th century. Early historians used

forty more as a symbolic number than as an accurate one. Thus, in the Bible, the Flood lasted forty days and nights; the Israelites wandered forty years in the wilderness; Moses listened to God for forty days and nights on Mount Sinai; David and Solomon each ruled for forty years; Christ spent forty days fasting in the wilderness (now Lent), forty months preaching, and forty days after Easter he ascended to heaven. In Egypt, Osiris disappeared for forty days, the period of religious fasting. Muhammad received the word of God at the age of forty. Many other Hebrew and Islamic rituals testify to the power of forty as a number symbolic of accomplishment or change.

Fountain

A fountain symbolizes the life force, and by extension rejuvenation or immortality, as in Van Eyck's *Adoration of the Lamb*. It can represent a symbol of the cosmic centre, the divine spirit, purification, inspiration and knowledge. Both Christian and Islamic traditions place a fountain or spring at the centre of paradise, at the foot of the Tree of Life, from which streams flow to the four cardinal points – an influential image for the layout of future garden and church architecture. Bernini's flamboyantly sculpted *Fountain of the Four Rivers* in Rome represents the continents. The fountain's "pure river of water" (Revelation 22:1) was equated with the Father and Son, so that the fountain became a symbol not only of purity, as in the legend of the unicorn, but of revelation and redemption. In Norse myth, the god Odin gives one of his eyes for a draught of water from the Fountain of Knowledge flowing from the world axis, the tree Yggdrasil. Greek Orphic tradition held that bypassing the Fountain of Forgetfulness and drinking from the Fountain of Memory at the entrance to Hades would ensure immortality. A popular 15th-century myth was the Fountain of Youth, which was painted by an anonymous artist (Castello, Mantua): it was thought that when aged people drank from it they were immediately rejuvenated. The theme dates back at least to the Roman myth of Jupiter turning Juventas into a fountain. An intertwining theme is the rejuvenating effects of love: ornamental fountains, surmounted by naked Cupids, flow in arcadian Gardens of Love and its jetting water has a sexual symbolism. The sealed fountain is a Christian image of virginity. Eastern legends located the Fountain of Life in the far north, although Florida in the US once seemed a likely site to Europeans.

Four
Comprehensiveness, ubiquity, omnipotence, solidity, organization, power, intellect, justice, stability, the earth. The symbolism of four is drawn primarily from the square and the four-armed cross. The square was the emblem of the earth in both India and China. The four-armed cross is the most common emblem of totality, the four directions of space.

The significance of these four cardinal points, traditionally thought to be ruled by powerful gods of wind and weather, led to the dominance of the number four in religion and ritual throughout much of pre-Columbian America. The four heavenly gods of the Mayan pantheon, the four creator gods of the Aztecs, the four worlds of creation in the Hopi tradition of Arizona, all point to this fundamental theme. As a symbol of universality, four was hardly less important in celestial geography elsewhere. The concept of the four rivers that flow from the Tree of Life in paradise and bring the gift of spiritual nourishment or immortality is common to Babylonian, Iranian, Christian, Teutonic, Nordic, Hindu and Buddhist traditions. Four-faced gods such as Amun-Ra in Egypt and Brahma in India symbolize their rulership of all the elements. As emblematic of terrestrial order and universality, four was also the number of castes in Hindu society. The four letters YHWH outlined the inutterable name of the Hebrew's God. The twelve tribes of Israel were grouped under four emblems: man, lion, bull and eagle. These became the Christian emblems respectively of the four evangelists, Matthew, Mark, Luke and John. The many other fourfold symbols in the Bible, such as the horsemen of the Apocalypse, similarly express the idea of universality.

Four was, in Pythagorean terms, the first number giving a solid – the tetrahedron with a base and three sides. Symbolizing the stabilizing force of religion as well as universality, the square was the basis of much sacred architecture.

The world or heaven was thought to be supported by four pillars (Egypt) or giants (Central America). Guardianship of the directions of space was another quaternary symbol. In the process of Egyptian mummification, four guardian-headed canopic jars held the entrails of the dead. A body lying in state is still conventionally watched over by four guards. As a "rational" number, four symbolized the intellect. In ancient Western tradition there were four elements – earth, air, fire and water – and four humours. Jungian psychology has continued this tradition by envisaging the human psyche in terms of four fundamental aspects: thought, emotion, intuition and the senses. Graphic symbols of four, apart from the square and cross, include the swastika and the quatrefoil.

Fox

A representative of guile – a symbolism soundly based on its cleverness and elusiveness but often extended, notably in European tradition, to more discreditable qualities such as malice, hypocrisy and evil. As a nocturnal predator difficult to trap, the fox became a Christian analogy for the wiles of the Devil. The red fox was a fire demon in ancient Rome. In North America, the fox was a morally neutral trickster figure, not unlike the coyote. Norse mythology linked the fox with the trickster Loki.

The Japanese rice-god Inari with the two foxes that act as his messengers and guard his rice sack.

Erotic associations appear in Chinese folk superstitions where "fox-women" were considered dangerous seducers and a fox's testicles were reputedly an aphrodisiac. Cunning and powers of transformation were also symbolic associations in Japan, although the white fox was the companion and messenger of the important rice god, Inari.

Francis of Assisi, Saint

Francis[1] (*c.*1181–1226) was the son of a wealthy merchant. He led an extravagant life but, aged about 20, after several illnesses and a military expedition, he became pious, solitary, and devoted to God. In 1210, Pope Innocent III sent him and 11 followers to preach under the name of the Friars Minor; their headquarters was established near his native Assisi. Many followed his example, particularly St Clare, and took the vows of chastity, poverty and obedience. Francis tried three times to preach to the Muslims. He set out on a pilgrimage to the Holy Land but was shipwrecked in 1212. Two years later sickness forced him to abandon a journey to the moors in Spain. In Egypt in 1219, he succeeded in preaching to the Sultan. In 1224, while praying in the Apennines, he received the "stigmata", the marks of the five wounds of Christ, which never left him.

St Francis is seen as a tonsured middle-aged man, wearing the brown habit of his Order, and a rope girdle with three knots representing the three vows. He may be depicted barefoot holding the lily of purity or showing his stigmata. In Spanish Counter-Reformation art he is often be shown at prayer. Zurbarán represents him kneeling in meditation, holding a skull.

Francis Xavier, Saint

Several panel paintings and cycles showing episodes from the life of St Francis are displayed in monasteries of his Order. Panels by Sassetta (*Scenes from the Life of St Francis of Assisi*) were originally painted for the altarpiece of the church of San Francesco in San Sepolcro. The most famous fresco cycle is that painted by Giotto and his assistants at San Francesco, Assisi.

Even as a youth Francis was worthy of veneration; a man from Assisi spread his cloak before him. He was dedicated to his "Lady Poverty" and gave alms whenever he could. At his conversion he gave his cloak to a poor soldier. The following night he dreamed of a fine palace containing weapons with crosses; he thought that this was a sign of a military career but later understood it to be a vision of the Order he would found.

At prayer in the church of San Damiano he heard the voice of Christ saying, "Francis, repair my falling house"; and he did so, paying for the work from his father's coffers. His father disinherited him and took him to the bishop of Arezzo. Francis immediately threw off his clothes to symbolize his renunciation of all worldly goods, and the bishop covered him with his own cloak.

To maintain his chastity Francis would throw himself into a thorny bush or roll about in the snow when tempted by the flesh. Initially Pope Innocent III had reservations about confirming Francis' Order because he thought the rules too severe, but after a dream that the Lateran Basilica was collapsing and that Francis held it up, he confirmed Francis' brotherhood.

Francis was renowned for preaching to the birds. When swallows were chattering he ordered them to be silent and they obeyed; he called all animals his brothers and sisters.

Other episodes painted from St Francis' life include his dream of beautiful thrones in heaven: a voice told him that riches were reserved for him there. He is said to have gone to Arezzo, where he saw demons enjoying civil strife, and ordered his companions to exorcize them. In Syria, Francis proved his faith by walking through fire, which left him unharmed. It was here also that he answered a cry for water by conjuring up a stream.

In order to illustrate the Nativity, he placed a doll in a humble straw manger and thus began the tradition of the Christmas crib.

He was invited to dine with a devout knight and, foreseeing the host's imminent death, suggested that he make his confession. The knight obeyed and promptly died. Francis then became a vehicle for the voice of the Holy Spirit and was even asked to speak before Pope Honorius III.

On Francis' death a friar saw the soul of the saint rise to heaven on a white cloud, and a doubting knight was converted by touching the saint's stigmata. Once dead, Francis was successfully invoked in order to heal a wounded man, to restore a woman to life to make her confession, and to free a penitent heretic.

Francis Xavier, Saint

Francis (1506–52) became a follower of St Ignatius Loyola while studying at the University of Paris, and was one of the first of seven Jesuits who dedicated themselves to God in 1534. In 1541 he went as a missionary to Portuguese India for seven years.

Then he went on to Japan for two years, and then to China, where he was taken ill and died. The patron saint of missionaries, Francis Xavier is seen in Jesuit habit tending the sick, or he is shown dying in ecstasy, as in Baciccia's altarpiece in Sant' Andrea al Quirinale, Rome.

Frea

The chief goddess of the early German pantheon and the consort of the god Wodan, who was the forerunner to Odin. Frea (Frig in Anglo-Saxon), gave her name to Friday.

Freyja

The great goddess of the Vanir, the Scandinavian deities of earth and water, one of the two divine races who dwelt in Asgard, the home of the gods. Freyja ("Lady") was clearly a powerful figure, venerated by women, heroes and rulers.

Freyja was the sister of the god Freyr and one tradition claimed that they were married (she may be identifiable with Freyr's bride Gerd). The goddess was associated with sexual freedom: she had many lovers among the gods and also among human rulers, whom she protected. Freyja brought fruitfulness to the land and sea and assisted in marriage and childbirth. This generosity explains one of the goddess's alternative names, Gefn, which derives from the verb *gefa*, to give. Freyja was also a goddess of magic and divination.

Like Freyr, Freyja was associated with wealth. She was said to weep tears of gold and to possess a magnificent necklace called Brisingamen.

Freyja had much in common with Frigg, the chief goddess of the Aesir, the race of sky deities. For example,

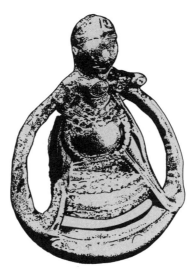

A Swedish pendant of the Viking age that may depict the goddess Freyja.

both were associated with childbearing and could assume the form of a bird. It is possible that they both developed from the early Germanic goddess Frea.

Freyr

The chief Scandinavian god of fertility and abundance. Freyr ("Lord") was one of the Vanir, the deities of earth and water. He was the son of Njord, a god of the sea and ships, and Skadi, a goddess of the mountain forests. Freyr's sister, and perhaps also his consort, was the goddess Freyja.

Freyr and the Vanir brought peace and abundance to the land and its rulers, so long as they kept his favour. The god's cult, which laid great emphasis on fertility and which may have involved sexual rites and orgies, was popular throughout Scandinavia during the Viking age. Divination played an important part in the cult.

Although Freyr was not one of the sky gods, he was associated with the sun as a source of fertility. According to one myth, Freyr wooed Gerd, the daughter of a giant, who lived in the underworld. She agreed to marry him when he convinced her that her refusal would arouse the anger of the gods, bringing sterility and destruction. The myth has been interpreted as the sun uniting with the earth to produce abundance.

One of Freyr's symbols was a golden boar, which passed through the sky and beneath the earth as, it was said, did the sun. Another symbol was the ship. Freyr possessed a vessel, *Skidbladnir*, able to carry all the gods, which he kept folded up in a pouch when he did not need it.

Frigg

The queen of heaven and chief goddess among the Scandinavian sky deities, the Aesir. Frigg was the wife of Odin, the head of the Aesir and ruler of Asgard, the home of the gods. She had much in common with the goddess Freyja and they may both have developed from the early Germanic goddess, Frea. Frigg features in myth as the grieving mother of Balder, whom she tried without success to fetch back from Hel, the underworld land of the dead.

Frog

A foetal symbol, linked with the Egyptian frog goddess of birth, Heket, and in other cultures also associated with the primeval state of matter, fecundity, germination, evolution, lunar phases, water and rain. Its embryonic symbolism, its amphibious transformation from egg and tadpole to a land-going creature with rudi-

mentary human features, helps to explain the Grimm fairy tale of the frog who turned into a prince. Frogs were mocked symbols of foolish aspiration. Identified in Revelation (16:13) as an unclean spirit, and sometimes associated with heresy, the frog appears widely as a fertility and resurrection symbol, and harbinger of spring rains and the reawakening of nature – particularly in ancient Egypt and Asia.

In Vedic myth, a Great Frog, as the primordial state of undifferentiated matter, supports the earth. Frog images were used to invoke rain in ancient China where, in folklore, frogs' spawn appeared with the morning dew. Frogs signify luck in Japan, especially for voyagers. Their croaking is a common metaphor for boring instruction. Their love-play led the Greeks to associate them with Aphrodite.

Fruit

Abundance, prosperity, earthly pleasures or desires – the food most often used to portray the paradisal state or the Golden Age of pastoral life. A cornucopia, represented as a horn or an ornamental bowl, offers an abundant supply of fruit and illustrates nature's bounty. It is often depicted with Ceres (in Greek myth, Demeter), the goddess of agriculture, and with personifications of Abundance, Peace or Summer. Various fruits (see individual entries) share some of the creative symbolism of the egg. Fruit may be included in still-life painting to illustrate the transience of life: Caravaggio's *Bacchus* includes a still-life detail of over-ripe fruit. Exotic or out-of-season fruit might suggest wealth. However, sometimes fruit is chosen as a subject purely to demonstrate the artist's skill.

Frum, John
The central figure of a Melanesian cargo cult which began in the New Hebrides (Vanuatu) during the Second World War. John Frum is said to be an incarnation of the supreme being worshipped in Vanuatu before the people were converted to Christianity. His coming is believed to herald a new age of *kago* ("wealth").

Fu Xi
A creator god who features in some of the most ancient Chinese myths, often

Fu Xi and Nü Gua, after a 7th-century CE Chinese painting on cloth.

alongside the creator goddess Nü Gua. From the 4th century BCE onward Fu Xi and Nü Gua appear frequently as the creators of the human race and its protectors against calamities, especially floods. During the Han dynasty (202BCE–220CE) they came to be presented as husband and wife. They were often depicted with the tails of serpents.

Han scholars reworked many myths as fact to fill in gaps in early Chinese history. Fu Xi was declared to have been the very first emperor, and to have ruled from 2852BCE–2737BCE. He was hailed as a great culture hero, inventor of musical instruments and the first Chinese script. He instructed on how to rear domestic animals and to fish with nets.

Furies, The
Fearsome female deities or spirits of the underworld. In most accounts, the Furies (Erinyes in Greek) sprang from the goddess Gaia, the earth, at the spot where the blood of the god Uranos fell after his castration. They were powerful agents of justice, who sought out transgressors on earth and administered and oversaw their torments in the underworld. Their names were said to be Furies: Alecto (which means "Relentless"), Megaira ("Resentful") and Tisiphone ("Avenger of Murder").

Alternatively, they were the daughters of the Roman god of the Underworld, Pluto. Their heads were covered with serpents and they breathed vengeance and pestilence. They are the usual attendants of Mars, the Roman god of war The Furies are seen dragging Mars away from Peace in Rubens' *Allegory of Peace and War*.

Frum, John: *see* Cargo Cults

Fu Xi: *see* CREATION; CULTURE HERO; Gourd Children, The; Nü Gua

Furies, The: *see* Hades, Mars

Gabriel, Archangel

Gabriel, Archangel

Gabriel was one of God's principal winged messengers and, in particular, brought news of birth. In the Bible, Gabriel explains the visions of Daniel;¹ in the New Testament he is identified with the angel who announced the birth of John the Baptist to Zacharias, and of Christ to the Virgin Mary. His words to Mary were, "Hail, thou that art highly favoured, the Lord is with thee; blessed art thou among women."² The Latin equivalent, "*Ave gratia plena Dominus tecum*" or "*Ave Maria*", may be written on paintings of the Annunciation – for example, Simone Martini's. Gabriel often offers the Virgin the lily of purity, which, therefore, may be considered his attribute.

Gaia

The Greek goddess personifying the earth, one of the primal deities which arose from Chaos in the beginning, according to Hesiod's *Theogony*. Gaia (or Ge) then played the most crucial role in the early stages of creation. She brought forth the god Uranos, the sky, and then the Mountains and the Sea before having intercourse with Uranos to produce the first divine races: the twelve Titans, three Cyclopes and three giants called Hekatoncheires, each with a hundred hands. But Uranos was dismayed by these offspring and forced them back into Gaia. This angered the goddess, who persuaded Kronos, the youngest Titan, to castrate his father and become the ruler of heaven. In some accounts Gaia predicted that Kronos, like Uranos, would be overthrown by one of his children. Kronos therefore devoured each of his offspring as his wife, the Titan Rhea, gave birth. But Rhea concealed the infant Zeus, who was nurtured by Gaia until he was old enough to dethrone his father and become the leader of the gods.

Gaia, causing life to spring from the earth, was also the sacred energy which endowed some sites with oracular powers. Delphi, believed by the Greeks to be the centre of the earth, was the site of Gaia's most famous oracle. It became the chief shrine of Apollo after he had killed the dragon Pytho, which Gaia had set to guard it.

The goddess had many offspring, who included Echidne, Erichthonius, the Furies and Nereus.

Galatea

In Greek myth,[1] the Nereid or sea-nymph Galatea lived in the sea off Sicily and was in love with the handsome shepherd Acis, but she was herself pursued by the giant Cyclops, Polyphemus, a savage monster who raised sheep on an island generally thought to be Sicily. Polyphemus climbed a hill overlooking the sea, and here he played his pipe of a hundred reeds and sang a pastoral love song to Galatea. Later, however, the Cyclops saw her lying in Acis' arms; so he chased the youth, hurling a huge lump of the mountainside fatally at him. Galateia turned her dead lover into a stream which sprang from the rock. Raphael's *The Triumph of Galatea* shows her fleeing on a cockle-shell chariot fitted with paddles and drawn by dolphins; Cupids fly in the air and Tritons and Nereids play in the waves.

Ganesha

The elephant-headed Hindu god, the offspring of the goddess Parvati, the wife of Shiva. Once she had married Shiva, Parvati desired a child to guard her from unwelcome visitors. As she bathed she created Ganesha from the rubbings of her own body and set him to watch the entrance to her chambers. When he tried to refuse entry to Shiva himself, the god angrily decapitated him. Parvati insisted that her son be revived, so Shiva replaced Ganesha's head with that of an elephant. He then

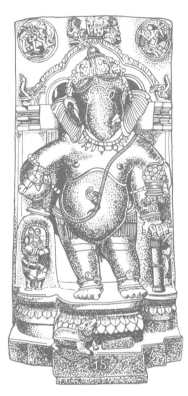

The elephant-headed god Ganesha, after a 13th-century Indian statue.

put Ganesha in charge of the *ganas*, his goblin-like attendants.

Ganesha was well-known for overcoming all obstacles and his name is traditionally invoked before the start of any enterprise. Hence his alternative title of Vighneshvara ("Lord of Obstacles").

Ganga

"Ganges", the goddess personifying the Ganges River and the holiest of Hinduism's three (or, in some accounts, seven) great river goddesses. Ganga descended from heaven and in order to cushion her descent the god

Galatea: *see* Cyclops; Nereus; Polyphemus
[1] Ovid, *Met XIII:738–897*

Ganesha: *see* Shiva; Skanda

Ganga: *see* Shiva

Shiva allowed her to land on his matted hair. Shiva divided Ganga into seven rivers (the Ganges and its tributaries) so that she could arrive on earth without causing catastrophic floods.

Ganga purifies those who bathe in her and the ashes of the dead are scattered on her waters. As a goddess she is often depicted on her mount, the *makara*, a water monster .

Ganymede

In Greek myth, a beautiful Trojan youth, the son of King Tros of Troy. The god Zeus fell in love with him and sent an eagle to abduct him (other accounts claim that the eagle was Zeus in transformed guise). The bird snatched Ganymede from the Trojan plain and carried him to the peak of Mount Olympus, where Zeus granted him immortality and eternal youth as cupbearer to the gods.

Garang

The first man, according to the Dinka people of southern Sudan. He was the husband of Abuk, the first woman, who caused death and illness on earth.

Garden

In ancient traditions, an image of the perfected world, cosmic order and harmony – paradise lost and regained. For all major world cultures, gardens represented both the visible blessings of God (the divine gardener) and the ability of humans themselves to achieve spiritual harmony, a state of grace or beatitude.

In Genesis the Garden of Eden is described as an earthly paradise, from which God expelled Adam and Eve for eating the forbidden fruit of the Tree of Knowledge. The Virgin may be depicted in a flowery garden, which is often walled – the *Hortus Conclusus* – in reference to the Immaculate Conception of Christ, the enclosed female principle intimating sealed fruitfulness. The Rhenish Master (15th century) shows this in *Paradise Garden*.

In the arid landscapes of Egypt and Iran, oasis-like formal gardens with their shading trees, flowers, scents, birds and flowing water, became symbols of refuge, beauty, fertility, purity and the springtime freshness of youth – a foretaste of the joys of immortality. The cross-like layout of the classic Persian garden, divided by four streams flowing from a central source or fountain, was modelled on the mythical image of paradise (a word etymologically synonymous with "garden"). In China, vast gardens with lakes and rocks and mountains created by the Han dynasty imitated the mythical Mystic Isles to which emperors hoped to go as immortals. Kyoto, the perfect example of Japanese garden art, is imbued with spiritual symbolism. Some Indian gardens take the form of mandalas. Aztec gardens, as images of the natural world in microcosm, included wild animals as well as plants. Roman banquets held in funerary gardens symbolized the companionable nourishments of the Classical paradise of Elysium.

Psychologically, the garden is a symbol of consciousness as opposed to the wilderness of the unconscious, and also of the enclosing female principle. A garden is often used as a metaphor for sexual paradise constituted by the loved one – the "fountain of gardens, a well of living waters" (Song of Solomon 4:15).

In medieval Europe the garden was confined within the precincts of castles and monasteries. In art it may be shown as a Garden of Love, embodying the pleasures and conventions of a courtier's life. Medieval gardens also appear in illustrations of the early 14th-century poem *Le Roman de la Rose*, in which the young poet is led to a Palace of Pleasure to meet Love, only to be obstructed by Danger, Fear and Slander.

In England, gardens laid out for royalty and the aristocracy were subject to fashion but also reflected social and political change. Until the 1750s geometrical designs, created with avenues, terraces and hedges, were to an extent a reflection of a hierarchical and authoritarian society. In the later 18th century, however, this regularity gave way to the open, gentle curves of Lancelot "Capability" Brown, who designed parks modelled on the Classically-inspired landscapes of the French artist Claude Lorrain, and on literary descriptions of classical gardens, with statues, fountains, grottoes and walks. With the onset of the Romantic movement in 19th-century literature and painting it became fashionable to imitate wild, remote landscapes, which were often the settings for contemporary Gothic novels.

Garlic
A superstitious emblem of protective power in southern and central Europe from Classical times. Apart from anti-magnetic properties (a Roman belief), it was said to deter snakes, lightning, the evil eye, and vampires.

The custom of hanging up bunches of garlic in the home had protective symbolism for centuries. In ancient Greece, where the smell of garlic was disliked, its chewing had more plausible value as a way for women to maintain their chastity.

Garuda
"The Devourer", a celestial bird and mount of the Hindu god Vishnu. Garuda, often depicted as part human and part eagle, was the offspring of the sage Kashyapa and Vinata, the mother of all birds. He was associated with fire and the sun, and was regarded as an incarnation of the fire god Agni. He was the enemy of the Nagas, the serpents. When Vinata was enslaved by her sister Kadru, mother of all snakes, she was promised her freedom if Garuda brought the elixir of the gods to the snakes. Garuda stole the elixir and placed it where sharp-bladed grass grew. Vinata was freed and the snakes licked the grass, splitting their tongues, which have been forked ever since. The god Indra retrieved the elixir.

A Buddhist form of Garuda, after a 16th-century depiction.

Gautama, Siddhartha *see* BUDDHA, THE

Gazelle *see* Antelope

Geb *see* Nut

Gefion
A Scandinavian fertility goddess. The Swedish king Gylfi promised Gefion as much of his kingdom as she could

Garuda: *see* Indra; Seven Sages, The; Vishnu

Gefion: *see* Freyja

Geminianus, Saint

plough in a day, so she transformed her four giant sons into oxen so powerful that their plough wrenched away a great area of the Swedish mainland. This became the Danish island of Zealand, the centre of the goddess's cult. Gefion may have been a manifestation of the goddess Freyja, who was also known by the name Gefn.

Geminianus, Saint

The bishop of Modena, Geminianus (4th century) was a friend of St Ambrose and was renowned as a healer. Legend has it that he went to Constantinople to exorcize a demon from the Emperor's daughter, and so he may be shown with a demon at his feet. Attila the Hun had a vision of the saint, as a result of which he halted his attack on Modena. Geminianus was also said to have saved Modena from floods. He is depicted by Sebastiano Mainardi as a bishop holding a model of San Gimignano, the many-towered town which adopted his name (church of Sant' Agostino, San Gimignano).

Geneviève, Saint

The devotion to God shown by Geneviève (*c.*420–500CE) was noticed when she was only eight years old and tending a flock of sheep. She was said to have performed several miracles during her childhood. Her prayers apparently repelled the advance on Paris of Attila the Hun. She arranged for food for the starving during the Frankish siege of Paris, and the enemy leader listened to her pleas for clemency for the captives. In 1129 an epidemic of ergot poisoning suddenly abated when her relics were carried in a procession. She is the patroness of Paris and may be shown holding the keys of the city. The Pantheon in Paris was once dedicated to her. Her story was illustrated on its walls by Puvis de Chavannes.

George, Saint

George (traditionally late 3rd or early 4th century CE) is said to have been martyred in Palestine. Carpaccio's cycle in the Scuola di San Giorgio, Venice, depicts the legend¹ of George as a soldier who travelled to Libya where a dragon was terrifying the populace. The people of Libya appeased the monster's fury by offering it every day a youth or maiden selected by lot. Eventually the king's only daughter was picked, but George, mounted on his horse, armed himself with the sign of the Cross and gave the beast a grievous wound, forcing it to the ground. The maiden's girdle was then tied around the dragon's neck, and it followed her, like a dog on a leash, back to the city. The king and all the people were baptized into Christianity, and George slew the dragon. George, often on a white horse, is usually shown slaying the winged beast, as in Paolo Uccello's *Saint George and the Dragon*. The theme was taken to represent the triumph of Christianity over evil. Like Christ of the Resurrection, George may hold a white banner with a red cross, which later became the national flag of England.

Later episodes from his life are less frequently painted. He is said to have fallen into the hands of persecutors and to have survived torture. He was subjected to the rack and fire, had salt rubbed into his wounds, was poisoned, and survived a wheel fitted with sharp knives, and a cauldron of molten lead. He is said to have prayed to God to destroy a pagan temple, whereupon the building immediately caught fire. Then he was dragged through the streets and finally he was beheaded. George's cult was brought to Europe by the Crusaders, and *c.*1348 his image was adopted by Edward III of England as the patron of the Order of the Garter. He is the protector of England.

In fact, no historical evidence of St George's life exists and his feast day (like that of St Christopher, among others) has recently been removed by the Pope from the calendar of the Catholic church.

Gerd

A princess of the underworld race of giants who became the bride of the Norse god Freyr. She may be identifiable with Freyr's sister Freyja, who, in one tradition, was also his wife.

Gesar Khan

The hero of a Tibeto-Mongolian cycle of myths which contain traces of

The divine warrior hero, Gesar Khan.

pre-Buddhist mythological traditions, such as references to numerous local deities. Gesar Khan ("King Gesar") was chosen by the gods to descend from heaven in human form in order to combat the evils arising from a curse laid on humanity by a bitter old woman and her three sons. Gesar was born on earth from an egg and set out on a heroic life of great adventures, defeating evil wherever he and his companions found it.

At the end of his life Gesar retreated to the holy mountain Margye Pongri with his followers for a period of meditation and ritual purification for the bloody deeds they had committed as warriors. After this period Gesar ascended to heaven, knowing that one day he would have to return to earth, since evil could never be wiped out completely.

Giant

An adversarial symbol with some similarities to the dragon in Western mythologies, probably sometimes drawn from memories of ancient tribal enemies who grew steadily more imposing as legends were woven about them. Usually portrayed as brutish, aggressive, stupid and clumsy, giants are vanquished in myth sometimes by a combination of divine and human effort, sometimes by the courage and cunning of a hero-figure. Ancient legends of giants can be seen as allegories of the struggle for social and spiritual evolution against barbarian forces or against the elemental forces of the earth – Norse giants, for example, directly personify the powers of fire and frost.

In several cosmogonies, the destruction of a race of Titans or giants is depicted as a primal stage in the

Gerd: *see* Freyr

Giant: *see* Arthur; Christopher, Saint; David; Dragon; Father; Fire. Flame; Gigantomachy, The; Hero, Heroine
Ovid, *Met 1:151–162*

Gideon

Gideon:
[1] *Judges 6:36–40*
[2] *Judges 7:5–21*

Gigantomachy, The: *see*
Gaia; Uranos; Zeus

process of creation – a sacrificial symbolism that may underlie the burning of giant wicker figures filled with animal and human victims that were a feature of some pagan midsummer rituals. Psychologically, owing to their exaggerated physical size, giants are symbols of parental authority, particularly of the father.

In Greek mythology, the giant Titans were the offspring of Uranos and Gaia. There are usually said to have been twelve of them, six males and six females, all of enormous size and strength. According to Ovid,[1] they sought to overthrow the gods of Mount Olympus. They piled two other mountains on top of each other to reach the summit, prompting Zeus (in Roman myth, Jupiter) to hurl his thunderbolts at them to halt their attack. The subject was popular in Baroque times: Giulio Romano's *trompe l'œil* frescoes in the Palazzo del Tè, Mantua, were an example to later artists of the dramatic possibilities offered by the episode.

In the Bible, David slew the giant Goliath in single combat during the war between the Israelites and Philistines, an act that ultimately led to his succession as king of Israel.

St Christopher, the patron saint of travellers, is often represented as a giant, carrying the Christ Child in his arms or on his shoulders.

Gideon

In the Bible Gideon was one of the divinely ordained judges of Israel. He was threshing wheat when an angel told him that he would save his people from the Midianites.

However, he needed repeated proofs of God's support, to confirm his own and his followers' faith, so he laid a fleece on the ground and asked God that the morning dew should fall only on the fleece and not on the ground. In the morning he wrung a bowlful of water from the fleece yet the ground had remained dry. The next night he asked for the reverse to happen, and indeed the following morning the fleece was dry while the ground was covered in dew.[1] Gideon did not wish to conquer with superior numbers so, with God's guidance, he carefully selected 300 men from his troops – numbering more than 30,000 in all – by leading them to water: those who drank like dogs – an unwise action when the enemy is nearby – were dismissed; those who drank from water cupped in their hands were enlisted. Gideon and his troops attacked at night, blowing on trumpets, crying, "The sword of the Lord, and of Gideon" and the Midianites fled.[2]

In *The Battle of Gideon Against the Midianites* Poussin painted a night scene in which the trumpeters are seen causing chaos; and in *The Sword of the Lord of Gideon* Stanley Spencer showed tents collapsing to reveal the startled Midianites.

Gigantomachy, The

"The Battle of the Giants", specifically the battle between the Olympian deities and a race of giants which sprang from the goddess Gaia, the earth, at the spot where she was spattered with the blood of the castrated god Uranos. The Olympians defeated the giants.

Gilding *see* Gold

Giles, Saint

Little is known of Giles (Aegidius), who may have been a hermit near Arles, in the south of France, some time before the 9th century CE. He was highly popular in the late Middle Ages, and over 150 churches in England were dedicated to him.

The Master of St Giles (*c*.1500) shows the episode when a deer, which had been wounded by hunters, came to Giles for protection. When the hunters eventually tracked down the deer, they found that the arrow had transferred itself from the animal to the saint. The deer is the attribute of St Giles, who may also be shown with an arrow in his arm.

Gilgamesh

An early king of Erech (or Uruk) in Sumer (modern Iraq) and the hero of the Babylonian (Sumerian-Akkadian) epic of Gilga-mesh, the world's oldest extant work of literature (*c*.2000BCE or earlier). The most complete version of the epic comes from the library of

Gilgamesh (left), from a baked clay plaque of the Old Babylonian period.

Assyria's King Asshurbanipal (*c*.669–627BCE). In this version, the people of the city of Erech begged the gods to send someone to restrain the repressive hand of their ruler, Gilgamesh, son of the goddess Ninsun and a mortal. So the gods created Enkidu, a hairy barbarian of superhuman strength who lived in the desert. Gilgamesh decided to capture Enkidu and sent a prostitute

to seduce him. Enkidu had intercourse with her and let her take him to Erech and civilization.

When Enkidu was brought before Gilgamesh, he at once engaged the king in a bout of wrestling. After this fight the two men became companions and journeyed together to slay the monster Humbaba (Huwawa to the Sumerians). When the two men returned in triumph, the goddess Ishtar (the Sumerian Inanna) attempted to seduce Gilgamesh, but she was rejected. The angry goddess sent a fierce bull to kill Gilgamesh, but Enkidu came to his aid and the two butchered the creature. The people of Erech rejoiced, but the deities decided that Enkidu must die for his role in killing Humbaba and the bull. He died in the arms of Gilgamesh.

Devastated by Enkidu's death, Gilgamesh set out on a vain quest to discover the secret of eternal life. He visited Utnapishtim, who was granted immortality after he alone had survived a great flood sent by the gods to destroy humanity. Utnapishtim told Gilgamesh of a plant growing at the bottom of the sea which was said to bring new life to whomever ate it. Accompanied by Utnapishtim's boatman Urshanabi, Gilgamesh found the plant but it was stolen by a snake. At last resigned to mortality, he returned to Erech.

Ginnungagap

"The Yawning (or Deceiving) Gap", the primeval emptiness which held all the potential energy of creation, according to ancient Norse myth.

Ginseng

An Oriental virility symbol, its masculine significance seemingly based

Gilgamesh: *see* Enkidu; Ishtar; Utnapishtim

Ginnungagap: *see* Ymir

Ginseng: *see* Phallus

on the phallic shape sometimes taken by the roots. Drugs made from ginseng have been used as reputed aphrodisiacs in China for centuries, and are also said to possess the "celestial" quality of promoting physical and mental equilibrium.

Girdle, Belt

Fidelity, chastity, strength, preparedness for action. In the older sense of a belt or sash, the girdle acquired a considerable and varied symbolism because it was used not only to hold garments together (hence an emblem of female chastity) but also to carry weapons, provisions, money, tools, and so on. Laying aside the girdle implied retirement from military service (in Rome, for example) – the opposite of warriors' or travellers' "girding up their loins". Its sexual symbolism ranged from marital fidelity (a girdle of sheep's wool given by Romans to their brides) to seductiveness (the magic girdle of the Greek goddess Aphrodite [Venus], said to make its wearer irresistible to men). Magic girdles appear in mythology as emblems of strength (the belt of Thor which doubled the power of his muscles).

Deriving from the ornate girdles of chivalry, ceremonial girdles were awarded as emblems of honour in England; hence the "belted earl". The rope girdles of monks allude to the binding and scourging of Christ; the Franciscan girdle has three knots signifying obedience to Christ and the vows of poverty and chastity. The priestly *cingulum* worn at the Roman Catholic Mass also symbolizes chastity. The Virgin is said to have given her girdle to St Thomas on her Assumption.

Circle symbolism makes the Hindu girdle an emblem of the cycles of

time, and may also account for the girdles of invisibility that sometimes appear in folklore more widely.

Gitchi Manitou

"Great Spirit", the name of the supreme deity of the Algonquian people of the northeastern United States and southeastern Canada. Gitchi Manitou conceived and governed the universe, but left its day-to-day running to more active divinities, such as Sun, Moon, Thunder and Wind. His omnipresence manifested itself in the interaction of all life forms, natural and supernatural.

Gla

"Knowing", the first thing to emerge from Fu, the primordial emptiness, according to the highly sophisticated creation myth of the Bambara people of west Africa. Gla (or Gla Gla Zo) was the prime force of creation. It uttered a "Voice of Emptiness" from which its twin, Dya, arose. From Gla and Dya sprang a damp matter like cold rust which hardened into icy, shining objects that filled the primal void. The twin beings caused a wind of fire to melt the icy bodies: in this melting all things became potential in silence and invisibility.

Gla and Dya withdrew their energy into themselves and everything solidified anew. Then they melted everything once more. After these two successive fusions, Gla set up a to and fro movement which is the soul of the universe. At the same time the contact between the twin beings caused a cosmic explosion from which a hard, powerful, vibrating matter was ejected. From its vibration emerged, one by one, the signs and names for all things as yet uncreated, each of which began to vibrate gently within itself, each in its own place. Then Gla produced "the foot of humanity", the symbol of human consciousness, which is the "seed" of the universe. This element communicated consciousness to all things, which were thus able to come into existence.

The process of bringing things into being was then assumed by two creator spirits, Pemba and Faro.

Glaucus and Scylla

In mythology,[1] the nymph Scylla was bathing in the cool water of a secluded cove when Glaucus appeared before her. Once a fisherman, Glaucus had been transformed into a sea-god when he had eaten a herb that rendered fish immortal: he is depicted with a rusty green beard, sweeping hair, huge shoulders, dark blue arms, and a writhing fish-tail for legs. He fell in love with Scylla, pursued her and appealed to her with his story. Scylla rejected him, so Glaucus turned to the sorceress Circe for help to win his love. However, Circe fell in love with him; when he rejected her, she turned Scylla into a sea-monster. In *Glaucus and Scylla*, Salvator Rosa shows Scylla shrinking from Glaucus as he rises from the waters.

Globe, Orb

World dominion or absolute authority – an emblem of power dating from at least the Roman Empire. Sharing with the sphere the symbolism of totality, it is a popular attribute in art of figures representing universal qualities from truth, fame, fortune and abundance to justice, philosophy and the liberal arts. The globe is also the attribute of omnipresent divinities, including the Greek deities Zeus (in Roman myth,

Jupiter), Eros (Cupid), Apollo and Cybele. In Christian iconography, God often holds or stands on a globe. An orb surmounted by a cross represents the dominion of Christ and was an emblem of the Holy Roman Emperors, as it still is of British sovereigns. Emperors, kings or spiritual leaders such as the pope usually hold the globe in the left hand. A crowned globe represented the Philosopher's Stone in alchemy. A globe with stars is an attribute of Urania, the muse of astronomy.

In Hans Holbein's *The Ambassadors* the inclusion of a globe with other learned objects may signify education. In the 17th century, a period of discovery and expansion, globes and maps reveal an interest in new territories; they may also refer to the absence of someone on a journey abroad. In Dutch painting a globe or map combined with other references to sensual delights often alluded to earthly desires, as in Willem Buytewech's *Merry Company*.

Glooskap

A divine culture hero and trickster figure of the Algonquian people. Glooskap, or Gluskap, was said to have created the stars and planets and humanity from the corpse of his mother, while his evil twin brother, Maslum, produced disease and other ills. The two brothers often conflicted as Maslum endeavoured to counter the benefits which Glooskap brought to the human race. In the end Maslum was defeated.

One myth relates how Glooskap first took the summer to the frozen lands of the north. Glooskap used his trickery to abduct Summer, the beautiful female chief of the little people.

Glaucus and Scylla:
[1] Ovid, *Met XIII:898–968* and *XIV:1–74*

Globe, Orb: *see* CROSS; crown; FAME; Fortune; God; Philosopher's Stone; sphere; star; TRUTH; VIRTUES, THE

Glooskap: *see* CULTURE HERO; TRICKSTER

He escorted her north and took her
into the tipi of Winter. Her warmth
caused the giant to melt away.
Glooskap then let Summer return to
her own people.

Glove

A symbol of the executive hand
itself, therefore often used as a pledge
of action in days when gloves were
more widely worn, especially by people of rank. The custom of throwing
down a glove as a challenge (later,
slapping someone in the face with a
glove) goes back to medieval trials
by battle.

Defendants who had lost cases
deposited a folded glove as security
that they would carry out the court
order. Gloves were also used by jousting knights as love pledges and by
rulers to confer commercial rights or
fiefs. In the ritual of status, removing
the right glove acknowledged the
superiority of an overlord or sovereign – and showed that no threat was
intended. White (pontifical) gloves
are used in the Roman Catholic
Church as symbols of purity.

Goat

Virility, potency, lust, cunning and
destructiveness in the male; fecundity
and nourishing care in the female.
Much of the ambiguous symbolism
of the goat resolves itself along these
sexual lines. The she-goat (or goat
nymph) Amalthea was thus the
revered wet-nurse of the Greek god
Zeus (in Roman myth, Jupiter), her
horn the cornucopia of abundance –
symbolism soundly based on the
quality and suitability of goat's milk
for babies. The vitality of the male
goat impressed the ancient world, as
its connection with several Sumerian-

*The god Agni riding a goat; after
an 18th-century Indian painting.*

Semitic and Greek gods shows. The
goat was also the fiery mount of the
Vedic deity Agni, drew the chariot of
Thor, and was closely linked with
Dionysos (Bacchus in Roman myth),
as well as providing many of the physical features of Pan and the lusty
satyrs. Male goats are particularly
active in winter (when the female
comes on heat), which may account
for images of straw goats used in
Scandinavian corn festivals held at
yuletide – a season sometimes personified in art by the goat. However, the
goat's virility was seen by the Hebrews
as lewd. Herodotus reported bestial
sexual practices in the Mendesian cult
of the goat among the Egyptians.
This may have influenced the Christian symbolism of the goat as a personification of impurity and vile lust.
Goats are analogous with sinners or
unbelievers in the gospel account of

Judgment Day when Christ is to divide them from the sheep and consign them to everlasting fire[1]. Hence, probably, the goatish physical characteristics of the medieval Devil, an association strengthened by the goat's reputation for malicious destructiveness. Goats can also personify folly ("acting the goat"). Among the Israelites a goat was sacrificed to the Lord, and the scapegoat ("escape goat") was set free into the wilderness bearing the sins of the community.[2] Holman Hunt painted a forlorn image of *The Scapegoat*.

In China, where "goat" and "Yang" are homonyms, the goat is a positive masculine symbol, as it is in India where, as a sure-footed climber, it was associated with superiority. In the Zodiac, Capricorn is a goat-fish.

God

In the New Testament, Christ told his disciples to "teach all nations, baptizing them in the name of the Father, and of the Son, and of the Holy Ghost",[1] from which the doctrine of the Holy Trinity derives.

In late medieval imagery, God may be shown as part of the Trinity: either as the Father, creating the world; or in the shape of Christ; or, as the Holy Ghost, in an Annunciation, represented by shafts of light or by a dove.

In the Renaissance God came to be depicted as a static, paternal figure with long white hair and a beard, as in Masaccio's *Trinity*. Michelangelo's representation of God creating the world (Sistine Chapel, Rome) has affinities with depictions of Jupiter (in Greek myth, Zeus).

The attributes of God may be a triangular halo representing the Trinity, a globe in order to represent his capacity as the creator of the world,

or an *alpha* and *omega* to signify his position as the beginning and the end of all things.

GODS AND GODDESSES OF CLASSICAL MYTHOLOGY see GREEK AND ROMAN DEITIES

Goibhniu

A divine smith and founder of craftsmanship of Irish myth. Goibhniu ("Smith") headed a group of three deities (the other two being Luchta and Creidhne) who were the craftsmen and armourers of the Tuatha Dé Danann. A weapon made by Goibhniu was said always to hit its target and cause a mortal wound. He was reputed to be able to forge a weapon with just three blows of his hammer.

Gold

A metal of perfection, symbolically divine through its universal association with the sun in the ancient world and also because of its remarkable lustre, resistance to rust, durability and malleability. Its associated emblematic qualities range from purity, refinement, spiritual enlightenment, truth, harmony and wisdom to earthly power and glory, majesty, nobility and wealth. Gold was the alchemical Great Work, the goal of the transformation process, and the preferred metal for sacred objects or for sanctified kings. In the Inca empire, acceding rulers were covered in resin sprayed with gold dust, the historical origin of the El Dorado (gilded man) legend. Gilding on the icons of Byzantine Christianity and of Buddhism symbolized divinity, as does the gold-leaf work of medieval art. In many traditions, gold was identified as the actual substance of

God: *see* Alpha and Omega; Hand; Trinity
[1] *Matthew 28:19*

Goibhniu: *see* Fomorian; Tuatha Dé Danann

Gold: *see* Alchemy; El Dorado; Fire, Flame; Light; METALS; Sun; TRUTH; WISDOM; Yellow

*Jason seizes the Golden
Fleece; after a detail
from an ancient Greek
red-figure vase.*

divinity – the flesh of Ra in Egypt, the faeces of the sun-god Huitzilopochtli in Aztec Mexico – or was thought to be a residue of the sun itself, its illumination left as threads in the earth, a mineral form of light, as in Hindu thought. Alternatively, it was a symbol of the spirit of enlightenment, as in Buddhism, or of Christ's message. By association with the sun, gold is a masculine symbol. Most of the metal's symbolism also attaches to the colour gold – sun, fire, glory, divinity, the light of heaven and of truth.

Golden Fleece, The
The famous symbol of the almost impossible goal, combining two sky or solar emblems of aspiration – the ram from which the fleece was shorn (sacred to the god Zeus) and gold, the solar metal. The golden ram, kept by King Aëtes of Colchis and guarded by an unsleeping dragon, was retrieved by the hero Jason. The epic journey of Jason and his Argonauts is often likened to the legend of the Holy Grail as an allegory of quest for the treasure of spiritual enlightenment and immortality. As an emblem of chivalrous protection, the Golden Fleece became an order of knighthood in Burgundy, Austria and Spain. (One suggested origin for the Golden Fleece tale is that wool was used to trap gold particles in early sluicing techniques.)

Goldfinch
The Christian soul or spirit – the bird most often seen in the hand of the Christ Child. Apart from its beauty and gentleness, which made it a popular children's pet, the iconography of this bird may allude to a legend that a goldfinch flew down and drew a thorn

from Christ's crown on the road to Calvary, hence the blood-red splash on the front of its head.

Gong Gong
The god of water, sometimes said to be the son of Zhu Rong, the benevolent god of fire and lord of the cosmos. In one myth, Gong Gong, a repellent creature with the body of a serpent and a human head with red hair, envied Zhu Rong's power. He tried to overthrow him, but the fire god's forces were too powerful.

Defeated, Gong Gong flew into a rage and demolished Imperfect Mountain, which supported the heavens in the northwest of the world. The collapse of the mountain left a hole in the sky and caused the world to tilt, causing floods and other disasters. Order was restored when the creator goddess Nü Gua filled in the hole in the sky and propped it up with the legs of a giant tortoise, then mended all the breached river banks.

Goose
Vigilance, loquaciousness, love, marital happiness and fidelity – a solar symbol, especially in Egypt, and also an emblem of freedom, aspiration and (through its migrations) the seasons of spring and autumn. The solar and beneficent symbolism of the wild goose is close to that of the swan, and the two are virtually interchangeable in Celtic tradition. Julius Caesar himself noted that the Gauls domesticated the goose for pleasure rather than for food. It was a masculine symbol of Celtic warriors. In Rome, too, it was linked with the war-god Mars, and became a celebrated emblem of vigilance after an incident in 390BCE when the honking of sacred geese at

the temple of Juno alerted defenders of the Capitoline Hill to an attack by the Gauls. The Greeks linked the goose with Hera, Apollo, Eros and with the messenger god Hermes. It was messenger to the gods in Egypt, too, as well as being the legendary bird that laid the cosmic egg. It became an emblem of the soul of the pharaohs (as representatives of the sun, born from the primal egg). At the accession of a new pharaoh, four geese were despatched as heralds to the cardinal points. Goose sacrifices at the December solstice symbolized the returning sun. The wild goose was a masculine solar emblem in China, but an important symbol as the lunar bird of autumn in the art of China and Japan, probably because of its migratory flights. It was the mount of Asian shamans, and of Brahma in India, representing the soul's yearning for release from *samsara*, the ceaseless round of existence.

A secondary symbolic theme, widespread in fable and folklore, is based on the domestic goose, going back to its association with the Sumerian goddess of the farmyard, Bau. Here its image is of a gossipy, mothering creature, sometimes foolish (the "silly goose" of idiom). The sexual symbolism of the goose – linked with Priapus in Greece – was also widespread, and survives in the term "goosing", suggested by the nudging outstretched neck of the amorous male.

Gorgons, The

Three sisters, Stheno, Euryale and Medusa, the monstrous offspring of Phorcys and Ceto. The Gorgons lived in the far west and were usually depicted as grotesque, grimacing monsters, although in some traditions they were beautiful. They were said to be immortal except for Medusa, who was killed by the hero Perseus. The Gorgons were the sisters of the three Graeae.

Gourd Children, The

The brother and sister who recreated the human race after its destruction in a great flood, according to the mythology of the Yao people of southern China. One day, a farmer captured the Thunder God, who was responsible for storms and floods. He warned his son and daughter not to give the god anything to drink, but the children were merciful. One drop of water revived the god and he burst free from his cage. He gave the children a tooth in gratitude and left.

The children planted the tooth and a few minutes later a plant sprouted producing an enormous gourd. In the meantime, a great flood began to cover the earth. The farmer told his son and daughter to shelter in the gourd while he built a boat and floated on the rising waters to heaven, where he appealed for an end to the deluge. The gods consented, but the flood subsided so rapidly that the farmer's boat plummeted to earth and he was killed.

The children, safe inside their gourd, were the only survivors of the flood. From this point they are referred to as Fu Xi ("Bottle Gourd"). When they were older they married and the sister adopted the name Nü Gua, which also means gourd or melon.

Later Nü Gua bore a ball of flesh which they cut into pieces and carried up the ladder to heaven. The pieces were scattered by the wind and as they landed they became people, populating the world.

Graces, The

In Greek myth the three Graces were female divinities embodying beauty, grace, charm, elegance and generosity, who attended a greater goddess, usually Aphrodite (the Roman Venus), the goddess of love, whose attributes they adopted. Their names are said to have been Aglaia ("Splendour"), Euphrosyne ("Good Cheer") and Thalia ("Jollity").

The Graces were usually said to be the daughters of the god Zeus and the sea nymph Eurynome. The depiction of three beautiful women, inspired by Classical prototypes, was popular with both painters and sculptors: famous examples are the painting by Rubens and the sculpture by Canova.

Graeae, The

Three malevolent hags, known as Deion (meaning "Terrible"), Enyo (which means "Bellicose") and Pemphredo (meaning "Spiteful"), the daughters of Phorcys and Ceto. The Graeae ("Old Women"), who lived at the foot of Mount Atlas, were said to have been born wizened and aged, possessing only one tooth and one eye between them, which they took it in turns to use. They were the sisters of the three Gorgons.

Grail, The

A romantic symbol of the heart's desire – for spiritual or physical nourishment, psychic wholeness or immortality. In the elaborate and charming medieval Arthurian legends of the Grail, its exact physical nature is as elusive as the prize itself. Originally (in France) the Grail appears as a simple serving dish with magical properties, not unlike the cornucopia of Classical myth or the Celtic magic

cauldron (the most probable pagan source for the legend). Here the Grail seems to refer to a magical restorative for the waning powers of a ruler (the Fisher King) or of Nature herself. It was also identified with the Philosopher's Stone sought by alchemists. Alternatively, it was a cup, a lance, a sword or a book.

Finally, in Christian versions, the Grail was the goblet used at the Last Supper or, in non-biblical legend, the cup of immortality once owned but lost by Adam, or the chalice in which Joseph of Arimathea was said to have caught Christ's blood as Christ was crucified. As such, the Grail became a symbol of the sacred heart of Christ, conferring divine grace. Jungian psychology has seen the Grail as a symbol of humanity's yearning to find its own centre, and as an essentially female symbol (the cup), both receiving and giving.

Grain *see* Corn

Gráinne

An Irish princess, the daughter of Cormac, the high king of Ireland. Gráinne was betrothed to the great hero Finn but eloped with Diarmaid, one of his warriors.

Grammar

One of the traditional Liberal Arts, Grammar was described as the "learned and articulate voice, spoken in a correct manner", and was traditionally depicted as a sage, or a teacher with a whip for discipline.

In the 17th century a new image emerged, showing Grammar as a woman watering plants: "Just as plants are nourished by moderate application of water in succession, in the same fashion, the mind is made to grow by properly adapted tasks."[1] This idea was taken up by Laurent de la Hyre in his painting *Allegorical Figure of Grammar*.

Granida and Daifilo

The first pastoral play written in Dutch, *Granida*, by Pieter Hooft, was performed in 1605 and inspired several artists during the 17th century. Granida, daughter of the king of Persia, lost her way while hunting and came across the shepherd Daifilo, who fell in love with her at first sight. He followed her back to court and became the page of Tisiphernes, a prince who asked for Granida's hand in marriage. Granida had several suitors and decided that the one who defeated all his rivals in a series of duels should become her husband. Daifilo fought in Tisiphernes' place and was the victor. Granida and Daifilo eloped but they were caught and taken prisoner. Tisiphernes, moved by their love, intervened and eventually Granida and Daifilo married. Gerrit van Honthorst, in *Granida and Daifilo* (1625), was perhaps the first artist to paint these lovers.

Grape *see* Vine; Wine

Grasshopper

A lucky emblem in China, linked with fertility. In countries where the natural balance is delicate, a symbol of cosmic disorder – notably in the Bible where a plague of locusts symbolizes the wrath of God.

Great Mother *see* Cybele

GREEK AND ROMAN DEITIES
see panel overleaf

Green

A generally positive symbol, as is evident even in its use as the "go" colour in modern traffic signals. Universally associated with plant life (and by extension with spring, youth, renewal, freshness, fertility and hope), green has acquired powerful new symbolic resonance as the modern emblem of ecology. Traditionally, its spiritual symbolism was most important in the Islamic world, where it was the sacred colour of the Prophet and of divine providence, and in China, where green jade symbolized perfection, immortality or longevity, strength and magical powers – a colour associated particularly with the Ming dynasty. Green is also the emblematic colour of Ireland, the "Emerald Isle", an epithet nicely linked with Celtic traditions in which good souls voyaged to the green Isle of the Blessed, the Land of Youth, *Tir nan Og*. Emerald green is a Christian emblem of faith, the reputed colour of the Holy Grail in Christianizing versions of the legend. Green appears as the colour of the Trinity, of revelation and, in early Christian art, of the Cross and sometimes of the Virgin Mary's robe.

In the pagan world, green is more widely linked with water, rain and fertility, with gods and sprites of water, and with female deities, including the goddess Aphrodite (Venus). It is a female colour in Mali and also in China. The Green Dragon of Chinese alchemy represented the Yin principle, mercury and water. The Green Lion of Western alchemy symbolized the primary state of matter.

A secondary stream of symbolism is more ambivalent. Many traditions make a distinction between dark green (a Buddhist life colour) and the

Gregory the Great, Saint

GREEK AND ROMAN
DEITIES: *see individual
names*

GREEK AND ROMAN DEITIES

The most important gods and goddesses of the Romans were adopted, directly or indirectly (for example, via the Etruscans) from the Greek pantheon. In many cases, the Roman names are those of old Italian deities whose characteristics were assimilated to those of the Greek divinities with which they came to be identified. These are some of the most important parallels:

Greek deity	Roman deity	Influences
Aphrodite	Venus	Love
Apollo	Apollo	Light; the arts; healing
Ares	Mars	War
Artemis	Diana	Hunting; chastity
Asklepios	Aesculapius	Healing
Athene	Minerva	Wisdom
Demeter	Ceres	Fertility; crops
Dionysos	Bacchus, Liber	Wine; ecstasy
Hades	Dis Pater	Ruler of the underworld
Hephaistos	Vulcan	Forge and fire
Hera	Juno	Queen of heaven; marriage
Hermes	Mercury	Commerce, communication
Hestia	Vesta	Home and hearth
Pan	Faunus	Woodlands
Persephone	Proserpina	Queen of the underworld
Poseidon	Neptune	Ruler of the seas
Zeus	Jupiter	Supreme deity; ruler of the skies

Gregory the Great, Saint: *see
Ambrose, Saint; Augustine,
Saint; Doctors; Jerome,
Saint; Michael, Saint; Trajan
Golden Legend. St Gregory*

pale greenish tinge of death. The green of the god Osiris in Egyptian iconography symbolizes his role as god both of the dead and of new life. In English idiomatic usage, green represents immaturity but also the hues of envy and jealousy – the "green-eyed monster" of Iago's warning to Othello. It is a colour of illness, but psychologically occupies a cool, neutral position in the spectrum and is often regarded as a calming "therapeutic" colour – hence its use as the colour of pharmacy. Although green is a predominant colour of nature and of the world of the sensations, it is often linked with otherworldliness – the mystic colour of fairies and little

people from outer space. Satan himself is sometimes represented as green. Perhaps this stems from the fact that green is the colour of death and putrefaction.

Gregory the Great, Saint

Gregory (*c*.540–604CE) was one of four Latin Doctors of the Church, the others being Saints Ambrose, Augustine and Jerome. Gregory was elected Pope in 590CE. He was a remarkable administrator and a prolific writer, and spent large amounts of money on those suffering through war, illness and hunger, sending missionaries throughout Europe. In 597 he sent a mission to England under St Augustine of Canterbury; according to legend Gregory saw some fair-haired Anglo-Saxon slaves in a Roman market and was struck by their handsome appearance; when he was told they were *Angli* ("Angles"), he replied, "*Non Angli, sed Angeli*" ("Not Angles, but Angels").[1]

In 590CE a plague swept through Rome. As Gregory led a procession past Hadrian's mausoleum he had a vision of the archangel Michael on the top of the tomb, who indicated that the plague would soon be over. A chapel was built on the spot and the structure was renamed the Castel Sant' Angelo. Gregory is also thought to have established what is known as the Gregorian chant. He also established the Gregorian calendar we use today, correcting the slight inaccuracy of the Julian calendar established by Julius Caesar 650 years previously.

Gregory is usually shown as an elderly pope, often with the three other Doctors of the Church. He may have a dove, which whispers in his ear, inspiring his writings. Some Flemish and German paintings of the Renaissance show him kneeling at an altar, relating to the legend that when Gregory prayed for a sign to convert a disbeliever in his congregation, Christ on the cross appeared above the altar, with the instruments of his Passion.

Grey

Abnegation, humility, melancholia, indifference and, in modern terminology, a simile for dull sobriety – possibly because in spite of its subtle beauties it is the hue that is most often thought of as colourless. Only in Hebrew tradition does it appear to be linked with the wisdom of age. As the colour of ash, it was sometimes associated with death, mourning and the soul. In Christian religious communities it symbolizes renunciation.

Griffin

A solar hybrid creature, combining the head, wings and claws of an eagle with the body of a lion. Because its two aspects symbolize rulership of air and land and together make a double emblem of the sun's power, the griffin was a forceful motif – popular at least from the second millennium BCE in western Asia, later in the Middle East, Greece and eventually Europe. It was a Hebrew symbol of Persia (the contending powers of Zoroastrianism), had demonic significance in Assyria, but seems in Crete to have played a protective role in palace decoration. In Greece, where the griffin was sacred to Apollo, to Athene as wisdom and to Nemesis as retribution,

A griffin, after an Islamic bronze statuette found in Italy.

*Detail of Guanyin, from
a decorative plate.*

legend said that griffins guarded the gold of India and of the Scythians. In early Christian iconography the griffin was used to symbolize the forces of persecution, vengeance or hindrance. But from the 14th century it emerges as an emblem of the dual nature of Christ – human and divine – and of courageous vigilance, which was its usual meaning in heraldry.

Gri-gum

The seventh human king of Tibet and the first not to return to heaven at his death. A shaman foretold that Gri-gum would die in combat. The king was furious at this prophecy and challenged his ministers to fight him so that he could prove himself the supreme warrior. The royal groom, Lo-ngam, accepted the challenge and Gri-gum prepared for the duel. To avert bad luck he wore a dead dog and fox about his shoulders and a black turban with a mirror on his brow. He was also accompanied by several yaks which were carrying bags of soot.

The duel commenced and almost immediately the yaks burst the bags with their horns, filling the air with clouds of soot. In the confusion, Gri-gum cut the divine cord by which he, like his royal predecessors, was linked to heaven. Lo-ngam could see nothing in the sooty clouds apart from the mirror on Gri-gum's forehead. He fired an arrow at it and killed the king. Because he had severed his heavenly rope, Gri-gum could not ascend to heaven and so became the first Tibetan ruler to be buried on earth.

Grotesque

The term, derived from the Italian *grotta* (meaning "cave"), originated at the end of the 15th century, when lavishly decorated chambers were discovered in the Golden House of Nero (1st century CE). This style of decoration interweaves humans, animals, flowers and foliage, classical urns and motifs. It was especially popular in the 16th century.

Gu

A divine blacksmith culture hero, the son of the twin creator deities Mawu and Lisa, according to the Fon people of Benin. Lisa, the male twin, took Gu to earth and gave him the task of assisting humanity. He instructed people in ironworking and toolmaking so that they could practise agriculture and make dwellings and clothes.

Guanyin

The Chinese Buddhist goddess of mercy. The deity Guanyin is derived from Avalokiteshvara, the Indian (male) bodhisattva of compassion, who in China was considered an embodiment of positive motherly qualities. Mothers also prayed to her to protect their children and she was the goddess of all those in distress.

Guarini, Giovanni (*Il Pastor Fido*)

The play *Il Pastor Fido* (The Faithful Shepherd) of 1590 by Giovanni Guarini, which combines tragedy and comedy, provided artists with pastoral scenes populated by beautiful nymphs. Mirtillo, disguised as a woman, joins the game of kissing the nymph Amarillis and at his turn falls in love with her. Amarillis awards him the crown of victory, but he places it on her head, saying that it was her kisses that had made his so sweet.[1] The scene was illustrated by van Dyck in *Amaryllis and Mirtillo*.

The play includes a satyr who grabs the nymph Corisca by the hair, accusing her of deceiving him, but she eludes him by wearing a wig. Meanwhile, the nymph Dorinda is in love with the rich, gallant and beautiful Silvio, who enjoys only the hunt and is unaffected by love. Dorinda, disguised as a shepherd to be near her love, falls asleep under a bush; Silvio unwittingly shoots her with an arrow.

Gucumatz *see* **Kukulkan**

Guilds of Florence, The
In the early Renaissance the guilds of mercantile Florence were leading patrons of the building and decoration of many of the city's principal monuments. For example, they commissioned statues of their patron saints to fill the niches of Orsanmichele, the guilds' church. These included St George, patron saint of the Guild of Armourers; the Four Crowned Martyrs, the Stonemasons and Woodworkers; St Philip, the Shoemakers; St Peter, the Butchers; St Luke, the Lawyers; St Joseph, the Furriers; St Mark, the Linen-workers; St Eligius, the Smiths; St Matthew, the Bankers; St John the Evangelist, the Silk Guild; and St Stephen, the Wool Guild. They also commissioned a statue of St John the Baptist, who was the patron saint of the Cloth Merchants' Guild, as well as of the city itself.

Gwydion
A magician of Welsh myth, the nephew of Math, lord of Gwynedd, and a prominent character in the fourth branch of the *Mabinogion*. Whenever Math was not at war he had to keep his feet in the lap of a vir-

gin. Gwydion's brother, Gilfaethwy, wanted to seduce the maiden, so Gwydion distracted Math's attention by conjuring up a war with neighbouring Dyfed. When Math returned and discovered his nephews' trickery, he transformed them into animals for three years.

Later, after Gwydion had become human once more, he assisted Math in creating a beautiful woman out of flowers as a wife for the hero Lleu Llaw Gyffes. The woman, who was called Blodeuwedd, was unfaithful to Lleu and with her lover, Gronw Pebyr, plotted to kill him. They succeeded only in wounding the hero and he escaped in the form of an eagle. Gwydion restored Lleu to human form before killing Gronw Pebyr and turning Blodeuwedd into an owl.

Gyges and Candaules
According to Herodotus, Gyges was the bodyguard of Candaules, king of Lydia in Asia Minor the 7th century BCE. Candaules thought that his wife was the most beautiful woman in the world. To prove her beauty, he asked Gyges to watch her undressing. Gyges was unwilling because "with the stripping off of her tunic, a woman is stripped of the honour due to her". The king, however, insisted. Jacob Jordaens' *King Candaules of Lydia Showing his Wife to Gyges* shows the naked queen about to climb into bed, while the two men peep around the curtain. The story continues that the queen noticed Gyges slipping away and later confronted him. She made him choose, to save his honour, either to die in disgrace or to kill the king and marry her. Gyges chose the latter course, thereby making himself master of Candaules' wife and kingdom.

Guilds of Florence, The: *see* individual names of saints

Gwydion: *see* Blodeuwedd; Lleu Llaw Gyffes; Math; *Mabinogion, The*

Gyges and Candaules: Herodotus, *I:8–12*

Habakkuk

The god Hachiman.

Habakkuk

In the biblical *Book of Habakkuk* the prophet prays to God for revenge on the oppressors of his people. Donatello's sculpture *Habakkuk* shows the prophet's harrowed features, while Bernini's of the same name depicts the story of him taking pottage to Daniel in the lions' den. Habakkuk was transported from Judea by an angel who "carried him by the hair of his head".[1] Habakkuk delivered his food to Daniel and was then returned to Judea by the angel.

Habit

A cowled robe symbolizing vows of poverty in Christianity and Islam. It has particular significance in Arabia: the *khirka* (a sacred woollen robe) of Sufi mystics marked the entry of the initiate after three years into the community of ascetics, judged able to follow the Law, the Way and the Truth.

Hachiman

The Japanese god of war, the deified Emperor Ojin (died *c*.AD394), who was renowned for his military prowess. In many parts of Japan, men still mark their coming of age by visiting one of the god's shrines.

Hades

The Greek god who ruled the Underworld, the son of Kronos and Rhea and the brother of Demeter, Hera, Hestia, Poseidon and Zeus. His Roman equivalent was called Pluto or Dis Pater. Hades had no home on Mount Olympus and was not generally counted among the Olympians. Hades, whose name means "The Unseen", rarely left the underworld, but his most famous excursion was to kidnap Persephone and make her his wife. Hades presided in grim-faced majesty over his domain, where dead mortals were judged and punished. However, he was also the lord of the riches within the earth, hence his alternative name Pluto ("Wealth"). His cult stressed this and was sometimes linked with that of the goddess Demeter, the mother of Persephone.

Hades later became the name of the

Hades with Persephone; after a Greek vase painting.

Underworld itself: a gloomy region whose entrance was guarded by the three-headed dog Cerberus. It was reached through natural chasms and was situated on the further shore of one of the five rivers of Hades, the Styx (hate), across which the souls of the dead were ferried by Charon. The other rivers of Hades were the Acheron (woe), Cocytus (wailing), Lethe (forgetfulness), and Phlegethon (fire). Minos was the judge of dead souls, directing them to their final abode, which for most was the dreary Plain of Asphodel. Virtuous souls were rewarded with the paradisal Fields of Elysium. However, gloomy Tartarus, where unbearable torments were only temporarily eased by Orpheus' music, was the destiny for those who had outraged the gods. It is this last area that equates with the Christian perception of hell, and was painted in Pieter Bruegel the Younger's *Rape of Persephone*.

Hair

Life force, strength – a deeply significant aspect of the human body both socially and personally, as can be seen from the wide range of symbolism attached to different hair styles. The power symbolism of hair growth is famously exemplified by Samson, a warrior of the ancient Hebrew Nazarite sect whose long hair was a sign both of charismatic holiness and physical strength. The Khalsa community of Sikhs let their hair and beards grow for similar symbolic reasons. In many societies long hair was a mark of royal power or of liberty and independence, as among the Gauls and other Celtic peoples. Long, loose hair in women signified the unmarried state, or virginity – as in Christian iconography of the Virgin Mary and virgin saints – compared with the braided hair of the courtesan. Alternatively, as in Russia, a single braid marked the maiden, double braids the wife. Letting down bound hair was a permissive sexual signal.

Whereas body hair was usually associated purely with physical virility or lower states of being (hairiness is a devilish attribute in Christian art), head hair was intimately linked with the individual spirit or vital force of a person – an idea that accounts for the custom of keeping locks of hair. In ancient Greece, taking a lock of hair from a dead person released its soul into the underworld. Scalping, in Native American warfare, removed an enemy's power, the braves daringly leaving a lock of hair on their shaven heads for this purpose. Islamic custom was to leave a tuft by which the faithful could be drawn upward into paradise. Although hermits traditionally let their hair grow, many religious orders have followed the priestly Egyptian custom of shaving the hair as a symbol of submission to God or renunciation of the material world.

Hair: *see* Black; Castration; Gold; Head; LIBERTY; Red; Scalp

Submission (to the Manchus) was also the original symbolism of the Chinese pigtail. Cutting hair was close to a castration symbol in ancient China – and remains a resented symbol of conformity to military discipline in some countries. In different traditions, cutting, growing or tearing out hair has symbolized grief. Hair colour has its own symbolism, red hair once having demonic associations and golden hair standing for solar or kingly power, black for terrestrial. Dishevelled hair can symbolize asceticism – an attribute of Shiva who appears with wild locks. Nowadays, long, cropped or bizarre hair styles are fashionable symbols of protest, non-conformity or clan identification.

Halo

A circular radiance around the head widely used in Christian art from the 5th and 15th centuries CE to symbolize the divinity or sanctity of the members of the Trinity, the Holy Family, saints and angels. The convention was based on the nimbus surrounding the sun's disc and was adapted from pagan images of sun gods or deified rulers, particularly from the iconography of Mithraism, which Christianity supplanted in the Roman Empire. The "floating ring" image of a halo was a later form.

Although they are commonly depicted as circular, those of Christ or God the Father may actually be triangular to represent the Trinity; Christ might also have a cross behind his head for a halo. An aureole or mandorla – a larger area of light, sometimes surrounding the whole figure – is reserved for God the Father, Christ and the Virgin. Haloes were little used after the Baroque period.

Hammer

A creative–destructive symbol of male strength, linked with the power of the sun and thunderbolts, with sovereign authority, gods of war and beneficent artisan gods. The hammer seldom appears as a symbol of brute force alone (although King Edward I of England was called "The Hammer of the Scots" for his savage treatment of them). Even the mighty stone hammer of the Norse god Thor, which he could throw unerringly to kill or use to smite valleys out of mountain chains, could be put to use as a protective emblem on gravestones or to suggest the authority by which contracts or marriages were solemnized.

In the hands of the Greek god Hephaistos (the Roman Vulcan), the hammer was an instrument of divine skill, an emblem of the creative vigour that drives the chisel or shapes metal. This is the meaning of its use in Freemasonry as an attribute of the Lodge Master, symbolizing creative intelligence. The hammer (industry) and sickle (agriculture) emblem of Soviet Russia was likewise chosen as a forceful image of productive work.

In China the hammer was a symbol of the sovereign power to shape society. There and in India, its destructiveness was linked with the conquest of evil. It was also a symbol of protection against fire. A noisy tool, the hammer was widely linked with thunder (as for example in the case of Thor) and by extension, owing to the rain that often follows thunder, with fecundity. This may explain the link between the Celtic Hammer God and fertility. In Japan the hammer is an emblem of wealth (linked with the recovery of gold), an attribute of the prosperity god Daikoku.

Christ with a halo combined with a cross, a popular form of halo in early medieval and Byzantine art.

Hammer God, The

The name given to a widespread Celtic god, particularly popular in Gaul. His Celtic name is uncertain, but one or two Gaulish representations bear the name Sucellus ("Good Striker"). One of these shows him as consort of the goddess Nantosuelta. He was usually depicted as a bearded man in a tunic and cloak, holding a long-handled hammer in one hand and a pot in the other. The Hammer God had attributes connected with fertility and the goodness of nature.

Han Xiang

One of the Eight Immortals of Chinese Daoist (Taoist) myth. Han Xiang was said to be the great-nephew of Han Yü, a philosopher and essayist of the Tang dynasty (618–907CE). He embarked on his search for the Dao, the Daoist principle of existence, as the pupil of the Immortal Lü Dongbin, who later escorted him to heaven to eat the peaches of eternal life. Han Xiang began to climb the peach tree, but slipped and plummeted to earth. As he was about to hit the ground he achieved immortality.

Han Zhongli

One of the Eight Immortals of Daoist myth. Han Zhongli was an elderly man who lived during the Han dynasty (202BC–AD220). He learned the Dao, the Daoist principle of existence, from Li Xuan, the first Immortal, and was the messenger of heaven.

Hand

Power (temporal and spiritual), action, strength, domination, protection – a general symbolism that reflects the hand's executive role in human life and the belief that it can transmit spiritual as well as physical energy. The hand was sometimes an image forceful enough to stand alone in iconography, as a motif in cave paintings, for example, or in Christian paintings of God's hand appearing from the clouds. In Islam, the open Hand of Fatima (the daughter of Muhammad) proclaims the five fundamentals: faith, prayer, pilgrimage, fasting and charity. The Hand of Atum was a fertility emblem in Egypt, stimulating the original life-giving semen from the body of the male–female creator god. Because the number five was linked with the underworld in ancient Mexico, a hand with fingers spread was a death icon. The Red Hand of Ulster became the badge not only of the province but of baronetcy (a title instituted to raise money for Ulster's defence).

Belief that the hands of kings, religious leaders or miracle workers had beneficial power existed from ancient times; hence the laying on of hands in healing or in religious blessing, confirmation and ordination. Talismanic use of the hands extended to the grisly practice of thieves, carrying the severed right hand of a hanged criminal for nefarious good luck.

Except in China and Japan, where the left hand signifies honour, the right hand is widely favoured; one Celtic ruler was deposed after he lost his right hand in battle. Christ sits on the right hand of God, who dispenses mercy with the right, justice with the left. In Occidental tradition, the right hand symbolized frankness, logic, the left duplicity (white magic versus black). Similarly, the right hand blesses, the left curses. The right is sometimes scaled up by artists, as in Michelangelo's *David* (1501).

Han Xiang: *see* Eight Immortals, The; Lü Dongbin

Han Zhongli: *see* Eight Immortals, The; Li Xuan

Hand: *see* Christ, The Life of; Eye; Five; Glove; Left and Right; Mudras; Pantocrator; Passion of Christ, The

Exodus 33:20

The Hand of Fatima, from an Islamic engraved pendant.

*Hanuman, from an
Indian stone sculpture.*

References to the hand of God are numerous in the Bible. A hand in painting often represents God the Father, because of an implicit prohibition on depicting his head: "Thou canst not see my face; for no man shall see me and live."[1] God's hand may be seen releasing the dove, a symbol of the Holy Spirit, at the Annunciation to the Virgin. A hand paying Judas the thirty pieces of silver or holding a bag of coins denotes the Betrayal of Christ. A hand also became an Instrument of the Passion owing to the scene in which Christ's face was slapped during his mockery; this incident is shown in a fresco by Fra Angelico in San Marco, Florence. Traditionally, the right hand was considered powerful, the left weak

Although the conceptual link between hand and power (words synonymous in ancient Hebrew) is overwhelmingly important in pictorial symbolism, it is only one aspect of the much more extensive and varied symbolism of hand gestures. These form in Hindu and Buddhist *mudras* an entire symbolic language involving hundreds of hand and finger shapes and positions deployed in religious ritual, dance and theatre.

Hand gestures of fairly widespread significance (more signals than symbols) include the following: clenched – threat, aggressive force, secrecy, power (the raised fist of Black Power); open and raised with the palm outward – blessing, peace, protection (the right hand of the Buddha is often shown thus); raised, three fingers open – the Christian Trinity; raised, thumb and two fingers open – pledge or oath; both raised (orant) – adoration, prayer, receptiveness to celestial grace, surrender (now, less humbly, a victor's

receptiveness to applause); covered or concealed – respect; folded – tranquillity; palms upward, laid on each other – meditation (the upward palm signifying both giving and receiving); palms together – prayer, supplication, greeting, humility; on breast – submission (also an attitude of the sage).

The left fist placed in the right hand was a submissive signal in parts of Africa. Placing both your hands in the hands of another person is a more widespread gesture of trust or submission (as in feudal contracts to serve a lord). Clasping hands is an almost universal symbol of friendship, fraternity, welcome, agreement, congratulation, reconciliation or, in marriage, faithful love.

Palmists claim to be able to read more of a person's character and destiny in the hands than in the face. In iconography, an eye in a palm is a symbol of clairvoyance or, in Buddhism, of compassionate wisdom.

Hannibal

A great Carthaginian leader, Hannibal (247–182BCE) marched an army reported to consist of 90,000 infantry, 12,000 cavalry and a number of elephants across the Alps in 218BCE during the second Punic War against Rome. In *Snow Storm: Hannibal and his Army Crossing the Alps* Turner shows how the mighty army, which astounded the Romans, also had to battle with the forces of nature.

Hanuman

A monkey who became the most loyal companion of the Hindu god Rama and his consort Sita. When Sita was abducted by Ravana, the evil king of Lanka, Rama and his brother Lakshmana set off to find her. They encountered Hanuman, a minister of the exiled monkey king Sugriva. Hanuman led a party of monkeys to hunt for Sita. He heard that she was imprisoned on the island of Lanka and leaped over the sea, where he found Sita and showed her a ring which Rama had given him as a token.

Hanuman allowed himself to be caught by Ravana's son. Ravana then ordered that the monkey's tail be set alight as a punishment for his actions, but Hanuman used his flaming tail to burn down Ravana's kingdom. When Rama and Lakshmana were injured in the ensuing battle, Hanuman went to the Himalaya to fetch healing plants. Hanuman's dedication to Rama knew no bounds: once he tore open his chest to show Rama and Sita in his heart.

HARES AND RABBITS *see panel overleaf*

Harp

Purity and poetry – the instrument of the angelic choirs, of King David, and pre-eminently of the Celtic world (hence the harp emblems of Wales and Ireland). The Daghda, the great father god, played a magic harp. Harpstrings formed a ladder symbol of ascent to paradise in the lays of Norway and Iceland. In the Hell panel of *The Garden of Earthly Delights* (*c*.1495), Bosch used the harp as a memorable image of spiritual anguish by showing a figure crucified on the strings.

Harpy

In mythology a harpy was a monster with a woman's face and breasts and the body, claws and wings of a bird. Harpies defiled everything they touched and were thought to be the grasping, greedy administrators of the gods, or the beasts that snatched the soul away at death. Mantegna's *Allegory of the Fall of Ignorant Humanity* shows them supporting a globe on which the fat figure of Ignorance sits holding a rudder, flanked by blindfolded Ingratitude and scrawny Avarice.

Hart *see* Deer

Harvest

Harvesting may be part of a scene representing August or summer, and may represent nature's abundance. However, Jean-François Millet's *The Gleaners* subverts the usual mood: the peasants are so poor that they have to collect the remains left by the harvesters.

Hate

Hate is the pale, filthy guide of Calumny, who is the personification of slander. Mantegna depicted Hate, Fraud, Malice, Jealousy and Suspicion in *Minerva Expelling the Vices from the Garden of Virtue*. In this painting, Hate is a monkey-like hermaphrodite with only one breast. Four bags containing the seeds of evil hang from the creature's shoulders.

Hathor

A powerful and complex Egyptian goddess with numerous attributes. Hathor was the protector of women, whom she assisted in conception and childbirth. As the guardian of children, she suckled the young god Horus in the form of a cow, and later restored his sight after the god Seth had torn out his eyes. Hathor was associated with death and rebirth. She greeted the souls of the dead in the underworld and offered them food and drink. She

Harp: *see* Angels

Harvest: *see* SEASONS; TIME

Hate: *see* Calumny

Hathor: *see* Bastet; Horus; Sekhmet; Taweret

Hathor, from a mural, c.14th century BCE.

HARES AND RABBITS

The hare or rabbit features in almost every mythology as trickster, culture hero or fertility symbol. The animals are noted universally for their swiftness and playful behaviour, and they occur in myth as cunning jokers who outwit bigger but less agile creatures. The American folklore character Brer Rabbit represents a fusion of a trickster hare brought to North America by West African slaves and a Native American rabbit trickster of the southeast.

The trickster's stratagems often backfire, as in the Japanese story of the White Rabbit, who tricked a family of crocodiles into forming a bridge for him to cross from an island to the Japanese mainland. As he approached the last crocodile in the line he gleefully boasted of his trickery, at which the angry crocodile caught him and skinned him alive.

Sometimes the rabbit or hare plays the part of a culture hero, employing trickery to bring benefits to humanity; the Muskogean Creek people of Oklahoma (originally of Georgia and Alabama) told how the Rabbit stole fire from the Fire People.

Rabbits and hares are often linked with fertility, lust and vitality. In ancient Greece rabbits were seen as the attributes of Aphrodite, the goddess of love and sexuality. The creatures are widely associated with the moon, itself a symbol of feminine fecundity. The Germanic fertility goddess known in Anglo-Saxon as Eostra (hence the word Easter) owned a hare in the moon which laid eggs, symbolizing renewed life, around the time of her springtime festival – hence Easter eggs and the Easter rabbit.

The sexual and tricksterish aspects of the rabbit are brought together in the group of Aztec deities known as the Centzon Totochtin or "Four Hundred Rabbits".

In many parts of Asia and the Americas the equivalent of "the man in the moon" is traditionally said to be a rabbit or a hare.

The hare in the moon of Chinese myth, mixing the elixir of immortality.

was also the protector of lovers. In later centuries she became indistinguishable from Isis, many of whose attributes she shared.

Hawk *see* Falcon, Hawk

Hawthorn
A tree and flower invested with magical properties in Europe from Classical times when hawthorn was linked with Hymen, the god of marriage. The flowers were used for wedding garlands, the wood for marriage torches. The link between the hawthorn's spring flowering and virginity led to folk superstitions that it protected chastity. However, the faintly fishy perfume of the flowers was said by some to augur death if brought indoors.

Hazel

Fertility, water, supernatural powers of divination and wisdom. In northern Europe and the Celtic world, the hazel wand was the instrument of wizards and fairies, diviners and seekers of gold. A Classical tradition suggested it to be the rod of Hermes, messenger of the gods. Its mystic symbolism may derive both from the deep roots of the hazel (mysterious powers of the underworld) and from the berries (secret wisdom).

Apart from its use in incantation, the hazel had strong fertility and rain symbolism, was thought to bring luck to lovers, and according to Norman folklore, drew abundant milk from cows struck with a hazel ring.

He Xiangu

The eighth of the Eight Immortals of Chinese Daoist myth and the only one who was unambiguously female. She attained immortality after eating a "mother-of-pearl stone" which a spirit told her was to be found on the mountain where she dwelt.

Head

The ruling organ of reason and thought, but also the manifestation of a person's spirit, power, or life force – a significance that accounts for the ancient value placed upon the severed head of an enemy. For many peoples, including Celtic warriors who wore heads as trophies, the head had fertility or phallic symbolism and was thought to transmit the strength and courage of the decapitated warrior to its new owner. In iconography, the head of a god, king or hero, mounted on a pillar, shown on a coin, or used as a funerary emblem, embodied his or her power to influence events.

For Plato, the sphere of the head represented a human microcosm. In many traditions the head replaces the heart as the presumed location of the soul. In monster or animal/god symbols, it may indicate which part of the hybrid is dominant. Artists could increase the force of an image by multiplying heads or faces, sometimes to indicate different functions. Thus in Roman iconography, three-headed Hecate moved between heaven, earth and the underworld, two-faced Janus watched over entrances and exits, past and future, travellers leaving and returning. The four heads of Brahma refer to the four Hindu Vedas, the four ram heads of Amun-Ra to his rulership of all the elements.

In art, the Greek twins Castor and Polydeuces (Pollux) shown one looking up and one down symbolized ascending and descending phases of heavenly bodies. Images combining male and female heads had protective symbolism in Egypt. Headdresses (crowns, wreaths or caps) and head movements – bowed in submission, raised in pride – have particular significance in human gesture.

Heart

The symbolic source of the affections – love, compassion, charity, joy or sorrow – but also of spiritual illumination, truth and intelligence. It was often equated with the soul. Many ancient traditions, did not make a sharp distinction between feelings and thought. A person who "let the heart rule the head" would once have seemed sensible rather than foolish. Symbolically, the heart was the body's sun, animating all. Ritual application of this belief led the Aztecs to sacrifice thousands of hearts to the sun each year to

Hebe: *see* Hera; Herakles;
ZEUS, THE CONSORTS
OF

Hecate: *see*
UNDERWORLDS
¹ Ovid, *Fasti I:141–144*

restore its power. As a symbol of what is most essential in a human being, the heart was left in the eviscerated bodies of Egyptian mummies. It would be weighed in the underworld to see if it was heavy with misdeeds or light enough to pass on to paradise.

A heart most commonly symbolizes divine love and understanding because "the Lord seeth not as man seeth; for man looketh on the outward appearance, but the Lord looketh on the heart".¹ The heart is an emblem of truth, conscience or moral courage in many religions – the temple or throne of God in Islamic and Judeo-Christian thought; the divine centre, or *atman*, and the Third Eye of transcendent wisdom in Hinduism; the diamond of purity and essence of the Buddha; the Daoist centre of understanding.

The "Sacred Heart" of Christ became a focus of Roman Catholic worship as a symbol of the Lord's redeeming love, sometimes shown pierced by nails and with a crown of thorns, in reference to the Crucifixion and mocking of Jesus as "King of the Jews". A heart crowned with thorns is

Hebe, after an ancient vase painting.

also the emblem of the Jesuit saint Ignatius Loyola; while a flaming heart is the attribute of SS Augustine and Antony of Padua. A heart on fire is a key symbol of the ardent Christian but also an attribute in art of Charity and of profane passion – as in Renaissance paintings of the Greek goddess Aphrodite (in Roman myth, Venus). The heart transfixed by Eros's (Cupid's) arrow was another Renaissance theme, which became the motif of St Valentine's Day – a mid-February festival with pagan rather than Christian roots. In iconography, the heart takes on a vase-like shape, or is graphically represented by an inverted

The weighing of the deceased's heart against the feather of truth; after an Egyptian papyrus.

triangle, symbolizing something into which love is poured or carried; in this sense it is linked with the Holy Grail.

Heaven *see* AFTERLIFE; God

Hebe

"Youth", the goddess of youth and daughter of Zeus and Hera (Jupiter and Juno to the Romans). Hebe (Juventas to the Romans) lived on Mount Olympus, where she looked after Hera's peacocks and was handmaiden and cupbearer to the gods. Adolph Diez shows the beautiful young girl as the cupbearer of Jupiter in *Juventas with Jupiter in the Guise of an Eagle*. She became the divine wife of the hero Herakles after his death.

Hecate

The Greek goddess Hecate was usually said to be the daughter of the Titans Coeus and Phoebe. She resided in the underworld, where she oversaw ritual purifications as well as magical invocations. Sorceresses such as Medea drew power from her. At night she was thought to hold burning torches at crossroads, accompanied by ghosts and hell-hounds. Later, she was depicted as having three bodies, which stood back-to-back looking in different directions.[1] She appears in Shakespeare's *Macbeth* with three witches and was illustrated by Blake in his engravings of the play.

Hector

A Trojan prince, the son of King Priam and Queen Hecuba and brother of Paris. Homer's *Iliad* portrays Hector, a leading Trojan warrior, as a man of great fortitude and compassion who is more decisive and righteous than his elder brother Paris.

Hector's rivalry with the hero Achilles, the best Greek warrior, is a central theme of the *Iliad* and forms its climax. When Achilles quarrelled with his commander, Agamemnon, and withdrew from the fighting, Hector took advantage of his absence to push the Greeks back to their ships, wounding and killing many heroes. Patroclus, Achilles' best friend, led a successful Greek counterattack but was killed by Hector, causing Achilles to return to the battle to avenge Patroclus' death. The Trojan warrior Polydamas advised Hector to avoid a confrontation with Achilles but Hector refused to retreat. Achilles pursued Hector three times around the city walls before finally killing him in single combat. He then desecrated Hector's corpse by tying it by the feet to his chariot and dragging it daily around the tomb of Patroclus. Achilles refused to give up the corpse until the gods angrily forced him to accept a ransom from Hector's father. The *Iliad* ends with Hector's funeral.

Hecuba

A queen of Troy, the wife of King Priam and the mother of Paris, Hector, Cassandra, Troilus and, according to some accounts, fourteen other children. Hecuba dreamed one night that she gave birth to a flaming torch which set the city on fire, so when Paris was born he was abandoned, setting in motion the events which culminated in the Trojan War. Hecuba remained largely in the background during the conflict except to mourn her son Hector's death. After the fall of Troy and the slaughter of her husband and sons, she was taken into slavery by the victorious Greeks.

Heh and Hehet *see* Ogdoad, The

Heimdall

A Norse deity, also known as the White God. Heimdall was the offspring of nine giant maidens who may have been personifications of waves, and so he probably belonged to the Vanir, the divinities associated with the waters and the earth. He was renowned for his vigilance and acute hearing – he could see at night and hear the sound of grass growing – and kept unceasing watch over Bifrost, the bridge leading to Asgard, home of the gods. Heimdall's chief opponent was the god Loki, who eventually killed him. This act heralded the beginning of Ragnarok, the cosmic battle ending the old divine order.

Hekatoncheires, The

"One Hundred Hands", the name given to three giants with a hundred hands and fifty heads each. Named Cottus, Briareus and Gyges, they were the offspring of the goddess Gaia, the earth, and the god Uranos, the sky. To prevent their births Uranos forced them back into the earth, together with their brothers, the Cyclopes and Titans. They were released by the

Hel

Titan Kronos when he overthrew Uranos, but Kronos then reimprisoned them in the underworld. Freed by Zeus, they assisted him in the defeat of the Titans, who, some say, they later guarded in the underworld.

Hel

The Norse goddess of the underworld land of the dead, which was itself often referred to as Hel. In some accounts she was the daughter of Loki and was a sinister figure, said to be half black and half flesh-coloured.

Helen of Troy

Outstandingly beautiful, Helen was believed to be the daughter of the Greek god Zeus and Leda, whom he ravished in the form of a swan. As a result of this coupling, Leda produced two eggs. From one sprang Polydeuces and Helen, and from the other Castor and Clytemnestra. In some accounts, Zeus was the father of only Polydeuces and Helen.

Helen grew up at the court of Leda's husband, King Tyndareos of Sparta. Her beauty attracted many princely suitors. One of them, Odysseus, persuaded Tyndareos to make all the suitors swear to uphold the honour of Helen's choice as a husband. She married Menelaus, brother of Agamemnon and adopted heir of Tyndareos.

A decade later the Trojan prince Paris, who had been promised the hand of Helen by the goddess Aphrodite for judging her more beautiful than Athene or Hera, visited Sparta. Menelaus was called away to Crete and returned to find that the visitor had eloped to Troy with his wife. He journeyed to Troy with Odysseus to demand Helen's return; his appeal was rebuffed, and Helen and Paris married.

Helen of Troy, after an 5th-century BCE Greek drinking vessel.

True to their oath, all Helen's former suitors determined to avenge the insult to Menelaus – and this series of events began the Trojan War.[1] According to most accounts, after the Trojan War, Helen was reconciled with Menelaus and together they returned to Sparta.

Helena (Helen), Saint

The empress Helena (*c.*255–330CE) was the mother of Constantine, the first Christian emperor of Rome. Toward the end of her life she made a pilgrimage to the Holy Land, where she donated large amounts of money to the poor and founded churches on holy sites. According to legend,[1] Helena brought to Rome the hay from the manger in which the Christ Child had lain. She also brought to Constantinople the bodies of the Magi, which were later taken to Milan and then Cologne. She is said to have discovered the wood of the True Cross on which Christ was crucified, and may be shown in scenes of the wood's discovery. In a painting by Cornelis Engelbrechtsz she appears beside Constantine, holding a cross and wearing imperial dress.

Heliodorous

In the Apocrypha,[1] Heliodorus, treasurer to the Syrian king, was sent to Jerusalem to sequester funds from the Temple of Solomon that had been collected for widows and orphans. Raphael's *Expulsion of Heliodorus from the Temple* (Stanza di Eliodoro, Vatican) shows how, once Heliodorus had taken the money, the priests prayed and God sent a horse and rider, with two companions, who charged, driving Heliodorus to the ground. This was seen by the Church as an example of divine intervention.

Helios in his chariot, from a relief of c.300BCE.

Helios

"The Sun", the Greek god personifying the sun, the offspring of the Titans Hyperion and Theia. From his palace beyond the eastern horizon, he was said to drive his chariot westward across the sky. He returned home at night in a great cup that sailed on Ocean, the great river surrounding the world. The daily arrival of Helios was announced by the dawn goddess Eos . Helios appears in few myths, most notably in the story of Phaëthon.

Heliotrope

Adoration – a meaning suggested by the plant's turning toward the sun. The heliotrope had solar symbolism in Roman and Asian imperial wreaths and was a Christian emblem of religious devotion, an attribute of saints and prophets. In Greek myth, the lovesick girl Clytie was transformed into a heliotrope – for ever following the object of her hopeless passion, the sun god Helios.

Hell

In the New Testament Christ speaks of the unquenchable fire reserved for unbelievers, proclaiming that he "will send his angels, and they will gather ... all the evil doers, and throw them into a furnace of fire and there shall be wailing and gnashing of teeth".[1] At the Last Judgment he will condemn those who have not lived according to the seven acts of mercy, saying, "Depart from me, ye cursed, into everlasting fire, prepared for the devil and his angels."[2]

In depictions of the Last Judgment hell is always to the bottom right of the composition – that is, on Christ's left – so that the good can rise on his strong right side. The entrance to hell may be depicted as the jaws of the gaping monster Leviathan. The infernal realm may be filled with flames and monsters or composed of successive circles of the damned, as described in Dante's *Inferno*, illustrated closely by Botticelli. Alternatively, groups of the damned are organized and tortured according to which of the seven deadly sins they have committed. In Michelangelo's *Last Judgment* (Sistine Chapel, Vatican, Rome) Charon, ferryman of the Underworld, and Minos, judge of the dead, are borrowed from Hades, the ancient Greek predecessor of hell.

Hellen

The mythical ancestor of the Greek nation, the Hellenes. He was the son of Deucalion and Pyrrha, the only survivors of a great flood sent by Zeus to destroy humanity. Hellen and his wife Orseis had three sons, Aeolus, Dorus and Xuthus, from whom it was said that the various Greek peoples were descended.

Helmet

Invisible power, in particular the power of death represented by the helmet of Hades. The helmet can also symbolize thought. More obviously, it is the protective attribute of warriors or warrior divinities such as the Nordic Odin, and the Greek Ares (in Roman myth, Mars) and Athene (Minerva), and of heroes such as Perseus, whose winged helmet of invisibility enabled him to escape after slaying the Gorgon Medusa. In art the figures of Fortune and Faith are usually shown helmeted.

Hen

In Africa, a guide to the underworld, sacrificially used to call up spirits. In Europe a symbol of fussy, mothering care. A hen with chicks was a Christian image of divine providence. More rarely, the hen represents the personification Charity.

Hephaistos

The god of fire and forge, the divine smith. Hephaistos (or Hephaestus; Vulcan to the Romans) was the son either of Zeus and Hera or, according to most accounts, of Hera alone. It was said that the goddess bore him without a father in retaliation for Zeus giving birth to the goddess Athene without a mother. However, in other versions Hephaistos, born before Athene, eased her birth by splitting Zeus' head open with his axe. Either way, the two deities were linked as patrons of the arts and crafts.

Hephaistos was born lame and ugly, and Hera felt such shame that she hurled him from Mount Olympus into the great river Ocean which encircled the earth. He was rescued by the sea nymphs Thetis and Eurynome and raised by them for nine years, during which time he acquired his knowledge of craftsmanship. The god

grew up and sent Hera a beautifully wrought golden throne, but as soon as she sat on it she was bound by invisible cords, which only Hephaistos could loosen. He refused to return to Olympus and free his mother unless he was able to marry the goddess of love, Aphrodite (Venus). Dionysos got him drunk and led him to Olympus on a mule. The other deities laughed at the sight – Hephaistos was often portrayed as milder than the other Olympians and often the butt of their mockery. Once home, he freed Hera and was permitted to wed Aphrodite.

Hephaistos, who was usually shown wearing a craftsman's tunic, created Pandora, the first woman, and made countless other beautiful and magical things. He made ingenious works of art in metal for the gods, and for mortals at the request of the gods; these included magnificently decorated shields for both Achilles and (according to Virgil) Aeneas.¹ Boucher illustrated this in *Venus at Vulcan's Forge Asking for Arms for her Son, Aeneas*. The god also made for Jupiter a complete set of armour, for which he was promised whatever he wanted as a reward. Hephaistos asked for the chaste goddess Athene, but Zeus warned her of impending trouble. Hephaistos tried to rape her, but she fought him off and his semen fell to the earth, from which Erichthonius was born.

Although Hephaistos succeedd in marrying Aphrodite, she was constantly unfaithful to him. One humorous story describes how Hephaistos fashioned an invisible net to trap her in an adulterous embrace with Ares (Mars). Hephaistos exposed them to the gods who, to his discomfort, were greatly amused. Hermes antagonized him further by saying how much he would like to take Ares' place.[2]

In paintings, Hephaistos's deformity is usually apparent; he often appears half-naked and dishevelled at his forge, holding a hammer about to strike an anvil, or with a thunderbolt held in pincers; or he may be blowing the flames, his face black with smoke.

The god's forge was located either on or near Mount Olympus, or underground (especially in volcanic areas), or on Lemnos, one of his cult centres. His assistants were the Cyclopes. The Romans claimed that his smithy was beneath Mount Etna. Appropriately, he appears above fireplaces, as in Peruzzi's *Vulcan at his Forge* (Villa Farnesina, Rome).

Hera

In Greek myth, the supreme goddess of Olympus, the sister and wife of Zeus. Hera (which may mean "Lady") was worshipped as the upholder of the sanctity of marriage and was also associated with fertility and childbirth. Called Juno by the Romans, she was a great goddess in her own right, but most myths about her concentrate on her tempestuous relationship with her often adulterous husband, Zeus (Jupiter). She is portrayed as jealous and angry, constantly watchful of Zeus and ready to persecute his lovers. Among the victims of Hera's wrath were Io, Leto and Semele. Pieter Lastman illustrated *Juno discovering Jupiter and Io*. She also persecuted any offspring of Zeus' affairs, most notably the hero Herakles.

Notwithstanding Zeus' adultery, the ancient Greeks called the union of Hera and Zeus the Sacred Marriage and it represented the importance of wedlock in Greek society. Hera

always remained faithful to her husband. Hera bore Ares (god of war), Eileithyia (goddess of childbirth) and Hebe (goddess of youth). She also bore the god Hephaistos, possibly without the participation of Zeus, in revenge for the motherless birth of Athene from Zeus's head.

Hera's attribute is a peacock: a pair of these birds drew her chariot. It was she who gave the peacock its marvellous tail: after Argos, the one-hundred-eyed monster guarding Io, had been slain by Hermes, Juno took his eyes and transferred them to the bird's tail.[1] Antonio Balestra illustrated this in *Juno Placing the One Hundred Eyes of Argus in the Peacock's Tail*.

An ancient Italian deity, Juno, was identified early on with Hera. She was the patron of women, marriage, childbirth and motherhood, and was the embodiment of Roman matronly values. A temple of Juno Moneta ("Juno., Giver of Counsel") was situated on the Roman Capitol. A mint was founded there, and the title Moneta is the origin of both "mint" and "money". As patron of commerce, Hera might appear in paintings about financial gain, as in Nicholas Maes' *The Account Keeper*.

Heraclitus *see* **Democritus and Heraclitus**

Herakles

The greatest of all Greek heroes. Herakles (whom the Romans called Hercules) was the offspring of Zeus' adultery with Alkmene, the queen of Tiryns and a descendant of the hero Perseus. Possibly because Alkmene was an unwitting adulteress (Zeus had assumed the form of her husband), the wrath of Zeus's wife Hera was

Hera: *see* Ares; Athene; Callisto; Eileithyia; Hebe; Hephaistos; Herakles; Hesperides, The; Io; Ixion; Leto; Paris; Semele; ZEUS, THE CONSORTS OF
[1] Ovid, *Met I:568–746*

Herakles: *see overleaf*

Hera, the Roman Juno, after an ancient bas relief in Rome.

Herakles: see Alcestis;
Alkmene; Amazons;
ARGONAUTS, THE
VOYAGE OF; Centaur;
Cerberus; Cornucopia;
Deianeira; Eurystheus;
Hebe; Hera; HERAKLES,
THE LABOURS OF;
Jason; Milky Way; Lapiths,
The; Nessus; Perseus;
Theseus; Zeus
¹ Philostratus the Elder,
Imagines II:23
² Ovid, Met IX:1–97
³ Apollodorus, The Library
II v 11
⁴ Hyginus, Fabulae XXX
⁵ Apollodorus, The Library
II.v.9
⁶ Ovid, Met IX:98–229,
Hyginus, XXIII–XXVI and
Philostratus the Younger,
Imagines 16
⁷ Ovid, Fasti II 303–359
⁸ Xenophon, Memorabilia
II.i.22–34
⁹ Virgil, Aeneid
VIII:193–272 and Ovid,
Fasti I: 543–587
¹⁰ Ovid, Met IX:229–273

directed towards their offspring. Hera sent two huge serpents to devour the infant Herakles and his half-brother Iphikles in their crib, but Herakles throttled them with his bare hands when he was just eight months old.

Herakles had superhuman strength and is depicted as a huge, muscular figure with a club, wearing the skin of the Nemean Lion. The Classical statue known as the *Farnese Hercules*, discovered in 1540, provided the prototype for numerous images of the hero. He may be a personification of strength, courage and endurance, and his story was also treated as an allegory of good vanquishing evil.

Herakles grew to be the strongest man and greatest fighter in the world. He was often in combat, for example against the Lapiths, Centaurs and Amazons. He fought with Death in the underworld to free Alcestis.

Herakles joined Jason on his quest for the Golden Fleece. When the expedition neared Bithynia in northern Asia Minor (modern Turkey), Herakles broke his oar and went ashore to make a new one. His squire and lover, Hylas, went to look for water and was captured by water nymphs who dragged him down into the pool where they lived. Herakles was frantic at his lover's disappearance and let the Argonauts sail on while he looked for him. But Hylas was never seen again.

Herakles defeated the enemies of Creon, king of Thebes, who in gratitude gave him his daughter Megara in marriage. But one day Hera drove the hero mad[1] and he slew Megara and their three sons. As penance Herakles served King Eurystheus of Tiryns for twelve years, when he accomplished the twelve dangerous tasks set for him by the king and known as the Labours

of Herakles (*see panel on page 234*).

Millennia later stories from the Labours of Herakles were selected to make an oblique reference to the power of the patron. For example, Vasari painted *Labours of Hercules* for Duke Cosimo I; and Guido Reni painted the same subject for Ferdinando Gonzaga, duke of Mantua. The depiction of Herakles resting from his labours was also popular. Other adventures often depicted are:

HERAKLES AND ACHELOUS
The river-god Achelous fought Herakles for the hand of the princess Deianeira. In the contest Achelous turned himself at first into a serpent, then into a bull. Herakles flung himself around the bull's neck and, forcing its head to the ground, broke off one of its horns, which according to some accounts became the Cornucopia.[2]

Herakles fighting Achelous, after a Greek vase painting.

HERAKLES AND ANTAEUS
On the quest for the apples of the Hesperides Herakles wrestled with the giant Antaeus, whose strength came from he earth. Herakles lifted him off the ground long enough to strangle him.[3]

HERAKLES AND EURYTION

According to the Latin author Hyginus (1st century CE), Herakles attacked and slew the centaur Eurytion, whom he found raping a girl.[4]

HERAKLES AND HESIONE

Laomedon, king of Troy, was ordered to assuage the gods' displeasure by sacrificing his daughter Hesione to a sea-monster. Herakles killed the monster and rescued Hesione.[5]

HERAKLES AND NESSUS

The Centaur Nessus tried to abduct Herakles' wife, Deianeira, for which Herakles shot him with a poisoned arrow and the Centaur ejaculated onto the ground. The dying Centaur told Deianeira to mix his semen and blood with olive oil to make a love charm that would retain Herakles's affection forever. Later, when Herakles fell in love with Princess Iole, Deianeira smeard the potion on a shirt and sent a messenger, Lichas, to throw it around Herakles. But the potion was a lethal pison, and drove Herakles into agony. Dying, he seized Lichas and flung him into the sea. As Lichas flew through the air, fear drained away the messenger's blood and he turned to stone (*see* THE APOTHEOSIS OF HERAKLES).[6]

HERAKLES AND OMPHALE

Herakles murdered his friend Iphitus in a fit of madness. In punishment, Mercury (Hermes) sold him to Omphale, the widowed queen of Lydia. Taking Herakles as her lover, they exchanged clothes. In such array they feasted and fell asleep side by side. Pan, smitten with love for the queen, crept into Hercules' bed, thinking the hero to be his love, and was ejected forthwith.[7]

HERAKLES AT THE CROSSROADS

When passing from boyhood to youth, Herakles had to choose between a life of virtue or of vice. Two women of great stature appeared: Virtue was fair to look upon; Vice was plump, soft and seductive. Each wanted him to follow her, but he chose Virtue.[8]

HERCULES AND CACUS

According to a Roman myth, the monster Cacus terrorized the country around the Aventine Hill, near the later site of Rome, and tried to steal some of Geryon's cattle from Hercules (Herakles). But the hero cornered the monster and strangled him, thereby making the founding of Rome possible.[9]

THE APOTHEOSIS OF HERAKLES

Racked with pain from the poisoned shirt, the dying warrior built his pyre and lay down on it, the skin of the Nemean Lion beneath him, his thead resting on his club. Zeus, proud of his son's exploits, made Herakles immortal and bore him away to Mount Olympus in his four-horse chariot; there he was reconciled with Hera and married her daughter, Hebe, the goddess of youth.[10]

HERAKLES, THE LABOURS OF

see panel overleaf

Herm *see* **Hermes**

Hermaphrodite *see* **Androgyne**

Hermaphroditus and Salmacis

Hermaphroditus[1] was a handsome young hunter, the son of the god Hermes and the goddess Aphrodite (Venus in Roman myth). Hermaphroditus travelled far afield and came across a

Hermaphroditus and Salmacis: *see* Aphrodite; Hermes

[1] Ovid, *Met IV:274–388*

HERAKLES, THE LABOURS OF

The TWELVE LABOURS accomplished by Herakles in the service of King Eurystheus of Tiryns were the great hero's most renowned exploits. The first six labours took place in the Peloponnese.

1 The Nemean Lion. Herakles was ordered to kill a monstrous lion that was terrorizing the land of Nemea. No weapon could penetrate its hide, so Herakles beat the creature senseless with a great club and then throttled it. He then skinned the lion with its own claws and donned the pelt to render himself invulnerable.

2 The Lernean Hydra. The hero was sent to kill the Hydra, a great serpent or dragon with nine heads that infested a swamp near Lerna. Whenever he chopped off one head, two more grew in its place. Iolaus, his nephew, solved the problem by cauterizing each neck immediately after Herakles had cut off the head.

Herakles fighting the Nemean Lion from a vase of c.550BCE.

3 The Cerynean Hind. Herakles was told to capture this beast, which had golden horns and bronze hooves and lived on Mount Cerynea. It was sacred to the goddess Artemis and the hero dared not cause it harm. He caught the hind after chasing it for a year and slightly wounding it. To escape the goddess's anger he blamed Eurystheus for the creature's injury.

4 The Erymanthian Boar. The hero had to bring back alive a monstrous boar that was devastating the area around Mount Erymanthus. He captured the boar in snow and returned to Tiryns. Eurystheus, terrified at the sight of it, hid in an urn.

5 The Augean Stables. Herakles had just one day to clean out the cattle stables of Augeas, the son of Helios. The stables had never been cleaned and were piled high with 30 years' worth of dung from Augeas' great 30,000-strong cattle herds. Herakles succeeded by diverting the rivers Alpheus and Peneus through the stables.

6 The Stymphalian Birds. Herakles was ordered to get rid of a flock of monstrous man-eating birds with iron claws, wings and beaks which infested Lake Stymphalos in Arcadia. He scared them out of their trees with bronze castanets and then shot them one by one with his bow.

7 The Cretan Bull. Eurystheus sent Herakles to Crete to capture a wild, fire-breathing bull which was terrorizing the island. The hero caught the bull and took it to Greece.

8 The Mares of Diomedes. Herakles went to Thrace to capture the vicious mares owned by Diomedes, king of the Bitones, who fed them the flesh of strangers. Herakles slew Diomedes, fed him to the mares (which tamed them), and took them to Eurystheus.

9 The Girdle of Hippolyte. The hero was commanded to fetch the beautiful girdle of Hippolyte, the queen of the Amazons, for Eurystheus' daughter. Herakles vanquished the Amazons, slew Hippolyte and took her girdle.

10 The Cattle of Geryon. Herakles borrowed the cup of Helios, the Sun, to sail beyond Spain to the island where Geryon, a three-bodied monster, kept red cattle. He passed through the Straits of Gibraltar (setting up the twin Pillars of Herakles on either side) and into the great river Ocean that surrounded the world. He killed Geryon, his giant herdsman Eurytion and the two-headed watchdog Orthus, and returned to Greece with the cattle.

11 The Apples of the Hesperides. Eurystheus sent Herakles to the far west once again to bring back the golden apples that grew on a tree tended by the Hesperides, nymphs who lived on Mount Atlas. Herakles killed Ladon, the 100-headed dragon that guarded the tree, and took the apples. They were later returned by Athene, since they had been a wedding present from Gaia to Hera.

12 The Descent to the Underworld. The hero had to capture Cerberus, the three-headed dog that guarded the gates of the underworld. After a struggle he dragged Cerberus before Eurystheus, then sent the dog back to the underworld.

crystal pool where a water nymph named Salmacis dwelled – the only one unknown to Artemis (Diana), the goddess of chastity. When Salmacis caught sight of Hermaphroditus she longed to possess him and offered herself to him, but he rejected her. Once Hermaphroditus was in the water, Salmacis entwined herself passionately around him. She prayed never to be separated from him, and their bodies fused to become one, joining both male and female as a hermaphrodite, with a woman's breasts and a man's genitals. As he died, Hermaphroditus prayed that all men who bathed in the pool would acquire both mále and female attributes.

Hermes

The son of Zeus and the nymph Maia, the daughter of the Titan, Atlas. Hermes was born at sunrise and by noon he had already displayed his divinity by inventing the lyre. In the evening of the same day he stole the cattle of his half-brother, the god Apollo. Apollo caught him and took him to see Zeus for punishment, but agreed to accept the lyre instead.

Hermes was responsible for motion, transfer and exchange. In fact, as the messenger of the gods he was usually depicted in a traveller's hat and wearing winged sandals. He carried a herald's staff which was also his magic wand, the *caduceus*, formed from two snakes entwined around a central pole and usually crowned by a pair of wings. Giambologna cast a potent image of the god in flight.

Hermes was the god of travellers and roads and herms – square or rectangular pillars surmounted by a bearded head or armless bust, thought to depict Hermes – often stood near crossroads, on street corners of Athens and outside the city as milestones. They may have a phallus. Hermes oversaw all transactions, both legal and illicit: he was the patron of both merchants and thieves. He carried the divine word of the gods but was also the purveyor of lies and false oaths. As a teacher he was entrusted with the education of Eros (Cupid), depicted by Correggio in *The Education of Cupid*.

One of the titles given to Hermes was Psychopompos ("Bearer of Souls"), because he was said to escort the souls of the dead to the underworld. He was also the god of dreams and sleep, and carried a "wand which he can use at will to cast a spell upon our eyes or wake us from the soundest sleep".[1]

According to Julius Caesar, a god he called "Mercury" was the most widely worshipped deity of the Gauls and Britons. Caesar called this Celtic Mercury the inventor of the arts and a god of commercial success. He may in fact have been referring to the god Lugus. In Roman Gaul and Britain, many shrines were dedicated to the Celtic manifestations of Mercury.

The Greeks equated the Egyptian god Thoth with Hermes, and ascribed to him a body of lost writings (called "Hermetic") on mysticism, magic and alchemy. In this form the god was known as Hermes Trismegistus ("Thrice Greatest"). The writings remained hidden until they were "discovered" in the early centuries CE (when, in fact, they were probably written) and became the basis for much Western alchemical and magical practice. By the Middle Ages and Renaissance the author was believed to be not a god but a great sage, a contemporary of Moses, and the writings

Hermes, from a Greek vase painting.

were deemed to contain wisdom close to God. An image of Hermes Trismegistus as a sage is inlaid on the floor of the nave in Siena Cathedral.

Hero, Heroine

In Jungian psychology, a symbol of psychic vigour, a celebration of the human spirit. According to this interpretation, the trials of the hero represent the challenges of self-discovery. In ancient Greece, the appearance in literature and art of heroic prototypes with superhuman or semi-divine powers appears to have developed out of earlier forms of ancestor worship.

Hero and Leander

In mythology the beautiful Hero, priestess of Aphrodite (Venus), fell in love with the handsome Leander.¹ At night he swam across the Hellespont (the strait linking the Aegean Sea with the Sea of Marmara) to reach her, guided by a lighted torch at the top of Hero's tower. One stormy night the light blew out and Leander drowned. In despair, Hero threw herself from the top of her tower into the sea below. In *Hero and Leander* Domenico Fetti shows nymphs carrying Leander's body to the shore as Hero is dashed on to the rocks.

Heron

A symbol of inquisitiveness, but also usually a bird of good omen, symbol of the morning sun in Egypt and the model for the phoenix-like Benu bird, revered as the creator of light. The heron was an ascensional symbol in China and sometimes appeared in allegories of Christians rising above the storms of life, as the heron surmounts rainclouds.

Herse

In Greek myth¹ the maiden Herse was returning home with her sisters from a festival of Athene (Minerva in Roman myth), still carrying the sacred symbols in flower-wreathed baskets on their heads, when Hermes (Mercury) saw her and was astounded by her beauty. He flew down to earth but her sister Aglauros, who had envy planted deep in her heart, blocked the threshold of Herse's room. Hermes turned Aglauros into a blackened statue. In *Mercury, Herse and Aglauros* Louis Lagrenée shows the lovers on a bed as Aglauros peers around the curtain.

Hesperides, The

In Greek myth, a group of nymphs, often said to be the daughters of the Titan Atlas. They lived in the far west of the world on Mount Atlas and tended a garden in which grew a tree bearing golden apples.

Hestia

The virgin goddess of the hearth, the eldest child of Kronos and Rhea and the sister of Demeter, Hades, Hera, Poseidon and Zeus. Despite being the most senior Olympian deity, Hestia ("Hearth") appears infrequently in myth. However, she was revered as the divine guarantor of domestic stability and prosperity, and was said to be present at the naming and legitimation of children. She was also revered as the protector of social stability.

In Rome, where she was known as Vesta, the goddess became the focus of an important official cult as the protector of the Roman homeland. Her highly respected virgin priestesses, the Vestals, tended a sacred eternal flame which was regarded as the "hearth" of the nation.

The 64 hexagrams of the I Ching *(or* Yi Jing)*, the ancient Chinese classic manual of divination.*

Hexagram

Two interlocking or overlapping triangles, one inverted, symbolizing union in duality. This is now known as the Star of David (who unified Judah and Israel) and is the emblem of the modern state of Israel. It was earlier called Solomon's Seal or Solomon's Shield – although originally this may have been the pentacle, a five-pointed star of which there is more ancient archaeological evidence in Palestine. Hexagram shapes also appear in Indian mandalas as meditative images and, with mysterious significance, in Central American rock carvings. In alchemy, the hexagram symbolized the male/female dualities of fire and water (the inverted triangle), later the union of the four elements or the "fifth element" (the quintessence). In magic, the hexagram device was associated with exorcism. Coded lines used in ancient Chinese divination, also called hexagrams, are groups of six broken or unbroken lines symbolizing archetypal qualities and yielding 64 possible permutations, each with different significance.

Hina

A woman who grew the first coconut, according to a Tongan myth. Hina was a noblewoman whose virginity was respected and protected by all the community. An eel had intercourse with her and made her pregnant. Her people caught the eel, chopped it up and ate it, apart from the head, which Hina asked to keep. She buried the head and from it sprouted the first coconut.

Hine-hau-one

The first human being, according to Maori myth. The creator god Tane, the son of Papa, mother earth, and Rangi, father sky, wanted a wife. His mother turned him down, and on her advice he made the first human, Hine-hau-one ("Earth-Created Maiden"), from the sand of Hawaiki Island. Hine-hau-one was responsible for the first human birth and for the arrival of human mortality: she bore Tane a daughter, Hine-titama, who later became Hine-nui-te-po, the giant goddess of the underworld and death.

Hippolyte *see* HERAKLES, THE LABOURS OF

Hippolytus

In Greek myth, Hippolytus[1] was desired by his stepmother, Phaedra, who tried to persuade him to sleep with her. Infuriated by his persistent refusal, Phaedra pretended to his father, the hero Theseus, that Hippolytus had in fact tried to seduce her, and so Theseus banished him. *The Death of Hippolytus* by Rubens shows how, as

Hexagram: *see* Alchemy; Mandala; Pentagram; Pentacle; Quintessence; Six; Triangle; Trigrams

Hine-hau-one: *see* DEATH, THE ORIGIN OF; Rangi and Papa; Tane

Hippolytus: *see* Theseus
[1] Ovid, *Met XV:479–546*, Philostratus the Elder, *II:4* and Euripides, *Hippolytus*

Hippolytus fled, a sea-monster sent by the god Neptune (in Greek myth, Poseidon) terrified his horses. His chariot struck a tree, throwing him out; and, with his limbs entangled in the reins, he was dragged to his death.

Hippopotamus

Hippopotamus-like beasts symbolize brute strength, destructiveness, fecundity – sharply ambivalent symbolism in ancient Egypt. Theban images of the hippopotamus-goddess Taweret – mild, human-breasted, swollen-bellied, holding the hieroglyphic rolled papyrus of protection, symbolized guardianship of women and children. But she was the consort of the destroying Seth and could herself turn vengeful. The *Book of Job* describes Behemoth as a voracious hippopotamus-like creature, symbolizing humanity's need for divine help to conquer its brutishness.¹

History

History was often personified as a female figure with books, tablets or scrolls. Anton Mengs, in *An Allegory of History*, shows her crowned with laurel in the company of Fame, Time and double-headed Janus.

Hive

Collective work – a protective and maternal symbol of ordered industry. In Christian art, the beehive appears as an image of the monastic community, the attribute of eloquent religious leaders and of the Golden Age.

Hog *see* Boar; Pig

Hole

In religious artifacts and in mystic thought, less a symbol of emptiness than of an opening – to physical life at birth and to spiritual life at death. The significance of ancient pierced stones is not always explained by female sexual and fertility symbolism. In China, for example, precious jade discs were carefully perforated with a central hole as symbols of the gateway to heaven, a void leading to timelessness.

Holly

A midwinter emblem of hope and joy. Holly was among the evergreens carried at the Roman midwinter festival of Saturnalia, but its use at Christmas is linked more directly with Germanic customs of decorating houses with holly in December. In Christian tradition, holly is associated with John the Baptist and with Christ's Passion (the crown of thorns spotted with blood).

Holy Family, The

During the Renaissance paintings of the Holy Family – Mary, Joseph and the Infant Jesus – grew out of maternal images of the Virgin and Child. Michelangelo's *Doni Tondo* is a notable example of this development. The subject emphasizes the human aspect of the Incarnation, as the Holy Family are seen doing domestic tasks. For example, in Correggio's *Madonna of the Basket* the Virgin has her sewing beside her, while Joseph, a carpenter, is busily at work. The Holy Family is also often seen in a landscape, as in the Rest on the Flight into Egypt, which tended to be a popular subject.

An extension of the theme, called the Holy Kinship, shows the extended Holy Family with Saints Anna, Joachim, Elizabeth and others

Homer

The Greek epic poet Homer is the author of *The Iliad* and *The Odyssey* (though some dispute whether the same poet composed both works) and probably lived some time before the 8th century BCE. He is said to have been born on Chios, an island in the Aegean. In *Parnassus* Raphael depicted him with Dante and Virgil as a dignified old man wearing a laurel wreath. Homer is traditionally said to have been blind, so is frequently shown dictating his works to a scribe.

Honey

The food of gods and immortals, seers and poets – a symbol of purity, inspiration, eloquence, the divine Word and God-given blessings. Honey was a principal source of sugar in the ancient world, and had valued medicinal properties. It was also the basis of mead, a sacred beverage in many cultures, equated with the ambrosia of the gods. Its celestial qualities seemed borne out by its golden colour and by the idea that bees collected honey by sipping dew from flowers. Thus the mystic sweetness celebrated by Coleridge in the closing lines of *Kubla Khan* (1797–8): "For he on honey-dew hath fed, / And drunk the milk of Paradise." The biblical land of Canaan flowing with milk and honey was an image of spiritual as well as physical plenty. Honey was used not only as a votive food but also as an anointing or cleansing fluid in many ancient Middle-Eastern cultures, and in the initiatory rites of Mithraism. Kings were embalmed with it in Sparta, Scythia and Egypt. It was equated with the bliss of nirvana in India and with heavenly pleasures in China as well as in the West.

In Greece, where honey was again used in initiation rites, poets such as Homer and philosophers such as

Pythagoras were reputed to have been fed on nothing else.

In addition to its use as a balm it was widely thought to be an aphrodisiac or to promote fertility (its erotic symbolism perhaps strengthened by the effects of drinking mead). Jainism forbade eating honey for this reason.

Ho-no-susori and Hiko-hoho-demi

Two famous brothers of Japanese myth, the offspring of Honinigi, the grandson of the goddess Amaterasu, and his consort Kon-hana-sakuya-hime. The elder brother, Ho-no-susori ("Fireshine"), was a sea fisherman while Hiko-hoho-demi ("Fireshade") was a hunter. Hiko-hoho-demi grew unhappy with hunting and suggested that they swap occupations. Ho-no-susori agreed, but Hiko-hoho-demi fared no better at fishing and lost his brother's prized fish hook. Ho-no-susori insisted on retrieving his hook, so Hiko-hoho-demi went on a long journey to the undersea palace of Watatsumi-no-kami, the sea god.

Watatsumi-no-kami found Ho-no-susori's hook in the mouth of a red-fish and gave Hiko-hoho-demi his daughter Toyotama-hime in marriage. Later Watatsumi-no-kami let his son-in-law travel home on the back of a crocodile with, as a parting gift, two magic jewels: one to make the sea rise and one to make it fall.

Hiko-hoho-demi arrived home and gave his brother his hook. However, Ho-no-susori continued to complain, so Hiko-hoho-demi threw the first jewel into the sea. As the sea rose, Ho-no-susori panicked and pleaded for forgiveness from his brother. Hiko-hoho-demi then threw the second jewel into the sea, causing the water to fall. This is the origin of

Homer: *see* Trojan War; Ulysses

Honey: *see* Bee; Dew; Gold; Initiation; Mead; Milk; Nirvana; Word

Ho-no-susori and Hiko-hoho-demi: *see* Amaterasu; Jimmu-tenno

the tides. Ho-no-susori promised to serve Hiko-hoho-demi for the rest of his life.

Toyotama-hime joined Hiko-hoho-demi and bore a son, Amasuhiko, before returning to her father.

Horatii and Curatii, The

Two families, the Roman Horatii and the Latin Curatii of Alba,[1] each had three sons matched in years and strength. To conclude the war between the Romans and Latins, their kings suggested that these young men should fight. Both sets of brothers took an oath that the losing side would submit peacefully to the other. In *The Oath of the Horatii*, Jacques-Louis David shows the brothers making this vow before their father.

In the combat, the first advantage fell to the Curatii who, although wounded, killed two of the Horatii. The remaining Roman knew that he could not take on three men at once so he ran a distance, followed by the three Curatii, each at a different speed. Fighting and defeating each of the Curatii brothers one by one, he emerged the victor.

Horatius Cocles

The heroism of the Roman soldier Horatius Cocles[1] saved his city from capture by the Etruscan army under Lars Porsena. With two comrades, Horatius held the enemy back at a wooden bridge across the Tiber, giving the Romans time to destroy it. Severely wounded, he then dived into the river and swam to the other side. He was rewarded for his courage with as much land as he could plough in a day. Held up in Roman times and later fine example of an ancient Roman hero, his image appropriately adorns public places – for example, Pietro Perugino's *Horatius Cocles* (Collegio del Cambio, Perugia).

Horn

Force, strength, virility, fertility, supremacy – the potent symbol of barbaric gods, rulers, heroes or warriors. To the ancients, the horns of bulls, cows, rams, goats or bison were a crowning expression of male fighting spirit and phallic vitality, and also of female protective and reproductive power. Hence the popularity and status of horned divinities, particularly in traditions based on cattle herding or on hunting. Earliest representations of horned figures in cave paintings probably record shamanistic invocations of hunting success. Sympathetic magic may also have been conjured up by Celtic and Germanic horned war helmets, designed to inspire animal ferocity as well as to terrify enemies. In the Roman army, a horned decoration, the *corniculum*, was awarded for distinguished bravery. Similarly, headdresses decorated with horns, as in Native North America, were reserved for courageous leaders.

Viewed as a container rather than weapon, the horn becomes feminine, but retains its underlying symbolism of power. Thus, the legendary Horn of Plenty (Cornucopia) could not be emptied. Drinking horns, used ritually for mead or wine, were thought to confer potency. Horns forming a crescent-moon shape often symbolize mother goddesses, such as Hathor in Egypt, shown with the head of a cow or with a horned human head. The curving horns of a bull or cow cradling the sun disc depict both lunar and solar power. Ram horns are specifically solar – as in images of Amun who became the chief god of Egypt and whose curling horns were adopted by Alexander the Great, "Son of Amun", as a symbol of his imperial power.

In the Jewish Temple, sacred horns upon which sacrificial blood was smeared stood at the four corners of the altar as emblems of Yahweh's all-encompassing power. The Hebrew *shofar* (ram's horn), used as a warning signal by the ancient Israelites, was another symbol of protective power, and the word "horn" often appears in the Bible as a synonym for strength or, in the New Testament, for salvation. However, Christianity soon turned against pagan worship of the horn which became, in medieval art, a mark of Satan and his followers. Horns also identified the cuckold – possibly by association with stags losing their does to stronger males. In psychology, horns can be linked with life choice – the "horns of a dilemma".

Horse

An archetypal symbol of animal vitality, velocity and beauty. With the notable exceptions of Africa and of North and South America, where horses mysteriously disappeared for some thousands of years until the Spanish reintroduced them, the horse was linked everywhere with the rise of dominant civilizations, and with superiority. The mastered horse is a prime symbol of power – hence the popularity of the equestrian statue. In cave art, as in Romantic painting, horses flow across the surface medium like incarnations of the force of life itself. They were widely linked with the elemental powers of wind, storm, fire, waves and running water. Of all animals, their symbol-

ism is the least limited, ranging from light to darkness, sky to earth, life to death.

Their role as emblems of the continuity of life is suggested in many rites. Each October the Romans sacrificed a horse to Mars, the god of war and agriculture, and kept its tail throughout the winter as a fertility symbol. In ancient belief, horses knew the mysteries of the underworld, the earth and its cycles of germination. This early chthonic symbolism was replaced by a more widespread association of the horse with sun and sky gods, although horses continued to play a part in funerary rites as guides or messengers in the spirit world. The riderless horse is still used as a poignant symbol in military and state funerals.

Death is usually represented by a black horse, but rides a pale horse in the *Book of Revelation*. The white horse is almost invariably a solar symbol of light, life and spiritual illumination. It is an emblem of the Buddha (said to have left his worldly life on a white horse), of the Hindu Kalki (the last incarnation of Vishnu), of the merciful Kannon in Japan, and of the Prophet in Islam (in which horses are emblems of happiness and wealth). Christ is sometimes shown riding a white horse (Christianity thus links the horse with victory, ascension and the virtues of courage and generosity). In England the white horse was a Saxon standard, perhaps linked with the Celtic horse goddess Epona, who was taken into the Roman world as the protector of horses. For the Celts, horses were regal emblems, enjoying the status of lions in other cultures.

The winged horse is similarly a solar or spiritual symbol. Horses draw the chariot of the sun in Classical, Iran-

Horse: *see* ANIMALS;
BEASTS OF FABLE;
Black; Centaur; Chariot;
Clouds; Darkness; DEATH;
Earth; Fire, Flame; Light;
SEVEN DEADLY SINS;
Sky; Storm; Sun;
VICTORY; White; Wind;
Wings

The Norse god Odin riding his eight-legged horse Sleipnir, after a stone carving.

ian, Babylonian, Indian and Nordic mythology, and are ridden by many other gods, including Odin, whose eight-legged mare Sleipnir represents the eight winds. Clouds are the horses of the Valkyries, Scandinavian priestesses of the goddess Freyja.

Although predominantly linked with elemental or instinctual powers, horses can symbolize the speed of thought. Legend and folklore often invest them with magical powers of divination. They are also associated with sexual energy, impetuous desire or lust – as in Fuseli's painting *The Nightmare* (1781), possibly a rape fantasy, in which a wild-eyed horse thrusts its head through bed curtains of a girl.

Horseshoe

An ancient talisman against the evil eye – but only if the ends pointed upward. This supports the theory that the supposed magic of the horseshoe relied on the protective symbolism of the horned moon, the iron forming a crescent shape. A more simple explanation is simply that the horseshoe itself protected the horse.

Horus

The falcon-headed Egyptian sky and solar god, the son of the goddess Isis and the god Osiris. Seth caused the death of his brother Osiris, the first king of Egypt, and seized his throne. Isis retrieved her husband's body and hovered over it in the form of a sparrowhawk, fanning enough life back into him for long enough for her to conceive a son, Horus. Osiris descended to the underworld as its ruler.

Isis knew Seth would seek to harm her child, so she fled to the marshes of the Nile Delta and gave birth to

Horus at Chemmis near Buto. With the assistance of other deities, such as the goddesses Hathor and Selket, Isis raised Horus until he was old enough to challenge Seth and claim the royal inheritance that was rightly his.

The sun god invited Horus and Seth to put their cases before the Ennead, the nine great gods. Seth declared that he should be king because only he was strong enough to defend the sun during its nightly voyage through the underworld. Some deities accepted this argument, but Isis persuaded them to change their minds.

Seth refused to proceed with Isis there, so he adjourned the tribunal to an island to which Isis was refused access. However, the goddess bribed Nemty, the ferryman of the gods, to take her across in disguise. Then she tricked Seth into agreeing that it was wrong for a son to have his inheritance stolen. Seth complained about her trickery and the gods punished Nemty by cutting off his toes.

Further confrontations between Horus and Seth proved inconclusive. In the end the gods wrote to Osiris in the underworld, who threatened to send demons to the realm of the gods if Horus was not made king. The gods duly found in favour of Horus.

Horus was seen as a sky god whose left eye was the moon and whose right eye was the sun. Every Egyptian king was regarded as the Living Horus, while his deceased predecessor was identified with Osiris. The Eye of Horus or Wedjat ("Whole One") was frequently depicted in Egyptian art.

Host

The wafer of unleavened bread given in the Christian Eucharist as a symbol of Christ's sacrificial body (from the

Horus, from a wall painting in the tomb of an Egyptian king.

Latin *hostia*, "victim"). A text attributed to St Thomas Aquinas commends the host's symbolic roundness (perfection) and whiteness (purity).

Hourglass

Mortality and the relentless passing of time. The hourglass often appears in devotional still lifes to illustrate the brevity of human life, and is an attribute of Father Time and sometimes of Death. It can also borrow the symbolism of two triangles, one inverted, symbolizing the cycles of creation and destruction (the shape of Shiva's drum in Indian art).

Hreidmar *see* Fafnir

Hrungnir

One of the race of giants who were the enemies of the Norse gods. Hrungnir challenged the god Odin to a horse race, but lost. Later, he entered Asgard, the home of the gods, and confronted the god Thor in a mighty duel. The giant hurled a massive whetstone at Thor, part of which lodged in the god's skull. Thor made light of his injury and the destroyed Hrungnir with his hammer.

Hubert, Saint

In legend, a wealthy Netherlander called Hubert (died 727CE) was hunting on Good Friday when he came upon a hart with a crucifix between its antlers. Christ spoke from the cross and commanded him to change his life. He became a hermit and later bishop of Maastricht. The patron saint of hunters, he appears in north European painting from the 15th century. *The Conversion of St Hubert* by the Master of the Life of the Virgin shows him kneeling before the stag.

Huehueteotl

"Old God", the Aztec god of fire and the hearth, probably in origin an Olmec deity (*c.*1500BCE–*c.*400BCE). Huehueteotl was revered by the Aztecs as the oldest god and the first companion of humanity. He appears to have been above all a domestic deity. From as early as *c.*500BCE he was depicted as a hunched toothless old man with a brazier on his head.

Huitzilopochtli

"Hummingbird of the South", the god of the sun and war, the national god of the Aztecs, also known as Blue Tezcatlipoca. Huitzilopochtli was a uniquely Aztec god and may have begun as a legendary hero, later deified. He was conceived by magic when a heavenly ball of down entered the womb of his mother, the goddess Coatlicue, at Coatepec (Serpent Hill, near Tula, Mexico). Her existing offspring, the goddess Coyolxauhqui and her four hundred brothers, were angry at her pregnancy and cut off their mother's head and hands. At the moment she died Coatlicue gave birth to the fully formed Huitzilopochtli, who avenged his mother's death by killing Coyolxauhqui and hurling her dis-membered corpse to the bottom of Coatepec. He then routed his brothers.

The god was said to have guided the Aztec people from their place of origin, Aztlan, on a great southward trek to the future site of Tenochtitlan, the capital of the Aztec empire (modern Mexico City). A historical migration in fact lasted from *c.*1150CE to *c.*1350CE.

Huitzilopochtli, the lord of the Fifth Sun, the current world epoch, was a forbidding deity who was closely associated with war and death (hummingbirds were said to be the souls of fallen

Hourglass: *see* DEATH; Drum; Father Time; Triangle; VANITY

Hrungnir: *see* Asgard; Odin; Thor

Hubert, Saint: *see* Eustace, St

Huitzilopochtli: *see* Aztlan; Coatlicue; Five Suns, The

Huehueteotl, after a stone sculpture found at the site of Tenochtitlan.

*Huitzilopochtli, after
the 16th-century Aztec
Codex Borbonicus.*

warriors). He was central to the Aztec cult of human sacrifice, which was believed necessary to feed Tonatiuh, the sun, with whom the god was identified. His most important shrine, at the top of the Templo Mayor in Tenochtitlan, was the site of human sacrifices, often on a massive scale.

HUMANITY, THE ORIGIN OF
see panel opposite

Hun Dun *see* **Chaos (1)**

Hunaphu *see* **Xbalanque and Hunaphu**

Hunter, Hunting
Hunting, the sport of rulers and the aristocracy, offered the opportunity to display wealth and power, as well as dynamic configurations of people and animals in a wooded setting.

In Classical myth, Artemis (Diana), goddess of hunting, was surprised while bathing by the hunter Actaeon, and turned him into a stag. Adonis too was killed while hunting. In Christian art the unicorn was hunted as a "type" of Christ. Saints Eustace and Hubert were hunters.

Hyacinthus
Apollo loved the Spartan youth Hyacinthus[1] beyond all other mortals. They were competing at the discus when Apollo's struck Hyacinthus, killing him. In an alternative version,[2] jealous Zephyr, the wind, who loved Hyacinthus, blew the discus at his head. Apollo transformed the youth's blood into the purple hyacinth, which returns to life every year. In Poussin's *Kingdom of Flora* Hyacinthus stares at the flower that bears his name.

Hybrid *see* **BEASTS OF FABLE**

Hydra
The offspring of Echidne and Typhon, the Hydra was a serpent or dragon with many heads that was slain by the Greek hero Herakles as the second of his twelve labours. The monster was sometimes said to have the body of a hound.

Hyena
In European tradition, a symbol of cowardly greed and hypocrisy, a medieval Christian metaphor for Satan, who feeds on sinners. However, the hyena had a place in West African animist rites as the acolyte of the lion; it took a guardian role in the symbolism of the Bambara people in Mali. In ancient Egypt the hyena was credited with powers of divination, perhaps from its night vision.

Hylas
Hylas,[1] who accompanied Herakles on his adventures with Jason, was looking for water when he found a spring where Naiads danced. One nymph was captivated by Hylas' beauty; as the youth filled his pitcher, she encircled his neck and pulled him underwater. In *Hylas and the Nymphs* J.W. Waterhouse shows him being drawn into their watery domain.

Hymen
The Greek god of marriage, the son either of Dionysos and Aphrodite (Bacchus and Venus to the Romans), or of Apollo and a Muse. He is usually depicted as a boy crowned with flowers, holding a burning torch. He appears in marriage scenes.

Hymir
A giant who, in Norse myth, sailed on a celebrated fishing expedition with

HUMANITY, THE ORIGIN OF

Surprisingly few mythologies recount the origin of humanity in great detail. One concept found almost worldwide is that humans were formed from earth or clay by a creator deity. For example, the Bible recounts how God created Adam (meaning "Man") "of the dust of the ground", and according to Chinese myth the goddess Nü Gua created humanity from drops of watery mud. In Rwanda the High God is believed to form babies from clay in the womb, and women of childbearing age are careful to sleep with a pot of water next to the bed for God to use in order to mould his clay.

Usually, but not universally, man is said to have arrived before woman, a mythic tradition that often goes hand in hand with the belief, seen in the story of Adam and Eve, that women also brought misfortune to humanity. The Greeks related how the first woman, Pandora, took into human society a jar (known as "Pandora's Box") in which were contained all the evils of the world. Myths like these have served to justify the inferior position of women in patriarchal societies. However, a number of cultures claim that the first human was, in fact, a woman. For example, in Iroquois and Huron mythology the ancestor of the human race was Ataentsic, a woman who fell from the heavens to earth. Maori myth recounts how the god Tane wanted a wife and created the first woman Hine-hau-one ("Earth-Created Maiden"), from the sand of Hawhaiki island.

A particular type of human origin story widespread throughout the Central and South Americas is the "emergence myth". For example, the Incas believed that the creator deity Viracocha created humans from clay. He then told them to descend into the earth and emerge from caves. Thus the ancestors of the Incas emerged from three caves at Pacariqtambo ("Place of Origin") near Cuzco, the Inca capital.

HUMANITY, THE ORIGIN OF: *see* CREATION; Hine-hau-one; Nü Gua; Pandora; Tane

the god Thor. Using the head of one of Hymir's oxen as bait, Thor hooked the World Serpent, a poison-spitting dragon which lived in the depths of the ocean. The god hauled the dragon's head out of the water but as he raised his hammer to strike it, Hymir, terrified at the sight of the creature, cut Thor's line. Thor was furious and hurled Hymir into the sea.

Hyperion

A Titan, the son of Gaia and Uranos. Hyperion married his sister Theia and their offspring were Helios (the Sun), Selene (the Moon) and Eos (the Dawn). In later tradition Hyperion ("Going Above") became another name for Helios.

Hypsipyle *see* ARGONAUTS, THE VOYAGE OF THE

Hyssop

Purification, humility – a symbolism based on biblical references to the herb used in purification rites in the Temple of Jerusalem, although this may in fact have been a caper plant with similar aromatic qualities.

Hyperion: *see* Eos; Helios; Selene; Titan

Hypsipyle: *see* ARGONAUTS, THE VOYAGE OF THE

Hyssop: *see* Water

*An ibis, after a papyrus
(13th–12th cent. BCE).*

I Ching (Yi Jing) *see* **Trigrams**

Ibex *see* **Goat**

Ibis
A bird revered in ancient Egypt as an incarnation of the lunar deity Thoth, the god of scribes and wisdom, who is often shown as an ibis or a man with an ibis head. The symbolism was perhaps based on its habits as an inquisitive wading bird with a curving beak somewhat like a crescent moon. Ibises were mummified by the thousand.

Icarus
In Greek myth, the son of the Athenian craftsman Daedalus and a slave woman. When Daedalus and Icarus were imprisoned by King Minos of Crete, their only possible escape was by air. Daedalus made two pairs of wings from wax and feathers. He warned his son not to fly too close to the sun, but Icarus forgot his advice and the sun's heat melted the wax in his wings. He plummeted into the sea and drowned. Daedalus retrieved his

body from the ocean, thereafter called the Sea of Icarus or Icarian Sea, and buried him on a nearby island, thereafter called Icaria. The story may be read as a warning against overambition. Icarus is usually depicted tumbling out of the sky; Pieter Breugel's *Landscape with the Fall of Icarus* shows a shepherd and a ploughman on a cliff, oblivious to the tiny figure falling to his death in the sea.

Icon
In Eastern Christianity, a representational sacred image used as a focus (but not object) of devotion. Byzantine icon painters followed strict conventions to maintain a boundary between the sacred world and the sensual human world. The icon is thus intended not to be lifelike but to represent a transcendent reality upon which the viewer can meditate.

Ifa
The Yoruba god of order and control, who was sent down to earth to teach humans the secrets of healing and

prophecy. Ifa (known as Fa among the neighbouring Fon) often appears as the companion of, and counterbalance to, the trickster god Eshu, who tries to disrupt the regular order of things. Before any important enterprise it is customary to make an offering to Ifa. However, the first taste of the offering is presented to Eshu in order to ensure that things proceed smoothly. Ifa is said to have established the Ifa oracle, a widespread traditional system of divination.

Ignatius of Loyola, Saint

The founder of the Jesuits, Ignatius of Loyola (*c.*1491–1556) was of noble Spanish birth and became a soldier, but dedicated himself to God after being seriously wounded. He studied in Paris, where he and seven others, including St Francis Xavier, formed the core of the Society of Jesus (the Jesuits), with *Ad majorem Dei gloriam* ("To the greater glory of God") as its motto. It received papal approval in 1540 and its missionaries travelled far and wide to spread the faith and counter Protestantism.

Loyola's *Spiritual Exercises*, meditations on the soul, enlightenment and union with God, was highly influential. He is depicted with the Jesuit emblems of the Sacred Heart crowned with thorns, the Flaming Heart, and the monogram IHS. He wears a black habit and a biretta, and may be shown as a missionary, taking his vows, studying or performing miracles.

IHS

The "sacred monogram", an abbreviation of the Greek for Jesus (ΙΗΣΟΥΣ). It is found on Byzantine coins and was adopted in the West, where it was sometimes taken to mean *In Hoc*

Signo ("By this sign [you shall conquer]"), the words accompanying a vision of the Cross in a dream of the emperor Constantine; and *Iesus Hominum Salvator* (Latin, "Jesus, Saviour of Mankind"). IHS forms part of the emblems of Saints Ignatius Loyola, Teresa and Bernardino of Siena and is often seen on the Cross in depictions of the Crucifixion and is gloriously celebrated in Baciccia's *Adoration of the Name of Jesus*.

Iliad, The

A great Greek verse epic written *c.*750BCE and traditionally attributed to Homer, a blind poet said to have lived on the island of Chios in the Aegean. *The Iliad* covers events in the Trojan War toward the end of the conflict, from the withdrawal of the Greek hero Achilles from the battlefield to the death and funeral of the Trojan hero Hector. The title of the epic is derived from Ilion or Ilium, an alternative name for Troy.

Ilyap'a

The Inca god of storms and weather, revered as the god of the fertilizing rains, which he drew from the Celestial River (the Milky Way). Ilyap'a's sister kept the water in a jug; when Ilyap'a smashed it with a lightning bolt hurled from his sling the water fell as rain. The crack of the sling was heard as thunder and Ilyap'a's gleaming attire was glimpsed as lightning.

Imhotep

A historical Egyptian architect and priest, builder of the Step Pyramid *c.*2650BCE for the pharaoh Djoser. Imhotep came to be revered as a god of wisdom, healing and magic, the son of the god Ptah and a human mother.

Immolation

IMPRESA

A personal heraldic device is known in Italian as an *impresa*. Such devices were often accompanied by a motto or proverb. By the end of the 16th century *imprese* were very fashionable and became highly inventive and complicated in design. They were developed from family emblems and decorated palaces throughout Italy. Some emblems were shared: the Gonzaga dukes of Mantua and the Este dukes of Ferrara both used the eagle of imperial Rome. Below are emblems of families who were significant patrons of the arts:

Family	Place of Origin	Emblem
Barbarini	Florence	Bees
Borgia	Spain	Bull
Chigi	Siena	Pyramids of mounds
Farnese	Rome	Fleur-de-lys
Medici	Florence	Balls
Pamphili	Rome	Fleur-de-lys/Dove and olive branch
Piccolomini	Siena	Crescent moon
della Rovere	Savona	Oak tree/Acorns
Rucellai	Florence	Billowing sail
Sforza	Milan	The Visconti Dragon, with eagles, fleur-de-lys and other heraldry
Strozzi	Florence	Crescent moon
Visconti	Milan	Dragon or serpent spouting humans

Immolation see **Fire, Flame; Sacrifice**

Impresa *see panel above*

Inanna *see* **Ishtar**

Inari

The Japanese god of rice and more generally of prosperity. The patron of rice farmers, he is said to ensure the success of the harvest. In ancient times Inari was also the patron of swordsmiths. He is depicted as a bearded old man with his messengers, two foxes.

Incense

A symbol of purity, virtue, sweetness, and prayer. From the earliest times, the burning of aromatic resins, woods, dried plants or fruits has been one of the most universal of all religious acts. Sacred literature and iconography suggest that incense was used originally to perfume sacrifices or funeral pyres but was later burned by itself as a purely symbolic offering, sharing the emblematic meaning of smoke as a visible link between earth and sky, humanity and divinity.

Frankincense and myrrh, two of the Magi's gifts to Christ, were highly valued throughout the ancient Near East and Mediterranean world. These and other forms of incense were burned for ritual purification, a tradition inherited by the Church. The more recent popularity of incense in the West derives from Eastern traditions of using it for purification and as an aid to meditation.

Incense, often copal resin, also had fecundity symbolism in Central America, invoking rain by the association of smoke and clouds.

Indra

In Indian myth, the warrior king of the ancient Vedic pantheon. The tawny-haired son of heaven and earth, Indra was huge and powerfully built, with massive arms for wielding his weapons, including the thunderbolt (*vajra*). Whenever he drank *soma*, an intoxicating drink central to Vedic ritual, he swelled to fill the heavens and the earth. *Soma* gave him the power to make the sun rise and to perform great deeds. The champion of the gods against evil and protector of the aristocratic class, Indra was often depicted riding a white elephant. Indra appears to have been a rival of the god Varuna, whom he may have ousted as ruler of the gods.

In one famous story Indra fought and killed the dragon-demon Vritra, lord of chaos and drought, thereby allowing the ordered world to exist.

Indra riding on his white elephant, from a 19th-century painting.

By killing the dragon, Indra separated the waters from the land, the lower regions from the upper, and caused the sun to rise every morning.

As Hinduism evolved, Indra's prestige declined. In the myth of Vritra, for example, the dragon became a Brahman, whom it was a grave sin to kill, and Indra had to do penance for his transgression. He lost his strength and fine appearance and the younger deities often humiliated him. Krishna persuaded Indra's followers to cease worshipping him. Indra's chief function in classical Hinduism was as the god of rain, a role derived from his ancient association with thunder.

Ing

An early Anglo-Saxon god also known (as Yngvi) to the Swedes. Apparently a fertility god, Ing travelled the land in a waggon. The Ynglings, a historical line of Swedish kings, claimed descent from him.

Initiation

A rite dramatizing the passage from one stage of life to another or (as in a rite marking entry into a group, cult or sect) from one status to another. Initiations may involve rites in which the old self "dies" and a new self is "born", usually after trials which may be either physical or symbolic.

INRI

The initials of *Iesus Nazarenus Rex Iudaeorum* ("Jesus of Nazareth, King of the Jews"),[1] the Latin inscription on the Cross. It appears at the top of the Cross in paintings of the Crucifixion.

Intemperance

In 17th-century Dutch art, Intemperance may be illustrated by a figure who has fallen asleep after too much smoking and drinking. In contrast, Temperance dilutes her wine with water. Jan Steen's *Effects of Intemperance* shows the folly of such behaviour: a boy steals from the drinker's purse; a maid gives drink to a parrot (that foolish imitator of humans); children feed a cat on food meant for adults; a foolish boy casts roses before a swine. As a reminder of the fate of those who lack self-discipline, the birch of punishment is placed in a basket above Intemperance.

Interlacing

In art, interlaced motifs symbolize unity and continuity. Celtic art, particularly in Ireland, is rich in complex interweaving linear designs. Like similar ancient traditions of decoration, these patterns expressed the idea that divine energy was manifested by an endless cosmic vibration, seen most clearly in the motion of waves.

Intestines

An organ believed in various traditions to be the seat of emotion and intuitive or magical knowledge (hence expressions such as "gut feeling"), and of positive qualities such as courage and compassion. Extispicy, divination by examining animal entrails, was practised by the Etruscans and Romans.

Inti

The Inca sun god and lord of life, revered by the Incas as their divine ancestor. Inti was held in great awe and solar eclipses were seen as a sign of his anger. He was the focus of many important rituals and his chief festival, Inti Raymi, took place annually at the June (midwinter) solstice. The centre of Inti's worship was the massive Coricancha or Temple of the Sun at Cuzco, the Inca capital. The god's shrine there contained the mummies of deceased emperors and its walls were covered with gold, a sacred metal considered to be the sweat of the sun. Inti was usually depicted as a great disc of gold with a human face, from which emanated sun rays.

Intoxication

In ancient and shamanistic cultures, a symbol of communion with spirits or possession by them. Wine, mead and other intoxicants may be used ritually to achieve ecstatic states in which drinkers are believed to become receptive to divine revelation or travel to the spirit realm. The Greek god Silenus is an example of the "drunken sage", also found in Daoist tradition.

Invasions, The Book of

A 12th-century Irish prose collection of myths which claim to relate the history of Ireland since the biblical Flood. *The Book of Invasions* (in Irish *Leabhar Gabhála*) probably relies on earlier works. As its fuller title, *The Book of the Conquest of Ireland*, suggests, it recounts the successive invasions of Ireland by six peoples: Cessair and her followers; Parthalón and his followers; Nemhedh and his followers; the Fir Bholg; the Tuatha Dé Danann; and finally the Milesians or Sons of Míl – the Gaels.

Inversion

The dynamics of opposites. They are sometimes interchanged in symbolism so that, for example, the fool alludes to the king, or death leads to life. The idea of inversion is often symbolized by perfectly symmetrical objects such as an hour-glass or double triangle.

Io

A princess of Greek myth, the daughter of King Inachus of Argos and his wife Melia. Io was a virgin priestess of the goddess Hera (Juno in Roman myth). Zeus, Hera's husband, had intercourse with Io in the guise of a cloud, robbing her of her virginity, hiding his adulterous deed from Hera by casting dark clouds over all the land. But the unusual clouds made Hera suspicious, so Zeus turned Io into a sleek white heifer as a further precaution against being found out.

Hera asked for the lovely heifer as a gift and set Argus, an unsleeping giant with a hundred eyes, to guard her. Straying near her family, Io conveyed who she was by writing in the dust with her hoof. They mourned together until Argus moved her on.

Zeus asked Hermes to help free Io. Hermes sent Argus to sleep with many stories, then cut off his head. But before Zeus could turn Io back into a woman, Hera sent a gadfly to plague her. It pursued her round the world as far as Egypt, where Zeus finally restored her. At once she conceived a son, Epaphos. Hera forgave Zeus and set Argus's eyes in the peacock's tail.

Scenes found in art include Io embraced by a cloud (Correggio, *Io*), Juno (Hera) discovering Jupiter (Zeus) with Io as a heifer, and Mercury (Hermes) lulling Argus to sleep.

Iolofath

A culture hero and trickster of Micronesian myth, also known as Olifat. Often identified with the sun, he is credited with bringing fire to humans. For example, in the central Caroline Islands, Olifat is said to have sent a bird to earth with fire in its beak. On Ulithi atoll, Iolofath is the sun, the son of the sky god Lugeilang and a woman called Thilpelap. Iolofath lived on earth but one day decided to visit the sky. Iolofath was killed in a battle with his sky relatives, but Lugeilang revived him and allowed him to stay among the gods.

Iphigenia

At the outset of the Trojan War, the Greek leader Agamemnon was preparing to sail from Aulis but his fleet was becalmed. The seer Calchas told Agamemnon that a deer he had slain was sacred to the goddess Artemis, who demanded Agamemnon's daughter Iphigenia in sacrifice.[1] The death of Iphigenia earned Agamemnon the hatred of his wife, Clytemnestra, who had him murdered on his return. However, in one account, just as Iphigenia was about to die, Artemis snatched her from the altar and substituted a stag. Thereafter Iphigenia served as a priestess of Artemis on the isle of Tauris.

Irik

One of two primordial bird spirits (the other being Ara) which, according to the Iban of Borneo, were the first beings to exist.

Iris (1)

The Greek goddess of the rainbow, on which she descended to give messages to mortals from the gods, especially Zeus and Hera. In Homer's *The Iliad* she takes Hermes' place as Zeus's principal messenger, and in Ovid and Virgil[1] she is the messenger of Juno (Hera). In art Iris is also seen in the realm of the dream god, Hypnos.

Iris (2)

A family of flowers named, on account of their range of colours,

Iron

from the Greek goddess of the rainbow. It is a symbol of purity and protection, but also, in association with the Virgin Mary, grief – a symbolism based on the sword-shaped leaves of the gladiolus. An iris may appear instead of the more usual lily in paintings of the Virgin, symbolizing the Immaculate Conception or the sorrow of Christ's Passion. An iris may be the flower of the fleur-de-lys. In Japanese folklore, the iris protects houses from harm.

Iron

A symbol of masculine hardness, rigidity, strength and also the destructive brutality of war. Iron was associated by the Egyptians with the bones of the destructive god Seth; by the Greek poet Hesiod (*fl. c.*700BCE) with the hardship of the present "Age of Iron"; and by Herodotus (*c.*484–*c.*425BCE) with "the hurt of man". This symbolism suggests that iron was traditionally seen as a vulgar metal compared with copper and bronze, let alone gold, all of which were preferred for the production of religious artifacts. Iron later became a symbol of slavery, by association with fetters. However, it can also appear with protective or fertility symbolism.

Isaiah

One of the four "Greater Prophets" of the Hebrew Bible (Old Testament), together with Jeremiah, Ezekiel and Daniel. Isaiah enjoys special eminence in Christian tradition for his prophecies of the coming of the Messiah, for example: "Behold, a virgin shall conceive and bear a son."¹ He prophesied that "there shall come forth a rod out of the stem of Jesse, and a branch shall grow out of his

roots".² In art, a "Tree of Jesse", the father of David, lists the ancestors of Christ. Isaiah is depicted as an old man with a long beard, holding a book or scroll that may bear his name.

Ishtar

The great Babylonian goddess of love, sex and fertility, the daughter of either the god Anu or the god Sin. Ishtar (called Inanna by the Sumerians) was also a great war goddess, often referred to as "the Lady of Battles". In this aspect she was presented as a formidable figure, for example in the epic of Gilgamesh. Ishtar was identified with the planet Venus.

In her most important myth, Ishtar descends to the land of the dead, possibly to seize power there. According to the longer Sumerian account, Inanna told her vizier Ninshubur to go to three gods for aid if she did not return. She travelled through the underworld, passing through seven gates, at each of which she had to remove a piece of clothing. When she finally arrived before her sister Ereshkigal, the queen of the underworld, Inanna was naked. She tried to overthrow Ereshkigal but failed and was executed, and her corpse was hung on a nail.

Realizing that a disaster must have occurred, Ninshubur went to Enki (the Babylonian Ea), the god of wisdom. He made two asexual beings which descended to Inanna and revived her, but she was only allowed to leave the underworld on condition that she sent a substitute. Back on earth, she declared that her substitute would be her husband Dumuzi. He tried to escape, but was captured by underworld demons. The poem ends with a speech, possibly by Inanna, declaring that Dumuzi would spend one half of the year in the underworld and his sister, Geshtinanna ("Lady of the Vine"), the other half.

Isis

An Egyptian mother goddess, the consort and sister of Osiris, the sister of Seth and Nephthys, and the mother of Horus. Isis, one of the nine great deities known as the Ennead, features in myth principally as the devoted wife of Osiris, the first king on earth, and mother of Horus. As the divine exemplar of the dedicated wife and mother, Isis was the centre of an important cult which in the Greco-Roman age spread far beyond Egypt.

The goddess's adversary was her brother Seth, who brought about the death of Osiris and usurped his throne. Isis retrieved her husband's corpse and protected it from Seth, using magic powers to halt or reverse its decay. In one account, Isis hovered over the body as a sparrowhawk and fanned enough life into Osiris with her wings to enable her to conceive a son, the god Horus. Isis protected Horus from Seth and assisted him to regain his birthright, the kingship, from his uncle.

Island

As symbols of heaven or havens, islands appears in countless myths and legends. An island is always a magical world set apart: sometimes a spiritual goal or a place reserved for the great and good after death (like the Isles of the Blessed in Greco-Roman myth and the Arthurian Avalon), sometimes an enchanted place like the Irish Tír Nan Óg. In Hinduism the island is an image of spiritual peace in the chaos of material existence. The number of legendary islands inhabited only by

women suggest that the island may also be a symbol of a female power. Jason landed on Lemnos, whose inhabitants had slain all their menfolk for insulting them; and Calypso detained Odysseus on her island for seven years. In a similar Polynesian myth, Kae left the Island of Women when he discovered that he was growing older while his wife Hine renewed her youth by surfing.

Islands of the Blessed, The

A region of the underworld in Greco-Roman myth, the home of dead heroes and other worthies. It is usually identified with Elysium but sometimes seen as a separate paradise.

Itzamna

The supreme deity of the Maya pantheon. Itzamna ("Lizard House") was the inventor of writing and learning and the first priest. He was also revered as a deity of medicine and his consort was Ix Chel, the goddess of medicine, childbirth and weaving. The god was variously represented as a king, a scribe, an old man, and sometimes a great sky serpent. Itzamna appears to have been associated with the sun god, Ahau Kin: representations of the two gods are very similar. He was also known simply as Zamna and may have been the deity known to scholars as "God K".

Ivan the Fool

A figure of Russian folklore, the guardian of the hearth and upholder of family tradition. According to one well-known tale, Ivan the Fool was the youngest and scruffiest of three brothers and lay on the stove all day. Shortly before his death, their father asked his sons to keep watch over his

The goddess Isis, from the temple of Abydos (13th century BCE).

Itzamna, the supreme god of the Maya.

grave for three nights. The two elder sons sent Ivan to guard the grave on his own. At midnight on the third night, the dead father appeared and rewarded Ivan for his vigil with Silver Roan, a magic horse that breathed smoke and flashed fire from its eyes.

Later, the Tsar announced that he would give his daughter in marriage to any man who could snatch her veil at a great height. Ivan summoned Silver Roan with a spell, climbed into his ear and became a handsome young man. He won the Tsar's contest then turned back into his usual dirty self and disappeared. The Tsar held a great banquet in order to find the youth who had earned his daughter's hand. Ivan, dirty and in rags, sat behind the stove in the feasting hall. He was recognized when he used the veil to wipe his tankard. To his brothers' annoyance, he was given his prize.

Ivory

A symbol of incorruptibility, purity, rank and protection. The symbolism of aloofness ("ivory tower") probably derives from the high status of ivory in almost all ancient cultures. Elephant (or walrus) ivory was credited with healing powers in the East. Its Christian association with purity and, in particular, with the Virgin Mary are linked to its whiteness.

Ivy

A symbol of immortality and tenacity – of life and of desire. Because ivy wreaths cooled the brow, they were also thought to prevent drunkenness, hence the wreaths worn by the Greek god Dionysos (the Roman Bacchus) and his retinue. Essentially, the evergreen ivy embodied the force of life in the ancient Near East and was the

attribute of gods of resurrection – Osiris in Egypt, Dionysos in the Greek world and Attis in Phrygia.

In Christian art, ivy was a symbol of fidelity, resurrection and eternal life (from the fact that ivy clings and continues to grow on dead trees). Ivy-wreathed skulls in still-lifes also refer to immortality. Arthur Hughes' *The Long Engagement* shows a curate and his fiancée condemned to a lengthy betrothal: next to them is a tree carved with initials that have been covered by the slow-growing climber.

Ix Chel

The Mayan goddess of fertility, childbirth, medicine and weaving, and consort of the supreme deity Itzamna.

Ix Chel, after a wall-painting in a temple in Tulum.

Ix Chel ("Lady of the Rainbow") was sometimes depicted as an old woman with serpents in her hair and occasionally with the eyes and claws of a jaguar. She was particularly revered by women, and was also known as Ix Kanleom ("The Spider's Web that Catches the Morning Dew").

Ixion

In Greek myth, a king of the Lapiths, a race of Thessaly. Ixion promised gifts to his father-in-law Eioneus; but when Eioneus came to collect them,

Ixion on the burning wheel, from a bowl.

IZANAGI AND IZANAMI

The primal creator couple of Japanese mythology, in full Izanagi-no-Mikoto ("August Male") and Izanami-no-Mikoto ("August Female"). According to the *Kojiki*, five primordial divinities, the Separate Heavenly Deities, came into existence when the world was young. Seven further generations of divinities culminated in Izanagi and his sister Izanami, also his wife. The other deities commanded the couple to form the land. They stood on the Floating Bridge of Heaven and stirred the oceans with a jewelled spear. The water drops that fell from the spear became the first land, the island Onogoro.

Izanagi and Izanami descended to the island and built a heavenly pillar and a palace. They devised a wedding ritual: they each walked around the pillar, Izanami from the right and Izanagi from the left. When they met they exchanged greetings and then had intercourse. As a result Izanami gave birth to a deformed child, Hiruko ("Leech-Child"), which they abandoned. An assembly of the gods decided that the birth was Izanami's fault because she had spoken first at the pillar. The couple repeated the ritual and Izanagi spoke first. Izanami then gave birth to many offspring, beginning with a series of islands (Japan). She bore gods and goddesses, including the gods of mountains, winds and trees. But as the fire god Kagutsuchi (or Homusubi) was born, Izanami was burned and died, producing more deities in her urine, excrement and vomit.

Izanagi wept tears of grief, from which sprang more divinities. Angry at his loss, he cut off the fire god's head: yet more deities arose from Kagutsuchi's body. Determined to bring his beloved back to life, Izanagi went to Yomi, the underworld realm of the dead. In the shadows, Izanami promised to ask if she could return with him, but warned Izanagi not to look on her. His desire to see his wife was too great, and he used the tooth of a comb to make a torch. He saw at once that Izanami was already a rotten corpse and fled in horror. His wife, furious that he had ignored her wishes, sent demons, fierce underworld gods, after him. Finally she became a demon and joined the chase. Izanagi shook off his pursuers and blocked the entrance to Yomi with a boulder. From either side of the boulder the couple declared themselves divorced.

Izanagi felt contaminated by his contact with Yomi and bathed in a stream in northeastern Kyushu island as an act of purification. Gods and goddesses sprang from his clothes as he undressed and others arose as he washed his body. Finally Izanagi produced three great deities: the sun goddess Amaterasu from his left eye; the moon god Tsuki-yomi from his right eye; and the storm god Susano from his nose. Izanagi divided his kingdom among them. Each of them accepted their father's decree except Susano, whom Izanagi banished for his defiance. Izanagi then withdrew to heaven, where he is still said to reside in the "Younger Palace of the Sun".

Ixion dropped him into a pit of burning coals. Zeus forgave him this crime, but then Ixion tried to rape Hera (the Roman Juno), queen of the gods and Zeus's wife – an act that made Ixion a notorious symbol of sexual transgression. However, Hera tricked him by making an image of herself from a cloud and putting it in her bed in her place. Ixion had intercourse with the cloud, which consequently gave birth to Centauros, another sexual transgressor and father of the Centaurs.

Zeus punished Ixion by condemning him to be tied to a burning wheel which would rotate in the underworld for eternity. He is shown courting Juno in van Couenbergh and Rubens' *Ixion Received by Juno*.

IZANAGI AND IZANAMI *see panel above*

IZANAGI AND IZANAMI: *see* Amaterasu; Kagutsuchi; *Kojiki, The*; Susano; Tsuki-yomi

J

Jackal: *see* AFTERLIFE

*The jackal-headed god
Anubis, from an ancient
Egyptian papyrus.*

Jackal

An evil-smelling scavenger, symbolizing destruction or evil in India, but in ancient Egypt worshipped as Anubis, the god of embalming, who led souls to judgment. Anubis is shown as a black jackal or a jackal-headed man.

Jacob

In the Bible,[1] Jacob was one of the twin sons of Isaac and Rebecca, and was born clinging to the heel of his brother Esau. This was a sign from God that they would head two tribes, and that Jacob, the younger, would be stronger than Esau, who would serve him.

Jacob became a herdsman and his mother's favourite, Esau a hunter and his father's favourite. One day, faint with hunger, Esau sold his birthright to his brother for food. When they were older, Rebecca disguised Jacob as his brother so that the old and nearly blind Isaac would mistake the younger son for the elder when giving his blessing. When Esau discovered this, he swore to kill his twin. In art, these episodes may form part of a cycle of images of biblical patriarchs.

Rebecca sent Jacob away to escape his brother's wrath and to marry one of the daughters of his uncle Laban, so that he would not have to marry a local Canaanite. On his way, he stopped to sleep in the open and dreamed of a ladder reaching from earth to heaven, with "angels of God ascending and descending on it." In the dream God told Jacob that he and his descendants would prosper.[2] Jacob's dream is a common theme in art and the ladder may appear as Jacob's identifying attribute. Tintoretto (*Jacob's Dream*) and others have depicted the ladder as a flight of steps.

Jacob met the beautiful Rachel, one of Laban's daughters, and offered to work for Laban for seven years to win her hand. Laban agreed, but when the time came for their wedding, he put his elder daughter Leah in Rachel's place, because the younger sister could not marry before the elder. But Jacob offered to work for seven more years so that he might marry Rachel, too; Laban agreed.[3]

Jacob had many children by his wives and their handmaids. After twenty years he resolved to return to Canaan with his family. They left in secret, Rachel taking her father's household idols. Laban caught up with them, but Rachel hid the idols by sitting on them.[4] In *Rachel Hiding the Idols from her Father Laban*, Giambattista Tiepolo shows her feigning ignorance as her father questions her as to their whereabouts.

The night before they reached Canaan, Jacob, alone by a brook, wrestled until dawn with a man who was unable to throw him. The man refused to tell his name, but gave Jacob a new name, Israel ("striving with God" or "God strives").[5] In early Christian art the man was sometimes depicted as God, but later tradition shows him as an angel, as in Gauguin's *Jacob's Struggle with the Angel*. The episode is often taken as an allegory of virtue against vice, or the spiritual struggle of the Christian.

When Jacob heard that Esau was approaching with four hundred men, he sent his brother part of his herd as a gift, and the two were reconciled.[6]

In old age, Jacob blessed the children of Joseph, his favourite son, a tranquil scene depicted by Rembrandt in *The Blessing of Jacob*.[7] He prophesied that his twelve sons would be the founders of the tribes of Israel. Zurbarán painted a series entitled *Jacob and his Twelve Sons*.

Jade

A symbol of cosmic energy, perfection, virtue, power, authority, incorruptibility and immortality. Chinese tradition associates jade with a whole spectrum of virtues: moral purity, justice, truth, courage, harmony, loyalty and benevolence. The supreme god of the Chinese heaven is the Jade Emperor, and the imperial jade seal symbolized a celestial mandate. Jade religious objects included the ancient *bi* (a blue-green jade disc with a circular perforation) and *cong* (a yellow tubelike object), the significance of which is uncertain. The hardness and durability of nephrite jade (the material of most Chinese jade carving) led to the belief that powdered jade could prolong life and that jade amulets could preserve the body after death – hence the number of jade objects found in Chinese tombs.

Green nephrite jade had similarly high value in ancient Mexico, where it was a symbol of the heart and of blood through its association with fertilizing waters. As in China, jade stones were sometimes placed in the mouths of the dead to ensure their resurrection. Among the Maori, the beautiful green nephrite *pounamu*, found on New Zealand's South Island, was used to make the sacred *mere*, a war club symbolizing authority, and the *hei tiki*, a pendant in the form of a stylized ancestor figure.

Jade Emperor, The

Yuhuang, the divine ruler of heaven in Chinese myth. He lived in a celestial palace and, like his earthly counterpart, the emperor of China, governed his realm through a vast civil service. The emperor was the only human being to deal directly with the Jade Emperor. All other humans were the responsibility of heavenly bureaucrats under the chief minister, Dongyue Dadi ("Great Ruler of the Eastern Mountains"). The Jade Emperor's consort was Wangmu Niang Niang, who was also known

Jacob: see Joseph, Son of Jacob
[1] *Genesis 25:20–34*
[2] *Genesis 28:11–14*
[3] *Genesis 29:1–28*
[4] *Genesis 31:3–35*
[5] *Genesis 32:24-30*
[6] *Genesis 32:6–32; 33:1–4*
[7] *Genesis 48*

Jade: *see* Amulet; Blood; Earth; Gold; Green; Heart; Hole; VIRTUES; Water; Yin and Yang

Jade Emperor, The: *see* Xi Wang Mu

Jaguar

as Xi Wangmu, the Queen Mother of the West, who lived on the sacred Mount Kunlun.

JAGUAR *see panel on opposite page*

Jambudvipa

The circular continent at the centre of the world, according to Hindu and Jain myth. At its centre stands Mount Mandara, or Meru, which was used by the Asuras and Devas to churn the ocean. Jambudvipa is ringed by the great Salt Ocean and by another seven continents and seven seas.

James the Great, Saint (Apostle, Disciple)

James (died *c.*44CE) and John, the sons of Zebedee, were fishermen who, with Peter, were the favourite disciples of Christ. They witnessed the Transfiguration and the Agony in the Garden, and they are usually shown in paintings of these scenes. According to legend, King Herod Agrippa ordered the martyrdom of James: he was decapitated by the sword.[1]

In the 7th century CE a legend arose claiming that James went to Spain and was a successful evangelist. This tradition is a relatively late one, but contributed to the growth of his Spanish cult; he became the patron saint of Spain. In the Middle Ages his shrine at Compostela was one of the major places of pilgrimage, where many miracles were said to have taken place; pilgrims wore his emblem, a cockle shell. St James is often shown as a pilgrim himself with a cockle shell on his hat or on his cloak.

James is believed to have appeared at the Battle of Clavijo in 844CE to help the Spaniards win their first victory against the Moorish invaders, and many artists have shown him as a warrior on horseback.

James the Less (Apostle, Disciple)

James (died *c.*62CE), called the Less to avoid confusion with James the Great, is usually identified as "the Lord's brother" James in the New Testament and in art he may, therefore, resemble Christ. According to Acts he was a leader of the Christians of Jerusalem, where he was martyred, probably in 62CE. Josephus records that he was stoned to death, but legend says that James was instructed to preach about Christ from the roof of the Temple and that for this he was thrown from the roof, stoned and clubbed to death.[1] One man snatched up a fuller's bat, used to beat cloth, and split his skull. James may be shown as a bishop, with a club or a flat fuller's bat.

Janaka

In Hindu myth, the king of Videha and father of Sita, the wife of Rama.

Janus

The Roman god of thresholds and beginnings, and hence usually the first deity invoked in any religious liturgy.[1] The god of entrances and exits, his image was set up by the principal door of a building, as well as on *jani*, the great triumphal arches and other ceremonial gateways. Janus had two faces so that he could look ahead and behind, and so was sometimes represented as a herm (a double-faced head or bust). He was associated with wisdom because he knew the past and could foresee the future. He gave his name to January, which saw the end of one year and beginning of the next. His festival took place on 9 January.

JAGUAR

The largest and most ferocious cat of the Americas, the jaguar was the dominant animal in the symbolism of Central and South America, linked with divination, royalty, sovereignty, power, sorcery, fertility and the earth, and, as a nocturnal animal, it was closely associated with the moon and the forces of the spirit world. This fierce cat is still important today in the beliefs of many indigenous peoples.

The ancient concept of the "werejaguar", a human being magically self-transformed into a jaguar, was widespread. There are countless images of snarling jaguar-human hybrids in the art and religion of many pre-Columbian civilizations. The belief links the part-man, part-feline sculptures of the Olmecs (c.1500BCE–c.400BCE) with the present-day South American tribal jaguar-shamans, each of whom are believed to be able to change into a jaguar. Jaguar-shamans conduct rituals in order to cure disease, to bring success at hunting or even to divine the future.

The jaguar itself is often revered as a divine figure and the possessor of

knowledge. For example, a mirror-eyed jaguar was an awesome incarnation of the supreme Aztec deity Tezcatlipoca, whose magic mirror revealed all things from the thoughts of humans to the mysteries of the future. The Maya sun god, Ahau Kin, was said to become the Jaguar God, the lord of darkness, when he travelled at night through the underworld from west to east. The Kayapo people of central Brazil relate how humans did not possess fire or the bow and arrow before the hunter Botoque stole these precious gifts from the jaguar.

More generally, reverence of the jaguar was marked by fear. For some cultures, the jaguar was the celestial swallower of the sun and moon, for others a predatory haunter of crossroads. Because the jaguar skins worn by shamans symbolized their power either to protect their own tribe or to destroy another, the jaguar was a dangerous apparition, perhaps the spirit of a dead or living shaman from a hostile village. Essentially, the jaguar is a symbol of unpredictable or capricious power.

South American tribal societies ascribe great powers to the jaguar, depicted above.

Jason: *see* Argonauts;
ARGONAUTS, THE
VOYAGE OF THE; Chiron;
Herakles; Hylas; Medea;
Sirens
[1] Apollonius of Rhodes,
 Argonautica

Jar *see* **Pitcher**

Jason

In Greek myth, Jason was a prince of Iolcus in Thessaly, the son of King

Aeson.[1] When the throne was usurped by Pelias, Aeson's brother, Jason was sent away for safety's sake to Mount Pelion, where he was cared for and educated by the wise Centaur Chiron.

Jephthah:
¹ *Judges 11:30–40*

Jason being rescued by Athene, from an ancient Greek red-figure vase.

At the age of twenty Jason set out for home. On the way he helped an old woman (the goddess Hera in disguise) across a river, and won the goddess's protection throughout his subsequent adventures. In helping Hera, Jason lost a sandal and arrived at Iolcus with one bare foot. Pelias was alarmed when he saw him, because an oracle had warned him to beware a stranger with one shoe.

To get rid of his nephew, Pelias said he would cede him his throne if he travelled to Colchis at the far end of the Black Sea and brought him the famous Golden Fleece. This precious fleece hung in a grove guarded by a dragon. Jason accepted the challenge and sailed there on a famous perilous voyage in the vessel *Argo* with his crew, the Argonauts.

King Aeëtes of Colchis agreed to surrender the fleece if Jason could perform certain difficult tasks. The king's daughter, Medea, fell in love with Jason and aided him with her sorcery. Jason successfully completed the tasks, and found the Golden Fleece hanging on a huge oak tree,

guarded by the dragon. Medea's sweet voice charmed the dragon, and she sprinkled a potion in its eyes so that Jason could remove his prize safely.

Jason returned to Iolcus, to find that Pelias had executed Aeson. In revenge Jason's wife, Medea, persuaded the usurper's daughters that if they chopped up their father and cooked him, he would become a young man once more. They followed her instructions, only to discover that she had tricked them into murdering Pelias.

The gruesome murder caused public outrage and Jason and Medea were forced to flee Iolcus. They settled in Corinth and had many children. Years later, King Creon of Corinth offered Jason his daughter's hand, and Jason, attracted by a good political alliance, proposed to divorce Medea. She was furious and sent Creon and his daughter poisoned robes that caused them to die in agony. She then slit the throats of her own children and fled to Athens, leaving Jason alone in his misery. He is said to have died many years later when part of the *Argo* that had been set up in a temple fell on his head.

The stories of the search for the fleece appealed to, among others, Gustave Moreau, who painted *Medea Enamoured of Jason*, and *The Return of the Argonauts*.

Jataka

"Birth", the Sanskrit name given to the many popular myths about former lives of the Buddha. Jataka stories occur in all Buddhist regions.

Jephthah

One of the biblical judges, Jephthah led the Israelites against the Ammonites.¹ Before the battle he vowed to

God that if he was victorious he would sacrifice the first creature he met on his return home. Victory was secured, but the first person to greet him, "with timbrels and with dances", was his daughter and only child. He tore his clothes in anguish but kept his vow. In *The Sacrifice of Jephthah*, Charles Lebrun showed him standing, knife in hand, about to kill her.

Jeremiah

One of the four "Greater Prophets" of the Hebrew Bible (Old Testament), together with Isaiah, Ezekiel and Daniel. According to the Book of Jeremiah, he denounced the sins of Judah and foresaw the great suffering of his people. Rembrandt depicted him as an old man lamenting the destruction of Jerusalem by the Babylonians in 587BCE. The Book of Lamentations, which deals with the ensuing captivity of the Jews, was later attributed to Jeremiah. A tradition claims that his gloomy prophecies led to his enforced exile in Egypt, where he was stoned to death.

Jeroboam

In the Bible, Jeroboam ruled the northern part of a divided Israelite kingdom. To avoid the need for his people to go to Jerusalem Temple, he set up altars in Bethel and Dan. As he was burning incense, an angel appeared and admonished him, causing his hand to wither. Jeroboam prayed to God and his hand was restored.[1] Jean-Honoré Fragonard's *Jeroboam Sacrificing to Idols* shows him worshipping a calf.

Jerome, Saint

Jerome (*c*.342–420CE) was one of the four Latin Doctors of the Church, with Saints Ambrose, Augustine and Gregory the Great. He studied in Rome then became a hermit in Syria, where he learned Hebrew. Between 382CE and 385CE he was in Rome as secretary to the Pope, who encouraged him to revise the Latin version of the New Testament. In 386CE Jerome settled in Bethlehem and by *c*.404CE he had rendered the entire Bible into Latin from Hebrew and Greek. His translation was known as the *Versio Vulgata* ("Version in the Common Tongue"), or Vulgate.

According to legend, Jerome took a thorn from the paw of a lion that became his constant companion.[1] Popular in the 15th century was the image of Jerome as an old hermit in the wilderness praying in front of a crucifix or beating his breast with a stone, with a lion nearby (Cosimo Tura). He may appear as a scholar in a study (Antonello da Messina), or as a cardinal – although the office did not exist in his day – holding the Bible, or a model of a church to represent his status as a Doctor of the Church. The Scuola di San Giorgio, Venice, has scenes from Jerome's life by Carpaccio.

Jester *see* Clown

Jesus Christ *see* Christ, The Life of

JEWELS *see panel overleaf*

Jezebel

In the Bible, Jezebel was the wife of Ahab, king of the northern Israelite kingdom. She has come to symbolize the archetypal wicked woman. Ahab coveted a vineyard owned by Naboth, whom Jezebel contrived to have stoned to death for blasphemy. When Jezebel and Ahab went to take possession of the vineyard, they encoun-

Jeroboam:
[1] *I Kings 12:27–33; 13:1–6*

Jerome, Saint: *see* Ambrose, St; Augustine, St, Gregory the Great, St
[1] *Golden Legend, St Jerome*

Jezebel: *see* Elijah
[1] *I Kings 21:1–23*
[2] *II Kings 9:30–37*

JEWELS

Minerals of luminous brilliance, embedded in the earth, were a source of wonder to ancients worldwide. In one widespread belief, they were formed from snake saliva. This link helps to explain why some jewel symbolism is similar to that of the serpent: jewels are often emblems of wisdom and, in many folk tales, jewels are found in the foreheads, eyes or mouths of serpentine guardian symbols such as dragons. A Christian parallel is the legend that jewels were scattered through the earth in the fall of Lucifer (Lightbearer, the name given to Satan when he resided in heaven), as fragments of his celestial light. Alternatively their origin is that they are evidence of divine energy, working in the darkness of the earth to produce from dull stone perfected jewels of light. In Jungian psychology, jewels symbolize self-knowledge won from the unconscious.

In addition to their obvious meaning of precious things, jewels (a word derived from Latin through French for "play things") have always been symbols of spiritual illumination, purity, refinement, superiority, durability, with magical powers of healing and protection. In Eastern religion, they embody the treasures of spiritual knowledge, or divine union. In Buddhism the *triratna* ("three jewels") are the Buddha, Dharma (his teachings) and Sangha (the monastic community). Jewels are linked with Vishnu in Hinduism; faith, knowledge and right conduct in Jainism; compassion and wisdom in Japan; truth in Judaism (twelve jewels in the breastplate of the high priest); and intellect and incorruptibility in Islam.

Specific virtues have been ascribed to different stones (see table). Some correspondences are based on colour – notably jet, one of very few stones associated with mourning, but also thought to be particularly protective against the evil eye because it reflects light. Reflective or transparent stones may also be associated with divination; red stones with ardour or vitality and, in the case of the carbuncle, war.

Symbolism	Jewel
Courage	agate, carnelian, jade, ruby, turquoise
Fertility	jasper
Fidelity	diamond, emerald, garnet, hyacinth, opal, topaz
Friendship	carnelian, lodestone, peridot, ruby, topaz, tourmeline
Joy	chrysoprase, jasper
Longevity	amber, catseye, diamond, jade, ruby
Love, passion	carbuncle, garnet, lapis lazuli, moonstone, ruby
Purity, chastity	crystal, diamond, jade, pearl, sapphire
Royalty, power	diamond, jade, ruby, sapphire
Sobriety	amethyst
Truth, honesty, sincerity	diamond, jade, lodestone, onyx, sapphire
Wisdom	chrysolite, diamond, jade, topaz, zircon
Youth	aquamarine, beryl, emerald

tered the prophet Elijah, who said: "Where dogs licked the blood of Naboth shall dogs lick thy blood … and the dogs shall eat Jezebel."[1] The scene was depicted by Frederic, Lord Leighton, in *Jezebel and Ahab*.

After Ahab's death Jezebel "painted her face and tied her hair" to seduce Jehu, Ahab's general; but Jehu ordered three eunuchs to hurl her out of her window. When she hit the ground she was trampled by horses and eaten by dogs.

Jimmu-tenno

The legendary first emperor of Japan, whose dates are traditionally 660BCE–585BCE. Jimmu-tenno (also known as Kamu-yamato-iware-biko) was the grandson of Hiko-hoho-demi ("Fireshade") and the great-great-great-grandson of the goddess Amaterasu.

Jimmu and his brother Itsu-se head-

Jimmu-tenno setting out to conquer new lands, from a 19th-century print.

ed eastward from the Hyuga region of northeast Kyushu island on a great expedition to conquer new lands. Japanese chronicles claim that the expedition began in 607BCE, but there is evidence to suggest that a historical invasion of Yamato from the west occurred *c*.300CE–400CE. After Itsu-se died in battle on Honshu, Jimmu and his army pressed on to pacify the Land of the Reed Plain (Yamato). Receiving the homage of local rulers as he went, Jimmu marched eastward, guided by a heavenly crow. Finally, when he reached Yamato, he called a halt to the expedition. He built a palace and married Isuke-yori-hime, a princess descended from the god Susano.

Jizo

A Japanese Buddhist deity, the protector of children, in particular of those who have died. Jizo looks after anyone in pain and is believed to bring souls back from hell. Together with Amida and Kannon he is one of the three most popular deities of Japanese Buddhism.

Joachim, Saint

According to legend,[1] Joachim and Anna, the parents of the Virgin, were married for twenty years without offspring. Joachim went to the Temple to make an offering but a priest ordered him away, declaring that it was not proper for a man who did not increase the people of God to approach the altar. Joachim was ashamed to go home and went to live among the shepherds. One day an angel appeared to him and told him that Anna would give birth to Mary, conceived not in carnal desire but as a sign of divine generosity. The angel then revealed the same to Anna. The couple were

Jimmu-tenno: *see* Amaterasu; Ho-no-susori and Hiko-hoho-demi; IZANAGI AND IZANAMI; Susano

Jizo: *see* Amida; Kannon

Joachim, Saint: *see* Anna or Anne, St; Virgin
[1] *The Protevangelium of James (2nd cent.)* and *The Golden Legend, The Birth of the Blessed Virgin Mary*

Job

told to meet at the Golden Gate of Jerusalem, where they embraced tenderly. Giotto recorded these stories, which contributed to the development of the doctrine of the Immaculate Conception, in a famous series of frescoes (Arena Chapel, Padua).

Job

A symbol of patience and longsuffering in extreme circumstances. In the Bible, Job was a blameless and upright man who prospered in the land of Uz. Without his knowledge, he became the subject of an argument between God and Satan as to the strength of his faith. To test that faith, his herds, children, servants and house were all destroyed, and he was afflicted with boils. But Job refused to renounce God in spite of everything, including the advice of three friends (ironically called "Job's comforters") who tried to convince him he must have deserved his fate. God finally restored Job's family, property and health. An 1828 edition of the Book of Job was illustrated by William Blake.

Jocasta

A queen of Thebes in Greek myth. She was the wife of King Laius and later, unwittingly, married her son Oedipus.

John the Baptist, Saint

An ascetic prophet (died *c.*30CE) who practised baptism. He preached the imminent coming of the Messiah and is known as the forerunner of Christ.

According to the gospels,[1] the elderly priest Zacharias and his wife, Elizabeth, who lived in the days of King Herod, had no children. But as Zacharias was burning incense in the Temple, an angel announced that he

would have a son, named John, who would be great in the eyes of the Lord. Zacharias doubted the angel and in punishment was struck dumb. When the child was born, Zacharias was asked what he should be called; he wrote "John", and his speech was restored. At the Annunciation to the Virgin, an angel told Mary about the miraculous conception of John, and Mary went to stay with Elizabeth, who was her cousin. Their meeting is known as the Visitation.

When he grew up, John preached in the wilderness that the kingdom of heaven was at hand. "And John was clothed with camel's hair, and with a girdle of a skin about his loins." He ate wild honey and locusts. He baptized many people, proclaiming: "He that cometh after me is mightier than I." When Jesus was baptized, John "saw the Spirit of God descending like a dove. And lo a voice from heaven, saying, This is my beloved Son, in whom I am well pleased."[2]

John preached that it was unlawful for the ruler, Herod, to have married his brother's wife, Herodias, and for preaching this John was imprisoned; but Herod was afraid to put John to death because of his large following. On his birthday, Herod promised his stepdaughter (called Salome according to the Jewish historian Josephus) anything she wanted if she would dance for him. She was instructed by her mother to ask for the head of the Baptist. John was decapitated, and his head brought to Herod on a charger. Then his disciples buried his body.[3]

Episodes from John's life are common in art, especially the baptism of Christ and Salome with the saint's head. He also appears as a child in paintings of the Virgin and Child and of the Holy Family. As a man, John is usually shown as wild and unkempt, wearing a shaggy tunic and holding a long, thin cross. He may carry a lamb, in reference to his words as Christ approached for baptism: "Behold the Lamb of God, which taketh away the sin of the world." The lamb may hold the banner of the resurrection (a red cross on a white background).

John Chrysostom, Saint

John Chrysostom (*c*.347–407CE) was born at Antioch in Syria and in 398CE was elected archbishop of Constantinople. One story tells how he had a child by a princess, for which he was required to do penance by crawling on all fours – a scene engraved by Dürer.

Renowned for his eloquence (Chrysostom means "Mouth of Gold"), the saint is counted as one of the four Greek Doctors of the Church, along with Saints Athanasius, Basil and Gregory of Nazianzus. He may also appear with the four Latin Doctors, for example, sculpted under Bernini's *Chair of St Peter* (St Peter's, Rome).

John the Evangelist, Saint (John the Divine)

The author of the Fourth Gospel and the Book of Revelation is traditionally identified with Christ's "beloved disciple" John. He appears as a young man in numerous scenes in the New Testament. The brother of James the Great, John was a fisherman, and they were both mending their nets when Christ bade them follow him.[1] With Peter, the brothers were present at the Transfiguration and at the Agony in the Garden.

John has been identified as the unnamed "disciple whom Jesus loved", who wept on his shoulder at the Last Supper, and to whom Christ entrusted the care of his mother after his death.[2] In the Acts of the Apostles, John is described preaching with Peter. They were imprisoned together, and eventually John is said to have been exiled to the island of Patmos. He is said to have spent his last years at Ephesus, where he died. Poussin painted him as an old man writing.

According to legend,[3] John returned to Ephesus at the same time as the body of his dear friend Drusiana was being carried out for burial. John said: "Drusiana, may my Lord Jesus Christ raise you to life! Arise, go to your house and prepare food for me!" As Filippino Lippi depicted, Drusiana rose from the dead as if from sleep (Strozzi Chapel, Santa Maria Novella, Florence). At another time, a priest of the temple of Artemis wanted proof of John's faith. Two criminals were ordered to drink poison and died instantly, but when John took the cup, he made the sign of the cross and suffered no harm. In art he may hold a chalice full of snakes, alluding to this episode, as in Jan van Eyck's Ghent altarpiece (Cathedral of St Bavo, Ghent). When John went to Rome, he was thrown into a vat of boiling oil, yet emerged unscathed.

John's attribute is an eagle, a representation of divine inspiration, which is found in John's Gospel.

John Gualbert, Saint

John Gualbert (Giovanni Gualberto) of Florence (*c*.985–1073CE) was said to have pardoned his brother's murderer. He later had a vision of Christ on the Cross bowing his head toward him. He founded the monastic Order of the Vallombrosans in Tuscany,

John Chrysostom: *see* Doctor

John the Evangelist, Saint: *see* Apocalypse; Christ, The Life of; Evangelists; James the Great; Martyrs; Passion of Christ; Peter, St; Virgin
[1] *Mark 1:19–20*
[2] *John 19:25–27*
[3] *Golden Legend, St John the Evangelist*

John Gualbert, Saint: *see* RELIGIOUS ORDERS

based on St Benedict's rule. In Tuscan art he wears the Vallombrosans' light grey habit, sometimes with a crucifix.

Jonah

According to the Book of Jonah in the Bible, God ordered the prophet Jonah to visit the corrupt city of Nineveh and warn it of its impending destruction. But Jonah feared the reaction of the city's people and took a boat in the opposite direction. God sent a great tempest, and although the sailors rowed hard, they could not bring the vessel to land. Believing him to be the cause, they cast Jonah into the sea and the storm ceased. A "great fish" swallowed him up, but after three days and nights he repented and the fish disgorged him unharmed.[1]

The story of Jonah was taken as a prefiguration of Christ and the Resurrection, because when the Pharisees demanded a sign from Christ, he said that, like Jonah, "so shall the Son of Man be three days and three nights in the heart of the earth".[2] Michelangelo's massive image of Jonah appears above the altar in the Sistine Chapel in the Vatican, Rome.

Joseph, son of Jacob

In the Bible, Joseph was the favourite of the patriarch Jacob's twelve sons, and the one to whom he gave "a coat of many colours" (the Hebrew phrase is now usually translated as "a long-sleeved coat").[1] With the exception of Benjamin (the only brother to have the same mother as Joseph), the other sons envied Joseph their father's favouritism. Joseph dreamed that his sheaf of corn stood upright while his brothers' bowed down; and that the sun, moon and eleven stars paid homage to his star. This fuelled the broth-

ers' jealousy, and one day, when they were tending their sheep, they stripped Joseph of his coat, threw him in an empty well, and sold him as a slave for twenty pieces of silver to merchants journeying into Egypt. The brothers smeared the coat in goat's blood to convince Jacob that Joseph had been devoured by a wild animal.

In Egypt, Joseph was sold to Potiphar, the captain of Pharaoh's guard, who made him overseer of his house. Potiphar's wife pressed Joseph to make love to her, and when he refused she accused him of trying to rape her. Potiphar threw Joseph into prison.[2] When Pharaoh's baker and butler were also imprisoned, Joseph interpreted their dreams.[3] On his release, the butler recommended Joseph as an interpreter of Pharaoh's strange dreams, in which seven lean cattle devoured seven fat ones, and seven thin sheaves of corn ate seven thick ones. Joseph understood the dreams to mean that seven years of famine would follow seven years of plenty, and advised that reserves be set aside for the famine. Pharaoh rewarded Joseph for his prophecy by making him viceroy and overseer of preparations for the famine, and loading him with honours.[4]

When the famine came, Jacob sent his sons, except for Benjamin, to buy corn in Egypt. The brothers bowed down in respect before Joseph, without recognizing him. In return for corn, Joseph demanded that Benjamin be brought to Egypt, while another brother, Simeon, stayed as hostage. The brothers were reluctant, fearing for their father's health if another of his sons should come to any harm, but eventually they agreed.

On their return to Egypt with Benjamin, Joseph tormented his brothers further. He placed a silver cup in Benjamin's sack then declared that there had been a theft. Joseph's steward found the cup, accused Benjamin, and brought the brothers before Joseph. At last Joseph revealed his identity. He was reconciled with his brothers and invited them and Jacob to live with him in Egypt.[5]

The stories of Joseph, his ill-treatment, rise to power, wisdom and magnanimity, were very popular, especially in late medieval and Renaissance art. They appear in canvases, frescoes, furniture and tapestries. Individual scenes were also depicted, as in the 17th-century Orazio Gentileschi's *Joseph and Potiphar's Wife*.

Joseph, husband of the Virgin
All that is known of Joseph appears in the gospels. He was descended from the house of David,[1] worked as a carpenter and became betrothed to Mary, who had already conceived "of the Holy Ghost". An angel appeared to him to dispel his fears about marrying Mary, and then again after Jesus' birth to tell him to flee into Egypt with Mary and the child in order to avoid Herod's slaughter of all infant boys in Bethlehem. When Herod died, the angel appeared to Joseph once more to tell him to return to Nazareth with his family.[2]

Joseph presumably died before the Crucifixion, because on the Cross Jesus entrusted Mary to the care of one of his disciples, most likely John. Joseph appears in fresco cycles of the Life of the Virgin and Christ, and in scenes such as the Flight into Egypt and the Holy Family. He is usually depicted as a modest, benevolent old man. The idea that Joseph was elderly

may have come from an apocryphal gospel which claims that he had been married previously, had six children and lived to 111.[3] His attribute may be the Virgin's lily of purity or the flowering rod, which is said to have blossomed miraculously in the Temple to show that he was chosen above all others to be the Virgin's husband.

Joseph of Arimathea
A wealthy follower of Jesus who, in to the gospels, asked Pilate's permission to remove Jesus' body after the Crucifixion. Joseph wrapped it in clean linen and laid it in his own rock-cut tomb before rolling a stone over the entrance.[1] Joseph is often shown at the Deposition, lowering Christ from the Cross with Nicodemus, and at the Entombment (or Lamentation), such as that by Rogier van der Weyden.

Joshua
In the Bible,[1] Joshua succeeded Moses as leader of the Israelites, bringing them into the Promised Land. Having conquered kingdoms and cities, he shared them among the twelve tribes of Israel. After Moses' death Joshua led his people to the River Jordan and ordered his priests to lead the Ark of the Covenant across. As their feet touched the water, it separated, letting the people through. In memory of this miracle, Joshua asked twelve men to take twelve stones from where the priests had stood on the water and set them up on the far bank.[2] On this side lay the city of Jericho in the land of Canaan which Joshua besieged for six days. Every day seven priests marched around the city with seven trumpets before the Ark of the Covenant, but on the seventh day they went around seven times, then blew the trumpets.

Joseph, Husband of the Virgin: see Holy Family; Virgin, Life of
[1] *Matthew 1:1–16*
[2] *Matthew 2:13–23*
[3] *The Apocryphal History of Joseph the Carpenter*

Joseph of Arimathea: see Lamentation
[1] *Matthew 27:57–60*

Joshua:
[1] *Deuteronomy 31:14*
[2] *Joshua 3* and *4*
[3] *Joshua 6:1–20*
[4] *Joshua 10:12–28*

At this the Israelites gave a great shout and the walls of the city collapsed.[3] These scenes were recorded in Ghiberti's *Joshua* door panel for the Baptistry in Florence. John Martin's huge and dramatic *Joshua Commanding the Sun to Stand Still Over Gibeon* shows how God allowed the Israelites time to avenge themselves on one enemy, the Amorites, of whom many were slaughtered.

Jotunheim
The "Home of the Giants" in Norse myth. It lay in the roots of Yggdrasil, the cosmic ash tree which united the earth, the heavens and the underworld.

Journey
A universal symbol of transition, change or evolution, expressed in countless myths and legends in which a hero undertakes a journey beset with physical and moral trials. Many religious traditions envisage the soul journeying to an afterlife, and rites of passage often enact a symbolic journey to the next phase of life. In psychology a journey may symbolize the quest for self-discovery.

Jubilee *see* NUMBERS

Judas Iscariot
In the gospels, Judas is the disciple who betrayed Christ for thirty pieces of silver. At the Last Supper, Christ declared to his disciples that one of them would betray him. Judas asked, "Is it I?", to which Christ replied, "Thou hast said".[1] In paintings of the Last Supper, Judas usually sits somewhat apart. He led Pilate's soldiers to the Garden of Gethsemane, where he singled out his master with a kiss.[2] After Christ had been condemned,

Judas returned the silver and hanged himself in shame.[3] Caravaggio's *The Taking of Christ* was one of many treatments of this episode.

Judas is usually unattractive and may wear a yellow cloak. He may, as in Giotto's *The Stirring of Judas*, have a demon goading him. His attributes may be a moneybag, or the rope with which he hanged himself.

Jude, Saint (Apostle, Disciple)
The disciple Jude, also identified as Thaddeus and as the author of the Letter of Jude, was the brother of James the Less (and so perhaps also of Jesus). He was also known as "the other Judas, not Iscariot".[1] According to legend,[2] he went with another brother, Simon, to preach in Persia, where they performed baptisms and miracles and were martyred. Jude was martyred with a club, halberd or lance, which he might hold as attribute. He is the patron of lost causes.

Judith
The Israelite heroine of the book of the same name in the Apocrypha of the Old Testament. Holofernes, the commander of the Assyrian army, led his troops to Judea and prepared to make war with the people of Israel. A Jewish widow, Judith, bathed and adorned herself in her finest clothes and jewels and, accompanied by her maid and bearing wine and food, entered the Assyrian camp on the pretext that she had come to betray her people.[1] Seduced by her beauty, Holofernes gave a feast in her honour and, left alone with her, fell asleep from too much wine. Taking his sword, Judith seized his hair and struck off his head, which she bore in triumph to her people.[2] Terrified, the Assyrians fled.

Judith is usually depicted holding the head of Holofernes and sometimes the sword; her maid may hold the sack in which they placed the head. Judith was popular in Renaissance and Baroque art: Michelangelo (Sistine Chapel), Cristofano Allori and Artemisia Gentileschi all painted famous interpretations.

Jujube Tree

In Daoism, a symbol of pure nourishment, its fruit the food of immortality. The tree also appears in the Islamic paradise, a symbol of the farthest limits of time and space.

Julian the Hospitaller, Saint

According to legend[1], a stag told the noble Julian that he would kill his parents. To avoid this tragedy, Julian fled from home. He later married a widow, whose dowry was a castle. His parents arrived at the castle in search of their son; he was not at home, but his wife let them sleep in the marriage bed. Julian returned and saw two people asleep in his bed; thinking his wife had taken a lover, he killed them.

To pay for his crime, Julian and his wife established a hospice for the poor and sick near a river, across which he ferried travellers. One night he took a poor leper home and put him to bed. The man was an angel and told Julian that he had served his penance. Castagno frescoed Julian as a humble young man, while Cristofano Allori depicted his hospitality. His attribute may be a stag. He is the patron of ferrymen, travellers and innkeepers.

Juno see Hera

Jupiter see Zeus

Jurupari

A child of the sun who overthrew the rule of women, according to the Tupi people of Amazonian Brazil. In their version of a myth found widely from the Amazon to Tierra del Fuego, the Tupi recount how women, not men, originally ruled the world. The sun grew angry at this and took a wife, Ceucy, a virgin whom he made pregnant by the sap of the cucura tree. Ceucy bore Jurupari, who transferred all power and sacred wisdom to men. Jurupari told men to celebrate their power by holding feasts from which women were excluded on pain of death; to set an example, he even caused the death of his own mother. To this day Jurupari is said to wander the world looking for the perfect wife for his father, the sun.

Justina of Antioch, Saint

In legend,[1] a sorceror of Antioch called Cyprian (3rd century CE) thrice invoked the Devil to help him seduce the Christian virgin Justina. But each time she made the sign of the cross and the Devil fled. Realizing that Christ was greater than the Devil, Cyprian was converted. Justina and he were martyred at Nicomedia and may appear together. A unicorn, symbol of chastity, is Justina's attribute.

Justina of Padua, Saint

Justina was greatly revered in Padua, where a church was dedicated to her in the 6th century CE. A medieval legend claimed that she was baptized by a follower of St Peter and martyred under Nero. She appears in Paduan and Venetian painting and, like Justina of Antioch, may be shown with a unicorn because she retained her virginity even when the Devil tried to tempt her.

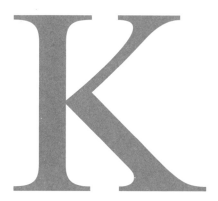

Ka

In Egyptian belief, the soul or spirit of an individual after death. Life-like funerary statues were believed to embody the *ka* of the person whom they represented.

Ka'aba

The cube-shaped building at the heart of Makkah (Mecca). In Islam it symbolizes the spiritual centre of the world, the origin of civilization, stability, totality and perfection. Pilgrims circumambulate the Ka'aba seven times and kiss the Black Stone at one corner – a meteorite said to have been given to Abraham by the archangel Gabriel.

Kachina

One of a class of ancestral spirits, according to the Pueblo Native American peoples of the southwestern United States, such as the Hopi and Zuni. Kachinas are revered as intermediaries between humans and the great elemental gods and as bringers of harmony and prosperity.

Kali

The Hindu goddess of death, the destroyer of demons and the most terrifying of all Hindu goddesses. Kali ("The Black One" or "Time") is dark-skinned and emaciated, with great fangs. She wears a tiger skin and a gruesome necklace of severed heads or skulls and appears most often on battlefields or at cremation grounds.

Kali, from a wall painting.

She is said to spring from the forehead of the warrior goddess Durga when she grows angry. Her ferocity is boundless and in battle she is liable to become so intoxicated with blood that she is in danger of causing the destruction of the world.

According to one myth Durga summoned Kali to kill the demon Raktabija, who produced replicas of himself from every drop of his blood that touched the ground. Durga and her companion goddesses, the seven Matrikas ("Little Mothers"), had wounded him many times, only to find themselves facing an ever-increasing number of Raktabijas. When Kali appeared she caught all his blood before it landed on the earth, devoured all the replica demons in a single mouthful and finally sucked Raktabija dry.

The goddess's most famous temple is at Kalighata in Calcutta.

Kalkin

The future tenth avatar (incarnation) of the Hindu god Vishnu. Kalki is a messianic figure whose advent will herald the end of the present cosmic age of evil, the Kali Yuga, and the beginning of a new golden age, or Krita Yuga. It is said that he will be manifested as a warrior on a white horse, or (according to South Indian popular belief) as the horse itself.

Kannon

The Japanese Buddhist *bosatsu* (bodhisattva) of mercy and wise counsel. Kannon is derived, like her Chinese equivalent Guanyin, from the Indian bodhisattva Avalokiteshvara.

Her cult was introduced from Korea a short while after Buddhism reached the Japanese archipelago.

Kannon, from a sword-guard dating from the late 19th century.

She is revered as the protector of infants and women in childbirth, as well as being the protector of the souls of the dead. In her popular manifestation as Senju Kannon ("Thousand-Armed Kannon"), she is said to dispense compassion from each of his thousand hands. She is often regarded as the companion of the Buddha Amida.

Karashishi

Symbols of strength and courage, a pair of chow-faced "lions" that guard Buddhist temples in Japan. The male has his mouth open, but is not terrifying. The stylized form is based on second-hand Chinese contact with the lion. The name "Dogs of Fo [Buddha]" is an apt description.

Karma

The Hindu and Buddhist term for retributive destiny; deeds or misdeeds in one life lead inevitably to good or bad consequences in the next. Karma (Sanskrit, literally "action"), which has been described as a moral balance sheet, links the

Kalkin: *see* VISHNU, THE AVATARS OF

Karashishi: *see* Dog; Lion

Kannon: *see* Amida; Avalokiteshvara; Bodhisattva; Guanyin

*St Peter holding the key
to heaven, after a 13th-
century relief sculpture,
Notre Dame, Paris.*

actions of the individual with the
forces of cause and effect in the
universe.

Kek and Keket *see* **Ogdoad, The**

Keret

A famous king of Ugaritic (Canaanite) myth. King Keret was anxious for
an heir and married seven times, but
each of his wives died childless.

In a dream, the supreme god El told
him to invade the neighbouring kingdom and marry Huray, the daughter
of its ruler. Keret embarked on his
mission and vowed to present the fertility goddess Ashera, the wife of El,
with several times Huray's weight in
gold if he succeeded. Keket won his
bride, and El promised that Huray
would have eight sons and that the eldest would be weaned by two goddesses, Ashera and Anath. Huray bore the
eight sons, but then Keret fell ill, probably because he had failed to fulfil his
promise to Ashera. He was unable to
administer justice and the land grew
dry and infertile. However, a ritual was
held in honour of the storm god Baal
and the rains returned. Keret recovered his health and suppressed a rebellion by one of his sons.

Key

Authority, power of choice, entry,
freedom of action, knowledge, initiation. Gold and silver keys, diagonally
crossed, are a papal emblem of
authority, the symbolic "keys of the
kingdom of heaven" which Christ
conferred on Peter. In Roman tradition, keys were similarly held in the
left hand of Janus, the guardian of
doors and gates, who was believed to
control the passage from day to night
and from winter to summer. Although

keys can lock as well as unlock, they
are nearly always visual symbols of
access, liberation or, in initiations,
progress from one stage of life to the
next (hence formerly and formally the
"key of the door" to adulthood at 21).
The Egyptian *ankh*, a key-like cross,
symbolizes passage to the afterlife.
Keys are often emblems of office or of
the freedom of a city. They were symbols of prosperity in Japan, signifying
the keys to the rice granary.

Khepry

A divine scarab beetle which was the
dawn manifestation of the Egyptian
sun god. Khepry is typically represented pushing the sun up into the sky, an
image derived from the scarab rolling
a ball of dung. To the Egyptians, the
scarab beetle was a symbol of rebirth,
regeneration and transformation.

Khnum

One of the four principal creator gods
of Egypt, the others being Amun-Ra,
Atum and Ptah. Khnum was envisaged as a potter who moulded deities,
humans and animals from clay on his
potter's wheel, and then breathed life
into them. He was usually depicted as
a man with the head of a ram, his
sacred animal and a symbol of male
creative power. Khnum was believed
to control the rising of the waters of
the Nile, an annual phenomenon crucial to the fertility of the land.

Khori Tumed

The name of a man who married a
swan maiden, according to the
mythology of the Buriat people of
Siberia. One day Khori Tumed saw
nine swans fly down to the island of
Oikhon in Lake Baikal, where they
undressed to reveal nine beautiful

maidens. As they bathed in the lake, Khori Tumed took away the feather dress of one swan, so that she could not fly away with the eight other swan maidens. She became his wife and bore him eleven sons.

They were happy, but one day she asked to try on her old swan dress, which Khori Tumed kept hidden. He agreed, thinking that he could stop her if she tried to escape through the door of their *yurt* (a round tent of skins). However, as soon as his wife donned the dress she flew up through the smoke hole in the *yurt*'s roof. Khori Tumed held her feet and asked her to name their sons before she went. She did so and they became men. She then flew around the *yurt* many times bestowing blessings, before finally disappearing into the sky.

Ki

The Sumerian earth goddess, the daughter of Nammu, the primeval sea, and the consort of An, the supreme deity. The coupling of Ki and An produced Enlil (the Akkadian Ea) and Enki, as well as the other great gods of the Sumerian pantheon.

Kikimora

A household deity of Russian folk myth. The *kikimora*, which takes the form of a small female being with flowing hair, is believed to be a manifestation of the soul of a dead person. It is said that if a housewife is lazy the *kikimora* will cause trouble and require propitiating. The appearance of the deity is sometimes taken as a portent of misfortune.

King

Often a symbol of divinely sanctioned power as well as of absolute temporal authority over a tribe, nation or region. The stronger the king's symbolic link with supernatural forces, the more crucial became his leadership qualities, intelligence and health – authority going hand in hand with responsibility for the happiness and health of his subjects. Hence ancient sacrifices of the king (or a scapegoat representing the king) when countries were overtaken by plagues or crop failures. Kings were symbols of fecundity, wisdom, military success and divine favour. The deification of emperors in Rome followed older traditions in which kings were symbolic delegates of the sun, a notion as alive in 17th-century France (when the Sun King, Louis XIV, guaranteed the eminence of his country) as it was in the empire of the Incas. Louis XVI was executed as a symbolic hostage to France's declining fortunes during the French Revolution two centuries later. In constitutional monarchies, despite ritual anointings and coronations, the ancient symbolism of kings as archetypes of human perfectibility, accountable to God rather than to the people, has been undercut, making their failings less dismaying. Traditional symbols of kingship include the sun (the queen is symbolized by the moon), gold, jade, the rod or sceptre, the throne or dais, the orb, the ruby, the sword and arrows.

Kingfisher

Fidelity, peace – a symbol of grace, nobility and conjugal devotion in China, and in Greece associated with mournful tranquillity through the myth of Alcyone (or Halcyone), in which she and her husband Ceyx were turned into kingfishers by the god Zeus. As kingfishers were thought to

Ki: *see* Anu (1); Enki; Enlil

Kikimora: see Bannik; Domovoi; Dvorovoi

King: *see* Arrow; Clown; Crown; Globe, Orb; Gold; Jade; Rod; Ruby; Sacrifice; Scapegoat; Sceptre; Sun; Sword; Throne; WISDOM

Kingfisher: *see* Birds; FIDELITY

nest at sea, Alcyone's father, Aeolus,
the god of wind, kept the waters calm
for seven days each year so that his
daughter could incubate her eggs.

Kingu

The son of the god Apsu, the sweet-
water ocean, and the goddess Tiamat, the salt-water ocean, according
to the Akkadian (Babylonian) creation myth. After the god Ea killed
Apsu, Kingu led his mother's demon
army against Ea's son Marduk.
Kingu was slain by Marduk, who
mixed his blood with earth to make
the first humans.

Kiss

Beyond its obvious personal significance, the kiss is a religious symbol of
spiritual union – the meaning behind
the custom of kissing church images
of saints. Kissing someone's hand was
a medieval sign of homage. The feet
or robes of kings were kissed both in
homage and in the belief that part of
their sanctity might transfer itself.

Kitchen God, The

The most important of all Chinese
domestic deities. The image of the

*The Kitchen God and his wife, from a
woodblock print.*

Kitchen God (alternatively known as
the Hearth God) usually stood above
the family stove, from where he would
observe the household.

Every New Year the god was said to
visit heaven to give an account of the
behaviour of the family in the past
year. Before he left, sweet paste or
honey was smeared over the mouth of
his image in order to prevent him
from speaking when he arrived (other
accounts say that this was done to
please him and to make him speak
sweet words). To speed the god on his
journey to heaven the image was ceremonially burnt.

Knee

Kneeling or bending the knee is a signal of submission and supplication in
all cultures, or of humility and homage, as in kneeling to pray, or curtsey-
ing to royalty.

Knife

A ritual instrument of sacrifice, circumcision and martydom, the knife is
usually a destructive symbol, particularly in the hands of Hindu divinities,
but in Buddhism it can signify severance from the ties of materialism. The
knife is the attribute of several Christian saints, including Bartholomew,
who is said to have been flayed alive.
Freud associated the knife with the
phallus in his interpretation of dreams.

Knight

In medieval legend, a symbol of mastery of the arts of horsemanship and
weaponry, the virtues of loyalty and
honourable service, and the sublimation of brutish desires. Knighthood
set before privileged young men a
symbolic ideal and generated a vast
literature of chivalry. In the colour

symbolism of knighthood, the Green Knight is the questing neophyte; the White Knight the chaste, conquering hero; the Red Knight the battle-tested warrior at spiritual maturity. The Black Knight is a more ambivalent figure, representing either evil or the anonymity of the man who has austerely withdrawn to expiate his sins. The symbolism of knighthood as a mission was taken up by St Ignatius Loyola who founded the Jesuits as an order dedicated to holy chivalry. The Knight Errant, by contrast, wanders in the vague hope that a worthy mission will present itself.

Knot

Tight knots are symbols of union, fixation or blockage, whereas knots shown as a loose, interwoven pattern represent infinity or longevity (a line without beginning or end). Incorporating ideas of tying or untying, capture or release, knot symbolism is remarkably complex. Curious fishermen's superstitions in northern Europe and Scotland attach magic significance to knots tied in pocket handkerchiefs or cords, thought to influence wind and weather. The Roman prohibition on wearing knotted garments in the temple of Juno Lucina, goddess of childbirth, reflects similar belief in sympathetic magic – knots representing blockage in a context where release was crucial. "Tying the knot", a Victorian synonym for marriage, was a popular motif in paintings of the Roman god of love Cupid. Union is also the symbolism of the knotted cord worn by Brahmins, binding them to Brahma in the same way as the thrice-knotted cord of the Franciscan friar binds him to his vows of poverty, celibacy and obedience.

Alternatively, knots often had protective symbolism, based probably on the idea of frustration. Thus, in Islam, beards were knotted to baffle demons, whereas in the presence of goodness knots were forbidden – as in the mosque at Mecca. The Gordian knot exemplified the principle of frustration. By slashing it apart, Alexander the Great found a short-term solution but never completed the conquest of Asia predicted for the man who could untie the knot.

The moral lesson Buddhism drew from this famous incident was that patience, not violence, unravels knots, specifically the knots tying humanity to the round of material existence. The open-weave knot pattern is one of the eight emblems of good luck in Chinese Buddhism. Similar ornamental patterns representing continuity appear in Hindu and Celtic art.

Kong Fuzi

"Master Kong", a Chinese philosopher better known in the West as Confucius, the latinized form of his name. Kong Fuzi (551BCE–479BCE) founded Confucianism, which stressed above all education, ritual, filial piety and devotion to the state and to members of one's family, particularly the elderly and ancestors.

Kong Fuzi himself came to be regarded as a divine figure who ranked after Heaven, Earth, the Imperial Ancestors and the Gods of Grain and Soil in the hierarchy of deities of the imperial Chinese state.

Krishna

A divine hero, the eighth avatar (incarnation) of the Hindu god Vishnu, but also an important figure in his

Knot: *see* Bonds; LONGEVITY

Krishna: *see* Indra; VISHNU, THE AVATARS OF

Lancelot, the most famous knight of the Arthurian legend; from a stained glass window by William Morris.

Kronos

*Krishna dancing on
the head of the snake
demon Kaliya, from
a 10th-century Indian
bronze.*

own right. When Kamsa, the evil king
of Mathura, heard a prediction that
the eighth child of his sister Devaki
would kill him, he imprisoned Devaki
and her husband Vasudeva, and
ordered each of their children to be
killed at birth. However, Vasudeva
smuggled the eighth child, Krishna
("Dark"), out of the birth chamber
and exchanged him for the newborn
daughter of the cowherds Nanda and
Yashoda, who lived across the river
Yamuna (Jumna). Outsmarted,
Kamsa ordered the terrible goddess
Putana to devour any newborn that
might be Krishna. But when she
offered Krishna her poisonous breast,
he sucked the life out of her.

As a child Krishna became
renowned for his pranks, especially
for stealing milk and butter. He
encouraged his foster-father to cease
worshipping Indra, who, in retaliation, sent a deluge to flood the land.
But Krishna lifted Mount Govard-
hana as an umbrella to protect the
cowherds and their cattle. He also
defeated Kaliya, a many-headed serpent infesting the Yamuna.

Krishna liked to play tricks on the
gopis, the young women of the
cowherd tribe. On one such occasion
he stole their clothes as they bathed
in the Yamuna. The *gopis* adored the
enchanting youth and left their
homes to join him by the river in an
ecstatic dance. The beautiful *gopi*
Radha captured Krishna's heart. Traditions vary as to whether she was
one of Krishna's wives, or his mistress, but their passion symbolizes the
intimate relationship between deity
and worshipper.

Eventually word of Krishna's deeds
reached King Kamsa, who summoned him. Krishna killed the bull-

demon Arishta, the horse-demon
Keshin and a champion wrestler,
before finally hurling Kamsa against a
wall and killing him. Then he led his
followers, the Yadavas, to a new city
called Duaraka.

Krishna had many wives. One, Ruk-
mini, bore a son, Pradyumna, who
also had a son Aniruddha. Aniruddha
was captured by the demon Bana. In
Krishna's fight to retrieve him it
seemed that the world would be dissolved, but Shiva, Bana's ally, recognized Krishna as the highest god.
Krishna spared Bana and freed his
own grandson.

Krishna's death was brought about
when some young Yadavas offended a
group of sages, by asking them what
sort of child they thought Samba
(another grandson who they had
dressed as a woman) would bear.
Incensed, the sages cursed Samba to
bear a pestle that would destroy the
Yadavas. The pestle was ground to
dust and thrown into the sea, where it
turned to reeds. One lance-like reed
was eaten by a fish and then caught
by a hunter. In a drinking bout,
Krishna, Balarama and the Yadavas
picked the reeds, killing each other
with them. As Krishna sat lost in
thought, the hunter, mistaking him
for a deer, shot him in the foot with
the reed he had found in the fish, and
killed him. Krishna then resumed his
divine nature.

Kronos

A Titan, the son of the Greek goddess Gaia, the earth, and Uranos, the
sky. When Gaia bore the Cyclopes,
Hekatoncheires and Titans, their
huge size alarmed Uranos, who
forced them back into her womb.
Gaia persuaded Kronos, the last-

born Titan, to castrate his father when he next had intercourse with her. Uranos died and Kronos became the ruler of heaven.

Kronos feared being overthrown by his children and devoured each of his offspring as soon as his wife, Rhea, gave birth. But Rhea concealed the sixth child, Zeus, and instead gave Kronos a rock wrapped in swaddling clothes. Zeus grew up in the care of Gaia and plotted the overthrow of Kronos. First, the goddess Metis ("Wise Cunning") gave Kronos a drink that made him regurgitate the brothers and sisters of Zeus (Demeter, Hades, Hera, Hestia and Poseidon). Zeus and his siblings fought Kronos and defeated him. Kronos went to the underworld and became, in some accounts, ruler of Elysium.

In the Orphic version of the creation myth, the name Kronos (which is of uncertain origin) was reinterpreted as Chronos ("Time").

Kukulkan
A Mayan deity (also called Gucumatz), equivalent to the Aztec Quetzalcoatl.

Kumarbi
The father of the gods, in Hittite mythology. In the beginning the ruler of heaven was Alalu, but he was deposed by the god Anu. Kumarbi (the equivalent of the Sumerian deity Enlil) in turn overthrew Anu and bit off his penis, but at the same time was impregnated by Anu's sperm. He gave birth to three "terrible gods", probably three different aspects of the weather god Teshub.

The sources are incomplete, but Teshub apparently overthrew Kumarbi, who then sought to avenge his downfall. He coupled with the Sea, representing the forces of chaos, and produced a son, Ullikummi, who grew to an enormous size on the shoulders of the sea-giant Upelluri. Ullikummi forced Teshub to abdicate. Teshub went to the wise god Ea, who separated Ullikummi from Upelluri, destroying his strength. The struggle between Kumarbi and Teshub was then renewed.

Kundalini
The Hindu image of latent or "earth" energy, symbolically represented by a sleeping serpent coiled at the base of the spine. Through spiritual discipline, the *kundalini* is roused so that a serpentine flow of life force moves upward through the etheric body via a series of *chakras* (wheels). These elements of the self, if properly developed, pass it on in steadily purified form to the crown *chakra*, there to blaze out as enlightenment.

Kurma
A tortoise, the second avatar (incarnation) of the Hindu god Vishnu. Kurma supported Mount Mandara on his back during the churning of the ocean by the Devas and Asuras.

Kusa-nada-hime
In Jaopanese myth, Kusa-nada-hime ("Rice Paddy Princess") was the youngest of eight sisters, seven of whom had been devoured by Yama-to-no-orochi, an eight-headed dragon. The creature was due to come for her when Susano arrived at the house of her elderly parents, on the river Hi in Izumo, Honshu island. The god killed the dragon and, with her parents' consent, married Kusa-nada-hime.

Labarum *see* **Chi-Rho**

Labyrinth
A labyrinth or maze is a structure or pattern of complex passages that is difficult to penetrate. The earliest known labyrinths, in Egypt and Etruria, were built to keep the tombs of kings inviolate. According to the Greek author Herodotus (*c*.484–*c*.425BCE), the greatest of these, near Lake Moeris in Egypt, had a baffling 3,000 chambers and twelve courts.

Remarkable plumbing conduits at the Minoan palace of Knossos on Crete may have been the origin of the legendary labyrinth of King Minos in which Theseus killed the Minotaur. The usual psychoanalytical reading of this myth is that Theseus, the saviour–hero, overcame the brutish aspects of his own character as well as the power of Minos. This meshes with the major religious and psychological meanings of passing through a labyrinth – that it represents an initiation, a symbolic return to the womb, a "death" leading to rebirth, the discovery of a spiritual

centre, the laborious and often perplexing process of self-discovery. A more obvious meaning of the labyrinth is that it symbolizes the manifold and difficult choices of life. Labyrinths formed by garden hedges turned this problem into a game.

But many labyrinths are unicursal, having no traps but leading sinuously along a single path. These were often used in early temples as initiation routes or more widely for religious dances that imitated the paths of the sun or planets. They reappeared on the floors of medieval Christian churches as "roads to Jerusalem" – paths symbolizing pilgrimage. At Chartres cathedral, France, penitents shuffled 650 feet (200m) on their knees along such a circular maze within an area only 40 feet (12 m) in diameter.

Lachesis
One of the three Fates of Greek myth, the sister of Clotho and Atropos. When a person was born, she held

the spindle of the thread of life, and may also be depicted measuring it out.

Laius

A king of Thebes in Greece, the father of Oedipus and husband of Jocasta.

Lake

Lakes are linked with rebirth and enchantment through the feminine symbolism of water, and also with the transition to death and other states. Priests bathed in the artificial "sacred lakes" of Egyptian temples, perhaps symbolizing the waters of creation, in order to become ritually pure. In Greek myth, the god Dionysos descended to the underworld through a lake. The Celtic custom of casting trophies to water spirits explains the connection between the Lady of the Lake and the sword Excalibur in Arthurian legend. Lakes may be the entrance to the Celtic Otherworld of enchantment and bliss, as in the Irish story of Oisín and Niamh, .

Lakshmana

In Hindu myth, the brother and companion of Rama, whom he assisted in many of his exploits.

Lamb

A symbol of purity, sacrifice, renewal, redemption, innocence, gentleness, humility and patience. In the Bible, a lamb or ram was frequently sacrificed to God. To protect themselves during the plague visited on the first-born of the Egyptians, the Israelites were instructed to kill a lamb "without blemish" and sprinkle their doorposts with its blood, an act which protected their own first-born.[1] This was the origin of Passover, when paschal lambs

were sacrificed in honour of God. Prophets such as Isaiah described the coming Messiah as a lamb. Because a lamb (or ram) was substituted for Isaac in the Sacrifice of Abraham, the Sacrificial Lamb or Lamb of God was taken as a prototype of Christ, the paschal lamb who shed his blood at Passovertide for the salvation of humankind. Hence John the Baptist proclaimed Jesus "the Lamb of God, which taketh away the sin of the world". A lamb may be the attribute of John the Baptist.[2]

Christ may carry a lamb in his role as the Good Shepherd, one of the earliest images of Christian art, adopted from pagan models. The Lamb of God is usually shown holding a cross or cruciform halo, or a banner with a red cross on a white background ("the Lamb and Flag") representing the Resurrection, the triumph over death. A lamb in early Christian and medieval art may also represent the Passion; its blood may flow into a chalice. In early Christian paintings, the disciples may appear as twelve sheep with the lamb in their midst.

A lamb with a book or seals refers to the Christ of the Book of Revelation, also described as a lamb with seven horns and seven eyes (seven spirits of God). The judging lamb of the Apocalypse is capable of wrath, at odds with the lamb's generally meek symbolism. In Revelation a lamb stood on Mount Sion; this lamb may be taken to represent the Church. Jan van Eyck's *Adoration of the Lamb* from the Ghent Polyptych illustrates another passage from Revelation[3]; it shows the lamb on an altar surrounded by angels holding the Instruments of Christ's Passion, while people gather from all corners of the world.

Laius: *see* Oedipus

Lake: *see* Mirror; Sea; Water

Lakshmana: *see* Krishna; Rama

Lamb: *see* Abraham; Agnes, St; Banner; Blood; Book; Christ, The Life of; CROSS; Fire, Flame; Halo; Isaac; John the Baptist, St; Passion of Christ; LION; Sacrifice; Sheep; Shepherd
[1] *Exodus 12:3–7*
[2] *John 1:29*
[3] *Revelation 14:1–4*
[4] *John 10:11*
[5] *Matthew 10:6*
[6] *John 21:16*

Lameness

As well as representing the sacrificial figure of Christ, a lamb may also symbolize one of Christ's flock, under the protection of the Good Shepherd.[4] This is illustrated in the early Christian mosaics in the Mausoleum of Galla Placidia in Ravenna. Christ sent his disciples out to preach to the "lost sheep of the house of Israel".[5] After the Resurrection, Christ twice instructed Peter to "feed my sheep".[6]

The lamb is also an important sacrificial and redemptive symbol in the Islamic rites of Ramadan.

Lameness

Lameness may be a warning symbol of divine power, a mark left upon the body of a demiurge or hero who has come too close to competing with a god on equal terms. Thus Jacob was made lame when he wrestled with the angel of God in Genesis. The Greek smith god Hephaistos (the Roman Vulcan) was lamed in his encounter with Zeus (Jupiter). Smith gods, masters of the creative secrets of fire, are nearly always represented in myth as men who have been maimed.

Lamentation

Although the scene known as the Lamentation does not appear in the Gospels, in art this tableau of mourners around the body of Christ follows the Deposition and precedes the Entombment. Christ is usually laid on the ground at the foot of the Cross and the Marys weep near the body. The Virgin Mary may be fainting, while Mary Magdalene may clasp the feet of Christ in a gesture reminiscent of her washing them at the Last Supper. Joseph of Arimathea, Nicodemus and John the Evangelist may also be present. A version of the Lamentation called the Pietà (Italian, "Pity"), usually depicts the Virgin alone with the dead Christ. Northern European artists emphasize the harrowing qualities of the subject, but Michelangelo's early *Pietà* conveys a gentle pathos, harmoniously placing Christ (as a fully grown man) in the lap of his mother. In other Pietàs, Christ may be on the ground to avoid compositional difficulties.

Lamp or Lantern

Spirit, truth, intelligence and life itself are all associated with the symbolism of light. In the Bible, a lamp signifies divine light: "thou art my lamp, O Lord; and the Lord will lighten my darkness".[1] It also symbolizes divine wisdom. Christ's words, "As long as I am in the world, I am the light of the world",[2] the inspiration for William Holman Hunt's popular painting, *The Light of the World*. Caravaggio often included a source of light external to the composition to suggest the divine illuminating the chosen.

In landscapes such as Albert Cuyp's *Milkmaid and Cattle Near Dordrecht*, a scene bathed in a golden glow evokes a rural idyll where humankind is in harmony with nature.

The *Arabian Nights* tale of Aladdin, who allowed his magic lamp to rust after it had brought him riches, is an allegory of neglecting the spiritual side of life. In Buddhism and Hinduism, the lamp, as a symbol of life, represents continuity from one state of existence to the next.

In shrines or on altars, lamps symbolize both devotion and the presence of divinity. In art, they personify vigilance and also night. The lamp is also a symbol of maternal care, associated with children and the sick. Florence

Nightingale was nicknamed "the Lady with the Lamp".

The lantern (an enclosed light) has more protective symbolism – the Chinese magic lantern supposedly wards off carp demons. The lantern was also used to cast propitious shadows. The Cynic philosopher Diogenes (4th–3rd centuries BCE) famously went about with a lantern in daylight looking for an honest man.

Lan Caihe

One of the Eight Immortals of Chinese (Daoist) mythology. Lan Caihe was sometimes depicted as a young woman or, as one writer expressed it curiously, "a man who did not know how to be a man". One day, when she (or he) was picking herbs in the hills, she came across a beggar covered in sores and tended his wounds. He turned out to be Li Xuan, an Immortal, who rewarded her with the gift of eternal youth. Thereafter she toured the country as a minstrel, telling people to seek the Daoist path.

Lance

The weapon of cavalry until the 20th century. Like the spear it symbolizes masculine, phallic and earthly power. It is associated with chivalry and also Christ's Passion. Its link with the Grail legend derives from a legend that the spear used to pierce Christ's side on the cross was the lance of a Roman centurion, traditionally called Longinus, who exclaimed: "Truly this man was the son of God." Longinus became the patron saint of Mantua, a city to which he was said to have returned with drops of holy blood. His lance, like that of Achilles, was credited with healing power. A broken lance is an attribute of St George and

symbolizes the experienced soldier. As an emblem of victory, the lance is an attribute of the Hindu war god Indra. The term "freelance" comes from medieval companies of knights whose lances were for hire.

LANDSCAPE *see panel overleaf*

Lang

The realm of the sky in the mythology of Ulith atoll in Micronesia.

Laocoön

Uttering the famous words "beware of Greeks bearing gifts", the Trojan priest Laocoön[1] warned his people that a huge wooden horse sent by the Greeks was treacherous – he rightly suspected that it contained soldiers who would bring about the downfall of their city. However, a Greek captive tricked the Trojans into believing that it was an offering to Athene.

As Laocoön was sacrificing a bull to Poseidon on the shore, two giant sea-snakes with monstrous coils swam up to him; first they twined themselves around his two sons before encircling the priest himself. Laocoön strove frantically to wrench the knots apart, but the snake's grip tightened and all were crushed to death. In 1506 a famous 2nd-century bCE marble statue of the scene, now in the Vatican Museum, Rome, was rediscovered and much admired and copied.

Laozi

"Old Master", the legendary founder of Daoism and supposed author of the *Dao De Jing* ("Classic of the Way and its Power"), the chief work of Daoist scripture. Laozi (Lao-tzu) is traditionally said to have been a royal archivist of the 6th century bCE and

Lan Caihe: *see* Eight Immortals; Li Xuan

Lance: *see* Blood; Grail; Longinus; PASSION; Phallus; Spear

Lang: *see* Iolofath

Laocoön: *see* Trojan War Virgil, *Aeneid II*

Laozi: *see* Eight Immortals

From an incense burner thought to show Laozi.

A Lar (Roman household deity), based on a statuette.

LANDSCAPE

Before the late 16th century, landscape painting did not exist as a subject in Western art, but was simply a backdrop for outdoor scenes. During the Renaissance, however, landscape details became increasingly naturalistic, and since then the interpretation of nature, whether as a subject in its own right or as an enhancement of a theme, has reflected various aims.

Seasons usually convey mood: winter may communicate bleakness and decay; spring and summer the optimism of renewal and vigour; autumn either harvest and plenty, or the onset of decline. Time of day and treatment of light are also evocative: dawn may suggest hope, while evening light casts ominous shadows.

Landscapes may be purely topographical or else picturesque views with arcadian or heroic connotations. Landscape may indicate humankind's relationship with nature: the pastoral image recalls the mythical Golden Age when humans and nature existed in harmony; cultivated fields and a clement sky may suggest humankind in control of its environment; while stormy scenes may show the superior forces of nature. Rural scenes may reveal an intimacy with nature or, from the late 18th century, consciously ignore the impact of the Industrial Revolution. The Impressionists chose to paint tamed and populated scenes, but Van Gogh, Cézanne and Gauguin presented a wilder nature, more akin to their particular temperaments.

to have instructed Confucius on matters of ritual. Legend has it that he grew disillusioned with court life and set off to the western mountains on an ox. At the frontier a guard asked him for teachings, and the result was the *Dao De Jing*. Also known as the *Laozi*, the work as it stands is believed to be by several hands. Laozi came to be regarded as a deity.

Lapis lazuli

A deep blue stone with celestial symbolism, particularly in Mesopotamia, Egypt and Mexico. Its association with divine forces helps to explain its value as an ornamental stone with talismanic value. To the Egyptians, only silver and gold were more precious. In Greece it was a love emblem and an attribute of Aphrodite, and in China it was linked with clearsightedness and success. All lapis in the Old World was mined in Afghanistan, hence the name ultramarine ("beyond the seas") for the expensive blue pigment derived from the stone.

Lapiths, The

A people of Thessaly in northern Greece. They appear in Greek myth most notably in the story of the Centauromachy (Battle of the Centaurs). The Centaurs disrupted the wedding feast of Perithous, the Lapith king, and attempted to run off with his bride, Hippodamia. The Athenian hero Theseus was among the guests and helped the Lapiths to victory in the ensuing battle, which was depicted on the Parthenon at Athens.

Lar

A Roman guardian divinity of the household. Roman houses often had a shrine to a Lar (plural Lares) depicting a small youth in a short tunic (*see* margin illustration, below right). Offerings were made to the Lar on family occasions, such as weddings and funerals.

Larch

One of the hardest and most durable of all pines (larch piles support much of Venice) and hence a symbol of immortality and also rebirth. A larch was the World Tree of Siberian shamanic cultures.

Last Judgment, The

The Nicene Creed was the first official statement of Christian belief, formulated in 325CE at the Council of Nicea in Asia Minor. It confirmed the doctrine of the Second Coming of Christ at the end of time, when the living and the dead would be judged: the "Last Judgment". The Gospels prophesied that all nations would come before Christ, and would divide the "sheep" (the righteous) from the "goats" (sinners and unbelievers).[1]

In late medieval and Renaissance churches the Last Judgment was traditionally depicted on or near the wall of the west entrance of churches as a reminder to departing congregations. Christ presides as judge, seated on a throne with the Apostles flanking him. Near him may be the Virgin as intercessor, St Peter with the keys to heaven, and angels bearing the Instruments of the Passion. Above Christ appear ranks of angels, martyrs or saints and, below him, St Michael holds the scales in which souls are weighed. Angels sound their trumpets to call up the dead. At the bottom of the composition graves open to release souls and the blessed soar up in a clockwise direction toward Christ's right. On his left the damned are sent to Hell. Here, among flames, Satan may devour and excrete sinners, while those suffering specific tortures may be grouped according to their punishment.

Michelangelo's *Last Judgment* in the Sistine Chapel, Rome, is unusual in being placed behind the altar. Christ is not passive but seems to storm out of the fresco with a condemning gesture, while saints wait anxiously for his blessing and, in the lower half, the elect throw off their shrouds. The damned sink in despair to be met by Minos, judge of Hades, whose coiled tail indicates which circle of hell awaits them, and by Charon, ready to ferry them to the kingdom of Satan.

Latinus

In Roman myth, a king of Laurentum in Latium who aided the hero Aeneas.

Latona *see* Leto

Laurel

A symbol of victory, peace, purification, protection, divination, secret knowledge and immortality. The aromatic bay species of laurel was the crowning emblem of the Greco-Roman world, a wreath of laurels being worn by those worthy of honour, especially poets; hence "poet laureate". Paintings of victorious generals of ancient Rome also show them crowned with laurel.

Laurel's honorific value derived from its association with the god Apollo, who is said to have purified himself with it in the groves of Tempe in Thessaly after slaying the Python at Delphi. The priestess of his Delphic cult, Pythia, chewed laurel before giving her prophecies. It was thought to

Larch: *see* Tree

Last Judgment: *see* Hades
[1] *Matthew 25:32–33*

Latinus: *see* Aeneas

Laurel: *see* Apollo; Crown; Daphne; Dragon; Hair; Lightning; PEACE; Tree; VICTORY; VIRTUES; Wreath, Garland

deter pestilence and lightning, a superstition believed by the emperor Tiberius who used to reach for his laurel wreath during thunderstorms. Associated with many deities including Dionysos (the Roman Bacchus), Zeus (Jupiter), Hera (Juno) and Artemis (Diana), laurel was an emblem of truce or peace as well as of triumph. A secondary symbolism of chastity derives from the myth that the nymph Daphne was turned into a laurel tree as she fled Apollo's advances. In art she is usually shown fleeing from the god as her arms metamorphose into branches.

Laurel had talismanic significance in North Africa, and in China is the tree beneath which the lunar hare mixes the elixir of immortality. It is a Christian symbol of eternal life.

Laurence, Saint

It is known that Laurence was a deacon, that he was martyred in Rome in 258CE, and that he was buried outside the city, where a church dedicated to him now stands. Legend[1] claims that he was entrusted by Pope Sixtus II with the church's treasure, which he then distributed among the poor. When Laurence was ordered by the pagan prefect of Rome to bring the treasure, he gathered together all the poor and sick and said to them: "See here the eternal treasure, which never diminishes but increases."

Laurence was martyred on an iron grid above roasting coals. Heated pitchforks were pressed on his body, whereupon he is said to have cried: "You have me well done on one side, now turn me over and eat!" The martyrdom is shown in Bronzino's 1569 painting. Fra Angelico also painted scenes from his life in the Chapel of

Nicholas V in the Vatican. Laurence was a patron saint of Florence and of the Medicis; he appears in many paintings commissioned by the family.

Laurence is usually dressed as a deacon with a censer, or he may hold a plate of coins in reference to the alms he distributed. However, his most common attribute is the gridiron of his martyrdom.

Lavinia

In Roman myth, the daughter of King Latinus and second wife of Aeneas. He founded a town, Lavinium, named after her.

Lead

The base metal of alchemy, and therefore a metaphor for humanity at the most primitive level of spiritual development. Its more general symbolism of dull heaviness is linked not only to its physical weight but to its ancient association with the god Kronos (Saturn to the Romans). Bellerophon put lead down the throat of the monstrous Chimaera, which died when its fiery breath melted the metal – an episode perhaps linked to the belief that lead had protective power.

Leaf

A Chinese emblem of happiness. Young leaves more generally share the symbolism given to green vegetation. Leaves often symbolize countless human lives – and their brevity. The falling leaves of autumn are an ancient metaphor for mortality and the passage of time.

Leda

In Greek myth,[1] Leda was the wife of King Tyndareus of Sparta. Zeus (the Roman Jupiter) fell in love with her

Leda and the swan.

and came to her in the form of a swan. Leda subsequently laid two eggs: from one hatched Clytemnestra and Castor, and from the other Helen of Troy and Polydeuces (Pollux). Accounts vary as to the paternity of these children as Leda is said to have slept with her husband on the same night as with Zeus; most often the latter pair are said to have been Zeus' offspring.

Michelangelo's cartoon and lost painting of 1530 showing Leda erotically embracing the swan provided the basis for several other works. Correggio's work of *c*.1534 similarly emphasizes the sexual nature of the encounter. Leonardo da Vinci's earlier treatment of the theme, which is also now lost but exists in copies by other artists, shows Leda standing with the swan, while her infants play on the ground, hatched from eggs.

Leech-child

The misshapen firstborn of Japan's primal deities Izanagi and Izanami.

Left and Right

Western and some other traditions assign more symbolic value to the right than to the left, probably for no better reason than that most people are right-handed. With few exceptions, the right is associated with precedence, action and the solar, male principle; the left with secondary position, weakness, passivity and the lunar, female principle. For the Romans the left (*sinister* in Latin) was linked with bad luck. Preference for the right is particularly marked in Christian symbolism, the left often being seen as the dark side, of sinners and black magic. In China the concept of Yin-Yang harmony made for a less rigid division of symbolic values. If anything, the left is usually given precedence, as in Japan: it is associated with honour, nobility, wisdom and the male, celestial and solar principle, while the right is linked with lunar and female qualities.

Attempts to explain the symbolism of left and right in relation to the movement of the sun or stars founder on this cultural inconsistency and suggest that attitudes are based simply on custom.

The political significance of "left-wing" and "right-wing" derives a precedent of 1789 when reformers sat on the left, reactionaries on the right in the first French National Assembly.

Leonard, Saint

Little is known of Leonard.[1] He was apparently a hermit, but founded a monastery near Limoges in France in the 6th century. He was held in such esteem that the king of France released any prisoners visited by the saint. His prayers for the queen's wellbeing and the safe delivery of her child were answered, and he performed many miracles, including freeing some prisoners bound in

Leech-child: *see* IZANAGI AND IZANAMI

Left and Right: *see* Black; Hand; Yin and Yang

Leonard, Saint:
[1] *Golden Legend, St Leonard*

chains. He is usually dressed as a monk. Fetters are his attribute, as he is the patron saint of prisoners.

Leonidas

A king of Sparta in Greece. At Thermopylae in 480BCE, Leonidas and his 300 men withstood the massive army of King Xerxes of Persia for two days, but on the following day they were attacked from the rear. Only one man survived.[1] In *Leonidas at Thermopylae* Jacques-Louis David shows Leonidas and his men before battle, depicted as idealized nudes.

Leopard

A symbol of ferocity, pitiless force, courage, pride, and speed. It was associated with evil both in ancient Egypt and in Christian tradition. Leopard skins worn by shamans in Asia and Africa symbolized their mastery over the demonic powers of this animal. In Egypt it was equated with the god Seth; priests dressed in leopard skins at funerary rites to demonstrate their ability to protect the dead from his malevolent influence.

In the Classical world, the leopard was an attribute of the god Dionysus (the Roman Bacchus) as creator–destroyer, and two leopards draw the chariot of Dionysos in art. The animal's spots were associated with the legendary multi-eyed Argus.

Negative Christian symbolism was based on the vision of a monstrous leopard in Daniel 7:6 and, more influentially, on God telling Jeremiah that evildoers could no more change their ways than a leopard could change its spots[1]. Hence the link between the leopard and Satan, sin and lust. All the same, the animal stood for courage in European her-

The Greek god Dionysos riding a leopard, from a mosaic found at Delos, c.180CE.

aldry, as well as in China where it also had lunar symbolism. The name "leopard" came from a fabled hybrid between a lion and a pard or panther (a name now applied to the black leopard or, in America, the puma).

Lernean Hydra, The

A many-headed dragon killed by the Greek hero Herakles as the first of his labours.

Leshii

A forest spirit of eastern Slav folk myth, the guardian of trees and forest animals. Resembling a peasant, he may be as tall as a tree or as short as grass, depending where he lives. He can change shape, such as into an animal or a relative, especially when he intends mischief. A peasant entering a forest would ward off the *leshii* by praying or turning his clothes inside out.

Lethe

"Forgetfulness", a river of the Greek underworld. The dead drank its waters to erase memories of their past lives.

Leto

One of the Titans of Greek myth, the daughter of Coeus and Phoebe and called Latona by the Romans. She had intercourse with Zeus[1] and became pregnant with the twins Apollo and Artemis. The jealous Hera, the wife of Zeus, caused Leto to wander the world in agony looking for a place to give birth. Johann Koenig's *Latona Changing the Lycian Peasants into Frogs* illustrates how she stopped to drink from a lake where peasants gathering reeds harried and insulted her. As punishment for their malicious behaviour she turned them into frogs, which even under water continued to bicker. She eventually bore the divine twins on the island Ortygia, later called Delos. In some accounts these were different islands and Artemis was born on Ortygia and Apollo on Delos.

Leviathan

This enormous sea-monster symbolizes a force of nature that only a super-human power could bring into being or control. It usually takes the form of a crocodile, whale or sea serpent (illustration opposite). Although often taken to mean a whale, the Hebrew word *liviatan* refers to any monster of the deep. Job 41 begins "Can you draw out leviathan with a fishhook?" and goes on to describe a creature with crocodile features. It is described in the Bible as a huge scaly monster that breathes fire and "out of his nostrils goeth smoke, as out of a seething pot, or cauldron".[1] With open jaws it may represent Satan and the descent into hell, as in El Greco's *Allegory of the Holy League*.

The symbolism of a creature so fierce that "none dare stir him up"

derives from Mesopotamian and Phoenician myths in which a hero god struggles to wrest order from a primordial chaos god of the deep. The English philosopher Thomas Hobbes (1588–1679), in his *Leviathan*, used the biblical monster as a symbol for the absolute state to which the individual is subordinate.

Lhatho Thori

A legendary king of Tibet (traditionally ruled 433CE–493CE). One day the sky filled with rainbows, and Buddhist images and texts fell onto his palace. Lhatho Thori worshipped the objects without understanding them: it was prophesied that their meaning would become clear after five generations: Tibet was converted to Buddhism by King Trisong Detsen in the 8th century CE.

Li Xuan

The first of the Eight Immortals of Chinese Daoist myth. Li Xuan ("Iron Crutch") had a club foot and was said to have learned the Dao, the principle of existence, from the goddess Xi Wang Mu, the Queen-Mother of the West, who gave him an iron crutch.

Liber

An ancient Italian agricultural deity. He was identified (like Bacchus) with the Greek god Dionysos.

Liberal Arts, The

During the Middle Ages and Renaissance the seven Liberal Arts were the subjects of secular education. They comprised the *trivium*: grammar, rhetoric and logic (dialectic); and the *quadrivium*: arithmetic, geometry, astronomy and music. In art, the sages of antiquity might accompany

Leto: *see* Apollo; Artemis; Eileithyia; Hera; Zeus
[1] Ovid, *Met VI: 313–381*

Leviathan: *see* Hell
[1] *Job 41*

Lhatho Thori: *see* Padmasambhava; Trisong Detsen

Li Xuan: *see* Eight Immortals; Xi Wang Mu

Liber: *see* Bacchus; Dionysos; GREEK AND ROMAN DEITIES

Liberal Arts: *see* Grammar; MUSIC/MUSICAL INSTRUMENTS
[1] *Genesis 4:22*

Leviathan in the form of a sea serpent, from a 12th-century English representation.

Liberalis, Saint: *see*
George, St

LIBERTY

Liberty is usually represented in art by a woman holding a sceptre and wearing a Phrygian cap – a reference to the Roman custom of presenting caps to freed slaves. The cap became a popular emblem of the French Revolution, as in Delacroix's painting *Liberty Leading the People* (1830). Light itself is a symbol of liberation (from darkness), and Bartholdi's *Statue of Liberty*, New York, holds a torch. Other symbols of liberty or freedom include the acrobat, bell, broken chains, cat, eagle, falcon, fish, long hair and wings.

personifications of the Liberal Arts or represent their subjects: Priscian or Donatus, grammar; Cicero, rhetoric; Aristotle, logic; Pythagoras, arithmetic; Euclid, geometry; Ptolemy, astronomy; and the bibli°cal character Tubal-Cain,[1] music. These are shown in Andrea da Firenze's frescoes in Santa Maria Novella, Florence. Female personifications of the subjects may each have a book and inscriptions to identify them. Examples are the enthroned figures depicted by Pinturicchio in the Room of the Liberal Arts in the Vatican, as follows: **Grammar**, the foundation of all subjects, may have writing instruments, a fountain from which scholars drink, fruit that she offers to a child, or a rod for chastisement, or she may point to the slim door of knowledge. **Rhetoric**, a subject learned in adolescence, may have a scroll, a sword and the globe of her universal domain. **Logic** may be shown with a scorpion or snake, perhaps signifying the penetrating nature

of the subject. **Arithmetic** is often seen holding her fingers up, to calculate with them, or holding an abacus or tables covered with figures. **Geometry** may be seen with a set square, pair of compasses, measuring rod or other instruments of the science. **Astronomy** may point to the sky and have an astrolabe or a globe marked with the constellations. **Music** may be shown playing instruments and singing.

Liberalis, Saint

An early Christian (*c*.4th century), Liberalis was venerated at Treviso and the surrounding Veneto, where he is said to have made many converts. He is usually depicted, as in Giorgione's altarpiece in San Liberale, Castelfranco, as a knight in armour with spear and banner. For this reason he may be confused with St George.

LIBERTY see panel, above

LIGHT see panel, right

Lightning

Universally a manifestation of divine wrath, power or fertilizing potency. Lightning was variously seen as the symbolic or actual weapon, arm or phallus of the supreme male sky god – or of his auxiliary. Alternatively, it was the blinding light of his eye – in Native American tradition the wink of the Thunderbird, the great sky spirit; in India the flashing third eye of Shiva, the light of truth.

Lightning is a phenomenon symbolically linked with both fire and water because it often preceded rain. As both creator and destroyer, it was viewed with a mixture of fear and reverence. Places struck by lightning became sacred ground, and people it

LIGHT

A metaphor for the spirit and the divinity, symbolizing inner enlightenment and the presence of a cosmic power of ultimate goodness and truth. By extension, light is a symbol of immortality, eternity, paradise, pure being, revelation, wisdom, intellect, majesty, joy and life itself. Although most philosophical traditions recognize light and darkness as a necessary duality, major religions of the Near East saw them as ethically contending forces, kingdoms of good and evil, as in Zoroastrianism and Manicheanism. Light became synonymous with "good" or "God". Thus, Christ is the Light of the World; Buddha the Light of Asia; Krishna the Lord of Light; Allah the Light of Heaven and Earth. In Judeo-Christian tradition, eternal light is the reward of the virtuous.

Genesis attempts to draw a clear distinction between divine light and the more ephemeral physical light of the sun, moon or stars, created only later. Candlemas, on February 2, took over the symbolism of more ancient pagan rites in which torches or candles were lit to invoke fertility and the spring renewal of crops. Similarly, Christmas has as its origins a midwinter festival of light, honouring the light and hailing its return in the darkest days; similar feasts are found in many cultures. In symbolism generally, the sun's light is linked with spiritual knowledge, the reflected light of the moon with rational knowledge.

touched bore the mark of God if they survived, or were thought to be translated instantly to heaven if they died. In Mexico, for example, Tlaloc used lightning to despatch souls to the Aztec heaven. The Classical master of lightning was Zeus (in Roman myth, Jupiter). Greek origin myths about Dionysos ascribe the first of his two births to a lightning flash from Zeus.

The phallic symbolism of lightning is particularly overt among the Australian Aboriginals where it symbolized a cosmic erect penis. Jewish tradition associated lightning with revelation, as in Exodus (19:16–18) where thunder and lightning announce the presence of God to Moses on Mount Sinai. Lightning was widely thought to be an augury, significant enough in Rome to cause public assemblies to close for the day. Striking from the left (the lucky east in relation to the position in which the Roman augur sat) lightning was a sign of Jupiter's favour; the Greeks took the reverse view.

In iconography, lightning is represented by the flashing axe, the forked trident, the sceptre, the hammer, the arrow and graphically by the zigzag. It was sometimes personified by a giant bird of prey not only in North America, but also in southern Africa, in myths of the Lightning Bird.

Lilith

The demonic first wife of Adam, according to Hebrew legend. Lilith may derive from the Mesopotamian fertility goddess Ninlil.

Lily

One of the most ambiguous of all flower symbols – identified with

Lilith, the legendary first wife of Adam.

Lime or Linden

A Shiva lingam.

Christian piety, purity and innocence, but having associations with fecundity and erotic love in older traditions through its phallic pistil and fragrance. The lily found in Christian art is the white lily named the "Madonna" in the 19th century after its association with the Virgin Mary (it was also the attribute of her husband Joseph and of many saints). It is often shown in a vase or is held by the archangel Gabriel in Annunciation paintings. It is also the attribute of those associated with the Virgin, especially Gabriel, Joachim and Joseph, the virgin saints and St Dominic. The beautiful lily of the valley has the same symbolism.

As a favourite garden flower of antiquity, the lily was fabled to have sprung from the milk of the Greek goddess Hera and was linked with fecundity not only in Greece but also in Egypt and the Near East generally, where it was a popular decorative motif. Lilies symbolized prosperity and royalty in Byzantium, and this, rather than the link with purity, may have been the original reason for the choice of the fleur-de-lis (heraldic lily or iris flower with three petals bound at the base) as the French royal coat of arms from the 12th century.

Its emblematic significance for Christian saints is taken largely from the Sermon on the Mount in which Jesus used the glorious "lilies of the field" as an allegory of how God provided for those who renounced the pursuit of wealth (Matthew 6:28–30); however, these flowers are now thought to have been poppy anemones. Another biblical reference (Song of Songs 1:2) compares the lips of the beloved to lilies, presumably red ones. The white lily can sometimes symbolize death as well as purity, and is often seen as a portent of death. The lotus, or water lily, is a botanically different flower with a much wider symbolism.

Lime or Linden
A tree of friendship or community, a symbolism going back to the classical world but relevant particularly in Germany where the linden (or European lime) was a popular focus of village life, as it is in some French villages. The main avenue of Berlin is Unter den Linden ("Under the Linden Trees"). Its gentle and beneficial associations may be linked with the honey made from its flowers.

Lingam
In Indian art and architecture, a stylized phallus representing the Hindu god Shiva as divine procreator. It symbolizes the male generative force in nature. In the cave of Elephanta at Bombay, the lingam – a thick, smooth cone of black stone – was the focus of circumambulation rituals, indicating its role as an axial symbol as well as a phallic one, somewhat like the classical *omphalos*.

In one myth, Shiva's lingam appears as a pillar of light, the upper and lower limits of which cannot be found by either the god Brahma as a wild goose or by Vishnu as a boar – proof of Shiva's power.

Although essentially a virility symbol, the lingam sometimes appears with a stone circle at its base representing the yoni (vulva) as a symbol of the sacred marriage of male and female. The lingam entwined by a snake refers to the yogic *kundalini*, the serpentine flow of vital energy through the body.

LION

A symbol of divine and solar power, royal authority, strength, courage, wisdom, justice and protection – but also cruelty, ferocity and death. The lion is a commanding personification of the sun, which passes through the zodiac sign of Leo, the Lion, in the hottest part of the year (July 23–August 23). As it is actually a shade-loving, mainly nocturnal hunter, its solar associations are based on the iconographic splendour of its golden coat, radiant mane and sheer physical presence.

In Egypt, the avenging lioness goddess Sekhmet was the Eye of Ra, sent by the sun god to destroy rebellious humankind. Her messengers were infectious diseases, for which reason her priests were also doctors. The lion was also

The lions of yesterday and tomorrow, from an illustration to an ancient Egyptian Book of the Dead.

a guide to the underworld, through which the sun was believed to pass each night. Lions were guardians of the dead in Greece, and also of palaces, thrones, shrines, doors or gateways, as at Mycenae. They were linked with Dionysos, Phoebus, Artemis and Cybele, whose chariot was drawn by lions.

A lion devouring a bull, horse or boar represents the complementary opposites of life and death, sun and moon, summer and winter – a symbolism found in Africa and Asia as well as the Near East. Victory over death is symbolized by the wearing of lion skins and by legends like that of Herakles slaying the Nemean lion or Samson tearing one limb from limb.

The lion was the emblem of the strength of Judah and came to be linked with salvation and the Messiah. Daniel in the lions' den represents God's redemption of his people. In Revelation (5:5–6) the Lion of Judah becomes Christ, the redeeming Lamb. Christian calmness in the face of peril is expressed in a number of symbolic stories, including the legends that St Paul tamed and baptized a lion and that St Jerome removed a thorn from a lion's paw. A lion lying peacefully with a lamb or other animals suggests an age without conflict. St Mark is identified as the winged lion, one of the four creatures of Ezekiel.

The lion has an ancient role as king of beasts and is widely a symbol of royal power and dominion, victory, bravery and fortitude. It has been included in many royal and aristocratic emblems since ancient Mesopotamia. Identified with the lion were Muhammad's son-in-law Ali, the "Lion of Allah"; King Richard I "the Lionheart" of England; and the emperor of Ethiopia, "the Lion of Judah". The lion is a royal emblem of Scotland and of England and a symbol of British imperial power.

The Buddha is a "lion among men", because the lion in India symbolized courage and wisdom, religious zeal and defence of the law. It was a symbol of Ashoka, who unified India in the 3rd century BCE.The Hindu god Vishnu became incarnate as Narasimha, a creature half-man, half-lion, to destroy a demon. The lion is the mount of the goddess Parvati and represents her more frightening aspect as the warrior goddess Durga. To overcome a lion may be seen as proof of superhuman strength, as in the stories of Gilgamesh, Samson, Daniel and Herakles.

The lion is renowned for its vigilance: in the Bible it is "the mightiest among beasts and does not turn back before any."[1], and hence is the guardian of church doorways or may support pulpits. In China and Japan the lion is protective, lion dances serving to frighten away demons.

The lion is not always supreme among beasts. In Africa, where it is otherwise revered for its royal status, lions in myth are often outwitted by smaller and more cunning creatures, such as the hare.

Lizard

The lizard shares some of the symbolism of its close relative, the snake, especially as an emblem of resurrection (deriving from its regular skin-shedding). This may explain its use as a motif on Christian candle-holders. It was a beneficial emblem in Egypt and the Classical world, sometimes linked with wisdom. It became an attribute of Logic in art. Lizards appear in Maori myth as guardian monsters. In Aboriginal, Melanesian and African folklore and decoration they are culture heroes or ancestor figures.

Llama

Llamas were among the Incas' most valuable sacrificial animals, and were closely associated with the heavens and rain. They were sacrificed to the new moon and, by tradition, black llamas were deliberately starved during the month of October so that the gods would hear their bleating as a plea from earth for rain. It was said that when the constellation Yacama (the Llama), near the Milky Way, disappeared from view at midnight, it was preventing flooding by drinking water from the earth.

Lleu Llaw Gyffes

"Shining One of the Skilful Hand", a divine warrior-magician of Welsh mythology, probably related to the old Celtic god Lugus and the Irish hero Lugh. According to the *Mabinogion*, Lleu's mother Arianrhod, daughter of the goddess Dôn and sister of the magician Gwydion, gave birth to twin boys. One was called Dylan but she vowed that the other would have no name until she decided to name him herself. His uncle Gwydion tricked her into calling him Lleu Llaw Gyffes.

She forbade Lleu to bear arms until she had armed him; again Gwydion tricked her. Finally, Arianrhod forbade Lleu to have a human wife and so Gwydion and his uncle, Math, made him a magic wife of flowers, Blodeuwedd.

Lleu was magically gifted in the arts, could also change shape at will, and it was almost impossible to contrive his death. Blodeuwedd and her adulterous lover, Gronw Pebyr, succeeded in doing so once, but Lleu escaped, wounded, in the form of an eagle.

Llyr

In Welsh myth, the divine head of a family which dominates the second branch of the *Mabinogion*. Llyr was the father of Branwen, Brân the Blessed and Manawydan. In Geoffrey of Monmouth's *History of the Kings of Britain* (1136), Llyr appeared as Leir, one of the mythical early kings of Britain. This Leir was the ultimate source of Shakespeare's *King Lear*.

Loki

A trickster deity of Scandinavian mythology. It is uncertain whether Loki is a god or a giant, one of the gods' enemies. He caused mischief among the gods, such as the death of Balder, but also assisted them, as when he helped Thor to retrieve his mighty hammer from the giants.

Loki was the father of Hel, the queen of the underworld land of the dead, and of Sleipnir, Odin's eight-legged horse. He also bore the monstrous wolf Fenrir and the venomous World Serpent that swam in the ocean surrounding the world.

In punishment for causing the death of Balder, the gods chained Loki to three rocks. He eventually broke free

Based on a Norse hearth stone, this image may depict Loki.

and led the giants against the gods at the apocalyptic battle of Ragnarok. Loki came face to face with the god Heimdall and both were killed in the ensuing duel.

LONGEVITY *see panel, right*

Longinus, Saint
Longinus was the name given in the Middle Ages to the Roman centurion who pierced the side of the crucified Christ and was immediately converted, saying: "Truly this was the Son of God."[1] His attribute is a spear. The weapon is one of the relics of St Peter's in Rome, where Bernini's sculpture of Longinus shows him at the moment of his conversion.

Lono
The Hawaiian god of the sky, peace and agriculture, the equivalent of the god known elsewhere in Oceania as Rongo. Lono came into the ascendancy in Hawaii every year during the four-month long Makihiki festival, which began with the appearance of the Pleiades on the evening horizon and the arrival of the autumn rains. During Makihiki, which the god was said to have founded, an image of Lono was taken around the Hawaiian islands and homage was paid to him in return for fertility and abundance. At the end of the Makihiki festival Lono was ritually "killed" at his chief temple and was then said to leave for Kahiki, his invisible land, until the following autumn. The remainder of the year was dedicated to Ku, the god of earth and warfare.

Loom
An instrument of cosmic creation and the structure upon which individual

LONGEVITY
Long life is a preoccupation of the traditional symbol system of the Chinese. Trees or their emblematic fruits are, not unexpectedly, the most common symbols of longevity, notably the peach, apple, bamboo, cedar, citron, cypress, myrtle, oak, palm, pear, pine and plum. The colour green and stones such as jade, diamond and ruby, and rock itself, also represent longevity. Other emblems include a basket of flowers, two Chinese bats, the carp, chrysanthemum, crane, deer, dove, elephant, hare, knot, marigold, mushroom, phoenix, stork, toad, tortoise and turtle. Many of these can also symbolize immortality.

destiny is woven – an ancient symbolism encapsulated in the three Fates of Greek myth, who span, measured and cut the thread of life. In another myth, Arachne was changed into a spider by the goddess Athene, who was jealous of her skill at the loom. Another figure depicted at a loom is the faithful Penelope during the long absence of her husband Odysseus.

Loretto
Loretto on the Adriatic coast of Italy became a major place of pilgrimage because, according to legend, the house of the Virgin Mary's birth was miraculously transported there from the Holy Land in 1291. Caravaggio's *Madonna of the Pilgrims* was commissioned to imitate a statue known as the Madonna of Loretto. Giambattista Tiepolo's *Holy House of Loretto* shows the house with the Virgin on its roof being carried by angels.

LONGEVITY: *see individual names*

Longinus, Saint: *see* Lance; Spear
[1] *Matthew 27:54*

Lono: *see* Ku; Rongo

Loom: *see* Spider; Weaving; Web

Lot

In the Bible, Lot accompanied his uncle Abraham into Canaan and then selfishly stated his own claim to the well-watered plain of the Jordan. This brought him into contact with the wicked inhabitants of Sodom and Gomorrah.¹ Lot played host to two angels but the people of Sodom threatened to violate his guests. Urged by the angels to "escape for thy life; look not behind thee", Lot and his family fled as God destroyed Sodom and Gomorrah, but his wife looked back and was turned into a pillar of salt. To preserve the seed of their father, Lot's daughters made him drunk and slept with him, giving birth to the ancestors of the Moabites and Ammonites.² In *Lot and his Daughters* Bonifazio de' Pitati, like many other artists, shows Lot in his drunkenness with his daughters, while Sodom and Gomorrah burn in the background.

Lotus

A flower with prolific symbolic meanings, particularly in the traditions of Egypt, India, China and Japan. Its unique importance is based both on the decorative beauty of its radiating petals and on an analogy between them and an idealized form of the vulva as the divine source of life. By extension, the lotus came to symbolize, among other things, birth and rebirth, as well as the origin of cosmic life, and the creator gods or the sun and sun gods. It also represented human spiritual growth from the folded bud of the heart, and the soul's potential to attain divine perfection.

In Egypt, the lotus, rising from bottom mud as a water lily to unfold its immaculate petals to the sun, suggested the glory of the sun's own emergence from the primeval water. A metaphor for creation, it was a votive symbol not only of solar and fecundity gods and goddesses but of the Upper Nile as the giver of life. The blue lily, more sacred than the white, was an emblem of modesty and cleanliness in Egypt and also Chinese Buddhism. Lotus wreaths for the dead took up the symbolism of rebirth.

As a decorative funerary motif symbolizing resurrection, the lotus appeared in ancient Greece and Italy, and in western Asia where decorative Egyptian lotus forms were the origin of the Ionic order of capitals in architecture. (The "lotus-eaters" of Greek myth, rapt in blissful oblivion, have nothing to do with the sacred flower: the fermented juice of a North African bush lotus is the probable source of this Homeric reference.)

In Hinduism the sacred lotus grew from the navel of Vishnu as he rested on the waters, giving birth to Brahma (a representation of spiritual growth). The lotus is a symbol of what is divine or immortal in humanity, and is almost a synonym of perfection.

Indian-derived iconography, both Hindu and Buddhist, is full of deities, Buddhas and bodhisattvas sitting cross-legged in the centre of flame-like lotus petals. The lotus is the attribute of sun and fire gods, and the leading symbol of Padma, the consort of the god Vishnu. It symbolizes the realization of inner potential or, in Tantric and yogic traditions, the ability to harness the flow of energy moving through the *chakra*s (often depicted as wheel-like lotuses) flowering as the thousand-petalled lotus of enlightenment at the top of the skull. A parallel concept is the "golden blossom" of Chinese Taoism, a Buddhist-

The Hindu god Brahma seated in a lotus flower.

inspired tradition in which the lotus is again a symbol of spiritual unfolding.

Veneration of the lotus is equally, if not more, marked in Buddhism. The lotus represents the nature of the Buddha himself and is the aspirational image of the spiritual flowering of knowledge that can lead to the state of awakening.

Echoing Egyptian symbolism of the birth of gods from the pure vulva of the lotus, the father of Tibetan Buddhism, Padmasambhava, was said to have been discovered at the heart of a lotus in his eighth year. In Tibetan and Chinese Buddhism the lotus is one of the Eight Auspicious Signs. In China further symbolic associations were added – rectitude, firmness, conjugal harmony and prosperity – especially the blessing of many children, represented by a boy holding a lotus. Sacred and profane symbolism mix in Chinese tradition – a courtesan was a "golden lotus", although the lotus is more generally linked with purity and virginity, and is a Japanese emblem of incorruptible morality. It appears also in Mayan iconography, apparently with rebirth symbolism.

Louis IX, Saint

King Louis IX of France (1214–70) was famed as a pious, just and merciful monarch.[1] In 1248 he led a crusade and returned with what were believed to be Christ's Crown of Thorns and a piece of the True Cross, which, with a sword and the fleurs-de-lys, may be his attributes. He died of plague on his second crusade. He is a national saint of France and may be dressed as a king with a crown or clad in armour as a knight. In place of a sceptre he may hold a staff surmounted by a hand, as in a painting by El Greco.

Louis of Toulouse, Saint

Descended from Louis IX of France, Louis (1274–97) was offered the throne of Naples, but renounced it in favour of his brother, Robert of Anjou, and entered the Franciscan order. He became bishop of Toulouse and devoted his short life to Christian works, dying at the age of 23. Simone Martini's *St Louis Altar* shows the young saint enthroned, dressed in his bishop's vestments and holding a crozier. Angels appear above, supporting the crown he refused, as he in turn crowns Robert, who kneels beside him. Surrounding the image are French fleurs-de-lys.

Lozenge

Graphically, a symbol of life, the vulva, fertility and, in some contexts, innocence. It takes on dual imagery when combined with the phallic symbolism of snakes in Native American decorative art. In Mali, a half-lozenge shape with a point at the other end was a symbol for a young woman. Lozenges appear with fertility symbolism on the jade skirt of the Aztec goddess Chalchiuhtlicue. In Christian art, the lozenge symbol of fertility goddesses was taken as a virginity symbol in the worship of the Virgin Mary.

Lü Dongbin

One of the Eight Immortals of Chinese Daoist mythology. Lü Dongbin dreamt that he enjoyed great prosperity for fifty years but then suffered disgrace and ruin. It convinced him that worldly ambition was futile and he followed Han Zhongli, whom he had met at an inn, into the hills to seek the Dao, the principle of existence. Among his disciples were the Immortals Han Xiang and Cao Guojiu.

Louis IX, Saint: *see* Fleur-de-Lys
[1] *John of Joinville, Life of Louis IX*

Louis of Toulouse: *see* Fleur-de-Lys; Louis IX, St

Lozenge: *see* Almond; Aureole; Mandorla; Snake; Virginity; Vulva; Woman

Lucretia: *see* Brutus; Lucius Janius
[1] *Ovid, Fasti II:721–853 and Livy, The History of Rome I 1.vii–1.ix*

Lucretia

The Roman story of Lucretia[1] is one of conjugal fidelity and virtue. Lucretia, the wife of Tarquinius Collatinus, served in the army of Sextus, son of King Tarquinius Superbus (Tarquin the Proud). One night, Sextus raped her. Lucretia confessed her disgrace to her husband before plunging a knife into her own heart. This incident was instrumental in persuading the Romans to overthrow Tarquin. Depictions of Lucretia commonly show either her rape, as in Titian's violent *Tarquin and Lucretia*, or her suicide. In Lorenzo Lotto's *A Lady with a Drawing of Lucretia*, the figure, probably herself called Lucretia, directs us to a drawing of the mythical Lucretia.

Lucy, Saint

Lucy (died *c*.304CE) was martyred in Sicily. Legend[1] claims that she persuaded her mother to pray at the shrine of St Agatha, where she was healed of an incurable disease. In gratitude Lucy gave all her goods to the poor but, angered by her faith, her suitor handed her over to the Roman consul. When she was condemned to a brothel to be violated, she was made miraculously immovable, even by oxen. She survived being drenched in urine and oil and set alight, only to be killed by a sword thrust into her throat. Her name, implying light, explains why her attribute is a lamp.

In another legend, one of her suitors ceaselessly praised her eyes, so she tore them out and sent them to him. Consequently, she may be shown with a pair of eyes on a dish. Giambattista Tiepolo shows her taking her last communion (Santi Apostoli, Venice).

Lueji

A legendary queen of the Lunda people, the descendant of the primordial serpent Chinawezi and wife of the hero Chibinda Ilunga.

Lugh

"The Bright One", the name of a divine Irish warrior-hero probably identifiable with the Welsh figure Lleu and the ancient Celtic deity Lugus.

According to the *Book of Invasions*, Lugh was the grandson of Balar of the Evil Eye, the leader of the monstrous Fomorians. Balar, it was foretold, would be killed by a grandson, so he imprisoned his only daughter, Eithne, in a cave on Tory island. Kian, one of the Tuatha Dé Danann, the enemies of the Fomorians, secretly seduced her and she had triplets. Balar drowned them all except Lugh, who was saved and reared by a smith.

Many years later Lugh, a handsome young warrior, arrived at the court of Nuadhu, the king of the Tuatha Dé Danann. His skills in all the arts – warfare, healing, prophecy, magic, music, poetry and others – made such a great impression that Nuadhu abdicated in his favour. Lugh led the Tuatha Dé Danann against the Fomorians at the second battle of Magh Tuiredh and killed Balar.

The old Irish festival of Lughnasad (August 1) was said to have been introduced by Lugh.

Lugus

A deity widely popular throughout the ancient Celtic lands., his name means "Bright" or "Shining" and he is related to the Irish Lugh and Welsh Lleu. Lugus was probably the Celtic god referred to by Julius Caesar as "Mercury", the chief deity of the

Gauls and "inventor of all the arts".

The Emperor Augustus chose Lugdunum ("Fort of Lugus", modern Lyon) as the capital of Gaul in 12BCE. He inaugurated a festival in his own honour on 1 August, the date of the festival of Lugus (and the same date as the Irish Lughnasad).

Luke, Saint

Author of one of the gospels and of the Acts of the Apostles, Luke was a physician and may have travelled with St Paul to Italy. Although in medieval tradition it was thought that he was martyred, there is no firm basis for this. Legend claims that he was a painter, who produced several portraits of the Virgin. 15th- and 16th-century Flemish artists such as Rogier van der Weyden show him in this role. St Luke is the patron saint of painters as well as doctors and pharmacists. As an evangelist Luke may be depicted writing his gospel. His attribute is a winged bull, one of the "four creatures" of Ezekiel.

Lute

In Renaissance art, an attribute of the personifications of Music and Hearing, and a popular emblem of the lover. Lutes or mandolins with broken strings appear in still lifes as symbols of discord. In China, the lute was an attribute of the scholar and, in common with many other musical instruments, of harmony – in marriage as well as in government.

Luxury

Luxury may be closely associated with Lust, one of the Vices. Dutch 17th-century paintings, which appear to be on the theme of "merry company", with richly dressed figures sitting at a dinner table covered with sumptuous objects, may contain warnings of the vanity of earthly possessions and of wastefulness. The etching *Death Surprising a Young Couple* by Jan van de Velde has the inscription: "We often sit in luxury, while Death is closer than we know".

Lynceus (1)

In Greek myth, a prince of Messenia, son of King Aphareus and Queen Arene. He was one of the Argonauts and was said to have such keen sight that he could see beneath the earth.

Lynceus (2)

A king of Argos in Greece, the son of Aegyptus and husband of Hypermnestra. He and Hypermnestra were ancestors of the hero Perseus.

Lynx

An emblem of vigilance, a symbolism soundly based on the animal's acute vision, superstitiously believed to enable it to see through obstacles and penetrate secrets. The lynx in art represents the sense of sight.

Lyre

A symbol of divine harmony, musical and poetic inspiration, and divination. The lyre is linked in Classical mythology with Hermes, its inventor, but more especially with Apollo (who famously defeated Marsyas in a musical contest) and Orpheus (whose music charmed beasts and stopped rivers). The lyre is the attribute of Erato, the Muse of lyric poetry; of Terpsichore, the Muse of dance and song; and of Poetry personified. A seven-stringed lyre symbolized the seven planets; a twelve-stringed one represented the signs of the Zodiac.

Luke, Saint: *see* Bull; Doctor; Evangelists; Paul, St

Lute: *see* Music; PEACE

Luxury: *see* VICES

Lynceus (1): *see* Argonaut; Dioscuri

Lynceus (2): *see* Danaïd; Perseus

Lynx: *see* VIGILANCE

Lyre: *see* Music; PLANETS; Zodiac

A musician (possibly the god Hermes) with a cithara, a type of long lyre, from a Greek vase.

Maat

The Egyptian goddess of truth and justice. Maat, the daughter of the sun god and sometimes paired with Thoth, embodied divine order and harmony. She was depicted standing or squatting, with her symbol, an ostrich feather, in her headdress. In the underworld, the heart (that is, the conscience) of a dead person was weighed against the feather of Maat. If the heart was burdened by sin and so heavier than the feather, the deceased was devoured by a monster. If the scales balanced, the deceased became a spirit among the gods.

Mabinogion, The

A collection of Welsh mythological tales. The *Mabinogion* is the principal source of ancient Welsh and British myths, even though these are overlain by many later elements. There are four sections or "Branches" to the main narrative of the *Mabinogion*. These deal with the stories of the families of Pwyll (First and Third Branch), Llyr (Second Branch) and Dôn (Fourth

Branch). Pryderi, the son of Pwyll, appears in each Branch, and there are numerous other interrelationships. Outside the main narrative are other tales, such as the story of Culhwch and Olwen.

Within the stories there are parallels with Irish myth, such as the families of the Irish goddess Danu (the Tuatha Dé Danann) and the Welsh goddess Dôn, and the figures of Lugh and Lleu.

Maccabees, The

According to the Old Testament Apocrypha, the Maccabee family rebelled against the Syrian high priests and kings dominating Judea.[1] Under a cruel regime, seven brothers and their mother were brought before the king and ordered to eat the forbidden flesh of the pig. When they refused they were dismembered one by one. In art they may be seen in a cauldron, their mutilated limbs in view.

Mace

An authority symbol. Originally a club-like weapon with flanges to penetrate armour, the mace was later carried by bodyguards and eventually became a purely ceremonial symbol of power. Because it was associated particularly with royal authority in England, the ceremonial mace acquired by the House of Commons in 1649 was a significant emblem of Cromwell's parliament's newly-won right to govern.

Mael Dúin

An Irish hero who went on a great sea voyage. Mael Dúin sailed away to kill the man who had slain his father. However, he took more crew members than a druid advised him to, and when the ship reached the murderer's island a storm blew it far off course. They encountered many fabulous lands and monsters, including ants the size of foals, blazing hot swine, vanishing maidens and the Land of Women, an island of perpetual feasting and pleasure where old age was unknown. Mael Dúin and his crew eventually returned to Ireland.

Magh Tuiredh, The Battles of

Two conflicts at Magh Tuiredh (Moytirra, County Sligo) which serve as the focal points of the *Book of Invasions*, the account of the mythical conquest of Ireland by successive races. The divine race, the Tuatha Dé Danann, defeated their predecessors, the Fir Bholg, in the first battle of Magh Tuiredh and the monstrous Fomorians in the second battle.

Magna Mater *see* Cybele

Magnet

To the ancients, an impressive symbol of cosmic coherence. Known mainly through the magnetic properties of lodestone, in Egypt the magnet was associated with the power of Horus, the god who regulated the movements of the heavenly bodies. Lodestone was sometimes used as a love charm.

Magpie

Joy, married bliss, sexual happiness – a happy emblem in the traditions of China where the cry of a magpie announced the arrival of friends, but in the West a bird linked with acquisitiveness, mischievous chatter and even witchcraft. The magpie's fondness for bright objects seems to be the origin of its association with a Chinese custom by which a parted husband and wife break a mirror and keep half each. If either is unfaithful, their half of the mirror will turn into a magpie and fly back to tell the other. A yang emblem and sacred bird of the Manchus, the magpie often appears on Chinese greeting cards.

Mahabharata, The

A great Sanskrit verse epic composed *c*.400BCE–*c*.400CE. Vast in extent and scope (Homer's *Iliad* and *Odyssey* combined are just a tenth of its length), the *Mahabharata* relates a dynastic feud between two related families, the Pandavas and the Kauravas. In the course of the narrative, many myths are recounted, alongside other aspects of Hindu religion, ritual and philosophy.

Mahadevi *see* Devi

Maia

One of the Pleiades, the seven daughters of the sea nymph Pleione and the Titan Atlas. Maia lived in a cave, where the Greek god Zeus had intercourse with her, without his wife Hera noticing, so Maia did not suffer Hera's jealous anger. The offspring of this coupling was the god Hermes. Maia and her sisters became the constellation bearing their name.

Maitreya

The bodhisattva embodying *maitri*, meaning "friendliness". He resides in the Tushita heaven and is the Buddha of the future age, but until its arrival he is said to visit earth in various guises to bring salvation and instruction.

Makara

A hybrid aquatic monster (shown usually as a fish-crocodile), in Hindu myth symbolizing the power of the waters. Because the makara is ridden by Varuna, lord of both physical and moral order as well as of the heavens and the deep, its image is generally beneficent, linked with the rainbow and rainfall, the water-born lotus, and the sun's return at the December solstice. In the Hindu zodiac, the makara replaces the goat-fish Capricorn, symbolizing rebirth into or release from the cycle of material existence.

Makosh

The goddess of fertility, abundance and moisture. Makosh, also spelled Mokosh, was the centre of a fertility cult that was widespread among the eastern Slav peoples (Belorussians, Russians and Ukrainians). Makosh was also revered as the protector of women's work, as well as the protector of maidens.

Mama Kilya

The Inca moon goddess, the sister and wife of the sun god Inti. She was revered as the mother of the Inca people and as the deity whose waxing and

*The bodhisattva Maitreya, after a
Chinese porcelain figurine.*

waning marked the passing of time. During an eclipse of the moon it was believed that Mama Kilya was being attacked by a mountain lion or giant serpent, which people would drive off by causing a great din.

Man

The paragon of animals, a symbol in most ancient cultures of what is perfectible in nature – being made in the image of God and containing both matter and spirit, earth and heaven. This mystic belief underlies the frequent depictions of humankind as a microcosm containing, at least symbolically, all the elements of the universe itself. The human body, in Pythagorean tradition a pentagram formed by arms, legs and head, was often taken as a model for temple architecture. The male principle itself

*An image, possibly of
Makosh, from an Slav
embroidery.*

is symbolized usually by sun, fire and lightning, and by phallic verticality or penetrative objects; these include the arrow, cone, lance, lingam, obelisk, pillar, or pole, plough, rod, spade, spear, sword, thunderbolt and torch.

Man of Sorrows

It was prophesied that the Messiah would be "despised and rejected of men; a man of sorrows, and acquainted with grief".[1] The image is not part of the narrative of the Passion of Christ, although in paintings it may include symbols from before and after the Crucifixion. Thus Christ may be standing in the sepulchre, crowned with thorns, displaying his wounds.

Manannán

An Irish divinity of the sea, the son of the sea god Lir and one of the Tuatha Dé Danann. Manannán was regarded as the protector of Ireland, which he embraced with the ocean. He had great magic powers and assisted some of the heroes of Irish myth. For example, he helped Lugh to secure a Tuatha Dé Danann victory against the monstrous Fomorian invaders by giving him a magic boat, horse and sword. Manannán was said to have been the first king of the Isle of Man, which was named after him (Mannin in Manx).

Manawydan

A Welsh hero-magician, the son of Llyr. Manawydan is the protagonist of the Third Branch of the *Mabinogion*, which relates how his homeland, Dyfed, was placed under a spell that caused all people and beasts to disappear. Manawydan travelled to England with his wife Rhiannon, stepson Pryderi (lord of Dyfed) and Pryderi's wife Cegfa. After many magical

adventures he discovered that the spell had been cast by a bishop, Llwyd, in revenge for a wrong done to a friend by Pryderi's father Pwyll. Eventually, Llwyd lifted the spell and Manawydan returned home. Manawydan may be identical in origin to the Irish Manannán.

Manco Capac

The mythical ancestor of the Inca emperors. Manco Capac was one of three brothers and three sisters who emerged into the world from caves at Pacariqtambo. After a journey of some distance with Mama Oqlyo, his sister and wife, Manco Capac came to an auspicious site. They founded a settlement there which became Cuzco, the Inca capital, and their offspring became the Inca imperial family. Later, Manco Capac became a stone – one of the Incas' most revered treasures.

Mandala

A design that symbolizes spiritual, cosmic or psychic order. Although Buddhist mandalas, particularly in the geometric form of the *yantra*, have become famous as aids in meditative exercises, ancient mandala forms in both Hinduism and Buddhism also had initiatory symbolism, orienting worshippers to a sacred space. They are attempts to provide an image of the supreme reality – of a spiritual wholeness that transcends the world of appearances. The Sanskrit meaning of *mandala* is "circle", and even when dominated by squares or triangles, mandalas have concentric structures. They symbolize progression toward a spiritual centre, either mentally or physically – as in the mandala structure of many temples or stupas.

The striking feature of all mandala

Man of Sorrows: *see* Passion of Christ, The
[1] *Isaiah 53:3*

Manannán: *see* Manawydan

Manawydan: *see* Branwen; Brân the Blessed; Llyr; *Mabinogion, The*; Manannán; Pryderi; Pwyll; Rhiannon

Manco Capac: *see* HUMANITY, THE ORIGIN OF; Pacariqtambo

Mandala: *see* Centre; Circle; Initiation; Lotus; Square; Stupa; Temple; Triangle

Mandorla

Mandorla: *see* Almond;
Aureole; Fire; Flame;
Lozenge; Transformation;
Virginity

Mandrake: *see* Devils;
Witchcraft

Manlius Torquatus:
¹ Livy, *The History of Rome*
VIII vii

A sacred mandala, based on an 18th-century Indian painting from the region of Rajasthan.

patterns is their careful balancing of visual elements, symbolizing a divine harmony beyond the confusion or disorder of the material world. To Jung, these patterns were archetypal symbols of the human longing for psychic integration. To others, the mandala represents a spiritual journey out of the self. The meaning of individual mandalas differs; some have figurative elements that invite contemplation of, for example, the specific virtues embodied by a particular Bodhisattva, often shown seated within a lotus. However, the sense of order is consistent, symbolizing a guiding intelligence, a supernatural structure, the serenity of enlightenment.

An almond-shaped mandorla surrounding Christ. After an Eastern Orthodox image.

Mandorla
An almond-shaped aureole used in medieval Christian art to frame the figure of Christ at his ascension, and also to enclose the Virgin Mary, Mary Magdalen or other saints borne to heaven. As the *vesica piscis* ("fish bladder"), the mandorla was an early symbol of Christ in glory. The mystic "almond" (*mandorla* in Italian) was associated with purity and virginity, its oval shape being an ancient symbol of the vulva. Graphically, it also resembles a flame, a symbol of spirituality. Another view is that it represents the duality of heaven and earth – depicted as two intersecting arcs. This would explain why mandorlas usually enclose emblematically ascending figures, symbolizing not only their sanctity but also their transfiguration.

Mandrake
A Mediterranean narcotic plant of the potato family with a forked root suggesting the human form, credited with magical powers and widely associated with sorcery and witchcraft. It was used to cast spells by the enchantress Circe in Greek mythology; as an aphrodisiac in Egypt; as an aid to conception in Israel; and as an anti-inflammatory herbal remedy in Rome.

Superstitions accumulating around the mandrake (or *mandragora*) in medieval times led to the idea that when it was uprooted its shrieks could kill or that "mortals hearing them run mad" (Shakespeare's *Romeo and Juliet*, Act 4:3).

The legend that mandrakes grew from the semen of hanged murderers illustrates a symbolic shift from the idea that a man-shaped plant could have sympathetic benefits to the fear that it represented demonic forces.

Manitou
The supreme deity of the Algonquian people. The name means "spirit".

Manjushri
"Amiably Majestic", the bodhisattva of wisdom, who in Vajrayana Buddhist tradition is said to eradicate ignorance from the world.

Manjushri, after an 18th-century gilded bronze Tibetan statuette.

Manlius Torquatus

During the war against the Latins in 340BCE, the Roman consuls, of whom Manlius Torquatus was one, forbade single combat with the enemy.[1] His son disobeyed the ruling and, although he defeated his opponent, Manlius ordered his execution. Ferdinand Bol illustrated this example of severe justice in *Manlius Torquatus Beheading His Son*, for the Council Chamber of the Admiralty in Amsterdam.

Manna

Divine grace – symbolism relating to the apparently miraculous nourishment that sustained the children of Israel for 40 years in the wilderness (Exodus 16). Its description as "honey wafers", has led to suggestions that the wafers were made up from the *Lecanora* lichen and from honey-like gum resins of the tamarisk or similar trees of the region. These are free foods of the Bedouin, and falls of wind-blown lichen are known in North Africa. Christianity adapted the symbolism of the Jewish "food from heaven" represented by Christ as "the bread of life" (John 6:31–35).

Mantis

An insect which appears widely as a trickster and culture hero. Both roles are evident in the fire origin myth of the Khoisan peoples of southwestern Africa. Originally, Ostrich kept fire tucked under his wing. Mantis persuaded him to reach for some fruit at the top of a plum tree. As Ostrich opened his wings to balance himself, Mantis took the fire. The Khoisan also claim that it was Mantis who was first to give everything its name.

Mantra

A word or syllable symbolizing an aspect of divine power in Hindu and Buddhist traditions. Whether spoken aloud, or pronounced simply in the mind of someone concentrating on it, the sonority of the sacred word has a quasi-magical value corresponding to a creative energy charge. The mantra is believed to align the worshipper with the vibration of the cosmos itself.

Maponus

A youthful god revered in ancient Gaul and Britain. Maponus ("Divine Son" or "Divine Youth") appears to have been associated with music, poetry and hunting. He was probably identical with the Welsh Mabon ("Son"), who figures in the story of Olwen and Culhwch as a boar hunter with divine powers, and the Irish Mac Óc ("Young Son"), otherwise known as Oenghus, the god of love.

Marcus Sextus

With his painting *The Return of Marcus Sextus* Pierre-Narcisse Guérin invented a figure from Roman history who returns from exile to find his wife dead. The artist no doubt intended to allude to the return of émigrés to France after the 1789 Revolution.

Marduk

The supreme god of Akkad and its capital, Babylon. The creation myth of the Akkadian people recounts how the primal deities Apsu and Tiamat coupled to produce a succession of divinities culminating in Ea, from whom sprang Marduk. A power struggle arose in heaven: Ea killed Apsu and in revenge Tiamat (who was envisaged as a dragon embodying primordial

Marduk and his snake-dragon; after an image on an Akkadian seal.

chaos) unleashed a host of monsters headed by her son Kingu against the younger deities. The latter elected Marduk as their champion. He killed Tiamat by cutting her body in two, forming the earth from one part and the sky from the other. Then he took from Kingu the Tablets of Destiny, the divine decrees which conferred supreme power on their possessor. He killed Kingu and mixed his blood with earth in order to form the human race. The gods acknowledged Marduk as supreme deity and built him a great sanctuary, Esagila, in Babylon.

After the conquest of Sumer by the Akkadians *c*.1900BCE, Marduk became the supreme god of Mesopotamia. His temple in Babylon contained a great *ziggurat* (stepped pyramid), perhaps the original of the Biblical Tower of Babel.

Margaret of Antioch, Saint

There is no historical evidence to prove that Margaret existed, yet her cult was popular in the later Middle Ages. Legend states that the Christian maiden was harassed by the prefect of Antioch; after refusing to become his concubine, she was tortured and thrown into prison.[1] Here, the Devil appeared to her in the form of a hideous dragon and swallowed her up, but the power of the cross she was wearing split the dragon in two, leaving her unharmed. She was subsequently beheaded, but not before she had prayed that, just as she had been safely delivered from the dragon's belly, so healthy children would be born to all women who invoked her aid when faced with a difficult labour. She consequently became the patron saint of childbirth. A dragon is her attribute, and she may be depicted trampling it underfoot. She is often shown as an attendant saint in paintings of the Virgin, frequently in the company of Catherine of Alexandria.

Margaret of Cortona, Saint

The daughter of a peasant family in Tuscany, Margaret (*c*.1247–97) became the mistress of a nobleman near Montepulciano. The man was assassinated, whereupon his dog found Margaret and led her to his murdered body. She repented her ways and joined the Franciscans. Baroque artists such as Lanfranco painted her ecstatic vision of Christ. Her attribute is her lover's dog.

Marigold

A solar flower, linked in China with longevity, in India with Krishna, and in the West with the purity and perfection of the Virgin Mary, after whom it was named ("Mary-gold"). The marigold is sometimes suggested as the flower (more usually the heliotrope) in the Greek myth of Clytia, who was hopelessly in love with Apollo.

Mark, Saint

One of the four Evangelists, Mark (died *c*.74CE) travelled to Rome, where he is thought to have written his gospel aided by St Peter. He then travelled to Cyprus and Alexandria, where he is said to have become the first bishop, and to have been battered and stoned to death. He is depicted as a middle-aged, dark-haired, bearded man, often shown writing his gospel, and his attribute is the winged lion.

According to legend, Mark was once caught in a storm off the Adriatic coast and was blown onto the islands of the Venetian Lagoon; an angel appeared to him and announced that he stood on the spot where a city would rise in his honour. Some 400 years later, settlers began to drive in the foundations of Venice. In 829CE two Venetian merchants induced priests to let them secretly remove St Mark's relics from Alexandria; they managed to conceal them from officials under a consignment of salted pork and transported them to Venice. A basilica was built, dedicated to the saint initially as the Chapel of the Doge's palace, Venice, and his relics were enclosed within a column of marble. With the passing of time their exact location was forgotten, which caused much distress; but one day, during a fast, stones bounced out of the column and revealed the holy casket of the saint's relics. St Mark is, therefore, particularly venerated in Venice, where scenes of his life were painted by Tintoretto and others, and the winged lion was adopted as an emblem of the city.

The Venetians popularized stories regarding the saint's miraculous intervention on behalf of those who invoked his help.[1] In one, a servant made a pilgrimage to the body of St Mark without his master's permission. Tintoretto, in his depiction of the tale, shows how, when the man returned, his master wanted his eyes put out, his feet cut off, his legs broken and his teeth smashed. He was thrown to the ground but, because he had prayed to St Mark, the sharp pointed sticks used to inflict his punishment broke into pieces and the iron tools melted or became blunt. Both master and servant repented.

St Mark is also said to have saved several victims shipwrecked during a storm. Some Venetian merchants had

Marigold: *see* FLOWERS; Heliotrope: Sun; Virginity

Mark, Saint: *see* Evangelists, The

Golden Legend, St Mark

Marriage

taken passage in a Saracen ship, and seeing that the ship was in imminent danger they climbed into the skiff towed by the vessel and cut the rope, whereupon a great wave sank the ship. One of the Saracens, struggling in the waves, invoked the saint and vowed that he would be baptized if rescued: he was instantly plucked out of the sea and deposited in the skiff. In another tale Saints Mark, Nicholas and George appeared to a fisherman at the height of a storm and told him to row out to sea. They came across demons threatening to destroy Venice and exorcized them, and St Mark gave the fisherman his ring; as Paris Bordone shows, the saint commanded him to tell their story to the Doge and present the ring as evidence.

Marriage

A rite of passage invested with sacred significance in most ancient societies. It symbolized a semi-divine state of wholeness – union between the opposite principles of male and female necessary to create and protect new life. The depiction in myth and art of the "marriage" of key dualities (gods and goddesses, sun and moon, heaven and earth, king and queen or, in alchemy, sulphur and mercury) likewise symbolized the continuation of cosmic order and the fertility of nature, a process in which human marriages were felt to be important religiously as well as socially. The idea of human–divine union was often expressed in terms of marriage, as in the description of nuns as "brides of Christ".

Wedding customs, full of symbolic meanings now largely forgotten, attempted to ensure that marriages were binding, fruitful and happy. Binding symbols still in use include the ring (a circular symbol of eternity, union and completeness); the joining of hands; and the tying of knots (as in the Hindu custom by which the bridegroom knots a ribbon around the neck of the bride).

Fertility symbols include the sprinkling of grain, rice or their substitute, confetti, over the couple; the wedding cake (food being a sexual symbol as well as a symbolic means of uniting the two families in a shared feast); the presence of small children around the bride (sympathetic fertility magic); and the breaking of glasses or other objects (successful defloration). An enormous number of other customs were devised to ward off evil influences, ensure good luck or harmlessly act out social tensions caused by the marriage or the couple's drastic change of lifestyle. A custom as peculiar as tying tin cans to the back of the couple's car may derive from the idea that bad spirits could be driven off by making a lot of noise.

Mars

Mars, the Roman god of war and agriculture, was said to be the son of Jupiter (in Greek myth, Zeus) and Juno (Hera). Mars was originally the god of agriculture and the divine guardian of the land. He presumably grew more warlike in character as the expanding Roman state became itself more aggressive and militaristic. Mars enjoyed far greater prominence than the Greek war god Ares, with whom he came to be identified, and not all his myths were adapted from Greek ones. According to the most important of these native myths, Mars was the father of Romulus and Remus, the founders of Rome.

Mars was the champion of the

The god Mars, embodiment of Roman military prowess, riding in his chariot.

Roman nation and its armies and his official cult was second in importance only to that of Jupiter. However, the god retained the role of the protector of farmers and herdsmen. He was popular in Gaul and Britain, where many Celtic protector deities (not only those of war and agriculture) were identified with him. His chief festivals took place in March, which is named after him (in Latin *Martius*)

In art Mars is depicted as a militant figure armed with a helmet and shield and a spear, sword or lance. He may be accompanied by the Furies or by his sisters, Strife and Bellona (the latter being his female counterpart). He appears in allegories illustrating the triumph of love or wisdom over war. Mars may also be used to emphasize, by contrast, the superior aim of peace, in his negative role of war trampling on civilized pursuits.

His most famous affair was with Venus (Aphrodite), goddess of love, a relationship shown in numerous paintings. Whenever Mars rested in her company he took off his armour and the world was at peace. Painters followed the Classical description of the couple together: "Mars potent in arms, rules the savage works of war, yet often casts himself back into your lap, vanquished by the ever-living wound of love."[1] The theme may also be treated humorously, with *putti* disrespectfully playing with Mars' discarded armour.

Marsyas *see* Apollo

Martha

Martha, sister of Mary and Lazarus in the gospels, represents the good housewife. The gospels describe how she hospitably received Christ into her house and busied herself serving him while Mary listened to his words. She reproached him for not encouraging Mary to help her, but Christ replied that Mary had chosen the faithful path.[1] Martha is usually shown at work, perhaps with a ladle or pot or wearing a bunch of household keys. Velázquez's *Kitchen Scene with Christ in the House of Martha and Mary* suggests she is somewhat disgruntled with her lot. According to legend,[2] Martha, Mary and Lazarus were set adrift on rafts without food but landed safely on the coast of France near Marseilles. At that time a ferocious dragon was terrorizing the neighbouring community of Tarascon, but Martha subdued it with holy water and a cross.

Martin of Tours, Saint

Martin (*c*.315–397CE) was a young officer in the Roman army who was born in Hungary. While billeted in France, he converted to Christianity. He became a recluse, then founded the first monastery in Gaul, and was made Bishop of Tours *c*.370CE. He made many converts and had a reputation as a miracle worker. A figure of great importance in France, Martin was one of the first to be venerated as a saint, although he was not a martyr.

Martha:
[1] *Luke 10:38–42*
[2] *Golden Legend, St Martha*

Martin of Tours, Saint:
[1] *Golden Legend, St Martin*

MARTYRS: *see* Saints

Legend[1] relates that one bitter night Martin came upon a naked beggar and divided his own cloak in two with his sword in order to cover the man; Christ then appeared to him, which led to his baptism. Martin asked for discharge from the army, saying, "I am a soldier of Christ and I am forbidden to fight." He was accused of cowardice, but offered to stand in the line of battle armed only with a cross. The following day the barbarian army surrendered. Martin hid when the people of Tours sought to elect him their bishop, as he wished to continue the solitary life, but a cackling goose gave away his hiding place. On one occasion Martin gave his clothes away to a poor man while on his way to Mass and instructed the archdeacon to fetch him a new tunic. The archdeacon meanly brought one that was far too small, but while Martin was conducting the service angels presented him with gold armlets set with jewels so that his bare arms were decently covered.

The cult of St Martin was widespread. Scenes from his life by Simone Martini (*c.*1317) decorate the chapel dedicated to him in San Francesco, Assisi. He is particularly venerated in France. He is depicted as a bishop with the French fleur-de-lys on his cope, or occasionally with a goose, or as a soldier on horseback in the act of dividing his cloak for the beggar.

Martyrs

The early Christian martyrs, who were persecuted by the Romans until the reign of Constantine, formed the subjects of altarpieces intended for churches and chapels dedicated to them or commissioned by patrons of the same name. Accounts of many of their lives are given in the *Golden Legend* (*c.*1260) by Jacobus de Voragine; many were converted at an early age, refused to worship pagan idols and were tortured but refused to renounce their faith. Their attributes are often the instruments with which they were tortured or killed, but common to all is the martyrs' palm. Following the Council of Trent (1545–63) images showing their torments were favoured in order to encourage piety.

A particularly gruesome series of frescoes was commissioned by Pope Gregory for the church of San Stefano Rotondo in Rome. The martyrs are also shown in divine rapture, experiencing visions of the Virgin and Child or of Christ, or receiving their last communion from Christ.

Under King Shapur II (310–379CE) the Persians made war against the Roman Empire, which by then had adopted Christianity. In *10,000 Martyrs on Mount Ararat* Carpaccio shows the crucifixion of Armenian Christians by the Persians; Dürer, in *The Martyrdom of the 10,000 Christians under King Sapor*, shows them being executed in a variety of ways.

Mary Magdalene

Mary Magdalene (1st century CE) was traditionally believed to be a reformed prostitute and is identified as the woman who "was a sinner" at the house of the Pharisee, who washed Christ's feet with her tears, wiped them with her hair and anointed them. Christ then forgave her sins.[1] She was present at the Crucifixion and found Christ's tomb empty after the Resurrection. Initially she mistook him for a gardener but then recognized him, and Christ bade her, "Touch me not, for I am not yet ascended to my Father; but go to my brethren and say to them, I ascend unto my Father."[2] This *Noli me tangere* theme was painted both as part of the narrative and as an episode by itself, for example, by Titian.

According to legend,[3] Mary was the sister of Martha and Lazarus, with whom she was set adrift at sea, landing in Marseilles. She made many converts and performed miracles, then retired into the wilderness where she ate nothing but was nourished by angels. A hermit witnessed how angels descended and lifted her up seven times a day, and at the appointed hour of her death a choir of angels brought her to church to be blessed.

In scenes from the Life and Passion of Christ, Mary is often painted with long blond hair, wearing red. Masaccio shows her distraught at the Crucifixion. Her most common attribute is her jar of ointment; Rogier van der Weyden shows her carrying this in his mid-15th-century *Braque Triptych*. Mary is also depict-ed as a penitent both young and old; Donatello carved her as a haggard elderly figure, her long hair covering her naked body. She may also be seen contemplating a skull, a crucifix or an open book, or in divine rapture.

Mask

Transformation, protection, identification or disguise. The primary ancient symbolism of the mask is that it embodied a supernatural force or even transformed its shaman wearer into the spirit depicted by the mask. The earliest animal masks appear to have been used to capture the spirit of a hunted animal and prevent it from harming the wearer. Later primitive masks had totemic significance, identifying the tribe with a particular ancestral spirit whose power could then be used to protect the tribe, frighten its enemies, exorcise demons or diseases, expel the lingering spirits of the dead, or provide a focus for worship. The Iroquois False Face society were professional exorcisers of disease demons, masked to symbolize the baleful twin brother of the creator god. Masks or face packs were also used in African, Native American and Oceanic initiation ceremonies to mark the transition from a childish to an adult appearance. Burial masks representing dead notables were widely used not merely to shield their decaying faces, as in the golden masks of Mycenae, but also to ensure that their souls could find their way back to their bodies, a point of concern in Egyptian and other funerary rites.

The tragic and comic masks, also the attributes of the comic and tragic muses Melpomene and Thalia, were worn to identify different characters. in ancient Greek drama. They developed from the use of religious masks to act out myths or to symbolize the presence of divinities, particularly in the fertility cult of Dionysos. The characters of the Commedia dell'Arte also wore masks. Demon-frightening masks in Asia (which survive in processional dragon and lion dances) may similarly have been the origin of the masks later used with stylized colour symbolism in the Japanese No theatre – red for virtue, white for corruption, black for villainy. The mask can also, more obviously, symbolize concealment or illusion. In Indian tradition the mask is *maya* – the world as a delusion projected by the individual who has not understood the divine *maya* or Mask of God. In Western art, the mask is an attribute

Mary Magdalene: *see* Martha; Passion of Christ, The
[1] *Luke 7:36–48*
[2] *John 20:17*
[3] *Golden Legend, St Mary Magdalene*

Mask: *see* ANIMALS; Black; Commedia dell'Arte; Dragon; Initiation; Lion; Muses, The; Night; Red; Totem; Transformation; White

of Deceit personified, and of Vice and Night.

Math

The magician-lord of Gwynedd and protagonist of the Fourth Branch of the *Mabinogion*. Math, the son of Mathonwy and brother of Dôn, had to keep his feet in the lap of a virgin whenever he was not at war. His nephew Gilfaethwy wanted to seduce one of these maidens, so his brother Gwydion got Math out of the way by conjuring up a war with Pryderi, lord of Dyfed. When Math returned and discovered his nephews' trickery, he transformed them into animals for three years.

Math needed a new virgin, so his niece Arianrhod, the sister of Gwydion and Gilfaethwy, submitted to a virginity test. She stepped over Math's magic wand and failed the test by giving birth at once to twins, Dylan and Lleu Llaw Gyffes. Among the prohibitions she imposed on Lleu was the stricture that he should never have a human wife. Later, Math and Gwydion created a beautiful woman out of flowers, called Blodeuwedd, as a wife for Lleu.

Matthew, Saint

The attribute of the Apostle Matthew, or Levi, is a winged angel or winged man. Matthew was a tax gatherer for the Roman government. One day, as he sat in the customs house, Christ called him, "and saith unto him, Follow me. And he arose, and followed him." There is no authenticated account of the rest of his life, but legend relates that he preached in Ethiopia, where the king lusted after a Christian virgin. Matthew reprimanded him for desiring to violate a

bride of Christ, and for this he was martyred by the sword or axe. Like the other Evangelists, Matthew may be shown writing his Gospel, usually guided by an angel. He may have the coins or purse of his former trade; in Florence he was the patron saint of money changers or bankers. Caravaggio depicted his Calling and Martyrdom in dramatic canvases in the Contarelli Chapel in San Luigi dei Francesi, Rome.

Maui

The most famous trickster and culture hero of Polynesian mythology. Maui was born prematurely and, some say, thrown into the sea by his mother, but the sun saved him. One of his first exploits was to slow down the sun with the jawbone of his dead grandmother, either to give people more time to cook their food, or to give his mother more light for making bark-cloth (*tapa*).

On a fishing trip with his brothers, Maui fished up the first land (that is, island), in one account the island of Hawaiki or Te-ika-a-Maui (which means "Fish of Maui"), New Zealand. He brought humanity fire, which he stole from its keeper, Mahui-ike, an ancestral heroine of the underworld. On another trip to the underworld Maui attempted to pass through the body of the sleeping Hine-nui-te-po, the goddess of death, because he believed that this would render him immortal. But the goddess awoke and killed him. Since then no human has been able to achieve immortality.

Maurice, Saint

Legend[1] claims that Maurice, who probably lived in the 3rd century CE, was the commander of the Theban

Legion (Christian soldiers from Thebes in Egypt who served the Romans in Gaul). They were ordered to offer sacrifice to pagan gods, and when they refused the entire troop was massacred. Maurice was particularly venerated in the area around the canton of Valais, Switzerland, where an abbey was dedicated to him. In a painting by Malthius Grünewald he is generally shown as dark-skinned or Moorish, and wearing armour. Maurice is patron saint of northern Austria, and may be represented carrying a banner bearing an eagle, the country's emblem.

Maypole

A spring emblem of fertility and solar renewal, linked to ancient agricultural and resurrection rites and to the axial symbolism of the World Tree. In England, the phallic symbolism of maypoles and wanton behaviour around them on May Day affronted the Puritans. Pagan sources of the maypole include the Greek and Roman spring rites of Attis, slain consort of the Earth Mother, Cybele. His symbol was a stripped pine tree, wound with woollen bands, around which dances were performed to invoke and celebrate his resurrection.

The Roman festival of Hilaria adapted this tradition, combined with other, existing spring rites as it spread into the Celtic world. English maypoles emphasized the symbolism of fecundity by attaching a feminine disk to the male pole. Dancers unwinding ribbons as they circle around the pole are said to symbolize the creation of the cosmos from the axial centre (this has similarity with the rites of Attis, suggesting a Roman source). More exhausting or painful circular dances performed by the Plains Indians in North America used a central pole as a linking symbol between earth and the supernatural forces above it. These dances invoked the power of the sun, sometimes by offering sacrificial pieces of flesh torn from the breasts of warriors.

Mead

The beverage of the gods in Celtic tradition, making it a symbol of immortality. Celtic legends told of deposed kings drowned in barrels of mead in their burning palaces. An alcholic drink made from fermented honey mixed with water and often spiced, mead shares the positive symbolism of honey.

Medea

A sorceress of Greek myth, the daughter of King Aeëtes of Colchis and the sea nymph Idyia, and the wife successively of Jason and Aegeus, the father of Theseus. When the Argonauts sailed from Iolcus to Colchis, Medea fell in love with Jason and helped him win the Golden Fleece. She assisted his escape by murdering her own brother, Apsyrtus. Later, Jason and Medea went to Medea's aunt, the

Medea deceiving King Pelias; after a 6th-century BCE vase painting.

Maypole: *see* Axis; Phallus; Pillar; Pine, Pine cone; Sacrifice; Sun; Sun dance; Tree

Mead: *see* Alcohol; Honey; Intoxication

Medea: *see* Alcestis; ARGONAUTS, THE VOYAGE OF THE; Circe; Jason; Talos; Theseus

Medhbh

witch Circe, to be purified for the murder of Apsyrtus, but Circe was
appalled at the crime and cursed them.

They returned to Iolcus, to find that
Jason's uncle, King Pelias, had executed Aeson, Jason's father and the right-
ful king. Medea brought Aeson back
to life and then convinced the usurper
and his daughters she could make him
young again too. In some accounts
she told them that they could rejuvenate their father by emptying his
veins, and she later pretended to fill
them with youthful essence; in others
she is said to have advised the daughters to cut Pelias up and boil him.
They followed her instructions, to discover that she had tricked them into
murdering Pelias.

The gruesome manner of Pelias'
death caused outrage and Jason and
Medea fled to Corinth. They had
many children. Later, King Creon of
Corinth offered Jason his daughter in
marriage. Jason agreed and told
Medea that he proposed to divorce
her. Furious at this betrayal, Medea
sent Creon's daughter poisoned robes,
killing both her and her father. She
then slit the throats of her children
and fled to Athens.

In Athens she married King Aegeus
and they had a son, Medus, Aegeus'
heir presumptive. But Aegeus had an
elder son, Theseus, whom he had
never seen, born to a princess of
Troezen. One day Theseus arrived in
Athens and Medea, who recognized
him through her magic powers, persuaded Aegeus that the stranger
planned to kill him. Aegeus agreed
that she should poison his wine, but at
the last moment he recognized Theseus and knocked the wine from his
hand. Realizing Medea's treachery,
Aegeus banished her and Medus.

According to one account, Medea
and Medus finally returned to
Colchis, where Aeëtes had been overthrown by his brother Perses. With his
mother's aid Medus killed Perses and
took the throne. Turner's *Vision of
Medea* shows Medea practising her
black arts.

Medhbh

A divine sorceress, who was the queen
of Connacht and the chief adversary
of the Ulster heroes Conchobar and
Cú Chulainn in the war in *Táin Bó
Cuailnge* (*The Cattle Raid of Cooley*).
She was the lover of many kings and
the only woman to satisfy the sexual
appetite of the hero Ferghus, said to
be seven times that of other men. She
died after being hit by a piece of hard
cheese hurled in a slingshot by her
nephew Furbaidhe, whose mother she
had murdered.

Medusa

Medusa was one of three Gorgon sisters, daughters of the sea divinities
Phorcys and Ceto, renowned for her
beauty, and especially her lovely hair.¹
Poseidon (in Roman myth, Neptune)

*Athene guiding Perseus to decapitate
Medusa; after a 5th-century BCE jug.*

robbed her of her virginity in a Temple of Athene (Minerva), and to punish her for violating the sacred spot, the goddess changed Medusa's hair into a mass of fearsome snakes. The hero Perseus was charged with bringing Medusa's head to King Polydectes of Seriphos, who held his mother Danaë captive. Medusa's direct glance turned anything living to stone, so Perseus cut off her head either while looking in a mirror or, in another account, by letting his protector, the goddess Athene, guide his hand. He put the head into a bag, later using it to turn his enemies to stone before finally giving it to Athene, who wore it on her *aegis* (breastplate). Caravaggio re-created this shield in paint. From Medusa's blood sprang a son, Chrysaor, and the winged horse Pegasus.

Megara *see* **Herakles**

Melancholia

In the Middle Ages a melancholic temperament was thought to be caused by an excess of black bile, and was associated with intellectual pursuits. Melancholia, daughter of Saturn (in Greek myth, Cronos) was of an introspective nature, and may appear in art in an attitude of gloomy contemplation. Dürer's engraving *Melancholia* shows a winged figure, heavily slumped. Scholarly objects – a sphere, a geometric block and tools – lie in disorder, while a book remains unopened in her lap and a pair of compasses unnoticed in her hand.

Meleager

In Greek myth, a prince of Calydon in Aetolia, the son of King Oenus and Queen Althaea.[1] When Meleager was born, the Fates told Althaea that he would die when a certain piece of wood on the fire had been burned up. To save her son Althaea removed it from the fire and hid it.

When Meleager was a young man, his father neglected to make Artemis (in Roman myth, Diana) an offering, and in her wrath she sent down a wild boar – the Calydonian boar – to ravage his lands. Meleager gathered a large band of heroes, huntsmen and hounds, and a great chase ensued. The fleet-footed huntress Atalanta joined the company and Meleager fell in love with her. She was the first to wound the boar, while Meleager drove in the fatal spear. He gave the boar's head to Atalanta as a trophy, but his mother's envious brothers tried to wrestle it from her and were killed by Meleager. Althea, remembering the prophecy, kindled a fire and flung on the log; Meleager died as it burned. Artemis, placated by this tragedy, turned the women who mourned for him into birds and dispatched them into the sky. *The Hunt for the Calydonian Boar*, one of a series of eight paintings by Charles Lebrun, depicts the best-known episode of the story of Meleager.

Menelaus

A king of Sparta. Menelaus was the son of Atreus, brother of Agamemnon and husband of Helen of Troy.

Menhir

A Neolithic standing stone, often set up near European burial sites and thought by some to symbolize the life force of a male divinity or hero and to memorialize him as a durable presence protectively watching over the living. Early standing stones appear to be astronomical markers, but later

Melancholia: *see* Temperaments, The

Meleager: *see* Atalanta
[1] Ovid, *Met VIII:260–546* & Philostratus the Younger, *Imagines 15*

Menelaus: *see* Atreus; Agamemnon; Helen; Paris; PELOPS, THE CURSE OF THE HOUSE OF; TROJAN WAR, THE HEROES OF THE

Menhir: *see* Phallus; Man; Stone

*In alchemy, the element
mercury was represented
as the god, as in this
figure taken from an
engraving of 1666.*

and smaller menhirs are sometimes
carved with figurative details supporting the idea of a more symbolic role.

Mercury (1)
Fluidity, liaison, transformation,
volatility and the intellect – a lunar
and female metal linked by
alchemists with "cold" energy. As the
only common metal liquid at ordinary temperatures, mercury was of
great interest to alchemists, especially
because it forms easy amalgams with
other metals – and was once used to
extract gold from ore for this reason.
Mercury (the metal, planet and
androgynous god) has unusually consistent and universal symbolism in
mythology, astrology and alchemy.
The planet Mercury, closest of the
planets to the sun, circles the sun
quickly and is elusive to observe,
hence its association with the winged
messenger of the gods (Hermes/Mer-
cury). The metal, also known as
quicksilver or "liquid silver", was
extracted by the ancients from roasted cinnabar and represented the second stage of alchemic purification
before "conjunction" with its symbolic opposite, sulphur. Its planetary
sigil, adopted by alchemists, is at least
3,000 years old. In China, mercury
was associated with the dragon and
with the liquid bodily elements –
blood, water and semen. It corre-
sponded to the yogic element in Indian tradition, associated with the
internal flow of spiritual energy, and
with the semen of Shiva.

Mercury (2) *see* **Hermes**

Meretsger
An Egyptian snake goddess of the
peak overlooking the royal tombs of

Thebes (modern Luxor). She was generally benevolent and had the power
to cure disease, but she could also
inflict sickness on sinners.

Merlin
A magician and prophet. The Merlin
of Arthurian legend derives ultimately from the figure of Myrddin or
Merddin, a seer or madman with
prophetic gifts who was said to have
lived in the Caledonian Forest in
British-speaking southern Scotland.

*The magician Merlin as a boy; after
an illustration to the 13th-century*
Prophecies of Merlin.

He is said to have gone mad after see-
ing a terrible vision in battle. Other
versions of the Myrddin story are the
Irish myth of the Frenzy of Suibhne
(Sweeney) and the Scottish myth of
Lailoken (or Llalogan).

The story of Myrddin was brought
to Wales after *c*.500CE by British
migrants from Strathclyde and developed in the 9th and 10th centuries.
The character of the Arthurian Merlin
was fixed by Geoffrey of Monmouth,

whose Latin *History of the Kings of Britain* (1136) introduced a seer-magician called Merlinus Ambrosius, based on another, unrelated, legendary character, the wonder-child Ambrosius. Parallels have also been drawn between the tales of Merlin and those of the Irish hero Finn.

Metals

Cosmic energy trapped in solid form – a symbolism that explains some puzzling aspects of ancient attitudes toward metals. Early extraction, purification and smelting techniques and, still more, the efforts of alchemists to transmute base metals to gold, made metallurgy an allegory of spiritual testing and purification. Metals, like humans, were earthly things with celestial potential. Hence the development of a cosmic hierarchy in which metals were paired with the seven known planets. In ascending order, least precious to the most precious, these were: lead with Saturn; tin with Jupiter; iron with Mars; copper with Venus; mercury with Mercury; silver with the moon; gold with the sun. In psychology, metals represented the human's sensuality, transcended only by spiritual development. In some initiation rites, metallic possessions were discarded to signify the shedding of impurities.

Meteorite

A divine spark or seed. In the ancient world, meteorites were thought to be fragments of the governing stars – virtually angels in material form, recalling humans to the existence of a higher life. Meteoric stone or metal thus had sacred value. The Ka'aba stone, focal point of Makkah (Mecca), is believed to be a meteorite.

Metis

An Oceanid (sea nymph) of Greek myth, the daughter of Okeanos and Tethys and first wife of Zeus. Metis ("Wise Cunning"), assisted Zeus in the overthrow of his father Kronos by serving Kronos an emetic drink that made him spew up Zeus' brothers and sisters, whom he had swallowed at birth. Together with Zeus they fought and defeated the Titans, establishing Zeus as lord of the heavens. Zeus then married Metis and she became pregnant by him.

The goddess Gaia predicted that Metis would bear a goddess equal to Zeus in wisdom as well as a god who would overthrow him and become lord of heaven and earth. Wishing to avoid the fate of his father, Zeus swallowed Metis and thereafter possessed her cunning wisdom, which meant that he could never be tricked as Kronos had been. Of Metis' predicted children, the god was never born, but the goddess – Athene – eventually sprang, fully formed and armed, from Zeus' head.

Michael, Saint (Archangel)

Michael, the heavenly messenger who was also adopted as a saint, was the prince of angels and the military leader who threw the Devil from heaven. "And there was war in heaven: Michael and his angels fought against the dragon; and the dragon fought and his angels, and prevailed not; neither was their place found any more in heaven."[1] He is depicted fighting the dragon by several artists including Dürer, or as a beautiful young man with wings (often in white or in armour, with lance and shield) standing over a dragon – for example, by Piero della Francesca. In scenes of the Last Judgment he holds scales on which he weighs the souls of the dead.

Mictlan

The Aztec land of the dead. Mictlan was a terrifying place but not solely a region of punishment, because everyone, sinner and virtuous alike, was destined to pass through it unless they had died violently (in which case they went straight to one of the celestial regions). The souls of the deceased encountered various perils, such as sharp knives and turbulent waters, on their way to Mictlan where the god Mictlantecuhtli and his consort Mictecacihuatl presided over the dead.

The god Quetzalcoatl was said to have travelled into the underworld to steal bones from which he fashioned a new race of humans. Mictlantecuhtli chased him, causing him to drop some of the stolen bones, a number of which broke. As a result of this, the new race of humans became all different sizes.

Midas

The Classical myth of Midas, the legendary king of Phrygia, represents human folly and greed.[1] Midas entertained the god Dionysos's companion, Silenus, at a festival lasting ten days and nights. The god was so grateful that he granted Midas a wish. The king asked that everything he touched be turned to gold. However, he had not anticipated being unable to eat and drink, as his food and wine were also transformed. Distraught, he begged for forgiveness for his greed. In *Midas Washing at the Source of the Pactolus* Poussin illustrates how Midas washed away folly in the River Pactolus, so that its sands became gold dust.

Now averse to riches, Midas retired to the country – but he had learned little wisdom. He worshipped Pan, who competed on his reed pipes against Apollo, the god of music. Apollo was pronounced the victor, but Midas foolishly objected; whereupon Apollo gave Midas ass's ears as a perpetual hallmark of his deafness to musical quality. Domenichino painted *The Judgment of Midas* as one of a series of rural scenes, several of which show Apollo in a vengeful mood.

Midnight

In Chinese tradition, the beginning of twelve hours of solar ascent – a moment charged with power and believed to be a propitious time for conception, particularly at the December solstice. It was also, in Christian legend, the hour of Christ's birth. India's independence on the stroke of midnight had added symbolic significance because it was in Tantric tradition an hour of spiritual zenith as well as initiation.

Milesians, The

The sixth and final race to conquer Ireland, according to the *Book of Invasions*. The Milesians (the Gaels), or Sons of Míl after their leader, Míl Espaine (Latin *Miles Hispaniae*, "Soldier of Spain"), landed in southwest Ireland from Spain on 1 May, the feast of Beltane. They defeated the Tuatha Dé Danann and the land was divided in two: the Milesians ruled Ireland above ground and Tuatha Dé established a new domain in the subterranean Otherworld.

Milk

The elixir of life, rebirth and immortality – a metaphor for kindness, care, compassion, abundance and fertility. In Indian tradition, the fundamental role of milk is expressed in a Vedic myth of the origin of the world, when gods and anti-gods churned the cosmic pail of the primeval ocean to create first milk, then butter, then the sun and moon, and finally the elixir of immortality, *soma*. A milk-giving tree grew in the Hindu paradise. Milk appears in many traditions, including Celtic, as a drink of immortality. Apart from the obvious links with nursing and motherhood or adoption, milk was an initiation or rebirth symbol in Greek Orphic rites, in Islam, and at early Christian baptisms.

It was poured as a libation for the resurrection of the god Osiris in Egypt, and in spring fertility rites elsewhere. More generally, it represented the drinking in of knowledge or spiritual nourishment. Its colour also made it a symbol of purity – milk rather than blood was said to have spurted from the decapitated St Catherine of Alexandria.

Milky Way

There are various accounts of the origin of the Milky Way, which stretches in a luminous band across the night sky.[1] One is that Zeus (Jupiter) held his son Herakles (Hercules) to sleeping Hera's (Juno) breast to secure his immortality. After the infant had drunk, the flow of milk continued, some splashing upward creating constellations, some falling to earth as lilies. In *The Origin of the Milky Way* Tintoretto shows Herakles waking his unwitting wet-nurse.

The Milky Way appears as a celestial serpent in Central American myth; the path travelled by souls to the afterlife in North America; a celestial river from which the thunder god draws rain in Peru; and as a symbolic boundary or bridge between the known world and the divine.

Milo of Croton

A Greek athlete of the 6th century BCE, Milo had remarkable strength.[1] However, he fell prey to wild animals when his hand caught in a split tree-trunk, which he was trying to prise open. Pierre Puget's sculpture *Milo of Croton* shows him screaming in agony as a lion sinks its teeth into him.

Mimi

A trickster being in the Aboriginal mythology of western Arnhem Land. The *mimi* are said to live in crevices in the rock face of the Arnhem Land escarpment and on the whole are benign: for example, they taught people the art of hunting. But *mimi* are hostile if surprised by the sudden presence of strangers. People who startle them may be punished with sickness. Ancient Aboriginal cave paintings are often said to be the work of the *mimi*.

Mimosa

The certainty of resurrection – a religious symbolism based on the solar colour of its golden flowers and on the idea that it was a mimic of sentient life, its leaves responding to stimuli and unfolding to the light everlasting.

Minakshi

A warrior goddess worshipped at Madurai as the consort of Shiva. She was said to have been born with three breasts and raised as a boy by her parents, who were a king and queen. She succeeded her father as ruler and con-

An image after a bark painting, thought to show mimi *tricksters.*

*The bull-man Minotaur,
after an ancient Greek
vase painting.*

quered the world, then went to the
sacred Mount Kailasa to challenge
the god Shiva. On meeting the great
god, however, she became shy and
reserved, losing her third breast. The
story contrasts with the myth of Parvati, whose gentler nature subdued
the fierce and warlike Shiva.

Minerva *see* **Athene**

Minia
A cosmic serpent of northern African
mythology. In the Sahara and Sahel it
is widely said that Minia was the first
thing made by the divine creator. The
serpent's head was in the sky and its
tail was in the waters beneath the
earth. Its body was divided into seven
parts. The god then used these parts
to form the world and all life.

Miniato, Saint
According to legend, Miniato was a
3rd-century Florentine Christian
martyr. He survived ordeals with wild
beasts in the ampitheatre but was
eventually beheaded; he then carried
his head from the bottom of a valley
to the summit of a hill above Florence
where the Romanesque church dedicated to him now stands. Here he can
be seen as a young man crowned and
holding the martyrs' palm in a 1390s
painting by Agnolo Gaddi.

Minos
A king of Crete, the son of Europa
and Zeus. After her affair with Zeus,
Europa married Asterius, king of
Crete, who adopted Minos, Sarpedon
and Rhadamanthys, her three sons by
Zeus. Minos succeeded Asterius fol-
lowing a quarrel with his brothers,
who left Crete. To affirm his power
Minos prayed to the sea god Poseidon

for a suitable sacrificial beast; a magnificent bull emerged from the sea.
But the beast was so beautiful that
Minos would not sacrifice it, angering
Poseidon, who caused Minos' wife
Pasiphaë to commit adultery with the
bull. In consequence, Pasiphaë bore
the Minotaur, a monster which was
half bull and half man.

During his reign Minos conquered
much of Greece. But, failing to take
Athens, he prayed for a plague to
strike the city. This epidemic was
relieved only by the payment, by King
Aegeus of Athens, of an annual tribute of seven boys and seven girls, who
were fed to the Minotaur in its lair, a
dark subterranean maze called the
Labyrinth. This subservience ended
when Aegeus' son, Theseus, sailed to
Crete and killed the Minotaur.

Minos employed the great craftsman Daedalus. Following imprison-
ment for his part in killing the
Minotaur, Daedalus fled to King
Cocalus of Sicily. Minos followed him
and demanded that Cocalus hand him
over. However, while staying at
Cocalus' palace, Minos was killed by
a contraption invented by Daedalus,
causing him to be drenched in boiling
water in the bath and scalded to
death. Minos went to the underworld
and became a judge of the dead.
Among his children were Euryale,
Orion's mother, and Phaedra, a queen
of Athens.

Minotaur, The
A monster, part bull and part man,
the offspring of Queen Pasiphaë of
Crete and a bull. King Minos, the
husband of Pasiphaë, prayed for a
bull to sacrifice to the god Poseidon.
The bull which appeared was so marvellous that he did not want to kill it,

angering Poseidon so much that the god made Pasiphaë fall passionately in love with the animal. To satisfy her lust she enlisted the help of the royal craftsman Daedalus, who constructed a hollow life-sized model of a beautiful heifer to attract the attentions of the bull. Pasiphaë positioned herself in this model to have intercourse with the beast. She became pregnant and bore the Minotaur (literally "Bull of Minos"), sometimes called Asterius or Asterion.

Furious at his wife and craftsman, Minos ordered Daedalus to make a prison for the savage hybrid. He built the Labyrinth, an underground maze of tunnels from which it was impossible to escape. In the centre of this was the Minotaur's lair.

Every year King Minos demanded tribute of seven boys and seven girls from Aegeus, the king of Athens, to be devoured by the Minotaur. One year, however, the victims were accompanied by the hero Theseus, the son of Aegeus. Ariadne, the daughter of Minos, fell in love with Theseus and when the terrified children were sent into the Minotaur's lair she gave the hero a ball of twine. With this he could enter the Labyrinth and later find his way out. Unravelling the twine as he went, Theseus followed the sound of the bellowing Minotaur and reached the centre of the Labyrinth. He wrestled with the Minotaur and beat it to death, then led the children out of the Labyrinth to safety.

The bull's head on a human body generally symbolizes the complete dominance of the animal instinct, but in the ominous times of the 1930s Picasso depicted a Minotaur to express the dual nature of man.

Mirror

Veracity, self-knowledge, sincerity, purity, enlightenment, divination – a predominantly positive symbol because of its ancient association with light, especially the light of the mirror-like disks of the sun and moon, thought to reflect divinity to earth. Hence the belief that evil spirits could not abide mirrors and, as spirits of darkness, had no reflection.

Although mirrors sometimes appear in Western art as disapproving attributes of Pride, Vanity or Lust, they more often symbolize Truth – the folk wisdom that the mirror never lies: "You may not go," Hamlet rages at his mother, "until I set you up a glass where you may see the inmost part of you." (Shakespeare's *Hamlet*, 3:4;). The Virgin Mary is sometimes shown holding a mirror – a reference to her untainted chastity and to the Christ Child as the mirror of God. The mirror (until the late Middle Ages usually a round disk of bronze or silver, polished on one side) was an emblem of the Greek goddess Aphrodite (Venus to the Romans) and of mother goddesses in the Middle East.

The philosophical significance of the mirror as a symbol of the self-examined life is widespread in Asian traditions and particularly important in Japanese myth and religion: the creator-god Izanagi gave his children a mirror, telling them to kneel and look into it morning and evening until they had shed evil thoughts and passions. In the Shinto hell, a giant mirror reflects the sins of new arrivals and determines the region of their punishment in ice or fire. The bronze mirror Yatano-Kagami, kept at Ise in Japan's most important Shinto shrine, symbolizes the sun goddess Amaterasu,

Mirror: *see* AFTERLIFE; CHASTITY; Heart; Karma; Lake; Light; Magpie; Marriage; Moon; SEVEN DEADLY SINS; TRUTH; Twins; VANITY

Missal

who was tempted by a magic mirror to emerge from the cave in which she had hidden her divine light. The mirror was an imperial solar emblem handed from emperor to emperor.

In both Hinduism and Buddhism it symbolizes the enlightened realization that the phenomenal world is an illusion, a mere reflection. Yama, the Hindu guardian of the underworld, also uses a mirror to judge the state of a soul's karma. The mirror is one of the Eight Auspicious Emblems of Buddhism. It is a Chinese emblem of sincerity, harmony and marital happiness linked with the magpie.

Almost everywhere, mirrors have been linked with magic and especially with divination because they can reflect past or future events as well as present ones. Shamans in central Asia aimed mirrors at the sun or moon in order to read the future. The mirror can also symbolize a mystic door into a parallel world, as in Lewis Carrol's *Alice in Wonderland.*

The widespread superstition that breaking a mirror brings bad luck is linked with primitive ideas that a person's reflection contains part of his or her life force, or a twin "soul". Equally widely, the brightness or dullness of a mirror is an allegory for the state of a person's soul. In both Islamic and Christian thought, the human heart is likened to a mirror that reflects God.

Missal

A missal, or book of the Mass, contains the services and prayers for the Roman Catholic liturgical year. It was often decorated with appropriate scenes; its frontispiece might be the Crucifixion or Christ in Majesty, sometimes surrounded by scenes from the Life and Passion of Christ.

Mist

A transition, evolution or supernatural intervention – the significance of mist in some Oriental paintings and in traditional symbolism generally. Mist stood for the indeterminate, a prelude to revelation or to the emergence of new forms, as in initiation rites.

Mistletoe

Fertility, protection, healing, rebirth, immortality – the magical "golden bough" of the Celtic world. As an evergreen parasite that produces yellow flowers, and white berries in midwinter, mistletoe symbolized the continuing potency of the deciduous trees on which it was found. Mistletoe clinging to an oak (a rare event) was a female fertility symbol to the Druids who, according to the Roman author Pliny (*c.*24–79CE), cut it with a golden sickle on the sixth day of the new moon (probably at the Celtic New Year in November) and sacrificed a young white bull beneath the tree. The berry juice (which was equated with the tree's semen and its connotations of power and wisdom) supposedly prevented sterility or disease in cattle and was credited with other healing properties.

Celtic reverence for mistletoe – thought to be produced by lightning – may have influenced the account in Virgil's *Aeneid* (*c.*29–19BCE) of Aeneas travelling safely through the underworld carrying a bough of it. The golden bough of life appears more unexpectedly as an instrument of death in the Nordic and Germanic myth of Balder, god of light, who was killed by an innocent dart made from mistletoe. This apparent inversion of its talismanic symbolism may signify the passage from mortal to immortal status through the agency of a sacred plant. Celtic tradition seems to account for Christmas kisses under a bunch of mistletoe, an augury of fruitful union.

Mithras
A Persian god of justice, war and the sun. Mithra was originally the divine personification of *mitra* ("contract") and the upholder of order and truth. As a god of war he rode in a golden chariot drawn by four horses to combat demons and their followers, and was associated with the sun (often being envisaged in myth, for example by the Greeks, as a deity riding a chariot through the sky).

Under the Roman Empire, Mithras became the focus of a mystery cult particularly popular among the Roman soldiery. Mithraic shrines were characterized by an image of Mithra slaying a bull in an ancient Persian rite said to have been established by the first man, Yima. For the followers of Mithraism this rite symbolized the renewal of creation. In killing the bull it was believed that Mithra brought back Yima's rule over a world where hunger and death were yet unknown. The rite bestowed immortality upon Mithra's worshippers, hence its appeal to troops facing the dangers of combat.

Miyazu-hime *see* Yamato-takeru

Mjollnir
The name of the magic hammer-axe that was the chief weapon of the Norse god Thor. Its blows were heard as thunder, the sparks it caused were seen as lightning. Neck pendants in the shape of the hammer were common amulets in Scandinavia.

Mnemosyne
In Greek myth, a Titan, the daughter of Gaia, the earth, and Uranos. Mnemosyne ("Memory") coupled with Zeus to produce the Muses, the nine goddesses of the fine arts, history and astronomy.

Model
A model of a church may be held by St Jerome as one of the Four Doctors of the Church, or by other saints who founded monastic Orders. Saints may hold a model of the town or city of which they are patron; an example is St Emidius, patron of Ascoli Piceno in the Italian Marches, seen in Carlo Crivelli's *Annunciation*. A model of a building shown with its patron and architect may illustrate the enlightenment and generosity of the patron and the genius of the designer. Thus Vasari painted *Cosimo de Medici Receiving the Model for San Lorenzo from Brunelleschi*.

Monica, Saint
Monica (332–387CE) was the mother of St Augustine.[1] Converted to Christianity in Africa, she led a saintly life and tried to bring up her son in her faith. After she was widowed, she followed Augustine to Italy, where they were strongly influenced by St Ambrose of Milan, and Augustine was converted. She died at the port of Ostia, near Rome, as they were setting out for Africa. Monica appears in scenes of the life of St Augustine.

Monkey
Like the ape, the monkey is an animal with a higher symbolic status in the East than in the West. Its imitative skills and wide behavioural range make its symbolism inconsistent, and

Mjollnir: *see* Hammer; Thor

Mnemosyne: *see* Muses, The; ZEUS, THE CONSORTS OF

Model: *see* Doctor; Geminianus, St; Jerome, St

Monica, Saint: *see* Augustine, St
[1] St Augustine, *Confessions* IX:8–13

Monkey: *see* Ape; Apple; SEVEN DEADLY SINS; WISDOM

Mithra, based on a marble sculpture of c.2nd century CE.

*The moon card from the
Tarot pack.*

enable it to be used variously to personify virtuous or foolish aspects of human behaviour. In Tibetan tradition, the bodhisattva Avalokiteshvara (incarnate in the Dalai Lama) originally entered the country in the guise of a saintly monkey, took pity on an ogress who had fallen in love with him, and with her fathered the six ancestors of the Tibetan race.

Stories of monkey-kings appear also in Chinese and Indian myth where they play agile and intelligent hero roles. Hanuman, the Hindu monkey god, was a fertility symbol as well as healer, warrior and loyal follower of the god Rama. The gibbon monkey symbolized maternal protection in Chinese art, and monkey dolls had similar protective symbolism in Japan. The famous *koshin* – three monkeys who see, hear and speak no evil, carved in wood on the shrine of the first Tokugawa shogun at Nikko – unexpectedly signify the wisdom of discretion, an inversion of the Western view of the monkey as inquisitive and chattering. The carving has been explained as a talisman against slander. Malice, lust and greed are attributes of the monkey in Christian art: monkeys often caricature the venial faults of human nature or represent the imitative arts.

Monkey King, The

The character, also called Sun Wukong, who stole the peaches of immortality from empress Wang Mu Niang Niang. He features in a 14th-century novel *Journey to the West*, also known as *Monkey*.

Moon

Fertility, cyclic regeneration, resurrection, immortality, occult power, muta-

bility, intuition and the emotions – ancient regulator of time, the waters, crop growth and the lives of women. The moon's appearances and disappearances and its startling changes of form presented an impressive cosmic image of the earthly cycles of animal and vegetable birth, growth, decline, death and rebirth.

The extent and power of lunar worship and lunar symbolism are partly explained by the moon's enormous importance as a source of light for night hunting and as the earliest measure of time – its phases forming the basis of the first known calendars. Beyond its influence on the tides, the moon was widely believed to control human destiny as well as rainfall, snow, floods, and the rhythms of plant and animal life in general and of women, through the lunar rhythms of the menstrual cycle.

Although primarily a symbol of the female principle, the moon was sometimes personified by male gods, especially among nomadic or hunting cultures. The great Sumerian-Semitic moon-god Sin, whose sign was a boat-shaped crescent, was Lord of Months, and of destiny. The moon was male in Japan, Oceania and the Teutonic countries as well, and also among some African and Native American tribes. Female moon deities vary in character, ranging from protective great mother goddesses to fierce, silvery defenders of their virginity such as the horned Greek hunter-goddess Artemis, who is identified by a crescent moon in her hair or in the sky. Chastity, mutability, fickleness or "cold" indifference are all qualities associated with the moon.

The moon was associated with the Virgin Mary, notably in paintings of the Immaculate Conception. Its best-known Classical personification, Diana, was a minor Italian woodland goddess, later identified with Artemis, who had absorbed elements of the Greek moon cults of Selene (Luna in Roman myth), lover of Endymion; and Hecate, representing the moon in its funerary aspect.

The "dark of the moon" (its three-day absence) made the moon a symbol of the passage from life to death as well as from death to life. In some traditions, the moon is the way to the afterlife or the abode of the honoured dead. Although generally a benevolent symbol, the moon is sometimes a witching presence associated with death and with occult figures such as the Egyptian god Thoth and the goddess Hecate in Greece. Apart from major fertility symbols like the hare or rabbit, lunar animals include the hibernating bear, amphibians such as the frog and toad, other nocturnal animals such as the cat and fox – and the snail with its appearing and disappearing antennae (the "horns" on the crescent moon).

The hare or rabbit and the toad were most often identified with the patches on the moon (alternatively thought to be an old man gathering sticks, a water-carrier or – in Africa – mud slung by the jealous sun). More often in myth (and alchemy), the sun and moon form a necessary duality as husband and wife, brother and sister, hot and cold, fire and water, male and female – notably symbolized by the Egyptian headdress which shows the sun disk enclosed by the horns of the moon. Together they may refer to the unity or cycle of time, to the universal, or to a marriage of dual natures. Both these heavenly bodies may be shown in

the sky at the Crucifixion. Astrology stressed the passive aspects of the moon as a mere reflector of the sun's light, hence its association with conceptual or rational thought rather than direct knowledge (although Daoism saw it as the eye of spiritual knowledge in the darkness of ignorance).

Psychology links it with subjectivity, intuition and the emotions – and with shifts of mood, which is a recurring symbolism.

Moon Spirit, The

One of the three great spirit forces in Inuit belief, together with the Air Spirit and the Sea Spirit. The Moon Spirit is a male deity and a great hunter. He dwells in the land of the sky, presiding over fertility, morality and, to the Inuit of Alaska, animals. The Moon Spirit is inherently benevolent but is perceived as threatening as he responds to human misdeeds by sending sickness, bad weather, and failure in hunting.

Morríghan, The

An Irish war goddess, who is sometimes manifested as three goddesses. The Morríghan (which means "Phantom Queen") was one of a number of powerful female Irish war deities. Like the others she was an awesome presence on the battlefield, although she did not participate in combat. Before a battle she could possibly be found by a ford. There she would wash the armour of those warriors whose destiny it was to die in the fray.

The goddess possessed magic powers and could change shape at will, especially into a raven or crow, which was regarded as a herald of death. In some accounts it was the Morríghan (rather than Badhbh) who landed on the corpse of the hero Cú Chulainn to show that he was dead. Also associated with fertility and sexuality, the goddess tried to seduce Cú Chulainn in the guise of a young maiden, and stood astride her ford to have intercourse with the Daghda, the father god of the Tuatha Dé Danann, on the feast of Samhain.

Moses

Moses, the great biblical prophet, led the Israelites out of captivity from Egypt, received the Ten Commandments from God, and organized the Jewish religion. He is invariably depicted as a vigorous elderly man, with a long flowing white beard. He is often shown with shafts of light radiating from either side of his head, for "the skin of his face shone" when he received the word of God.[1] These shafts are sometimes represented as horns, owing to an early mistranslation from Hebrew into Latin, in which "shone" was taken to mean "horned". He may also hold the tablets on which the Commandments were written, or a staff. The best-known episodes from his life are as follows:

THE FINDING OF MOSES

The populous Israelites were the slaves of the Pharaohs. Fearing their numbers, the Pharaoh resolved to kill all male Jewish children. To escape the massacre, his mother hid the infant Moses in a basket by the edge of the Nile; he was found by the Pharaoh's daughter, who adopted him.[2]

THE PHARAOH'S CROWN

In Jewish legend the Pharaoh placed a crown on Moses' head when he was a boy.[3] Moses trampled on it, and the scene came to represent the salvation of his people. This was interpreted as an omen that Moses would overthrow the king; so a trial was ordered whereby Moses had to choose between eating a bowl of burning coals and one of cherries. He would be exonerated if he chose the former. Moses grabbed the coals and put them into his mouth, an act which indicated his future greatness.

THE DAUGHTERS OF JETHRO

As a young man, Moses killed an Egyptian for beating a Jew and fled to the land of Midian. Here he met the seven daughters of Jethro, who were prevented from watering their flocks by shepherds. Moses drove off the shepherds and in reward was given one of the daughters as his bride.[4]

THE BURNING BUSH

As Moses watched over Jethro's flock, an angel appeared from a bush that was in flames without actually burning. From the bush God told Moses to lead his people out of Egypt into a land flowing with milk and honey.[5]

THE STAFF OF MOSES

Moses asked for a sign to prove that he was acting on God's command. God told him to cast his staff on the ground: it became a serpent but when he picked it up it became a staff again.[6] Returning to Egypt with his brother Aaron, Moses begged the Pharaoh to free their people. The ruler was unmoved either by pleas or by the sign given by the miraculous staff.[7]

THE PLAGUES OF EGYPT

Moses, with God's help, brought down ten plagues on the land of Egypt.[8] With each one, however, the Pharaoh's resolve was strengthened. Finally Moses threatened that all the first-born of the Egyptians would die unless the Israelites were released. The angel of death "passed over the houses of the children of Israel" and smote the "firstborn of Pharaoh that sat on his throne unto the firstborn of the captive in the dungeon, and all the firstborn of cattle".[9]

For seven days the Israelites ate unleavened bread according to God's command, thus initiating the celebration of the Passover. After this the Pharaoh agreed to let the Israelites leave Egypt.

MOSES DIVIDES THE RED SEA
When the Pharaoh heard that Moses was leading his people to the Promised Land, he pursued them with an army. At the Red Sea the Lord told Moses to raise his staff, and the waters parted to allow the Israelites through. When the Egyptians tried to follow, the waters covered them.[10]

THE FALL OF MANNA
In the wilderness the Israelites became lost and were without food. God told Moses that he would "rain bread from heaven", and the following morning the ground was covered with manna, described as being like coriander seed, white and tasting like wafers made with honey. This was their food for 40 years.[11]

MOSES STRIKES THE ROCK
When the Israelites were thirsty the Lord commanded Moses to strike the rock of Horeb with his staff. Water poured forth, quenching the thirst of the people and their flocks.[12]

THE VICTORY OVER THE AMALEKITES
In the wilderness the Amalekites fought the Israelites. Moses instructed Joshua to fight while he himself watched the battle from the top of a hill. "And it came to pass, when Moses held up his hand, that Israel prevailed: and when he let down his hand, Amalek prevailed." As Moses' arms grew weary, Aaron and Hur held them up for him.[13]

THE TEN COMMANDMENTS
On Mount Sinai God instructed Moses on the Ten Commandments.[14] Moses informed his people and returned to Mount Sinai for 40 days and nights to be instructed in making an elaborate Ark to hold the covenant. Then God "gave unto Moses, when he had made an end of communing with him upon Mount Sinai, two tables of testimony, tables of stone, written with the finger of God".[15]

THE GOLDEN CALF
While Moses was on Mount Sinai, the Israelites asked Aaron to make a false god. Aaron took their jewelry and fashioned a golden calf, which the people worshipped. God instructed Moses to return from the mountain, for his people had "corrupted themselves". He went down with the two tables of testimony, and "saw the calf, and the dancing: and Moses' anger waxed hot, and he cast the tables out of his hands, and brake them beneath the mount".[16]

THE BRAZEN SERPENT
The Israelites, weary of their nomadic wandering, complained, whereupon "the Lord sent fiery serpents among the people, and they bit the people; and much people of Israel died". They begged Moses to rid them of the serpents, and "the Lord said unto Moses, Make thee a fiery

serpent, and set it upon a pole; and it shall come to pass, that every one that is bitten, when he looketh upon it, shall live".[17]

Episodes from the life of Moses were depicted along with other biblical prophets, such as Bartolo di Fredi's frescoes (Collegiata, San Gimignano). He was seen as a type of Christ, with the Brazen Serpent prefiguring the Crucifixion.[18]

Other scenes from the life of Moses were also paired with those from Christ's, such as Tintoretto's *The Fall of Manna* and *The Last Supper* flanking the High Altar of San Giorgio Maggiore, Venice. As Moses set down the law of the old covenant, so Christ dispensed the new. This was clearly indicated in frescoes by a number of artists, including Botticelli (Sistine Chapel, Vatican, Rome) and Perugino. As God's appointed representative on earth, the chief apostle St Peter was often likened to Moses.

Isolated incidents from the life of Moses might be chosen for artistic reasons; in *Moses Defending the Daughters of Jethro* Rosso Fiorentino had the chance to show muscular figures wrestling; the elegance of Pharaoh's daughter finding the infant Moses appealed to both Poussin and Giambattista Tiepolo; Turner's *The Fifth Plague of Egypt* shows the dying Egyptians against a stormy landscape.

Mot

The Ugaritic (Canaanite) god of death, a primal deity embodying the earth. Mot, who represented the destructive power of sterility and drought, features in the important cycle of Ugaritic myths about the storm god Baal. When Baal, who represented the life-giving power of rain and water, became king on earth, his rule was challenged by Mot. Even after a protracted struggle Baal was unable to vanquish Mot, who as the personification of death could never be defeated. However, the supreme god El intervened and persuaded Mot to accept Baal's overlordship.

Mother

Linked with nature, the earth and its waters, fertility, nourishment, warmth, shelter, protection, devotion – but also with stifling love, mortal destiny and the grave. Paleolithic carvings, perhaps 30,000 years old, suggest that swollen-breasted maternal figures were the earliest of all fertility symbols. And although many cosmogonies identify male or dual-sex creator divinities as the original source of life, it is possible that they were predated by worship of mother goddesses personifying Nature, the Earth or the Creative Force itself.

In Native American mythology, Mother Earth (or Earth Mother), with her male counterpart and consort Father Sky (or Sky Father), is usually the offspring of the remote supreme divinity or "Great Spirit".

Mother Earth (left) and Father Sky (right), after a Navajo ritual sandpainting.

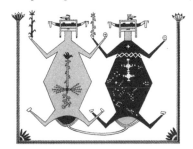

Once Mother Earth and Father Sky appeared, the supreme divinity withdrew from the world and left them to continue with the task of creation. According to some peoples of the American southwest, Mother Earth and Father Sky coupled to produce the first living beings, including the first humans who emerged from within the earth.

Hesiod (fl. *c.*700BCE), the poet who systematized Greek mythology, placed Ge or Gaia (the earth) first in his genealogy of the gods as the "universal mother, firmly founded, the oldest of divinities". She bore the gods and, according to Attic myth, the first human, Erichthonius. In the Greco-Roman world, worship of maternal nature symbols including Rhea and Demeter culminated in the veneration of the Phrygian Great Mother, Cybele, whose cult was an early rival to Christianity in the Roman world.

The Christian cult of the Virgin Mary is unique, not only because Mary was a young woman (the human element in Christ), and not a goddess, but also because she represented a complete break with the long tradition of venerated mothers who were essentially nature symbols. Her symbolic link with earlier mother goddesses is that her son was killed. The death, emasculation or dismemberment of the mother goddess's loved ones is a great recurring theme in the mythic symbolism of the mother – representing the death–rebirth cycle that is the iron rule of nature.

Mothering–devouring symbolism is attached to both earth (the darkness of germination and of the grave) and sea (the primeval waters of life, represented by the great Sumerian goddess Nammu, and the dread abyss). Kali, the "Dark Mother" of Hindu mythology, is the most alarming image of the creator–destroyer. The "terrible mother" of psychology is a symbol of possessive love and the danger of an infantile fixation persisting and blocking development of the self. Mother–witch symbolism can reflect this tyranny as well as ancient ties between the mother and secret earthly lore. The mother is linked psychologically with instinct, emotions, sentiment, tenderness and moodiness.

Multiple aspects of the mother were sometimes represented in iconography by triform or triple goddesses, as with Hecate and in Celtic carvings. Celtic mother goddesses were usually protective, especially of animals, including wild beasts. Their attributes included boats or rudders, as well as more familiar emblems of fertility and prosperity such as baskets of fruit, sheaves of corn or cornucopias.

Other mother symbols include the bear (especially in dreams), cow, dove, goose, partridge and swallow in addition to other productive animals and some wild beasts, especially the lioness; fountains, lakes, oceans, rivers and the moon; gardens, gates, houses and ships; containers, especially baskets and cups; the crescent of the waxing moon; the labyrinth sign known as the "mother and child" pattern; or, in graphic representation the lozenge or the spiral; and founding or nurturing entities such as Church, university, or country of birth.

Mound

In Egyptian tradition, the intermediate state of matter. According to Egypt's creation mythology, the first form to arise from the primeval state

Mound: *see* Axis; Heron; Sun

Mountain

of chaos (Nun) was a mound providing a perch for the Benu bird, personifying the creator sun god.

Mounds also had sacred axial symbolism for lowland peoples as mediating places between the natural and supernatural worlds.

Mountain

The spiritual peak and centre of the world, the meeting place of earth and heaven – a symbol of transcendence, eternity, purity, stability, ascent, ambition and challenge. The belief that deities inhabited mountains or manifested their presence there was universal in countries with peaks high enough to be veiled by clouds. Such mountains were often feared as well as venerated – as in Africa. They were associated with immortals, heroes, sanctified prophets and gods. The Bible is full of references to sacred mountains. God's revelations to Moses on Mt Sinai were paralleled in Christianity by Christ's Sermon on the Mount. It was on Mt Carmel that Elijah triumphed over the priests of Baal, on Mt Horeb that he heard the word of God, and on the Mount of Olives that Christ ascended into heaven according to the Acts of the Apostles. In medieval legends of the Grail, the elixir of life is guarded in a castle on Montsalvat. In China, the World Mountain, Kunlun, thought to be the source of the Yellow River, was a symbol of order and harmony, the dwelling-place of immortals and of the Supreme Being. Fujiyama, almost an emblem of Japan itself, was and is a sacred place of Shinto pilgrimage. In Central Mexico, Mt Tlaloc was a personification of the great fertility and rain god. From Mt Olympus, the Greeks were subject to the whims of

their quarrelsome gods. Sacred mountains could be figurative as well as real, as in the Celtic White Mountain, the emerald-based Qaf of Islam, or Mt Meru, the Hindu World Mountain at the North Pole. In Hindu cosmogony, Mt Mandara is used as a pivot to churn the cosmic waters.

The polar mountain is both centre and axis of the world, spreading out from its peak like a great inverted World Tree. The peak could be seen both as a navel and as a hole or point of departure from terrestrial life. Sometimes the mountain was hollow, and contained sleeping immortals. Figurative mountains were usually envisaged as layered, representing the progressive stages of spiritual ascent. (The risks of scaling mountains unprepared were well understood.) Mountain-shaped temples express the same idea in the great ziggurats of Mesopotamia or Central America and in the stupas and pagodas of Asia. Psychologically, climbing the mountain symbolizes a great challenge, the stages toward self-knowledge. Verticality makes the mountain a masculine symbol, although the great mother Cybele was specifically a mountain deity. In art, twin-peaked mountains symbolize dual powers. Other mountain symbols include the triangle, the cross, the crown, the star and steps or ladders. Muhammad reputedly used the immutability of mountains as an allegory of the need for humility when he ordered Mt Safa to move: when it refused to budge he went to the mountain to thank God that it had stayed put.

Mouse

Timidity – an ancient symbolism, judging from the legendary insult of the Egyptian king Tachos, disappointed by the puny appearance of a Spartan ally: "The mountain laboured, Jupiter stood aghast, and a mouse ran out." The secret depredations of mice made them a Jewish symbol of hypocrisy and a Christian symbol of wicked destructiveness. In folk superstition, mice were souls that had slipped from the mouths of the dead (red if good, black if corrupted) – rather as doves were said to fly from the mouths of saints as their souls departed. Mice were used for divination in Africa because they were believed to understand the mysteries of the underworld.

Mouth

Open mouths in iconography may be symbols of devouring (as in the many images of gaping-jawed monsters representing the gates of hell) or of spirits speaking (as in primitive masks or carvings). They can also symbolize the breath of life.

In Egyptian funerary rites, the mouths of the dead were opened to enable their *ka* to give evidence in the judgment hall of the afterlife – and to receive the gift of new life. Solar disks were placed in the mouths of the dead, as were jade objects (symbolizing immortality) in China and Mexico. Jung saw a symbolic link between the mouth – as red and consuming – and fire, expressed in fire-breathing dragon legends. More commonly, the mouth is associated with the vulva, as in Chinese symbolism.

Moyang Melur

A moon spirit, who was half tiger, half man, who kept the rules of society in a bag, according to the Ma'-betisék people of Malaya. In the beginning, humans lived like animals with no rules of behaviour. They were constantly found committing incest, cannibalism and murder.

Moyang Melur enjoyed leaning out of the moon to watch the chaotic state of human society. One night he leaned too far and fell out. When he landed on earth, he encountered a hunter, Moyang Kapir. He vowed to the hunter that he would kill all humans unless he could return at once to the moon. Moyang Kapir threw a liana rope up to the moon and the pair climbed up to Moyang Melur's dwelling. The spirit's wife, Moyang Engko, invited the hunter to stay for dinner, but Moyang Kapir suspected that she intended to cook him.

While she was preparing the meal he escaped back to earth with the bag containing the rules of behaviour, which he had found under a mat. Moyang Kapir cut the rope to the moon to prevent Moyang Melur from following him, and gave out the rules to his kinsfolk.

From that time humans knew how to behave and were punished when they broke the rules.

Moytirra

The location in County Sligo, Ireland, of the first and second battles of Magh Tuiredh. Moytirra is an anglicized spelling of Magh Tuiredh.

Mucius Scaevola

A legendary hero of the Roman republic, Mucius risked his life for his people.[1] When Rome was besieged by the Etruscans, Mucius disguised himself and entered the enemy camp of Lars Porsena, intending to assassinate him. Instead he stabbed a secretary, mistaking him for the king, and was

Mouth: *see* AFTERWORLDS; breath, Breathing; cicada; disk; dragon; fire, Flame; jade; ka; mask; red; vulva; whale

Moytirra: *see* Magh Tuiredh, The battles of

Mucius Scaevola:
[1] Livy, *The History of Rome* *II xi*

seized. To prove the fearlessness of
the Romans, he thrust his right hand
into a fire and held it there. Greatly
impressed, Porsena made his peace
with Rome. Mucius was thereafter
left-handed (*scaevola*). His image, a
symbol of constancy, was used in the
decoration of public places, as in
Ghirlandaio's *Mucius Scaevola*
(Palazza Vecchio, Florence).

Mudras

An extensive system of subtle and
symbolic hand gestures used in
Hindu and Buddhist iconography, in
ritual religious dancing and also,
with adaptations, in dance and the
theatre generally throughout much
of Asia.

Mudungkala

A blind old woman responsible for
the arrival of the first people, according to the Tiwi people of Melville and
Bathurst islands off northern Australia. In the creation period or
Dreamtime, Mudungkala emerged
from the ground at the southeastern
end of Melville island. She was carrying three children, the first people,
who populated the islands.
Mudungkala crawled across the fea-
tureless primeval landscape and, as
she went, water sprang up in her
track. Eventually the water level rose
so much that the islands were cut off
from the Australian mainland.

Mule *see* Ass

Muromets, Ilya

"Ilya of Murom", a Russian folk epic
hero, or *bogatyr*. He was the son of a
peasant and was said to have been a
weak, sickly child. For thirty-three
years Ilya was so poorly he could not

even stand, but then one day a pair of
travelling musicians offered him a
draught of honey which conferred
great strength upon him. With the
blessing of his ageing parents Ilya
went off to become a great hero, protecting his people against monsters
and other perils. He was said to possess a horse which flew through the
air and a magical bow and arrows
which could shatter a tree into small
many pieces. These possessions link
Ilya with Perun, the old Slav god of
lightning and war.

One famous episode recounts how
Ilya overcame the monster known as
Nightingale the Brigand, a creature
half bird and half human which lived
in a tree and waylaid travellers on the
road to Kiev. Nightingale could conjure a great screaming wind which
could kill humans as well as flatten
trees and plants. Ilya urged his horse
to ignore the noise of the wind and
shot Nightingale in the head. He tied
him to his stirrup and carried him triumphantly into Kiev.

When Ilya knew that it was time to
die he ordered the construction of a
great cathedral at Kiev. When it had
reached completion, he died and his
body was transformed into stone.

Muses, The

In Classical mythology, the Muses
presided over and inspired music,
poetry, dancing and the Liberal Arts.
They were protected by Apollo, with
whom artists often show them on
Mount Parnassus as young and beautiful virgins. Raphael's fresco *Parnassus* (Stanza della Segnatura, Vatican,
Rome) shows Apollo and the muses
along with poets, both ancient and
modern. There were traditionally
thought to be nine Muses: Clio (the

Mushroom: *see* fairies; phallus; LONGEVITY; ring; soul; witchcraft

MUSES, THE

Name	Meaning	Branch of the arts
Calliope	Beautiful voice	Epic poetry
Clio	Fame	History
Erato	Lovely	Lyric poetry
Euterpe	Joy	The flute
Melpomene	Singing	Tragic drama
Polyhymnia	Many Songs	Mime
Terpsichore	Joyful Dance	Dance
Thalia	GoodCheer/Plenty	Comic drama
Urania	Celestial	Astronomy

muse of history), Euterpe (music), Thalia (comedy), Melpomene (tragedy), Terpsichore (dancing), Erato (lyric poetry), Polyhymnia (sacred song), Calliope (epic poetry) and Urania (astronomy). As attributes they may be shown with books, musical instruments or other related objects. They were the children of Jupiter (in Greek myth, Zeus) and Mnemosyne (Memory).

The home of the Muses was the wooded Mount Helicon where they were visited by Athene (in Roman myth, Minerva), who wished to see the miraculous Hippocrene, a fountain which a blow from the winged horse Pegasus' hoof had caused to flow from the earth.[1] Their symbolism was based on the association between springs or fountains and inspiration. Hence their origin as Greek nymphs of mountain streams, the daughters of the god Zeus and his adultery with Mnemosyne.

A *museum* (literally, a home or seat of the Muses) was originally the term applied to an institution dedicated to learning, literature and the arts; an example was the Academy at Alexandria in the 3rd century BCE. A museum still suggests a place where antiquities are housed, as distinct from a gallery, also of ancient origin, where colonnades were used for the display of pictures.

The Muses appear in art as companions of Apollo or alone with a variety of attributes including books, scrolls, tablets, flutes, viols, tambourines, trumpets, lyres, harps, horns, crowns, laurel wreaths, masks, or, in the case of Melpomene a sword or dagger.

Mushroom

Life from death – an important symbol of longevity and happiness in China, and the legendary food of the immortals in Taoist tradition. Mushrooms personify souls of the reborn in some parts of central Europe, and Africa. Their magical sudden appearance, and possibly the use of some varieties as hallucinogens, may account for folklore associations with the supernatural, leading to the notion of pixie houses or witches' rings. The shape of the mushroom, once linked with phallic potency, has become the most powerful apocalyptic symbol of the nuclear age.

Music, Musical Instruments *see panel opposite*

Mweel

The sister and consort of Woot, mythical ancestor of the Kuba kings and people of southeastern Congo-Kinshasq. Woot and Mweel had intercourse, as a result of which she bore Nyimi Lele, ancestor of the neighbouring Lele people.

Mwetsi

"Moon", the first man, according to the creation mythology of the Shona people of Zimbabwe. Mwari, the high god, created Mwetsi, who lived at first beneath the waters. Mwetsi went to live on earth, but it was a desert and he started to lament. Mwari sent him a wife, Morning Star, who gave birth to all the trees and plants of the earth. The trees touched the sky and it began to rain, making the land fertile. Mwetsi and Morning Star made a house and tools and cultivated the land.

When two years had passed, Mwari replaced Morning Star with a second wife, Evening Star, and warned Mwetsi that he faced disaster. That night Mwari and Evening Star had intercourse and produced goats, sheep, cattle, chickens and antelopes, then girls and boys who grew to adulthood in a single day. On their fourth night together Evening Star warned Mwetsi that his life was in peril, but still he had intercourse with her and on the following day she gave birth to lions, leopards, scorpions and snakes. That evening, however, she did not want intercourse with Mwetsi and suggested that he take their daughters. He took this advice and coupled with his daughters, who the next morning had babies who became adults by evening.

In this way Mwetsi became king of a populous nation. But Evening Star had intercourse with a serpent and became barren. The snake bit Mwetsi and he fell ill from its poison. As Mwetsi's health grew worse, so too did the health of the land: the rains stopped, the rivers and lakes dried up and death stalked the nation. To put an end to all the suffering, Mwetsi's children strangled him and chose another king.

This myth probably served to account for the ritual murder of the Mambo (king) of Monomotapa in medieval Zimbabwe. To ensure the uninterrupted prosperity of the land, the Mambo was not permitted to grow old but was ritually slain after ruling for four years and a replacement chosen.

Myrrh *see* Incense

Myrtle

Sensual love, marital happiness, longevity and harmony. Perhaps because of its purple berries, this fragrant evergreen shrub, growing wild in the Mediterranean and sometimes used for victors' wreaths, was widely associated with love goddesses, especially the Greek Aphrodite (in Roman myth, Venus), and with rituals surrounding marriage and childbirth: it crowns the bridal figure in Titian's Sacred and Profane Love. In the Underworld, Aeneas saw a myrtle-wood which hides all those broken by love. Aphrodite once covered herself in its leaves to hide from satyrs.. Myrtle was revered by the Mandaean sect as a life symbol. It was a Chinese emblem of success. The crackling of its leaves was thought to show whether a lover would be faithful.

MUSIC, MUSICAL INSTRUMENTS

Seen as a mystical order, music was linked with the origin of life in some traditions, notably in Indian religious traditions where sound is regarded as the primordial vibration of divine energy, invoked in sacred chanted mantras such as *Om*. From this idea comes the legend of Krishna's flute, which brought the world into existence.

The earliest music, probably based on rhythms and imitations of the sounds of humans (the heartbeat, sex), animals and the natural world, was essentially an attempt to communicate with the spirit world. With the development of sophisticated instruments and harmonics, music became a symbol of cosmic order and was associated in China and in Greece with number symbolism and with the planets ("the harmony of the spheres"). Plato believed that the cosmos formed a number, and that the planets would create a divine harmony by moving at different speeds to one another, just as musical pitch changed when strings were vibrated at differing rates.

Yin or Yang qualities were allocated to the semitones of the earliest Chinese octave, music thus becoming a symbol of the vital duality holding together disparate things.

The Greek word for "music" literally means "the art of the Muses", and musical instruments are the attributes of these nine deities of the arts. In European traditions, certain instruments have special associations through their sound and appearance: the trumpet is heraldic, proclaiming a messenger, announcing the famous

or calling up the dead; the harp suggests the divine, and is often played by choirs of angels, as well as being the instrument that King David is said to have played. It is similar to the lyre, sacred to Apollo, god of music and lyric poetry, and played by Orpheus, enchanter of the animals. The rustic bagpipe was played by shepherds; medieval pipes and the small round-backed lute were minstrels' instruments and accompanied folk dances; and tambourines and cymbals provided the accompaniment to orgiastic Bacchanalian dancing. The syrinx (reed pipes of varying lengths) was sacred to Pan.

In allegory, the civilized lyre may be contrasted with weapons of war, and musical instruments may represent the sense of hearing. In paintings, the inclusion of certain instruments could indicate modernity: as with, for example, the small portable organ, popular during the 14th century; and the viol, which was developed during the Renaissance, and appears in Giovanni Bellini's *San Zaccaria Altarpiece*. Orpheus, or the figure of Musica, a woman playing or singing, may personify music, as may St Cecilia, the patron of saint of music.

Music was once an important part of family life and in art may indicate domestic harmony. It has also long been associated with love, exemplified by a 17th-century Dutch saying, "Learn on the lute, learn on the virginals to play, for strings have the power to steal the heart away." In art, flirtatious couples playing duets may allude to sexual pleasure, and a flute or pipe has a phallic connotation.

Naga

In India, a *naga* is one of the race of serpents, the offspring of Kadru, the daughter of the god Daksha. The *nagas* often appeared as malign, for example the multi-headed serpent Kaliya who was subdued by the god Krishna. However, not all *nagas* were hostile or destructive. Among the kings of the *nagas* was the many-headed Vasuki, whom the gods and demons used to twist Mount Mandara during the churning of the ocean. Elsewhere the world is said to rest on his many heads (however, when he moves he causes earthquakes). Another *naga*, Ananta, is the resting place of Vishnu in the periods between the absorptions and emanations of the cosmos. The *nagas* were the particular enemy of Garuda, whose mother Vinata, the ancestor of all birds, was Kadru's sister. *Nagas* are often depicted as cobras.

Nail

Protection – as in the Chinese custom of hammering superfluous nails into

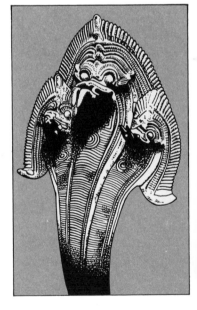

A naga, *based on a bronze figure from* Angkor Wat *in Cambodia.*

houses to ward off demons, or the annual ceremonial hammering of a nail into the temple of Jupiter in ancient Rome.

A binding or fastening symbolism is thought to explain nails driven into some African fetishes (to keep their resident spirits fixed on the task for which their help was invoked). In art, three nails symbolize the Crucifixion. They also appear as the attributes of figures associated with legends about Christ or the Cross – notably Helena, mother of Constantine the Great, who was said to have discovered the True Cross and the nails themselves.

Nakedness

Innocence, freedom, vulnerability, truth and, in the idealizations of Greek art, divinity itself. Although nakedness can also symbolize carnality, shame or wickedness – as in the huddled naked figures of a Bosch painting depicting hell (c.1490) – the unadorned human body was, in most traditions, a symbol of openness, simplicity and the purity of the new born. Hence the disrobing of initiates and sometimes of priests in some ancient religious rites.

The Bible's depiction of Adam and Eve as naked before the Fall associated nakedness with the primal state of innocence. Ascetics have sometimes gone naked for this reason. In medieval art, naked witches symbolized the fleshly temptations of Satan, but modern witch covens use the term "sky-clad" (naked) to suggest their openness to supernatural forces. Similarly, naked Indian ascetics are "clothed in air". In civilizations where nudity was frowned upon, such as China and ancient Rome, nakedness symbolized primitiveness or poverty.

Nambi

The woman responsible for the arrival of death on earth, according to the Ganda people of Uganda. Nambi was the daughter of the High God, who gave her in marriage to Kintu, the mythical founder of the royal dynasty of Buganda. The High God warned Kintu that he must hurry back to earth, or Nambi's brother Walumbe (Death) would follow them.

On the journey Nambi insisted on returning to heaven to fetch grain for the chicken that they had received as a wedding gift. Death duly followed her home and since then all people have been mortal.

Nammu

The Sumerian goddess embodying the primeval ocean. Nammu was the first deity and origin of all things. She gave birth to the earth goddess Ki and the sky god An, who in turn coupled to produce the great gods of the Sumer, including Enlil and Enki.

Namorodo

A race of trickster beings in the Australian Aboriginal mythology of western Arnhem Land. Frightening figures with long claws, their bodies consist only of bones and skin held together by sinew. The creatures move at night, flying through the air with a swishing sound. They may kill anyone they hear with one of their claws: particularly the injured and the ill. If the Namorodo captures the spirit of a dead person, it can never join the clan's totemic ancestors, but instead turns into a hostile being that wanders through the bush. The Namorodo have also been linked with sorcery and shooting stars.

Nanna (1)

The Sumerian moon god. Nanna (the Akkadian Sin) was greatest of the trinity of astral deities, comprising himself and his offspring Inanna and Utu. He was revered as the god who measured time and, because he shone in the night, also as the enemy of dark forces and of wrongdoers. Nanna was renowned for his wisdom by the other gods, who would visit him regularly for advice.

Nanna (2) *see* Balder

Narcissus

A flower of spring, but also a symbol of youthful death, sleep and rebirth. The range of plants belonging to this genus (which include daffodils and jonquils) may account for its wide variety of symbolism. In Greek

A detail showing Narcissus, after Narcissus *by Nicolas-Bernard Lépicté.*

mythology, Narcissus was a youth who was so beautiful that many nymphs, including Echo, fell in love with him.¹ Yet he scorned them all, and one cried, "May he himself fall in love with another, as we have done with him! May he too be unable to gain his loved one!" In the heat of the day Narcissus came to a sheltered spot with a clear pool and as he leaned down to drink he became enchanted by his own reflection. No thought of food or sleep could draw him from the spot, so he wasted away. Nymphs mourned his death, but when they came for his body they found in its place the flower that bears his name.

The story is usually taken to be an allegory of vanity, self-love or, in psychological terms, morbid introspection, but its original symbolism may have been more straightforward. The narcissus blooms and dies early, and self-reflections were feared in the ancient world as omens of death.

The narcissus was also the flower that Persephone was gathering when the chariot of Hades erupted from the earth and carried her off to the underworld. It was used in the rites of Demeter and planted on graves to symbolize the idea that death was only a sleep (the Greek name for the flower has the same root as "narcotic": *narké*, "numbness").

The theme of Narcissus has attracted artists since the Renaissance. He is usually shown gazing into the pool, or lying dead on the ground while Echo mourns him. Dalí created a memorable image of Narcissus metamorphosing into the flower.

The fragrance of the narcissus symbolized youth in Persia. Its upright stem also made it an Islamic emblem of the faithful servant or believer. As it bloomed at the Chinese New Year, it was a symbol of joy, good luck or a happy marriage in Oriental tradition. A white narcissus was the sacred lily of China, and sometimes replaces the lily in Christian art as the attribute of the Virgin Mary.

Nataraja *see* Shiva

Naunet *see* Ogdoad, The

Nauplius

In Greek myth, a king of Nauplia, a port city founded by his ancestor (also called Nauplius) who was a son of the god Poseidon. Nauplius the younger was an Argonaut and the father of Palamedes, a Greek warrior at Troy who was stoned to death by his comrades after being framed for treachery by Odysseus. In revenge for his son's death, Nauplius urged the wives of the Greeks to commit adultery. He later lit beacons which lured many Greek ships returning from Troy onto rocks during a storm. The ensuing outrage forced Nauplius to flee Nauplia. According to one account, he drowned after he too was lured onto rocks by a bogus beacon.

Navel

Creative force, origin of life and spiritual and psychic centre. In Vedic tradition, the lotus of creation grew from the navel of Vishnu as he rested on the cosmic waters, giving birth to Brahma. In Greek myth, Delphi was the navel of the world, represented by a stone called the *omphalos* (navel, umbilicus). In Norse myth, the Pole Star was the cosmic navel. As a life symbol, the navel is sometimes exaggerated in African statuary. A prominent navel was also a Chinese emblem of strength and beauty.

Nechtan

An Irish water god and the husband of Boann, the goddess of the river Boyne. Nechtan was said to possess a sacred well of knowledge, which only he and his three cupbearers were permitted to approach.

Necklace

Linking and binding. A symbol with sexual significance in cultures where the neck had erotic associations. In parts of Africa, extravagant neck ornaments were status symbols.

Needle

A Yin-Yang symbol in China: the eye female, the point male. Needle pricks were often associated with bad luck in folk tales, leading to superstitions against sewing on certain days, as in the Chinese notion that a needle could pierce the Buddha's eye if used in the first five days of New Year.

Nehalennia

An ancient sea goddess of the coastal Netherlands. Nehalennia was particularly revered as the goddess of seafarers and was worshipped at two sanctuaries, one on the island of Walcheren and one (now submerged) at Colijnsplaat. Here many altars were erected, upon which offerings were made both to ensure a good voyage and to thank the goddess for a safe return. There is some debate over whether Nehalennia was in origin a Celtic or Germanic goddess. However, her cult flourished in the 3rd century CE, when the region was occupied by a Celtic tribe under Roman rule. Her worshippers appear to have come from all over the western Roman Empire.

Neith

A great Egyptian mother goddess. According to one account, she emerged from the Nun, the primordial waters, and created deities and humans. When she spat into the Nun her spittle became Apep, the serpent of chaos. She was also the mother of Sobek, the crocodile god.

During the struggle of Horus and Seth over the kingship, the gods and goddesses wrote to Neith seeking her advice. She replied that to compensate for giving up the throne to Horus, Seth should receive Anat and Astarte, two goddesses of foreign origin, as

The great Egyptian mother goddess Neith, based on a figurine.

Nekhbet: *see* Eileithyia

Nemesis: *see* Nyx

Nemhedh: *see* Fir Bholg; Fomorian; *Invasions*, The *Book of*; Parthalón; Tuatha Dé Danann

Nephthys: *see* Anubis; Isis; Osiris; Seth

wives. This judgment probably implies that Neith considered Seth unworthy of marriage to native goddesses.

Neith was a formidable figure who was also associated with hunting and warfare. Her emblem was a shield displaying two crossed arrows. The centre of her cult was at Sais (modern Sa el-Hagar) in the Nile delta.

Nekhbet

The Egyptian vulture goddess of the southern city of Nekheb (modern el-Kab) and the patron goddess of Upper Egypt. With Wadjet, the patron goddess of Lower Egypt, Nekhbet was the protector of the Egyptian king (pharaoh) and was often depicted as a vulture hovering with her wings spread above the royal image. She was also the goddess of childbirth, and was identified by the Greeks with the goddess Eileithyia.

Nemesis

In Greek myth, Nemesis, daughter of Nyx (Night), punished those insolent to the gods, and so she was the goddess of vengeance or retribution. Like Fortune, she may stand on a wheel or globe and have a scourge hanging from her girdle. In Dürer's engraving *Nemesis*, she is shown naked, holding a bridle in one hand for the undisciplined and a cup in the other with which to reward the virtuous.

Nemhedh

The leader of the third people to conquer Ireland, according to the *Book of Invasions*. Nemhedh, the son of Agnomen of the Scythian Greeks, arrived with four women thirty years after the destruction through plague of the second race of invaders, whose leader was Parthalón. The newcomers settled and multiplied, and cleared more plains for settlement and cultivation, a process begun by Parthalón. More lakes arose and the land of Ireland became fully formed.

Nemhedh fought the monstrous Fomorians successfully until plague wiped out most of the Nemedians. The Fomorians forced the survivors and their descendants pay a heavy tribute every year, but eventually the Nemedians attacked the Fomorian stronghold on Tory Island and killed the Fomorian king, but most of the Nemedians were slain, except for thirty men – one boatload – who went into exile. Some settled in Britain, some in the "Northern Islands of the World", and some in their ancestral homeland, Greece. The descendants of those who went to Greece (the Fir Bholg) and to the northern isles (the Tuatha Dé Danann) subsequently returned to Ireland as the fourth and fifth races of invaders respectively.

Nephthys

An Egyptian goddess, the daughter of Geb and Nut, sister of Isis, Osiris and Seth. Nephthys, less prominent in myth than her siblings, married Seth

The goddesses Nephthys (right) and Isis adore the sun god Khepry.

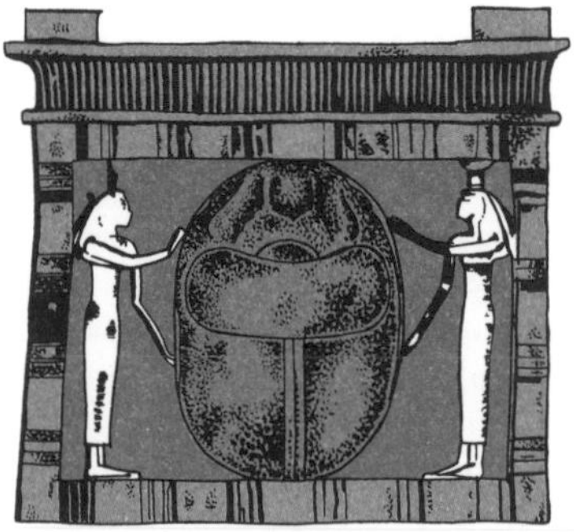

but produced no children, so she committed adultery with Osiris and consequently bore the god Anubis. She deserted Seth after he had brought about the death of Osiris and then she lamented with Isis over their brother's corpse. It was the custom at Egyptian funerals for two women to impersonate Nephthys and Isis and lament over the mummy of the deceased.

Neptune *see* Poseidon

Nereus and Nereids

A Greek sea god, the son of the god Pontos, the sea, and the goddess Gaia, the earth. He was older than the god Poseidon, the Olympian ruler of the oceans, and hence was known as "The Old Man of the Sea". Nereus had the gift of prophecy and could change shape at will. He married the Oceanid (sea nymph) Doris and was the father of fifty sea nymphs known as the Nereids. Among the more famous Nereids were Amphitrite (the wife of Poseidon, although in some accounts she is one of the Oceanids), Galateia (the lover of the shepherd Acis) and Thetis (the mother of Achilles).

Nerthus

Meaning "Mother Earth", Nerthus was an early Germanic earth and fertility goddess worshipped by a number of tribes in Denmark. According to the Roman historian Tacitus, the effigy of Nerthus was kept in a sacred grove in a wagon that was covered with a cloth and touched only by her priest. Whenever he sensed the goddess's presence he would conduct the wagon, which was drawn by cows, through the countryside.

The visitation of Nerthus would bring a rare period of peace among the warring tribes. Wherever she came the people would hold joyful celebrations for several days. After her tour she was returned to her sanctuary and her wagon, vestments and perhaps her effigy were cleansed in a hidden lake by slaves. These slaves were then drowned immediately afterwards so that no outsiders would ever learn what the wagon contained.

Nessus *see* Herakles

Nestor

In Greek myth, a king of Pylos in the southern Peloponnese. The elderly Nestor was the oldest of the Greek leaders to take part in the Trojan War. He was treated with great respect by his compatriots, to whom he would recount long tales of his younger days and offer advice that was often, but not always, reliable. After the defeat of Troy he reached home safely and lived for many years longer.

Net

Magical capture – a symbolism based on the ability of an apparently flimsy device to ensnare. As described in Luke's gospel, Christ used a net to catch both a miraculous draught of fishes and, through this demonstration of his power, to "capture" the disciples Peter, James and John, who were themselves to become "fishers of men". As a stealthy snarer of souls, Satan was popularly believed to possess a great net.

An earlier mythic symbol of the net's power was its use by the Babylonian hero god Marduk to subdue Tiamat, chaos goddess of the primeval ocean. Islamic tradition deriving from Iran envisaged a mystic net as the means by which men could apprehend God. Still

Nereus and Nereids: *see* Amphitrite; Gaia; Galatea; Nymph; Oceanid; Pontos; Poseidon; Thetis

Net: *see* Devils; Fish; Sea

more poetic is the Daoist image of the stars as the "net of heaven", arranged in a wide mesh through which nothing can escape – a symbol of cosmic unity.

In art, nets are usually attributes of sea gods, including the Norse goddess Ran, who gathers drowned souls in her net. The Greek goddess Aphrodite (in Roman myth, Venus) and the god Ares (Mars) are sometimes shown under a net, in reference to the myth that Hephaistos (Vulcan) caught them with a net of bronze wire when he found his consort Aphrodite cuckolding him with the god of war.

Ngandjala-Ngandjala

One of a race of tricksters that are found in the Aboriginal mythology of the western Kimberleys. Similar to the Wurulu-Wurulu and *mimi*, the Ngandjala-Ngandjala are said to roam the bush in search of mischief such as ruining the harvest or destroying cave paintings made by ancestral heroes. However, some believe that the beings may at times be helpful, for example by cooking edible fruit in order to ripen it. In the rainy season the Ngandjala-Ngandjala are sometimes visible in the clouds, and the mist rising after a downpour indicates the location of the camp fires where they cook fruit.

The trickster Unguramu steals edible roots from the fires of the Ngandjala-Ngandjala, who grab hold of his tail and pull it until he relents and tells them where he has put the stolen food.

Niche

In Christian, Islamic and Hindu architecture, a symbolic cavern formed by a horizontal (earth) beneath an arch (sky) – the dwelling-place of God. A lamp or candle in a niche signifies the divine presence or Word.

Nicholas of Bari or Myra, Saint

All that is known of Nicholas is that he may have been a bishop of Myra in Asia Minor during the 4th century. Legend[1] tells how a noble but poor man was thinking of prostituting his three virgin daughters because he was unable to provide them with a dowry; Nicholas threw three golden balls or bags of gold through the window of their house and withdrew unseen, thereby saving them from their fate.

Once, seamen threatened by a violent storm invoked Nicholas, and he appeared, and assisted them with the rigging until the storm died down. When famine spread through his bishopric, Nicholas learned that several ships were anchored in the harbour laden with grain. The saint promised the fearful sailors that if they gave the grain to his starving people, the customs men would not find their cargo short. Nicholas was also said to have saved three soldiers from decapitation; had an innocent prince released from prison; and brought to life three children who had been murdered by their innkeeper father to feed to his guests during a plague.

The cult of Nicholas grew after the 11th century when his relics were taken from Myra to Bari in Italy. Scenes of his rescuing the three daughters and of the sailors' rescue were particularly popular, as seen in Fra Angelico's predella to the Perugia Polyptych. He is usually painted as a bishop, and his attribute is three golden balls at his feet, as shown in Raphael's *Ansidei Madonna*.

He is a patron saint of Greece and of sailors and children, and also the origin of Father Christmas (Santa Claus being a derivative of St Nicholas), an identification probably derived from his patronage of children and his charitable acts of presenting gifts by night. Despite his popularity, he was removed from the Catholic church calendar in 1969 owing to a lack of evidence about his existence; but the Church permits his veneration locally.

Nicodemus

Nicodemus was the Pharisee told by Christ that his spirit would be born again in the faith.[1] When the Pharisees were deliberating over the fate of Christ, Nicodemus asked that Christ should be heard before he was judged.[2] He was present at the Deposition, tending the dead Christ, and he brought a mixture of myrrh and aloes to embalm him at the Entombment.[3] he often appears in simple dress accompanying Joseph of Arimathea.

Night

As darkness, Night is associated with primeval fears of the unknown, concealment, evil and the Powers of Darkness, witchcraft and haunting spirits, despair, madness and death – but also with germination, the passive, female principle, sexuality, rest, peace, sleep, dreams and renewal. The positive symbolism of "silent night, holy night" is as universal as the negativity of "the dark night of the soul".

Nightingale

The anguish and ecstasy of love – a symbolism based on the beauty of the song poured forth by the nightingale cock during its spring mating season. The "immortal Bird" of Keats' *Ode to a Nightingale* (1819) is a metaphor for both singers and poets. Its song has often been linked with pain as well as joy, as in the Greek myth of Philo-

mela, whose brother-in-law Tereus cut out her tongue so that she could not reveal that he had raped her; she was turned into a nightingale by the pitying gods. Usually a good omen, the bird was variously said to sing of love, loss, yearning for paradise or, in Japan, holy scripture. It was once eaten in the superstitious belief that it would promote a musical or eloquent voice.

Nihonshoki, The

The *Chronicle of Japan*, the title of a work compiled by scholars and completed in 720CE. The *Nihonshoki* is an important source of Japanese myth, but less reliable than the *Kojiki*, which was composed at about the same time. Written mainly in Chinese script, the text is heavily influenced by Chinese and Korean mythical and historical traditions and dynastic chronicles.

Nikkal *see* Yarikh

Nimbus *see* Halo

Nine

As the triple triad, a supremely powerful number in most traditions, notably in China, in Buddhism and in the Celtic world. The most auspicious Chinese number and most potent Yang number, it was the basis of much Daoist ceremonial and of ritual divisions in architecture and property. In mysticism, it represented the triple synthesis of mind, body and spirit, or of the underworld, earth and heaven.

Nine is a Hebrew symbol of truth and a Christian symbol of order within order – hence, perhaps, the organization of angels into nine orders. There are nine heavens or celestial spheres in many traditions and, in Central America, nine underworld regions. Often

Nicodemus: *see*
Lamentation; Passion of
Christ, The
[1] *John* 3:1–9
[2] *John* 7:51
[3] *John* 19:39

Night: *see* Chariot;
Crescent; Darkness;
DEATH; Mask; Mother;
Nyx; Owl; Ox; PEACE;
Poppy; Rat; Witchcraft

Nightingale: *see* Birds;
Tereus

Nihonshoki, The: *see* *Kojiki,
The*

Nine: *see* AFTERLIFE;
Angels; NUMBERS; Three;
VIRTUES

associated with male courage or
endurance, nine was a key number in
the shamanistic rituals of northern
and central Asia. The nine days and
nights during which the Norse god
Odin hanged himself on the World
Tree Yggdrasil symbolized the ritual
period required for his magical resurrection or rejuvenation.

It impressed early mathematicians
that multiplication by nine always
produced digits that added up to nine.

Niobe, Niobids

In Greek myth[1], a queen of Thebes, the
wife of King Amphion and daughter
of Tantalus and Dione. Niobe bore
seven daughters and seven sons (the
Niobids) and was immensely proud of
them. Niobe rashly boasted that she
had more children than the goddess
Leto, mother of Artemis and Apollo,
and that the Niobids were more beautiful than Leto's pair. Leto was outraged and commanded Artemis and
Apollo to avenge the insult. One by
one, Apollo and Artemis shot Niobe's
children under a relentless hail of
arrows, Artemis killing all the girls and
Apollo all the boys (in some accounts
one son and one daughter survived).

In the 18th century, Richard Wilson
depicted Apollo and Diana shooting
the Niobids from the clouds in *The
Death of Niobe's Children*. Niobe's
husband, Amphion, king of Thebes,
drove a sword into his heart to end his
grief. Niobe was overcome with distress and remorse. The god Zeus,
father of Artemis and Apollo, took
pity on her, turning her into a marble
statue that wept unending tears.

Nirvana

In Buddhism, the state attained by
one who has become enlightened and
ceased to accumulate *karma*, and
hence won release from the cycle of
birth, death and rebirth, with its
attendant endless human sufferings.
This blissful state of undifferentiated
being or pure illumination lies beyond
objective description. Its clarity has
been likened in Buddhism to the brilliance of the full moon revealed by
parting clouds.

Njord

A Scandinavian god of the sea and
ships, the husband of the mountain
goddess Skadi and the father of Freyr
and Freyja. In one verse fragment, the
marriage of Njord and Skadi failed
because Njord was unhappy away
from the sea and Skadi could not bear
to be far from the mountains.

Noah

A biblical patriarch descended from
Adam and Eve, Noah alone won
God's favour when he saw "that the
wickedness of man was great on the
earth". God regretted that he had
made humankind and resolved to
destroy it in a great flood. But he
instructed Noah to build an ark into
which he should take his wife, his
three sons Shem, Ham and Japheth
and their wives, and a male and
female of every living creature.[1] The
rains lasted for 40 days and nights.[2]
When the waters abated Noah sent a
raven and a dove to find dry land, but
they found none.[3] When he sent out
the dove a second time it returned
with an olive branch in its beak.[4] The
ark landed on Mount Ararat, and
God commanded Noah to replenish
the earth and multiply.

Noah and his sons burned sacrifices,
and God sent a rainbow as a reminder
of his renewed covenant with

humankind.[5] Noah began to farm and planted a vineyard. On one occasion he became drunk on wine and fell asleep naked and uncovered. Ham saw Noah naked but did not avert his eyes or cover his father. He told Shem and Japheth, who at once took up a cloak and covered Noah, walking backward to avoid looking at his nakedness. When Noah learnt of Ham's disrespect, he cursed Ham's son, Canaan, condemning him to be for ever the servant of Shem and Japheth.[6]

When Noah entered the ark he was in his 600th year, and he has been consistently portrayed as an elderly man with a white beard. In late medieval and Renaissance art, scenes from the story of Noah appear in Old Testament cycles by Ghiberti (Baptistery, Florence), and by Michelangelo (Sistine Chapel, Vatican, Rome). Isolated scenes were also painted, particularly the animals entering the ark, as in Jan Bruegel the Elder's *The Entry of the Animals into Noah's Ark*. The dove returning with the olive leaf, a sign of peace and reconciliation between mankind and God, was painted with affection by John Everett Millais in *The Return of the Dove to the Ark*.

Nommo

A creator spirit, according to the Dogon people of Mali. The myth says that in the beginning, there was a heavenly being called Amma, an egg which was the seed of the universe. Amma vibrated seven times before bursting open to reveal the first Nommo or creator spirit. This was followed by a female twin and then four more Nommo pairs. The Nommos created and organized the sky and earth, the succession of day and night, the seasons and human society.

Noon

The hour of revelation in Jewish and Islamic tradition and, more generally, the moment of naked confrontation. The positive spiritual significance of midday comes from the absence of shadows (which, symbolically, are considered harmful) and from ancient rituals of sun worship at the zenith when the sun appeared in its full power and glory.

Norn

A Norse goddess of fate. There were sometimes said to be three Norns, although their number varied, and it was unclear whether they belonged to the race of giants or gods. Like the Fates of Classical myth, they determined the destiny of humans and deities, deciding the fate of princes as they were born. The Norns were linked with a spring called the Well of Fate under Yggdrasil, the World Tree.

North see CARDINAL POINTS, THE

Nü Gua

A great creator goddess who figures in some of the oldest Chinese creation myths. Her origin is obscure, but her name (like that of the god Fu Xi, with whom she is often associated in myth) is derived from words for gourds or melon, fruits which occur widely in the creation and fertility myths of other peoples. Nü Gua and Fu Xi may have begun as separate deities, but under the Han dynasty (202BCE–220CE) they were often presented as husband and wife, with human heads and interlaced serpents' tails.

Myths about Nü Gua and Fu Xi describe the creation of humans and their early struggles involving ancient warfare and disasters, especially

Nü Gua with serpentine body, from an early 20th-century Chinese illustration.

floods. Nü Gua was esteemed as the creator and protector of humanity. She descended from heaven after the earth and heavens had become separated and hills, rivers, plants and animals had appeared. Lonely on earth, she formed a number of small beings from mud: the first people. Pleased with her creation, she decided to speed up the process. She dipped a vine in muddy water and shook it so that drops flew everywhere. Every drop became a new human and the world was soon populated. When the first humans grew old and died, she taught people how to procreate and raise children.

Nudd

A royal figure in Welsh mythology. Nudd is etymologically related to the British god Nodens or Nodons, the focus of an important healing shrine at Lydney in Gloucestershire. Other shrines link Nodens with the Roman Mars, widely revered by the Celts as a protector deity.

Nudd's name is also etymologically identical to that of the mythical Irish king Nuadhu, and also appears in the alliterative form Lludd Llaw Eireint, "Nudd or Lludd Silver-Hand", an exact equivalent of Nuadhu's title, Airgedlámh. Lludd Llaw Eireint is said to have ruled Britain, which was saved from invaders through the intervention of his brother Llefelys: this episode parallels the assistance given to Nuadhu against the Fomorians by Lugh. In Geoffrey of Monmouth's *History of the Kings of Britain* (1136), Nudd/ Lludd became the mythical King Lud, after whom Ludgate in London and the city of London itself were once said to have been named.

NUDE *see panel opposite*

Nuliajuk *see* **Sea Spirit, The**

Numa Pompilius

The legendary successor (7th century BCE) of Romulus as king of Rome . A philosopher and poet, he presided over a golden age, when temples were built and religious rites established.[1] He appears in public settings, such as Perugino's frescoes *Numa Pompilius* (Collegio del Cambio, Perugia), as an example of a virtuous ruler.

NUMBERS *see panel overleaf*

Nun

The dark primeval waters of chaos, which existed before the first gods, in one Egyptian account of creation. The chaotic energy within the waters of the Nun held the potential of all life forms. It also contained the spirit of the cre-

NUDE

The nude in art, whether male or female, can be a representation of power, delight, fecundity or shame. Sculpted or painted, the nude was intended to transport the viewer into a world of the imagination. The nude occurs in both mythological and biblical narratives. Venus (the Greek Aphrodite), the goddess of beauty and love, is often shown unclothed but Minerva (Athene), goddess of wisdom, only rarely so. Elsewhere a nude might signify poverty or truth.

Inherited from ancient Greece was the idea of a "Golden Age" when humankind was in harmony with nature and clothes were not needed. Similarly, in the Bible, Adam and Eve wandered in the Garden of Eden and "they were both naked, the man and his wife, and were not ashamed."[1]

The female nude may express the abundance of nature and the source of life. However "natural" the result appears, the artist has often perfected the form. Inspired by Classical prototypes, the idealized male may be given strength and grace, and the female charms that accord with taste and fashion. Even if the subject warns against the dangers of love, the figure may still be profoundly sensual. From the Renaissance until the second half of the 19th century, the female nude was painted in innumerable ways to delight primarily the male spectator.

To be without clothes is also to be vulnerable. When Adam and Eve were expelled from Paradise, "the eyes of them both were opened, and they knew that they were naked; and they sewed fig leaves together, and made themselves aprons."[2] They knew shame for the first time. Moreover, the Bible deemed that "the nakedness of thy father or the nakedness of thy mother, shalt thou not uncover", hence the embarrassment felt by Shem and Japheth at their father Noah's nakedness. Most shaming of all is the nakedness of those who suffer in hell.

Christ's nakedness or near-nakedness at the Flagellation and Crucifixion, or in a Pietà, presents him as defenceless and thus heightens the sense of sorrow.

NUDE: *see* Acteon; ADAM AND EVE; Noah; Pygmalion; Truth
[1] *Genesis 2:25*
[2] *Genesis 3:*

ator, but the creator had no place in which to become embodied. Time and creation began when a mound of land rose from the Nun (an image doubtless inspired by the annual receding of theh Nile flood in former times). The creator was able to come into existence on this primeval mound, which he did in the form of a bird (variously depicted as a falcon, heron or wagtail). In another account, a primeval lotus grew out of the Nun and opened to reveal the infant deity. The primeval waters of chaos were also embodied as a god, Nun, and a goddess, Naunet. They formed part of the eight primal divinities referred to as the Ogdoad.

Nut

The Egyptian sky goddess, the daughter of Shu and Tefnut and sister of Geb, the earth god. According to the most detailed version of the Egyptian creation myth, Nut and Geb had

Nut: *see* Ennead, The; Isis; Nephthys; Ogdoad, The; Osiris; Seth; Shu (1)

NUMBERS

Divine order, the cryptic keys to cosmic harmony. The greatest mathematical philosophers of ancient Babylonia and Greece, and later, India, believed that numbers could reveal the principles of creation and the laws of space and time. In the interplay of odd and even numbers the Greek philosopher Pythagoras (*c*.580BCE–*c*.500BCE) saw the workings of a dualistic universe of opposites – limit and unlimited, straight and curved, square and oblong. "All things are numbers," he said. In Hinduism numbers were the basis of the material universe. The Aztecs assigned to each fundamental number a god, a quality, a direction and a colour. Because numbers were used by gods to regulate the world, they were thought to have particular symbolic significance. Numbers were seen as fundamental in music, poetry, architecture and art.

Jewish Cabbalists allocated number values to letters of the Hebrew alphabet and used the system to reinterpret the Hebrew Bible, a forerunner to numerology. Number superstition is often based on the traditional symbolism of numbers (sacred seven, unlucky 13). The sequence one, two, three almost universally represented unity, duality and synthesis. In Pythagorean terms, 1, 2, 3, 4 symbolized the flow from point to line to surface to solid. In Greece, odd numbers were masculine and active, even numbers feminine and passive. In China, odd numbers were yang, celestial, immutable and auspicious; even were yin, terrestrial, mutable and

sometimes less auspicious. Numbers with archetypal significance ran from one to ten (or one to 12 in duodecimal systems). Higher numbers in which important archetypes reappear (17 in Islamic tradition; 40 in the Semitic world) often reinforce number symbolism.

In many traditions 13 was considered unlucky, possibly because early lunar-based calendars needed the intercalation of a 13th "month", thought to be unfavourable; advice not to sow on the 13th of any month goes back at least to Hesiod (8th century BCE); Satan was the "13th figure" at witch's rites. In the Tarot, Death is the 13th card of the major arcana. In Central America, 13 was sacred (13-day weeks in the religious calendar). The "left over" five days of the Mayan 20-month solar calendar were unlucky.

Twenty was a sacred number in Central America, associated with the sun god. In Hebrew tradition 21 was associated with wisdom, as was 50, the year of jubilee because it followed 49 years (sacred seven times seven), and was when debts should be forgiven, slaves freed and property returned. Shavuot, the Feast of Weeks (on the Pentecostal 50th day) is similarly linked with seven because it follows the end of the seventh week after Passover. Sixty was used as the basis for the Chinese calendar. Seventy, the biblical life span, represented totality or universality. For many, 10,000 symbolized infinite numbers or infinite time – the Greeks called the 10,000 élite warriors of Persia, the "Immortals".

intercourse but embraced so tightly that Nut had no room to bear their children, Isis, Osiris, Nephthys and Seth. Aided by the eight deities of the Ogdoad, Shu parted the couple, lifting Nut high above Geb.

Nut, the sky, was at times portrayed as a naked woman arching over Geb, the earth, and sometimes as a star-covered cow. She was said to swallow the sun every evening. Sometimes it was said that she wanted to devour her own offspring: then she was depicted as a sow, which will also eat its farrow.

Nymph

In Greek myth, a young woman (*nymphe*) usually of divine or semi-divine parentage. They came in many forms, including sea nymphs (such as the Nereids and Oceanids), freshwater nymphs (naiads), wood nymphs (dryads), nymphs of individual trees (hamadryads), and nymphs associated with local features. They were often portrayed as beautiful young women, who fell in love with mortal men.

Nymphs were mortal, but had long lives and prophetic gifts. Desired by satyrs, and sometimes by mortals, they were chaste and attended gods such as Artemis. Nymphs raised the gods Zeus and Dionysos. Nymphs were sometimes shown with a satyr, as in Watteau's *Nymph Surprised by a Satyr*. Such subjects provided the perfect opportunity to show beautiful women bathing naked.

Nyx

"Night", the darkness of the earth, one of the primal Greek deities which arose from Chaos at the beginning of creation. According to Hesiod, Nyx and Erebos (the darkness of the underworld) had intercourse to produce Aither (the Ether, or bright upper air) and Hemera ("Day"). Nyx was the mother of the Fates, Eris (Discord), Thanatos (Death) and Hypnos (Sleep). Even Zeus feared her black-winged figure. Nyx was associated with inflexible destiny and was shown clad in a robe or cloak of stars, riding in a chariot pulled by black horses, or by nocturnal creatures such as owls and bats, while wearing a crown of poppies and carrying two of her children, Sleep and Death. She is personified in Western art by a maternal figure with a white child (Sleep) and a black one (Death), an image that conveys the ambivalent symbolism of night. Usually depicted as a calm figure with folded wings, she may be presented with a mask, a crescent moon or an owl: all are seen in Michelangelo's *Night*. In Renaissance illustration, Night and Day are depicted as black and white rats gnawing at Time.

In the Orphic creation myth Nyx was the daughter and consort of Phanes, the creator god, and gave birth to the deities Gaia and Uranos.

Nyx (Night, left) and Eos (Dawn, right) disappear as Helios (the sun) appears. After a Greek vase.

Oak

Oak

Might, endurance, longevity, nobility.
The oak was sacred to the thunder
gods of Greece, Scandinavia and the
Slavic countries, possibly because it
was thought to bear the brunt of
lightning strikes.

In Celtic Druidic rites it served as an
axial symbol and natural temple,
associated with male potency and wisdom. Although predominantly a male
emblem (the acorn was equated by the
Celts with the glans penis) Cybele,
Juno and other Great Mother Goddesses were also linked with the oak,
and the Dryads were oak nymphs.
In Greek myth, Herakles' (to the
Romans, Hercules') club was of oak,
and according to some traditions
Christ died on an oak cross. Oak-
leaves are used as military insignia, for
example in Germany and the USA.

Oar

For some seafaring peoples, a rod-like
symbol of royal power, executive
action or skill, probably by association with its propulsive and guiding
force. According to the Roman poet
Virgil (70–19BCE), an oar was ceremonially carried around the site of the
city of Troy to dedicate its rebuilding.
River gods sometimes carry oars in
iconography.

Obelisk

An Egyptian symbol of the sun god in
the form of a rectangular, tapering
pillar topped by a reflective pyramid
designed to catch and concentrate
the light. Obelisks were used as funerary pillars or memorials, perhaps
emblematic of the penetrative potency of sunbeams and of immortal
power. They were also erected as temple pylons, often in pairs.

Ocean *see* Sea

Oceanid

One of the three thousand sea nymphs
who were the daughters of the Titan
Okeanos (or Oceanus) and Tethys.
The Oceanids were deities who tended
all the waters of the world. Among
the more famous of them were

Amphitrite (the wife of Poseidon, although she may have been a Nereid), Calypso (a lover of Odysseus), Clymene (the wife of Helios, the sun god), Doris (the wife of Nereus, the Old Man of the Sea), Metis (the first wife of Zeus) and Perseis (the mother of Aeëtes, Circe and Pasiphaë).

Oceanus *see* **Okeanos**

Octagon

In religious architecture, and particularly in baptisteries, a symbol of rebirth to eternal life. Eight is a number emblematic of renewal, and eight-sided forms were felt to mediate between the symbolism of the square (earthly existence) and the circle (heaven or eternity). In temples, a dome supported by eight pillars in square plan – representing the cardinal and intercardinal points – was a similar image of totality.

Octopus

A vortex and underworld symbol, linked with the spiral, whirlpool, spider and sea serpent. The octopus shown on Mycenaean medallions with decoratively coiled arms may have been a seafarer's amulet against the dangers of the deep or the evil eye. There are intriguing similarities with the round-faced, snake-haired, paralyzing-eyed Medusa of Greek legend (so close that the similarly tentacled jellyfish is called the "medusa"). A sinister or infernal symbolism may also have been suggested by the inky cloud ejected by a frightened octopus. The Zodiac sign Cancer, which is linked with the moon, the waters and the June solstice, was sometimes represented by the octopus rather than the crab.

Odin

The ruler of Asgard, home of the Norse gods, and the supreme deity of the Norse pantheon. His antecedent was the ancient Germanic god Wodan. Both gods were associated with battle, magic, inspiration, the underworld realm and the dead.

Odin was the upholder of kings and the protector of brave heroes, to whom he gave magic weapons, such as Sigmund's sword Gram, and other assistance. However, he would destroy his heroes when he felt the time was right. When Sigmund was old, Odin decided that it was time for him to die; he then appeared before Sigmund in battle and caused Gram to break in two. Disarmed, Sigmund fell under his opponent's blows.

Odin was a shape-shifter, manifesting himself, for example, as a hooded old one-eyed man, a snake and an eagle. He was generally accompanied by wolves and ravens and rode on a magic eight-legged horse, Sleipnir.

Odin was said to summon kings and fallen heroes to Valhalla, the Hall of the Slain, in Asgard. In Viking literature the dead warriors are described as entering Valhalla with great pomp, accompanied by the Valkyries, fearsome goddess-warriors whom Odin sent to determine the course of battles and to select those who would die. In Valhalla the fallen would indulge in feasting and combat, and be ever ready to defend Asgard. The god's warrior devotees, the Berserks (which probably means "Bear Shirt"), wore bear or wolf pelts in battle and were renowned for falling into ecstatic battle-frenzies that made them totally impervious to pain.

The ecstasy associated with Odin made him a god of inspiration,

An octopus; after a Minoan vase.

Odysseus

Odin, after a 12th-century tapestry.

revered by poets and orators. One myth recounts how the dwarfs made the gods a magic mead of inspiration from the blood of a giant mixed with honey. It was stolen by another giant, Suttung, and hidden in a mountain. Odin turned into a snake and slid into the mountain, where he tricked Suttung's daughter into giving him the mead to drink. But he did not swallow it and flew back to Asgard with it, in the form of an eagle.

He was a god of wealth, represented by the divine gold ring Draupnir, from which dropped eight new gold rings every nine nights. Odin also presided over magic and was the possessor of the secret of the runes, mystical symbols used in divination. Prisoners of war were sacrificed to him, and it was said that the course of the battle could be divined from the death movements of the victim. Odin himself was able to travel to the realm of the dead.

Odin was killed at the apocalyptic battle of Ragnarok by the monstrous wolf Fenrir.

Odysseus

A king of Ithaca, an important figure in Homer's *Iliad* and the central figure of the *Odyssey*, which is named after him. Odysseus, whom the Romans called Ulysses or Ulixes, was the son of Laertes and Anticlea, the king and queen of Ithaca. But, some accounts made him the illegitimate son of Sisyphus, a famous trickster, from whom Odysseus was said to have inherited the trickery and guile for which he was renowned. He featured in much Greek tragedy as a cunning and pragmatic politician, and philosophers contrasted his complex, calculating and often deceitful nature with the

directness and nobility of the great hero Achilles.

Odysseus first employed his cunning when he was a suitor for the hand of Helen, the beautiful daughter of King Tyndareos of Sparta. Odysseus advised Tyndareos that, to prevent a riot among Helen's unsuccessful suitors, he should make them swear to uphold the honour of the man eventually chosen as her husband. Tyndareos agreed and selected Menelaus for his daughter's hand. As suggested, Odysseus and the other princes undertook to defend Menelaus if his honour was slighted. As a reward for his counsel, Tyndareos then secured Odysseus the hand of his niece Penelope in marriage.

When Helen eloped with the Trojan prince Paris, all her former suitors came to Menelaus' aid and organized a military expedition against Troy under Agamemnon, Menelaus' brother. Odysseus, however, was reluctant to fight and pretended to be mad and plough the seashore. But the warrior Palamedes exposed the pretence forcing Odysseus to admit his sanity. As a result, Odysseus schemed to bring about Palamedes' death. At Troy he planted gold under Palamedes' tent claiming it was his payment as a Trojan spy. Palamedes was found guilty of treason and stoned to death by his comrades. Later in the siege of Troy, Odysseus designed the famous hollow wooden horse in which the Greek warriors hid and gained entry to the city.

After the fall of Troy the returning Greek fleet was scattered by storms, and Odysseus' ships became separated from the main body. Thus began the wanderings recounted in the Odyssey. After the storms Odysseus and his crew came to the city of the Cicones,

The Sirens trying to lure Odysseus and his crew. From a red-figure jar of the 5th century BCE.

which they sacked. Another storm drove them into a region of sorcery and monsters. They landed first on the island of the Lotus Eaters, whose inhabitants gave some of the crew lotus flowers to eat, wiping out their memories and making them so lethargic that they had to be carried back to their ships.

The next land was inhabited by the Cyclopes, the monstrous one-eyed shepherds. One of them, Polyphemus, took Odysseus and some of his crew captive in his cave and began to eat them. Odysseus got the monster drunk and told him his name was "Nobody". As Polyphemus lay in a drunken stupor, the hero and a few others drove a hot wooden stake into his eye, causing him to scream. Other Cyclopes came to see what was the matter, but on hearing Polyphemus groan "Nobody is hurting me!" they assumed nothing was wrong and left. When the blinded Cyclops rose the next morning, he unsealed the cave to let out his sheep and the Greeks escaped by holding on to the undersides of the animals. Polyphemus' son, the sea god Poseidon, cursed Odysseus to wander the seas for ten years, for blinding his father.

Next, Odysseus came to the island of Aeolus, the lord of the winds, who gave him a sack containing unfavourable winds. He had sailed on to within sight of Ithaca when a crewman opened the sack while Odysseus was sleeping, releasing the winds, which then blew the voyagers onward to the land of the Laestrygonians. These giant cannibals sank all the ships but one, and ate their crews. Odysseus, in the one remaining ship, then landed on the island of the sorceress Circe. Half of the crew went to her palace, where she turned them into pigs and locked them in a sty. Aided by the god Hermes and a magic plant, Odysseus became immune to Circe's spells and compelled her to release his men. The Greeks stayed for a year with Circe, who advised Odysseus to consult the blind prophet Teiresias. Teiresias told him to go to the underworld and make an offering to Poseidon. In the underworld Odysseus met great former heroes, including his old colleagues Achilles and Ajax.

From the underworld Odysseus sailed past the islands of the Sirens, monsters with birds' bodies and women's heads. Their singing was irresistible and lured sailors onto rocks. Odysseus wanted to hear their song, so, following Circe's advice, he ordered his men to plug their ears with wax and strap him to the mast. The crewmen rowed safely past, deaf to their captain's bewitched demands to steer towards the beautiful voices.

The ship successfully negotiated the sea monsters Scylla and Charybdis and came to Thrinakia, the island of Helios, the sun, where it was becalmed. Ignoring Circe's advice, the starving crew killed some of Helios' cattle to eat. Helios, outraged,

Oedipus

destroyed the ship and all its crew except for Odysseus. He was washed up on the island of the beautiful Oceanid (sea nymph) Calypso, who kept him as an unwilling lover for eight years, but Odysseus longed for home. She finally released him after the intervention of the goddess Athene, and Odysseus sailed on a raft to the luxurious land of the Phaeacians. Their king, named Alcinous, sent Odysseus home to Ithaca in a magical ship full of marvellous gifts.

Before announcing himself when they arrived home, Odysseus found Penelope, who had never believed him dead, surrounded by unwanted suitors. In disguise he discovered that his family and people were still faithful, then killed the suitors with the aid of his son Telemachus. He was happily reunited with Penelope after twenty years. The prophet Teiresias foretold that Odysseus' death would come from the sea. In some accounts Telegonus, the son of Odysseus and Circe, later came to Ithaca and accidentally killed his father.

Odyssey, The *see* **Odysseus**

Oedipus

A king of Thebes, particularly famous for sexual transgression in Greek myth. According to one account of his story, the Delphic oracle told King Laius and Queen Jocasta of Thebes that their child would kill his father and marry his mother. So when Jocasta gave birth to a son, Laius pierced and bound the baby's feet and abandoned it on a hillside. However, a shepherd found the child and took him to Corinth, where he was adopted by King Polybus and Queen Merope. They named the boy Oedipus ("Swollen Foot").

Years later, during a feast, a stranger claimed that Polybus was not Oedipus' father. Annoyed by the charge, Oedipus went to Delphi, where the oracle told him that he would kill his father and marry his mother. He then fled Corinth, in the belief that Polybus and Merope were his real parents. On the road to Thebes he got involved in a fight in which he killed a stranger who had ordered him to make way for his chariot; unknown to Oedipus, this was his father. In Thebes he vanquished the Sphinx, a monster which devoured anyone unable to answer her riddle, an act for which the Thebans hailed him as their saviour and offered him the vacant throne and the

Oedipus and the Sphinx, from a kylix *(shallow drinking cup) of* c.*450BCE.*

hand of Queen Jocasta. Thebes prospered under Oedipus and he and Jocasta had four children; Antigone, Ismene, Polyneices and Eteocles.

Some years later Thebes was hit by drought, disease and famine. Creon, Jocasta's brother, went to Delphi and was told that the plagues would end only when Laius' killer had been expelled. The prophet Teiresias declared that Oedipus was the guilty man. Then a messenger from Corinth – the shepherd who had handed him as a baby to Polybus and Merope – came to tell Oedipus that Polybus had died and that he should return to Corinth to become king. Oedipus refused to go to Merope because of the old oracle, but the shepherd told him that she was not his real mother. The terrible truth dawned: Laius and Jocasta were his real parents, and it was Laius whom Oedipus had killed on the road to Thebes. Jocasta hanged herself in distress and Oedipus blinded himself with her brooch and went into exile in Attica, led there by his daughters Antigone and Ismene. He died at Colonus near Athens.

Oenghus

An Irish deity, one of the Tuatha Dé Danann, often said to be the god of love. Oenghus was the son of the Daghdha and Boann. His modern description as god of love derived principally from the assistance he lent to lovers, especially Diarmaid and Gráinne. Another myth recounts how Oenghus himself fell in love with a beautiful swan-maiden called Caer. Every two years she changed into a swan at Samhain (31 October –1 November). One year Oenghus took the form of a swan and flew off with her to his palace, Brugh na Bóinne (the prehistoric tombs of Newgrange, County Meath). Oenghus bore the title Mac Óc (meaning "Young Son") and was probably identical in origin to the British and Gaulish deity Maponus.

Ogdoad, The

A group of eight primal deities personifying the forces of chaos. The Ogdoad (from the Greek *okto*, eight) was made

Seven of the eight Ogdoad pictured around the sun god Ra-Harakhty, from a papyrus of c.*1350BCE.*

up of four couples, each pair an embodiment of an aspect of the primal world: Nun and Naunet (the primeval waters); Amun and Amaunet (unseen forces); Heh and Hehet (infinity); and Kek and Keket (darkness).

The deities of the Ogdoad were sometimes represented as frogs and serpents, which lived in the primordial slime, or as eight baboons hailing the dawn. The principal cult town of the Ogdoad was Khemenu (meaning "Town of Eight", known as Hermopolis to the Greeks, and now called el-Ashmunein). This was said to be where the sun first rose on a mythical "Island of Fire" after hatching from a cosmic egg that had been formed by the Ogdoad.

Oghma

An Irish divine warrior, the son of the Daghda and one of the Tuatha Dé Danann. Oghma was famous for his strength, eloquence and poetic gifts and was credited with the invention of Ogham, the early Irish alphabet, which consisted of lines and notches.

Oenghus: *see* Boann;
Daghdha, The; Diarmaid;
Maponus

Ogdoad, The: *see* Amun;
Ennead, The; Nun

Oghma: *see* Daghdha, The;
Herakles

He was probably identical to the Gaulish Ogmios, who, in turn, was identified with the semi-divine Classical hero Hercules (Herakles), except that Ogmios was an old man and revered as the god of eloquence.

Oil

Spiritual grace, illumination and benediction – associations traditional in the Near East where olive oil was used for light and nourishment, and was also a medicinal balm. Anointing kings symbolized their consecration as rulers with divine authority. In many parts of the world, oil was given protective and fertility symbolism.

Oisín

An Irish warrior and poet, the son of the hero Finn and Sadhbh, a woman of the Otherworld who sometimes took the form of a deer. Oisín ("Fawn") was raised by his mother in the wilderness and later found by Finn. He became one of the greatest warriors of the Fian, Finn's followers.

Oisín was put under a spell by the goddess Niamh, and went with her to her father's kingdom, the Otherworld or Tír na Nóg ("Land of Youth"). He dwelt there for a long time, but eventually became homesick for Ireland. Niamh allowed him to visit his homeland on horseback, on condition that he never set foot on Irish soil. Oisín returned to Ireland only to discover that the world he knew had long gone, and he had been in Tír na Nóg for three centuries without ageing. Soon afterward he fell off his horse, touched the ground, and at once aged three hundred years. Before Oisín died, he was visited by St Patrick, to whom he recounted all the tales of the Fian for posterity.

Okeanos, from a 1st-century CE mosaic.

Okeanos

A Titan, the son of Gaia and Uranos, who personified Ocean, a great river which, in Greek cosmology, surrounded the world. Okeanos married his sister Tethys, who bore the sea nymphs known as the Oceanids.

Olive

A blessed tree in Judeo-Christian, Classical and Islamic traditions, famously associated with peace but also with victory, joy, plenty, purity, immortality and virginity. As an early, important and exceptionally durable crop in the Mediterranean world, the olive was sacred in Greece to the warlike goddess Athene, who is said to have invented the tree for Athens, thereby winning a contest with Poseidon for the patronage of the city. The tree was associated also with Zeus, Apollo, Hera and Cybele.

Brides wore or carried olive leaves (signifying virginity), and olive wreaths crowned victors at the Olympic Games. The peace symbolism of the olive became dominant under the *Pax Romana* when olive branches were presented by envoys submitting to the imperial power. The Roman emblematic meaning was later taken up by Jewish and Christian symbolists who saw the olive as a sign of peace between God and humanity, for the bible said it was an olive twig that was brought back to Noah by a dove sent out to see if the waters had receded from the earth and dry land could be found. The olive tree is an attribute of Peace, Concord and Wisdom in Western art.

In Islamic tradition it is a Tree of Life, associated with the Prophet and also Abraham – one of the two forbidden trees of Paradise. In Japan it is an emblem of friendship and success, in China of calmness.

Olwen

The daughter of Ysbaddaden, a chieftain of the giants, and the heroine of a Welsh story which is part of the *Mabinogion*. The warrior Culhwch, Arthur's nephew, wanted to wed Olwen and was set a number of difficult tasks by Ysbaddaden before he would grant his consent. With the assistance of some men with extraordinary gifts, such as Arthur and Mabon, Culhwch succeeded and won the hand of Olwen. His most important task was to capture a magic boar, called Twrch Trwyth, and retrieve a wondrous comb and shears kept between its ears. The hunt ranged over southern Wales, Cornwall and Ireland.

Olympia

A city in the Peloponnese which was the site of the greatest Greek religious festival, held every four years (an Olympiad) in honour of the god Zeus, the chief of the Olympian gods (hence the city's name). At the end of every Olympiad all wars ceased for the July festival and the best athletes of the Greek world converged on Olympia to participate in the great games. The foundation of the games, traditionally

A reconstruction of the temple of Zeus at Olympia, with a statue of the enthroned god in the centre.

said to have begun in the 8th century BCE, was sometimes attributed to mythical figures such as the hero Herakles or King Pelops. The games were abolished in 393CE by the Christian emperor Theodosius, presumably because of their pagan associations.

The temple of Zeus at Olympia contained a chryselephantine (ivory and gold) statue of the god that stood 13 metres (42 feet) high. Sculpted by the great Pheidias, it was completed *c.*430BCE, and was one of the seven wonders of the ancient world.

OLYMPIANS, THE *see panel overleaf*

Olympus, Mount

A mountain in northeastern Greece, said to be the home of the gods.

Om (Aum)

The sacred Hindu and Buddhist syllable representing the primordial sound that created the existential world – the divine Word or mantra of mantras. Its three phonetic elements (*ah-oo-mm*) symbolize fundamental triads, including Brahma, Vishnu and Shiva as creating, sustaining and destroying principles in the cycle of being.

Olwen: *see* Arthur; *Mabinogion*, The; Maponus; Twrch Trwyth

Olympia: *see* Herakles, OLYMPIANS, THE; PELOPS,THE CURSE OF THE HOUSE OF, Zeus

Olympus, Mount: *see* OLYMPIANS, THE

Om (Aum): *see* Mantra; Triad; Word

The sacred mantra OM (AUM), written in Sanskrit script, is a common Hindu and Buddhist amulet.

OLYMPIANS, THE

The highest mountain in Greece, Mount Olympus, was said to be the residence of Zeus and the other twelve principal deities of the Greek pantheon, who were therefore known as the Olympians. Their names were as follows:

Name	Parentage	Main functions
Aphrodite	Uranos	Goddess of love and sexuality
Apollo	Zeus and Leto	God of light and the arts
Ares	Zeus and Hera	God of war
Artemis	Zeus and Leto	Goddess of hunting and childbirth
Athene	Zeus and Metis	Goddess of wisdom
Demeter	Kronos and Rhea	Goddess of fertility and crops
Dionysos	Zeus and Persephone and Semele	God of wine and ecstasy
Hephaistos	Hera	God of craftsmanship; divine smith
Hera	Kronos and Rhea	Goddess of marriage; queen of Zeus
Hermes	Zeus and Maia	God of communication; divine messenger
Hestia	Kronos and Rhea	Goddess of the hearth
Poseidon	Kronos and Rhea	Ruler of the seas
Zeus	Kronos and Rhea	Supreme deity; ruler of the heavens

Omphalos

A sacred zone or object symbolizing the cosmic navel or centre of creation – a focus of spiritual and physical forces and a link between the underworld, the earth and the heavens. The original *omphalos* at Delphi in Greece – a white standing-stone with a tracery of carving – was sacred to Apollo and may originally have been a focus of Earth Mother worship and divination. In one myth, Rhea (the earth) wrapped the stone in a swaddling cloth and, in place of her newborn son Zeus, gave it to her husband Kronos, who was devouring his children at birth. According to tradition, the site of Delphi was sacred to Gaia before being usurped by Apollo.

Omphalos symbols ranged from stones of phallic shape or ovoids with serpentine carving symbolizing generative forces to sacred trees or mountains. The holes in sacred Chinese jade *bi* discs may have somewhat similar significance.

One

A number symbolizing primordial unity, the deity or creative essence, the sun or light, and the origin of life.

In Western tradition, the Arabic numeral had phallic, axial, aggressive and active symbolism. It was the symbol of God in all the great monotheistic religions, and particularly in Islam.

In Pythagorean thought, the number one was the point, the common basis for all calculation. It was the Confucian perfect entity, the indivisible, the mystic centre from which everything else radiated. More obviously, one is an emblem of the beginning, of the self, and of loneliness.

Oni

Demons believed to inhabit the earth and Jigoku, the Japanese hell. Oni are usually invisible, although some are able to adopt the form of a human or an animal. They are responsible for all kinds of misfortune, such as famine and disease, and may possess a person or steal his or her soul.

Ops *see* **Rhea**

Orange

Fertility, splendour, love. Orange blossom was an ancient token of fertility, used in bridal wreaths – a custom continued in Christian countries but with the symbolism shifted toward purity. Oranges were possibly the "golden apples" of the Hesperides, a link with the setting sun. In art, the Christ Child sometimes holds an orange, a redemption symbol because the orange was thought by some to be the forbidden fruit of the Tree of Knowledge. Oranges are eaten as emblems of good fortune on the second day of the Chinese New Year. The colour is associated with fire and luxury, except in Buddhist countries where the saffron robes of monks symbolize humility.

Orb *see* **Globe, Orb**

Orchid

A Chinese fecundity symbol and charm against sterility, and an emblem of beauty, scholarship, refinement and friendship. In Chinese paintings, orchids in a vase symbolize harmony.

Orestes

In Greek myth,[1] a king of Argos (or Mycenae) and Sparta, the son of Agamemnon and Clytemnestra. After Agamemnon had been murdered by Clytemnestra and her lover Aegisthus, the boy Orestes escaped from Argos with the aid either of his nurse or of his sister Elektra. He was raised at the court of his uncle, King Strophius of Phocis, and became the best friend of Strophius' son Pylades. After nine years Orestes consulted the oracle at Delphi about how to avenge his father's death and was told to return to Argos to slay the murderers.

Orestes and Pylades went to Argos and contacted Elektra, who helped them gain entry to the royal palace in the guise of travellers seeking hospitality. Unrecognized by Clytemnestra, he claimed to have heard that Orestes was dead. Clytemnestra joyfully called for her husband, who had feared his return. Aegisthus came, unarmed, and Orestes killed him on the spot before cutting off his mother's head with one blow.

One version of the myth says that for committing matricide Orestes, tormented by grief, was forced to wander all over Greece, pursued by the Furies. Eventually, however, after consulting the Delphic oracle, he went to Athens to face trial by the Areopagus, the name given to the court of Athenian elders. Orestes was exonerated of his crime with the casting vote of the goddess Athene, who argued that the murder of Agamemnon was a graver crime than that of Clytemnestra.

Orestes returned home to become king of Argos and later, after the death of his grandfather Tyndareos, he also became king of Sparta. Additionally, he conquered a large part of Arcadia in the central Peloponnese. Orestes married Hermione, the daughter of Menelaus, his uncle, and

Oni: *see* Emma-ho; Jigoku

Orange: *see* Apple; COLOURS; Fire, Flame; Yellow

Orchid: *see* FLOWERS; Vase

Orestes: *see* Aegisthus; Agamemnon; Athene; Clytemnestra; PELOPS, THE CURSE OF THE HOUSE OF; Tyndareos
[1] Aeschylus, *Oresteia* and Euripides, *Iphigeneia*

Orestes killing Aegisthus, after a red-figure vase of the 5th century BCE.

Helen. Pylades married Elektra. Orestes was said to have died in old age from a snake bite.

Orgy

A symbol of primeval chaos and the supremacy of instinct and passion as elemental creative forces. Apart from specific orgiastic cults, many ancient cultures institutionalized periods of licence in which social norms were rejected or reversed. In Babylonia, twelve days of anarchy acted out a mythic struggle against the chaos goddess to establish cosmic order.

The Roman Saturnalia was similarly an authorized twelve-day carnival at the December solstice to celebrate the rebirth of the vegetation god. The symbolism of the religious orgy, as in the frenzied pagan rites of the Greek god Dionysos (Bacchus), was the annihilation of the difference between the human state – limited by time, morality, social convention or physical stamina – and the timeless, unlimited, ever-energized state of divinity.

Orientation

The orientation of mosques, temples and churches toward the east is almost universally linked with the symbolism of light as divine illumination. In many Christian churches the eastern window was precisely aligned with the east to allow the rising sun to strike the altar. Alternatively, it faced the direction of the rising sun on the day of the saint to whom the church was dedicated. Islamic worshippers face east to signify that their spirits are turned to the divine source.

Orion

A giant hunter of Greek myth,¹ the son of the god Poseidon and of Euryale, the daughter of King Minos and Queen Pasiphaë of Crete. According to one of the numerous accounts of his fate, Orion cleared the island of Chios of wild beasts in return for the hand of Merope, the daughter of Oenopion, the island's king. After Oenopion reneged on his promise, Orion raped Merope in a drunken rage. In revenge, Oenopion put out his eyes.

In one account, Orion went to the forge of Hephaistos (the Roman Vulcan) and set Cedalion, one of the god's assistants, on his shoulders to guide him toward the sunrise, so that its rays might restore his sight – a scene Poussin illustrated in *Landscape with Orion*. In a different version, Orion waded through the sea – he was so tall the water only came up to his chest – and over land toward the home of the god Helios, the sun, who restored his sight. The hunter then had an affair with Helios' sister, the dawn goddess Eos.

Eos and Orion went together to Delos, where the goddess Artemis (Diana) invited Orion to go hunting with her. The god Apollo was afraid that his chaste sister, like Eos, might fall for the huge hunter, so he told the goddess Gaia, the earth, that Orion had boasted he could kill every beast in the world. So Gaia sent a monstrous scorpion to kill Orion, who swam off to seek the protection of Eos on Delos. Apollo convinced Artemis that the swimming figure in the distance was a brigand who had raped one of her followers. The goddess shot Orion in the head and killed him. On discovering his true identity, she set him among the stars as the constellation that bears his name, pursued for ever by the scorpion (the constellation Scorpio).

A different story states that Orion was killed by a scorpion's bite delivered by Artemis because he had tried to violate her. Both Orion and the scorpion were then transformed into constellations.

Orpheus

According to Greek myth,[1] Orpheus was the greatest mortal musician. He was the son of King Oeagrus of Thrace and Calliope, the Muse of epic poetry. His paternity was also ascribed to the god Apollo.

Orpheus became famous for his singing and playing of the lyre. It was remarked that he played the lyre so beautifully that animals were charmed, rivers ceased flowing, and mountains and trees moved to hear his music. He was said to have charmed the waves when he sailed with Jason and the Argonauts. He also drowned out the voices of the Sirens when the ship *Argo* sailed close to their island, where they lured sailors on to the rocks with their haunting singing.

He fell in love with Eurydice, a dryad (tree nymph) or naiad (water nymph). But at at their wedding omens foretold an unhappy outcome and even Hymen, god of marriage, was gloomy. As the innocent new bride wandered in the meadows with her band of Naiads, a serpent bit her ankle and she fell lifeless to the ground (Poussin painted the ill-fated wedding in *Landscape with Orpheus and Eurydice*).

Orpheus was overcome with grief. He took his lyre and entered the underworld, the land of the dead, where his laments for Eurydice were so beautiful that Cerberus, the monstrous guard dog of the underworld, was charmed and let him pass. Hades (Pluto) and Persephone (Proserpina), the king and queen of the dead, were also greatly moved by his pleas to change Eurydice's destiny. They released Eurydice from death and allowed her to follow Orpheus back to earth – but on condition that he did not look at her before reaching the entrance of the underworld. But just before they emerged into daylight, Orpheus could no longer resist and turned to see his beloved following behind. At once, Eurydice slipped back down into the depths,

Orpheus singing, from a bowl of the 5th century BCE.

Orpheus: *see* Apollo; Cerberus; Hades, MUSES, THE; Nymph; Orphism; Persephone
[1] Ovid, *Met X:1–85*

Orphism

her last farewell hardly reaching his ears as she disappeared into the underworld forever.

Orpheus' sorrow was boundless. He refused all advances from women, preferring to lament his loss in song. Some Thracian women became so angry at his lack of interest in them that they tore him to pieces in a frenzy. Even then Orpheus' head and lyre brought forth their beautiful music. A temple, constructed above his head, became the site of a famous oracle. Orpheus was the traditional founder of a mystic cult, named Orphism.

Orphism

A mystery religion supposed to have been founded by the musician Orpheus after his return from the underworld. Its adherents, the Orphics, were concerned with the immortality of the soul, seeing death as welcome because it liberated the soul from the impure body. They always wore white and avoided contact with dead flesh, be it human or animal. They were vegetarians and opposed to animal sacrifice.

The Orphic creation myth is more philosophical and abstract than the one more widely known in Hesiod's *Theogony*. In the beginning Chronos (meaning "Time") was accompanied by Adrasteia ("Necessity"). From Chronos sprang Aither ("Bright Upper Air"), Erebos ("Underworld Darkness") and Chaos ("Yawning Void"). Chronos fashioned an egg in Aither and from the egg hatched Phanes (literally "Light"), the creator of everything, a deity both male and female with four eyes and golden wings. He had many names, including Eros ("Desire"). Phanes had a daughter, Nyx ("Night"), whom he married.

Their offspring were the goddess Gaia, the earth, and Uranos, the sky. The myth hereafter is similar to the Hesiodic account. However, the Orphics believed that Zeus created everything anew, swallowing Phanes and coupling with the goddess Persephone, queen of the underworld, to produce Dionysos-Zagreus.

Osiris

A great god of Egyptian myth and the first king, the son of the earth god Geb and the sky goddess Nut and the twin brother of Isis. As the eldest child of Geb and Nut, Osiris became the first ruler (pharaoh) on earth. He was a good and wise sovereign, revered as the god who taught humanity the secrets of farming and civilization. But his rule came under threat from chaotic powers, chiefly in the form of his brother, the god Seth, who ultimately brought about his death.

There are numerous accounts of the death of Osiris, a central episode in Egyptian myth. In one version, Seth grew jealous of his brother and plotted to take his throne. He ordered a beautiful painted chest to be made and declared that it would be given to whoever fitted inside it. Osiris tried it and found it a perfect fit, but Seth at once closed the chest and sealed it with lead. It was dropped in the Nile and drifted out to sea. Seth became king in his brother's place.

Most accounts relate how Isis, the devoted widow of her brother Osiris, retrieved the corpse and used her magic powers to revive it for long enough to conceive Horus, who later defeated Seth and recovered his father's throne. Anubis embalmed the body of Osiris and created the first mummy. But Seth later found the

The mummification of Osiris by Anubis, from a Roman-period papyrus.

body and tore it to pieces. Each piece was buried at a different place throughout Egypt.

After death Osiris became ruler of Duat, the underworld. In early times he was the lord of a demonic kingdom. Later, however, he was seen as the just judge of the dead, one who welcomed virtuous souls to paradise. Every dead pharaoh was identified with Osiris, just as the living king was identified with his son Horus.

Osiris was said to cause the annual growth of crops. The cutting and threshing of the harvest was compared to the killing of the god and the dismemberment of his body.

Ostrich
An ostrich feather was the attribute of Ma'at, the Egyptian goddess of justice and truth: the mythological feather against which the hearts of the dead were weighed to ascertain if they were heavy with sin. The even length of ostrich feathers is given as a reason for this symbolism of equity. More probably, the feathers had special status because they came from Africa's largest bird. The decorative impact of large ostrich eggs may also explain why they (rather than other eggs) were hung in Eastern Orthodox churches as resurrection symbols. The idea that

the ostrich hides its head in the sand (giving us the modern idiom meaning "not facing facts") seems to have come from its habit of stretching its neck out close to the ground when threatened.

Other World, The
A magical and fantastic land of Slavic folk tales. The Other World, or "Thrice Tenth Kingdom", lies beyond this world and is variously located above the earth or beneath it, or under the sea, or on the other side of a dense forest bounded by a flaming river. It is often the destination of a hero on a quest, who may have to climb a steep mountain or penetrate deep caves to reach it. The way to the Other World may be guarded by terrifying monsters, dragons and other perils. The land was said to be fabulously wealthy, with palaces that glittered with gold and silver. The object of the hero's journey was usually made of gold, for example golden apples or a golden bird.

One theory behind the heroic quest to the Other World and back is that it reflects the ancient Slav belief in shamanistic trance-induced journeys, through which a shaman was said to acquire both wisdom and power.

Otherworld, The
In Celtic myth, a fabulous enchanted land of pleasure, wisdom and plenty. In this magical land, time stands still, and disease, old age and death are unknown. The Otherworld features in both Irish and Welsh myths and is referred to by various names, such as Tír na Nóg (the Irish for "Land of Youth"). It is a land of happiness, peace and revelry, where food and drink are dispensed from never-emp-

Ostrich: *see* Birds; Egg; Feathers; Heart

Other World, The: *see* ANCESTORS; COSMOLOGY; Otherworld, The

Otherworld, The: *see* Arthur; Conla; Mael Dúin; Oisin; Other World, The; Tuatha Dé Danann

tying magic cauldrons. However, it is also a land fraught with perils for uninvited visitors from the visible world. One Old Welsh poem, "The Spoils of Annwn", describes how Arthur and three boatloads of his followers travelled to Annwn, the Otherworld, to steal the magic cauldron of the king of Annwn. The mission was nearly disastrous, as only seven men returned safely. This story may have been the origin of the Arthurian quest for the Holy Grail.

The Otherworld may be beyond the sea, beneath the ground, or within one of the numerous topographical features that in Ireland were once believed to be *sidhe* or fairy dwellings, such as a hill or ancient burial chamber. It was reached through lakes or caves or through encounters with one of its inhabitants, who included gods and goddesses, spirits, heroes and ancestors. The ancient Celtic festival known in Irish as Samhain (31 October–1 November) was said to be a time when the boundaries between this world and the Otherworld became fluid and Otherworld spirits walked abroad.

Otter

A lunar animal, linked with fertility and cult initiations in both Africa and North America. The Chinese associated the friendly and playful otter with a high sexual drive, and there are folk tales of otters disguising themselves as women to seduce men.

Ouroboros

The circular image of a snake swallowing its own tail – an emblem of the eternal and indivisible, and of cyclic time. The image has been variously interpreted, combining the creation symbolism of the egg (the space within the circle), the terrestrial symbolism of the serpent and the celestial symbolism of the circle. In its original Egyptian religious form, the *ouroboros* is thought to have symbolized the sun's daily return to its point of departure, passing through sky and underworld. In Greece, death and rebirth symbolism seems indicated by its use in Orphic iconography. Gnostics saw it as an image of self-sustaining Nature, endlessly recreating itself, and of unity in duality, the essential oneness of life, the universal serpent moving through all things. The maxim "One is all" sometimes accompanies the symbol. As an emblem of eternity, it was associated in the Roman Empire with Saturn, as the god of time, and Janus, the god of the New Year.

Oval *see* Lozenge

Oven, Furnace

A matrix or womb – an instrument of spiritual purification or regeneration. The "burning fiery furnace" into which Nebuchadnezzar cast the Jewish administrators of Babylon, Shadrach, Meshach and Abednego is a biblical symbol of spiritual trial. To the king's astonishment, they came out unscathed, proving the superiority of their God over the golden idol that they had been asked to worship. The purification symbolism of the oven or furnace derives from the processes of metallurgy and alchemy.

Owl

Now an emblem of sagacity and bookish erudition, the owl had sinister, even ferocious symbolism in some ancient cultures, particularly in China. Its silent, predatory night

The ouroboros, after a medieval Greek alchemical manual.

flights, staring eyes and eerie cry linked it widely with death and with occult powers, particularly of prophecy – perhaps from its ability to see in the dark. It was the bird of death in ancient Egypt, India, Central and North America, China and Japan, but in some traditions it appears as a guardian of the night or guide to the afterlife – among the Native American Plains' Indians, for example, where owl images or ritually worn feathers had protective significance.

In China, young owls were fabled to peck out their mother's eyes. It was an ancient emblem of destructive yang forces, linked with thunder and the June solstice. As a creature of the dark, the owl was a Christian symbol of the Devil or witchcraft, and an image of the blindness of non-belief. Its association with intelligence comes from the Athenians who made the owl sacred to their goddess of wisdom and learning, Athene Pronoia ("the foreseeing"). Greek coins of Athene show an owl on the reverse side. It is from this that the wise owl of European fables is derived, hence the common motif of owls perching on books, and the use of the term "owlish" to describe scholars blinking behind their bifocals. The owl also appears as an attribute of the personifications Night and Sleep.

Ox

Strength, patience, submissiveness, steady toil – a universally benevolent symbol. As the power that drove the ancient plough, the ox was a valuable animal, often used as a sacrifice, especially in cultic rituals connected with agricultural fertility. The ox is a Christian symbol of the sacrificial Christ

and also the emblem of St Luke and of the priesthood. Now identified with slow-witted brawn, the epithet "dumb ox" was once applied by the theologian Albertus Magnus to his bulky but formidably intelligent student Thomas Aquinas (1225–74): "One day the dumb ox will fill the world with his lowing."

As an image of humanity's animal nature mastered, the ox is a Daoist and Buddhist attribute of the sage and of contemplative learning in China. The white ox was a forbidden food in several traditions. White oxen were sacrificed to the Greek god Zeus (in Roman myth, Jupiter) and black ones to Hades (Pluto). Black oxen pull the chariot of Death in art and are also an attribute of Night. Lunar associations often distinguish the ox from the solar bull.

Oyster

Female sexuality and reproduction – a symbolism taken both from the general fertility symbolism of water and from the association between bivalves and the vulva. Pistol's famous boast, "Why then the world's mine oyster, which I with sword shall open" (Shakespeare's *The Merry Wives of Windsor*, 2:2) refers not to this symbolism but to the idea that wealth can be found anywhere, like pearls in oysters – a misconception, as the mollusc that produces true pearls is not the edible oyster.

Oysters were considered an aphrodisiac (and indeed they contain large amounts of zinc, which is beneficial to male sexual health) and in 17th century Dutch art they often appear in brothel scenes and may denote a prostitute: oyster-selling was regarded as one of the lowest forms of trade.

Ox: *see* Ass; Baptism; Black; Cow; DEATH; Night; Sacrifice; White

Oyster: *see* Pearl

The wise owl, an attribute of the goddess Athene, from an ancient Greek coin.

Padmasambhava

Padmasambhava

An Indian mystic and Tantric practitioner who brought Buddhism to Tibet at the invitation of the Tibetan king Trisong Detsen in 762CE. Many myths arose about him: for example, it was said that he was not born but appeared miraculously as an eight-year-old within the heart of a lotus flower. Raised by the king of Uddiyana, Padmasambhava was condemned to a life of penitence and asceticism after killing a royal minister. He became a Buddhist and attained great spiritual power; it was said he could communicate with supernatural beings.

Padmasambhava in wrathful guise, riding a tiger.

While he was staying in Tibet, Padmasambhava enlisted the aid of local spirits to counter demons hindering work on the king's new temple. With the aid of these spirits the monastery of Samye, Tibet's oldest, was soon built. When Padmasambhava left Tibet, he promised to return in spirit once a month to bless those who had invoked his name. Worshipped by Tibetan Buddhists as "the second Buddha", he is said to have lived for more than a thousand years.

Pagoda

A Buddhist reliquary tower, an architectural development of the stupa found at Buddhist temples and monasteries in southeast Asia, China, Korea and Japan. It was a development of the tall tiered finial spire of the classic Indian stupa.

Pairs *see* Doubles; Twins

Palamedes

In Greek myth, A warrior prince, the son of Nauplius the younger, king of Nauplia. While the Greeks were organizing their expedition against Troy, Odysseus was reluctant to fight and pretended to be mad, but Palamedes forced him to admit his sanity. Odysseus avenged this humiliation by claiming that Palamedes was a Trojan spy. Palamedes was arrested, found guilty and stoned to death.

Pale Fox

A trickster and culture hero in the mythology of the Dogon people of Mali. According to the Dogon creation myth, the creator god Amma made the fox bring both order and disorder into the world. Pale Fox stole seeds from Amma and planted them in the earth, which was Pale Fox's mother. However, this was an act of incest, and as a result the soil became dry and had to be purified. So Amma gave people seed that had not been stolen and they sowed it in the ground. This is how the practice of agriculture became established.

Pale Fox became an outcast from human society and lived in the wilderness. Wherever he went people followed and planted new fields with seeds. In this way human civilization spread through the world. The paw marks left by Pale Fox in sand are used for divination: they are said to be his way of communicating with the world.

Palm

Victory, supremacy, fame, longevity, resurrection and immortality. The majestic palm with its huge, radiant leaves was a solar and triumphal symbol. In antiquity palm leaves were used to hail victors. Personifications of Victory or Fame are shown in many paintings bestowing palm leaves on the illustrious. The palm was equated with the Tree of Life in both Egypt and Arabia. As a food source, the date palm, also had feminine, fecundity symbolism both in western Asia and China. Thus, palm motifs are associated not only with the sun cult of Apollo but also with the goddesses Astarte and Ishtar – and later with the Virgin Mary. In Islamic tradition, Mary bore Jesus under a date palm in the desert, which miraculously dropped dates to feed her.

During the Flight into Egypt the fruit of the palm tree fed Joseph and the Virgin, who is shown at her death being presented with a palm. The palm is also associated with Christ's Entry into Jerusalem, when the people "took branches of palm trees, and went forth to meet Him, and cried Hosanna; 'Blessed is the King of Israel that cometh in the name of the Lord'".[1] This event is remembered in the Christian celebration of Palm Sunday, the start of Holy Week.

Christianity adopted the palm for martyrs who had triumphed over death. It is thus the attribute in art of many Christian saints as well as of Victory, Fame and (through the Virgin Mary) Chastity. St Paul the Hermit (*c*.249–341CE) wears a loincloth of woven palm leaves. Pilgrims who had visited the Holy Land were "palmers". Palm forms on lamps or other funerary objects symbolize resurrection.

Palamedes: *see* Nauplius; Odysseus

Pale Fox: *see* CULTURE HERO; TRICKSTER

Palm: *see* Joseph, Husband of the Virgin; Martyrs; Passion of Christ, The; Virgin, The
[1] *John 12:13*

Pan

The god Pan, after a mosaic pavement.

Pan

In Greek myth, Pan was the god of woodlands and pastures, shepherds, flocks, and those who dwelled in the country. In Roman myth he lived in the woods and mountains of Arcadia and was associated with Faunus or Silvanus, chief of the satyrs. He was of uncertain parentage, but Hermes (Mercury in Roman myth) or Zeus (Jupiter) were often said to be his father. He had a human torso and arms but was born with the hindquarters of a goat and horns on his head, and was raised by nymphs.

In *The Triumph of Pan*, Poussin depicts Pan as a garlanded herm surrounded by revellers. Often in the company of Dionysos (in Roman myth, Bacchus) he was a figure of lust and enjoyed cavorting with the nymphs, who were frequently subjected to his unwanted attentions. Among those he pursued was Syrinx, a beautiful wood-nymph of Arcadia, who fled until she reached a river. She prayed to be transformed, and just as Pan thought he had caught her, he found he was clasping the marsh reeds. As Pan sighed in disappoint-

ment, the reeds produced a sweet sound that delighted him. He cut unequal lengths of reed, bound them together and named his pipes after the nymph: *syrinx* ("Pan pipes").

Some said that Pan caused unidentified noises which startled humans and beasts in the countryside. He came to be seen as a god who spread alarm, hence the word "panic".

In one Greek account, Pan coupled with Aphrodite, who bore their child Priapus, a rustic fertility god.

Pan Gu

A primal creator god who features in the most important Chinese creation myth. According to this account, which had acquired its present form by 300CE, Pan Gu was the offspring of the Yin and Yang, the two fundamental forces of the universe. He came into existence within a great cosmic egg, where he grew for 18,000 years, until the egg hatched. The dark heavy parts of the egg sank to become the earth, while the light translucent parts rose to become the skies. Pan Gu grew taller and pushed the earth and sky farther apart by ten feet (three metres) a day until finally, after another 18,000 years, they became fixed in their present positions. Exhausted, Pan Gu lay down and died. Wind and cloud sprang from his breath, thunder from his voice, the sun from his left eye, the moon from his right eye, the stars from his hair and whiskers, rain and dew from his sweat. All other natural features arose from the parts of his body.

The cult of Pan Gu still persists in certain parts of southern China.

Panathenaia, The

A great annual festival in honour of the goddess Athene, the most important religious event in the calendar of ancient Athens. At the climax of the festival, sacrifices were made to the goddess and a new robe (*peplos*) was presented to her statue in the Parthenon on the Acropolis. The public re-enactment of myth was an important feature of the Panathenaia.

Pandora

In Greek myth, the first woman. She was created by the Olympian gods to counter the aid given to men by the Titan Prometheus. After Prometheus had stolen fire from the forge of the smith god Hephaistos, Zeus asked Hephaistos to fashion the first woman out of clay.[1] Athene then brought this new creation, Pandora, to life and adorned her with finery. Aphrodite gave her beauty, Apollo taught her to sing and Hermes taught her the art of deceit.

Pandora was given a jar or chest (the so-called "Pandora's Box") and was sent as a wife for Epimetheus, the brother of Prometheus. Ignoring his brother's warning never to accept a gift from the gods, Epimetheus took Pandora into the society of men. Curious to see inside the jar she unstopped it, and in doing so released its contents: all the evils to beset humanity, including toil, sickness and conflict. Hope alone remained in the jar. The myth of Pandora, who was created after men and the cause of many ills, served to justify the inferior position of women in Greek society.

Pandora and Epimetheus were the parents of Pyrrha, who became the wife of Deucalion, and with whom she survived the great flood sent by Zeus.

Pandora's story became the counterpart of Eve's temptation and the Fall of Man, and in *Eva Prima Pandora*

the 16th-century painter Jean Cousin shows Pandora with both an apple and an urn of troubles. Pandora was also portrayed in the 19th century; Rossetti depicted her several times as a troubled beauty holding her casket from which an evil vapour escapes.

Pansy

Fond remembrance, hence its common name "heartsease". The word pansy comes from the French *pensée* ("thought"). Some symbologists have proposed a tortuous link between this and the number five, the number of petals that the flower has. The symbolism of the petals is more plausibly based on their heart-like shape and the "thoughts" of the heart.

Panther *see* Leopard

Pantocrator

The Pantocrator (Greek, "Ruler of All") was the name given to the image of Christ enthroned in majesty, and originated in Byzantine iconography. According to this convention Christ usually looked straight at the viewer, his expression stern. He blesses with his right hand and may hold the Gospel in his left. The influence of this image is seen in the late 13th-century mosaics in the Baptistery, Florence, in which Christ sits in judgment: he draws up those who are chosen with his right hand and with his left hand he condemns the sinful.

Paolo and Francesca

In Dante's *Inferno* (the first part of his epic *Divina Commedia*) Francesca da Rimini tells the poet her story.[1] She was the daughter of a friend of Dante, and married the deformed Gianciotto, son of the lord of Rimini. However,

Pandora: *see* Aphrodite; Athene; Deucalion; Epimetheus; Hermes; HUMANITY, THE ORIGIN OF; Prometheus; Zeus
[1] Hesiod, *Works and Days* 60–142

Pansy: *see* Five; FLOWERS; Heart

Paolo and Francesca: *see* Dante
[1] Dante, *Inferno* V:88–142

Hephaistos forming Pandora, from a vase of the 5th century BCE.

she fell in love with Paolo, her husband's younger brother, and they became lovers. Gianciotto discovered them together and stabbed them to death. Their punishment was to drift for ever on the wind in the second circle of hell. This tragic theme was taken up in the 19th century. In *Paolo and Francesca* Rossetti shows Paolo kissing Francesca as they read together.

Papa

The Maori creator goddess of the earth, the consort of the sky god Rangi and mother of the great gods of the Maori pantheon. Later, when her son Tane, the god of trees, was looking for a mate, he approached his mother first. She refused his advances and advised him to create a wife from the sand of Hawaiki island. This creature, Hine-hau-one ("Earth-created Maiden"), was the first human.

Paradise *see* AFTERLIFE

Parasol

Sovereignty, spiritual dominion, ascension, dignity, wealth, protection – a solar and royal emblem throughout India and Asia. In India the parasol was an attribute of Vishnu and of the Buddha.

On a terrestrial level, the parasol both protected dignitaries from the sun and acted as an elaborate symbol of their high status, its domed top representing the sky, its radiating struts the sun's rays, its shaft the world axis. The same symbolism appears in the parasol-like discs surmounting stupas, representing heavenly spheres. The struts of the parasol also symbolized wheels of energy (*chakras*) in Indian and Tantric Buddhist thought.

Paris

A Trojan prince, the son of King Priam and Queen Hecuba of Troy. While she was pregnant with Paris, Hecuba dreamed that she would bear a firebrand that would destroy the city of Troy. The baby Paris was therefore abandoned at birth on Mount Ida. However, he was suckled by a bear and found by a shepherd, who raised him as his son. In Roman myth he too became a shepherd, and the nymph Oenone fell in love with him. Later, as a handsome young man, he defeated his royal brothers in a boxing match and his identity was revealed by his prophetess sister, Cassandra.

Paris set in motion the events which culminated in the Trojan War when he attended the wedding on Mount Ida of the hero Peleus and the Nereid (sea nymph) Thetis, who later became the parents of the hero Achilles. One goddess, Eris (Strife), was not invited to the wedding, and in revenge she sent to the wedding feast a golden apple addressed simply "For The Fairest". The three great goddesses Aphrodite (in Roman myth Venus), Athene (Minerva) and Hera (Juno) were guests at the nuptials and each of them claimed that the apple was for her.

To settle the dispute, Zeus (Jupiter in Roman myth) asked Paris to choose the fairest goddess.[1] In order to judge them thoroughly, he asked them to undress. Hera told Paris to make Aphrodite take her girdle off as it would bewitch him, and Aphrodite encouraged Athene to remove her helmet. Athene promised the Trojan wisdom and military prowess if he chose her; Hera promised royal power; and Aphrodite promised the most beautiful woman in the world. Paris chose Aphrodite, and in doing so earned

Parrot: *see* Birds

Troy the unending enmity of Athene and Hera.

Paris's reward from Aphrodite was Helen, the beautiful wife of King Menelaus of Sparta who was reputedly the fairest woman in all Greece. Paris visited Sparta and Helen fell in love with him. While Menelaus was absent in Crete the pair eloped back to Troy. Menelaus and the hero Odysseus later visited Troy to request her return, but Paris, despite the misgivings of Hector, refused. All the leading princes of Greece, who had once sworn to uphold the honour of Menelaus, formed a military coalition under his brother Agamemnon, and sailed for Troy.

During the ensuing Greek siege of Troy, Paris faced Menelaus in single combat and was defeated, but before Menelaus could drag him from the field Aphrodite transported him to Helen's chamber. Later, Paris killed the Greek champion, Achilles, not in close combat but by shooting him in the heel (his only vulnerable spot), with a bow and arrow, which was considered a more cowardly

Paris (left) receives the three contending goddesses, who are led by Hermes.

weapon than a sword. Paris was mortally wounded by the Greek archer Philoctetes with a poisoned arrow that had once belonged to the hero Herakles.

In art Paris may be seen with Helen, bewitched by Venus, but the Judgment of Paris, in which he is painted as a shepherd, was a more popular subject, allowing the depiction of three beautiful female nudes. In such treatments, the disastrous outcome of his choice is usually ignored.

Parrot
A messenger or link between humanity and the spirit world, an obvious symbolism in view of its talkativeness. Parrots were associated with prophecy and thought to be rain-makers both in India and Central America. The parrot is also an attribute of the Hindu god of love, Kama. In Chinese folk tales, parrots inform on adulterous wives.

Parthalón

Parthalón

The leader of the second people to invade Ireland, according to the *Book of Invasions*. Parthalón, said to be a mythical descendant of Noah's son Japheth, arrived in Ireland nearly three hundred years after the Biblical Flood with a retinue of four leaders and five thousand followers. They led a settled existence, clearing and making habitable four plains in place of the previous one, rearing cattle, brewing ale, practising crafts and establishing legal surety. The enemies of Parthalón were the monstrous Fomorians, a race descended from Noah's son Ham. In the end Parthalón's people were annihilated, not by the Fomorians, but by plague. Only one man survived, Tuan mac Sdairn.

Partridge

Fecundity, love, feminine beauty. The partridge was associated with the goddess Aphrodite in Greece and with grace and beauty in Indo-Iranian tradition; folk superstition credited its flesh with aphrodisiac qualities. Adverse analogies by early Christian writers, particularly St Jerome, led to the bird being linked in Romanesque iconography with ill-gotten gains, and its cry with the temptations of Satan.

Passion of Christ, The

The Passion (Latin *passio*, "suffering") of Christ follows on directly from the Life of Christ and is described by all four gospels, although not always in exactly the same detail and sequence. In art the scenes are depicted individually as devotional images or as entire narrative cycles. The central episodes have given rise to the "Instruments of the Passion", including the Cross, the column of the Flagellation, Crown of Thorns, the spear or lance and the thirty pieces of silver (paid to Judas for betraying Christ). Other symbols of the Passion include the chalice, cock, dice, the goldfinch, hammer and nails, ladder, lamb, pelican, purple or red robe, red poppy, red rose, reeds, rope, skull, sponge, sword and vinegar.

CHRIST IN JERUSALEM

The narrative usually begins with the **Entry into Jerusalem**, in which Christ, riding on a humble donkey leading a colt, was greeted by a multitude. Some spread their garments in his way, others cut down branches from olive and palm[1] trees, strewed them in his path and praised him. Some artists have also included the story of Zaccheus, who climbed a tree in order to see Christ, and later gave half his goods to the poor; this may have taken place as Christ entered Jericho.[2]

In a famous scene, **Christ Driving the Money Lenders out of the Temple**, Christ is depicted outraged and indignant, expelling the merchants who are trading there illegally.[3]

Christ disputed with the chief priests, and they wished to arrest him but feared the multitude, who viewed him as a prophet. He denounced the Pharisees as hypocrites[4] and foresaw that their temples would be destroyed. They gathered at the house of the high priest, Caiaphas, and plotted Christ's downfall. One of the 12 disciples, Judas Iscariot, went to them and said, "What will ye give me, and I will deliver him unto you?", and they offered him thirty pieces of silver.[5]

THE LAST SUPPER AND BETRAYAL

To celebrate the Passover, Christ gathered the disciples together. At this, the

Last Supper, Christ announced, " 'one of you shall betray me,' and they were exceedingly sorrowful, and began every one of them to say unto Him 'Lord is it I?' " He instigated the sacrament of Holy Communion by blessing the bread and wine, which were thereafter to represent his flesh and blood, sacrificed to redeem humankind.

The Last Supper was an appropriate subject for monastic refectories; the moment usually chosen was the breaking of bread and drinking of wine: the theme of the transubstantiation.[6] However, Leonardo da Vinci's *Last Supper* shows the instant of Christ's announcement of his betrayal and the various emotional reactions of the disciples. After the supper Christ poured water into a basin and began **Washing the Feet of the Disciples**, a humble act against which Peter protested.[7]

Just before his arrest Christ went with the disciples to the Garden of Gethsemane and took Peter, James and John aside, asking them to keep watch while he prayed. However, they fell asleep. Paintings of the **Agony in the Garden** often show the three sleeping disciples, while Christ has a vision of the Chalice of the Eucharist or the Instruments of the Passion; in the middle distance Judas may be seen leading an armed multitude toward Christ. In the **Betrayal of Christ**, Judas went straight up to him and, with the words "Master, Master", gave him the **Kiss of Judas**. In anger, Peter cut off the ear of a servant of the high priest.[8]

The disciples deserted Christ but Peter followed him and sat with the servants of the high priests. Then came the **Denial of Christ**, as Christ had foretold, in which Peter was asked three times if he had been with Christ and denied it three times, saying, "I do not know that man." Thereupon the cock crowed and he remembered the words of Christ's prophecy and wept bitterly.[9] Judas discarded his pieces of silver and hanged himself.[10]

THE TRIAL OF CHRIST

In the **Trial of Christ** Christ was brought before four judges: the high priests, Annas and Caiaphas; Herod, tetrarch of Galilee; and Pontius Pilate, Roman governor of Judea, who examined him twice. Before Caiaphas Christ avowed that he was the Son of God. At this Caiaphas rent his own garments in anger, accused him of blasphemy and condemned him to death. The **Mocking of Christ** followed, in which Pilate's servants spat on his face, buffeted him and hit him with the palms of their hands.[11]

The high priests and elders then took him to Pontius Pilate for trial by Roman civil law.[12] **Before Pilate**, Christ said not a word that could condemn him. He also appeared **Before Herod** (Herod Agrippa, the ruler of Galilee, who was in Jerusalem for Passover). Again he remained silent and was mocked by Herod's soldiers before being returned to Pilate. According to tradition (not supported historically), at Passover Pilate would free a prisoner chosen by the people. He brought Christ to them, saying, **Ecce Homo** ("Behold the man"),[13] and asked them whom they would choose to release: Jesus or the thief Barabbas. According to the gospels, the chief priests incited the crowd to reply, "Barabbas", and they demanded that Christ be crucified. Pilate washed his hands before them, saying "I am innocent of the blood of this righteous man."

Passion of Christ, The

Pilate ordered Christ to be whipped, which has inspired many scenes of the **Flagellation**. Pilate's soldiers then dressed him in a scarlet (or purple) robe, gave him a reed, placed a mock crown on his head and hailed him "King of the Jews" (**Crowning with Thorns**). They spat on him and took the reed and hit him around the head.[14] This scene has sometimes been combined with the Mocking of Christ. John describes it as occurring before the Ecce Homo episode, so in some depictions of the latter, Christ wears the attributes of mock king-ship, such as the Crown of Thorns.

THE CRUCIFIXION, DEPOSITION AND ENTOMBMENT

The **Road to Calvary** (the *Via Dolorosa*) presents Christ carrying the Cross to the place of his **Crucifixion**, accompanied by a great crowd. As they crucified him, he said, "Father forgive them; for they know not what do." Soldiers cast lots for his garments and put a placard above his head that said: "Jesus of Nazareth, King of the Jews" (INRI). Two thieves were crucified with him, a penitent one on his right, an impenitent on his left. The impenitent thief mocked him along with the crowd, but was rebuked by the other, to whom Christ said, "Today thou shalt be with me in paradise."[15]

Among the holy women who watched near the Cross were his mother Mary, Mary Magdalene and Mary, the mother of James and Joseph. John, the disciple most loved by Christ, was also present. All these characters may be seen in depictions of the Crucifixion. Just before he died, a sponge soaked in wine and water was offered to Christ. After-wards a soldier pierced his side; blood and water flowed from the wound.[16]

In scenes of the **Deposition** or **Descent from the Cross** Joseph of Arimathea and the Pharisee Nicodemus are present and minister to him. They are also seen at the **Entombment**, placing Christ's wrapped and anointed body in the sepulchre. After this, Mary Magdalene and another Mary sat and kept vigil by the tomb.[17]

THE RESURRECTION AND ASCENSION

The **Resurrection** of Christ was confirmed by his appearance, first to Mary Magdalene and then to his disciples. On the third day after the Crucifixion the holy women, without the Virgin, went to the tomb and found that the stone had been rolled away. On entering they discovered two angels clothed in brilliant white, who asked, "Why seek ye the living among the dead? He is not here but has risen."[18] Mary Magdalene turned around and saw Christ, but mistook him for a gardener. He revealed himself to her saying, "Touch me not." The Latin version of these words has given the scene its name – *Noli me tangere*. Christ told her to go to the disciples and tell them that he was risen.[19]

That same day two disciples, one Cleopas, the other anonymous, went to the village of Emmaus, and Christ joined them on the journey. They did not recognize him until that evening at supper when he broke the bread and blessed it.[20] The scene is rendered as the **Supper at Emmaus**. As he had commanded, the 11 remaining disciples went to Galilee, and when they saw him they worshipped him. To Thomas, who doubted, he said, "Reach hither thy finger ... and thrust it into my side; and be not faithless, but believing."[21] Thomas reached out and touched Christ's stigmata, and only then was he convinced. This formed the basis for the popular image of **Doubting Thomas**. Christ commanded his disciples to teach all nations and baptize them.

Apart from Luke's brief mention of Christ being carried up to heaven, the following events do not appear in the Gospels but were often included in narrative cycles of the Passion. The **Ascension** occurred forty days after the Resurrection. Christ was with his disciples outside Jerusalem when he was taken up in a cloud, and as they watched, two angels appeared to tell them that they too would be received in heaven.[22]

At **Pentecost**, the apostles were all gathered together when "there came a sound from heaven as of a rushing mighty wind and it filled all the house where they were sitting. ... And they were all filled with the Holy Ghost, and began to speak with other tongues."[23] The **Descent of the Holy Ghost** marks the end of the Passion and the beginning of the Acts of the Apostles and so the establishment of the Christian church.

Passion Flower

The passion flower was probably named in the 16th century by missionaries to southern Africa who likened its composition to the instruments of Christ's Passion: its leaves represent the spear, its tendrils the scourges, its petals the disciples, without Peter and Judas, and its anthers the five wounds. The stem of the ovary was seen as the column of the Cross, or of the Flagellation, the stigmas represented the three nails, and the filaments within the flower were the Crown of Thorns. The 19th-century painter Charles Collins, in *Convent Thoughts*, shows a young nun contemplating the flower.

Patroclus

In Homer's *Iliad* Patroclus is the companion of the Greek hero Achilles, whose place he took against the Trojans when Achilles refused to fight. He was slain by Hector, which stirred Achilles into rejoining the Greek warriors and seeking revenge on Hector. In paintings Patroclus may be seen escorting Briseis, Achilles' concubine, to Agamemnon. Other depictions show the huge funeral pyre built for him by Achilles, as in Jacques-Louis David's *Funeral of Patroclus*.

Paul, Saint (Apostle)

Paul is the most important of the Apostles who spread Christianity to the Gentiles and, with Peter, founded the Church. Images and scenes from their lives often appear paired in painting. Paul (died *c*.67CE) may have a high forehead and a bushy beard, and hold the sword of his martyrdom or a book, the doctrine of his missionary work.

Paul (whose Hebrew name was Saul) was a Greek-speaking Jew with Roman citizenship, before his conversion a strict Pharisee. He witnessed the martyrdom of St Stephen, following which he "made havoc of the church and entered every house, he dragged off men and women and committed them to prison".[1] To continue his persecutions, he travelled to Damascus. On the road there he had a vision: "suddenly there shined round about him a light from heaven; and he fell to the earth and heard a voice saying unto him, 'Saul, Saul, why persecutest thou me?' "[2]

Patroclus: *see* Achilles; Trojan War, The

Paul, Saint: *see* Peter, St; Martyr
[1] *Acts 8:3*
[2] *Acts 9:3–4*
[3] *Acts 13:6–12*
[4] *Acts 14:8–18*
[5] *Acts 17:16–34*
[6] *Acts 28:1–6*

Peace

Peace: *see* Cornucopia;
Dove; Olive *and individual
names*

Blinded, his sight was restored after three days by a disciple who, in a vision, heard Christ say that Saul was "a chosen vessel". Saul was later converted and baptized. In 1621 Caravaggio painted a dramatic picture of the conversion of Paul for the church of Santa Maria del Popolo in Rome.

Paul had to escape by night from his Jewish enemies in Damascus and was lowered over the city wall in a basket. In Jerusalem he met St Peter and the disciples and began his life as a missionary. Raphael's cartoons for tapestries for the Sistine Chapel in Rome show some episodes from the acts of Peter and Paul. For example, Raphael shows how Paul and Barnabas were preaching in Cyprus when they were called by the Roman deputy Sergius Paulus, who wished to hear the word of God. However, the sorcerer Elymas sought to prevent the encounter. Paul struck him blind and Sergius Paulus was converted.[3]

In Lystra Paul and Peter cured a cripple who had never been able to walk, and when the people saw the miracle they believed that the gods had come down in the likeness of men and hailed the apostles as Zeus and Hermes (Jupiter and Mercury). The priest of Zeus brought garlands and an ox to sacrifice, but Paul and Barnabas tore their clothes and, crying out, prevented the sacrifice.[4]

In Athens Paul saw a city devoted to idolatry. He disputed daily in the market, where he encountered philosophers who took him to the tribunal in order to hear his doctrine. Paul's sermons converted some of the crowd, including Dionysius the Areopagite.[5]

In Macedonia Paul was preaching with Silas, when they were flogged

and thrown into prison for exorcizing a demon from a woman. The jailer made their feet fast in the stocks, but at midnight there was a great earthquake and their shackles unlocked and the doors burst open.

At Ephesus, Paul's preaching caused pagans to bring out their books and burn them, but in Jerusalem he was imprisoned by the Roman governor, and after two years he appealed for a trial before the emperor himself in Rome – to which, as a Roman citizen, he was entitled.

Paul was sailing to Rome with other prisoners when they were shipwrecked on Malta. The inhabitants kindled a fire for them against the cold and rain. As Paul gathered sticks and laid them on the fire, a viper came out of the heat and wrapped itself around his hand; Paul shook it off and suffered no harm, and the Maltese took him for a god:[6] Adam Elsheimer set the scene on a stormy night.

Paul's activities in Rome are uncertain, but he is thought to have written his epistles while in prison there. He was believed to have been beheaded at the site of the Tre Fontane in Rome at the same time as St Peter's martyrdom. He is buried on the site where the church of San Paolo Fuori le Mura now stands in Rome.

Peace

A personification of Peace may have a cornucopia, sheaves of corn or garlands of flowers, or be surrounded by the fruits of the bountiful earth which she nurtures. Children also may be nearby. She may be invoked preventatively to illustrate the benefits of peace, but she was also celebrated at the end of war. Peace is also represented in art by a dove carrying an olive sprig or by a winged figure holding an olive branch or wearing an olive wreath, accompanied by a dove. Other symbols of peace include the paired lion and lamb, broken arrows or other weapons, the lyre and other musical instruments, the colour blue, the amethyst, apple, caduceus, calumet, cornucopia, egg, elephant, flower, island, kingfisher, laurel, night, plough, saddle, sapphire, sky, white flag and wings. The sculptor Adrian Jones shows Peace riding in triumph in a *quadriga*, a chariot drawn by four horses harnessed abreast, surmounting the Arch of Wellington at Hyde Park Corner, London (1912).

Peach

One of the most favourable of all Chinese and Japanese symbols, its wood, blossom and fruit linked with immortality, longevity, spring, youth, marriage and protective magic. In Chinese myth, the peach Tree of Immortality, tended by the Queen of Heaven, Xi Wangmu, fruits every 3,000 years. Shou Lao, god of longevity, holds a peach or is depicted within the fruit. Peachwood was used to make miraculous bows, exorcism rods, talismans, oracular figures and effigies of tutelary gods; and peach boughs were laid outside houses at New Year. This apotropaic significance appears in Japan too, as in the story that Izanagi routed eight thunder gods by hurling peaches at them. In both countries, peach blossom is an emblem of purity and virginity. The peach is one of the Three Blessed Fruits of Buddhism.

In Western Renaissance art, a peach with a leaf attached was an emblem of truthfulness – a reference to an ancient use of this image as a symbol of the tongue speaking from the heart.

Peacock

Solar glory, immortality, royalty, incorruptibility, pride. The shimmering majesty of the male peacock's display is the origin of the bird's association with immortality through its link with the sun as an undying entity. In the ancient traditions of India and later in Iran, the wheel-like radiance of this display was a symbol of the "all-seeing" sun and of the eternal cycles of the cosmos. Because snakes were enemies of the sun in Iranian symbolism, the peacock was said to kill them and use their saliva to create the iridescent bronze–greens and blue–gold "eyes" of its tail feathers. To this legend was added the idea that the peacock's flesh was incorruptible. As the fame of the bird spread and it was put on show in the Mediterranean world, it became an emblem not only of rebirth (as in early Christian symbolism) but also of the starry firmament, and therefore of cosmic totality and unity. Unity in duality (the sun at zenith and the full moon) is depicted by the Islamic motif of two facing peacocks beside the Cosmic Tree.

In Classical tradition, the peacock was sacred to the Greek goddess Hera (in Roman myth, Juno), who was said to have bestowed on it the 100 eyes of the slain Argus Panoptes ("all-seeing"). Peacocks were widely held as emblems of royalty, spiritual power and apotheosis. In Rome, the peacock was the soul-bird of the empress and her princesses, as the eagle was of the emperor. The Persian court was the "Peacock Throne", and peacocks are also associated with the thrones of the Hindu god Indra, Amitabha (who presides over the Buddhist Western paradise) and the wings of the cheru-

Peach: *see* Bow; FRUIT; Heart; LONGEVITY; Rod; Tongue; Tree; VIRTUES; Wood

Peacock: *see* Argus; Birds; Chalice; Dance; Eye; Io; Pheasant; SEVEN DEADLY SINS, THE; Snake; Sun; Throne; Tree; Wheel

A peacock; after a medieval Persian painting.

Pear

bim who support the throne of Yahweh. The peacock is the escort or mount of several Hindu deities, notably Sarasvati (of wisdom, music and poetry), Kama (of sexual desire) and the war god Skanda (who could also transform poisons into the elixir of immortality).

As a Buddhist emblem of Avalokiteshvara (Guanyin in China) the peacock represents compassionate watchfulness – and had similar meaning in the Christian church. Peacocks sometimes appear in Christian art at the Nativity or drinking from a chalice – both motifs of eternal life. However, Christian doctrines of humility led to an analogy between the peacock and the sins of pride, luxury and vanity (associations instigated by the *Physiologus*, a 2nd-century-CE naturalist text froom which many medieval bestiaries were later derived).

Although the peacock thus chiefly personifies pride in Western art, most other traditions saw it as a wholly positive symbol of rank and dignity, especially in China. Peacock dances of southeast Asia draw on the original idea of the bird as a solar emblem, its enacted "death" bringing rain.

The peacock's decorative qualities have been much admired and utilized, especially in the Arts and Crafts and Art Nouveau movements.

Pear

A mother or love symbol, its erotic associations probably taken from the swelling shape of the fruit, suggesting the female pelvis or breast. Linked in Classical mythology with the Greek goddesses Hera (in Roman myth, Juno) and Aphrodite (Venus), the pear was also a longevity symbol in China, because the tree itself is long-lived. However, white symbolized mourning in China, and so pear blossom was a funerary token.

Pearl

Among jewels, the quintessential symbol both of light and of femininity – its pale iridescence associated with the luminous moon, its watery origins with fertility, its secret life in the shell with miraculous birth or rebirth. Hidden light also made the pearl a symbol of spiritual wisdom or esoteric knowledge. The pearl is an emblem both of fecundity and of purity, virginity and perfection. To the ancients, the pearl – an image of fire and water unified – was a marvel and a mystery, conjuring up theories of celestial impregnation by rain or by dew falling into the open shell, by thunder and lightning, or by trapped moonlight or starlight. Hence the appearance in Chinese art of the pearl (lightning) in the throat of the dragon (thunder).

As a form of celestial light, the pearl is the third eye (spiritual illumination) of Shiva and of the Buddha. It is the Islamic word of God, the Daoist mystic centre, the Christian "pearl of great price" from the waters of baptism. It is also a metaphor for Christ in the womb of the Virgin Mary. Spiritual symbolism persisted even after the Chinese found a non-celestial explanation for the production of pearls. They formed nacreous Buddhas by placing small metal images inside the freshwater molluscs used to produce cultured blister pearls.

The transfiguration of matter into a "spiritual" jewel made the pearl a widespread symbol of rebirth and led to the expensive Asian funerary custom of placing a pearl in the mouth of the dead, and of pearl-decorated tombs in Egypt. In the afterlife, pearls formed the individual spheres enclosing the Islamic blessed – and the gates of the new Jerusalem (in Revelation). They were thought to be medicinal as well as sacred. The Romans, who wore pearls in homage to Isis, used them as talismans against everything from shark attacks to lunacy, and powdered pearl is still an Indian panacea.

The sexual symbolism of the pearl is ambivalent. In classical tradition it was worn by the foam-born love-goddess Aphrodite (in Roman myth, Venus). Yet it is also a symbol of purity and innocence. Its association with tears (of sorrow and of joy) made it an unlucky bridal jewel – a broken pearl necklace was particularly ominous. Yet it was a propitious jewel in the East – one of the Eight Jewels of China and Three Imperial Insignia of Japan. In the ancient world, pearls were also, of course, straightforward symbols of wealth. Cleopatra reputedly dropped a pearl earring in her wine and drank it to show Antony how rich she was.

Pegasus

A winged horse, the offspring of the Greek god Poseidon and the Gorgon Medusa. When the hero Perseus cut off Medusa's head, Pegasus sprang from her blood. According to one account Perseus then flew on Pegasus to rescue the beautiful princess Andromeda from a sea dragon. However, it was more usually said that Pegasus had remained wild until the Corinthian prince Bellerophon tamed him after performing rites in honour of Athene and Poseidon.

Bellerophon later rode on Pegasus to kill the Chimera, a monster that infested the land of Lycia. However,

Pegasus, after a Greek dish painting.

when Bellerophon subsequently tried to fly on Pegasus to the peak of Mount Olympus, the home of the gods and goddesses, Zeus was angered by his presumption and sent a gadfly to sting his mount on the backside. Pegasus reared and threw Bellerophon to earth, crippling the errant hero for life. In some accounts, Pegasus itself was welcomed to Mount Olympus.

Pelasgus

The first man, according to one Greek account of creation. Pelasgus is said to have risen from the soil of Arcadia in the central Peloponnese. He founded the race of Pelasgians, who were an ancient non-Greek people who still inhabited some villages as late as *c*.450BCE.

Peleus *see* **Achilles**

Pelias

In Greek myth, a king of Iolcus in northern Greece, the son of the god Poseidon and a mortal, Tyro, and the uncle of the hero Jason. Pelias overthrew his half-brother, King Aeson, and sent Aeson's son, Jason, on a mission to retrieve the Golden Fleece

Pegasus: *see* Andromeda; Athene; Bellerophon; Chimera; Gorgons, The; Medusa; Muses, The; Perseus; Poseidon

Pelasgus: *see* HUMANITY, THE ORIGIN OF

Pelias: *see* Alcestis; Jason; Medea

of Colchis. Jason returned to find that Pelias had put Aeson to death. But Medea, Jason's sorceress wife, revived Aeson and then convinced Pelias and his daughters that if they cut him up and cooked his body he would become a young man again. One daughter, Alcestis, loved her father too much to contemplate harming him, regardless of the motive. Two other daughters, Evadne and Amphinome, carried out the deed – only to discover that Medea had tricked them into brutally murdering their father.

Pelican

Self-sacrificing love – a symbolism based on an old legend that pelicans tore their breasts to draw blood to feed their young. The earliest Christian bestiary drew an analogy between the pelican's reviving its young with its blood and Christ's shedding his blood for humankind. The pelican sometimes appears in Crucifixion paintings with this meaning, and can represent Charity in still lifes and filial devotion in heraldry. It represents Christ's human nature when paired with the phoenix.

PELOPS, THE CURSE OF THE HOUSE OF *see panel opposite*

Penates, The

The Roman household gods of the larder or storehouse (*penus*). The Penates, who usually operated in pairs, were said to look after the sustenance of the family. Their images were offered food before meals and their altars were maintained near that of the hearth goddess Vesta. In Rome there was a shrine in honour of the Penates of the Roman state.

Penelope

In Greek myth, the queen of Ithaca, daugher of King Icarius of Sparta and the naiad (water nymph) Periboea. A symbol of conjugal devotion, she was the wife of the hero Odysseus (Ulysses), remaining faithful to him throughout his twenty-year absence, at the Trojan War and on his long voyage home. Believing him dead, many suitors came to Ithaca to press for her hand, and she claimed that she would marry as soon as she had finished weaving a shroud for Laertes, her father-in-law. True to her husband she span by day and unpicked her work by night, fooling the suitors for three years. Odysseus at last returned and the couple were reunited.

In art Penelope is seen weaving, often at a loom with handmaids and

Penelope pining for Odysseus; after a Roman copy of a Greek statue.

A pelican; after a woodcarving on a tabernacle (in a church, a container for the sacred Host).

PELOPS, THE CURSE OF THE HOUSE OF

In Greek myth, a curse afflicted many of the descendents of King Pelops, a powerful monarch of much of the Peloponnese, which was said to have been named after him (literally "Isle of Pelops"). Pelops was the son of King Tantalus of Lydia, himself the victim of a famous curse, and Pelops' descendents, known as the Pelopids, were involved in the most notorious and bloody family feud to be found in Greek mythology.

Pelops was one of several suitors of Hippodameia, the daughter of King Oenomaus of Pisa in Elis. In order to find her a suitable husband, Hippodameia was required to accompany each suitor in a chariot race against Oenomaus. If victorious the suitor would win her hand. Despite the fact that he gave his opponents a head start, Oenomaus' own horses were a gift of the gods and he easily beat the suitors each time, whereupon he killed them with his spear.

According to one account, Pelops promised Oenomaus's charioteer Myrtilus (a son of the god Hermes), that he could spend a night with Hippodameia if he betrayed the king. Myrtilus replaced his master's axle pins with wax ones. During the race against Pelops, Oenomaus was closing on his rival when his chariot collapsed and he was killed in the tangled wreckage. As Oenomaus died he cursed Myrtilus to die at the hands of Pelops.

As was his right, Pelops married Hippodameia. During a chariot ride on the wedding night, Myrtilus claimed his reward from Pelops, who responded by hurling him into the sea. As he drowned, Myrtilus cursed Pelops and his descendants.

Pelops became king of Pisa and later of all Elis, Arcadia and other areas of the Peloponnese. He died with a reputation for piety, wisdom and wealth. The foundation of the Olympic Games at Olympia in Elis was sometimes attributed to him. He was said, in some sources, to have atoned for killing Myrtilus by building a temple to Hermes.

The curse on Pelops fell more heavily on his children. Two of his sons, Atreus and Thyestes, vied for the throne of Argos (or Mycenae). Atreus was successful, and in revenge Thyestes seduced Atreus' wife Aërope. Atreus put Aërope to death and invited his brother to a feast, at which he served him up some of his own children. When Thyestes discovered what he had eaten, he fled in horror and vowed revenge.

The oracle at Delphi told Thyestes to have a son by his own daughter. He assumed a disguise and raped his daughter Pelopia. He fled at once, losing his sword as he did so. Shortly afterwards, Atreus fell in love with Pelopia and married her. When she bore Thyestes' son, Aegisthus, Atreus assumed the child was his and raised him in his own palace.

Seven years later, Atreus sent his sons Agamemnon and Menelaus to fetch Thyestes back to Argos. He was flung into prison and Atreus ordered the boy Aegisthus to kill him as he slept. Thyestes woke just in time and recognized his own sword in the boy's hand. He realized that this was his son, who had received the sword from his mother. He sent Aegisthus to fetch Pelopia, who stabbed herself as soon as he told her that he, Thyestes, had raped her and fathered her child. On Thyestes' orders Aegisthus then assassinated Atreus and Thyestes became king of Argos.

With the aid of King Tyndareos of Sparta, Agamemnon later expelled Thyestes (who died in exile on Cythera) and regained the throne of Argos. Menelaus then succeeded Tyndareos at Sparta. Agamemnon and Menelaus were both betrayed by their wives, Clytemnestra and Helen. Helen eloped with Paris of Troy, an event which sparked off the Trojan War. During her husband's absence at the war, Clytemnestra became the lover of Aegisthus and conspired with him to assassinate Agamemnon on his return from Troy. She and Aegisthus were subsequently killed by Orestes, who was her son by Agamemnon.

The curse of Myrtilus finally ended when the elders of Athens, persuaded by the goddess Athene, exonerated Orestes of the crime of matricide, on the grounds that in having killed Clytemnestra he had avenged the even greater crime of parricide.

servants – for example in Giovanni Stradano's depiction of the theme in the Palazzo Vecchio, Florence.

Pentacle, Pentagram

A geometric symbol of harmony, health and mystic powers – a five-pointed star with lines that cross to each point. When used in magic rituals, this sign is usually called the pentacle. The pentagram seems to have originated in Mesopotamia 4,000 years ago, probably as an astronomical plot of the movements of the planet Venus. It became a Sumerian and Egyptian stellar sign, is thought to have been the figure used on the seal of King Solomon of Israel (although the hexagram is also proposed). In Greece, the Pythagoreans adopted it as an emblem of health and mystic harmony, the marriage of heaven and earth, combining the number two (terrestrial and feminine) with three (heavenly and masculine). The resulting number five symbolized the microcosm of the human body and mind.

From this point on, the pentagram steadily acquired mystic meaning. Gnostics and alchemists associated it with the five elements, Christians with the protective five wounds of Christ, medieval sorcerers with Solomon's reputed powers over nature and the spirit world.

Magicians sometimes wore pentacle caps of fine linen to conjure up supernatural help. In casting spells, special powers were credited to pentacles drawn on virgin calfskin, but they were also protectively inscribed in wood, on rocks and on amulets or rings. Goethe's Dr Faust draws a pentacle to prevent Mephistopheles from crossing his doorway. With one point upward and two down, the pentacle

The mystic pentagram or pentacle – a five-pointed star also known as the "Seal of Solomon".

was the sign of white magic, the "Druid's foot". With one down and two up, it represented the "Goat's foot" and horns of the Devil – a characteristic symbolic inversion. Latin or Cabbalistic Hebrew lettering often appears on talismanic pentacles drawn within protective circles. The pentacle was also a Masonic aspirational symbol, the "flaming star".

Penthesilea

In Greek myth, a queen of the Amazons, the daughter of the war god Ares and the Amazon queen Otrere. Penthesilea and her comrades fought on the side of Troy during the Trojan War. During the conflict she was slain by the Greek hero Achilles. However, as she died the pair fell in love.

Pentheus

In Greek myth, a king of Thebes, the son of Echion, one of the Spartoi or "Sown Men", and of Agave, the daughter of Cadmus, the first king of Thebes. Pentheus figures in a celebrated myth which concerns the worship of the god Dionysos (Bacchus). He learned that all the women of Thebes had left the city and gone into the hills, following ecstatically in the wake of an "Eastern Stranger" claiming to bring the new cult of Dionysos. The stranger (in fact Dionysos in disguise) was captured on Pentheus' orders, but he easily escaped. He persuaded Pentheus to go into the hills and spy on the orgiastic revels of the maenads or Bacchants (female followers of Dionysos). But Pentheus was spotted by the women, who in their Dionysiac frenzy mistook him for a lion and, led by his mother Agave, tore him to pieces.

Peony

An imperial flower of China, associated with wealth, glory and dignity because of its showy beauty. It was a Japanese fertility symbol, linked with joy and marriage. In the West its roots, seeds and flowers had an ancient medicinal reputation, hence its name, taken from the Greek word for "physician" and from the Paeon who healed those of the gods who had been wounded at Troy. The peony is sometimes identified as the "rose without a thorn".

Persephone

A Greek fertility goddess and the queen of the underworld. Persephone (Proserpina to the Romans) was the daughter of Zeus and his sister, the fertility goddess Demeter, and was often referred to simply as Kore (meaning "Maiden"). One day, Persephone was in a field picking flowers with the Oceanids (sea nymphs). Suddenly, on a rare visit to the living world, the god Hades, ruler of the underworld, abducted her in his chariot and returned with her to his kingdom. Bernini's statue *The Rape of Proser-*

pina in the Borghese Gallery, Rome, captures the horror of the abduction. Zeus had agreed to allow him to marry Persephone and make her his queen.

Furious at the kidnap of her daughter, Demeter left Mount Olympus and searched everywhere for Persephone. In the end she stopped the crops from growing, threatening humanity with famine unless Persephone returned. Zeus eventually gave way and sent the god Hermes to escort Persephone from the underworld. Before she left, Hades induced her to eat some pomegranate seeds. Demeter welcomed her daughter joyfully, but warned her that if she had consumed the food of the underworld she must return to Hades for ever. Persephone remembered the pomegranate seeds, but Zeus declared a compromise: Persephone would spend two-thirds of the year with her mother and the remaining third with Hades.

Persephone and Demeter were the focus of the Eleusinian Mysteries, a famous cult based at Eleusis near Athens. Unusually, the cult was open to all: men, women and even slaves were among its initiates, who were attracted by the promise of a special afterlife in the underworld.

Perses *see* **Perseus**

Perseus

A great Greek hero, the son of the god Zeus (in Roman myth, Jupiter) and his mortal lover Danaë, the daughter of King Acrisius of Argos. An oracle warned Acrisius that a son of Danaë would kill him, so he locked her in a bronze tower or dungeon. However, the god Zeus entered her room in the form of a shower of gold and had intercourse with her. Their child was Perseus, whom Danaë con-

Peony: *see* FLOWERS; Rose

Persephone: *see* Demeter; Hades; Hermes; ZEUS, THE CONSORTS OF
¹ Ovid, *Met V 346–571*

Perseus: *see* Danaë; Medusa; Pegasus; ZEUS, THE CONSORTS OF
¹ Ovid, *Met V 1–249*

Persephone with Hades in the underworld, from a red-figure vase.

Perseus escaping with Medusa's head in his bag. From a water-jar of the 5th century BCE.

cealed for four years. Discovering the truth, Acrisius locked his daughter and grandson in a chest and hurled it into the sea. They were saved by a fisherman, Dictys, whose brother, Polydectes, ruled the isle of Seriphos.

Perseus then lived and grew to manhood on Seriphos. Polydectes fell in love with Danaë, but she refused his advances. To be rid of Perseus, who was her protector, Polydectes sent him on a seemingly impossible mission: to bring back the head of the Gorgon Medusa, a monster whose stare turned living creatures instantly to stone. With Perseus gone, Polydectes locked Danaë in a chamber and refused her food until she agreed to marry him.

Perseus was aided on his mission by the god Hermes (in Roman myth, Mercury) and goddess Athene (Minerva). Paris Bordone illustrates the scene in *Perseus Armed by Mercury and Minerva*. Three monstrous hags, the Graeae, directed him to their sisters, the Gorgons, but told him to go first to certain nymphs who would give him winged sandals, a "cap of darkness" (a cloak to render him invisible) and a leather bag in which to carry the head. Hermes gave the hero a curved sword and he proceeded to Medusa's lair. In order to avoid looking on her directly

Perseus watched her reflection in his shield (or, in some accounts, Athene guided his hand while he looked away). He struck off her head and put it in the bag. From her blood sprang the winged horse Pegasus.

As Perseus flew home with Medusa's head, drops of her blood scattered on the earth and became deadly serpents. On the way, Perseus spotted a beautiful girl chained to a rock and immediately fell in love with her. She was Andromeda, a princess of "Ethiopia" (Joppa in Palestine), who was to be sacrificed to a sea-monster sent by the sea god Poseidon (Neptune) after her mother Cassiopeia had boasted that she was more beautiful than the Nereids.

Perseus vanquished the monster, and a luxurious wedding banquet was prepared for the couple. At this event a riotous mob entered the palace, led by Phineus,[1] Andromeda's suitor, who had come to avenge the theft of his bride. A furious fight ensued, at the end of which Perseus held up Medusa's head and turned Phineus and his men to stone. Since the Renaissance, scenes of Perseus rescuing Andromeda have been popular, exemplified by Piero di Cosimo and Joachim Wtewael. Another scene represented is the fight at the wedding, as in Luca Giordano's *Phineus and his Followers Turned to Stone*. Perseus also used the Gorgon's head to turn Atlas to stone, thus creating the Atlas Mountains in Morocco.

On returning to Seriphos, the hero promptly revealed Medusa's head to Polydectes and his supporters, turning them to stone. He rescued Danaë and went with her back to Argos. Acrisius, who remembered the old oracle, fled to Larissa in Thessaly. One day Perseus attended games in the same city and accidentally struck Acrisius with a discus, fulfilling the prophecy. Perseus became king of Argos but, because he was the murderer of its former monarch, chose instead to rule Tiryns. He did so for many years, founding many cities. The several children of Perseus and Andromeda includedPerseus. He was raised by his grandparents, Cepheus and Cassiopeia, and became a great conqueror. He was said to have given his name to Persia.

Perun

The ancient eastern Slavic god of thunder, lightning and warfare. His statue stood in shrines at Kiev, the first city of Russia (modern Ukraine) and Novgorod, the second city. In the late 10th century, Perun began to replace Rod, who represented light, fertility and creation, among aristocratic worshippers. Traces of the cult of Perun havebeen detected among the western Slavs. His name in Polish, Piorun, is also the word for thunder.

Peter, Saint (Apostle, Disciple)

Peter (died *c.*64CE), the "Prince of the Apostles", held a unique position among the disciples of Christ, and in painting he stands in the favoured place on Christ's right. Peter was missionary to the Jews, as St Paul was to the Gentiles, and both were founders of the church. Like many other Jews of the time, he had a Greek name (Peter) in addition to a Hebrew one (Simon). Peter (Petros) is from Greek *petra*, rock: Christ said "thou art Peter, and upon this rock I will build my church; and the gates of hell shall not prevail against it. And I will give thee the keys of the kingdom of heaven".[1] After the Resurrection, Christ appeared to St Peter and instructed

him to "feed my sheep".[2] His unique position was confirmed when Christ agreed to let him walk upon the water.

Peter is considered in Roman Catholic tradition to have been the first bishop of Rome, hence the "Apostolic Succession" of the popes, who inherited his office. He is represented as a vigorous elderly man with curly white hair and beard, and he often wears a golden-yellow cloak over green or blue. His most common attribute is a pair of keys.

Peter appears frequently in the gospels. He was present at the Transfiguration and the Agony in the Garden, and he is painted in numerous scenes of the Life and Passion of Christ. He was one of the first to be called: "and Jesus, walking by the sea of Galilee, saw two brethren, Simon called Peter, and Andrew, casting a net into the sea; for they were fishers. And he said unto them, Follow me, and I will make you fishers of men. And they straightway left their nets and followed him."[3]

Reference to Peter's future missionary work was also made during the episode known as the Miraculous Draught of Fishes. Christ asked Peter to take him on board so that he could preach to the multitude gathered on the shore. Peter informed him that, although they had toiled all night, they had caught nothing; and Christ told him to cast their nets out into the deep water once more. They caught so many fish that their nets began to break, and Christ said, "fear not; from henceforth thou shalt catch men".[4] As the cartoon by Raphael shows, Peter fell to his knees, as this was the moment when he recognized Christ as the Messiah. As part of a cycle of the Life of St Peter, Masaccio

Perun: *see* Rod

Peter, Saint: *see* Christ, The Life of; Martyrs; Passion of Christ, The; Paul, St
[1] *Matthew 16:18–19*
[2] *John 21:16*
[3] *Matthew 4:18–20*
[4] *Luke 5:1–10*

Peter Martyr, Saint

frescoed the episode of the Tribute Money (Brancacci Chapel, Santa Maria del Carmine, Florence). At Capernaum the tax-gatherer asked Peter if Christ had paid the tribute money. Christ told Peter to cast his line into the sea: the first fish he hooked would have a coin in its mouth to pay the tax.⁵

Before the Last Supper, Peter was reluctant to let Jesus wash his feet. At Christ's arrest he cut the ear off one of the servants in the crowd. As Jesus had predicted, he denied knowing Christ three times that same night, before the cock crowed.⁶

After the Ascension, Peter was an active missionary, preacher and performer of miracles: "they brought forth the sick into the streets and laid them on beds and couches";⁷ and the very shadow of the saint passing by cured them. In Jerusalem, with St John, he healed a cripple at the gate of the Temple,⁸ and they persuaded the rich to sell their land and give the proceeds to the poor. Ananias and his wife Sapphira, however, kept back part of the money, for which Peter struck them dead.⁹ At Joppa he performed a miracle by raising Tabitha from the dead, a woman "full of good works and almsdeeds".¹⁰ During the persecutions of Herod, Peter was thrown into prison. Raphael's fresco in the Stanza d'Eliodoro in the Vatican, illustrates how an angel put the guards to sleep, the chains fell from Peter's hands, and he was led to freedom.¹¹

Tradition claims that Peter went to Rome, where he met Paul and organized the first Christian community. Apocryphal legend¹² tells of how the sorcerer Simon Magus followed him, and his black arts won favour with the emperor Nero. Simon boasted that he

could raise the dead and could fly from the top of a tall tower; the painter Solimena shows him tumbling to his death (San Paolo Maggiore, Naples). Nero then ordered Peter's arrest, but the apostle converted his jailers and was set free, whereupon his followers begged him to flee.

As Peter was walking out of Rome on the Appian Way, Christ appeared, burdened with his cross. Peter asked Domine, quo vadis? ("Lord, where goest thou?"), to which Christ replied "To Rome, to be crucified again." Annibale Carracci shows the surprised saint with Christ pointing the way. Peter returned to Rome, where he was arrested and imprisoned. As portrayed by Michelangelo, legend has it that he insisted on being crucified upside down, to differentiate himself from Christ. He was buried in the Christian catacombs directly below the site of the dome of St Peter's.

Peter Martyr, Saint

Peter (1205–52) heard St Dominic preach and joined his Order, himself becoming an outstanding preacher. He became Inquisitor General and vigorously suppressed heresy, but he made enemies as a result of this. As Giovanni Bellini shows, he was assassinated along with a friar who accompanied him on his way from Como to Milan.¹ An important saint for the Dominicans, Peter Martyr wears the black and white habit of the order and often has an open wound in his head, or a knife in his skull, as depicted by Cima da Conegliano (Brera, Milan).

Phaedra

In Greek myth, a queen of Athens, the daughter of King Minos and Queen Pasiphaë of Crete, the sister of

Ariadne, and the second wife of the hero Theseus. Hippolytus, the son of Theseus and his Amazon wife Antiope, followed the goddess Artemis and preferred hunting to amour. He thereby offended the love goddess Aphrodite, who in revenge made Phaedra fall in love with him. She tried to hide her passion for her stepson, but her nurse revealed it and he fled in revulsion. Phaedra committed suicide but left a note in which she accused Hippolytus of raping her. Theseus discovered this note and invoked a curse on Hippolytus. When his son rode along the seashore in his chariot, a sea dragon suddenly sprang from the waves causing his horses to bolt, and drag him to his death.

Phaethon

The son of the Greek sun god Helios (Phoebus in Roman myth) and the Oceanid (sea nymph) Clymene. When Helios promised to grant his son any request, Phaethon (also spelled Phaeton) asked to drive his father's chariot of the sun for a day. Helios reluctantly agreed, knowing that this was a foolhardy venture because only he could control the fiery steeds, illustrated by Poussin in *Apollo and the Chariot of Phaethon*.

Dawn turned the sky pink, the stars fled, and Phaethon leaped eagerly into the chariot. He drove near the constellation of Scorpio and its menacing tail frightened him so much that he dropped the reins. The horses bolted and plunged so near the earth that it caught fire, woods blazed and springs dried up. At one point he drove the sun chariot so close to the ground that the people there were scorched black (and this was why some nations had dark skins). The earth cried out for

help to Zeus (in Roman myth, Jupiter), who hurled a thunderbolt at Phaethon and dashed him from the chariot. Phaethon fell headlong into a river, and his charred body was buried by nymphs. His mother and his friend Cygnus mourned him and his sisters flung themselves on his tomb. They were turned into trees and their tears, hardened by the sun, became amber.

A theme of human pride and folly, the Fall of Phaethon was popular in Baroque art and was a suitable subject for ceilings, as in Sebastiano Ricci's *The Fall of Phaethon* (Palazzo Fulcis Bertoldi, Belluno).

Phallus

Creation, generative force, the source of life – a solar and active fertility symbol widely believed to be protective and lucky. Overscale erect phalluses in art were often more symbolic than erotic. Figures of Priapus, the hideous but enormously–phallused (hence "priapic") son of the god Dionysos (Bacchus, in Roman myth) and goddess Aphrodite (Venus) were placed in Greek and Roman gardens, vineyards and orchards to encourage growth and scare off thieves as well as crows with his red-painted phallus. Many upright or penetrative objects used as symbols in the ancient world had phallic significance. Phallic funerary objects symbolized the continuity of life after death. Phallic-shaped talismans were popular with farmers and fishermen, and were also used as charms against sterility.

Pheasant

An imperial and Yang emblem in China, associated by its beauty and colour with the sun, light, virtue and the organizing ability of high-ranking

Phaethon: *see* Swan; Zeus
Ovid, *Met I: 747–779; II: 1–400*

Phallus: *see* Head; Lingam; Man; Omphalos; Pillar; Rod

Pheasant: *see* Birds; Peacock; Phoenix; Sun; Thunder

civil servants. The Chinese also linked it with thunder, presumably from its clapping wings. In Japan it was a messenger of the great sun-goddess Amaterasu. The Chinese pheasant and Indian peacock (members of the same family) were exotic birds in ancient Europe, and their shining plumage may have influenced artistic depictions of the fabled phoenix.

Philemon and Baucis

In mythology¹ Zeus and Hermes (in Roman myth, Jupiter and Mercury) disguised themselves as mortals to observe good and evil in humankind.¹ In the hills of Phrygia they looked for somewhere to rest, but were turned away from a thousand homes until they came to the tiny cottage of the elderly Philemon and his wife Baucis. This couple treated their guests with kindness, and were amazed to find that their flagon of wine refilled itself. They had a single goose, which they wanted to kill in honour of their guests, but the bird took refuge with the travellers.

The gods then revealed themselves and announced that they would destroy the inhospitable land. Philemon and Baucis climbed up a steep mountain with them and watched their country drown in marshy waters. Their home, however, was turned into a temple with marble columns and a golden roof. They asked to serve as priests at the shrine of the gods and requested that, when their time came to die, they should do so together. Both wishes were granted and they were turned into trees growing side by side. Artists have focused on the hospitality of the old couple, and have shown the gods sitting at

table and the goose being chased or standing nearby, as in *Philemon and Baucis* by a painter of the School of Rubens.

Philip, Saint (Apostle, Disciple)

Philip (died *c.*80AD) appears rarely in the gospels. He doubted that Christ could feed five thousand people with only five loaves of bread and five fishes,¹ and he may be shown holding the loaves or in close proximity to them. At the Last Supper, Philip asked Christ to "show us the Father", and Christ replied "I am in the Father and the Father in me." Philip was present at the gathering of the disciples after the Ascension.² Details of his later life are unknown, but legend³ tells that he preached to the pagans of Hierapolis who thrust him in front of a statue of the god Mars and ordered him to make a sacrifice. Filippino Lippi illustrates Philip vanquishing a dragon that emerged from the base of the statue. The infuriated crowd seized Philip and nailed him to a cross.

Philip of Neri, Saint

Known as the "Apostle of Rome", Philip (1515–95) was an important figure in the Counter Reformation. Aged 18, he abandoned his father's business to study philosophy and theology in Rome, where he founded a brotherhood of laymen, known as the Oratorians, to look after pilgrims and the sick. In recognition, the pope granted him the church in Rome, which he rebuilt as the Chiesa Nuova. Philip of Neri is shown as an Oratorian in black with a biretta, sometimes in the company of his friend St Carlo Borromeo. However, Piazzetta shows the saint with a vision of the Virgin and Child: he is wearing a bishop's mitre and cardinal's hat, honours that he rejected in his life (Santa Maria della Fava, Venice).

Philosopher's Stone

The key to spiritual enlightenment. In the physical processes of alchemy, the "stone" was a mysterious substance which, once created, could be used as a powder or tincture at the final stage of the Great Work to turn base metals into gold. Symbolism based on this belief made the Philosopher's Stone the elixir of life, the Grail itself – the spiritual wholeness that human beings strive to find.

Philosophy

Philosophy was praised as the highest intellectual pursuit because it investigated through reasoned argument and was concerned with the cause and nature of things. Through the application of wisdom, truth and knowledge, it gave rise to true judgment. Philosophy may be personified as a woman enthroned with a book or represented by the great philosophers of antiquity.

Phineus

In Greek myth, a Thracian king and prophet. According to one account, Phineus blinded his two sons after their stepmother Idaea falsely accused them of attempting to seduce her. In punishment, the god Zeus offered him death or loss of sight and Phineus chose the latter. However, his decision to live in darkness offended the sun god Helios, who sent the Harpies, monsters with the faces of hags and the claws and bodies of birds, to plague him by constantly snatching his food or defecating on it. Phineus nearly died of starvation before being rescued by two of the Argonauts, Calais and Zetes.

Phlegethon

"River of Fire", one of the five rivers of the underworld, also known as the Puriphlegethon. The river was said to consist of liquid fire.

Phocion

The Athenian general Phocion (died *c.*318BCE) led a virtuous life of self-control, modesty and patriotism.[1] He was accused of treason, however, and was forced to take a dose of the deadly poison hemlock. As a posthumous humiliation he was not allowed to be buried in Athens. Poussin depicts the scene in *A Landscape with the Body of Phocion Carried Out of Athens*; a pendant picture shows his wife gathering his ashes and taking them back to Athens for an honourable burial.

Phoenix

One of the most famous of all rebirth symbols – a legendary bird that endessly renews itself in fire.[1] The phoenix legend had its origin in the city of Heliopolis, ancient centre of Egyptian sun worship, where sacrifices were made to the heron-like Benu Bird as the creative spirit of the sun. Based on these fire rituals and on descriptions of gorgeous exotic birds such as the golden pheasant, Greek writers wove stories which vary in detail but have an overall coherence. The phoenix (a Greek word that may derive from Benu) was a unique male bird of miraculous longevity – 500 years, or more by some accounts. At the end of this period, the phoenix built an aromatic nest, immolated itself, was reborn after three days, and carried the nest and ashes of its previous incarnation to the altar of the sun in Heliopolis.

Philosopher's stone: *see* Alchemy; Gold; Grail

Phineus: *see* ARGONAUTS, THE VOYAGE OF THE; Calais and Zetes; Harpy; Helios

Phlegethon: *see* Acheron; Cocytus; Hades; Lethe; Styx

Phocion:
[1] Plutarch, *Lives, Phocion*

Phoenix: *see* Alchemy; BEASTS OF FABLE; Birds; Eagle; Fire, Flame; Heron; LONGEVITY; Palm; Pelican; Pheasant; Ra; Red; Salamander; Sulphur; Sun
[1] Pliny the Elder, *Natural History X:3*

A representation of the Philosopher's Stone, after a 17th-century alchemical manual.

*The phoenix rising from the ashes,
after a 14th-century herbal.*

Initially a symbol of the cyclic disappearance and reappearance of the sun, the phoenix soon became an emblem of human resurrection – and eventually of the indomitable human spirit in overcoming trials. Because artists were never quite sure what it looked like, its iconography is easily confused with the general solar (and soul) symbolism of other birds – especially with the eagle released from the pyre of a Roman emperor.

On Roman coins the phoenix symbolized the undying empire. It appears in early Christian funerary sculpture as a symbol of Christ's resurrection and the hope of victory over death. In medieval paintings the bird represents the divine nature of Christ when paired with the pelican (a symbol of his human nature). The phoenix can also appear as an attribute of Charity. A common motif in alchemy, it symbolizes the purifying and transforming fire, the chemical element sulphur, and the colour red. A Jewish legend attributed the bird's longevity to its refusal to eat the forbidden fruit of paradise.

Analogies are sometimes made between the phoenix and other fabled birds. These include the Persian Simurgh, the Chinese Feng-huang (a symbol of conjugal interdependence) and the Central American Quetzal bird. Only the Simurgh shares enough of the phoenix's symbolism to suggest that the two myths might have enriched one another. There are closer links with Arabic legends of the salamander that lives in fire.

Phrygian cap

A conical cap of soft felt which became an emblem of liberty during the French Revolution – as in Delacroix's painting *Liberty Leading the People* (1830). This style of cap was worn in ancient times by the freemen of Phrygia in Asia Minor under the reign of Midas. It was also worn by Persians and Trojans.

In art, the youth Paris can be shown wearing it – perhaps a reference to the phallic significance of its pointed cone. Traditionally the cap was red, suggesting sacrificial symbolism, aptly so in the French Revolution.

Pig

Gluttony, selfishness, lust, obstinacy and ignorance – but also motherhood, fertility, prosperity and happiness. The affectionate view of pigs in much myth contrasts with their generally negative symbolism in world religious traditions. In earlier cultures, sows were venerated as Great Mother emblems of fecundity. The Egyptian sky-goddess Nut was sometimes depicted as a sow suckling her piglets (the stars). The sow was linked also with Isis and with mother goddesses in Mesopotamia, Scandinavia and the Celtic world, where Ceridwen was a sow goddess. The Celtic legend of Manannan, who had a herd of miraculously self-renewing pigs, expressed a general symbolism of abundance.

In some accounts of Greek myth a sow nourished the infant Zeus (in Roman myth, Jupiter), and pigs were prestigious fertility sacrifices, offered to the agricultural deities Demeter (Ceres), Ares (Mars) and Gaia. The pig was also a fertility (and virility) symbol in China.

Jewish and Islamic distrust of eating scavengers' meat changed all this. According to the Old Testament, God told Moses and Aaron to "speak unto the children of Israel, saying: These are the beasts which ye shall eat among all the beasts that are on the earth." The meat of the pig was not included as it was deemed unclean.[1]

There is also a more general associations between pigs and animal passions (as in the Greek myth of Circe who turned her suitors into pigs). In Western art the pig symbolizes Gluttony and Lust (spurned by the figure of Chastity) as well as Sloth. The gospel story of how Christ cast out demons into the Gadarene swine[2] symbolized the need for humanity to sublimate its sensual greed. A similar theme appears in Buddhism where the pig, symbolizing ignorance, is one of the three animals that tie humankind to the endless wheel of birth, death and rebirth.

Pigeon see Dove

Pilgrimage

A journey to a spiritual centre, symbolizing trial, expiation or purification, and the achievement of a goal or ascension to a new plane of existence. In an emblematic sense, the pilgrimage is as much an initiation as an act of devotion. Its rationale is the ancient belief that supernatural forces manifest themselves most powerfully at particular localities. In the Islamic faith, the location is Mecca, birthplace of the Prophet. In Hinduism it is Benares on the Ganges. For Buddhists and Christians it is key sites in the life of the Buddha and Christ.

In the early 13th century the Inquisition imposed pilgrimages as a punishment upon penitent heretics, who were expected to return with evidence that they had reached their destination. In the Middle Ages the principal places of pilgrimage were the Holy Land, Rome and Santiago de Compostela. Pilgrims would bring back a Cross and palm from the Holy Land, and a cockle shell from the shrine of St James at Santiago. Typically, a cockle shell in the hat denotes a pilgrim, who would also wear a simple cloak and carry a staff.

Pillar

An obvious general symbol of support, but also a sacred axis and emblem of divine power, vital energy, ascension, steadfastness, strength and stability – terrestrial and cosmic. A broken pillar or pole was a symbol of death or chaos not only in Western art but for the Aboriginal peoples of Australia. Freestanding pillars in the ancient world often had specific emblematic meanings, and architectural columns sometimes did also. At a primitive level, pillars of wood or stone often represented either World Trees (like the German Irmensul) or supreme gods. Two pillars engraved with eagles were a focus of the worship of Zeus on Mount Lycaeon in Arcadia. In Egypt the *djed* (a pillar eventually embellished with four capitals) was said to represent the spinal

Pilgrimage: *see* Centre; Initiation; James the Great, St *and other individual names*

Pillar: *see* Axis; Crown; Eagle; Fire, Flame; Liberty; Maypole; Moon; Obelisk; Ram; Sun; Thyrsus; Tree; VIRTUES, THE

Pine, Pine cone

column of the god Osiris, symbolically canalizing his flow of immortal life. Mesopotamian and Phoenician gods were similarly represented by pillars, sometimes topped by emblems such as the ram's head of the great Ea. At Carthage, three pillars symbolized the moon and its phases. The role of the pillar as a symbol of communication with supernatural forces is also clear in Pre-Columbian cultures, as at Machu Picchu where Inca priests ritually "tied" their sun god to a pillar.

In the *Book of Exodus*, the God of the Israelites guides his people through Sinai as a pillar of fire. The fiery pillar is likewise a symbol of the Buddha. In Hinduism a pillar with a crown symbolizes the Way. Wisdom has seven pillars according to the *Book of Proverbs*. Five devotional pillars mark the true follower of Islam. Two giant pillars, called Jachin and Boaz, flanked the porch of Solomon's Temple, a symbol of stability in duality – later taken as a Masonic emblem of justice and benevolence. In art, the pillar is the attribute of Fortitude and Constancy, and it is with this symbolism that Christ appears tied to a pillar in scenes of his flagellation.

Heroes of legendary strength and courage are associated with pillars – the Irish Cúchulainn belts himself to one so that he can die upright; Samson dies wrenching down the pillars of the Philistine temple; Herakles sets up the rock of Gibraltar and the citadel of Ceuta as pillars of the civilized world, keeping monsters out of the Mediterranean and prudent men in. The boastful heraldic device of Charles V showed the Pillars of Herakles with the words *plus ultra* ("farther beyond"), a reference to Spanish dominions in the Americas.

Pine, Pine cone

In Oriental symbolism, the most important of all resinous evergreens, representing immortality or longevity. Like the cedar, it was linked with incorruptibility and was planted around Chinese graves with this symbolism. Its resin was fabled to produce the mushrooms on which the Daoist immortals fed. The Scots pine is a favourite motif in Chinese and Japanese art, either singly representing longevity or in pairs representing married fidelity. It appears often with other emblems of longevity or renewal including the plum, bamboo, mushroom, stork and white stag.

The pine is also an emblem of courage, resolution and good luck – the tree of the Shinto New Year. As the fir, it is similarly propitious in Nordic tradition, sacred to Odin (Wodan), and the centre of the Yuletide rites that led to its adoption as the Christmas tree. Its general symbolism in the West was linked to agricultural fertility, particularly in the Roman spring rebirth rites of Cybele and Attis (represented by a pine wound around with wool). The pine was sacred also to the Greek gods Zeus (Jupiter) and Dionysos (Bacchus), whose emblem is the *thyrsus* (rod) tipped with a pine cone. The cone itself is a phallic and flame symbol of masculine generative force. Surmounting a column (and sometimes mistaken for a pineapple), it was an emblem of the Mesopotamian hero god Marduk.

Pipe *see* **Calumet**

Pitcher

Like other vessels, a maternal womb symbol, associated in iconography with the source of life or (in Egypt where it is an attribute of Isis and

Osiris) the fertilizing waters. In art, Temperance pours water from one pitcher to another. Hebe, handmaiden of the gods, carries a pitcher. It is the attribute of Aquarius and of the Star in the Tarot pack.

PLANETS, THE *see panel overleaf*

Plants *see* **Vegetation**

Pleiades, The
The seven daughters of the Oceanid (sea nymph) Pleione and the Titan Atlas. In one account, the Pleiades were pursued by the giant hunter Orion until Zeus turned them all into stars to save them. The Pleiad Maia was the mother of the god Hermes.

Plough
An biblical symbol of the peaceful arts of agriculture, and more generally a male fertility symbol – the phallic plough entering the female earth. Ritual ploughing by a new Chinese emperor symbolized his responsibility for the fertility of his country. The plough is an emblem of the Silver Age, the descent into labour. Nomadic peoples in western Asia (and in America, where the plough was unknown before Europeans came), once saw ploughing as an affront to the integrity of Mother Earth. The Plough group of seven bright stars in the constellation Ursa Major) was taken as a symbol of the celestial energy that created diversity from primal unity.

Plum
In China, where the hardy Oriental plum blossoms early, an important symbol both of longevity and of virginity or nuptial happiness. Because its flowers appeared in late winter, it joined the pine and bamboo as one of the Three Friends of Winter. Legend said that the great sage Lao-tse was born under a plum, and the tree was a samurai emblem in Japan.

Pluto *see* **Hades**

Point
In mystical thought, the centre and origin of life – a symbol of primordial creative power, sometimes conceived as being so concentrated that it could be represented only in a non-material way – as a hole. This ancient symbolism of infinitely compressed energy, widespread in mystical writing, comes close to the central theories of modern astronomy and physics.

Pole Star
Constancy, the axis of the wheeling firmament. Polaris, visible as the bright unmoving North Star in the constellation Ursa Minor, was of enormous importance in navigation. Many traditions revered it as the zenith of a supernatural pole or pillar linking the terrestrial and celestial spheres. It was sometimes thought to be the shining Gate of Heaven. The ancient Egyptians associated the pole star of their era (Thuban in Draco) with the souls of their pharaohs (who were said to rise to the never-setting circumpolar stars after death), the Chinese with a supreme being.

The North Pole itself – sometimes depicted as a plumbline, as in masonic symbolism – was connected to a spiritual centre individual to each culture, often a sacred mountain or World Tree.

Pollux *see* **Dioscuri, The**

PLANETS, THE

The ancient belief that the planets were powerful living gods has profoundly influenced the evolution of symbolism. For more than two thousand years after the Greeks incorporated this belief into their myths, leading thinkers in the fields of science, philosophy and religion accepted the principle that all the planets presided over events on earth – as the sun and moon unarguably do. Although astrology and science had parted company by the 18th century, planetary symbolism had by then become an inextricable part of human life. The days of the week are themselves based on the seven "planets" which the ancients could see moving busily against the vast backcloth of the stars. Taking the earth as the unmoving centre, these seven (a mystic number in consequence) were the moon, Mercury, the sun, Venus, Mars, Jupiter and Saturn (the other three planets were as yet unknown). To each were assigned characteristics based partly on their colour and motion, and a system of "correspondences" linking them to specific directions of space, colours, metals, bodily organs, jewels, flowers and so on. The theory underlying this complex symbol system was that the "planets" and all aspects of terrestrial nature, including humankind, were interconnected. Of the seven "planets", the moon, Mars and Saturn had potential for evil, the others were perceived as generally beneficial.

Set out below are the distinguishing features that identify the planets in the cosmology and myth of Western tradition.

Mercury Personified by an androgynous, lissom youth: Mercury (Roman), Hermes (Greek) or Nabu (Mesopotamian). He has a caduceus, a winged cap and sandals, and is associated with mobility, mediation, reason, eloquence, free will, adaptation, commerce, Wednesday, quicksilver (mercury); purple or grey-blue, the centre, Virgo and Gemini.

Venus Personified by a beautiful woman: Venus (Roman), Aphrodite (Greek), Ishtar (Mesopotamian). Attributes include laurel, myrtle and rose, the shell or dolphin, the torch or flaming heart and a chariot drawn by doves or swans. Associated with love (sacred or profane), desire, sexuality, pleasure, rebirth, imagination, harmony and happiness as the evening star (in Mesopotamia, war as

Left to right: Jupiter, Mars, Sun, Saturn, Moon, Mercury, and Venus. From the Dijon Bible.

morning star), Friday, copper, green/pale yellow, west as the evening star, Libra and Taurus.

Mars Personified by an aggressive man: Mars (Roman), Ares (Greek), Nergal (Mesopotamian). Helmeted with a shield and sword or spear, perhaps mounted, sometimes with a wolf. Energy, violence, courage, ardour, tension, fire, Tuesday, iron, red, south, Aries and Scorpio.

Jupiter Personified by an imposing, godlike man: Jupiter (Roman), Zeus (Greek), Marduk (Mesopotamian), often bearded. Attributes include the eagle, sceptre and thunderbolt. Power, equilibrium, justice, optimism, organizing ability, Thursday, tin, blue, east, Sagittarius and Pisces.

Saturn Usually personified by a man with a grey beard: Saturn (Roman), Kronos (Greek), Ninib (Mesopotamian). He has a sickle and often a crutch. Once associated with agriculture but generally with pessimism, rigidity, morality, religion, chastity, contemplation, inertia, death, melancholy, Saturday, lead, black, north, Capricorn and Aquarius.

In **Chinese astrology**, Mercury was linked with north, water and black; Venus (male) west, metal and white; Mars south, fire and red; Jupiter east, wood and blue; Saturn the centre, earth and yellow.

Polybus *see* **Oedipus**

Polydeuces *see* **Dioscuri, The**

Polyneices

In Greek myth, a king of Thebes, the son of Oedipus and Jocasta and the brother of Antigone, Eteocles and Ismene. Polyneices and his brother Eteocles inherited Oedipus' throne as joint rulers but quarrelled soon after and Eteocles, supported by Jocasta's brother Creon, seized the throne for himself. Polyneices fled to Argos and, with the aid of seven warriors known as the Seven Against Thebes, returned to attack Eteocles. Creon routed the Argives, but Polyneices and Eteocles killed each other in single combat.

Creon assumed the Theban throne and ordered a magnificent funeral for Eteocles. He declared that Polyneices had been a traitor and that anyone who sought to carry out any burial rite would be put to death. Antigone gave her beloved brother's corpse a token funeral and as a result was arrested. She was imprisoned in a cave where she committed suicide.

Polyphemus

In Greek myth, one of the Cyclopes, a race of one-eyed giants. Polyphemus is a shepherd in the two famous myths in which he appears. In one story, Polyphemus fell in love with a beautiful sea nymph, Galatea. However, she loved Acis, a handsome young shepherd. When Polyphemus crushed Acis to death beneath a boulder, Galatea turned her dead lover into a stream. In an account that excludes Acis, Polyphemus wooed the nymph and eventually won her heart.

On his wanderings after the fall of Troy, the hero Odysseus (Ulysses to

Blinding Polyphemus, from a black-figure kylix *(cup), 6th-century* BCE.

the Romans)[1] came to the island, probably Sicily, where Polyphemus looked after his flocks. Taking twelve men and some potent wine, Odysseus entered the monster's cave and awaited his return. Polyphemus drove his flock into the cave and sealed the entrance. He discovered the strangers and promptly feasted on two of them; in the morning he ate two more. That evening Odysseus persuaded the Cyclops to drink the wine, until the giant fell down senseless. Odysseus drove a burning stake into the giant's eye and escaped next morning by clinging to the bellies of Polyphemus's sheep as he let them out to pasture.

In revenge for killing his son, the god Poseidon made Odysseus' journey home lengthy and hazardous. Turner's *Ulysses Deriding Polyphemus* shows Ulysses' boat pulling away, guided by phosphorescent Nereids.

Polyxena

The beautiful daughter of King Priam of Troy. She and the Greek hero Achilles fell in love, but her brother Hector refused to let her marry an

Pomegranate

enemy of the Trojans. Achilles killed Hector during battle and was himself killed by Paris. After the fall of Troy the ghost of Achilles requested that Polyxena be sacrificed to honour his tomb. In *The Sacrifice of Polyxena* Giovanni Battista Pittoni shows her being led with dignity to the tomb where she asks Neoptolemus, Achilles' son, to kill her, preferring death to enslavement by the Greeks.

Pomegranate

Fecundity, abundance, generosity, sexual temptation. The multicellular structure of the pomegranate with its many seeds bedded in juicy pulp within a leathery casing also led to subsidiary emblematic meanings – the oneness of the diverse cosmos, the manifold blessings of God, the Christian church protecting its many members. An ancient Persian fruit, known to the Romans as the "apple of Carthage", the pomegranate was predominantly a fertility symbol linked with love, marriage and many children both in the Mediterranean world and in China, where it was one of the Three Blessed Fruits of Buddhism.

It was sacred to love goddesses such as Astarte and Aphrodite (Venus in Roman myth), and also to the maternal and agricultural goddesses Hera (Juno), who holds a pomegranate as a marriage symbol, and Demeter (Ceres) or her daughter Persephone (Proserpina, Proserpine). Hades gave a pomegranate (symbolizing indissoluble wedlock) to Persephone when she asked permission to return to the earth's surface. By eating it, she condemned herself to spend four months each year with her underworld lord – a sexual symbolism exploited in D G Rossetti's painting of her holding a

bitten pomegranate (*Proserpina*, 1874).The myth represented the bleakness of autumn and winter and the regeneration of spring and summer, symbolized by the pomegranate. The fruit was said to have sprung from the blood of Dionysos. This tradition accounts for paintings in which Christ holds a pomegranate as a resurrection symbol, for example, in *Madonna della Melagrana* by Botticelli. Muhammad recommended the fruit to purge envy and hatred.

Pomona and Vertumnus

In Roman myth[1] Pomona was a wood nymph who was devoted to the cultivation of fruit trees, from which she derived her name (*poma* meaning "fruit" in Latin). She carried a curved knife for pruning, and watered the plants from trickling streams. To keep satyrs out she fenced herself inside her orchards, but Vertumnus (a satyr, though he may not be depicted as such) fell in love with her and adopted various disguises to approach her: as a rough harvester, a vineyard worker, a soldier and a fisherman.

Dressed as an old woman, he entered her garden and lavishly praised Pomona's fruit trees. Disguised, he tried to persuade her to court Vertumnus, likening marriage to a tree that supports a vine, but to no avail. Finally, he threw off his disguise and the nymph, entranced by his beauty, was smitten with a passion equal to his own.

This bucolic subject was chosen for the decoration of villas: for example, the Villa Medici, which was adorned by Pontormo; while other artists chose the scene of the disguised Vertumnus wooing Pomona, such as Domenico Fetti in his *Vertumnus and Pomona*.

The Christ Child fed from a pomegranate; after a detail of Botticelli's Madonna della Melagrana *(1480s).*

Pontos

"The Sea", a primal Greek deity embodying the waters. Pontos sprang from the goddess Gaia, the earth, and coupled with her to produce the sea deities Nereus (the Old man of the Sea) and, according to one account, Phorcys and Ceto.

Poplar

A duality symbol in China because the leaves of the white poplar are dark green on the upper (solar) side but appear white on the lower (moon) side, where they are covered with soft down. The Greeks explained this colour change in the myth of Herakles (Hercules to the Romans) who bound a poplar branch around his head for his descent into the underworld. Smoke darkened the top of the leaves while his sweat blanched their lower surfaces.

The poplar was sacred to Sabazius and to Zeus (Jupiter), but is usually funerary in its symbolism.

Poppy

In art, an emblem of the Greek gods of sleep (Hypnos) and dreams (Morpheus); and in allegory, of Night personified – a symbolism based on the properties of the opium poppy which grows as a wild flower in Greece and the eastern Mediterranean, and was used for herbal infusions from ancient times. The poppy was linked also with the Greek fertility goddesses Demeter (Ceres in Roman myth) and her daughter Persephone (Proserpina) as a symbol of the winter "sleep" of vegetation. Christianity borrowed aspects of this older tradition, making the red poppy an emblem of Christ's sacrifice and "sleep of death". The First World War battlefields of Flanders gave fresh poignancy to the sacrificial symbolism of the red poppy. Its use as a memorial to the war dead was inspired by the the Canadian war poet John McCrae (1872–1918) who wrote: "In Flanders field the poppies blow / Between the crosses, row on row."

Poseidon

The Olympian Greek god of the sea, the son of Kronos and Rhea and brother of Demeter, Hades, Hera, Hestia and Zeus. Like his brother Zeus, who assigned to him the rule of the oceans, Poseidon was a god of awesome power and violence, which was manifested in thunderstorms and

Poseidon; after a red-figure wine cup of the 6th century BCE.

earthquakes. In ancient art he closely resembled Zeus, except that Poseidon wielded not a thunderbolt but a trident, a three-pronged fork.

Poseidon married Amphitrite, a sea nymph, and she bore their son Triton, a merman-like creature. The sea god was renowned for adultery, for example with the goddess Gaia, the earth; she bore him a monstrous daughter, Charybdis, and a giant son, Antaeus. Another of his lovers was the Gorgon

Priam

Medusa, with whom the god (in the form of a horse or bird) had intercourse in a temple of the goddess Athene. For this sacrilege Athene turned Medusa into a snake-haired monster. Poseidon often appears as Athene's rival in myth, most notably in the account of their contest for the protectorship of Athens, which Athene won.

Poseidon's other loves included Amymone, Caenis and Coronis. To escape his attentions the Nereid (sea nymph) Amphitrite fled to the farthest limits of the sea but was persuaded to marry him by a dolphin; their son was the merman Triton. Poseidon was also the father, by the sea nymph Thöosa, of the Cyclops Polyphemus. Amphitrite tolerated most of Poseidon's infidelities, but when he fell for the nymph Scylla she turned her into a hideous sea monster.

Poseidon's emblems were his trident, with which he would whip up winds and tempests, the horse (which in one account he invented) and the bull.

Poseidon was known to the Romans as Neptune. According to the *Aeneid*, after the Trojan War, Juno (Hera) commanded the winds to unleash a storm to deter Aeneas' fleet, but Neptune rose from the waves and made the ocean calm.

In art the god commonly appears as a slightly dishevelled, but vigorous and majestic with cascading locks. His attribute is the trident and he usually rides a chariot, sometimes made from a shell, drawn by sea horses (*hippocampi*) or dolphins. He is often accompanied by mermaids and mermen blowing conches, and sea nymphs or naiads (freshwater nymphs). In allegory he may represent water, and his figure commonly decorates fountains.

Precious stones *see* **JEWELS**

Priam

In Greek myth, a king of Troy in northwestern Asia Minor (modern Turkey), the son of King Laomedon and Queen Strymo. Under King Priam's wise rule, Troy became powerful and prosperous. He married Hecuba, a princess of Phrygia, who bore many children, including Paris, Hector and Cassandra.

Following Hecuba's dream that her child would destroy Troy, Priam had the baby Paris exposed on a mountain. But he survived and later eloped with Helen, the queen of Sparta, thereby setting off the events leading to the war between Troy and the Greeks, which ended in the deaths of Priam and his sons, and the destruction of Troy.

During the war, Priam's Greek enemies treated him with more dignity and respect (he was by then very old) than they did other Trojans, particularly when he entered the Greek camp in order to plead for the corpse of his son Hector, who had been slain by the hero Achilles. However, after the fall of the city he was slain on the altar of Zeus by Neoptolemus, the son of Achilles.

Priam imploring Achilles to release the body of Hector, after a Greek vase.

Priapus

A rustic Greek fertility god and the protector of orchards and gardens, Priapus was the son of Aphrodite (in Roman myth, Venus) and, variously, Dionysos (Bacchus), Hermes (Mercury), Pan or Zeus (Jupiter). He had enormous genitals, and his mother banished him to the mountains because of his deformity. He was a comic and obscene figure, usually portrayed as an ugly, squat old man with an enormous erection, hence the word "priapic".

Priapus attended a feast of Dionysos where he lost his heart to the nymph Lotis, but she scorned him.[1] When night came Lotis fell asleep on the grass and Priapus was about to ravish her when an ass belonging to a companion of Silenus (the son of Pan) brayed raucously and Lotis awoke. In terror she pushed Priapus away and fled. The gods took pity on her and transformed her into the lotus tree to protect her from further advances by Priapus.[2] Giovanni Bellini shows this scene in *Feast of the Gods*.

Primrose

Wanton pleasure – as in Ophelia's warning to her brother not to tread "the primrose path of dalliance" (Shakespeare's *Hamlet*, 1:3). This early budding perennial was a European emblem of youth, linked to the "little people" of Celtic folklore.

Prince, Princess

The ideal young man or woman – a persistent symbol of all that is most beautiful, gentle or heroic. The prince, in particular, was a hopeful emblem of renewed national vigour or fertility. Public disappointment with the visible defects of princes may help to account for the popular fairy stories of frog princes transformed by love into something closer to the ideal.

Procession

A purification ritual or demonstration of power in many early traditions. Sacred objects or sacrificial animals were carried in processions around newly sown fields to protect crops from disease or to ensure successful growth. The paper dragons still carried in Chinese processions invoked rain. Processional marching around an enemy symbolically bound and weakened them, as when the Israelites marched around the walls of Jericho with the sacred ark. Roman triumphal processions not only displayed military heroes to the public but asserted their power over the captives they led.

Procrustes

In Greek myth, an innkeeper who killed travellers on the road between Athens and Eleusis. Procrustes ("The Stretcher") made all those who came his way lie down on a bed; if they were too short for it he would rack them to the right length; if they were too tall he would chop them down to size. The hero Theseus killed him by cutting off his head.

Prometheus

A Titan, the divine protector of the human race. Prometheus ("Forethought") was either the son of the Titans Iapetus and Themis, or of Iapetus and the Oceanid (sea nymph) Clymene. He did not oppose Zeus (in Roman myth, Jupiter) and the Olympians during their battle against Kronos and the Titans, but he resented the defeat of his race. He decided

Priapus: *see* Aphrodite; Bacchus; Dionysos; Hermes; Pan; ZEUS. THE CONSORTS OF
[1] Ovid, *Fasti* I:393–441
[2] Ovid, *Met* IX:346–348

Primrose: *see* FLOWERS

Prince, Princess: *see* Frog

Procession: *see* Ark; Dragon; Sacrifice

Procrustes: *see* Theseus

Prometheus: *see* CULTURE HERO; Hephaistos; Herakles; HUMANITY, THE ORIGIN OF; Pandora; TITAN; Zeus
[1] Apollodorus, *The Llibrary I vii 1*
[2] Apollonius, *Argonautica II:1242–1261*

*Prometheus creating the first man;
after a relief from Naples, Italy.*

to spite Zeus by promoting the interests of men, created as equals in the time of Kronos but treated as inferior by Zeus, according to Hesiod's *Theogony*. (In an alternative account, Prometheus himself created the first man, Phaenon, from clay, as depicted by Piero di Cosimo in two paintings of the story of Prometheus).

Zeus and men met to decide how to divide up their food. The men prepared a sacrificial animal, and Prometheus told them to pour fat over the bones, so that they glistened temptingly. Zeus saw the tasty-looking bones and, as Prometheus had predicted, decided that they must always be given to the gods.

However, he soon discovered that Prometheus had tricked him into leaving men the succulent meat. As punishment, Zeus deprived mankind of fire. But, with the help of Athene (Minerva to the Romans) Prometheus stole a flame from the god Hephaistos and, hiding it in a stalk of fennel, took it to men (in an alternate myth he climbed to the heavens and retrieved a spark from the chariot of the sun). Prometheus also taught men how to use fire in skills such as metalworking

In retribution for this theft Zeus spread evils over the world, released via Pandora's box, and chained Prometheus to a rock on Mount Caucasus. Each day an eagle came and devoured his liver, and each night the organ regenerated, to be eaten anew. After many years of this torment, Herakles set Prometheus free.[1] As Jason and the Argonauts sailed through the steep crags of the Caucasian mountains they saw the eagle and heard the Titan's anguished cries.[2] The torment by the eagle was the most popular theme in art from the story of Prometheus, especially in the 17th century. Rubens, for example, shows his muscular body racked with pain.

The story has various resonances: the courage needed to disobey the gods; the "fire" of intelligence distinguishing man from the beasts; and the way in which Prometheus ended the Golden Age, bringing wisdom to humankind.

Prose Edda, The
A collection of old Scandinavian myths gathered *c.*1230CE by the Icelandic poet Snorri Sturluson.

Proserpina, Proserpine *see* Persephone

Proteus
A Greek sea god, the son of the Titans Okeanos and Tethys. Proteus possessed the gift of prophecy, but disliked being asked questions and would take any form to avoid his questioners, hence the word "protean" ("shape-shifting").

Psyche
In an ancient Roman tale,[1] Psyche's beauty rivalled that of Venus (in Greek myth, Aphrodite), and the angry goddess commanded Cupid (Eros) to make her fall in love with an idiot.[1] However, Cupid himself fell in love with Psyche and took her to an

enchanted castle. He forbade her to look at him and came to her only at night, vanishing at daybreak. Psyche's jealous sisters tricked her into looking at her sleeping lover by the light of a lamp. When she saw his beauty she too fell in love, but a drop of scalding oil woke the god, and he angrily soared away.

A distraught Psyche roamed the earth looking for Cupid until she found the house of Venus. Here she became Venus' slave and her mistress set her a series of almost impossible tasks: to separate a pile of mixed grain, which she achieved with the help of ants; to procure golden wool from dangerous sheep, in which a reed from the sacred waters instructed her; to fetch water from a sacred stream guarded by dragons, in which the eagles of Jupiter (Zeus) came to her aid; and to collect some of Proserpina's (Persephone's) beauty from the underworld, in which a tower guided her safely to Hades. At last Cupid begged Jupiter to take pity on Psyche; a council of the gods was held, and Psyche was given a cup of nectar to make her immortal. The great wedding feast of Cupid and Psyche was arranged, and she later bore him a daughter called Pleasure.

The story of the beautiful couple was a popular and happy romantic tale. Its numerous episodes and final wedding scene have been used to cover large areas or fill the many vaults of a ceiling, as in Raphael's frescoes in the Loggia (Villa Farnesina, Rome). Episodes from the story were also painted as a series, such as the twelve canvases of Luca Giordano's *Cupid and Psyche*. Alternatively, artists painted isolated scenes, such as Fragonard's *Psyche*

Showing her Sisters her Gifts from Cupid, and François Gérard's *Psyche Receiving her First Kiss*.

Ptah

A great Egyptian creator god, revered as the divine craftsman. He was said to have made gods and humans from precious metals. He created deities by thinking of them in his heart and speaking aloud their names.

Pulang Gana

The earth spirit of the Iban, one of the Dayak (non-Muslim) peoples of Borneo. It is said that long ago, people tried to clear a patch of jungle for the first rice farm, but could not do so because Pulang Gana kept reviving all the cut trees. The spirit allowed them to grow rice if they offered him beads, jars and shells.

Puranas, The

A group of Hindu religious texts, composed over the period *c.*250CE–*c.*1700CE. The group forms the greatest source of Indian myth. There are eighteen "Great" *Purana*s and many "Minor" *Purana*s.

Purgatory

Spiritual refinement or purification – a symbolism suggested by the processes of metallurgy and alchemy but transferred to early Christian concepts of the afterlife. In the Roman Catholic faith, the souls of those with venial (less than mortal) sins may need to pass through the fiery (but temporary) state of Purgatory on their way to heaven.

Purple

The colour of royalty and dignity in the ancient world. Its emblematic

Ptah: *see* Amon; Atum; Khnum

Purgatory: *see* AFTERLIFE; Alchemy; Fire, Flame

Purple: *see* COLOURS

The Egyptian god Ptah, based on a Late Period bronze statuette.

Purukupali

meaning was based on the high value of cloth dyed purple by the secretions of two species of molluscs, which was an expensive process. Purple was worn by priests, magistrates and military leaders in the Roman world but was associated particularly with emperors. The children of Byzantine emperors were born in a room with purple drapes, hence the phrase "born in the purple". Cardinals are still said to be "raised to the purple" although their robes are actually red.

Purukupali

The ancestral figure responsible for human mortality, according to the Tiwi people of Melville and Bathurst islands. Purukupali was one of the first people, the son of Mudungkala, a blind old ancestral heroine of the Dreamtime. Purukupali married and his wife had a son. They lived in the same camp as the Moon Man, Tjapara, a bachelor who desired Purukupali's wife. He went into the forest with her one day, leaving her son under the shade of a tree. But while they were gone, the shade moved and the child died in the scorching heat.

This made Purukupali angry and he announced that from that time on all people would die. Tjapara promised to bring the son back to life. They fought over the body but eventually Purukupali seized it and walked into the sea. Tjapara turned into the moon: the features of the moon are the scars that he sustained from his fight.

Putto

A *putto* (plural *putti*) is a very young, winged boy, also known as an *amoretto* or "little Cupid". *Putti* may be little angels or cherubs in religious paintings, or add a humorous note to secu-

lar paintings about love. They often accompany Venus (Aphrodite) or may worship her statue. In Titian's *The Worship of Venus*, countless *putti* gather apples, sacred to the goddess, from the floor of the orchard or fly up to pick them from the trees and tumble about playing ball.

Pwll

A lord of Dyfed in Wales and the protagonist of the First Branch of the *Mabinogion*. Pwll went hunting and attempted to steal the kill of Arawn, the king of the Otherworld (Annwn). Furious at Pwll's behaviour, Arawn declared eternal enmity unless both men exchanged identities and realms for one year, after which Pwll must slay Arawn's enemy, Hafgan. Pwll agreed and went to Annwn in the form of Arawn, leaving the latter to rule Dyfed. A year later Pwll completed his side of the bargain and met up with Arawn. The two hailed each other as friends and left for their own lands. After this Pwll was often referred to as "Lord of Annwn".

Another myth recounts how Pwll won the hand of Rhiannon, a supernatural woman. She and Pwll were the parents of the hero Pryderi.

Pygmalion

In Greek myth, the race of Propoetides denied the divinity of Aphrodite (the Roman Venus) and in her anger she turned their women into prostitutes.[1] When Pygmalion saw their wicked lives he vowed to remain celibate. He carved a snowy ivory statue, more beautiful than any living woman, and fell in love with his own creation. He would stroke and embrace it, and wooed it as if it were alive. At the festival of Aphrodite, he prayed to the goddess to bring his statue to life, and she consented, and was present at their marriage. The subject interested artists of the 18th and 19th centuries: François Boucher painted *Pygmalion*; in a painting of the same title Jean-Léon Gérôme shows Pygmalion embracing his statue; and Edward Burne-Jones painted the series *Story of Pygmalion*.

Pyramid

In Egypt, a symbol of the creative power of the sun and the immortality of the pharaoh whose tomb it was. Pyramidal constructions elsewhere, notably Babylonian ziggurats rising to temple sanctuaries, had different symbolic aims. The Egyptian pyramid was developed from the conventional flat-topped *mastaba* tomb by Imhotep, the high priest of the sun-god Ra. Although his pyramid for the pharoah Djoser at Saqqara was stepped, later architects perfected the form of the true pyramid, facing it with limestone to reflect the light, clarifying its symbolism. It represented the primal mound which, in Egyptian cosmogony, first caught the light of the creator sun. The mass and power of the structure were "material for eternity" – a building whose permanence negated death and whose height and reflective surfaces symbolized the perfect union between the buried pharaoh and the sun god. Apart from concentrating the light, the sloping triangular sides have more structural than symbolic purpose, providing the stability that made these stupendous monuments possible.

Pyramus and Thisbe

In Greek myth, Pyramus and Thisbe grew up next door to each other and fell in love.[1] But their parents forbade their marriage and the lovers communicated through a slender chink in the wall between their houses, cursing the wall for preventing their embrace.

They determined to escape at night and planned to meet outside the city, near a mulberry tree by a tomb. Thisbe slipped out first, but, near the appointed tree, was frightened by a bloodied lion arriving from a recent kill.

As she fled to a cave, her veil slipped from her shoulders and the lion tore it to shreds. Pyramus came upon the bloodstained garment and, thinking his beloved dead, plunged a sword into his side. Thisbe found him dying and took her own life. Their blood turned the fruit of the mulberry tree red for evermore. In *Landscape with Pyramus and Thisbe* Poussin shows Thisbe rushing across to the fatally wounded Pyramus, against a stormy landscape.

Pyrrha

In Greek myth, the daughter of Epimetheus and Pandora and wife of Deucalion. She and her husband were the only two survivors of a great flood sent by the god Zeus to destroy the human race.

Pythagoras

A celebrated Greek philosopher and mathematician, Pythagoras (*c*.582–507BCE) held that all relationships could be expressed in numbers and discovered that there was a numerical relationship between the length of a string and the sound it made when plucked. Pythagoras may appear as a personification of arithmetic in representations of the Liberal Arts.

Pytho, Python *see* **Gaia**; **SNAKE**

Pyramid: *see* Light; Mound; Obelisk; Sun; Ziggurat

Pyramus and Thisbe:
[1] Ovid, *Met IV:55–166*

Pyrrha: *see* Deucalion; Epimetheus; FLOOD MYTHS; Pandora; Zeus

Pythagoras: *see* LIBERAL ARTS

Quail

Warmth, ardour and courage – a symbolism based on the bird's reddish-brown colour, its combativeness, and its migratory appearance in early summer. Quails were linked with the Greek island of Delos, mythical birthplace of the god Apollo and his sister Artemis. The quail was an emblem of military valour in both China and ancient Rome. The Chinese linked it with the south, fire and summer. Its association with light seems confirmed by the Hindu myth of the twin Ashvin deities who released a quail (symbolizing spring) from the mouth of a wolf (winter). As a night flyer the quail has been linked with witchcraft in Europe, but in general it was a good augury. In the Bible, God sent a host of quails to the Israelites, for whom the birds provided food in the desert during their flight from captivity in Egypt.[1]

The quail was also once supposed to be an extremely amorous bird, and hence courtesans came to be known as "quails".

Qudshu

An Egyptian goddess of good health and consort of the fertility god Min. Of Syrian origin, Qudshu was seen at times as a form of the goddess Hathor. She is depicted naked, holding lotus flowers and snakes, standing on the back of a lion.

Queen

Like the king a celestially ordained archetype of her sex; a human symbol of the moon. The two were linked in a duality seen as necessary for the prosperity and happiness of the realm. In alchemy, the sacred marriage of the white queen (mercury) and red king (sulphur) symbolized the union of male and female principles to produce the Philosopher's Stone.

As consorts, queens were subordinate to the dynastic male, but as sovereigns in their own right they could rapidly acquire symbolic importance or even semi-mythic status, as did Queen Elizabeth I of England (on whom the poet Edmund Spenser based Gloriana in his *Faerie Queen* of 1596).

In the ancient world, mother goddesses were Queens of Heaven (a title also accorded the Virgin Mary), lunar goddesses Queens of the Night. Symbolic attributes included the blue robe, chalice, turreted or starry crown, orb and sceptre, and the metal silver.

Quetzalcoatl

One of the most important Aztec deities, although he has his origins in pre-Aztec cultures. For example, Quetzalcoatl (which can mean both "Feathered Serpent" and "Precious Twin") was revered by the Toltec people, whose civilization flourished from the 9th–12th centuries CE, who worshipped him as the god of the morning and evening star. The Aztecs adopted Quetzalcoatl as the patron of priests, learning and crafts and the inventor of the calendar.

He appeared in numerous other guises, such as the god of twins and, especially, as the god of the wind, Ehecatl. As a great creator god, he played an important part in the myth of the Five Suns (he presided over the second Sun or world era). With his twin brother, the dog-headed god Xolotl, Quetzalcoatl descended to the underworld land of the dead to steal bones from which the human race was recreated, after having been destroyed in the four cosmic upheavals.

The mythical doings of the god Quetzalcoatl became confused with those of a historical Toltec priest-king called Topiltzin-Quetzalcoatl. It was said that Quetzalcoatl disliked the blood sacrifices demanded by Tezcatlipoca and the two gods argued. In the end Quetzalcoatl was expelled from Tula, the Toltec capital, in 987CE. He reached the Gulf of Mexico and immolated himself, to be

The god Quetzalcoatl, from the 16th-century Aztec Codex Telleriano-Remensis.

reborn as the planet Venus. According to another account, the god is said to have sailed away on a raft, but it was predicted that he would come back one day. This prophecy was exploited by the conquistador Hernán Cortés, who was initially hailed as the returning god Quetzalcoatl when he landed in Mexico in 1519.

Quintessence

Perfected matter. Western alchemists said that the four elements (earth, air, fire and water) were surrounded by a purer, mystic element, the "fifth essence" (this is the literal meaning of "quintessence"), similar to the Indic notion of *prana*, the energizing etheric spirit, or the Chinese *qi* (*ch'i*).

The animal symbols eagle (air), phoenix (fire), dolphin (water) and man (earth), were grouped to represent the quintessence.

Quirinus

A Roman god of war, in origin possibly the Sabine equivalent of Mars. After his deification, Romulus came to be identified with Quirinus. The Quirinal, one of the seven hills of Rome, was named after him.

Quetzalcoatl: *see* Ehecatl; Five Suns, The; Tezcatlipoca; Tlaloc

Quintessence: *see* Air; Alchemy; Dolphin; Eagle; Earth; Fire, Flame; Man; Phoenix; Water

Quirinus: *see* Mars; Romulus

Ra

Ra

The creator sun god and supreme deity of Egypt. As the solar god, Ra took numerous forms. The morning sun was a child, or else Khephry, the scarab. The noonday sun was Ra-Harakhty ("Ra, Horus of the Horizon"), a human figure with a falcon's head surmounted by a sun disc. In most accounts of the sun's rule on earth he is called by this name, which represents a fusion of Ra and the ancient god Harakhty, a manifestation of Horus. The evening sun was Atum or Ra-Atum, depicted in human form wearing the royal crown of Egypt. The night sun had no precise name but his image (in human form with a ram's head) bore the caption "Flesh (of Ra)".

The sun was said to be born each dawn from Nut, the sky goddess. He was mature at noon and old in the evening. At night he passed through the underworld land of the dead on his barque, and the god Seth and the myriad spirits of the blessed dead would help defend him against the constant attacks of Apep, the serpent of chaos. The sun was reborn at dawn.

According to one myth, Ra once lived on earth as the ruler of gods and humanity. However, he grew weary and withdrew into the heavens.

Rabbit *see* **HARES AND RABBITS**

Radha *see* **Krishna**

Radiance

The white light which, together with its counterpart Black Misery (black light), was the first thing to exist, in pre-Buddhist Tibetan myth. From a huge cosmic egg Radiance brought forth blessings such as happiness, long life, prosperity and benevolent deities.

Ragnarok

"The Twilight of the Gods", the apocalyptic battle between the gods and their enemies which resulted in the destruction of the old divine order, according to Norse myth. In one account, the trickster Loki broke free from the fetters in which the gods had put him and mustered an army of giants to attack Asgard, the gods' home. His followers destroyed Bifrost, the bridge leading to Asgard, and the giant army arrived in a ship.

The monstrous wolf Fenrir, son of Loki, broke free and devoured Odin, who was the chief of the gods. Odin's son Vidar then tore Fenrir apart. The god Thor killed the World Serpent which lurked in the waters surrounding the world, but was overcome by its venom and died. Loki faced his old enemy Heimdall, the sentry of Asgard, and the pair slew each other. Then Surt, the fire giant, set the world aflame. The heavens collapsed and the earth was overwhelmed by the seas.

The old world vanished, but a new one appeared, green and beautiful, with a new sun. From the surviving children of the old deities, such as Vidar, sprang a new generation of gods. A human couple, who had survived the calamity by hiding in the branches of Yggdrasil, the World Tree, repopulated the earth.

Rain

A vital symbol of fecundity, often linked in primitive agricultural societies with divine semen, as in the Greek myth in which the god Zeus impregnated Danaë, the mother of Perseus, in the form of a golden shower. The traditional belief that the gods determine whether to withhold rain, unleash it with punishing force, or sprinkle it sweetly like a blessing, has never entirely disappeared. Gentle rain (likened to mercy by Portia in Shakespeare's *The Merchant of Venice*; *c.*1596) was widely seen as a sign of divine approval or, in China, Yin-Yang harmony in the celestial

sphere. The supreme fertility god of the Aztecs, Tlaloc (or Chac in the Mayan pantheon), was a rain god whose motif was a bar with comb-like teeth representing falling rain. To him, children were sacrificed on mountain tops, their blood and tears propitious signs of coming rainfall.

A similar link between blood and rain appears in Iranian mythology where the rain-god Tishtrya, as a white horse, is sustained by sacrifices as he fights the black horse of drought. The heavenly origin of rain made it an emblem of purity, and purification rituals were often carried out to invoke its fall. In the straightforward sympathetic magic of rain dancing, stamping feet imitated the patter of drops striking the earth. Apart from the axe, hammer and thunderbolt (a rain of fire or light), symbols of rain include the snake or horned serpent, the dragon in China, frogs and other amphibians, lunar creatures such as the crab and spider, dogs (associated with wind gods) and, more unexpectedly, the cat, chameleon, cow, elephant, parrot and turkey.

Rainbow

A bridging symbol between the supernatural and natural worlds, usually optimistic. In Judeo-Christian tradition, a rainbow was the sign of God's reconciliation with humankind after the Flood: "I have set my bow in the clouds, and it shall be a sign of the covenant between me and the earth".[1] In Greece, the rainbow goddess Iris, robed in iridescent dew, carried messages to earth from the supreme god Zeus and his wife Hera. In India the rainbow was the bow of the hero god Indra (a tradition paralleled in the Pacific where the rainbow is the

Rain: *see* Axe; Black; Blood; Bull; Cat; Chameleon; Clouds; Comb; Cord; Cow; Crab; Dance; Dog; Dragon; Dwarf; Elephant; Emerald; Feathers; Frog; Green; Hammer; Hazel; Incense; Lightning; Makara; Moon; Parrot; Rainbow; Snake; Spider; Storm; Tamarisk; Tambourine; Thunder; Toad; Tongue; Triangle; Turkey; Water; Yin-Yang

Rainbow: *see* Bridge; Dew; Flood; Iris; Ladder; Light; Noah; Rain; Seven; snake; Trinity
[1] *Genesis 9:13*

Tlaloc, the Aztec rain god; after an illustration in an Aztec manuscript.

emblem of Kahukara, the Maori war god). In Tibetan Tantric Buddhism the "rainbow body" is the penultimate transitional state of meditation in which matter begins to be transformed into pure light.

The beneficial symbolism underlying all these traditions is not universal. As a solar and water emblem, the arc of the rainbow touching the earth usually suggested fertility and treasure – the folklore "pot of gold". But in some cultures, an underworld symbolism appears. The rainbow was associated with a serpent in parts of Africa, India, Asia and Native North America, as well as in Australia, and its powers were unpredictable. In some central African myths, Nkongolo, the Rainbow King, is a cruel tyrant. This perhaps relates to the African and Asian superstition that it is provocative and risky to point at a rainbow.

In Central Asia, rainbow-coloured ribbons were a shamanistic aid to sky travel, but there were folklore warnings against treading on the end of a rainbow and being whirled upward. More often, the ladder symbolism of the rainbow is positive. It is the seven-coloured ladder of the Buddha, and in many traditions the path to paradise.

In Western art, Christ sometimes sits in judgment on top of a rainbow, which can also appear as an attribute of the Virgin Mary and (with three bands) the Trinity.

Ram

Solar energy, impetuous ardour, virility, hot-headedness, obstinacy – a symbol of fire as both a creative and a consuming, or sacrificial, force. Its spiral horns were an emblem of the increasing solar power of Amun-Ra in Egypt who took over the symbolism of the ram-headed creator god Khnum. In iconography the ram was a popular symbol of potent gods including Ea and Baal in the Middle East, Zeus and Apollo in Greece, Indra and Agni in India, and, by association with its battering power, thunder gods such as the Scandinavian Thor whose chariot is drawn by rams. A ram-headed serpent (virility and renewal) is the companion of the Celtic god Cernunnos.

As the first sign of the Zodiac, Aries the ram symbolizes the renewal of fertility and returning warmth of the sun at the March equinox. It is an astrological sign of the choleric temperament and the fiery planet Mars. As a fire and solar emblem the ram was also an important sacrificial animal – in Hebrew tradition it was God's last-minute replacement for Isaac when Abraham obediently prepared to sacrifice his son.[1] Christian iconography sometimes makes Christ the sacrificial ram. More often, Christ with a ram has significance as protector of his flock. The ram was an attribute of the Greek god Hermes (in Roman myth, Mercury). The Golden Fleece came from the marvellous ram of Hermes, which was sacrificed to Zeus. The *shofar*, or Hebrew sacred ram's horn, is a protective emblem.

Rama

A divine warrior hero, the seventh avatar (incarnation) of the Hindu god Vishnu and, like Krishna, an important figure in his own right. According to the *Ramayana* (composed between *c.*200BCE and *c.*200CE), there was once a childless king called Dasha-ratha, the ruler of the holy city of Ayodhya. He performed a sacrifice in order to be granted male offspring.

Rama, the divine hero of Hindu myth, with his consort Sita and devotees.

At the gods' request, Vishnu became incarnate as Dasharatha's four sons, in order to destroy Ravana, the demon ruler of the island kingdom of Lanka. The greatest of these four sons were Rama and Bharata. Their brothers Lakshmana and Shatrughna became their respective loyal aides.

A great sage, Vishvamitra, enlisted the help of Rama on a mission against the Rakshasas, a race of demons. He was successful and the sage took Rama and Lakshmana to the court of King Janaka of Videha. Part of Rama's purpose while there was to marry Sita, Janaka's beautiful daughter, who had sprung from a furrow ploughed by Janaka. King Dasharatha chose Rama as his heir, but Rama was exiled for fourteen years and left with Sita and Lakshmana. During this time, Bharata was persuaded to rule in Rama's place as his regent. A female Rakshasa, Shurpanakha, tried to seduce Rama and Lakshmana, but the latter drove her off. In revenge she induced her brother, the evil King Ravana, to kidnap Sita and carry her off to Lanka. Rama and Lakshmana at once launched a search for Sita. With the devoted support of the monkey Hanuman, they destroyed Ravana's kingdom and his army of Rakshasas, and Sita was recovered. Rama fought and killed the demon king.

Rama greeted Sita coldly, convinced that she must have been unfaithful during her captivity. She underwent an ordeal by fire and the gods appeared to Rama to tell him he was an incarnation of Vishnu. The god of fire presented Sita, unhurt and exonerated, and the two were happily reunited. Dasharatha appeared and blessed his sons, telling Rama to return to Ayodhya and assume the kingship.

***Ramayana, The* see Rama**

Rangda

A fierce sorceress queen of Balinese myth. Rangda ("Widow"), who is depicted as near-naked with long hair and nails. Her immortal opponent is the spirit king Barong. The combat between Rangda and Barong, acted out in Balinese dance, always ends in Barong vanquishing Rangda. Rangda may have originated in a notorious 11th-century queen of Bali.

Rangi and Papa

The primal creator deities of the Maori pantheon. Rangi, the sky god, and Papa, the earth goddess, embraced so tightly in the primordial void that none of their six children could escape after they had been born. Tu, the god of war, proposed killing their parents, but Tane, the god of forests, said it was better to force them apart. Each god in turn tried to separate the deities but only Tane succeeded. Then Rangi and Papa assumed the positions they have kept to this day.

Raphael, Archangel (Saint)

Like the other archangels, Raphael is often shown as a winged youth. He acts as a guardian angel and is traditionally a protector of the young and of travellers. He acted as a guide for Tobias; in art Tobias may hold a fish and Raphael a jar containing the fish's gall, with which he restored the sight of Tobias's father (Raphael means "God heals"). He is shown with these attributes in Francesco Botticini's *The Three Archangels and Tobias*.

Rat

Destructiveness, avarice, foresight and fecundity. As nocturnal raiders of granaries, rats were usually perceived as harmful in the ancient Middle East.

They were linked with the underworld and, in Christianity, with the Devil.

A different symbolism based on their knowingness, fecundity and bread-winning abilities is evident not only in folklore (their legendary foreknowledge of doomed ships) but also in their association with Asian gods of wisdom, success or prosperity (including the "riches" that comprise many children). A rat is the steed of the elephant-headed god Ganesha in Indian myth, and the companion of the Japanese god of wealth Daikoku. In the mythology of southern China, a rat brought rice to humankind. The rat is the first sign of the Chinese Zodiac. Some Renaissance paintings show a black and white rat, representing night and day gnawing at time.

Raven

Like its close relative the crow, a bird associated with death, loss and war in western Europe but widely venerated elsewhere. Its Western reputation was influenced by its association as a soothsayer with Celtic battle goddesses such as the Morríghan and Badhbh

Raven (left) with the sun disc; after a Native American headdress.

and with the Norse war god, Odin, who was accompanied by two ravens, Hugin and Munin. However, these two, apart from reporting events on earth, symbolized the constructive principles of mind and memory.

Hebrew symbolism is also ambivalent. As a scavenger, the raven was unclean. But it was the astute bird released from the ark by Noah which flew to and fro until the earth dried. Ravens also fed Elijah and several Christian hermit saints.

In general, the raven is a solar and oracular symbol, its glistening black plumage perhaps suggesting an ability to survive a close relationship with the sun. It was the messenger bird of Apollo as well as of the goddess Athene in Greece and was linked with the sun cult of Mithras. In China, it was the three-legged emblem of the Chou dynasty, symbolizing the rising, zenith and sinking of the sun (in which a legendary raven was said to live). In both China and Japan, ravens are emblems of family love. The raven appears in Africa and elsewhere as a guide, warning of dangers.

In Native North America it features prominently as a culture hero and trickster. The Inuit believe that Raven was born by magical means, the offspring of a woman who swallowed a feather or, in other accounts, a stone. Other native peoples, such as the Tlingit of southern Alaska, envisage two Ravens, one a trickster and the other a culture hero. Usually, however, the character has both tricksterish and creator qualities, as in the Tsimshian story of how Raven stole the heavenly bodies from a greedy chief and hurled them into the sky.

Rays *see* **Sun**

Rebecca

In the Bible,[1] Abraham asked his servant Eliezer to find a wife for his son Isaac. At a well where women came to fetch water, Rebecca gladly drew water for Eliezer and his camels, and so was chosen. The scene was popular among 17th- and 18th-century artists.

Red

The active and masculine colour of life, fire, war, energy, aggression, danger, political revolution, impulse, emotion, passion, love, joy, festivity, vitality, health, strength and youth. Red was the emblematic colour of sun and war gods, and of power generally. In its destructive aspect it was sometimes linked with evil, notably in Egyptian myth where it was the colour of Set and of the chaos serpent, Apep. Death was a red horseman in Celtic tradition. As the colour of arousal, it was also linked with sexuality – with the phallic god, Priapus, in Greece and with the "scarlet woman" of prostitution.

More often, however, its symbolism was positive. In China, where it was the emblem of the Chou dynasty and of the south, it was the luckiest of all colours, associated with life, wealth, energy, and summer. Red on white could symbolize lost blood and the pallor of death, but the Asian red beauty spot is protective. In the Chinese theatre, red paint on an actor's face marks them out as holy. Red ochre was used in early burials to "paint life" into the dead.

Even in Christianity, where the main symbolism of red is sacrificial (Christ's Passion and the martyrdom of saints), it was also an emblem of God's soldiers – crusaders, cardinals and pilgrims. Calendars marking

Reed: *see* CROSS;
PASSION; Water;
Witchcraft

Religious Ceremonial
Objects: *see* Aaron; Blood;
Christ, The Life of; John the
Evangelist, St; Laurence, St
¹ *Mark 14:23–25*

Religious Dress: *see* Jerome,
St; Religious Ceremonial
Objects; RELIGIOUS
ORDERS

feasts and saints' days in red are the origin of the "red-letter" day. Red is also traditionally linked with the occult arts and is a dominant colour in the Tarot. In alchemy it symbolizes sulphur and the fire of purification.

Reed

A Japanese emblem of purification in the creation myth of Izanagi, perhaps by association with water. "The Reed Plain" is a Japanese metaphor for the mortal world, and the reed for manifestation. The reed also had purification symbolism in the Celtic world and was superstitiously thought effective against witches. It had fertility symbolism in Mesoamerica and was an emblem of the god Pan (from his invention of the reed "pan pipes") and music in Greece.

More generally, the reed is a symbol of weakness, as in the biblical reference to Egypt as a weak ally, a "broken reed" (Isaiah 36:6).

The reed cross is an emblem of John the Baptist who, Christ said, was not a reed shaken in the wind. The reed is also a symbol of Christ's Passion because a sponge, soaked in vinegar, was put on the end of a reed to reach Christ's mouth as he was crucified.

Reindeer *see* Deer

Religious Ceremonial Objects

Many religious objects have gathered significance from Old and New Testament teaching, and are related to particular sacraments, incidents or people. A **censer**, or thurible, is the vessel in which incense burns, and may be the attribute of Aaron or of deacon saints such as Laurence. A **chalice** is the sacramental cup of the Eucharist. At the Last Supper, Christ

"took the cup, and when he had given thanks, he gave it to them; and they all drank of it. And he said unto them, This is my blood of the new testament, which is shed for many. ... I will drink no more of the fruit of the vine, until that day that I drink it new in the kingdom of God."¹ The cup of salvation is, therefore, an important feature in painting illustrating the service of the Eucharist, and is shown with various saints or priests officiating. It may be presented to Christ by an angel during the Agony in the Garden. A chalice with snakes is the attribute of St John the Evangelist. A **corporal** is the cloth on which the chalice is placed during the Eucharist before consecration.

A **ciborium** is a cup with an arched cover which is reserved for the Host. A ciborium may also be a canopy covering an altar or shrine. A **pyx** is a small portable receptacle for the Host. The Host is preserved in a **tabernacle**. A **monstrance**, an open or transparent receptacle, holds the consecrated Host for display at the service of benediction. It is also carried in processions, especially at the Corpus Christi – a celebration of the Sacrament of the Eucharist, founded in 1264 by Pope Urban IV. Similar containers termed **reliquaries**, usually highly ornate, hold holy relics and were used to perform miracles. They are seen carried in procession, as in the *Stories of the Relic of the True Cross* by Bellini and artists of his studio.

Religious Dress

The dress of bishops, priests and deacons of the Catholic Church denotes their rank and the office they are performing. When celebrating Mass, they wear a **chasuble**, a highly decorated outer garment; a **maniple**, a band of silk worn on the arm; and a **stole**, a narrow embroidered band worn around the neck and crossed over the chest. A **cope** (a large semi-circular cape with a deep collar) is worn in processions and on important occasions. Otherwise, a **cassock** and **biretta** (a square, ridged hat) are worn; these are usually purple for bishops and black for priests and deacons.

Some elements of the liturgical dress may be common to all ministers. For example, a bishop's mitre is also worn by the pope as bishop of Rome.

In paintings, churchmen are usually depicted in the highest office they attained. Early saints such as St Jerome, who is depicted as a cardinal, were given these offices posthumously.

The Church hierarchy is recognizable from the following attire: the Pope has a **tiara**, a conical hat with three crowns, or wears a white cassock with a short red cloak; cardinals wear a scarlet cassock and broad-brimmed hat; Bishops wear a chasuble or cope, and a **mitre** (a tall, tapered head dress with a cleft) and carry a **crozier** or staff. Deacons may be seen carrying a **censer**. The regular clergy belong to a religious order, and therefore they are seen wearing the habit of their order.

RELIGIOUS ORDERS *see panel overleaf*

Rémi (Remigius), Saint

The son of a count of Gaul, Rémi (*c.*438–*c.*533CE) was appointed Bishop of Rheims at the age of 22. According to legend[1], Clovis I, king of the Franks, vowed to follow his wife's faith if he became glorious in battle. This ambition fulfilled, he was baptized by Rémi but, when he arrived at the font, the sacred oil was found missing; a dove flew down with a phial in its beak and from this the king was anointed. The Master of St Giles shows Rémi as a bishop baptizing the king, and also his conversion of many heretics.

Remus *see* Romulus and Remus

Resin

Immortality – a symbolism based on the belief that resin was an incorruptible substance of long-lived trees such as the cypress, and that it could ensure life after death. Resin was used in embalming and was mixed with incense.

Rhadamanthus *see* Europa

Rhea

A Titan, the daughter of the Greek earth goddess Gaia and the sky god Uranos and the mother of Demeter, Hades, Hera, Hestia, Poseidon and Zeus. Rhea (Roman, Ops) married her brother Kronos, the chief of the gods, who had overthrown their father. Gaia prophesied that Kronos would also be overthrown by one of his offspring, so he devoured each of his children as they were born. But Rhea saved her youngest child, Zeus, by concealing him the moment he was born and presenting Kronos with a rock wrapped up in swaddling clothes, which he swallowed. Zeus later fulfilled Gaia's prophecy. Rhea was sometimes identified with Cybele, the Great Mother.

Rhiannon

A princess of Welsh myth, the daughter of the king of the Otherworld. Rhiannon appears in the *Mabinogion* as the wife of the hero Pwll, lord of Dyfed. She was associated with hors-

RELIGIOUS ORDERS: *see* COLOURS: Religious Dress *and individual saints*

RELIGIOUS ORDERS

Monasticism was in existence before the legalization of Christianity in the Roman Empire(313CE). Hermits formed communities dedicated to prayer and the Christian doctrine, but St Anthony is usually considered to have been the founder of monasticism in the 3rd century. The different orders were distinguished by the habits their members wore. An abbot or abbess is shown with the pastoral staff, which signifies office, but otherwise wears the dress of his or her order. The following is a brief description of some of the most frequently painted orders and their identifying attributes:

The **Benedictines**, founded by St Benedict *c.*529CE at Monte Cassino, are the oldest order in Europe, The abbey founded in 910CE at Cluny, became a major religious centre in the Middle Ages. The rule stressed communal living, physical labour and learning. Their habit is black.

There were also several reformed versions of the Benedictine order, resulting in: the **Camaldolese**, founded by St Romuald in the early 11th century, who wear white; the **Vallombrosians**, founded by St John Gualbert *c.*1038, who wear light grey; the **Carthusians (Charterhouse)**, founded by St Bruno *c.*1090, who wear white; and the **Cistercians**, founded by St Bernard of Clairvaux *c.*1115, who also wear white. The **Olivetians** and **Oratorians** were also reformed Benedictines, and paintings for these orders may show their founder wearing white.

The **Augustinians** were founded *c.*1060 and were named after St Augustine of Hippo, whose example they followed. He had lived in a community and looked after the material needs of the church and of the poor. Noted Augustinians included Martin Luther. Their habit is black.

The order of **Franciscans** was founded in 1210 by St Francis of Assisi. These friars were called *frati* (brothers) instead of *padri* (fathers) to emphasize their humility, and St Francis added the term *minori* to members of his community. They were noted as missionaries and preachers and took vows of poverty, chastity and obedience. They renounced all forms of ownership and were mendicants, living solely on alms. Their hooded habit was first grey, hence the name "grey friars", but two centuries later it changed to brown and was bound at the waist with a knotted cord. They are shown barefoot or wearing only simple sandals. With St Clare, St Francis also established the **Poor Clares** in 1212, the first community for poor women.

The **Dominicans** were founded in 1216 by St Dominic. Like the Franciscans they took vows, particularly of poverty, and were mendicant. They were preachers but were also known for emphasizing study and teaching. Their habit is a white gown with a black hooded cloak.

The **Jesuits (Society of Jesus)** were founded by St Ignatius Loyola and approved by the Pope in 1540. Active missionaries, the Jesuits place emphasis on education, charity and moderation. Their habit is black with a high collar.

The princess Rhiannon; after a relief.

In myth, either it was the gift of a culture hero or it appeared in the primeval gourd with human life itself. Rice wine was drunk ritually in China as a form of ambrosia, and rice grains, which had protective symbolism, were placed in the mouths of the dead. Balinese veneration of the Rice Mother, a figure made from a long (male) and shorter (female) corn sheaf, expressed southeast Asian folk beliefs that rice plants, like humans, contained within them a vital spirit. In Japan, Inari was a god not only of rice but also of prosperity.

Right *see* **Left and Right**

Rinaldo

A Christian hero who features in the epic poem *Jerusalem Delivered* by Torquato Tasso (1544–95), which describes the siege and capture of Jerusalem from the Saracens during the First Crusade. Rinaldo was lulled to sleep by the Saracen sorceress Armida, who planned to kill him but was suddenly overcome by his beauty.[1] In *Rinaldo and Armida*, Poussin shows Cupid (Eros) holding back the hand in which she clutches a dagger; and in another version he depicts her carrying Rinaldo away to her enchanted castle.

The companions of Rinaldo, Carlo and Ubaldo, set out to rescue the knight, fighting a dragon and savage beasts on their way. Nymphs bathing naked tried to lure them into laying down their arms, but they passed on unmoved. They found Rinaldo in Armida's thrall, gazing into her eyes as she held up a mirror so that each could see the passion of their love. In his *Rinaldo and Armida* Giambattista Tiepolo shows this moment, and the subject may be used to illustrate men's

es and is probably identifiable with the Celtic horse goddess Epona. For example, she first appeared to Pwyll on a magic white mare which no horse could ever catch. Later, she was falsely charged with devouring her son Pryderi, and forced to carry Pwyll's guests from the horse block into his palace in punishment. She was released from this when Pryderi, who had been kidnapped, reappeared several years later.

Rhinoceros

A lucky emblem in China, curiously linked with scholarship. Folklore said its horn could detect poison. Superstitiously, powdered rhinoceros horn is thought to improve virility, and its medicinal use in India may have contributed to the legend of the unicorn.

Rice

A fecundity symbol at weddings – a custom taken from India. In Asia, rice is the emblematic equivalent of corn, a symbol of divine nourishment, both bodily and spiritually.

Rhinoceros: *see* Horn; Unicorn

Rice: *see* Corn; Fox; Inari; Marriage; Rat

Rinaldo: *see* Tancred
[1] Tasso, *Jerusalem Delivered* XIV:1xvi–1xx
[2] Tasso, *Jerusalem Delivered* XVI:xx–xxxiv

The Rice Mother, from a 19th-century northern Balinese figure.

enslavement by women. When Armida departed, Ubaldo stepped forward and showed Rinaldo his true image in his shield, at which Rinaldo threw off his crown of flowers.[2] Charles van Loo painted episodes from the poem (Palazzo Reale, Turin), including the warrior listening to Armida's pleas as he returned to the Crusade with Carlo and Ubaldo.

Ring

Eternity, unity, wholeness, commitment, authority. The circular symbolism of the ring makes it an emblem of completion, strength and protection as well as of continuity – all of which help to give significance to engagement and wedding rings. The oldest surviving rings (from Egypt) are signets bearing either personal seals or amulets, usually in the form of a scarab beetle symbolizing eternal life. Thus from the earliest times the ring has been an emblem of authority or delegated authority, of occult protective power and of a personal pledge.

Roman betrothal rings were tokens of legal vows. The later custom of giving a wedding ring was based probably on ecclesiastical use of signet rings. Wedding rings were originally worn, like episcopal rings, on the third finger of the right hand. The Pope's Fisherman's Ring (showing Peter drawing in a net), broken at his death, is the supreme Roman Catholic seal. The plain gold nun's ring is a binding symbol of her marriage to Christ. The Doge's ring, thrown into the Adriatic at Venice on Ascension Day, was a token of perpetual Venetian sea power, a mystic ceremony initiated by Pope Alexander III after the city helped him to humiliate Emperor Frederick Barbarossa in 1176.

Rings are associated with magical force or hidden treasure in many legends. An ancient belief held that King Solomon's ring was the source of his supernatural powers and wisdom.

River, Stream

The flowing away of all things – a powerful natural symbol of the passage of time and life. For the many great civilizations dependent on their irrigating fertility, rivers were important symbols of supply as well as purification and removal. The common image of four streams in paradise flowing from the Tree of Life to the cardinal points was a metaphor for divine energy and spiritual nourishment coursing through the whole universe.

In Hinduism, the Ganges, personified by the supreme river goddess Ganga, was an axial symbol, depicted in myth as falling from heaven to cleanse the earth (cushioned by Shiva) and penetrating also to the underworld. Purification in the Ganges is a central ritual in Hinduism. A cruder example of purification symbolism appears in the Greek myth of Herakles (in Roman myth, Hercules) who diverted a river through the Augean stables. Because they were unpredictable, rivers were propitiated with sacrifices to local gods or, more usually, goddesses. They often appear as boundaries, particularly dividing the worlds of the living and the dead. The Celts thought that confluences of rivers were particularly sacred. In China, the drowned were thought to haunt rivers, hoping to find living bodies that they could inhabit.

Robin

An alternative to the goldfinch in the legendary story of a bird that plucked a thorn from Christ's crown and was splashed with his blood. This may have led to European superstitions that the robin announces death by tapping at a window pane, and that it is bad luck to kill one.

Rock

Dependability, integrity, steadfastness, stability, permanence, strength and, in China, longevity. Rock, the most common biblical metaphor for reliability, is often equated with the living force of God, manifested by water springing from the rock struck by the rod of Moses. Christ is the "Rock of Ages", the source of eternal life. The Church itself was founded by the disciple Peter (Greek *petros* "a stone", *petra* "a rock"). In Chinese painting, rock is a Yang (male and active) symbol. Rock sculptures, notably on Easter Island, in Egypt, and more recently in Borglum's monumental presidential carvings at Mount Rushmore in the USA, convey the same emblematic meaning of power. Gods were reputedly born from living rock in several Near Eastern religions, notably Mithraism.

Rod

An ancient emblem of supernatural power, symbolically associated with the potency of the tree or branch, the phallus, the snake and the hand or pointing finger. The creative and fertility symbolism of the rod is clear in the biblical story of Aaron's rod, which flowered and produced almonds as a sign of divine blessing on the house of Levi – endorsing the authority of Aaron, the brother of Moses, as the founder of the Jewish priesthood.[1] In religion, myth, legend and folklore, the rod, especially from particular trees such as the hazel, is an emblem of personal authority or gives its holder power over the natural world – to transform, prophesy, arbitrate, heal wounds, find water and summon or dismiss spirits.

ROME, THE KINGS OF *see panel overleaf*

Romulus and Remus

Twin brothers and founders of Rome (traditionally in 753BCE), with the city said to have been named after Romulus, its legendary first king. According to legend[1] the boys were descendants of Aeneas, the Trojan hero destined to be the forefather of the Romans.

King Numitor of Alba Longa, a descendant of the hero Aeneas, was overthrown by his brother Amulius, who ordered Numitor's only child, Rhea Silvia, to become a Vestal virgin. One day, in a sacred grove, the god Mars raped her as she slept. When she bore twins, Romulus and Remus, Amulius commanded that they be abandoned on the River Tiber. They were cast adrift in a basket saved by a she-wolf, who suckled them, and they were adopted by a shepherd, Faustulus.

Romulus and Remus suckled by a she-wolf; after an Etruscan bronze, with the twins added in the Renaissance.

ROME, THE KINGS OF:
see Romulus and Remus and
individual names

The legendary second king of Rome, Numa Pompilius (left); after a Roman coin.

Rood screen: see CROSS;
Veil

Rope: see Bonds; Cord;
Snake

ROME, THE KINGS OF

There were said to have been seven kings of Rome between the traditional date of the city's foundation (753BCE) and the establishment of the republic (510BCE). The names of these legendary kings were as follows:

King	Traditional dates of reign (all BCE)	Deeds
Romulus	753–715	Founder of the city
Numa Pompilius	715–673	Founded important religious institutions
Tullius Hostilius	673–642	Celebrated soldier
Ancus Marcius	642–616	Built first Tiber bridge
Tarquin the Elder	616–579	Built first stone walls; began temple of Jupiter and Minerva; annexed territory
Servius Tullius	579–534	Constitutional reform
Tarquin the Proud	534–510	Annexed territory; despot

Eventually, Faustulus explained the truth about their origins. Romulus killed Amulius and restored his grandfather Numitor to the throne. The twins decided to found a new city where the she-wolf had found them. They argued over the exact spot and Romulus, acting on a sign from the gods, began to mark out a boundary ditch on the Palatine Hill. Remus jumped over it to show how ineffective it was as a defence. Considering this an act of sacrilege, Romulus killed him, becoming the sole ruler of the new settlement, Rome. He drew many men to the city by declaring it a safe-haven for runaways. However, there were no women, so Romulus invited the chiefs of the surrounding Sabine tribes to a festival, during which his men abducted all the unmarried Sabine women. A war ensued between the Romans and the Sabines which ended after the Sabine women appealed for peace to their fathers and new husbands.

The two peoples were united and Romulus ruled jointly with Titus Tatius, the Sabine monarch, until the latter's death shortly after the war. Romulus ruled alone, the first king of Rome, for a further thirty-three years.

The she-wolf was a symbol of Rome; an Etruscan bronze of one (late 6th or early 5th century BCE) originally stood on the Capitol; Romulus and Remus were added to the statue by Antonio Pollaiuolo in the late 15th century (see illustration).

Rood screen

A carved and decorated partition of wood or stone between the chancel and the main body of the medieval Christian church, originally carrying a cross (rood) of the Crucifixion. It symbolized the division between worldly and priestly spheres, earth and heaven.

Rope

Bondage, but also ascension – the spiritual symbolism of the Indian rope trick. The idea of a rope or cord forming a ladder from earth to heaven was widespread in the ancient world and was sometimes linked with the umbilical cord – specifically among the Australian Aboriginals. In Hindu mysticism, the rope is an emblem of the inner path to spiritual illumination. Ropes and serpents were often linked, as in the Vedic myth of the cosmic serpent acting as a rope to twirl the mountain that churned creation from the sea of milk. In art, looped rope is a sinister attribute of Nemesis, the goddess of retribution, and of St Andrew, who was bound to the cross. Medieval penitents wore ropes around their necks as emblems of submission and remorse.

Rosary

A rosary (literally, a "rose garden") is a string of beads, divided into five sections, and each one having one large bead and ten small. Rosary was the name given by Christian mystics in the 13th century to a sequence of prayers and meditations addressed to the Virgin Mary as the Rose of Heaven, which needed to be counted off on a string of beads. Known as the Mysteries, the prayers are divided into three groups of five: Joyful, Sorrowful and Glorious. A rosary may be included in paintings of the *Virgin and Child*, such as Bergognone's Virgin and Child; or of St Dominic, who was said to have instituted its use as an emblem of devotion.

Prayer beads were used much earlier in India, and with more specific symbolism. The fifty beads of the Hindu rosary are the number of letters in the Sanskrit alphabet and the rosary is linked with the creative power of sound, and in particular with the god

Brahma and his consort Sarasvati, as well as with Shiva. In Buddhism, the beads number 108 – referring to the legend that 108 Brahmins were present at the Buddha's birth. The circle of beads symbolizes the Wheel of Life and Time.

The Islamic rosary, the *mala*, has 99 beads representing all the names of God. A mystic 100th bead, unsounded and non-existent, symbolizes the name that is known only in paradise. Rosaries are superstitiously thought to have talismanic power.

Rose

The paragon of flowers in Western tradition – a symbol of the heart, the centre and the cosmic wheel, and also of sacred, romantic and sensual love. The white rose is an emblem of innocence, purity and virginity; the red symbolizes passion and desire, voluptuous beauty. Both are symbols of perfection and images of the cup of eternal life. With this meaning, rose petals were scattered on graves at the Roman festival of Rosaria, and Roman emperors wore rose wreaths as crowns.

The Pope sent a golden rose to sovereigns whom the Church esteemed, and since the Middle Ages roses have played an important part in heraldry. The wars that racked England during the 14th century gained the name the Wars of the Roses from the white rose of the House of York and the red rose of the House of Lancaster. With peace restored, the flower was adopted by the Tudor dynasty and became a royal device.

Mortality is symbolized by the blown rose, and the red rose can signify spilt blood, martyrdom, death and resurrection. Classical myth linked the red rose through its colour with

The "Rosy Cross" of the Rosicrucians – a cross with a central rose symbol.

Rosemary

the war god Ares and his consort Aphrodite (Mars and Aphrodite in Roman myth), whose birth from the sea was said to be the occasion for the flower's first bloom; and with her slain lover Adonis. According to one account, Adonis was fatally attacked by a wild boar. As Aphrodite ran to her wounded lover's side, she tore her foot on the thorns of a white rose, the drops of her blood turning it red. The rose was also a sun and dawn emblem and was linked with the Greek god Dionysos, the goddess Hecate, the Graces and the Muses.

In medieval Christianity the petals of the flower were taken to represent the five wounds of Christ; a blood-red rose growing among thorns signified the suffering of Christ and of his love for humanity, and the early martyrs and their persecutors; and a white rose reflected the spotless purity of the Virgin. In the Garden of Eden the rose grew without thorns, and its fragrance and beauty were a reminder of the glory of Paradise. Saints and angels often hold roses as an indication of the heavenly bliss they have entered.

The rose became the focal image of the occult and Cabbalistic Rosicrucian society in the 17th century, whose emblem was a cross formed by a rose itself or a wooden cross with a central rose or roses at the intersections of the arms. Multilayered petals symbolized stages of initiation, the central rose representing the point of unity, the heart of Christ, divine light, the sun at the centre of the wheel of life.

The rosette (the flower seen from above) and the Gothic rose also have wheel symbolism, connoting the unfolding of generative power – a Western equivalent of the emblematic lotus. In the related symbolism of Freemasonry, three St John's roses represent light, love and life. The Virgin Mary is the Rose of Heaven and the sinless Rose Without Thorns, a reference to her faultless purity. Rose garlands were also a symbol of virginity in Rome.

An important secondary symbolism of the rose is discretion. Various tales account for this. In a Roman myth, Cupid stops rumours about the infidelities of Venus by bribing the god of silence with a rose. Another explanation is that rose garlands were worn at Dionysian (Bacchanalian) revels in the belief that they would moderate drunkenness and loose talk. Roses were later hung or painted above council or banqueting tables as signs that conversation was *sub rosa* – private not public.

Rosemary
"There's rosemary, that's for remembrance," says Ophelia in Shakespeare's Hamlet (4:5). This aromatic herb was chosen as an ancient marriage token, perhaps for its lingering fragrance. Its Latin name, *ros marinus* literally means "sea dew"; hence it was connected with the sea-born goddess Venus (Aphrodite in Greek myth), and with fidelity in love

Round Table, The
Unity, coherence, and completeness. According to Arthurian legend, the famous table with an empty place for the Holy Grail was designed by Merlin to seat 150 knights without wrangling over precedence. The magical power of the Round Table derives from Celtic reverence for the circle, probably based on earlier worship of

sky gods. Cosmic significance is similarly suggested by the Hindu round table constructed in twelve segments and linked with the Zodiac and the months of the year.

Ruby

Ardent love, vitality, royalty, courage – the stone of fortune and happiness (including longevity) in India, Burma, China and Japan. Its colour, ranging from red to the purplish "pigeon's blood" hue of the most valuable rubies, linked it in the classical world with the fiery Ares (in Roman myth, Mars), but also with Kronos (Saturn), who controlled passion. It was said to inflame lovers and was believed to glow in the dark. Its habit of looking paler under some lights was read as a warning – of poison or other dangers. (Catherine of Aragon's ruby reputedly lost colour as she lost favour with England's Henry VIII.) Homeopathically, the ruby was a medicinal jewel, thought to be effective for loss of blood as well as low spirits. Fire is the symbolism of its appearance on the foreheads of legendary dragons.

Rudder

As the instrument of guidance, an emblem of responsible authority, sometimes shown on official medallions. In Western art it is an attribute of Fortune, as well as Abundance.

Rue

A bitter herb sometimes used in church to sprinkle holy water, and in Hebrew tradition associated with repentance. Thus it became the "herb of grace" mentioned by Ophelia in Shakespeare's *Hamlet* (4:5). As a homophone of the verb "rue", it is also a symbol of sorrow in English tradition.

Runes

Early Germanic lettering which acquired quasi-magic symbolism as this form of alphabet spread from southern Europe north to Scandinavia and Britain. The linking of specific runes to the sun, moon and other sky gods, and the art of funerary rune carving, led to the belief that runes embodied supernatural powers – to protect, to avenge and particularly to foretell the future.

Runes inscribed on stone, wood or leather were shamanistically used to cast spells or in divination to convey oracular messages. The zigzag sign of Adolf Hitler's SS, based on the double Sigrune ("victory rune", or runic "S", associated with the sun, victory and the yew from which bows were cut), was an example of Nazi attempts to co-opt runes as so-called "Aryan" symbols.

Ruth

In the Bible,[1] Ruth was from the land of Moab, but married into a Jewish family who had settled there. When her husband and father-in-law died, she left her country to accompany Naomi, her mother-in-law, to Bethlehem. Naomi begged her not to stay but Ruth refused to abandon her. They arrived at the beginning of the harvest and Ruth asked the Israelite Boaz if she might glean in his fields. He granted her permission, telling his reapers to leave her extra corn from their sheaves. Eventually they married, and from their union evolved the line of David and, therefore, in Christian tradition, of Christ.

In his painting *Summer* or *The Meeting Between Ruth and Boaz*, Poussin chose this subject to illustrate the season of summer.

Ruby: *see* Blood; Dragon; Fire, Flame; JEWELS; LONGEVITY; Purple; Red

Rudder: *see* FORTUNE

Rue: *see* Water

Runes: *see* Sun; Swastika; VICTORY; Yew; Zigzag

Runic symbols being read from a stick; after a medieval woodcut.

Sabbath

The Jewish symbol of God's Creation and of the covenant between God and the Israelites, commemorated in a festive day of rest on Saturday. Christianity initially followed the established tradition of resting on the seventh day (Saturday), but with less strict prohibitions. However, the Christian Sabbath was moved to Sunday, the day on which Christ rose from the dead. The Islamic holy day of rest is Friday. Behind these common Semitic customs perhaps lies an earlier seventh-day tradition based on the four quarterly phases of the moon. The Babylonian seventh day was dedicated to the moon-god Sin, and was a time at which important state functions were suspended. This has suggested to some scholars the symbolism of an unpropitious "day out of time".

The "witches' sabbath" of medieval and later imagination was an inversion of the Christian Sunday, suggesting that while God rested, demons were abroad.

Sabine Women, The

According to Roman legend[1] Romulus founded Rome in 753BCE. Since there were few women in the settlement, he was concerned about the future growth and greatness of Rome, so he invited the neighbouring Sabines to a festival and, at a given signal, the Romans raped the Sabine women. They were careful to choose unmarried women, for the intention was to unite with their neighbours "by the greatest and surest bonds"; only one married woman was mistakenly chosen. The Rape of the Sabine Women was treated by numerous sculptors and painters, such as Giambologna (Loggia dei Lanzi, Florence) and Pietro da Cortona.

Romulus refused to let the women return, so their dishonoured fathers and brothers marched against Rome. During the battle, the women came running out "with miserable cries and lamentations, like creatures possessed, in the midst of the army and among the dead bodies, to come at their husbands and their fathers, some with their young babes in their arms, others with their hair loose about their ears, but all calling, now upon the Sabines, now upon the Romans, in the most tender and endearing words." Jacques-Louis David drew upon this dramatic account in *The Intervention of the Sabine Women*. Both armies melted with compassion and the women ended the fight by pleading with both sides to unite.

Sacra Conversazione

The *sacra conversazione*, or "holy conversation", is a type of devotional altarpiece that was developed *c*.1440, in which various saints flank the Madonna and Child, with the Madonna often shown enthroned, in the same pictorial space, rather than in separate panels. An example is Domenico Veneziano's *St Lucy Altarpiece or Madonna and Child with Saints*.

Sacraments, The

The seven sacraments of the Catholic church are Baptism, Confirmation, the Eucharist, Penance, Ordination, Matrimony and Extreme Unction. They were painted only occasionally in the Renaissance, Rogier van der Weyden's *Seven Sacraments Triptych* being a rare example. Later, Poussin executed two large series of seven separate paintings, both series entitled *The Seven Sacraments*. Five of the subjects were taken from the lives of Christ and the Virgin: *Baptism* is represented by John the Baptist and Christ; *Penance* by Mary Magdalene washing Christ's feet; *Ordination* by Christ giving the keys of heaven to St Peter; *Matrimony* by the marriage of the Virgin and Joseph; and the *Eucharist* by the Last Supper. *Extreme Unction* is a man receiving the sacrament as he lies dying surrounded by mourners. *Confirmation* is set in the catacombs, and evokes the atmosphere of the early Christian age.

Sacrifice

A means of communion between a god and a person or persons in which something prized is sanctified and then destroyed as a symbolic offering. The high status and value of domestic animals in the ancient world made them the most common sacrifice.

Forms of sacrifice are extensive and varied across cultures, ranging from rituals of atonement or purification to offerings made in propitiation or gratitude – and even to funerary customs in which human victims were killed to become tutelary spirits or to provide companionship or services in the afterlife. At its deepest level, sacrifice was a creative act mimicking the death of all living things, particularly vegetative life in winter, as a necessary prelude to rebirth or the renewal of fertility.

Saddle

An emblem of family life in ancient China where the word for "saddle" is a homophone of "peace". Hence the custom by which a bride steps over a saddle at the gateway of her husband's parental home. On the steppes of central Asia, dying shamans were pillowed on their saddles – symbols of their journey to a celestial afterlife.

Sail

A full sail or billowing drapery may illustrate what could not otherwise be shown – the element of air, wind, vital breath and the soul, as in medieval paintings where sails represented the advent of the Holy Spirit. In mythological painting a sail may suggest

Sacrifice: *see* Blood; Bull; CROSS; Lamb; Ox; Ram

Saddle: *see* AFTERLIFE

Sail: *see* Air; Breath; Breathing; FORTUNE; Soul; TRIUMPHS; Wind

prosperity and success, as in works depicting triumphs. Because the winds are not constant, a sail may also be the attribute of Fortune, because she was inconstant, and of the Greek goddess Athene (Minerva to the Romans).

Saints

Saint was the title given to the Apostles, the Evangelists, and the numerous martyrs who died during the Roman persecutions. Pope Alexander III (1159–81) gave the Papacy the exclusive right to canonize others, such as popes and monarchs.

Saints are shown with haloes, and their attributes usually relate closely to their lives. They can appear in paintings together regardless of the period in which they lived. In visions of Paradise, such as that by Nardo di Cione (Strozzi Chapel, Santa Maria Novella, Florence), saints, accompanied by angels, surround the throne of Christ, according to their hierarchy. Like a jury, they may also flank Christ at the Last Judgment.

The reasons for the choice of a particular saint in art are manifold. The saint could be the patron of the city or the titular saint of the church or chapel for which the work was commissioned. Paintings for a monastic order often include its founder.

The saint may be the namesake of the patron or the protector of the patron's family. The image of a saint may also be commissioned for the significance of particular episodes in his or her life; for example, St Sebastian recovered from his wounds and was therefore invoked against the plague.

Salamander

A legendary lizard which lived in the heart of fire, therefore taken as an

The legendary salamander in the flames, which do not harm it.

emblem of fire itself. Pliny reported the belief that the salamander survived fire by quenching it with its cold body, a story perhaps based on the damp-loving amphibians called fire salamanders because of their bright yellow-and-black markings. The salamander, said to be born in fire, is a common symbol in alchemical drawings, symbolizing the purifying agents of fire and sulphur. It is a Christian symbol of the pure-spirited believer who resists the flames of temptation, and sometimes a symbol of chastity. As the device of Francis I of France, the salamander symbolized the patronage of good things, the destruction of bad. More usually, in heraldry, it symbolizes courage.

Salmon

Virility, fecundity, courage, wisdom and foresight – a symbolism common to coastal peoples of northern Europe and of the American northwest. Salmon battling their way upstream became totemic images of nature's bounty and wisdom. For the Celts, transformation and phallic symbolism mingle in the story of Tuan mac Cairill who, in salmon form, was said to have impregnated an Irish queen to whom he was served after being caught. The Irish hero Finn scolded his thumb as he cooked the Salmon of Knowledge. He sucked his thumb to ease the pain, and in tasting the salmon's juice acquired powers of prophecy and wisdom.

Salome

Salome was the daughter of Herodias, the wife of Herod Agrippa, ruler of Galilee and Perea. In the New Testament[1] (which does not give her name; it is known from the Jewish historian Josephus), she danced at a banquet to celebrate the birthday of her stepfather. Her dance pleased him so much that he promised to give her whatever she requested as a reward. John the Baptist had preached against Herod's marriage to Salome's mother, Herodias, and Herodias instructed her daughter to demand John's head.

In cycles of the life of the Baptist the episode of the dance of Salome often occupied a prominent position, as in Filippino Lippi's frescoes (Prato Cathedral, Florence). Salome's story of intrigue and murder also inspired many other artists, notably Aubrey Beardsley, who made illustrations to the play *Salome* by Oscar Wilde (1856–1900).

Salt

A key symbol of hospitality and friendship in the ancient Middle East, where salt was an important and valuable commodity. Because it was used as a preservative as well as for its savour, sharing salt and bread also implied a lasting relationship. The association between salt and incorruptibility made it a covenanted offering in Hebrew sacrifices and an emblem of purification in religious rituals from Greece to Japan. The

Christian elect were the "salt of the earth" according to Christ's Sermon on the Mount.

Greeks and Romans both credited salt with protective qualities. Hence the superstition that it is bad luck to spill it and that a pinch should be thrown over the left shoulder to avert this. (Judas Iscariot has ominously spilt the salt in Leonardo da Vinci's *The Last Supper*, c.1495). Salt is also associated with the bite of sharp wit and wisdom.

Salvator Mundi

Salvator Mundi, or Saviour of the World, was the name applied to a type of devotional image showing Christ holding a globe, as in a painting of c.1510 by Carpaccio. Christ may be making the sign of benediction, pointing above to the divine, wearing a Crown of Thorns, or any combination of these.

Samson

A biblical leader, Samson had great physical strength, and is shown as muscular with long hair. His attribute is often a broken pillar.

The Israelites had been ruled by the Philistines for forty years when an angel announced to Manoah and his barren wife that they would conceive a son, to be named Samson, who would liberate their people. He warned that Samson's hair must never be cut. Manoah made an offering to the Lord, and as he lit the altar fire the angel ascended to heaven in the flames.[1] Like the mythological Hercules, the young Samson slew a lion with his bare hands.[2] He was captured by the Philistines, but he broke the ropes binding him and killed 1,000 men with the jawbone of a don-

Salome: *see* John the Baptist, Saint
[1] *Matthew 14:1–11*

Salt: *see* WISDOM

Samson: *see* Cassone; Hercules
[1] *Judges 13:1–20*
[2] *Judges 14:5–6*
[3] *Judges 15:13–19*
[4] *Judges 16:1–30*

Sand

Sand: *see* Hourglass;
Washing

Sap: *see* Soma; Vine; Wine

Sapphire: *see* Blue;
JEWELS; Sky; VIRTUES

Sappho:
¹ Ovid, *Heroids XV*

Sardanapalus:
¹ Diodorus of Sicily, *II.27*

key. This weapon also provided him with a stream of water to quench his thirst.³

Samson fell in love with Delilah who, bribed by the Philistine kings, sought to discover the secret of his strength. At last he revealed the truth, and Delilah, having lulled him to sleep in her lap, called upon the Philistines to shave his head. This done, they bound him, put out his eyes, set him in bronze chains and put him to work at a prison mill. There, however, his hair began to grow again.

When brought out to entertain an audience of Philistines, including their five kings, he was placed between pillars supporting the building. Samson asked God to restore his strength, and he brought down the pillars and whole building, killing himself, as well as more Philistines than he had ever killed during his life.⁴

The most commonly painted episode of his life is the sleeping Samson betrayed by Delilah to the Philistines, as in Rubens' *Samson and Delilah*. The subject illustrates how even the strong can be rendered powerless by a woman. Other episodes were also favoured, such as the annunciation of Samson's birth, or the angel ascending in the flames of Manoah's sacrifice. Rembrandt depicted the gory scene of *The Blinding of Samson*.

Sand

A symbol of multiplicity because of its countless grains. In arid regions, particularly in North Africa and the Near East, sand was a substitute for water as a cleansing medium and was associated with purification. More generally, it symbolizes instability, obliteration and the erosion of time (through its use in hour glasses).

Sap

The vital force that permeates all life – symbolically an agent of renewal, spiritualization and immortality. Plant juice was widely equated with the cyclic storing and flow of semen, with the death and renewal of vegetative life, and with growth toward divine light. The Dionysian cult of the grape and the Vedic cult of *soma* (with which it was possibly connected) are the most significant expressions of these ideas.

Sapphire

A jewel of heaven (from its cerulean colour) and, in stone lore, an emblem of celestial harmony, peace, truth and serenity. The sapphire was sacred to the planet Saturn in Hindu tradition and was therefore associated with self-control.

Sappho

The Greek poetess Sappho (7th century BCE), lived on the island of Lesbos and was famous for her poetry, beauty and the violence of her passions.¹ She fell in love with Phaon, who refused her, whereupon she threw herself into the sea. The Lesbians honoured her as a goddess after her death. Sappho and Phaon are shown together in Jacques-Louis David's *Sappho and Phaon*, and Gustave Moreau painted *Sappho Leaping into the Sea*.

Sardanapalus

A 7th-century BCE king of Assyria, Sardanapalus was besieged in his capital and ordered his wives, favourite concubine Myrrha, servants and treasures to be burned on a funeral pyre with him.¹ Delacroix's extravagant *Death of Sardanapalus* was based on Byron's play *Sardanapalus* (1821).

Sarpedon

A warrior king of Greek myth, the son of Europa and Zeus and the brother of Minos and Rhadamanthys. He and his brothers ruled Crete jointly until all three of them fell in love with the same beautiful youth, Miletus. Sarpedon was the one to win his love, and as a result caused Minos to expel them, as well as Rhadamanthys.

In a full and eventful career, Sarpedon assisted in the foundation of the kingdom of Lycia in southwestern Asia Minor. He married and had a son, Evander, later king of Lycia. Finally, when he died he became a judge of the dead in the underworld.

Satan

In the Christian faith, Satan was a rebel angel who rose up in pride against God, and fell from heaven, vanquished by St Michael and his armies. Thereafter his sole aim was to foster evil. As an angel, his name had been Lucifer.[1] He was also associated with the false god Beelzebub, called by the Gospels "the prince of the devils".[2] In images of the Last Judgment Satan is represented as the Lord of Hell, an incarnation of evil, who feeds on sinners and is surrounded by demons and the condemned, as in Taddeo di Bartolo's fresco (Collegiata, San Gimignano).

The Book of Revelation describes how "the great dragon was cast out, that old serpent called the Devil, and Satan, which deceiveth the whole world; he was cast out into the earth, and his angels were cast out with him."[3] Thus the Devil may take on the guise of a dragon, in the fights with Saints Michael and George; or a serpent, in the Temptation of Eve. After the Crucifixion, Christ descended into Limbo and vanquished the Devil. Satan may also be represented as a hybrid with horns, pointed ears, a tail, claws, cloven hoofs, the wings of a bat and the face of an animal.

Sati

A Hindu goddess, the daughter of Daksha and the first wife of Shiva. According to one account, when Shiva was excluded from a horse sacrifice arranged by her father, Sati was so overcome with shame that she burned herself to death. She was reincarnated as Parvati or Uma, the god's second wife.

Saturn

An Italian agricultural deity later identified with the Greek god Kronos.

Satyr

A goatish symbol of male lust and the life of sensual pleasure. In classical mythology satyrs accompany nature gods such as the Roman Silvanus, the Greek Dionysos (in Roman myth, Bacchus) and Pan (Faunus). They ravish nymphs and naiads, drink copiously, play pipes, and pour their unbridled energy into ecstatic dancing. Attributes include ivy wreaths, bunches of grapes, fruit, cornucopias and snakes – a reference to the legend in which Faunus turned himself into a snake to violate his own daughter.

Medieval Christianity took a stern view of satyrs, associating them not with the Golden Age of carnal delights but with evil. They remained favourite subjects for erotic art, usually depicted as semi-human with a goat's beard, hairy legs and hoofs, and sometimes a horse's tail, often naked with an erection. However, a satyr appears with peasants in Jacob Jor-

Sarpedon: *see* Bellerophon; Minos; Rhadamanthys

Satan: *see* ANGELS; Descent in Hell; Passion of Christ, The
[1] *Isaiah 14:12*
[2] *Matthew 12:24*
[3] *Revelation 12:9*

Sati: *see* Shiva

Saturn: *see* Kronos; TIME

Satyr: *see* Dance; Devils; Dionysos; Faunus and Fauns; Goat; Pan; Snake; Wreath, Garland

Satyrs drinking from a wineskin; after a 5th-century BCE wine cooler.

Saul

*Venus riding in a
scallop, after Botticelli's*
The Birth of Venus.

daens' *Satyr and the Peasant*, pointing
out the incongruity of blowing on
soup to make it cool and on hands
to warm them.

Saul

In the Bible, Saul[1] was chosen by God
and anointed by Samuel as the first
king of the twelve tribes of Israel. He
waged war on the Philistines and
Amalekites, but God rejected him for
his leniency to his enemies. Saul found
comfort with David, the court musician, who played the harp so beautifully that Saul made him his
armour-bearer.[2] Rembrandt's *David
Harping Before Saul* shows sympathy
with the melancholic king. On the eve
of battle with the Philistines, Saul
consulted the Witch of Endor, from
whom he learned that his army would
be defeated and his three sons killed.
When this happened, he fell on his
own sword, as shown in Bruegel's
panoramic *The Suicide of Saul*.

Scales

Justice, impartiality, equilibrium, harmony, truth, divine judgment. Scales
represent the Zodiac sign of Libra at
the balancing point of the year when
the sun crosses the equator southward.
They are the most common emblem
not only of Justice but of the causal
link between sin and punishment in the
afterlife. In Western art, scales are the
attribute of Themis, the Greek goddess
of law and order; the messenger-god
Hermes (in Roman myth, Mercury);
the archangel Michael; and Logic and
Opportunity personified. Empty scales
may be carried by Famine.

Judgmental scales are associated
with Christ and, in Egypt, with Osiris
and the truth goddess, Ma'at. In
Tibetan art, good deeds and bad were

symbolized by white and black stones
in the balancing pans. They may be
seen in art with relevant trades, for
example in Quentin Metsys' *The
Moneylender and his Wife*.

Scallop

Like other bivalves, a symbol of the
vulva, but particularly significant
through its association with the birth
of the Greek goddess Aphrodite (in
Roman myth, Venus). The painter
Sandro Botticelli famously shows her
coming ashore in a scallop shell
blown by the West wind (*The Birth of
Venus, c.*1484–6).

Christianity took over this pagan
sexuality and fertility myth to make
the scallop shell a symbol of the hope
of resurrection and rebirth. The scallop is the particular symbol of the
Apostle James, son of Zebedee, reputed to have voyaged to Spain; his
shrine at Santiago de Compostela was
a focus of medieval pilgrimage. The
scallop shell became an emblem first
of this pilgrimage and then of pilgrims in general, thirsty for the waters
of the spirit.

Scalp

Among Native North Americans a
symbol of life force. Scalping was
equivalent to head-hunting as a
means of capturing the power or vital
energy of an enemy. Among some
tribes, warriors left a scalp lock as a
sign of confidence and a challenge to
men of other tribes.

Scapegoat

The symbolic discharger of other people's sins or shortcomings. A scapegoat or "goat for Azazel" (a desert
demon) was sent into the wilderness
by the Hebrews on the Day of Atone-

ment, Yom Kippur, emblematically bearing away the transgressions of the Israelites. In Christianity, Christ made himself a scapegoat by taking on himself the sins of the world. According to J. G. Frazer in *The Golden Bough* (1890), earlier traditions in Asia Minor involved the beating and burning of a human victim as a scapegoat for the ruler in countries afflicted by drought, plague or crop failure.

Scarab

An Egyptian solar and male emblem of genesis, rebirth and the eternal life force – the most popular amulet of ancient Egypt. This little dung beetle was associated with Khepry, the Egyptian god of the rising sun. All scarabs were thought to be male and to produce larvae by incubating their semen in balls of dung which they rolled along in microcosmic imitation of the sun's passage through the sky. Protective scarab amulets or signet rings, funerary pendants and seals symbolized generative energy, cyclic renewal and, in early Christianity, resurrection. In China, the scarab was thought to be a model of autogenesis.

Scáthach *see* Cú Chulainn

Sceptre

Like the rod, a fertility emblem of creative power and authority, but more ornately decorated and associated with supreme gods or rulers. The sceptre often implies royal or spiritual power to administer justice, including punishment. Thus the pharaonic sceptre of Egypt was topped by the head of the violent god Set. Other sceptres are specifically linked with the creative–destructive force of the thunderbolt – in particular the "dia-mond sceptre" or *vajra* of Hindu and Buddhist tradition and the Tibetan *dorje*. They symbolize both indestructible spiritual dominion and compassionate wisdom or illumination. The ivory sceptre of Rome was surmounted by the eagle of supremacy and immortality. Spherical tops symbolized universal authority, as in the sceptre of British monarchs with orb and cross. In China, the Buddhist sceptre, the *ju-i*, was employed as a symbol of heavenly blessings – the meaning of its presentation to a bride's family – or of the honour due to elders..

Scholastica, Saint

Little is known of Scholastica[1] (*c*.480–*c*.543CE) except that she was St Benedict's sister. She probably founded a Benedictine nunnery near Monte Cassino and became the chief female saint of that order. At her last meeting with her brother she asked him to delay his departure from the nunnery; when he refused, her prayers brought on a thunderstorm that prevented him from leaving. They spent the whole night in holy conversation and mutual edification. Three days later she died, and Benedict saw her soul rising to heaven in the form of a dove. Scholastica may appear in pictures beside her brother. She generally wears the black of the Benedictine order, and holding a lily and accompanied by the dove of the legend.

Scio

In 1822, during the Greek wars of independence, patriots on the island of Scio (or Chios) attacked the Turkish garrison. The Turks retaliated by massacring men, women and children. This inspired great sympathy in

Scarab: *see* Amulet; Khepry; Ring; Sun

Sceptre: *see* CROSS; Eagle; Globe; Orb; Religious Ceremonial Objects; Rod; Thunder

Scholastica, Saint: *see* Benedict, Saint; Dove; Lily
*Golden Legend,
St Benedict*

The god Khepry as a scarab pushing the sun over the horizon; after an Egyptian pendant.

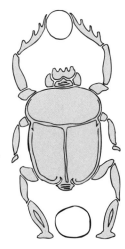

Scipio

the West and the subject was notably painted by Delacroix in *The Massacre of Scio: Greek Families Awaiting Death or Slavery*.

Scipio
General Cornelius Scipio Africanus (235BCE–183BCE) was so named after his victories over Hannibal and the destruction of Carthage (in Africa), which ended the Punic Wars. His Roman family was awarded great honours during the years of the Republic. He was the subject of the historical poem *Africa* by Petrarch (1304–74). Scenes of his triumph may allude to contemporary victories, and may be used for public decorations to accompany a dignitary's ceremonial entry into a city. The virtuous Scipio also had a bust of the mother goddess Cybele brought to Rome, as it had been prophesied that the presence of this bust was necessary for the defeat of Hannibal. The theme was shown in Mantegna's *Introduction of the Cult of Cybele into Rome*.

The Continence of Scipio was a popular theme in art.¹ After a victory at New Carthage, Scipio captured a beautiful young girl who was betrothed to the young Allucius. Hearing of this, Scipio restored the girl to her betrothed and requested only that Allucius be a friend to Rome; he gave the girl's ransom to the couple as a wedding gift. The theme was painted to signify self-control, as well as the generosity of a noble and virtuous general toward the innocent. Artists such as Sebastiano Ricci in *The Continence of Scipio* chose to set the scene before Scipio's magnanimous act to enhance the suspense.

Sciron *see* **Theseus**

Scissors *see* **Shears, Scissors**

Scorpion
Death, chastisement, retribution, vindictiveness, treachery. In Greek mythology, the hunter Orion was stung to death by a scorpion, either for his boastfulness or for forcing his attentions on the goddess Artemis.

Like the serpent, the scorpion was sometimes a guardian emblem: in Egypt it was sacred to Selket, protector of the dead. Because it was thought to secrete a medicinal oil against its own sting, it had an ambivalent wounding/healing symbolism in Africa. The scorpion is a demonic creature in the Bible, and appears in medieval art as an emblem of deadly treachery and sometimes of envy or hatred. In art it is an attribute of Africa and also of Logic, perhaps as a symbol of conclusive argument.

Scroll
In iconography, usually an emblem of ancient wisdom, prophecy or canonical law. In Judeo-Christian tradition, scrolls are attributes not only of great prophets such as Isaiah and Jeremiah but also of the Apostles, especially James, son of Zebedee.

Scylla and Charybdis
In Greek myth, a pair of female sea monsters, located in the Straits of Messina, between Sicily and mainland Italy. Charybdis, the daughter of the god Poseidon and the goddess Gaia, became a giant whirlpool, which sucked in water three times a day with force enough to swallow a ship.

Scylla was originally a beautiful sea nymph. In one account, Poseidon fell in love with her, so Amphitrite, his jealous wife, put magic herbs into the pool where she bathed, turning Scylla into a six-headed monster. Its home was a cave opposite Charybdis. It often snatched sailors off their ships to eat them.

Sea

In many traditions, the primeval source of life – formless, limitless, inexhaustible and full of possibility. In Mesopotamian myth, life arose from the mingling of Apsu, the sweet waters on which the earth floated, and the salt waters, personified by the chaos-goddess Tiamat who gave birth to all things and whose destruction led to the organized world. In Genesis, God moves upon the face of the primordial sea. The Hindu creator-god Vishnu sleeps on a serpent coiled upon the sea. The sea is a maternal image even more primary than the earth, but implies also transformation and rebirth. It is also a symbol of infinite wisdom and, in psychology, of the unconscious.

Sea Spirit, The

The most important of the three principal spirits in the belief of the Inuit of Canada and Greenland, the others being the Air Spirit and the Moon Spirit. The Sea Spirit, who is called Sedna and Nuliajuk among other names, presides over all the creatures eaten by humans. She takes the form of a woman and lives at the bottom of the sea, sending forth the creatures to be hunted for food.

Seal

Associated by the Greeks with transformation. Virginal nymphs, turned into seals to escape importunate men, formed part of the train of the sea-god Proteus (who could himself

change shape at will). Hence, perhaps, mermaid legends and fairy tales of seals who shed their skins and wander the shore as alluring women, such as the selkies of Scottish legend.

SEASONS, THE *see panel overleaf*

Sebastian, Saint

Sebastian (3rd century CE) was an early martyr, venerated from the 4th century onward. In legend,[1] he was a Christian officer in the Roman Praetorian Guard who persuaded two fellow officers to die rather than renounce Christ.

When his faith was discovered, the emperor ordered that he be executed. He was shot with so many arrows that "he looked like a porcupine", and the soldiers left him for dead. He miraculously survived and was nursed by a Christian woman, Irene. Georges de la Tour shows her tending the saint.

A few days later, when Sebastian stood on the steps of the imperial palace to rebuke the emperor, he was recognized and stoned to death. As Carracci illustrates, his body was tipped into the Cloaca Maxima, the main Roman sewer. Sebastian revealed the location of his body to a Christian woman in her dream; it was retrieved and buried on the Via Appia Antica, Rome, near the basilica now dedicated to him.

Sebastian was invoked against disease because he survived his wounds, and the image of him pierced with arrows is shown far more often than his martyrdom. He was particularly popular with painters of the Italian Renaissance, who frequently portrayed him as a handsome naked youth, riddled with arrows, looking

A sea spirit, based on a wood carving found in the Solomon Islands.

SEASONS, THE

Like the phases of the moon, the seasons were universal symbols of birth, growth, death and rebirth, the orderly cycles of nature and of human life. Since antiquity the seasons have been likened to the four ages of humankind[1] The theme of the seasons as the ages of man was illustrated by David Teniers in *Spring, Summer, Autumn, Winter*.

Most traditions recognized four seasons. Native American myths held that these were caused by the struggle of contending gods who controlled the four directions of space. Egypt and some other cultures recognized only three seasons – winter, spring and summer.

The four seasons of the year are often represented in art by the agricultural activities and the weather with which they are associated. Giuseppe Arcimboldi ingeniously transformed the agricultural produce of the seasons into faces.

Poussin inventively included scenes from the Old Testament in his series of the four seasons: *Adam and Eve in Paradise* is spring; *The meeting of Ruth and Boaz* is summer; *Spies returning from the Promised Land* are autumn; and *The Flood* is winter.

Pieter Bruegel painted six panels, each of which illustrates a two-month period; for example, *Hunters in the Snow* is thought to represent January and February.

In Western art and astrology, **Spring** is represented by a child or young woman with sprigs of blossom. It is linked with the Greek goddess Aphrodite (Venus in Roman myth), the god Hermes (Mercury), the Roman Flora, the lamb or kid, and the Zodiac signs Aries, Taurus and Gemini.

Summer is shown by a woman crowned with ears of corn, carrying a sickle. It is linked with the Greek fertility goddess Demeter (Ceres) or the god Apollo, the lion or dragon belching flame, and the signs Cancer, Leo and Virgo.

Autumn is a woman with vine leaves, grapes and other fruit, perhaps in a cornucopia. It is linked with Dionysos (Bacchus), the hare, and Libra, Scorpio and Sagittarius.

Winter may appear as an old man by a fire or a bare-headed woman in a winter landscape. It is linked with Hephaistos (Vulcan) or Boreas, the salamander or wild duck, and Capricorn, Aquarius and Pisces.

SEASONS, THE: see Corn; Cornucopia; Dragon; Fire, Flame; Flora; FLOWERS; Hare, Rabbit; Lion; Salamander; Sickle, Scythe; Vine; Zodiac

Sekhmet: see Bastet; Ra

heavenward for inspiration. Mantegna's painting is a typical example.

Sekhmet

"The Powerful", the Egyptian lioness goddess. In contrast to the other important feline goddess, Bastet, she was a terrifying deity and, as the Eye pf Ra, often the agent of divine retribution. For example, she was sent by the sun god Ra to punish the rebellious human race but proved so successful that she had to be restrained from wiping out humanity entirely. Infectious disease was believed to be the goddess's messenger, and criminals were occasionally sacrificed in her honour. Sekhmet was depicted in human form as a woman with the head of a lioness.

The fierce lioness goddess Sekhmet.

Selene

The Greek goddess of the moon, the daughter of the Titans Hyperion and Thea. She is most notable as the lover of Endymion, a king of Elis in the Peloponnese, by whom she had fifty sons. In one story, Selene did not want Endymion to age and die. She put him into a magic sleep so that he remained young for ever.

Selket

The Egyptian scorpion goddess, who presided over childbirth and whose task it was to watch over mummified bodies during burial. She was one of the deities who protected the goddess Isis from her hostile brother Seth as she nursed the infant Horus. Selket was depicted as a woman with a scorpion on her head, or as a scorpion with the head of a woman.

Semele

In Greek myth,[1] a princess of Thebes, the daughter of King Cadmus and Queen Harmonia. The god Zeus (Jupiter in Roman myth) became the lover of Semele in the guise of a handsome mortal, arousing the jealousy of his wife Hera (Juno) when Semele became pregnant. So the goddess disguised herself as an old woman and told Semele that her lover was none other than Zeus, and that to prove it, all she had to do was to ask him to show himself in all his glory.

Semele therefore persuaded Zeus to promise her a favour. After he had agreed, she requested to see him in his full majesty. The god was reluctant, but his promise bound him to do as she wished. Finally, he appeared in his entire divine magnificence, riding in his celestial chariot accompanied by a brilliant display of thunderbolts and lightning. However, as he (and of course the cunning Hera) had foreseen, this sight was too much for any mortal, and Semele was burned to a cinder. From her ashes Zeus retrieved their unborn child, the god Dionysos (Bacchus), and sewed him into his thigh until his birth. In *Jupiter and Semele* Gustave Moreau painted a youthful Jupiter on his throne, with a nude Semele in his lap, gazing at his brilliance.

Semiramis

In Near Eastern and Classical legend, perhaps based on a historical figure, the beautiful Semiramis was the wife of Menones, who hanged himself when Ninus, the reputed founder of Nineveh, demanded her from him. Through Ninus she acquired the crown of Nineveh. She then had Ninus put to death, and henceforth

Selene: *see* Eos; Helios; Hyperion; TITAN

Selket: *see* Anubis; Horus; Isis; Seth

Semele: *see* Cadmus; Dionysos; Hera; ZEUS, THE CONSORTS OF
[1] Ovid, *Met III:253–315* and Philostratus the Elder, *I:14*

Semiramis:
[1] Valerius Maximus, *9:III*

Seneca:
[1] Tacitus, *Annals* XV:60–64

Sennacherib:
[1] *Isaiah* 37:36

Separate Heavenly Deities,
The: *see* IZANAGI AND
IZANAMI

Sephiroth: *see* NUMBERS;
Tree

Seraphim: *see* Angels;
Cherubim; Fire, Flame

displayed a warlike disposition. Once, on hearing news of a revolt in Babylon, she took up arms immediately, though her hair was undone and she was only half dressed.[1] As empress of Assyria she travelled throughout her kingdom building monuments. She was eventually killed by her son. The composer Gioacchino Rossini (1792–1868) made her the subject of an opera, *Semiramide*, which in turn inspired Degas's *Semiramis Constructing a Town*.

Seneca

The celebrated Roman Stoic philosopher Seneca (4BCE–65CE) was tutor to the emperor Nero. However, Nero later accused Seneca of conspiring against him, and he was ordered to take his own life.[1] Seneca's wife wanted to die with him but was prevented from doing so.

Jacques-Louis David's *Death of Seneca* depicts how, with calm dignity, he opened his veins. The philosopher's animated last words were recorded by his friends. To hasten his death, Seneca drank poison as well, but to no effect, so he asked to be placed in a hot bath in order to make his blood flow more freely.

Sennacherib, King

In the Bible, Sennacherib and his Assyrian warriors had conquered all the cities of Judah and were about to attack Jerusalem. One night, however, an angel of the Lord entered their camp and smote dead 185,000 soldiers as they slept.[1] Rubens' *The Defeat of Sennacherib* shows the king and his army not asleep but mounted on horseback, plunged into chaos as a host of angels swoops down in a blaze of heavenly light.

Senses, The

The depiction of the five senses – hearing, sight, smell, touch and taste – was particularly popular with artists of the 17th century, for example Gonzales Coques' series of *c*.1650. The senses are often represented by relevant objects, such as musical instruments for hearing and flowers for smell. In Coques' *Touch* a man is seen letting blood from his arm. The senses may also be suggested in paintings such as Willem Buytewech's *Merry Company*, or in still lifes, to act as a reminder of the vanities of the material world.

Separate Heavenly Deities, The

Five primal Japanese deities who were the first gods to exist. They included Amanominakanushi-no-kami ("The Lord of the Centre of Heaven"), who was the oldest deity.

Sephiroth

A Hebrew symbol system, usually depicted as a Tree of Life with 10 branches, through which medieval Cabbalists hoped to understand the mysteries of creation and the inner life of God. Although the symbolism of the *sephiroth* is complex and esoteric, its underlying idea is that the whole of Creation reveals the nature of God who sought to behold in it His own attributes. Cabbalists believed that these attributes were set out in coded form in the scriptures. Spiritual illumination could be achieved by understanding their precise relationships, charted in a sinuous path from *keter* (meaning "crown") to *malkhut* (which means "kingdom").

Seraphim

The highest of the nine orders of angels, symbolizing the purifying fire of the spirit. Isaiah 6:2–6 describes the seraphim as six-winged creatures standing above the throne of God and singing his praises. One brought Isaiah a live coal to purge his lips of sin.

Serpent *see* SNAKE

Seth

The Egyptian god personifying the forces of disorder and sterility, the son of the sky goddess Nut and the earth god Geb, and the brother of Osiris, Isis and Nepthys. Osiris became the first king on earth, but Seth was jealous, so brought about his brother's death and took the throne. He was later challenged by the god Horus, son of Osiris and Isis, and their struggle for the kingship is a central episode of Egyptian mythology. In the end the gods who arbitrated in their conflict decided in favour of Horus, and Seth had to accept their judgment. In compensation he went to live in the divine sky realm as the god of storms with two foreign goddesses, Anath and Astarte, as new wives. His first wife, Nephthys, had left him after the death of Osiris. Many myths present the followers of Seth perpetually struggling against those of Horus, the god who symbolized order.

Seth was often represented as a hybrid animal, part pig and part wild ass. His earthly domain was the barren desert and most animals of the desert were associated with him. Oxen and asses were also linked to Seth, because they threshed barley and thus trod on the body of Osiris, who was believed to be manifested in the crops. For this reason, it was said, Horus condemned these beasts to suffer constant beatings.

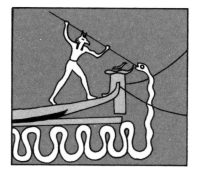

Seth in the sun god's barque, spearing the underworld serpent Apep; after a papyrus, c.1050BCE.

As the strongest of the gods, Seth fulfilled the positive role of defending the sun god on his nightly journey through the underworld. During this journey the sun's barque was attacked by Apep, the serpent of chaos. Seth was often depicted in ancient art in the act of spearing Apep.

Seven

A sacred, mystical and magic number, especially in the traditions of western Asia, symbolizing cosmic and spiritual order and the completion of a natural cycle.

The importance of the number seven is based on early astronomy – in particular the seven wandering stars or dynamic celestial bodies (the sun and moon, Mars, Mercury, Jupiter, Venus and Saturn) after which the days of the week in many cultures were named. Another influence was the four seven-day phases of the moon that made up the 28 days of the lunar calendar. Arithmeticians further noted that the first seven digits added together came to 28.

Seven was fundamental in the Mesopotamian world, which divided

Seth: *see* Anath; Astarte; Apep; Ennead, The; Geb; Horus; Isis; Nephthys; Nut; Osiris; Ra

Seven: *see* AFTERLIFE; COLOURS; Dragon; Initiation; Kaaba; Lyre; Moon; Mountain; Music; NUMBERS; PLANETS; Pillar; Rays; Sabbath; Square; Tree; Triangle; Week

both the earth and heaven into seven zones and depicted the Tree of Life with seven branches.

In the Bible, God's blessing on the seventh day is followed by scores of other references to seven. It was the number of Jewish feasts, festivals, purifications and years between sabbaticals. Seven was also the number of the Pillars of Wisdom and in other cultures it was often linked with intellectual mastery.

Seven was sacred to the god Osiris in Egypt (a symbol of immortality); to the god Apollo in Greece (the number of strings on his lyre); to Mithras, the Persian god of light (the number of initiatory stages in his cult); and to the Buddha (his seven emblems).

In Hindu tradition, the world mountain has seven faces, the sun seven rays. The seventh ray is a symbol of the centre, the power of God. In Islam, where the number seven symbolizes perfection, there are seven heavens, earths, seas, hells and doors to paradise. Pilgrims walk seven times around the sacred Ka'aba at Makkah.

In Arabic and other folklore customs, seven had protective power, associated particularly with childbirth. Legends are full of sevens, as in the widespread tales of seven-headed dragons or the story of the Seven Sleepers of Ephesus – young Christians, reputedly walled up in a cave during the reign of Diocletian, who were resurrected 200 years later.

Seven Against Thebes, The
Seven warriors who, in Greek myth, took part in the civil war between Polyneices and Eteocles, the sons of Oedipus. After Oedipus left Thebes to go into exile, Polyneices and Eteocles, who (in one account) had expelled

him, inherited his throne as joint rulers. Each agreed to rule alternately for one year at a time, but after the first year Eteocles refused to give up the throne for his brother's turn. Polyneices fled to Argos and assembled seven contingents of troops, each under one of the following commanders: King Adrastus of Argos; Amphiaraus; Capaneus; Hippomedon; Parthenopaeus; Tydeus; and Polyneices himself.

During the ensuing siege of Thebes, each contingent assailed one of the city's seven gates. The expedition was a failure, as Oedipus had cursed both his sons. They killed each other in single combat and the Seven were annihilated, except Adrastus who escaped back to Argos on his swift horse.

SEVEN DEADLY SINS, THE see panel opposite

Seven Sages, The
Seven men of great wisdom and spiritual power who appear frequently in Hindu mythology. The Seven Sages are: Atri; Bharadvaja; Gautama; Jamadagni; Kashyapa; Vasistha; and Vishvamitra.

Seven Sisters, The
Seven wandering ancestral heroines of the Dreamtime, also referred to by their Aboriginal name of Kungarankalpa. The complete route of the sisters has been pieced together from stories told about them by different Aboriginal clans living along its course. The sisters fled southward from the centre of Australia to escape from a lecherous man called Nyiru. Various features of the landscape mark the course of the chase: for example, a low cliff was the wind-

SEVEN DEADLY SINS, THE

In art, particularly Renaissance and Baroque painting, the Seven Deadly Sins of Christian tradition – Anger, Avarice, Envy, Gluttony, Lust, Pride and Sloth – are depicted to represent the "moral" lesson of good against evil.

Anger In Renaissance art this vice is often represented as a woman tearing her clothes in furious rage.

Avarice A favourite subject of medieval sculptors, and later of painters. Avarice is usually symbolized by a sinner holding or wearing a purse or by a harpy whose claws tormented misers, who might be shown hoarding money or golden apples. Among the other symbols of avarice are the rat and toad.

A satyr symbolizing Lust, after Pallas Expelling the Vices from the Garden of Virtue, *by Andrea Mantegna (c.1500).*

Envy A sin usually portrayed as a woman eating the heart torn from her own breast (the origin of the colloquialism "eat your heart out") or sometimes her entrails. Her familiar attribute is a snake, sometimes shown as her protruded, poisonous tongue. Other symbols of envy include the scorpion, the "evil eye" and the colour green (hence "green with envy").

Gluttony Personified in art either by corpulent and voracious figures or by the animals most commonly linked with this fleshly vice – the pig, bear, fox, wolf or hedgehog.

Lust This vice was a popular subject for medieval artists. Lust is usually represented in Western art by snakes or toads that are shown feeding on the breasts or genitals of women (whose sexual urges seemed more shocking to the Church than those of men).

Other emblems of lust include the ape, ass, basilisk, bear, boar, cat, centaur, cock, Devil, goat, hare, horse, leopard, the Minotaur, mirror, monkey, pig, rabbit, satyr, torch and witch.

Pride This sin is usually personified in Western art by a woman with a peacock. She may also be shown with a lion and an eagle as dominant emblems of earthly and celestial nature. The biblical saying "pride goes before destruction and an haughty spirit before a fall" (Proverbs 16:18) led to medieval allegories of pride as an unseated horseman. This symbolism influenced Caravaggio's masterpiece *The Conversion of St Paul* (*c*.1600), which shows the apostle-to-be thrown from his horse on his way to Damascus to persecute Christians. Other symbols of pride are the cock, fallen angel, leopard, mirror and ziggurat or Tower of Babel.

Sloth A sin that is usually personified in Western art by an overweight man or a pig, or by a scene of physical or mental idleness, the latter said to lead to melancholy. Sloth often rides, or is accompanied by, a beast of burden such as the ass or ox. The snail was another emblem of sloth.

SEVEN DEADLY SINS, THE: *see* Angels; BEASTS OF FABLE; Green; Mirror; Ziggurat; *and names of individual animals*

Shadow

break that they built when they camped one night. On reaching the southern coast (near modern Port Augusta), the seven sisters went into the sea and then leapt into the sky and became the Pleiades.

Shadow

In primitive traditions, the soul or alter ego, associated particularly with the spirits of the dead. In China, the Immortals, as beings wholly penetrated by light, had no shadows, whereas in Western folklore people who cast no shadow were suspected of having sold their souls to the Devil and of being, in a sense, "unreal" (shadows being proof of material reality). As the antithesis of light, the Devil was himself a shadow. In psychology, the shadow symbolizes the intuitive, selfish side of the psyche, often repressed.

Shango

A divine ancestral king of the Yoruba people of West Africa. Shango, one of the most important Yoruba deities, was famed for his martial prowess and as a magician. His oppressive rule led to his overthrow, after which he is said to have hanged himself on a tree. Then he ascended to heaven and became the god of rain and thunder. Representations of him show him wielding a twin-headed axe, the symbol of thunder. His wife, Oja, was a lake which after Shango's death became the river Niger.

Shashti

A Hindu goddess of childbirth and protector of newborns. Her name means "sixth", because she is venerated on the sixth day after childbirth, said to mark the end of the most dangerous time for mother and baby.

Shears, Scissors

Mortality, the unpredictability of life. With this symbolism, shears or scissors are the attribute in art of Atropos, one of the three Fates, who in Greek lore severs the thread of human life.

Sheba, The Queen of

In the Old Testament the Queen of Sheba came to Jerusalem to see if the rumours she had heard about King Solomon's wealth were true. Like the Magi worshipping the Christ Child, she brought a magnificent array of spices, gold and precious stones as gifts.[1] He in return gave her "all she desired". Their meeting was depicted by Ghiberti (Baptistery, Florence).

In legend,[2] on her way to visit Solomon, the queen recognized and worshipped the wood of the True Cross.

Sheep, Shepherd

Meekness – a Christian symbol of the laity, needing spiritual leadership and easily led astray. "Feed my sheep" were among the last words said by Christ to Peter before his ascension, according to the gospel of John (21:15). The "lost sheep" is a misled sinner, the "black sheep" an incorrigible one. .Shepherds symbolize spiritual leadership. Christ is commnly portrayed as the Good Shepherd in early Christian art, with a ram or lamb on his shoulders, an image based on Classical images of the Orpheus or Hermes (Mercury). Hermes also shepherded the souls of the dead, and the Egyptian pharaohs caried a crook as part of their regalia.

Shell

Auspicious, erotic, lunar and feminine symbol, linked with conception, regeneration, baptism and, in many traditions, prosperity – probably through fecundity symbolism based on its association with the vulva. Prized shells were a form of currency in Oceania. The shell is one of the eight symbols of good luck in Chinese Buddhism. As underworld and resurrection symbols, shells were sometimes funerary tokens. More recently, the shell has become a symbol of introspection or withdrawal.

In Classical mythology a scallop shell was the attribute of Aphrodite (in Roman myth, Venus), who was born from the sea. Shells were also the chariots of Poseidon (Neptune) and Galatea. Conch shells may be used as trumpets by Tritons (mermen) and other figures, such as the impudent satyr in Botticelli's *Mars and Venus*. In Dutch 17th-century still lifes, such as that of Abraham van Beyeren, exotic shells allude to the newly discovered territories, and display the artist's skill.

Ship

A symbol of security, representing a female (or lunar) womb or cradle. Also a symbol of quest and passage to other states of being. In the ancient world, ships often symbolized the voyaging of heavenly bodies – the crescent of the Babylonian moon god navigating space, or the Egyptian barque of the sun on its nightly passage through the underworld. Funerary ships were provided for the dead in Egypt, and other traditions, notably in the Viking custom of immolating chieftains in longships. The ship with mast and anchor as a cryptic sign of the Cross was an early Christian symbol of Christ. The idea of the Church as a secure place amid the storms of

life derived from biblical ships such as Noah's ark, and the "Navicella" in which the disciples were sailing on the Sea of Galilee, in the incident of Christ walking on the water.[1] Churches themselves were symbolic ships, with the nave (Latin *navis*: "ship") carrying passengers, buttresses as oars and a spire as a mast. In art, the ship is an attribute of St Peter and of Fortune, ships being emblems of uncertain prosperity – as in the expression, "when my ship comes in".

Shiva

One of the *trimurti*, the Hindu trinity of Brahma, Shiva and Vishnu, and among the most complex of all Indian deities. He originated as the early Vedic god Rudra ("Ruddy" or "Howler"), a malign storm god, who was later addressed as Shiva (meaning "Auspicious") in order to propitiate

Shiva on his mount, the bull Nandi, from a 19th-century Indian painting.

Ship: *see* Anchor; Ark; Boat; Crescent; CROSS; Spire; Woman
[1] *Matthew 14:24–27*

Shiva: *see* Brahma; Churning of the Ocean, The; Daksha; Ganesha; Ganga; Nataraja; Sati; Skanda; Vishnu

The Hindu goddess
Shri, or Lakshmi.

him. Shiva is a destroyer and angry avenger, but also a benign herdsman of souls. With similar ambivalence, he is associated with asceticism and yoga (he meditates on Mount Kailasa) but also with the erotic.

Shiva is worshipped in the form of a linga or lingam (sacred phallic pillar). According to one myth, Vishnu and Brahma were disputing who was the greatest when Shiva appeared in the form of a fiery column, the linga. Brahma took the form of a goose and flew to find the top, while Vishnu became a boar and sought the bottom. Both failed and were forced to concede to Shiva's authority.

Both ascetic and erotic aspects are found in a myth that relates how Shiva smeared himself in ashes and visited a forest where many sages lived a life of asceticism. The sages feared he would seduce their wives and cursed the god to lose his penis. Shiva was castrated, but with his own complicity. The world then grew dark and cold and the sages lost their virility until they had placated Shiva by erecting a linga.

Shiva is depicted with a pale or ashen face and a blue neck caused when, in a protector role, he consumed the poison which sprang from the churning of the ocean (the poison threatened to destroy humanity). Another instance of the god as protector is the myth of how he broke the fall of the goddess Ganga, the Ganges, when she descended from heaven to cleanse the world with her waters. Other attributes of Shiva are a necklace of skulls, coiled locks like those of an ascetic, and in the middle of his forehead, a third eye (*shakra*) of enlightenment and destruction. He is also Nataraja, "Lord of the Dance", the source of all movement in the cosmos. Shiva's wife appears variously as Sati, the daughter of the creator god Daksha, and Uma or Parvati, the daughter of the mountain Himalaya. His marriage brings an element of domesticity into the god's austere life, and he is often portrayed in a family group with Parvati and their children, Skanda and Ganesha.

Shri

The Hindu goddess of prosperity (*shri*), also called Lakshmi ("good fortune"). According to some accounts, Shri arose from the ocean when it was churned by the gods (Devas) and demons (Asuras). Shri found herself immediately attracted to Vishnu, who, as the god who presided over the churning, had first claim on the beautiful goddess. The pair were frequently associated, although earlier myths sometimes linked her with the god Indra. As the consort of Vishnu, Shri came to represent the perfect Hindu wife because she was loyal and submissive to her husband.

Shu *see* Tefnut

Sibyl

In antiquity Sibyls were prophetesses, believed to be inspired by the gods. There were believed to be ten in all: the Ancyran, Cumaean, Delphic, Erythraean, Libyan, Marpessan, Persian, Samian and Tiburtine. The most famous were the Delphic and the Cumaean oracles of Apollo. Their prophecies were written down, and these "Sibylline Verses" were carefully preserved. Some of the verses, probably composed by Christians in the 2nd century, "foretell" Christ's Passion. The emperor Augustus was said to have been told of the advent of Christ by the Tiburtine Sibyl, at the place where the Church of the Aracoeli (Altar of Light) now stands next to the Capitol in Rome. In *Augustus and the Tiburtine Sibyl* Antoine Caron shows the emperor kneeling to the Sibyl while she points to a vision of the Virgin and Child. Seen as female counterparts to the biblical prophets, Sibyls were portrayed as matronly figures, and commonly have inscriptions to identify them. They fill spaces in polyptychs, such as Jan van Eyck's *Ghent Altarpiece*, and in chapels, as in Raphael's *Sibyls* (Chigi Chapel, Santa Maria della Pace, Rome). Their images decorate the floor of Siena Cathedral, and Michelangelo placed them, with the biblical prophets, around scenes from the Book of Genesis (Sistine Chapel, Vatican, Rome).

Sickle, Scythe

Death, but also fertility. The curved sickle was a lunar harvest symbol of the agricultural-god Kronos (in Roman myth, Saturn). With this meaning the sickle was also an attribute of the fertility-god Priapus and of summer. In early Greek myth, Kronos used a sickle to castrate his father, Uranos (Uranus) – symbolizing the separation of earthly creation from the sky. In art, Death (sometimes personified as Father Time or the Grim Reaper) carries a scythe.

Sida

A wandering culture hero of Papua, also known as Sido, Soido, Sosom, Souw and other variations. Sida features in the mythology of communities along the rivers Fly and Purari of southern Papua and in the mountainous interior. This figure travelled through the world, leaving various

features of the landscape to mark the places where he passed. For example, a small lake denotes the spot where he urinated. Each community knows the incidents that took place in its own territory. In most places the myths are part of a secret male cult and become known only to initiates. The hero is represented as possessing a very long penis and he was shamed on account of his desire for sex. According to the Daribi, Souw's penis tried to enter a young woman, but she cried out and it withdrew. Souw was furious at being humiliated in this way and gave humanity war, death and witchcraft. But then he wandered into the highlands and deposited hairs that became dogs and pigs, which were useful domestic animals. Elsewhere he is said to have given people their first vegetables and stocks of fish.

Sieve

Discernment, conscience, purification – a biblical emblem of God's coming judgment. Because of its ancient associations with purification, in art the sieve is an attribute of Chastity.

Sigmund

A hero of Norse myth, the son of Volsung and a descendant of the god Odin. One night, Odin appeared in the warriors' hall in the guise of a one-eyed old man and plunged a magnificent sword into the tree trunk supporting the roof. Whoever removed the sword, he declared, would possess it. Then he vanished. In turn, all the warriors tried to pull out the sword, but only Sigmund succeeded.

With this divine sword, Gram, Sigmund became famous for many heroic exploits. When Sigmund was old, Odin decided that it was time for him

Sigurd

to die. A one-eyed old man appeared before him in battle and caused Gram to break in two. Disarmed, Sigmund fell under his opponent's blows. His widow, Hjordis, kept the fragments of Gram for their son Sigurd.

Sigurd

A great hero of Norse myth, the son of Sigmund and Hjordis and a descendant of the god Odin. Sigurd, known as "The Volsung" after his grandfather Volsung, was raised at the court of his stepfather Hjalprek, where Regin, a clever but malign smith, fostered him and taught him many skills. Aided by an old man (the god Odin in disguise), the hero chose a wonderful horse, Grani, descended from Sleipnir, Odin's eight-legged steed.

Regin told Sigurd of a great horde of treasure guarded by his brother, Fafnir the dragon. Regin forged a weapon of unsurpassed sharpness from the pieces of the magic sword Gram, which the god Odin had once given to Sigurd's father Sigmund. The smith advised Sigurd to dig a pit, hide

Sigurd (right) roasting Fafnir's heart; after a 12th century woodcarving.

in it, and stab Fafnir as he crawled over it. But Odin, disguised as an old man, warned Sigurd that Regin wanted the horde for himself and expected Sigurd to drown in Fafnir's blood. To survive, he must dig a number of pits to catch the blood. Sigurd complied and killed Fafnir. Later, when the hero was roasting Fafnir's heart, he poked it to see if it was cooked and burned his finger. He sucked the finger and when Fafnir's blood touched his tongue he could understand the speech of birds. He overheard them saying that Regin intended to kill him. He beheaded the evil smith and rode off with the treasure.

However, the hoard contained a gold ring, upon which the dwarf Andvari (from whom the treasure had originally been stolen) had laid a curse that promised death to its possessor. This curse later fell on Sigurd. He was loved by a Valkyrie, Brynhild, whom he promised to marry but whom Odin had imprisoned in an enchanted sleep within a ring of flame. However, another warrior, Gunnar, wanted to marry her and so Sigurd, who had lost his memory, impersonated Gunnar to cross the ring of fire (this was an initiation ceremony). Brynhild married Gunnar but later discovered the trick and had Sigurd assassinated before immolating herself.

Sigyn *see* Loki

Silenus

In Greek myth, Silenus was the companion of Dionysos (Bacchus) in revelry. Sometimes described as the son of Pan or Hermes (Mercury), he is depicted as a fat, merry, old man riding an ass, in varying degrees of drunkenness. Rubens' *Drunken Silenus Supported by Satyrs* shows him inebriated to the point of helplessness.

Silver

Purity, chastity and eloquence. In the symbolism of metals, silver was lunar, feminine and cold, and is the attribute of moon-goddesses, in particular the Greek Artemis (in Roman myth, Diana), and of queens. Through its link with the moon it was equated also with the light of hope and with wisdom – orators are silver-tongued. Hence the Oriental proverb: "Speech is silver, silence golden." The Silver Age was emblematic of lost innocence, perhaps because, as the malleable metal of much ancient coinage, silver had some negative associations – famously so as a symbol of Christ's betrayal for "thirty pieces of silver".

Simon, Saint (Apostle, Disciple)

Little is known of Christ's disciple Simon (1st century CE), who was called the Zealot or the Canaanite. According to legend,[1] he preached with St Jude in Egypt and in Persia, where they performed miracles, baptized the converted, and were martyred. In some accounts Simon was crucified, in others sawn in two; he may therefore be shown with either a cross or a saw.

Siren

In Greek myth, one of a group of three (sometimes two) female monsters usually depicted with the bodies of birds and the heads of women. The Sirens lived on an island identifed with Sicily. It was said that their song was so irresistibly beautiful that any mariner who heard it would immediately sail toward the creatures – only

A Siren, with the head of a woman and the body of a bird.

to be shipwrecked on the rocks. In another account, those who fell under the Sirens' seductive spell would land on the shore, where they would sit and listen until they wasted away and died. The Sirens were said to live among the skeletons of men whom they had bewitched. Both Jason and Odysseus had to sail near them on their homeward journeys. Odysseus escaped by plugging his crew's ears with wax and having himself bound to the mast until they had safely passed.[1] After Odysseus had sailed past safely, the defeated Sirens are said to have leaped into the sea and drowned. In art, although the Sirens were usually thought to be monsters, Gustave Moreau presents them, in *The Sirens*, as three beautiful maidens with crowns.

Sisera

In the Bible, Sisera was the captain of the armies of Jabin, king of Canaan, who ruled over the Israelites. Jael, who belonged to tribe at peace with Jabin, invited Sisera into her tent,

Simon, Saint: *see* Martyrs
[1] *Golden Legend, SS Simon and Jude*

Silver: *see* CHASTITY; METALS; Moon; Queen

Sirens: *see* Jason and the Argonauts; Odysseus; Orpheus
[1] Homer, *Odyssey XII*

Sisera:
[1] *Judges 4:21*

gave him a drink and let him rest. Then she "took a nail of the tent, and took a hammer in her hand, and went softly unto him, and smote the nail into his temples, and fastened it into the ground."[1] Like Judith, Jael was seen as a heroine and liberator of the Israelite people.

Sisyphus

In Greek myth the founder and first king of Corinth. Before he died, Sisyphus told his wife Merope (one of the Pleiades), to leave him unburied and accord him no funeral rites. After Sisyphus' shade had descended to the underworld, Merope did as he had instructed, much to the annoyance of the god Hades, the ruler of the underworld. Hades told Sisyphus to leave the underworld temporarily in order to ensure that Merope gave him a proper funeral.

Sisyphus came back to life in Corinth and resumed his reign, defying the orders of Hades. When he finally died in advanced old age, Sisyphus was sentenced in the underworld to the eternal torment of having to push a rock up to the top of a hill, only to see it roll back down again to the bottom every time he was about to send it toppling over the crest.[1] In his *Sisyphus*, Titian shows him struggling with the rock on his shoulder.

Sita *see* Rama

Six

The number of union and equilibrium, graphically expressed by the hexagram combining two triangles, one pointing up (male, fire, heaven), one pointing down (female, water, earth). This figure, now known as the Star of David, symbolized the union

of Israel and Judah and is sometimes also taken as an ideogram for the human soul. It was a Greek symbol of the androgyne.

The Chinese oracular *Book of Changes*, the *Yijing* (*I Ching*), is based on the symbolism of six broken or unbroken lines making up an overall system of 64 linear "hexagrams".

In the Pythagorean system, six represented chance or luck – as it does in modern dice. As the cube with six surfaces, the number six represents stability and truth.

In Genesis, and in earlier Sumerian-Semitic tradition, the world was created in six days. According to the book of Revelation, the number of the Beast (Satan) was "666"[1]. Most likely, though, it is a reference to the emperor Nero, the letters of whose name in Greek (*Kaisar Neron*) have the numerical value of 666 (Greek letters, like Hebrew ones, also had a numerical value). Another theory is that this number was chosen because it falls short repeatedly of the sacred number seven. Alternatively, it is suggested as a monastic number that identifies Simon Magus, a forerunner of Gnosticism, whom the writer of Revelation may have regarded as a dangerous influence in early Christianity.

Skadi *see* Njord

Skanda

The son of Shiva and Parvati. When Shiva and Parvati first had intercourse, the gods interrupted them for fear that Shiva's offspring might be too powerful. Shiva spilled his fiery semen, which was too hot to hold and was passed around the gods until it came to Ganga, the Ganges, where it was incubated. Skanda was born with

Skanda between Shiva and Parvati; based on a bronze sculpture of the 2nd century CE.

six heads and was suckled by the Krittikas (the Pleiades), whence his alternative name of Karttikeya. He vanquished a demon called Taraka and saved the world from destruction, becoming the leader of the armies of the gods. When Parvati first saw him, milk flowed from her breasts, and she accepted him as her own son.

Skeleton
Like the skull, a symbol of the death of the flesh, often used as a *memento mori* in art (and, according to the 1st-century CE Greek author Plutarch, at Egyptian banquets).

Death personified often appears as a skeleton with a scythe, the Grim Reaper. So do some gods of death, as in Mayan iconography. Skeletons are often shown dancing or making love, often as a satire on carnal pleasures but sometimes as a symbol of life to come, the skeleton (like the spirit) outlasting death.

Skin
A husk enclosing fresh life – the grim meaning of Aztec rites in which the priests of the vegetation-god Xipe Totec wore the skins of flayed victims

to symbolize the shell, pod or husk enclosing spring plants. The snake shedding its skin was a similar emblem of regeneration. Similarly, shamans put on animal skins to acquire their powers.

Skull
In its most self-evident form, a skull is a reminder of death, a *memento mori*, and is a symbol of mortality. A skull was used as an aid to meditation by monks, especially Franciscans and Jesuits, and by saints, especially the hermit St Jerome and the penitent Mary Magdalene, thus it is a frequent attribute of saints in medieval and Renaissance art, calling attention to the vanity of earthly things or the passing of time, as in Frans Hals' *Young Man Holding a Skull*. A cleverly foreshortened skull appears in Hans Holbein's *The Ambassadors*.

Paintings of the Crucifixion may have a skull at the foot of the Cross. The site of the Crucifixion was named Golgotha, or "Place of the Skull", possibly because bodies were left here to be pecked by the birds. Legend also claimed that Christ was crucified on the spot where Adam had been buried. In depictions of the Crucifixion, Adam's skull is thus shown as uncovered to indicate that Christ's sacrifice was for the redemption of humankind; or it could allude to Christ's Descent into Hell to resurrect the redeemed dead, of whom the first was Adam.

The skull had richer significance in many cultural traditions as the seat of intelligence, the spirit, vital energy, and the part of the body most resistant to decay – the symbolism underlying pagan cults of the skull in Europe. Renunciation of life is symbolized in

A Native American shamanic depiction of a skeleton.

Hindu iconography by a skull filled with blood. The piratical skull with crossed thighbones was designed to terrify and is now a universally understood warning signal.

Sky

Universally associated with supernatural forces, a symbol of superiority, dominion, spiritual ascension and aspiration. The fertilizing influence of sun and rain, the eternal presence of the stars, the tidal pull of the moon, the destructive forces of storms, all helped to establish the sky as the source of cosmic power. With few exceptions, notably in Egyptian myth, the sky was a masculine or yang symbol, often thought to have separated from the female earth in order to allow terrestrial life to develop. Heaven (usually but not always imagined as being located above the earth) was in most traditions a region of the sky arranged in layers through which the soul could ascend toward ultimate light and peace.

Sleep

In mythology Sleep dwelled in a silent cave, where poppies bloomed in abundance; from here he dispatched his son, Morpheus, to deliver dreams through the night.[1] Dreams may be depicted as visions of delight or horror. In art, Goya transformed irrational ideas into owls, bats and a cat in *The Dream of Reason Produces Monsters*. Death was the brother of Sleep, and both were the children of Night. They may be personified as dark- and light-skinned respectively.

Smith

A symbol of divine or magical creative skills in most early traditions,

linked with the natural forces of thunder, lightning, fire and volcanic activity, and with initiations into earth mysteries. In Greek myth the smith is the lame god Hephaistos (in Roman myth, Vulcan). Typically, he acts as demiurge or technician to the creator god and is benevolent despite his links with the underworld.

Smoke

An ascension symbol – of prayers or of purified souls. In Native North America, smoke was a means of communication on a cosmic as well as a mundane level. Less often, it appears as a symbol of concealment or of the transitory nature of life.

Snail

Now simply a metaphor for slowness, but in older traditions – especially in Africa and Central America – a lunar and fertility symbol. Periodically showing and hiding its horns like the moon, the snail also suggested by its helical shell the spiralling processes of cyclic continuity. It thus became an emblem of rebirth or resurrection, and of fecundity generally, as in Aztec iconography. The shell and uncoiling body also combined female and male sexual symbolism.

SNAKE *see panel opposite*

Sobek

The Egyptian crocodile god, the offspring of the mother goddess Neith. Sobek presided over rivers and lakes and was a protector of the pharaohs. He was particularly venerated at the city on Lake Fayum known to the Greeks as Crocodilopolis (Medinet el-Fayum). Many crocodiles were mummified as offerings to the god.

SNAKE

The most significant and complex of all animal symbols, and perhaps the oldest. Snakes carved on Paleolithic antlers in Africa or drawn on rock faces were primarily fertility or rain symbols, and sexual or agricultural fertility symbolism remained a basic element in most later snake cults. But obvious analogies between the snake and the penis, the umbilical cord or the humid processes of birth (for the snake combines male and female symbolism) do not fully explain the almost universal importance of the serpent in mythology. The snake was above all a magico-religious symbol of primeval life force, sometimes an image of the creator divinity itself. The *ouroboros* motif of a snake swallowing its own tail symbolizes not only eternity but a divine self-sufficiency.

An Aztec sculpture of a double-headed rattlesnake, perhaps related to the earth goddess Coatlicue.

Emblematically, the snake was in touch with the mysteries of the earth, the waters, darkness and the underworld – self-contained, cold-blooded, secretive, sometimes venomous, able to glide swiftly without feet, magically swallow large creatures, and rejuvenate itself by shedding its own skin. Its serpentine form was as allusive as its other characteristics, suggesting undulating waves and landscapes, winding rivers, vines and tree roots, and in the sky the rainbow, the lightning strike, the spiralling motion of the cosmos. As a result, the snake became one of the most widespread of all animist symbols – depicted on a gigantic scale in the 400-metre-long Great Serpent Mound in Ohio.

The snake coiled around its eggs suggested the analogy of a great serpent coiled around the world, supporting it or holding together the waters surrounding it. Thus the Hindu creator-god Vishnu rests on the coils of a great snake, Ananta (Shesha); Indra slays a chaos snake, Vritra, to release the fertilizing waters it enclosed; and the great earthquake snake, Vasuki, is used to churn the sea of creation. In African and other myths, a rainbow snake reaches from the watery underworld into the heavens. In Nordic myth, the great tempest serpent of Midgard holds the world in his unpredictable coils. In South America, eclipses were explained as the swallowing of the sun or moon by a giant serpent. In Egypt, the barque of the sun that travels through the underworld waters at night is threatened by the serpent Apep. In Mexico, Quetzalcoatl, the Aztec version of the bird-snake divinities known throughout Central America, unites the powers of earth and heaven.

The protective–destructive symbolism that runs through these and other serpent myths illustrates the degree to which the snake is a dualistic force, a source of strength when mastered but potentially dangerous and often emblematic of death or chaos as well as of life. The snake was often used as a curative symbol. In the ancient world, the snake's rejuvenation symbolism linked it specifically with the Classical god of healing, Asklepios. On the other hand, the snake was blamed for humanity's losing the gift of immortal life – not only in the story of Adam and Eve, the source of the connection between Satan and serpets, but also in the Babylonian *Epic of Gilgamesh*, where the magic plant of eternal life is stolen by a snake.

The snake's duality, the balance between fear and veneration in its symbolism, accounts for its appearance as either progenitor or aggressor, culture hero or monster. In its fearsome aspect, it gave birth to the dragons and sea serpents of Western tradition and to snake hybrids that symbolized the multiple perils of human existence. In this tradition the snake became a dominant symbol of chaos, evil, sin, temptation or deceit. It appears at the foot of the Cross as an emblem of the Fall, redeemed by Christ, and is shown being trampled by the Virgin Mary.

Solomon

Sol *see* **Helios; Solstice**

Solomon

In the Bible, Solomon was the son of David and Bathsheba, and king of Israel. He was renowned for his wisdom, a gift from God, which was exemplified in the Judgment of Solomon,[1] when two harlots who had given birth claimed to be the mother of the one surviving child. The king ordered the baby to be cut in two, whereupon in the appalled reaction of one woman he at once recognized the true mother. Solomon had a long and prosperous reign, preferring to amass wealth than wage war. He built a palace and the Temple of Jerusalem, which was covered with gold and sumptuous ornaments. Its spiral columns, in the Solomonic style, were brought to Rome and provided the inspiration for Bernini's canopy over the high altar of St Peter's, Rome.

Solomon had 700 wives and 300 concubines.[2] Many of these were foreign and worshipped pagan gods, whose cults Solomon also followed, stirring up divine displeasure.

Solstice

Significant in solar rituals, particularly those marking the northern winter solstice on December 21/22, the shortest day in the Northern hemisphere, after which the sun was symbolically "reborn". In 274CE, the emperor Aurelian sought to unite the Roman Empire around the cult of the Sol Invictus ("Unconquered Sun", the Persian god of light, Mithras) and fixed December 25 as the sun's birthday. Sixty years later, the Christian Church borrowed this date to commemorate the birth of Christ as the new prince of light.

Soma

An intoxicating drink symbolizing in Vedic and Hindu ritual the divine life force. There are close affinities with the symbolism of ambrosia, sap, semen and wine. *Soma* was personified by a Vedic god, identified in later Hindu tradition with the moon, from whose cup the gods drank *soma* (replenished each month from solar sources). In mystic rites, *soma* was drunk as a symbol of communion with divine power. In Hindu iconography, emblems of the exhilarating strength of *soma* include the bull, eagle and giant.

Soul

A symbol of the spiritual or non-bodily aspects of individual human existence. Most traditions envisaged one or more souls inhabiting the body, sometimes wandering from it during dreams and persisting in some form after death. In Egypt the soul that left the body was depicted as a human-headed hawk. In Greece it was shown as a butterfly leaving the mouth, or sometimes a snake. The Greek personification of the soul as the beautiful Psyche may have influenced the Christian iconography of souls as little winged figures. Doves flew from the mouths of saints, eagles from the pyres of emperors. In later Western art, souls often appear as naked children. In Semitic and other mystic traditions, souls were sparks of light.

South *see* **CARDINAL POINTS, THE**

Spark

A soul symbol in Orphic, Gnostic, Cabbalistic and other mystic traditions, conceived as a fragment of divine light separated from the Godhead in the dualistic universe of light and darkness, but able to rejoin it once freed from the material world.

Sparrow

A perky and prolific bird linked in China with the penis and sometimes eaten for its supposed potency. Sexual symbolism appears in Greece too, where the bird was an attribute of the goddess Aphrodite, and in Western art, where a woman holding a sparrow represents a wanton.

Spear

Male potency. The spear's phallic symbolism is clear in the Japanese myth in which the creator-god Izanagi stirs the ocean with a jewelled spear, drops from which form the first solid land. Fertility symbolism also linked the spear with lightning, as in Phoenician iconography of the storm-god Hadad who thrusts a spear with a zigzag shaft into the earth.

Sphere

The sphere shares the symbolism of perfection with the circle and totality with the globe. The Greek symbol for the sphere was the gamma cross (a cross in a circle), an ancient emblem of power. The armillary sphere, a skeletal globe composed of metal rings demonstrating the earth-centred Ptolemaic theory of the cosmos, was an old emblem of astronomy.

Sphinx (1)

Iin Egypt, a monumental human-headed lion symbolizing the power and majesty of the sun and the eternal glory of the ruler whom it protected and commemorated. A sphinx's head may bear the features of a particular monarch, such as the 4th-Dynasty

pharaoh Khephren (*c*.2600BCE), whose portrait appears on the Great Sphinx of Giza. The Sphinx has entered popular symbolism as an enigma or source of ancient wisdom.

Serene Egyptian sphinxes such as the ram-headed guardians at Karnak evolved into the winged protective sphinxes of the Near East and, perhaps, to the monstrous Greek Sphinx.

Sphinx (2)

"The Strangler", a monster of Greek myth, with with the head of a woman, the wings of a bird and the body of a lion. One of the monstrous offspring of Echidne and Typhon, the Sphinx was sent by Hera to plague Thebes after either the citizens or its king, Laius, showed disrespect for the gods.

The monster would devour anyone, who, when challenged, could not answer her riddle: "Which animal walks on four feet in the morning, on two at noon and on three in the evening?" No one knew the answer, and the Sphinx was well fed on Theban flesh. Help came in the form of Oedipus, who gave the Sphinx the answer to the riddle: a man, who

The Theban Sphinx, after an ancient Greek relief.

A spider from a 1,000-year-old disc of shell discovered in Illinois. For some Native American peoples the spider was a protector against storms.

crawls on all fours as a baby, walks on two legs until old age, and then hobbles with a stick. On hearing the answer, the Sphinx threw herself to her death.

Spider

A lunar and female symbol associated with the weaving of human destiny and therefore with divination. In India, the spider's web is a symbol of *maya* ("illusion") – the fragile and mortal world of appearances. Spiders often appear elsewhere in mythology as attributes of moon goddesses, and as culture heroines or demiurge creators of the world.

They can symbolize either ensnarement (by the Devil in Christian symbolism) or protection from storms, as among some Native North Americans. Folklore associations of the spider with good luck, wealth or coming rain are widespread, a symbolism that may be suggested by the spider descending its thread, emblematically bringing heavenly gifts.

Spinario

This ancient bronze statue (Musei Capitolini, Rome) of a boy pulling a thorn from his foot was often cited and copied from the Renaissance on. It was said to represent the diligence of a messenger who plucked out the thorn only after giving his message.

Spindle

A lunar symbol of the transitory nature of human life, but with more positive creative aspects, particularly in folklore. The spindle is an attribute of the mother goddess and of women generally. In art it is held by Clotho, the Fate who spins the thread of life.

Spiral

From the earliest times a dynamic symbol of life force, cosmic and microcosmic. Spiral forms are seen in nature from celestial galaxies to whirlwinds and whirlpools, from coiled serpents or conical shells to human fingertips – and (as science has discovered) to the double helix structure of DNA at the heart of every cell.

In art, spirals are one of the most common of all decorative motifs, ranging from Celtic double spirals in northern Europe or the volutes on Roman capitals, to the whorls in Maori carving and tattooing in the South Pacific. Maori whorls, based on fern forms, show the close link between spiral motifs and natural phenomena. Although this sometimes provides a key to their symbolism, spirals are so allusive that other clues are needed before specific meanings can be read into them. The symbolism of decorative spiral motifs is more often unconscious than conscious.

Carved on megaliths, spirals suggest a labyrinthine journey to the afterlife, and perhaps a return. The spiralling snakes on the caduceus – and double spirals in general – suggest a balance of opposing principles – the meaning of the Yin-Yang motif, which is itself a form of double spiral. Vortex forces in wind, water or fire suggest ascent, descent or the rotating energy that drives the cosmos.

By adding wheeling momentum to a circular form, the spiral also symbolizes time, the cyclic rhythms of the seasons and of birth and death, the waning and waxing of the moon, and the sun (often symbolized by the spiral). Like the yogic "serpent" at the base of the spine, the spring-like coil of a spiral suggests latent power. The uncoiling spiral is phallic and male, the involuted spiral female, making the double spiral also a fertility symbol.

The spiral as an open and flowing line suggests extension, evolution and continuity, uninterrupted concentric and centripetal movement, the very rhythm of breathing and of life itself.

Spire

A symbolic expression of the aim of Gothic architects to create churches that appeared to soar toward heaven. Gothic cathedrals sought to "render immaterial all that is material".

Spittle

A bodily fluid often thought to have special power to harm or heal, depending on the way it was used. Thus John (9:6) reports that Christ healed a blind man by mixing spittle with clay to anoint his lids. The habit of spitting for good luck uses the old offensive symbolism of spitting in the face of demons or witches.

Spleen

Once thought to be the ruling organ of emotion, but symbolizing ill humour in the West, good humour and laughter in the East. In ancient China, the spleen was one of the Eight Treasures, associated with yin energy.

Spring *see* SEASONS, THE

Spring (water)

Purity and fertility – a source of spiritual wisdom, salvation or healing. In myth, folklore and religion, springs are magical or spiritually significant places, an idea based partly on the general symbolism of water and partly on the spring as the unpolluted origin of water.

In pagan cults, springs were linked with the wisdom or gifts of benevolent underworld spirits. The healing properties of mineral springs may have added to the curative symbolism of springs in general. A spring flowing from the Tree of Life fed the four rivers of paradise – a Christian symbol of salvation.

Square

The ancient sign for the earth, particularly important in the symbol systems of India and China. Based on the order implied by the four directions of space, and on the stabilizing "female" symbolism of the number four, the square symbolized permanence, security, balance, the rational organization of space, correct proportion, limitation, moral rectitude and good faith (the "square deal"). As opposed to the dynamism of the circle, spiral, cross and triangle, the square is the most static of the graphic shapes frequently used as symbols. Combined with the circle, as in many Hindu mandalas, it stands for the union of earth with heaven – the symbolic basis of domed temples built on square ground plans. In many traditions, the square was an emblem of the perfect city, built for eternity – an extension of the symbolic difference between the "permanent" four walls of the house and the circular base of the nomadic tent.

The square was once an emblem of the Chinese emperor as lords of the Earth, which was conceived in Chinese cosmology as square. In more recent times the square has become the symbol of the Lodge Master in Freemasonry, the square's right-angle symbolizing a mason's duty to uphold moral rightness, justice and truth.

Spire: *see* Stupa; Tower

Spleen: *see* Yin and Yang

Spring (water): *see* fountain; tree; water; well; WISDOM

Square: *see* CARDINAL POINTS; Circle; Earth; Four; Mandala; Temple; VIRTUES, THE

*An eight-pointed star
representing the great
Near Eastern goddess
Ishtar (identified with
the planet Venus).*

Squirrel

A fertility symbol in Japan, in Europe it is an animal that shares the destructive, voracious symbolism of other rodents. Its darting journeys up and down trees suggested the Scandinavian myth of a squirrel go-between fostering enmity between the eagle at the top of the World Tree, Yggdrasil, and the serpent at the bottom.

Staff

Like the rod and sceptre, a male symbol of power and authority, often held as an emblem of office or carried ahead of high priests in ecclesiastical processions. The shepherd's staff, or crook, was, with the flail, the main emblem of the god Osiris as shepherd and judge of Egyptian souls. As a weapon, the staff can have punitive meaning, but usually appears in art as the attribute of pilgrims and saints.

Stag

In Christian art, stags may drink at the spring of life-giving waters, an allusion to the Psalms¹, as seen in early Christian mosaics (Galla Placidia, Ravenna). A stag is the attribute of Saints Eustace, Giles, Hubert and Julian. Stags were also frequently used by royalty and by the aristocracy as a heraldic device; the white hart of England's Plantagenet dynasty was used by Richard II as a royal emblem and is seen on the badges of the angels in the *Wilton Diptych*.

Star

Supremacy, constancy, guidance, guardianship, vigilance and aspiration. Ancient beliefs that the stars ruled or influenced human life, either as divinities or agents of divinity, account for much of the symbolism of the star, as well as underlying the hugely influential symbol system of astrology. Greek stellar myth peopled the sky with starry gods and heroes. In religion, stars formed the crowns of great mother goddesses, notably Ishtar in the Near East, and the Virgin Mary. Stars were cosmic windows or points of entry to heaven. They were the eyes of Mithras, Persian god of light. In the Bible, the "star out of Jacob" is a Messianic symbol, recalled in the New Testament description of Christ as "the bright and shining morning star".

Moving or shooting stars presaged the death of great men or the birth of gods, as in the Christmas story of the birth of Christ or Indian myths of Agni and the Buddha. In general symbolism, the most significant stars are the Pole Star, symbolic pivot of the universe, and the "star" of Venus – the aggressively bright, emblem of warfare and life-energy as the morning star, and of sexual pleasure and fertility as the evening star.

Among star images, the five-pointed pentagram and six-pointed hexagram (drawn with internal lines connecting each point) have major symbolism, discussed in their individual entries. The four-pointed star is the sun star of Shamash, the Mesopotamian solar god. The five-pointed star was the Sumerian emblem of Ishtar in her warrior aspect as the morning star. As an emblem of ascendancy, it is the star with the Islamic crescent, and the star most widely used on flags and in military and police insignia today. It is also the most common form of Bethlehem star or birth star. In Freemasonry, the five-pointed "blazing star" symbolizes the mystic centre and regeneration. The six-pointed star is the Star of David, the Pole Star, and sometimes appears as a birth star. The Gnostic mystic star has seven points. The eight-pointed star, linked with creation, fertility and sex, was the emblem of Ishtar in later Near-Eastern symbolism, and of Venus as the evening star. This is an alternative form of Bethlehem star.

Stations of the Cross, The

The Stations of the Cross record significant moments of the Passion of Christ on the road to Calvary (*Via Dolorosa*). In the Middle Ages, images appropriate to these moments were ranged at intervals in a church for devotional purposes. Later, scenes from the Crucifixion were added, so that the whole series comprised twelves scenes: Christ condemned to death; Christ carrying the Cross; his three falls; his encounter with the Virgin; Simon the Cyrenian helping him to carry the Cross; Veronica's veil; Christ speaking to the daughters of Jerusalem; Christ stripped of his garments; Christ nailed to the Cross; the release of his spirit; the Deposition; and lastly the Entombment.

Stentor

A Greek herald during the Trojan War who was renowned for his astonishingly loud voice, hence the word "stentorian".

Stephen, Saint

Stephen (died *c*.35CE) was venerated as the first Christian deacon and martyr. As the number of Christ's disciples grew, Stephen was appointed deacon with six others to minister to the Greek-speaking widows in Jerusalem. He disputed with the blasphemous and worked "great wonders and miracles among the people".[1] Brought before the Jewish council, he argued that the coming of Christ had been foretold by the prophets and that the Crucifixion was an act of murder. The elders "cast him out of the city and stoned him".[2]

In legend,[3] some 300 years after Stephen's death, Lucian, a priest in Jerusalem, was told in a dream where to find the saint's grave. His relics found their way to Rome, where they were placed in the tomb of St Laurence in the church dedicated to him outside the city walls. Apparently, when the tomb was opened, Laurence moved to make room for Stephen.

In Italian and French art of the Renaissance, Stephen is generally seen as a young deacon with his attribute of a stone, the instrument of his martyrdom. Scenes from his life were painted by Carpaccio, originally for the Scuola di San Stefano in Venice. In Fra Angelico's narrative cycle in the Nicholas V chapel (Vatican, Rome) he is paired with St Laurence.

Steps, Stairs

Symbols of progress toward enlightenment, esoteric understanding or heaven itself. Steps and terraces were often used in religious architecture and altar design, or in the rites of mystery cults, to symbolize the marked difference between earthly and spiritual planes, the gradually ascending stages of initiation, and the slow and difficult process of spiritual transformation. The number of steps often had specific meaning, as in the nine steps leading to the god Osiris (the completed cycle) in Egyptian tradition or the seven steps (the planets represented as diferent metals) in Mithraic initiations.

Stigmata

Stigmata

These five marks, representing the wounds Christ received at the Crucifixion in the hands, feet and side, were said to have manifested themselves on the bodies of various saints, including St Francis of Assisi and St Catherine of Siena, on account of their exceptional devotion.

Stone

Once a compelling animist symbol of magical powers thought to exist within inanimate matter. In nearly all ancient cultures, the general symbolic qualities of rock – permanence, strength, integrity – were heightened and given sacred significance in individual standing stones, sacrificial stone axes or knives, and stone objects such as amulets. Stones stored heat, coldness, water and (as jewels) light. They could appear as giant, lifelike presences. In Native North America, they were the metaphoric bones of Mother Earth, as also in Greece and in Asia Minor where the great mother goddess Cybele was worshipped in the form of a stone, later carried to Rome.

Stones could come from the sky as meteorites, like the sacred black stone of the Ka'aba at Makkah (Mecca). Thus they were linked with both earth and sky. As durable symbols of life force, they were used to mark sacred places and to act, like the altar, *omphalos* or lingam, as a focus of worship, or sacrifice or an invocation of fertility. Sacrificial victims were bound to them or (in Fiji) had their brains dashed out on them.

In funerary memorials, stone symbolized eternal life. In a number of coronation rituals, it signified authority over the land. To symbolize his claim to suzerainty over Scotland, King Edward I of England removed the Coronation Stone, or Stone of Destiny, from the abbey at Perth, on which Scots kings were crowned until 1296, and installed it at Westminster Abbey under the Coronation Chair (it was returned to Scotland in 1996).

The tradition of kissing a stone at Blarney Castle, Ireland, to acquire "the gift of the blarney" is based on the oracular symbolism of stone not only in Celtic tradition but also elsewhere. Thrown stones are associated both with death (especially in Hebrew tradition) and with life. In Greek myth, Deucalion and his sister restore the human race after the Deluge by throwing over their shoulders stones which become men and women.

Stone fights were superstitiously thought to promote fertility and bring rain in China. Stone chimes were Chinese fertility emblems. The use of stones and stone objects as phallic cures for sterility was widespread. With the decline of animist beliefs, stone became primarily a symbol of unfeeling coldness.

Stork

In the Orient, a popular emblem of longevity and, in Daoism, of immortality. There and elsewhere, the stork symbolizes filial devotion because it was thought to feed its elderly parents as well as its own children. Its nursing care and association with new life as a migratory bird of spring made it sacred to the Greek goddess Hera (in Roman myth, Juno) as a protective divinity of nursing mothers – the basis of the Western fable that storks bring babies. In art, storks draw the chariot of the god Hermes

(Mercury) and are often shown killing snakes. Christian iconography links the stork with purity, piety and resurrection.

Storm

Although associated with divine anger or punishment in most parts of the world, the storm was a symbol of creative energy and fecundity. Hence the name "house of abundance" for the temple of the great rain-bringing Mesopotamian storm-god Hadad. Most storm gods depicted wielding axes, hammers or thunderbolts have dual creative–destructive symbolism.

Strawberry

A symbol of carnal pleasure in the paintings of Bosch, who shows giant strawberries growing in *The Garden of Earthly Delights* (*c*.1495). Fruits eaten in the afterlife can symbolize the end of any chance of returning to the living, as in one Native Canadian myth.

Stupa

A domed reliquary originally built to house cremated relics of the Buddha and as a symbol of his teaching, the Dharma. In its classic form, derived from Indian temple design, a square base symbolizes the terrestial plane, a dome the cosmic egg, surmounted by a balcony representing the 33 heavens ruled by Shiva. The whole is surmounted by an axial spire with rings or parasols, taken to symbolize the Buddha's ascent and escape from the round of existence. From this spire developed the pagoda, the Chinese Buddhist version of the stupa.

Stymphalian Birds, The *see* HERAKLES, THE LABOURS OF

Styx

"Hateful", one of the five rivers of the Greek underworld, land of the dead. According to some accounts the Styx was a branch of the great river Ocean which surrounded the earth. On its course through the underworld it was said to encircle the land of the dead nine times, and the other underworld streams were its branches or tributaries. Styx was governed by a divinity of the same name. She was a daughter of Okeanos and Tethys.

Sujata

The heroine of a popular Buddhist myth of Thailand. Sujata, the daughter of a rich landowner, had a baby son and wished to make a thanks-offering of rice mixed with rich milk to the god of the bo or peepul tree (*ficus religiosa*). She approached someone sitting under the tree whom she assumed was the god. In fact it was the Buddha on the first of the forty-nine days of his enlightenment.

A relief of a stupa from Amaravati.

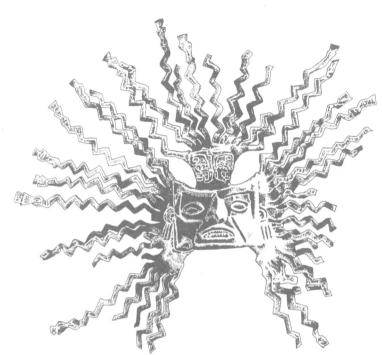

The god was sustained throughout this time by the rice and milk that Sujata joyfully offered him.

The sun with zigzag rays, after a golden Inca mask.

Sulphur

In the symbolism of alchemy, the active, fiery, male generative principle. Sulphur in reaction with the female principle of mercury would, it was thought, steadily purify base metals. Chinese superstition credited sulphur with magical powers against evil, whereas in Christian tradition Satan is himself a sulphuric figure controlling an infernal world of brimstone.

Summer *see* SEASONS, THE

Sun

The dominant symbol of creative energy in most traditions, often worshipped as the supreme god or a manifestation of his all-seeing power.

In spite of the geocentric (earth-centred) basis of ancient astronomy, some of the earliest graphic signs for the sun show it as the symbolic centre or heart of the cosmos. As the source of heat, the sun represents vitality, passion, courage and eternally renewed youth. As the source of light out of darkness, it symbolizes knowledge, intellect and Truth personified, who, in Western art, sometimes holds a sun in her hand. And as the most brilliant of the celestial bodies, it is the emblem of royalty and imperial splendour.

The sun represents the male principle in most traditions, but was female in Germany and Japan and for many tribes in the Celtic world, Africa, Native America, Oceania and New

Zealand. It was an imperial yang emblem in China but was never seen as supreme in the Chinese pantheon of gods. Like a number of other peoples, the Chinese symbolized the destructive aspects of solar power in a myth about how multiple suns made the world too hot. The ten original suns refused to share their solar duties on a rota basis and entered the sky together. The divine archer Yi had then to kill nine of them to restore cosmic balance. A distinctive solar emblem in China is a red disk with a three-legged black raven or crow symbolizing the three phases of the sun (rising, zenith, setting).

The most elaborate sun cults were those of Peru, Mexico and Egypt. Emphasizing the Inca claim to be "children of the sun", the Peruvian sun deity was depicted in human form with a disk-like golden face. In the Aztec cult of the Fifth Sun, the war god Huitzilopochtli required continuing human sacrifices to sustain the strength of the sun as guardian of the contemporary era. This charmless story, masking Aztec blood lust, is far from the Nordic legend of the death of the handsome young Nordic god of light, Balder, but is one of countless myths and rites based on the symbolic theme of the sun's eclipse, nightly disappearances or seasonally waxing and waning power.

Thus Egyptian solar myth depicts the barque of the sun travelling each night through underworld perils before emerging triumphantly from the mouth of a serpent each morning. In a farcical treatment of the theme, the Japanese sun goddess Amaterasu hides herself in a cave and has to be tricked to come out again. Personi-fications of the sun are multiple in some cultures, as in Egypt where Khepri is the scarab god of the rising sun, Horus the eye of day, Ra the zenith and Osiris the setting sun. In Greece, Helios personified the sun, whereas the Roman Sol was desultorily displaced by Apollo, representing the brilliance of its light.

Alternatively, the sun is the son of the supreme god or symbolizes his vision or radiant love. It was the eye of Zeus in Greece, of Odin in Scandinavia, of Ahura Mazda (alternatively called Ormuzd) in Iran, of Varuna in India and of Allah to Muhammad. It was the light of the Buddha, of the Great Spirit in Native North America, of God the Father in Christianity. In the Roman Empire, Christ, the Sun of Righteousness, replaced Mithras, who was venerated as Sol Invictus, the "Unvanquished Sun".

In iconography the sun is represented by a vast range of emblems. These include the gold disk, the rayed or winged disk (most common in the Near East), the half-disc with rays (in Japan, where Nihon, "Japan", means "Land of the Rising Sun" – literally "sun-source"), the circle with central point (a symbol of the conscious self in astrology), and a star, spiral, ring, wheel, swastika (or other turning cross forms), heart, rosette, lotus, sunflower and chrysanthemum.

The sun could be further represented by bronze, gold, yellow, red, diamond, ruby, topaz, a winged or feathered serpent, an eagle or an eagle with a serpent, or a falcon, phoenix, swan, lion, ram, cock or bull. Golden or white horses or swans draw the solar chariot. The "black sun" was an alchemical symbol of unworked primal matter.

SUN, MOON AND STARS IN MYTH

Its importance to the sustenance of all life often earns the sun the position of head of the pantheon and supreme creator. The sun is most often seen as a male god, as in ancient Egypt and among the Inca, but it may be female, as in Japan where it is manifested as the sun goddess Amaterasu.

The moon is generally female, with notable exceptions, such as the Egyptian god Thoth. An example of a supreme creator moon is Nyame, the mother goddess who created the universe, according to the mythology of the Akan people of Ghana. The moon is male in most of Oceania: in parts of New Guinea it is associated with nocturnal hunting, a male activity, while the sun is female, because women's work is carried out mainly in daylight.

The male moon figures in southern Africa, often as the consort of the planet Venus. The sun and moon are seen as married in other regions, while in the Americas they are often seen as a brother and sister who are incestuous lovers. They come together in the dark, and the female sun paints dark patches on her brother's cheek so she will know him later: this explains the features of the moon visible from earth. Other accounts of the lunar features include the Western idea that it is a face (the Man in the Moon) and the Chinese and Central American one that it is a hare. The phases of the moon are also accounted for in various ways. In Maori myth, the (male) moon is constantly fighting a god called Rona, and wanes as the moon grows

weary. At the new moon the two pause to restore their strength, and begin fighting again at full moon.

The sun and moon are sometimes seen as the eyes of a great creator deity. The Egyptians envisaged the moon as the right eye of Horus and the sun as his left eye. Similarly, in Chinese myth the left eye of the cosmic giant Pan Gu became the sun and his right eye became the moon.

Certain heavenly constellations are personalized in myth, with strikingly similar perceptions occurring in different cultures. The Greeks conceived of the Pleiades as the seven daughters of Atlas and Pleione. In the Southern Hemisphere, the Pleiades are also widely seen as a group of sisters. Here, their appearance heralds the onset of the rains. The Greeks claimed that Ursa Major, the Great Bear, was a nymph, Callisto, who had been turned into a bear. That part of Ursa Major which we call the Plough or Big Dipper is known to Native Americans as the Heavenly Bear.

The most significant individual star in most mythologies is Venus, the Morning or Evening Star. Venus is usually female, and in the Mediterranean and Near East is often identified with goddesses of love, sexuality and fertility, such as the Greek Aphrodite (Venus) and the Babylonian Ishtar and Inanna. Ishtar-Inanna formed part of a great heavenly triad of deities consisting of the sun, moon and Venus. For the Aztecs, Venus was identified with the god Quetzalcoatl and associated with death, resurrection and war.

The Inuit moon spirit, Tarqeq; after a mask.

SUN, MOON AND STARS IN MYTH *see panel opposite*

Sun Dance

The most important ritual of the Native North American Plains, symbolizing the power of the sun as a manifestation of the Great Spirit. To become shamans, to avenge insults or for other reasons, "pledgers" drew on this power by dancing in a circle around a forked world axis pole, staring at the sun and tearing from their chests cords binding them to the pole to symbolize release from ignorance.

Sun Wukong

The Monkey King, the protagonist of the 14th-century Chinese novel *Journey to the West* by Wu Cheng'en. After causing mischief on earth, Sun Wukong was lured to heaven by the promise of a post in the celestial civil service. But the post was only to allow the rulers of heaven to keep an eye on the mischievous monkey. Sun Wukong soon began to misbehave. In the end he was given the job of overseeing the garden of the heavenly empress Wang Mu Niang Niang, in which grew the peaches eaten by the gods and goddesses to replenish their immortality. The monkey devoured as many peaches as he could before slipping away to earth.

Angered by this, the entire celestial government soon sought Sun Wukong. Eventually he was caught by the Buddha, who locked him in a mountain for five hundred years until the merciful bodhisattva Guanyin interceded on his behalf. He was freed on condition that he accompanied a Buddhist pilgrim (the narrator of the novel) on a journey to India to acquire Buddhist texts. After the journey Sun Wukong was deified and returned to heaven.

Sunflower

Solar adoration – a symbolism used by Anton van Dyck (1599–1641), who painted himself with a sunflower to ingratiate himself with Charles I of England, his royal "sun". The sunflower, a plant brought to Europe from North America, is sometimes confused with the heliotrope, source of a Greek myth of solar infatuation.

Surabhi

In Hindu myth, the divine cow of plenty, the mother of all cattle. Surabhi is said to be one of the treasures which arose from the Churning of the Ocean by the gods and demons.

Susannah and the Elders

In the Old Testament Apocrypha, Susannah was married to the wealthy and honourable Joachim, in whose house two judges spent much time. They lusted after Susannah, and together they conspired to watch her bathing in her beautiful garden.[1] She commanded her maids to fetch her oils, and once she was alone, the two judges appeared and told her to lie with them or they would accuse her of adultery. She replied that she would prefer to be falsely accused than to sin in the eyes of the Lord. At her ensuing trial she was condemned to death. As she was led away, the Lord sent a youth, Daniel, who brought the truth to light, the elders were sentenced and Susannah was set free. From the Renaissance on, artists chose to show Susannah bathing, an opportunity to paint a beautiful female nude. One example is Tintoretto's *Susannah and the Elders*.

Susano

Susano

The Japanese god of storms and the divine embodiment of the forces of disorder. Susano was a fierce but not always malevolent deity who sprang from the primal father god Izanagi as he bathed in a stream. Izanagi divided the world among his three most powerful children; he gave Amaterasu the heavens, Tsuki-yomi the night and he assigned Susano the overlordship of the oceans. But Susano felt that he had done badly out of the division, became angry, and was banished by his father for his defiance.

Susano then became engaged in a long struggle with his sister Amaterasu, the sun goddess. His stubborn attempt to overthrow Amaterasu nearly brought catastrophe to the world precipitating the "Divine Crisis" during which the terrified Amat-

The god Susano, with Kusa-nada-hime behind him; after a Japanese print.

erasu withdrew into a cave, depriving the world of sunlight and causing many calamities. In the end, however, she emerged from the cave to continue her reign and Susano was expelled from heaven. On earth he found himself in the land of Izumo in southern Honshu island. Near the river Hi he won his wife, Kusa-nada-hime, by rescuing her from the eight-headed dragon Yamato-no-Orochi.

The god eventually took up residence in the underworld. Later Susano assisted his descendant Okuninushi in the defeat of his eighty jealous brothers.

Svarog

The supreme elemental deity of the ancient Slavs, the divine personification of the sky. Svarog's most famous shrine was at Rethra in the area of the Polabians ("People on the Elbe"), a western Slavic people living in what is now northeastern Germany. The temple contained a golden effigy of the god wearing a helmet resembling a bird with outstretched wings. Svarog had two sons: Dazhbog, the sun god, and Svarozhich, the god of fire. The veneration of Svarozhich (also called Ogon, "Fire") was the most marked expression of the ancient Slavic reverence for the forces of light.

Swallow

The traditional messenger of spring and so a renewal or resurrection symbol in many traditions, as well as an emblem of childbirth. In China, where the bird's arrival coincided with fecundity rites at the March equinox, swallows nesting in a house presaged early marriage with many children. The swallow was sacred to the goddess Isis in Egypt and to other mother goddesses elsewhere.

Swan

A romantic and ambiguous symbol of light, death, transformation, poetry, beauty and melancholy passion, especially influential in Western literature, music and ballet. As a solar and male emblem of light, the white swan became the shining hero of Wagner's opera *Lohengrin* (1848) and other tales of the swan knight. As an emblem of female softness, beauty and grace, it became the heroine of Tchaikovsky's ballet *Swan Lake* (1876). The Greek fable that swans sing a last song of unearthly beauty as they die linked the swan with death, as in the Finnish legend of the Swan of Tuonela in which it personifies the waters of the underworld.

The persistent theme of transformation in swan symbolism is prefigured in the myth in which the Greek god Zeus (Jupiter) disguised himself as a swan to ravish Leda. Through such myths the swan evolved into a symbol of achieved passion and the ebbing or loss of love.

Cygnus was a youth who was transformed into a swan. He was a close friend of Phaethon, the son of Helios, who died when he drove his father's chariot too close to the earth. As Cygnus mourned the death of Phaethon, his voice became thin and shrill; mistrusting the skies and hating fire, he chose to inhabit rivers, where he was changed into the swan.

A swan is associated with the Muses and with Apollo; one Greek legend claims that the soul of Apollo, and therefore of all good poets, turned into a swan. The swan is also linked with bardic inspiration in Celtic tradition (where it is almost interchangeable with the goose) and is often associated in iconography with the

Leda and the swan (Zeus in disguise), with the Dioscuri; after a copy of a lost work by Leonardo da Vinci.

Swan: *see* Apollo; Leda; MUSES; Phaethon; Venus

Swastika: *see* Axis; CARDINAL POINTS; Centre; Circle; cross; Foot, Footprint; Four; Hammer; Light; Lightning; NUMBERS; Sky; Sun; Wheel

harp and the otherworld of spiritual beings. A pair of swans, linked by a gold or silver chain, draw the Celtic barque of the sun.

These beautiful birds may be shown drawing Aphrodite's (Venus) chariot. Jan Asselijn's *The Threatened Swan* was retitled *Netherlands Defending her Nest Against the Enemies of the State* when the artist acquired the Grand Pensionary of the Dutch Republic as his new patron.

Swastika

An ideogram representing cosmic dynamism and creative energy, one of the most ancient and widespread of all linear symbols. Named from the Sanscrit *su* "well", and *asti* "being", its traditional significance was always positive. Nazi use of its power symbolism made it the most infamously successful emblem of the 20th century and the one most altered from its ancient meaning. The swastika is an equal-armed cross

Sword

with the end of each arm turned at a right-angle to give it whirling momentum. Pictorially it can suggest a solar wheel with light trailing from each turning spoke, and its appearance in many primitive cults was linked with sun or sky gods, particularly Indo-Iranian. It can rotate in either direction. The swastika with the top bar turned to the left – a Buddhist symbol of the cyclic round of existence – is sometimes, but not always, identified with the principle of male energy and was an emblem used by the emperor Charlemagne (742–814CE).

The reversed swastika (used by Hitler) was linked with female generative power in upper Mesopotamia and appears on the pubis of the great Semitic goddess Ishtar, equated in the classical world with the Greek Artemis (in Roman myth, Diana). Similarly in China, the reversed swastika is a yin symbol. The swastika's essential meaning of life force, solar power and cyclic regeneration is often extended to signify the Supreme Being, notably in Jainism. It appears on the footprint or breast of the Buddha (unmoving heart of the Wheel of Becoming). It is also a sign of Christ (moving in the world) in catacomb inscriptions, of Vedic and Hindu gods (Agni, Brahma, Surya, Vishnu, Shiva, Ganesha); of Zeus, Helios, Hera and Artemis in Greece; and of Thor, the Scandinavian god of thunder whose hammer may appear in swastika forms suggesting twin lightning bolts. The winged disk on a swastika was used as a symbol of solar energy in Egypt and Babylonia, but the swastika appeared widely elsewhere, on icons or artifacts and with a variety of subsidiary meanings.

A cosmic swastika motif, from a Native American sandpainting.

Apart from its rotative force, the swastika's other notable graphic feature is that its whirling arms quarter space around a pole or static centre. In Native American symbolism, the swastika was associated with the sacred number four – the four wind gods, the four seasons, or the four cardinal points as in China (where it was the symbol of the "infinite" number 10,000). Its use as a polar symbol survives in the Masonic order. It was a Gnostic secret symbol and the cross of the Manichean Christian sect. The use of the swastika as an emblem of "Aryan" racial purity dates from just before World War I, among anti-Semitic socialist groups in Germany and Austria. The Finnish Air Force adopted it as a military emblem in 1918. Hitler, master of mass psychology, recognized its dynamism as a party emblem and put it on the Nazi banner in August 1920, tilted to give it a bent-legged forward drive. "The effect was as if we had dropped a bomb," he wrote.

Swine *see* **Pig**

Sword

Beyond its obvious aggressive/protective function, an important symbol of authority, justice, decisive judgment, insight, penetrative intellect, phallic power, light, separation and death. One explanation for the unusually rich symbolism of the sword is that the arcane skills of sword-making meant that swords stronger, sharper and better balanced than others were credited with supernatural powers. Hence the many legends of magic swords such as the Arthurian Excalibur, and the frequent appearance of the sword as an emblem of magic.

Cults of the sword, particularly in Japan and in religious rituals of the Crusades, gave it a ceremonial as well as a military role, as in the conferring of knighthoods. A sword (said to have been drawn from the tail of an eight-headed dragon) is one of the Three Treasures of the Japanese emperor.

In art, the sword is the attribute of Justice, Constancy, Fortitude and Wrath personified – and of St Paul who called the word of God "the sword of the spirit". The two-edged sword is a particular symbol of divine wisdom or truth, notably in Revelation where it protrudes from the mouth of Christ (1:16). Similarly, Buddhism refers to the sword of wisdom cutting through ignorance. Vishnu is shown with a flaming sword of knowledge. The flame-like shape of the two-edged sword also links it with purification, as in alchemy where the sword is an emblem of fire. Purity is implied by the biblical cherubim with flaming swords who guard the way back to Eden (Genesis 3:24). The sword laid between man and woman in bed suggests purity as well as separation. The sword of Damocles, in legend suspended by a hair by Dionysius, tyrant of Syracuse, over the head of an over-ambitious courtier, symbolized the precarious nature of power. As an emblem of justice the sword often appears with the scales. It is carried by the archangel Michael, and appears with retributive significance opposite the lily in paintings of the judgmental Christ. A broken sword symbolizes failure. In Chinese dream symbolism, a woman drawing a sword from water will have a son; a sword falling into water presages a woman's death. Avoidance of death is the symbolism of sword dancing.

Sylvester, Saint

Sylvester (died 335CE) was an early popes, elected in 313, the same year that Christianity was legalized in the Roman Empire. Little is known about him, but legend[1] tells that he was highly eloquent. He disputed with 12 learned Jewish doctors about Christianity and finally, as proof, restored a bull to life. He also closed the throat of a dragon whose breath had killed two wise men in the Roman Forum.

In another legend, the emperor Constantine caught leprosy and ordered the slaughter of 3,000 children so that he could be cured by bathing in their blood. Saints Peter and Paul appeared to him in a dream and told him to summon Sylvester instead. Sylvester baptized the emperor, immersing him in a pool from which he emerged restored to health, and the children were returned to their mothers unharmed.

In 1248, in the Chapel of San Sylvestro (Quattro Coronati, Rome), scenes of Sylvester and Constantine were frescoed as an assertion of papal primacy. Scenes from the life of Pope Sylvester by Maso di Banco can be seen in the Bardi di Vernio Chapel, Santa Croce, Florence. In art Sylvester is usually dressed as a Pope; his attributes may be a chained dragon or a bull.

Syrinx

In Greek myth, a nymph of Arcadia in the Peloponnese, one of the retinue of the hunter goddess Artemis. The god Pan fell in love with Syrinx and tried to catch her, but she fled his advances and asked some river nymphs to turn her into a bed of reeds. Pan cut some of the reeds to make the first syrinx or pan-pipes.

Sylvester, Saint: *see* Bull; Constantine, Saint; Dragon
[1] *Golden Legend, St Sylvester*

Syrinx; *see* Nymph; Pan

Tabernacle

In Hebrew tradition, the earthly throne or dwelling place of God – a sanctuary, originally established by Moses in the wilderness according to precise geometric rules, symbolizing the cosmos and centred upon a Holy of Holies containing the Ark of the Covenant and approached through a series of veiled spaces of increasing sanctity. In the Christian church, the term "tabernacle" is also applied to a container in which is kept the pyx, the vessel that holds the sacred Host.

Tablet, Table

Linked through its durability with non-mortal or eternal powers, frequently a symbol of communication with them. In the ancient world, law codes, funerary inscriptions and other important documents were inscribed on tablets (sometimes called "tables") of bronze, marble or other metals and stones. Particularly in the Middle East, this led to the idea that divine commandments should be handed down on tablets – as in the Mosaic Tables of the Law. Mesopotamian and Islamic traditions held that tablets of fate or destiny existed on which the future, as well as the past, was inscribed. Funerary tablets usually symbolized the consecration of tombs to the spirits of the dead. In China they prevented ancestral spirits from wandering. Greek tablets bearing curses on enemies were probably addressed to underworld divinities.

Táin Bó Cuailnge, The

The *Cattle Raid of Cooley*, an Irish epic probably composed *c*.700CE but known from manuscripts of the 12th–14th centuries. The central work in a great cycle of Irish heroic myths from Ulster, it focuses on the war between Queen Medhbh of Connacht and "The Men of Ireland", and their opponents King Conchobar of Ulster and "The Men of Ulster". The war is sparked by the theft, on Medhbh's orders, of the magnificent Brown Bull of Cooley in Ulster. The leading character in the story is the Ulster hero Cú Chulainn, Conchobar's champion.

Talos

In Greek myth, a bronze giant made by the god Hephaistos for King Minos of Crete. Talos ran around the island's coastline looking out for foreign invasion. If he encountered intruders he would hurl rocks at them or make himself red hot and then hug his victims to death. When the Argonauts attempted to land on Crete, the sorceress Medea killed Talos by sending him to sleep and then removing a plug in his ankle to drain his single vein, which ran from head to foot through his body.

Tamarisk

A resin-giving tree with sacred significance in desert regions, including Mesopotamia, Palestine (where it was possibly a source of manna, as it still is for the Bedouin) and Egypt, where it was associated with the resurrection of the god Osiris. The tamarisk was linked with immortality in China and rain in Japan.

Tambourine

The drum of dancers, associated particularly with orgiastic agricultural fertility rites. Maenads or Bacchantes carry tambourines in the rites of the Greek god Dionysos (in Roman myth, Bacchus). The tambourine's percussive sound, suggesting thunder and rain, made it a fecundity symbol from Africa to Asia and also in Central America. In Indian art, it signifies cosmic rhythms in the hand of Shiva, war in the hand of Indra.

Tancred

The hero of the popular epic poem *Jerusalem Delivered* by Torquato Tasso (1544–95), Tancred, like Rinaldo, was a romantic subject in painting. He fell in love with the pagan Clorinda, who fought for the Saracens, but fatally wounded her in battle, not recognizing her in armour. As she lay dying she asked Tancred to wash away her sins with water. He ran to fill his helmet from a nearby stream so that she could die in peace.[1]

Erminia, a Saracen princess who also secretly loved Tancred, escaped the besieged city of Jerusalem wearing armour and fell asleep in the woods. Domenichino's *Erminia with the Shepherds* shows how she awoke to the sound of a shepherd and his young sons singing. While they explained the delights of country life, she briefly considered abandoning war for a life of rural peace.[2]

Tancred accepted a challenge to fight the Saracen giant Argantes, but although he killed his opponent he was himself heavily wounded. Filled with fear for her lover, Erminia ran to his side with his squire Vafrino. At first they believed him dead, as Guercino's *Tancred and Erminia* shows. Seeing his lips give a sigh, however, Erminia cut off her amber hair to stop the flow of his blood, and they carried him back alive to the Crusaders' camp.[3]

Tane

The Maori god of trees and forests, one of the six offspring of the primal deities Rangi, the sky, and Papa, the earth. Tane succeeded in forcing apart his parents, who had been locked in a tight embrace, but in doing so incurred the jealousy of his siblings. Tawhiri, the god of the elements, blew down all Tane's trees and caused Tane's offspring, the fish, who until then had lived in the forests, to flee to the sea, the domain of the god Tan-

Talos: *see* ARGONAUTS, THE VOYAGE OF THE; Hephaistos; Medea; Minos

Tamarisk: *see* Manna; Resin

Tambourine: *see* Drum; Rain; Thunder

Tancred: *see* Rinaldo; Olindo and Sophronia
[1] Tasso, *Jerusalem Delivered* XII:lxiv–lxviii
[2] Tasso, *Jerusalem Delivered* VII:vi–xv
[3] Tasso, *Jerusalem Delivered* XIX:ciii–cxii

Tane: *see* Hine-hau-one; Rangi and Papa; Tangaroa; Tawhiri; Tu

*A possible depiction
of Tangaroa; after
a Maori woodcarving.*

garoa. It is said that Tane, furious at
the loss of his offspring, has been at
loggerheads with Tangaroa ever since.

Tane wanted a wife and went first to
his mother Papa. She rebuffed his
advances and told him to create a
female version of himself from the
sand of Hawaiki island. This creation,
Hine-hau-one ("Earth-created Maid-
en"), was the first human.

Tangaroa

The Maori god of the sea, the son of
Rangi and Papa. Unsurprisingly, the
sea god was very important throughout Polynesia and was known by various forms of the same name, such as
A'a in the Tubuai or Austral islands
and Ta'aroa in Tahiti. Outside New
Zealand, on the smaller islands, he
was widely revered as the supreme
creator deity.

According to Maori myth, most of
the things in the sea were the creation
of Tangaroa and those on land the
creation of his brother Tane, the god
of trees and forests. However, all fish
were the progeny of Tane and lived in
the forests until Tawhiri, the god of
the elements, blew down the trees and
drove them in panic into the sea. The
loss of all the fish to his brother Tangaroa annoyed Tane. They have been
in conflict ever since: Tane's trees fur-
nish wood for canoes, with which men
overcome the waves, while the ocean
of Tangaroa tries to overwhelm the
forests of the islands.

Tantalus

In Greek myth,[1] a king of Lydia in
western Asia Minor (modern Turkey),
the son of the god Zeus (Jupiter in
Roman myth) and the Titan Pluto.
According to one account, Tantalus
asked the gods of Olympus to dine

with him and then cooked his son
Pelops in order to test their omniscience. To their anger, the deities knew
at once what they had been served
and restored Pelops to life. Tantalus's
eternal punishment was to stand in a
pool "tantalized" by its refreshing
waters, which nearly reached his chin;
whenever he stooped to drink, the
water receded. Trees dangled fruits
over his head, but the wind always
blew them just out of his reach. In
variations of the myth, Tantalus
earned his punishment when he stole
ambrosia and nectar, the food of the
gods, or when he gave away their
secrets.

Tantalus and his descendants (he
was the father of Niobe and ancestor
of the Pelopids) were renowned for
suffering terrible curses.

Alternatively, Tantalus is described
as being eternally prevented by the
Furies from enjoying a sumptuous
banquet. He was a warning to the
subjects of a monarch who ruled by
divine right, and was painted as a
companion to the others who suffered
in hell: Ixion, Sisyphus and Tityus.
Most notably, there are copies of lost
paintings by Titian and Ribera.

Tarot

In occult tradition, a symbol system
charting human progress toward spiritual enlightenment or psychic wholeness. The Tarot deck, which drew on
the general currency of symbolism at
the end of the 14th century, may well
have been the origin of modern playing cards' four suits of numbered and
court cards. In Tarot, these corre-
sponded to a "minor arcana" of 56
cards (essentially the modern deck
plus four knights – except that hearts,
diamonds, clubs and spades were rep-

resented as cups, coins or pentacles, wands and swords); and to this were added 22 Greater Trumps, called the "major arcana", which were later discarded as playing cards but had enough allusive power to become the most poetic medium of Western divination and fortune-telling. Esoteric influences included Cabbalistic lore based on the 22 letters of the Hebrew alphabet, and perhaps some elements of Greco-Egyptian Hermetic lore.

As with all oracular systems, the mystique of the Tarot is based on its interpretative flexibility. The cards of the major arcana have been redesigned many times and have accumulated a vast range of meanings and interpretations. The following skeleton key lists only a handful of traditional associations.

The **Fool** is the only unnumbered card of the major arcana (sometimes alloted zero or XXII) – Everyman, the outsider, the microcosm, the independent seeker. Card I is the **Magician**, **Juggler** or **Minstrel** – skill, the transformable self, the manipulator of human personality, the creative spirit. Card II is the **Archpriestess** – discrimination, moral law, feminine insight. Card III is the **Empress** – security, fecundity, growth, desire. Card IV is the **Emperor** – action, temporal power, virility, leadership. Card V is the **Archpriest** – enlightenment, spiritual energy, the soul, philosophy. Card VI is the **Lover** – union, the choice between love and passion. Card VII is the **Chariot** – success, self-control, vitality. Card VIII is **Justice** – balance, duality, right judgment. Card IX is the **Hermit** – truth, self-sufficiency, morality, solitude. Card X is the **Wheel of Fortune** – movement, major change, precarious balance.

The Fool, *the unnumbered card of the Tarot pack; from a 15th-century French pack.*

Card XI is **Strength** – confidence, courage, inner powers. Card XII is the **Hanged Man** – expiation (enforced or voluntary), realignment. Card XIII is **Death** – transition, severance from fleshly desires. Card XIV is **Temperance** – self-control, dilution, the flux of emotional life. Card XV is the **Devil** – trial, self-examination. Card XVI is the **Tower** – misfortune, revelation, emotional release. Card XVII is the **Star** – hope, replenished spiritual energy. Card XVIII is the **Moon** – illusion, the power of imagination. Card XIX is the **Sun** – joy, successful integration. Card XX is the **Judgment** –

transformation, the voice of God. Card XXI is the **World** – completion, wholeness, reward.

Tarpeia

A famous traitor in the mythical early history of Rome. When the Romans were fighting the Sabines, Tarpeia, the daughter of a Roman commander, fell in love with the Sabine king Titus Tatius. In one account, she offered to let him into Rome if he gave her "what the Sabines wear on their left arms" – meaning their gold bracelets. With her aid the Sabines entered the city, but Titus Tatius regarded her treason with contempt. His warriors were ordered to hurl at her "what the Sabines wear on their left arms": their shields. Tarpeia was crushed to death under their weight. The Tarpeian Rock, from which traitors were thrown to their deaths, was said to have been named after her.

Tartaros

A primal Greek deity embodying the darkest regions of the underworld. According to Hesiod, Tartaros, Gaia, Eros, Erebos and Nyx were first to arise after Chaos came into being. However, Tartaros features little in myth as a deity. As a region Tartaros was described in early accounts as an even deeper land than the realm of Hades, but the name later came to be used more or less as a synonym for the underworld, especially the part of it where the dead were punished.

Tarvaa

A famous shaman of Mongolian myth. Tarvaa lived in ancient times. When he was fifteen, he grew sick and fell unconscious. His family thought that he was dead and quickly put his body outside the house, where crows pecked out his eyes. Tarvaa's soul, upset that his family should be so hasty to consider him dead, travelled to the land of spirits. As he was not dead, the judge of the dead turned his soul away, but offered him any gift he wanted. Tarvaa chose to have eloquence and knowledge of the wonders of the spirit world. When his soul returned to his body, Tarvaa, who was by now blind, awoke and became a great wise shaman.

Tattoo

Usually a symbol of close allegiance to or identification with a social or cultic group. Some tattoos, particularly those depicting animals, were applied as talismans to borrow a specific animal's powers.

Taweret

An Egyptian protector goddess of women and children. Taweret also assisted in the rebirth of the dead in the primal waters of the Nun. She was often depicted as a fearsome beast, part crocodile, part lion and part hippopotamus, with pendulous breasts. She was sometimes said to be the consort of the god Seth, who could also be manifested as a hippopotamus.

Tawhaki

A famous hero of Maori myth. Tawhaki and his brother Kariki were the sons of the semi-divine Hema and a sky goddess. After Hema was killed by monsters, Tawhaki journeyed to the place where his father died to avenge his death. On the journey the hero had numerous adventures which form the bulk of the myth cycle. In many of them the rather stupid and bumbling Kariki is compared unfavourably with his heroic and noble brother. During their travels Tawhaki married and had a son, Wahieroa, whose son Rata is another hero of Polynesian myth.

Tawhiri
The Maori god of the elements, the son of the sky god Rangi and earth goddess Papa. The Maori creation myth recounts how Tawhiri, jealous of his brother Tane, god of forests, sent great storms that blew down all his trees. All the fish, who at that time dwelt in trees, sought refuge in the ocean and since then the two have been at loggerheads.

Tea
In Zen Buddhism, a ceremonial drink associated with intense meditation, a symbolism supported by a Japanese legend that the first tea plant grew from the eyelids of the meditating Bodhidharma who cut them off to stay awake. Qualities emphasized in the etiquette of the tea ceremony are purity, harmony, tranquillity and the beauty of simplicity.

Teeth
Primordial emblems of aggressive or defensive power. In Greek myth the dragon's teeth sown by Cadmus, a prince of Thebes, were symbols of generative vitality: they sprouted from the ground as warriors. In contrast, the drawing or loss of teeth is a castration or impotency symbol. The association between teeth and power explains why shamans wear necklaces of animals' teeth.

Tefnut
The primal Egyptian goddess of moisture, the offspring of the creator deity Ra-Atum and the sister of the air god Shu. Tefnut and Shu coupled to produce the sky goddess Nut and the earth god Geb, who in turn were the parents of the deities Osiris, Isis, Seth and Nephthys.

Teiresias
In Greek myth, celebrated blind prophet of Thebes, also spelled Tiresias. According to one account, Teiresias came across two copulating snakes and hit the female with his stick. He immediately turned into a woman. Eight years later he encountered the same snakes and struck the male, at once becoming a man again.

Later, the god Zeus claimed that women had more pleasure during intercourse than men, but his wife Hera disagreed. They consulted Teiresias, the only person who could know the truth, and he declared that women had nine times the pleasure of men. Hera, who was furious at this answer, struck him blind. However, Zeus compensated Teiresias for his blindness by granting him the gift of prophecy. The prophet was said to have lived for seven generations.

Telemachus
In Homer's *Odyssey* Telemachus, the son of Odysseus (Ulysses to the Romans), went in search of his father, who had not returned from the Trojan War. The French writer Fénelon (1651–1715) retold the story in a romance, *Télémaque*, in which the hero was protected by Minerva (in Greek myth, Athene), disguised as his old guardian, Mentor. In *Telemachus and Mentor*, Giambattista Tiepolo shows the two striding out together. Telemachus was detained, as his father had been, by the goddess Calypso. However, he fell in love with one of her nymphs, and her companions burned

Telepinu

his boat to further prolong his stay on their island. He finally escaped when Mentor threw him into the sea and he was rescued by a passing boat.

Telepinu
The Hittite god of agriculture, the son of the weather god Teshub. According to one myth, Telepinu went into hiding and made the land, animals and people barren. When the gods found him he flew home on an eagle and fruitfulness was restored.

Temperaments, The
In the Middle Ages it was taught that the body contained four fluids or "humours", which related to the temperaments. To sustain well-being the humours had to be held in a natural balance, and the dominant humour would determine a person's character. An excess of blood made a person sanguine (hot-headed); of phlegm, phlegmatic; of yellow bile, choleric; and of black bile, melancholic. The balance could be thrown by planetary movements as well as diet, leading to illness and emotional upset. Melancholia is probably the temperament most often seen in art, as in Dürer's engraving of 1514.

Temple
The earthly house of a deity or God, the cosmic centre linking underworld, earth and heaven, or the ascending path toward spiritual enlightenment – concepts that have profoundly modified the functional forms of sacred buildings throughout history. In the spirit of the Greek *temenos* ("sacred enclosure"), temples could be as simple as an altar or shrine to a nature divinity sited beside a river, on a mountain top or in a grove of trees.

At the other end of the architectural spectrum are the great temples of Greece and Rome; the pyramids and ziggurats of Egypt, the Near East and Central America; the "cosmic mountain" and complex mandala forms of Hindu temples in India and southeast Asia; the magnificent interior spaces of Islamic mosques; and the glories of Christian churches from the late Roman period to the present day.

Ten
Inclusiveness, perfection – the mystical number of completion and unity, especially in Jewish tradition; hence the number of the Commandments revealed to Moses by God, summarizing the most important Hebrew religious obligations. In the Pythagorean system, ten was a symbol of the whole of creation, represented by a star of ten points, the holy *tetraktys* – the sum of the first four numbers: 1, 2, 3 and 4. As the number of digits on the human hands, ten was a symbol of completeness even on the simplest level. The Egyptians based their calendar on the decans, 36 bright stars divided by intervals of ten days. Each decan was thought to influence human life – a significant concept in the development of Greek astrology.

A tenth was almost universally the percentage of spoils, property or produce owed to a god or king in the ancient world – the basis of the tithes system. In China, ten was the perfectly balanced number, represented by a cross with a short central bar. As a combination of male and female numerals, ten was sometimes used as a symbol of marriage. The decade symbolizes a turning point in history or a completed cycle in myth, as in the Fall of Troy after a ten-year siege.

Teresa, Saint

Teresa of Avila (1515–82) entered a Carmelite convent in her native town aged about 20, and in 1562 founded the first of many convents of reformed or "discalced" (barefoot) Carmelites. Teresa frequently had mystical visions, which she recorded. In one heavenly rapture she described how an angel appeared: "In his hands I saw a great golden spear, and at the iron tip there appeared to be a point of fire. This he plunged into my heart several times ... and left me utterly consumed by the great love of God. The pain was so severe that it made me utter several moans."[1] This divine experience was famously sculpted in the 17th century by Bernini (Cornaro Chapel, church of Santa Maria della Vittoria, Rome).

Tereus

A Thracian king who, in some accounts, was the son of the war god Ares. He lent military assistance to King Pandion of Athens and received the hand of his daughter Procne as a reward but their wedding feast was attended by the Furies, whose presence doomed the marriage. Later, Tereus accompanied Pandion's other daughter, Philomela, from Athens to Thrace to visit Procne. Before they reached his city, he raped her and cut out her tongue so that she could not say what had happened. He then imprisoned her and told Procne that she was dead.

However, Philomela wove a tapestry which recounted everything and had it smuggled to Procne, who came to her at once and freed her. The two sisters took their revenge by killing Itys, the son of Tereus and Procne, and serving him up as a meal to his unwit-

ting father. Tereus ate what he was served, then asked for his son to be brought in. In reply, Philomela thrust the child's bleeding head before him. Rubens depicts Tereus recoiling in horror, in *The Banquet of Tereus*. Tereus was horrified and pursued the sisters, but before he caught them the gods turned all three into birds. Tereus became the hawk, Procne the swallow and Philomela the nightingale (the "Philomel" of the poets).

Tethys

A Titan, the daughter of the goddess Gaia, the earth, and the god Uranos, the sky. Tethys married her brother Okeanos and bore the sea nymphs known as the Oceanids.

Tetramorphs

The term given to the four creatures described in the first chapter of Ezekiel, which have the heads of a man, lion, ox and eagle. Following the same order, this vision is linked in Christianity with the evangelists Matthew, Mark, Luke and John, and with Christ's incarnation, resurrection, sacrifice and ascension.

Tezcatlipoca

"The Lord of the Smoking Mirror", the greatest god of the Aztec pantheon. Every other creator divinity was regarded as an aspect of Tezcatlipoca. According to the Aztec creation myth, the primal divinities Ometecuhtli and Omecihuatl coupled to produce the four great deities who were known as Tezcatlipoca, Huitzilopochtli, Quetzalcoatl and Xipe Totec, who are referred to as the "Four Tezcatlipocas". Xipe Totec ("Red Tezcatlipoca") ruled over the First Sun or world epoch.

Tezcatlipoca; after an Aztec codex.

The cult of Tezcatlipoca came to central Mexico *c.*1000CE with the Toltecs and by the time of the Aztecs (*c.*1325CE) the god had accumulated the greatest number of manifestations and titles of any deity. Among his titles were Yoalli Ehecatl ("Night Wind"), Yaotl ("Warrior") and Titlacuan ("He Whose Slaves We Are"). Tezcatlipoca was associated with darkness, war and death, and was said to confront warriors at crossroads at night. The Aztecs venerated him as the protector of magicians and royalty. He was thought of as an omnipresent, invisible, god of the shadows, who possessed a magic mirror that enabled him to foretell the future and look into people's hearts. He brought bravery, riches and good fortune, but also death and misery.

Reflecting Tezcatlipoca's supreme position was his identification with the jaguar, which was revered as the king of beasts and lord of the night. Probably the most important of all his jaguar manifestations was the jaguar deity Tepeyollotli ("The Heart of the Mountain").

Thalia *see* **Graces, The**

Theagenes and Chariclea

The ancient romance *Theagenes and Chariclea* by Heliodorus of Syria was published in Basel in 1534. Chariclea, princess of Ethiopia, was born white owing to the effect of a marble statue of Andromeda on her mother while pregnant. Fearful of being accused of adultery, the mother had Chariclea brought up elsewhere. As a youth, Chariclea awarded Theagenes the palm of victory after an athletic race, and they immediately fell in love; the incident is shown in Abraham Bloemaert's *Theagenes and Chariclea*. After several adventures Chariclea returned to Ethiopia, where she was accepted as the king's daughter.

Thecla, Saint

According to Christian legend, Thecla (1st century CE) was said to have been converted to Christianity by St Paul;[1] breaking off her engagement to a young man, she became a bride of Christ. Persecuted for her faith, she survived torture by fire and exposure to wild beasts in the amphitheatre, eventually becoming a hermit. In her old age a chasm opened up to save her from further persecutions. She is honoured as the first female martyr by the Greek Church, although she is of doubtful historical authenticity. Churches were dedicated to her in Italy, such as the Cathedral of Este, where a painting by Giambattista Tieoplo shows her interceding on behalf of the town for release from the plague.

Theia

In Greek myth, a Titan, the daughter of the goddess Gaia and the god Uranos. Theia married her brother Hyperion and from this union she became the mother of the divinities Helios (the Sun), Eos (the Dawn) and Selene (the Moon).

Themis

In Greek myth, a Titan, the daughter of the goddess Gaia and the god Uranos. According to some accounts, Themis ("Order") was the wife of the Titan Iapetus and the mother of Titans Atlas and Prometheus, and of Epimetheus and Menoetius. She became the second consort of the god Zeus and bore a number of important goddesses: Dike ("Justice"); Eirene ("Peace"); the Fates; and the Seasons.

Theodore, Saint

Legend cites Theodore (4th century CE) as a Roman soldier who, converted to Christianity, set fire to a pagan temple, for which he was cruelly tortured with iron hooks and burned to death.[1] Like St George, Theodore was also thought to have slain a dragon, and his attribute is a crocodile. Dressed as a knight, he stands over a dragon as the first patron saint of Venice in a sculpture in the Piazzetta of San Marco.

Theogony, The

An account of the origin of the universe and its divinities by Hesiod, a Greek writer of the 8th–century BC. The first important attempt to systematize the many prevailing Greek myths about the beginnings of the cosmos, it became the most widely accepted account. Hesiod relates the genealogy of the Olympian gods and goddesses of myth from Chaos (meaning "Yawning Void").

Theseus

A king of Athens and one of the greatest heroes of Greek myth. Theseus was the son of King Aegeus of Athens and Aethra, a princess of Troezen in the Peloponnese. The childless Aegeus visited King Pittheus of Troezen, who got his guest drunk and gave him Aethra as a concubine. Aethra became pregnant, and Aegeus told her that if the child was a boy he was to come to Athens as soon as he could lift a certain rock. Under this rock Aegeus had left a sword and sandals by means of which he would know his son.

The child was Theseus. Led by his mother, he lifted the rock and discovered the objects, as Poussin shows in Theseus Finding his Father's Arms. Now a young man he set out for the Athenian court with the tokens of recognition. By the time he reached Athens he was already famous, because on the way he had vanquished a series of notorious brigands, such as Pityocamptes, Sciron and Procrustes. Aegeus welcomed the valiant stranger, but the sorceress Medea, whom Aegeus had married in the intervening years, recognized the youth through her magic powers. Considering him a threat to the succession of her son Medus, the sorceress persuaded the king that the newcomer planned to kill him. He gave her permission to poison the stranger's wine at a banquet. However, as Theseus was about to drink, Aegeus spotted the tokens of recognition and knocked the cup from his hand. He hailed his son and banished Medea and Medus.

At his father's request Theseus went to Marathon and killed a wild bull (father of the Minotaur of Crete) that was terrorizing the countryside. The hero then went to Crete and killed the Minotaur. He sailed away with the

Cretan king's daughter, Ariadne, but later abandoned her on the island of Naxos. His triumphant return home was tempered with tragedy. Aegeus had requested that when Theseus returned, he should hoist a white sail if all had gone well and a black one if the mission had been a disaster. Forgetting this instruction, Theseus returned with the black sail hoisted. Believing his son to be dead and stricken with grief, Aegeus threw himself into the sea, hence the Aegean Sea.

Now king of Athens, Theseus fought alongside the hero Herakles in order to defeat the Amazon warriors, taking the Amazon Antiope as his prize. She gave birth to a son, Hippolytus, and was killed in battle against Theseus when the Amazons invaded Attica. Theseus was consistently unsuccessful; he married Phaedra, sister of Ariadne, but she fell in love with Hippolytus instead. When the beautiful youth rejected her, she told Theseus that he had tried to seduce her, a scene depicted by Pierre-Narcisse Guérin in *Phaedra and Hippolytus*. Theseus then sought Neptune's help in punishing the boy, and Hippolytus was dragged to death by his horses.

The Athenians revered Theseus as a just and fair king who established legal institutions and brought all Attica under Athenian rule.

Among his other adventures, Theseus fought off the Centaurs who invaded the wedding of his friend Pirithous, king of the Lapiths. Theseus and Pirithous also descended into the Underworld to carry away Persephone (in Roman myth, Proserpina), but were stopped by Hades (Pluto). In punishment Pirithous was placed on his father Ixion's wheel, and Theseus was tied to a huge stone until

he was rescued by Herakles. On his return to Athens, Theseus discovered his throne had been usurped by a certain Menestheus, and he fled to the island of Scyros. Here he was said to have been pushed down a steep precipice to his death by the king of the island, who feared possible usurpation from such a powerful hero. His supposed bones were reburied in a temple in Athens in the 5th century BCE. He appears in art as a muscular figure, sometimes with a club, not unlike Herakles.

Thetis

In mythology it was prophesied that Thetis, the most beautiful of the Nereids and one of the daughters of Nereus and Doris, would bear a child who would surpass his father. This deterred the supreme god Zeus (in Roman myth, Jupiter) from pursuing her, and so he ordered Peleus, a mortal, to become her lover instead. Thetis tried to avoid the union by changing into a bird, a tree and a tiger, but Peleus held her by force.

All the deities but Eris (Discord, Strife) were invited to their wedding of Peleus and Thetis. She turned up and threw down a golden apple, inscribed "For the Fairest"; Zeus asked the Trojan prince Paris to judge which of the goddesses Aphrodite (Venus), Athene (Minerva) and Hera (Juno) should have it. The Judgment of Paris – he chose Aphrodite – ultimately led to the Trojan War. Achilles, the hero of that war, was the son of Thetis and Peleus. Homer's *Iliad* relates, how, when the hero was insulted by Agamemnon, Thetis rose from the depths of the sea to Mount Olympus and begged Zeus to avenge him. Ingres illustrated this scene in

Jupiter and Thetis. Thetis also asked Hephaistos (Vulcan) to make Achilles a magnificent suit of armour.

Thistle

Retaliation – the symbolism of the thistle as the heraldic emblem of both Scotland (with the royal motto *Nemo me impune lacessit* – "No one strikes me with impunity") and Lorraine. Adam is punished with thistly ground in Genesis. However, like some other spiny plants, the thistle was associated with healing or talismanic powers and the white-spotted Lady's thistle is linked with the milk of the Virgin Mary. In art, thistles are emblems of martyrdom.

Thomas, Saint (Apostle, Disciple)

Thomas, or "Didymus" the twin (1st century CE), is known for doubting the Resurrection: he declared that unless "I shall see in his hands the prints of the nails, and put my finger into the print of the nails, and thrust my hand into his side, I will not believe". Christ instructed him to do so, saying: "Be not faithless but believing."[1] The Doubting Thomas theme appears in many cycles of post-Resurrection stories, including Duccio's *Maestà*, and in single episodes such as Caravaggio's vivid *The Incredulity of St Thomas*, in which Christ draws Thomas' finger to the wound in his chest.

According to legend[2] Thomas also doubted the Assumption of the Virgin, but "suddenly the girdle that had encircled her body fell intact into his hands", and he believed. The supposed girdle was preserved and in 1141 brought to the cathedral of Prato in Tuscany, where relevant scenes were frescoed by Agnolo Gaddi in the 1390s, and Donatello and Michelozzo carved a pulpit to display the relic.

Other apocryphal writings claim that Thomas took the Christian message to India, where he was martyred.[3]

Thomas Aquinas, Saint

One of the great Doctors (Teachers) of the Medieval Church, Thomas (1225–74) was educated at the University of Naples, where he joined the Dominican order *c.*1244. His noble family was outraged that he chose to be a mendicant friar and had him imprisoned for a year, but this only reinforced his resolve. Released, he studied at Paris and Cologne, then devoted the rest of his life to teaching in Paris and several cities in Italy, and to writing his *Summa Theologica* (1266–73), which became the basis of much of later Catholic doctrine.

He is depicted in the Dominican habit, and his importance as a theologian is represented in the chapter house known as the Spanish Chapel in the Dominican church of Santa Maria Novella in Florence, painted by Andrea da Firenze in the mid-14th century. He may be seen at his books and have a star on his chest, or hold a lily. Velázquez shows him supported by angels in front of a fire, a reference to the episode in which he used a burning log to chase off a woman who had come to tempt him.

Thor

The Norse god of the sky and thunder, and the divine protector of the community. He was derived from the earlier Germanic sky and thunder deity Donar, called Thunor ("Thunder") by the Anglo-Saxons. Thursday was named after him. Thor, said to have been the son of Fjorgyn (a name for the earth), was of immense stature, with a red beard, flaming eyes

Thomas, Saint:
[1] *John 20:25–29*
[2] *Golden Legend, The Assumption of the Virgin*
[3] *Acts of Thomas*

Thomas Aquinas, Saint: *see* RELIGIOUS ORDERS

Thor: *see* DRAGON; Hymir; Jupiter; Loki; Ragnarok; Thrym

*Thor fishing for the world serpent with
the giant Hymir, after a stone carving.*

*Thoth, the Egyptian
god of the moon and
the patron of scribes.*

and a huge appetite. He was hearty
and blunt and had a furious temper,
which he often took out on the giants,
enemies of the gods. Thor's weapon
was a great magic axe-hammer, which
symbolized thunder and lightning. It
had tremendous destructive power,
shattering giants and mountains at a
single blow. The hammer was also an
instrument of life and healing: after
Thor had devoured his own goats for
supper he restored their bones to life
with his hammer.

Thor was a highly popular deity,
especially in western Norway and Iceland. He was venerated as the protector of farmers and of the councils of
the people. There are many stories of
his adventures, and the highly pre-
dictable fate of the giants and monsters who crossed his path was often
recounted with robust humour. One
myth tells how Thor went fishing with
the giant Hymir for the World Serpent,
a dragon that lived in the sea surrounding the earth. Using an ox head
as bait, Thor hooked the monster,
which put up a fierce struggle. As the
serpent's head appeared above the
waves, Thor prepared to bludgeon it
with his hammer, but Hymir was so
terrified that he cut the god's line and

the monster escaped. Incensed, Thor
hurled Hymir into the sea. Thor finally killed the serpent at the apocalyptic
battle of Ragnarok, but in doing so he
was poisoned by its venom and died.

Thorn

Affliction or protection. The thorny
acacia tree appears with both these
symbolic meanings in the ancient
Middle East – as the attribute of the
protective Egyptian goddess Neith
and of the mocked Christ with his
Crown of Thorns.

Thoth

The Egyptian god of the moon and
wisdom. In one account, the sun god
Ra created the moon as a light for the
night sky and placed it under Thoth's
supervision. Thoth was said to have
invented hieroglyphic writing and was
venerated as the patron of scribes. He
was associated with knowledge and
also wrote the first book of magic.
Thoth recorded the judgments on the
deceased in the underworld. The god
was depicted as a baboon, an ibis or a
human with the head of an ibis. He
was identified with the Greek god
Hermes (Mercury).

Thread

Continuity in space and time, linkage,
destiny – a symbolism linked always
with the delicate fabric of human life.
In Classical mythology the three Fates
spin, measure and cut the thread of
life. In Eastern tradition, two threads
woven together symbolized the common destiny of a married couple.

Three

Synthesis, reunion, resolution, creativity, versatility, omniscience, birth
and growth – the most positive num-

ber not only in symbolism but in religious thought, mythology, legend and folklore where the tradition of "third time lucky" is very old. The Christian doctrine of the Trinity, which enabled a monotheistic God to be worshipped through the Holy Spirit and the person of Christ, is an example of the way in which three can replace one as the symbol of a more versatile and powerful unity. Three-headed or threefold gods such as the Greek Hecate or the Celtic Brighid had multiple functions or controlled several spheres. The Egyptian god of wisdom, Thoth, was called by the Greeks Hermes Trismegistos: "Thrice Greatest Hermes".

Religious triads are common – the Hindu Trimurti of Brahma (creator), Vishnu (sustainer) and Shiva (destroyer); the three brothers, Zeus (Jupiter in Roman myth), Poseidon (Neptune) and Hades (Pluto), who controlled the Greek world with their triple attributes, the three-forked lightning, the trident and the three-headed dog Cerberus; the three great Inca deities of sun, moon and storm; the three brothers who controlled the heavens in China.

Other mythological and allegorical figures also frequently come in threes, such as the Fates (in both Classical and Norse traditions), the Furies, the Graces, the Harpies, the Gorgons, or the Christian theological virtues of Faith, Hope and Charity. Three is a much repeated number in the New Testament: the three Magi; the three denials of Peter; the three crosses on Golgotha; the Resurrection after three days.

Three was the number of harmony for Pythagoras, of completeness for Aristotle, having an end as well as a beginning and middle. In other traditions, including Daoism, three symbolized strength because it implied a central element. Politically, three was the first number to make possible executive action by a majority, as in the Roman triumvirates. In China, it was the auspicious number symbolizing sanctity, loyalty, respect and refinement. It was the number of the Japanese sacred "treasures" – the mirror, sword and jewel. In Buddhism it is the number of holy scriptures in the canon, the *Three Baskets* or *Tripitaka*. In Hinduism, it is the number of sounds in the mystic word *Om* (*Aum*), expressing the ternary rhythm of the whole cosmos and of divinity.

Three is, significantly, the smallest number of a family unit or "tribe". It symbolized the individual body, soul and spirit. In Africa it was the number of maleness (penis and testicles). In sexual relationships, it is an emblem of conflict ("three's a crowd"), the eternal triangle. Otherwise, three is usually seen as a lucky number, possibly because it symbolizes the resolution of a conflict – a decisive action that may lead to success or disaster. In folk tales, wishes are granted in threes. Heroes or heroines are allowed three choices, set three trials or given three chances to succeed. Ritual actions are often performed thrice, as in Islamic daily ablutions, in salutations or in making auguries.

The graphic symbol of three is the triangle. Other triform symbols include the triskele (a form of triple-armed swastika), the trefoil, the Chinese trigram, the trident, the fleur-de-lys, three fishes with a single head (representing the Christian Trinity) and three-legged lunar animals (representing the phases of the moon).

Throne (seat)

*The thumb-sucking
figure on this Celtic
stone cross is probably
the Irish hero Finn.*

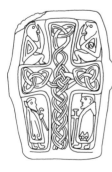

Throne (seat)

Power, stability, splendour. Psychologically, rulers have always projected confidence by seating themselves while others stand. Their thrones, which have become increasingly elaborate throughout history, came to symbolize their authority, so much so that the throne itself became a symbol of glory, as in Buddhist, Hindu and Eastern Orthodox Christian traditions, which sometimes represented the radiant presence of a divinity by depicting an empty throne. The diamond throne is a Buddhist image of the centre. Christ told his Disciples that they would sit upon twelve thrones to judge the twelve tribes of Israel. Steps or a dais (elevation) and canopy (heavenly protection) often support the power symbolism of the seat itself. Jewels, precious metals and effigies of solar creatures such as the lion or peacock were popular decorative features. In Egyptian iconography, the goddess Isis is identified with the throne as great mother.

Thrym

A giant who stole the hammer of the god Thor, according to Scandinavian myth. Thrym insisted on the hand of the great goddess Freyja before he would return the hammer. Thor disguised himself as Freyja, and went to Jotunheim, the home of the giants. A wedding feast was prepared and when the hammer was laid in the lap of the "bride" (a traditional act of blessing in pagan Scandinavia), Thor seized it, annihilated Thrym and the other giants present, and returned to Asgard, home of the gods.

Thule

A Classical term for the farthest limit of the known world, hence *Ultima Thule*, "Farthest Thule". In legend and symbolism, Thule represents the mystic threshold of the otherworld. Like the Hyperboreans beyond the North Wind, its people were thought to be wiser and longer-lived than ordinary mortals. It is often described as a white island, perhaps a reference to Iceland.

Thumb

Power – a meaning derived from the thumb's key role in manual skill and gripping strength, and from its phallic symbolism. In Irish myth, the hero Finn scalded himself while roasting the Salmon of Knowledge; he sucked his thumb and gained the fish's power of prophecy; a similar episode involving a finger occurs in the story of the Norse hero Sigurd.

Thunder

Divine might – equated in Semitic and some other traditions with the sounded word of God (lightning represented the written word) – "God thunders wondrously with his voice" (Job 37:5). Thunderbolts (often depicted as jagged arrows of fire hurled from the clouds) are attributes of the most powerful sky gods in many traditions, notably the weapons of the Greek god, Zeus (in Roman myth, Jupiter). The thunderbolt was a creative-destructive symbol, associated with an impregnating force as well as with chastisement or justice. Thus in Hindu and Buddhist tradition, Indra uses the *vajra*, a thunderbolt in the form of a diamond sceptre, to split the clouds (in Tantric symbolism representing ignorance). The Inca rain god Ilyap'a releases the celestial waters with his thunder sling, symbolism in common with the projectile force usually associated with thunder in the ancient world. In Native North America, the Thunderbird is chiefly a protective sky god. Bird symbolism also appears in Siberian mythology.

Although predominantly linked elsewhere with male gods such as the Norse Thor, or with divine smiths (often lame), thunder was sometimes associated through its fecundity symbolism with earth or moon goddesses. In Asia, it was linked with the dragon (especially in China), the drum, the rumbling wagon of dead souls and the anger or laughter of the gods. Other associations include the hammer, mallet, chisel, axe, the bellowing bull and bullroarer, rain-linked animals such as the snake, and graphic signs such as the arrowed zigzag, the fleur-de-lys and the spiral of rolling thunder. Some thunder gods, as in Japan, were earth and sky deities, speaking from the volcano as well as from the clouds.

Thunderbird

A great eagle-like creature which, in many Native American traditions, embodies the spirit of thunder and the elemental forces of creation and destruction. Lightning is said to flash from the animal's eyes or beak and thunder is the sound of its beating wings. The Thunderbird is believed to have awesome creative and destructive power, and anything struck by lightning is said to possess special spirit force. In the Northwest Coast region of North America, the Thunderbird is a great sky god that preys on whales, which it can carry off in its talons. The Lakota of the Plains see the creature (Wakinyan) as a manifestation of the supreme being Wakan Tanka and there is a cult based upon personal encounters with the beast. In traditions of the western

A Native American Thunderbird; after a Northwest Coast culture depiction.

USA there is said to be one Thunderbird in each of the four quarters of the world.

Thyrsus

A rod (originally a hollow fennel stalk) intertwined with vine leaves and ivy, the attribute of the Greek god Dionysos (Bacchus) and his followers. It may be tipped with a pine cone or a bunch of grapes. It symbolized impregnating and fertilizing power. Fermented pine resin may have been mixed with wine in Dionysian (Bacchanalian) rites, heightening the significance of the thyrsus as an emblem of orgiastic release.

Tiamat

The goddess personifying the primal salt-water ocean, according to the Babylonian (Akkadian) myth. Tiamat coupled with Apsu, the sweet-water ocean, to produce many great gods, including Ea, who in turn fathered Marduk. Ea killed Apsu and, in revenge, Tiamat attacked Ea and the other younger gods using a horde of

Thunderbird: *see* Wakan Tanka

Thyrsus: *see* Dionysos; Fennel; Ivy; Orgy; Pine, Pine cone; Resin; Rod; Staff; Vine

Tiamat: *see* Apsu; DRAGON; Ea; Marduk

Tian

fierce monsters. The gods then chose Marduk as their champion. He slew Tiamat and cut her in two: one half of her corpse became the sky, the other half the earth. Depictions of the slaying of Tiamat portray her as a dragon or similar monster, which represents the embodi-ment of the primordial chaos which must be overcome before the ordered cosmos can arise.

Tian

A Chinese god, literally "Heaven", the divine embodiment of the heavens. Venerated under the Zhou dynasty (1050BCE–221BCE), Tian was eventually supplanted by the Jade Emperor.

Tiara, Papal

The triple-tiered, beehive-shaped papal crown developed in the 14th century as a non-liturgical headdress symbolizing three aspects of the Pope's sovereignty – spiritual authority in the world, temporal authority in Rome and Italy, and pre-eminence among other Christian rulers. The modern symbolism of the papal tiara is that the pope is Father of the Church, terrestrial prince and Vicar of Christ.

Tiger

Feline power, ferocity, cruelty, wrath, beauty and speed – a symbol both aggressive and protective, bestial and royal in the traditions of Asia and India, where the tiger largely replaces the lion as the supreme animal image of the great and terrible in nature. William Blake's poem *The Tyger* (1794) takes up the same symbolism of a fearful symmetry, the dangerous force of elemental desire. Like the lion, the tiger can represent both death and life, evil and evil's destruction. Several gods show their power

by riding tigers, including Durga in India. More unexpectedly, the god of wealth rides a tiger in China, and here it is also an emblem of gambling or perhaps of its risks (a "tiger" was slang for the lowest hand in poker in the USA). The tiger is particularly linked with military valour and was an emblem of warriors in India. In China, five legendary tigers protected the directions of space: blue in the east, black in the north, red in the south, white in the west and yellow in the centre.

The tiger's protective symbolism also accounts for the stone tigers on graves and doorways in China, and for the ancient custom by which children wear tiger caps. Shiva and his destroyer consort Kali frequently appear in tiger skins in Hindu iconography. Although tigers were rarely seen west of Persia, they are sometimes substituted for leopards as the animals drawing the chariot of the Greek god Dionysus (Bacchus) in Western art. In southeast Asia, the tiger appears as an ancestral figure, and folk tales of ferocious tiger-bodied men and women are known from India to Siberia. The tiger is the third sign of the Chinese Zodiac and personifies Anger in Chinese Buddhism (one of the Three Senseless Animals).

Time

Time has been represented in art in two distinct ways. Commonly it is personified as a winged old man with an hour-glass or scythe. He may convey a message, as in Pompeo Batoni's *Time*, who sits pointing to a young girl while an old woman loses her beauty. This representation of Time is finite. His daughter is Truth. The transience of time may be represented by things such as flowers, smoke or bubbles, or by objects that are reminiscent of death, such as a skull.

Time may also be shown as cyclical, denoted by the recurring months and seasons, represented by agricultural pursuits. This agricultural association gives Time his attribute of the scythe. Times of the year may also be suggested by the signs of the zodiac. Michelangelo interpreted Time as the figures of *Dawn*, *Dusk*, *Night* and *Day*, identified by their forms or movement – except that Night is given attributes of an owl, a mask, a star and a crescent moon.

Tintiya

The male supreme being of Balinese myth. In Balinese cosmology, Tintiya resides in the highest of the six heavens that lie above Mother Earth.

Tirawa

"Arch of Heaven", the supreme being of the Pawnee. In the beginning, in Pawnee myth, Tirawa created Shakuru (the Sun), Pah (the Moon), the Morning Star, the Evening Star, a Star of Death, and four stars to hold up the sky. He assigned to each heavenly body its place in the heavens and gave it a portion of his power.

TITAN *see panel overleaf*

Tithonus

In Greek myth, a Trojan prince, the brother of King Priam. Eos, the goddess of dawn, became his lover (or wife) and asked the god Zeus to grant Tithonus eternal life. However, she forgot to ask for eternal youth and eventually Tithonus became so wizened that Eos, digusted at the sight, imprisoned him in her palace.

Tityus

In Greek myth, Tityus was the giant son of Gaia, the earth, and his body stretched over nine acres. He was condemned to Tartaros, the depths of the in the underworld for assaulting Leto, the mother of Apollo and Artemis (the Roman Diana). In the underworld a pair of vultures continually plucked out his liver, while he was powerless to drive them off.[1] Images of his torture, such as Michelangelo's drawing *Tityus*, may be confused with Prometheus, who suffered a similar fate.

Tiv'r

The ancestral culture hero of the Trans-Fly area of Papua New Guinea. One day Tiv'r heard a faint roaring inside his wife's womb. This was the first bullroarer, a length of wood spun around the head on a line to produce a roaring sound that is believed to be the voice of the bullroarer spirit. Bullroarers are widely used in Melanesia during secret male initiation rituals.

Tiwaz

The ancient Germanic god of war and lawgiving, who was identified with the Roman god Mars. According to the Roman author Tacitus, a great god and "ruler of all" was worshipped in a sacred wood and all entering the wood had to be bound. This god may have been Tiwaz, who became the Norse Tyr. Known to the Anglo-Saxons as Tiw or Tig, Tiwaz gave his name to Tuesday, in imitation of the Roman *Martis dies* ("Mars day").

Tlaloc

The Aztec lord of rain and chief fertility god. In origin Tlaloc was an ancient pre-Aztec rain deity. He had close affinities with the Maya rain god, Chac

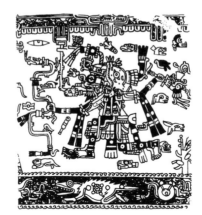

Tlaloc; after an Aztec codex.

but it was under the Aztecs that his cult spread to the whole of Mexico. An ambivalent deity, Tlaloc brought the gentle rain that fertilized the soil but also devastating storms. His divine assistants were the Tlaloque and their sister, Chalchiuhtlicue, was Tlaloc's wife. The god presided over many lesser fertility deities, such as the maize gods Chicometeotl and Centeotl.

Tlaloc was particularly associated with mountains, where rain clouds gathered and the sources of rivers were to be found. During his festival, young children were sacrificed on mountain tops. The Aztec heavenly paradise, Tlalocan, was named after him. Only Tlaloc's victims – such as those who had drowned or been struck by lightning – could enter Tlalocan.

Toad

In European superstition, a loathsome familiar of witches, suggestive of death and the torments of the damned – a demonic symbolism that stems from the ancient Near East, based perhaps on the toad's toxic secretions. These were used medici-

nally in China where the toad was a lunar, yin and humid symbol, a rainbringer and therefore associated with luck and riches. In folklore, a three-legged toad lived in the moon: it was said that a lunar eclipse was the act of the toad swallowing the moon. Rain and fertility symbolism appear in Mexico and in parts of Africa where the toad is sometimes given the status of a culture hero.

Curiously, the toad's link in medieval Europe with darkness and evil, avarice and lust was mixed with birth and rebirth symbolism (through its amphibian transformations) and with the idea of longevity and riches. The notion that the toad, like the snake, had a jewel in its forehead was widespread; the jewel symbolizing happiness. Alchemy associated the toad with the primal elements of earth and water. The "toady" was originally a mountebank's apprentice who pretended to swallow toads so that his master could "cure" him of the ingested poison.

Tobias

In the Old Testament Apocrypha, Tobit was a Jew who lived in the Assyrian capital of Nineveh and defied the law by helping his fellow Jews in exile. For this all his goods were taken away. When Tobit gave a Jew a proper burial one night, he slept in his courtyard and was blinded by sparrow droppings.[1]

Fearing imminent death, Tobit remembered some money that he had deposited with a man in Media and sent his son Tobias to reclaim it.[2] The Archangel Raphael appeared in disguise to guide him, and Tobias's dog accompanied them.

One evening they came to the river Tigris, and when Tobias "went down to wash himself, a fish leaped out of

TITAN

One of a race of deities of Greek myth, the offspring of the earth goddess Gaia and the sky god Uranos. The first generation of Titans were six brothers (Coeus, Crius, Iapetus, Hyperion, Kronos and Okeanos) and six sisters (Mnemosyne, Phoebe, Rhea, Theia, Tethys and Themis). Their offspring were also called Titans, except Zeus and his siblings (the first Olympians) and the daughters of Okeanos and Tethys (called the Oceanids). The Olympian goddess of love, Aphrodite was also a Titan, born from Uranos alone.

In one account, Uranos hated the Titans and their brothers, the monstrous Cyclopes and hundred-handed Hekatoncheires, and forced them back into their mother. Insulted, Gaia gave the youngest Titan, Kronos, a stone sickle with which he cut off his father's genitals the next time Uranos and Gaia had intercourse. Uranos' severed genitals fell into the ocean and turned to white foam, from which sprang Aphrodite.

Kronos, now supreme in heaven, freed his Titan siblings, but left the Cyclopes and Hekatoncheires. He married his sister Rhea. Fearing being overthrown like his father, he devoured each of his offspring as Rhea gave birth. But Rhea saved the youngest, Zeus, who was later to plot the downfall of his father. Metis, (an Oceanid), gave Kronos an emetic that made him vomit out Zeus' siblings who were Demeter, Hades, Hestia, Hera and Poseidon. They joined forces with the Cyclopes and Hekatoncheires (freed by Zeus) and fought Kronos and his supporters in a battle called the Titanomachy ("Battle of the Titans"). Not one female Titan, nor Okeanos, Prometheus nor the sun god Helios, joined the battle against Zeus, who was victorious.

Kronos and his allies were confined in the underworld with the Hekatoncheires as jailers. In some accounts Kronos later became the ruler of Elysium in the underworld.

TITAN: *see* Cyclops; Hekatoncheires, The; Oceanid; OLYMPIANS, THE; Zeus; *and other individual names*

the river, and would have devoured him." Raphael told him to catch the fish and to keep its heart, liver and gall while they ate the rest.[3]

They arrived at the house of Tobias's cousin Raguel, where it was arranged that Tobias would marry Raguel's daughter, Sarah. The heart and liver of the fish were burned and their aroma banished a demon which had caused the death of Sarah's seven previous husbands on their wedding night. Raphael was sent to collect Tobit's money, the wedding was celebrated, and they returned to Nineveh, where Raphael cured Tobit's blindness with the gall of the fish.[4]

The young Tobias with his angelic protector was a popular subject in 15th-century Florence, where the Compagnia di Raffaello had been formed. In paintings, therefore, the principal figure is often the archangel, as in *Tobias and the Angel* by a follower of Verrocchio. The work includes elements from the narrative which may be considered attributes: The angel Raphael, with a dog and pot containing the fish's gall, leads Tobias holding a fish.

The happy outcome of the story must have appealed to travellers: Tobit had announced as Tobias set off that "the good angel will keep him company, and his journey shall be prosperous and he shall return safe".[5] A number of later artists also illustrated scenes from the story of Tobit and Tobias; for example, Rembrandt painted *The Angel Leaving Tobias*.

Tobit *see* **Tobias**

Tonalpohualli
The Aztec sacred calendar. It consisted of 260 days which were divided into twenty weeks of thirteen days, each week and day having a presiding deity. The calendar, which was used for religious purposes, ran alongside the regular solar calendar in cycle that lasted fifty-two years. At the end of this period a great ceremony called "New Fire" marked the recommencement of the cycle and the symbolic rebirth of the world.

The Mayan version of this calendar was known as Tzolkin.

Tongue
Often shown protruding in carvings and paintings, the tongue has a variety of symbolic meanings. As the only internal organ of the body that can be so startlingly displayed, the tongue is a forceful aggressive–defensive symbol. The protruding tongue in Maori carvings and *hakas* (war dances) expresses challenge and defiance (as does everyday tongue-poking). Sexual symbolism is common in tribal art, as in fertility "pole figures" with extended tongues in Borneo.

The protective god Bes in Egypt appears with a protruding tongue, often believed to ward off evil. In India, Kali's tongue, similarly extended, symbolizes her consuming power. The fire god Agni is shown with seven tongues and there is a strong symbolic link between tongues and flames – both are red, active, consuming and creative–destructive (through the tongue's powerful role in speech). In the book of Isaiah, the Lord's tongue is "a devouring fire", and in the *Acts the Apostles* the assembled apostles receive the gift of languages in the form of cloven tongues "as of fire".

The tongue often represents language itself, and also eloquence or wisdom; the Buddha's tongue, for example, is long. In Egyptian funerary art, extended tongues allowed the dead to speak to the gods. Displayed tongues may also have a demonic, carnivorous or frightening symbolism, as in Greek and other stage masks. Some animal effigies with protruding tongues invoke rain.

Tonsure
A hairstyle symbolizing a monk's renunciation of the material world. The medieval Christian style of tonsure, in which the top of the head was shaved to leave a circle of hair, is thought to have commemorated Christ's crown of thorns.

Torch
In the old sense of a burning brand, a symbol of the flame of life, desire and the light of truth, intelligence or the spirit. In art, the Greek Eros (in Roman myth, Cupid), Aphrodite (Venus) and their attendants often carry torches of sexual desire. Burning love is the theme of the "torch singer" and the open secret of the man who "carries a torch" for someone. As a fertility symbol, the flaming torch is

usually phallic and male, especially in the ritual of weddings. As a symbol of life it is often carried in art by female mythological figures such as Demeter (Ceres), Persephone (Proserpine) and Hecate, who are all connected with the underworld life, beyond death.

The torch is also an attribute of Prometheus, who stole fire for humankind, and Herakles, who used a torch to cauterize the heads of the Hydra in order to kill it. On graves, the flaming torch lights the way for the dead to guide them to the afterworld. Extinguished or reversed, it symbolizes death, as it did in Mithraic ritual. The torch can also symbolize an undying tradition, as in the Olympic ceremonies.

Torii

The symbolic gateway to a Japanese Shinto shrine. Literally a "bird perch" it is essentially a sun symbol, identified as one of the birds which helped to tempt the sun goddess Amaterasu from her hiding place, thus restoring light to the world. It also represents the entrance to spiritual light.

Tortoise, Turtle

Strength, patience, endurance, stability, slowness, fecundity, longevity. The tortoise or turtle (members of the same reptile group) is an important and ancient symbol of cosmic order in many traditions, especially those of China. Stone tortoises supporting the pillars of imperial graves allude to the legendary Ao who supported the world on its four legs. Associated with the north, water and winter, the animal also appeared on imperial banners as the Black Warrior. It was protective against fire as well as in war. In Japan, it supported the world

mountain, and the marine turtle was the emblem of Kumpira, god of sailors – as it was of Ea, the Sumerian-Semitic Lord of the Deep. With a domed shell on its back and the squarer shell protecting its belly, the tortoise or turtle was widely used as a tripartite cosmic image of the vaulted heaven, the body (humankind) and the earth, underworld or waters. In India, the symbolism of stability was emphasized by the notion that an elephant supported the world by standing on the legs of the cosmic turtle. Alternatively, the cosmic tree is shown growing from the turtle Kurma, which is an avatar of the sustainer god Vishnu. Creator hero symbolism appears again in Native American mythology where the turtle lifts the earth from the deep.

Although mainly a female, lunar and water symbol, the tortoise is linked both with female and male fertility, as in parts of Africa where the emerging head is seen as penile. As protective emblems, tortoises are a popular household pets there.

Western symbolism is less extensive, best summed up in the *Festina lente* ("Make haste slowly") emblem of Cosimo de' Medici – a turtle with a sail on its back, voyaging slowly but surely. In alchemy, the tortoise symbolizes matter at the beginning of the evolutionary process.

Totem

An animal or other natural object that acts as the identifying symbol of a closely knit clan. In primitive art, the most impressive examples are the giant totem poles of America's northwest coast, which serve almost as heraldic status symbols. The ravens, bears or other animals carved into them represent mythical ancestral

The god Vishnu as Kurma the turtle; after a Hindu painting.

spirits in animal guise or symbolize qualities admired by the clan. In initiation rituals, the totem may be a more personal tutelary spirit.

Tower

Ascent, ambition, strength, watchfulness, inaccessibility, chastity. Biblical writers felt that the Tower of Babel (an allusion to the monumental ziggurat at Babylon) carried the axial earth–heaven symbolism of the tower to insolent heights. Tower myths symbolizing human presumption are common in southern Africa too. As emblems of aspiration, towers were retained as status symbols in the architecture of the Loire châteaux long after towers ceased to have a defensive function as donjons. In Greek myth, Danaë was imprisoned ina tower to protect her from suitors, a theme echoed in the German folktale of Rapunzel. In medieval Christian symbolism, the Virgin Mary was the "Tower of Ivory", both pure and impregnable. In art, the figure of Chastity sometimes appears in a tower, as do many distressed maidens in fairy tales.

Trajan

According to legend[1] the Roman emperor Trajan was on his way to war when he was stopped by a widow demanding justice for the death of her son. Moved with compassion, Trajan postponed his affairs and saw to it that the innocent boy was avenged. In another legend (possibly simply a variant of the first), the emperor's own son was recklessly galloping through the city and ran down and killed the son of a widow. When Trajan of heard this, he handed over his son to the widow to replace her loss.

Many years after the emperor's death, St Gregory the Great, walking through the Forum of Trajan, was reminded of Trajan's kindness, and God's voice told him that the soul of the emperor, a pgan, was pardoned. The subject of Trajan and the widow was painted as an example of justice.

Transformation

Transformations of all kinds symbolize liberation from the physical or mortal limitations of nature. Supernatural beings in most mythologies transmogrify at will into animals; wine is transubstantiated into blood; Christ is transfigured into a being of light under the eyes of his Apostles, and souls transmigrate into other bodies after death. Cross-dressing (transvestism) symbolizes liberation from the constraints of a single sex, a return to the primal perfection of the androgyne.

Tree

The supreme natural symbol of dynamic growth, seasonal death and regeneration. Many trees are held to be sacred or magic in different cultures (see individual names of trees).

Reverence for the power of trees goes back to primitive beliefs that gods and spirits inhabited them. Animist symbolism of this kind survives in European folklore of the tree-man or Green Man. In fairy tales, trees can either be protective and grant wishes, or appear as frightening, obstructive, even demonic.

As mythologies developed, the idea of a mighty tree that formed a central axis for the flow of divine energy linking the supernatural and natural worlds took symbolic shape in the Tree of Life or cosmic tree, rooted in the waters of the underworld and passing through earth to heaven. This symbol is almost universal. The Tree of Life often becomes a metaphor for the whole of creation. In many traditions it grows on a sacred mountain or in paradise. A fountain of spiritual nourishment may gush from its roots. A snake coiled at its base can represent spiralling energy drawn from the earth; alternatively, the serpent is a destructive symbol. Birds nest in the upper branches, emblems of celestial messengers or souls. Through the Tree of Life, humanity ascends from its lower nature toward spiritual illumination, salvation or release from the cycle of being. Medieval images of Christ crucified on a tree rather than a cross relate to this more ancient symbolism. To be hanged from a tree was the fate of a man cursed, according to Deuteronomy. A tree crucifixion thus heightened the symbolism of salvation through Christ, scapegoat for the sins of the world. The image unifies the Tree of Knowledge (the Fall) with the Tree of Life.

By its very form, the tree is a symbol of evolution, its branches suggesting diversity spreading out from the trunk (unity). In Indian iconography, a tree sprouting from the cosmic egg represents Brahma creating the manifest world. Alternatively, the cosmic tree is reversed to show its roots drawing spiritual strength from the sky and spreading it outward and downward – a favourite image in Cabbalism and other forms of mysticism and magic (also frequently used in drawing genealogical charts). In many traditions, the Tree of Life bears stars, lights, globes or fruit symbolizing the planets, or cycles of the sun or moon. Lunar symbolism is common, the moon drawing up water as sap rises

up the tree. The fruit of the Tree of Life can also symbolize immortality – represented in China, for example, by the peach. Many other food-bearing trees appear as Trees of Life – the sycamore fig in Egypt, the almond in Iran, the olive, palm or pomegranate in other Middle-Eastern or Semitic traditions. Their cosmic symbolism seems to have developed out of simpler cults in which the trees were embodiments of the fecund Earth Mother. For this reason, in spite of their phallic verticality, trees are usually feminine in symbolism. Thus, in Egyptian iconography, the sacred fig is identified with the goddess Hathor who is shown in tree form, providing food and drink.

Earth Mother fertility rites were usually centred upon deciduous trees, whose bare winter branches and spring flowering provided apt symbols of the seasonal cycles of death and regeneration. A notable exception was the worship of Attis in Asia Minor and the later Greco-Roman world. The emblematic tree of Attis was a pine, a leading symbol of immortality. His death (by emasculation) and rebirth were celebrated by stripping the pine and winding it in wool – the probable origin of the maypole tradition, a tree-based fertility rite. Dualism in tree symbolism is usually represented by paired trees or trees with divided trunks. In the story of Tristan and Isolde, entwined trees grow from their grave. In the dualist symbolism of the Near East, the Tree of Life is paralleled by a Tree of Death. This is the biblical Tree of the Knowledge of Good and Evil, whose forbidden fruit, when tasted by Eve in the Garden of Eden, brought upon humankind the curse of mortality.

TRICKSTER

In most mythologies of the world there are figures known as "tricksters", whose principal characteristics are cunning, quick-wittedness and a propensity for mischievous or humorous behaviour. Such characters may be human (whether mortal or divine) in form, as for example Hermes, Eshu, Maui and Loki, but they are very often anthropomorphized animals, such as hares and rabbits (which are

The West African trickster Eshu in various forms, from a Yoruba shrine.

particularly popular trickster figures), monkeys, tortoises and spiders. The effects of their activities may be creative or destructive, or both.

In North America the trickster is frequently the same as the "culture hero". For example, the Raven trickster of the northwest coast employs his trickery to outwit the adversaries of humanity, and steal fire and the heavenly bodies for the benefit of humankind and the world. The Maori trickster Maui falls into much the same category.

Elsewhere the trickster may be more purely subversive or even dangerous, a bringer of chaos without any compensating benefits for the human race and the cosmic order. The West African trickster Eshu (or Legba) and the Chinese Monkey King, Sun Wukong, spread disorder indiscriminately among humans and the gods until they are brought to book. (Tricksters – who are usually male – often fall victim to their own antics.) Few tricksters can surpass the notoriety of the Norse god Loki. His mischief-making was said to have brought about not only his own death, but also the destruction of the world.

Tree of Jesse, The

In the Bible, Isaiah prophesied that "there shall come forth a rod out of the stem of Jesse and a branch shall grow out of his roots: And the spirit of the Lord shall rest upon him."[1] In the Middle Ages, therefore, the ancestry of Christ, stretching back to Jesse, father of David, was shown as a genealogical tree, the names of his forebears appearing on the numerous branches. Luke[2] traces Christ's ancestry right back to Adam.

Jacobus de Voragine (1230–98), author of the *Golden Legend*, claims that both the Virgin and Christ were descended from the house of David.[3] The maternal line of Christ's ancestry is shown in paintings of St Anne (Anna, the legendary mother of the Virgin) and the Holy Kinship. Taddeo Gaddi's *The Tree of the Cross* shows branches growing from the Crucifixion, decorated with medallions of the four evangelists and twelve prophets.

Triad

A group of three, often used in iconography to symbolize closely linked ideas such as body/soul/spirit or divinities sharing functions such as the Fates or Graces in Greek mythology. In Hinduism, the triad Brahma, Vishnu, Shiva symbolizes three aspects of divine power represented by separate gods who are not fused into a single godhead as in the Christian Trinity. Like many Celtic triadic carvings of gods, they can appear as a single three-headed figure. Medieval artists also sometimes portrayed the Trinity in this way until the Church banned such images.

The tortoise often appears as a triadic symbol, especially in Daoist art where it is an emblem of the triad of earth-humankind-heaven – a symbolism central to the Chinese secret societies known as Triads.

Triangle

One of the most powerful and versatile geometric symbols. The equilateral triangle sitting on its base is a male and solar sign representing divinity, fire, life, the heart, the mountain and ascent, prosperity, harmony and royalty. The reversed triangle – possibly a more ancient sign – is female and lunar, representing the great mother, water, fecundity, rain, heavenly grace. The symbolism of the female pubic triangle and vulva is sometimes made more specific by the addition of a short interior line drawn from the bottom point. In China, the triangle appears to be always female. Male and female triangles meeting at their points signify sexual union. Interpenetrating to form a hexagram, they symbolize synthesis, the union of opposites. Horizontally, with bases meeting, two triangles represented the waxing and waning moon. As the simplest plane figure, based on the sacred number three, the triangle was the Pythagorean sign for wisdom, linked with Athene.

In both Judaism and Christianity, the triangle was the sign for God. The God of the Christian Trinity is sometimes represented by an eye within a triangle or by a venerable figure with a triangular halo. Alchemy used upward- and downward-pointing triangles as the signs for fire and water. More generally, linear triangles or triangular-shaped compositions can refer to triads of gods or other threefold concepts.

TRICKSTER *see panel opposite*

Trident

Sea power – an emblem of the ancient Minoan civilization (as well as of Britannia ruling the waves). The trident was most famously the authority symbol of Poseidon, Greek god of the sea (Neptune in Roman myth). Its appearance in the hands of some gods of storm supports the view that its prongs represent forked lightning. Others who carry a trident in art include Satan, for whom it serves the same function as the pitchfork, and the figure of Death.

In India the similar *trisula* symbolizes the three aspects of Shiva (creator/sustainer/destroyer), and is a forehead mark of his followers. Its Christian use as a symbol of the Trinity is rare.

Trigrams

Symbols consisting of three solid (Yang) or broken (Yin) lines. Eight trigrams (the *ba gua* or *pa kua*) form the basis of the great Chinese book of divination, the *Yi Jing (I Ching)*. They symbolize the Daoist belief that the cosmos is based on a constant flux of complementary forces – the masculine and active Yang balancing the female and passive Yin. Permutated groups of two trigrams make up the

Triangle: *see* Alchemy; Eye; Fire, Flame; Halo; Heart; Hexagram; Man; Moon; Mountain; Three; Triad; Trinity; WISDOM; Woman

Trident: *see* DEATH; Devils; Lightning; Poseidon; Three; Trinity

Trigrams: *see* Three; Yin and Yang

*The creator god Pan Gu devising
the eight trigrams used in Chinese* Yi
Jing *divination.*

64 hexagrams of the *Yi Jing*, the
insightful interpretation of which provides a guide to wise action.

Trimurti, The

The Hindu divine triad of the great
gods Brahma, Shiva and Vishnu, symbolizing the three cycles of manifestation: Brahma is seen as the originator
of the cosmos, Vishnu as its preserver,
and Shiva as its destroyer. In spite of
its similarities with the Christian Trinity, the *Trimurti* is not a three-in-one
monotheistic concept. In later Hindu
tradition, Shiva can himself represent
the three aspects of the trimurti.
Recent Hinduism has shown a ten-
dency to prefer five gods: Shiva, Vishnu, Devi, Ganesha and Surya.

Trinity, The

In Christianity, the three Persons that
form the single godhead – God the
Father, God the Son and God the
Holy Spirit. The doctrine of the Trinity – the evolutionof which was characterized by centuries of theological
debate regarding the interrelationship
of the three Persons – symbolizes the
indivisible essence of a divinity revealing itself in different forms.

Figuratively, the Trinity is most
directly represented by the figure of

God behind and above the crucified
Christ with the hovering dove of the
Holy Spirit, or by the dove with two
enthroned figures. Other trinitarian
symbols include a throne, book and
dove (power, intellect, love); three
fishes entwined or sharing a single
head; three eagles or lions; three suns;
a triangle enclosing an eye or with
three stars; three overlapping circles
or arcs within a circle; a three-leafed
clover or trefoil cross.

Triskele, Triskelion

A three-legged symbol of dynamic
energy, somewhat like a swastika but
with three instead of four bent limbs
rotating in a circle. As a motif in Celtic
art or on Greek coinage and shields, it
appears to relate less to solar cycles or
lunar phases (one suggested meaning)
than to power or physical prowess. It
remains an emblem of the Scilly Isles
and the Isle of Man.

Triumphs

In ancient Rome a triumph was a
great procession granted to a victorious emperor or general and his
legions after a successful military
campaign. Their booty would be
paraded along the Via Sacra, followed
by the captives taken in the campaign,
who would afterward be executed or
else become slaves.

During the Renaissance the idea of
the triumphal procession was revived
both in practice and as a subject to be
depicted in art. The triumphs of historical contemporary and Classical
figures, and of personifications of the
virtues and mythological figures were
all represented.

Trionfi by Petrarch (1304–74) also
became the inspiration for Italian
artists. In the first of these six poems,

the poet has a vision of Love on a chariot of fire, which is pulled by four white horses and which holds lovers captive. In each successive poem, the protagonist is seen to conquer his or her predecessor, so that in the second, Chastity overcomes Love after a battle between reason and passion. There follow the triumphs of Death, of Fame, of Time and of Eternity, but the most popular triumphs in art were those of Love and of Chastity.

Trojan Horse, The *see following entry*

Trojan War, The

The *Iliad*, attributed to the poet Homer (8th century BCE), and other later works describe how the Greeks (or Acheans) laid siege to the city of Troy in a war that lasted nine years. The principal Greek heroes were King Agamemnon, his brother Menelaus, Achilles, Odysseus, Patroclus and Diomedes; the Trojan heroes were Hector and Aeneas, the son of Aphrodite (in Roman myth, Venus). The battle arose because Paris, a prince of Troy, had abducted Helen, wife of Menelaus, after a competition in which Paris had to choose the most beautiful of the three goddesses Athene (Minerva), Aphrodite and Hera (Juno). He chose Aphrodite, who granted Helen as his prize.

The gods took an active part in the war: Hera, Athene and Poseidon (Neptune) supported the Greeks; Apollo, Aphrodite and Ares (Mars), the Trojans. Zeus (Jupiter) both incited and checked each side, sending thunderbolts and lightning, and intervening in the destinies of those involved.

The *Iliad* recounts events near the end of the conflict. At the outset of Homer's epic, the greatest Greek war-rior, Achilles, was insulted when Agamemnon appropriated his mistress, Briseis, and he withdrew from battle.[1] His mother, Thetis, begged Zeus to avenge him and take action against Agamemnon. The Greeks suffered a series of defeats, and Hector, King Priam's favourite son, breached their defences and set fire to their encampment and one of their ships.

Still sulking, Achilles agreed to let his closest friend, Patroclus, lead his force to the Greeks' aid, but Patroclus fought too long and was killed by Hector. Achilles, in magnificent armour fashioned by Hephaistos (Vulcan), returned to the war and avenged the death of Patroclus by slaying Hector.

Subjects drawn from the *Iliad* were particularly popular in the 18th and early 19th centuries; an example is Giambattista Tiepolo's *Room of The Iliad*. The scenes most often chosen were: The Wrath of Achilles, in which Achilles is about to draw his sword against Agamemnon when Athene held him back by his golden locks;[2]

Athene helping to build the wooden horse of Troy; after a red-figure drinking cup of the 5th century BCE.

Trowel: *see* Initiation

Troy: *see* Trojan War, The;
TROJAN WAR, THE
HEROES OF THE

Briseis being taken away from Achilles or led to Agamemnon by Patroclus;[3] Thetis asking Zeus to avenge Achilles;[4] Aphrodite wounded by Diomedes as she tries to save her son, Aeneas;[5] Hector reproaching Paris for failing to take part in the war; Hector making a tender farewell to his wife, Andromache, and their baby son;[6] Achilles dragging the body of Hector, tied by the ankles to his chariot, around the walls of Troy;[7] King Priam, protected by Hermes (Mercury), in Achilles' camp, kneeling and kissing Achilles' hand, pleading for the body of his slain son Hector;[8] and Andromache and her son grieving over Hector's corpse, which had been saved by Apollo from decay and damage.

The Greeks won a decisive victory in the Trojan War by means of the Trojan Horse. This episode, perhaps the most famous of the war, is related in both the *Odyssey* and Virgil's *Aeneid*, although the account in Virgil is fuller.[9] In order to penetrate the city of Troy, Odysseus proposed that the Greeks built a hollow wooden horse which they would pretend was an offering to Athene to ensure their safe homeward voyage. The carpenter Epios set to work, aided by the goddess Athene herself. In *The Building of the Trojan Horse* Domenico Tiepolo shows the Greeks constructing the horse.

When it was finished, the Greeks best men were installed inside it, and it was left at the city gates while the rest of the Greek army broke camp and sailed a short distance offshore, as if leaving for home. The Trojans rejoiced at the disappearance of their enemy. They ignored the warnings of the prophetess Cassandra and the priest Laocoön (who uttered the famous phrase "Beware of Greeks bearing gifts" and was later crushed to death with his two sons by a sea serpent), and were tricked by Sinon, a Greek captive, into believing that the horse was dedicated to Athene and should be brought to her temple. The horse was dragged into the city and, that night, Sinon released the Greeks. They cut down the sentries on the city gates, let in the rest of the Greek army, and set Troy ablaze.

The Greeks viewed the story of the Trojan War, in which most of the rulers of the various Greek states took part, as the history of the heroic deeds of their ancestors. The Romans adopted this tradition, claiming that many of the Trojan heroes ended up in Italy, where they founded numerous cities. The most famous of these was Aeneas, whose descendants founded Rome itself.

TROJAN WAR, THE HEROES OF THE *see panel opposite*

Trowel

An important initiation symbol in Freemasonry, binding new brothers to the fraternity and to its rules of secrecy. More generally, as the tool used to join building-blocks, it can appear in art as the attribute of the Creator.

Troy

A city in northwestern Asia Minor besieged and destroyed by the Greeks under Agamemnon, according to Greek myth. The myths about the Trojan War and its aftermath were first recounted in a series of epic poems, of which the most celebrated were the *Iliad* and the *Odyssey*, attributed to the blind bard Homer, who

TROJAN WAR, THE HEROES OF THE

Many great heroes fought in the Trojan War. The chief warriors on each side were as follows:

Greeks	Status	Characteristics
Achilles	Prince of Phthia	Greatest Greek warrior; slain by Paris
Agamemnon	King of Argos or Mycenae	Commander-in-chief; brother of Menelaus
Ajax (1)	Prince of Salamis	Greatest warrior after Achilles
Ajax (2)	Prince of Locris	Swift runner and expert spear thrower
Calchas	Seer of Megara or Mycenae	Chief prophet of the Greeks
Diomedes	Prince of Argos	Refused to fight Glaucus owing to family ties
Menelaus	King of Sparta	Husband of Helen: her elopement caused the war
Nestor	King of Pylos	Elder statesman and raconteur
Odysseus	King of Ithaca	Chief Greek schemer; devised Trojan Horse

Trojans and Allies

Aeneas	Prince of Troy	Son of Aphrodite; ancestor of the Romans
Glaucus	Prince of Lycia	Lycian commander; slain by Ajax (1)
Hector	Prince of Troy	Greatest Trojan warrior; slain by Achilles
Paris	Prince of Troy	Elopement with Helen caused the war
Priam	King of Troy	Father of Hector and Paris
Sarpedon	King of Lycia	Grandson of Zeus; slain by Patroclus

TROJAN WAR, THE HEROES OF THE: *see individual names*

True Cross: *see* Constantine, Saint; Helena, Saint; Queen of Sheba, The; Solomon
[1] *Golden Legend, The Finding of the Holy Cross*
[2] *Golden Legend, The Exaltation of the Holy Cross*

lived *c.*750BCE. Archaeological evidence has shown that there were several ancient cities on the site of Troy, one of which was indeed destroyed by fire and then abandoned *c.*1100BCE, at the end of the Bronze Age: in the epic poems of Homer the warriors are described as using weapons both of bronze and iron. The town was also called Ilion (Latin *Ilium*), hence the title of Homer's *Iliad*.

True Cross, The

According to legend,[1] when Adam grew old, his son, Seth, went to the gates of Paradise and begged for some healing ointment. The Archangel Michael appeared and gave him a branch, supposedly from the Tree of Knowledge. Seth returned to find his father dead and planted the branch over his grave. It grew into a tree which was cut down to build a house for King Solomon, but the trunk could not be accommodated, and so was laid across a stream to serve as a bridge. On her visit to Solomon, the Queen of Sheba, who had had a vision that the Saviour would one day hang upon this trunk, approached the "bridge" and knelt to worship it. She told Solomon that a man would come to destroy the kingdom of the Jews, and Solomon ordered the wood to be buried deep in the earth. When the time of Christ's Passion drew near, the wood floated to the surface of a pool and was used to make his Cross.

The legend then leaps to the 4th century CE, when the emperor Constantine was converted to Christianity and baptized. His mother, Helena, went to Jerusalem to seek a relic of the True Cross, but Jewish scholars refused to tell her where to find it. One Jew was thrown down a dry well

and, after six days without food, he capitulated and led Helena to the site of the Cross on Golgotha. Three crosses, however, were found, and since they could not distinguish Christ's from those of the two thieves, Helena and her companion placed them upright in the city and waited for the Lord to give a sign. A young man was restored to life when the True Cross was held over him, and Helena returned home with part of the supposed relic, now preserved in St Peter's, Rome.

Some two centuries later,[2] Chosroes (Khusraw), king of Persia, conquered Jerusalem and captured another part of the True Cross. He sat on a throne as the Father, put the wood in place of the Son, a cock in place of the Holy Ghost, and decreed that all should call him God. In the name of the Cross the emperor Heraclius defeated him and ordered the Persians to embrace the Christian faith. On his victorious return to Jerusalem, Heraclius was told by an angel to humble himself. In *The Emperor Heraclius Carries the Cross to Jerusalem* Michele Lambertini shows how he entered the city barefoot, carrying the Cross.

The story of the True Cross links the Fall of Man to the Redemption. It was painted in the late Middle Ages and early Renaissance, especially in churches that possessed a relic of the Cross, such as Santa Croce, Florence. Here Agnolo Gaddi painted frescoes of the narrative in the Chancel.

The story provided artists with a cast of celebrities, a variety of settings and a token piece of anti-semitism. Episodes were not necessarily painted in sequence. Piero della Francesca, in his *Legend of the True Cross*, put the battle scenes of Heraclius against the

Persians opposite each other in the lowest tier of the cycle to create a balanced decorative scheme.

Trumpet

Of all musical instruments, the most portentous – a traditional symbol of significant events, momentous news or violent action. In art, the trumpet is the attribute of Fame personified, and of the seven angels of the Last Judgment. The Romans popularized the shock effect of blowing trumpets before cavalry charges, as well as at important rituals and state ceremonies. Trumpets announced news brought by heralds and introduced knights in medieval jousting – hence the bragging meaning of "blowing your own trumpet".

Truth

A solar virtue, personified in Western art by a female figure who may hold a golden disk or mirror and wear a laurel wreath. In Renaissance paintings she often appears naked, with the attribute of the sun's rays or the sun itself, or a book in which truth is written. She is the daughter of Time, revealer of all. She may be standing on a globe to signify that she is superior to worldly concerns; Bernini used this idea in his sculpture of *Truth*.

Other symbols of truth include a peach with one leaf (symbolizing the union of heart and tongue), the colours blue, white and gold, the numbers nine and six, weapons such as the sword, and precious metals or jewels, especially gold, jade, silver, diamond, lodestone, onyx and sapphire. Truth is also closely identified with light in general – the day, lightning, the lamp, the lantern and torch. Among other emblems are the acorn, almond, bamboo, bell, crown, cube, globe, heart, ostrich feather, scales, set square, well or spring of water and wine.

Tsuki-yomi

The Japanese moon god, and the son of the primal creator Izanagi and brother of the sun goddess Amaterasu and storm god Susano. According to the *Nihonshoki*, Tsuki-yomi killed the food goddess Ogetsu-no-hime in disgust after she served food produced from her bodily orifices. The moon god told his sister Amaterasu, and she was so angry that she swore never to lay eyes on him again. This is why the sun and moon live so far apart.

Tu

The Maori god of war, the son of the earth goddess Papa and the sky god Rangi. In the Maori creation myth, Tu was attacked by his brother Tawhiri, the god of the elements. However, none of Tu's other brothers came to help him, so Tu turned on them. He trapped fish and animals, the offspring of Tangaroa and Tane, and ate the wild plants and crops, the offspring of Haumia and Rongo. Tu acquired magical knowledge that enabled him to control all his brothers' progeny: the weather, animals, plants and material possessions.

Tuatha Dé Danann

The fifth race of invaders to rule Ireland, according to the *Book of Invasions*. The Tuatha Dé Danann ("People of the Goddess Danu"), or simply Tuatha Dé, were descended from followers of Nemhedh, the leader of the third race of invaders, who had gone into exile to "the northern islands of the world". During

Trumpet: *see* FAME; Knight; Music

TRUTH: *see* TIME *and individual names*

Tsuki-yomi: *see* Amaterasu; Izanagi and Izanami; Susano

Tu: *see* Rongo; Tane; Tangaroa

Tuatha Dé Danann: *see* Daghdha, The; Danu; Dian Cécht; Goibhniu; *Invasions, The Book of*; Lugh; Milesians, The; Nemedh

their exile, the Tuatha Dé had acquired a great knowledge of supernatural lore, and became skilled in all arts. The progeny of a mother goddess, Danu, they were regarded as possessing divine natures and some of the more famous Tuatha Dé have clear links with ancient Celtic divinities (for example, Lugh is related to the Welsh Lleu and Gaulish Lugus).

The Tuatha Dé under their king, Nuadhu, defeated the Fir Bholg (the fourth race of invaders) at the first battle of Magh Tuiredh and later vanquished the monstrous Fomorians at the second battle. They were defeated by a sixth race of invaders, the Milesians (the Celts). The kingdom was then divided, the Tuatha Dé Danann ruling the Otherworld below ground (entered through lakes and *sidhe* or "fairy mounds") and the Milesians ruling the world above.

Tuccia

An example of abstinence, the Vestal Virgin Tuccia was, in legend, accused of breaking the laws of chastity. To prove her innocence, she carried water in a sieve from the Tiber to the Temple. In *Tuccia* a follower of Mantegna paired her with Sophonisba, another example of virtuous womanhood.

Tunnel *see* Cave; Labyrinth

Turban

A traditional emblem of the faithful in Islamic countries and among the Sikhs. Considerable ritual may surround the style of turban, which in Arab countries takes on some of the symbolism of the crown and is closely associated with the Prophet. His descendants may wear his sacred colour, green.

Turkey

A traditional thanksgiving food in Mexico long before it acquired the same symbolism in Massachusetts. Native North Americans linked the turkey with female fertility as well as male potency (suggested by its neck-swelling), and the Toltecs with impending rain.

Turquoise

A solar and fire symbol in Mexico, associated with the Aztec fire-god Xiuhtecuhtli, who is shown with turquoise plumes in his youthful aspect as Lord of Turquoise. The stone's blue-green colour suggested to the Aztecs a turquoise serpent linking heaven and earth, sun and fire. In gemstone lore, turquoise is a stone of courage, success, royal protection and the astrological sign Sagittarius.

Turtle *see* Tortoise

Twelve

The base number of space and time in ancient astronomy, astrology and calendric science, and therefore of considerable symbolic importance, especially in Judeo-Christian tradition where it was the number of the chosen. It represented cosmic organization, zones of celestial influence, and an achieved cycle of time (the twelve calendar months, the twelve hours of day and night, twelve groups of years in China). As the product of the two powerful numbers three and four, it symbolized a union of spiritual and temporal planes. In the Bible, twelve is the number of the sons of Jacob, and therefore of the tribes of Israel, the number of jewels in the high priest's pectoral. Christ had twelve senior disciples, symbolizing the role of Christianity as the faith of the New Israel. There were twelve fruits of the Tree of Life, gates of the Holy City and stars in the crown of Mary.

Twelve was also the number of disciples of Mithras and, for Shia Muslims, the number of Imams (succesors of the Prophet). Solar astrology was based upon the movement of the sun through the twelve signs of the Zodiac.

The ancient Greek author Hesiod (c.700BCE) said that there were twelve Titans, who were succeeded as supreme deities by the twelve Olympians. There were also twelve prominent Knights of the Round Table. Calendric symbolism underlies the twelve days of Christmas, a tradition developed from the period of Yuletide and Saturnalia festivity at the December solstice – a day representing each coming month.

Twilight

The half-light of decline and shadowy border of death. In northern Europe, accounts of the "twilight of the gods" – the meaning of Ragnarrok, the name given to the final cosmic cataclysm of Norse myth – symbolize the melancholy ebbing of solar warmth and light in a powerful image of the end of the world and the prelude to a fresh cycle of manifestation.

The link between twilight, the setting sun, and the west accounts for many myths of gods, heroes or sages disappearing in a westerly direction, such as Quetzalcoatl in Mexico and Laozi in China.

Twins

Harmonious dualism – or dualistic tension. Perhaps the most famous inseparable twins, who act as beneficial guides, are Castor and Polydeuces (Pollux to the Romans) of Classical mythology (called the Dioscuri, "Sons of God", because their father was, in some accounts, the Greek Zeus, or Jupiter in Roman myth). Another beneficent pair are the Vedic Asvins, born of the sun and the cloud goddess. Both sets represent the positive, powerful aspects of twin symbolism. The Asvins (perhaps symbols of the morning and evening star) work together to usher in the day and night. Castor and Pollux as warriors also symbolize strength in unity – and unity is the motive for their translation to the sky as the constellation Gemini after Castor is killed in battle. Twin disunity is exemplified by Romulus and Remus. The story in which Romulus kills his brother symbolized the dangers of divided responsibility. In some early societies, including China and parts of Africa, twins were ill omens and one or both were left to die. Elsewhere, they were often objects of awe, hence the number of legends in which one or both twins are fathered by divinities. Native American and Mesoamerican traditions include both twin heroes and twins with radically different characters. In Iroquois myths, for example, one twin is good, the other evil.

Twins can symbolize other dualities such as spirit–body, action–thought, and perhaps most commonly the duality of light–dark.

Tyr

A Scandinavian god, one of the Aesir or sky deities. Tyr, apparently a later form of the ancient Germanic god Tiwaz, appears to have been a battle god. He figures in myth chiefly as the only god who would dare to bind the monstrous wolf Fenrir.

Twilight: *see* AFTERLIFE; CARDINAL POINTS; Darkness; DEATH

Twins: *see* Doubles; Zodiac

Tyr: *see* Aesir, The; Fenrir; Loki; Odin; Tiwaz

Ugarit

A city in northwest Syria that flourished *c*.1500BCE–*c*.1200BCE. Tablets discovered there reveal much about the myths of the ancient Canaanites, often referred to as "Ugaritic".

Ugolino

In the *Divina Commedia* by Dante (1265–1321), Count Ugolino, a political leader, was imprisoned with his two sons and grandsons in a tower, and the key was thrown away. They all starved to death.[1] In *Ugolino*, Rodin shows an emaciated Ugolino kneeling over his barely living grandsons.

Ull

A Norse god, the stepson of the god Thor. In one myth, the god Odin was banned from heaven for seducing a maiden unfairly and Ull was chosen to rule over Asgard, the home of the gods, instead. However, after ten years Odin returned and expelled Ull, who fled to Sweden. A great hunter, Ull was depicted with skis or snowshoes and a bow.

Uluru

The Aboriginal name for the sandstone outcrop in Australia also known as Ayer's Rock. It is of great spiritual significance in Aboriginal tradition.

Ulysses *see* Odysseus

Umashiashikabihikoji-no-kami

One of the five "Separate Heavenly Deities", primordial Japanese gods.

Umbrella

An umbrella or parasol can represent protection or sovereignty. The Holy Roman Emperor might hold one over the pope as an indication of their alliance. An umbrella or parasol is one of the Eight Auspicious Emblems of Chinese and Tibetan Buddhism and is said to symbolize the royal life renounced by Siddhartha Gautama. Chinese and Japanese pagodas are developments of the parasol found atop Indian Buddhist stupas.

UNDERWORLDS
See panel overleaf

Unicorn

The unicorn is among the most ambiguous and poetic of all beasts of fable, usually portrayed in medieval art as a graceful white animal with a single, twisted horn on its forehead. It has the body, mane and head (sometimes goat-bearded) of a horse or pony, an antelope's cloven hoofs and a lion's tail. The symbolism of the unicorn in medieval Christian art weaves several strands, notably a pagan tradition that this strong, swift and fierce creature could be captured only by a virgin, whose purity it sensed and in whose lap it rested. Tapestries now in

From The Lady and the Unicorn, *a 15th-century French tapestry.*

New York's Metropolitan Museum show it being hunted and captured; others at the Cluny Museum, Paris, may be an allegory of the five senses.

The phallic and spear symbolism of the horn, combined with a mythology of purification, made the unicorn an elegant symbol of spiritual penetration, specifically the mystery of Christ's entry into the virgin's womb. This is the allegorical meaning of Gothic miniatures and later paintings and tapestries in which a unicorn lays its head in a woman's lap, attends her in an enclosed garden or rose bower, or is guided to her by a huntsman (the angel of the Annunciation, Gabriel).

The unicorn was associated with courtly love: it was likened to a man who becomes the helpless servant of the lady he loves. In chivalry, it symbolized the virtue of pure love and the power of a chaste woman to tame and transform the horn of desire. In art, unicorns draw the chariot of Chastity.

In alchemy, the unicorn represents mercury alongside the lion of sulphur. The animals can represent other dualities, such as the sun and moon, and are popular in heraldry.

Uraeus *see* Cobra

Uranos

A primal Greek deity embodying the heavens (Greek *ouranos* "sky"). Uranos was the son of the earth goddess Gaia (he had no father), with whom he produced eighteen offspring: three Hekatoncheires, three Cyclopes and twelve Titans. He despised his mighty progeny and forced them back into Gaia's womb. Offended, Gaia gave her last-born, the Titan Kronos, a stone sickle with which he castrated Uranos. The severed genitals fell into the sea and turned to white foam, from which sprang the love goddess Aphrodite. Blood spattered onto Gaia and spawned a race of giants and, in some accounts, the Furies.

Urn

A symbol of the female and fecundity; an emblem or attribute of water or river gods and of the astrological Aquarius. In Chinese and Tibetan Buddhism an urn or vase is one of the Eight Auspicious Emblems and can represent victory over death. An urn with a rising flame denotes resurrection in Western funerary art.

Ursula, Saint

Ursula was venerated by the early 5th century. According to legend,[1] she was a princess of Brittany. Conon, the pagan son of the king of Anglia, sought her hand and she agreed on condition that he was baptized; that she received ten virgin companions; that all eleven each had a retinue of 1,000 virgins; and that they all made a pilgrimage to Rome.

These terms were agreed and a great crowd watched Ursula's retinue set sail. At Cologne an angel told her in a dream that she and all her virgins would be martyred. From Basel they continued to Rome on foot where the pope blessed them. Accompanied by cardinals and priests, he returned with them, as he too had been told he would receive the martyr's palm. On the journey they were all slain by the Huns, whose leader tried to persuade Ursula to marry him. She refused and was shot with an arrow.

Usually shown as a young girl, Ursula may hold a martyr's palm, an arrow, a pilgrim's staff, or a white flag with the red cross of resurrection. Reflecting her royal birth, she may wear a crown or ermine-lined cloak, with which she may protect her virgins. Scenes from her life were painted in the late Middle Ages and Renaissance, particularly in Germany, Venice and the Veneto (notably *c*.1495 by Carpaccio). In 1641 Claude Lorrain depicted *Ursula's Embarkation*.

Utnapishtim

In the Akkadian *Epic of Gilgamesh*, Utnapishtim is the sole survivor of a

UNDERWORLDS

In the mythologies of many peoples a lower region is said to exist beneath this one. Usually a place of darkness, the "underworld" is often envisaged as a land inhabited by the dead, either permanently or as a place through which they pass en route to heaven or rebirth. In Mictlan, the grim underworld of Aztec belief, all but a few must undergo many perils before ascending to one of the heavens.

Elsewhere the dead are said to undergo judgment to determine whether a soul is sinful and if so what penalty it will suffer.

A soul being led into the Underworld, based on an Etruscan wall painting.

The ancient Egyptians believed that after death the soul of the deceased journeyed to the throne room of Osiris, lord of the underworld, where his or her heart was weighed in a balance against a feather of Maat (Truth). If, owing to its burden of sin, the heart tipped the balance, the soul would be annihilated. If not, it would join the blessed spirits.

The Celtic Otherworld, which was often located underground, was an enchanted parallel universe. In Norse myth, the home of the earth gods, Vanaheim, and that of the giants, Jotunheim, were both underground. According to the Chewong of Malaya, there are parallel worlds both below and above this one, the underside of each world being the sky of the world beneath.

---

deluge sent by the gods to destroy the human race. The story strikingly parallels that of Noah. The god Enlil was displeased with humanity and decided to destroy it in a flood. Utnapishtim survived by building a cube-shaped boat. As the waters receded, he sent a dove, a swallow and a raven to find land. He emerged from his boat to offer a sacrifice to the gods. Taking the wise god Ea's advice, Enlil agreed not to destroy humanity, but to punish it when necessary. He then bestows immortality on Utnapishtim.

Utu

The Sumerian sun god, the son of the moon god Nanna and brother of the love goddess Inanna. They constitute a great divine triad, equivalent to the Akkadian Shamash, Sin and Ishtar.

Uzziah

King Uzziah of Judah conquered the Philistines but his victories made him proud and he tried to take the priest's place in the Temple. In punishment he was struck down with leprosy. Rembrandt shows him as a resigned figure.

Vajrapani

"Thunderbolt-Wielder", a bodhisattva of Tantric Buddhism venerated as the annihilator of evil.

Valkyrie

"Chooser of the Slain", a Norse goddess of destiny. The Valkyries selected which warriors would die in battle and accompanied them to Valhalla, the feasting hall of the slain in Asgard, the home of the gods. Valkyries were also protective spirits, instructing young warriors and watching over them in battle. They are generally described as mounted female warriors, but in some sources they are bloodthirsty giants.

Vamana

A divine dwarf, the fifth avatar of the Hindu god Vishnu. When a demon called Bali conquered the world, Vamana asked him for as much land as he could cover in three strides. Bali consented and the dwarf at once turned himself into a giant, whose three strides took him from one end of the earth to the other.

Vampire

One of the undead of Slavic folklore (*vampyr* is a south Slavic word). Social

The Hindu god Vamana.

"undesirables" such as murderers, thieves, whores, heretics and witches, may become vampires, leaving their coffins at midnight to have sex with the living or feed off their blood. A sharp stake of aspen or hawthorn stake driven through a corpse would ensure that it rested in peace, or a corpse might be beheaded, dismembered or mutilated to prevent it from walking.

Vanir, The

One of two races of Norse gods and goddesses (the other being the Aesir). Mainly associated with the depths of the earth and water, they guaranteed the prosperity of land and were the guardians of its rulers. Symbols of the Vanir included the boar and the ship. The chief divinities of the Vanir were Freyr and his sister Freyja, the children of the sea god Njord and the mountain goddess Skadi. The Vanir and Aesir were enemies at first but made peace and lived together in Asgard, the home of the gods in the sky. The Vanir also had their own residence, Vanaheim, under the earth.

VANITY *see panel, above right*

Varaha

A divine boar, the third avatar of the Hindu god Vishnu. When the earth, envisaged as a woman, became submerged in the ocean, Varaha lifted her out of the water with his tusks.

Varuna

A Vedic Indian god emboding sovereignty. He was the rival of the martial Indra, who appears to have ousted him from the position of chief of the Vedic gods. Varuna was the guardian of cosmic order (*rta*) and symbolized

VANITY

Conceit is usually allegorized in art as a reclining nude preoccupied with her hair, a mirror symbolizing her self-regarding nature. In the older meaning of futility or emptiness, *vanitas* is a major field for symbolism in Western still lifes. Material possessions such as coins, gold or jewels, and trappings of power such as crowns or sceptres, are shown with symbols of emptiness such as overturned cups or emblems of mortality – a skull, clock or hourglass, flowers or a guttering candle. Animals associated with vanity are the ape, peacock and, less often, butterfly.

the more passive aspects of sovereignty, while Indra was a more active representative of kingship.

Vase

Often a feminine symbol, particularly in Western art where a vase with a lily refers to the Virgin Mary. In Egyptian funerary art, vases symbolized eternal life. A vase of flowers signifies harmony in Chinese Buddhism, and the vase appears as one of the Eight Auspicious Emblems in China and Tibet.

Vayu

The Persian and Vedic Indian god of air and wind.

Vedas, The

The earliest Indian religious texts. The *Vedas* (*veda* means "knowledge") were composed *c.*1000BCE in Sanskrit, the ancient sacred language of India, but were considered so sacred that they were transmitted only orally for many centuries. The oldest text is the *Rig Veda*. "Vedic" is used of the deities and myths alluded to in the *Veda*s.

Vegetation

In all cultures, a fundamental symbol of the living earth and of the cycle of birth, death and regeneration. Vegetation gods and goddesses were among the earliest divinities, often worshipped as sources of human as well as plant life. Plant–human transformation myths symbolize cosmic unity; the life force animating all things.

Veil

A veil symbolizes separation, reticence, protection, modesty, withdrawal, secrecy, sanctity. For nuns, "taking the veil" symbolizes their separation from the world. The veil of the Temple in Jerusalem screened off the Holy of Holies, marking the division between the material and spiritual realms. The veil being "rent in two

A woman lifts her veils in a gesture symbolizing the end of innocence; from an Indian costume design.

from top to bottom" at the moment of Christ's death[1] symbolized the end of the Old Covenant and beginning of the New.

In mysticism, the veil is often used as a metaphor for illusory existence – the *maya* of Buddhist tradition. Alternatively, a veil hides ultimate reality, the blinding light of divinity. In Islamic tradition, 70,000 veils of light and darkness hide the face of God. The bridal and widow's veil both symbolize states of transition. Chastity wears a veil of modesty in medieval art, and it is the attribute of St Veronica.

Veles

The ancient Slavic earth god, also called Volos. He was revered as the protector of herds and trade and also as the guardian of the dead. With the advent of Christianity, Veles became a saint, Vlas or Blasius.

Venus *see* Aphrodite

Veronica, Saint

In the apocryphal gospels[1] Veronica is named as the woman with the issue of blood who was cured by touching the hem of Christ's robe. She was said to possess a portrait of Christ, obtained when she dabbed the sweat off his face with a piece of linen as he carried the Cross to Calvary; his image was miraculously imprinted on the cloth. This so-called Veil of Veronica found its way to Rome and became an important relic in St Peter's basilica. The saint may be seen holding up the veil, as in El Greco's painting of her; or she may be in the ugly crowd pressing around Christ before his Crucifixion, standing out because of her elegance, as depicted by Bosch.

Vessantara

In Buddhist legend, the last incarnation of the Buddha before Siddhartha Gautama. Vessantara was astonishingly generous, but gave away so much that the people forced his father, King Sanjaya, to exile him.

The prince distributed all his possessions and settled in a Himalayan valley with his family. An old Brahman, Jujaka, asked for his children as servants and Vessantara obliged. He might have given his wife, too, but the god Sakka prevented it. Jujaka complained to Sanjaya, who, after paying a ransom for Vessantara's children, felt remorse for exiling his son. He revoked his banishment and the family was reunited.

Vesta and the Vestal Virgins

Vesta, the Roman equivalent of the Greek Hestia, was the goddess of the hearth and home. A fire burned constantly in her circular temple, guarded by the Vestal Virgins, whose honoured office survived for a thousand years. Entrusted to a high priest, Vestals were selected at the age of about six. In the first ten years they learned their sacred duties; in the next ten years they performed them; and in their final ten years they taught the novices. Then they were free to marry.

If they allowed the sacred fire to go out they were whipped by the high priest, but if they broke their vow of chastity they were walled up alive.

VICES *see panel, above right.*

Victory

Victory is personified in Western art by the Greek goddess Nike (Roman Victoria). The winged goddess is usually seen flying down with a palm

VICES

There are many vices, including Idolatry, Infidelity, Inconstancy, Folly, Injustice, Cowardice, Vanity and Ignorance, but the best-known vices are the Seven Vices or Seven Deadly Sins, being Pride, Anger, Envy, Lust, Gluttony, Sloth and Avarice, of which the Church held Lust and Avarice to be the worst. Those guilty of these various sins would be condemned to Hell at the Last Judgment.

Vices were personified in art. Fra Angelico's *Last Judgment* shows transgressors suffering punishments relevant to their crimes. Mantegna's *Minerva Expelling the Vices from the Garden of Virtue* shows Avarice leading a group of banished Vices. Accompanied by Ingratitude, she carries an obese crowned figure of Ignorance. Following them are a lusty satyr and a Centaur with a shameless nude on his back; a monkey called "Immortal Hatred" comprising Jealousy and Suspicion; and the armless figure of Idleness led by Sloth. The Vices are normally identified in art by varying attributes: Avarice usually holds a purse, while Anger may be a woman rending her clothes.

branch in one hand and a wreath of laurel (or olive, myrtle, ivy or parsley) in the other to crown a warrior, athlete or poet. She appears in Ingres' *Apotheosis of Homer*. Fame may accompany her. Other symbols of Victory include the triumphal arch, banner, crown, eagle, elephant, falcon, hawk, horse, lance, lion, palm, phoenix, wolf and zigzag sign (sigrune).

Vessantara: *see* Buddha; Indra

Vesta and Vestal Virgins: *see* Claudia; Romulus and Remus; Tuccia

VICES: *see* Dante; Luxury; SEVEN DEADLY SINS, THE; Sloth; VIRTUES

Victory: *see* Fame; Laurel; Palm *and individual names*

The Egyptian goddess Isis shown holding a vine, from the inside of an ancient coffin lid.

Vigilance

Birds, particularly domestic fowl such as the goose and cockerel, are the most common emblems of vigilance – the symbolism of the cock on church steeples. A popular baroque symbol of vigilance was a crane holding a stone in its mouth. Other emblems include the dog, dragon, griffin, hare, lion and peacock (from the eyes on its tail), eye motifs, a lamp and the watchful stars.

Vila

In Slavic myth, one of a race of female spirits of the dead. She is described as forever young and beautiful, with long, fair hair. The Bulgarians said that she and her companions represented the souls of young women who had died unbaptized. The Poles claimed that the *vila* was condemned to float between heaven and earth because she had been frivolous in life. Prominent in southern Slavic folk myth, she was beneficial and loved to dance and sing. There are stories of *vilas* marrying mortal men.

Vincent Ferrer, Saint

Born in Spain, Vincent (*c.*1350–1419) joined the Dominicans in 1367 and served as a missionary among the Muslims. His apocalyptic preaching drew crowds and he had a following of penitents. The polyptych by Giovanni Bellini in SS Giovanni e Paolo in Venice shows him in the Dominican habit. The predella depicts scenes of his legend, including saving a woman from drowning and reviving the dead.

Vincent of Saragossa, Saint

In legend,[1] Vincent (3rd century CE) was a deacon of Saragossa in Spain. He suffered a series of horrible tortures but refused to deny his faith. His body was left in a field and a crow drove off the wild beasts that came to devour it. It was then thrown into the sea, weighted down by a millstone, but it returned to the shore faster than the sailors who had tossed it overboard. Vincent commonly appears as a young deacon, accompanied by a millstone, a crow or the instruments of his torture, including a gridiron. He is the patron saint of Lisbon.

Vine

Vine and grapes are among the oldest symbols of fecundity and regeneration. They were life emblems in Egypt (linked with Osiris, the god of earthly fertility and regeneration). Like other Near Eastern agricultural divinities, the Greek Dionysos (Bacchus to the Romans) became identified with the vine. Throughout the Hebrew Bible, the vine is a happy emblem of the fruits of the earth. It was the first plant grown by Noah after the Flood, and in Exodus a branch with grapes is the first sign that the Israelites have reached the Promised Land.

In the New Testament, Jesus says "I am the true vine, and my Father is the vinegrower"[1]. The vine became a symbol of regeneration and the Resurrection and in the Eucharist, the fermented juice of its grapes is literally or symbolically (depending on denomination) Christ's blood. Vine motifs are common in Christian art and architecture. Christ may appear as a lamb surrounded with thorns and vines. In Botticelli's *Madonna of the Eucharist*, grapes appear alongside sheaves of corn (the wine and bread). Bunches of grapes are redemption and resurrection symbols in funerary art.

Associated with revelry, vines are also emblems of hospitality, youthfulness, the Golden Age and the bounty of autumn. Unsurprisingly, they can also symbolize excess, as in 17th-century Dutch paintings.

Violet

The colour is linked with temperance, moderation, spirituality and repentance, or a transition from active to passive, male to female, life to death. These interpretations are based on the mingling of red (passion, fire or earth) with blue (intellect, water or heaven). Christ and Mary wear violet robes in some paintings of the Passion. The little violet flower is also associated with modesty or humility, as in paintings of the Adoration, where they refer both to Mary's chastity and to the meekness of the Christ Child.

Viracocha

"Lord", the supreme Inca creator deity. He had no name but was referred to by titles reflecting his status as the omnipresent primal god who bestowed life on all beings, earthly and divine. His most frequent title was Ilya-Tiqsi Wiraqoca Pacayacaciq, ("Ancient Foundation, Lord, Teacher of the World"), hence Viracocha (the usual hispanicized spelling).

Viracocha created the world and populated it with giants. However, they disobeyed the creator, who wiped them out (in one account) with a great flood. He then created a new race of humans from clay and brought them all to life. He sent them into the earth, and they were told to emerge through caves into their respective lands.

The world was still dark, so Viracocha commanded the sun, moon and stars to rise from Lake Titicaca. He bestowed tokens of royalty on Manco Capac, who became the first king of

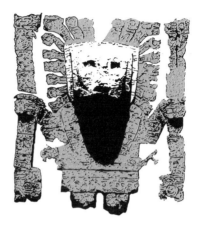

Viracocha, the Inca creator god; an image based on a sculpture.

the Incas. Then Viracocha journeyed through the world, shaping the landscape and teaching. In one account, when he reached the sea he sailed away to his divine domain, leaving the world to his divine progeny such as Inti, Mama Kilya and Ilyap'a.

Virgil

The great Roman poet Virgil (Publius Vergilius Maro, 70–19BCE) is famous for his epic *The Aeneid* which recounts the wanderings of Aeneas from the fallen Troy to Italy, where he became the ancestor of the Romans. In *Virgil Reading* The Aeneid *to Augustus and Octavia*, Jean-Joseph Taillasson shows the poet reading the epic to the emperor and his sister. Virgil also wrote pastoral poems and was considered the prince of Latin poets. Dante made Virgil his guide to the Gates of Paradise in the *Divina Commedia*.

Virgin, The

Images of the Virgin Mary, the mother of Christ or Madonna ("My Lady"), are countless and richly varied. Her

Virgin, The

popularity in Christian art and devotion is second only to Christ himself, a fact partly explained by her role as Mother of God and intercessor; partly by Christianity's need to venerate a female, maternal figure; and partly by the doctrine of the Church, which emphasized her virginity as a foil to the sin of lust. She was the subject of fresco cycles and altarpieces as well as small private devotional works.

EARLY LIFE OF THE VIRGIN

According to legend[1] Mary was born to Joachim and Anna, who conceived her by divine intervention (the Immaculate Conception), not conjugal intercourse. From the age of three she behaved like an adult, dedicating herself to prayer and weaving. She was taken to the temple to be brought up by priests and made a vow to God that she would remain a virgin. When she was about twelve, Joseph and other suitors laid rods on an altar; miraculously, Joseph's rod flowered and brought down the Holy Ghost in the form of a dove. Joseph and Mary celebrated their betrothal, and Mary returned to her parents.

Cycles of the early life of the Virgin, which may include the lives of Joachim and Anna, were illustrated in mosaics, panels and frescoes, most notably by Giotto (Arena Chapel, Padua). Isolated scenes were also chosen, as in *The Presentation of the Virgin in the Temple* by Titian, or the *Sposalizio* (or *Marriage of the Virgin to Joseph*) by Raphael.

ANNUNCIATION AND VISITATION

The gospels[2] relate the story of the **Annunciation**, the angel Gabriel's announcement to Mary that she would miraculously conceive Jesus by the Holy Ghost, and the moment of the conception itself. This is one of the most frequently depicted scenes in Christian art. Often with the lily of purity nearby, she is usually seated or kneeling in meditation, or reading a holy book, sometimes explicitly Isaiah's prophecy of a virgin birth.[3] The Virgin may recoil in humility from the angel's words: "Hail thou that art favoured, the Lord is with Thee."[4] God's hand may be seen dispatching rays of light and the dove of the Holy Ghost at the moment of conception.

Immediately after the Annunciation, was the **Visitation**, when Mary visited her cousin Elizabeth, who had miraculously conceived John the Baptist. They are usually shown embracing.[5]

THE VIRGIN AND THE LIFE OF CHRIST

The many scenes in this part of the Virgin's life may be depicted singly or in cycles of her life or of the life of Christ: the **Nativity, Adoration of the Shepherds, Adoration of the Magi, Circumcision of Christ, Purification, Presentation in the Temple, Flight into Egypt, Massacre of the Innocents** and **Dispute with the Doctors**. From this point the Virgin is mentioned little in the gospels apart from at the **Wedding Feast of Cana** and at the **Crucifixion**. After the **Ascension**, Mary was in the "upper room" at Jerusalem when the disciples gathered to pray at Pentecost and the Holy Ghost descended.

DORMITION AND ASSUMPTION

The stories of the death (**Dormition**) of the Virgin and her **Assumption** into heaven both derive from apocryphal legends.[6] When she died the Holy Ghost told the apostles to place her body in a cave near the Mount of Olives. On the way, a Jew tried to shake Mary off her litter but an angel severed his hands and they remained stuck to the bed. The Virgin restored his hands and he was converted. At the tomb, angels appeared with Enoch, Moses, Elijah, and Christ, and Mary was assumed (taken up) to heaven. In some accounts Mary did not die but simply slept for three days before the Assumption, hence the term Dormition ("falling asleep").

Depictions of the Assumption are far more common than the Dormition. The Virgin rose to become the **Queen of Heaven**, where she is enthroned in majesty. The **Maestà**, or **Virgin and Child in Majesty**, may include smaller figures of saints and angels. Duccio's side-panels to his *Maestà* include the scene of an angel before her with a gleaming palm announcing her imminent death. The **Coronation of the Virgin**, in which she is usually crowned by Christ, appeared in late medieval art.

LESSER EPISODES
One apocryphal episode tells how Joseph brought two midwives to Mary, only to find Christ already born. One of the midwives, Salome, doubted the miracle of the virgin birth but when she examined Mary, her hand withered up. She repented, and an angel told her to touch the infant Christ to restore her hand. The midwives may appear as attendants of Mary in pictures of the Adoration of the Magi. Another early legend relates how, during the Flight into Egypt, Christ tamed the beasts of the desert; and, when the Virgin was hungry and thirsty, commanded the branches of a palm tree to bend down so that she could eat, while a stream sprang from its roots to quench her thirst. This is shown in Correggio's *Madonna della Scodella*.

Later medieval legend tells of an emotional scene when Christ told his mother of his sufferings to come and bade her farewell before entering Jerusalem for the last time. The subject was particularly popular in Germany (depicted, for example, by Altdorfer).

DEVOTIONAL IMAGES OF THE VIRGIN
The Virgin as Mother of God is a central Church doctrine and images of the **Virgin (Madonna) and Child** stress her motherhood. This was also apparent in the **Tree of Jesse**, which emphasized Christ's descent from the father of David via the Virgin rather than Joseph. A most maternal image was the **Virgin Suckling the Christ Child**, depicted until the Council of Trent (1545–63) registered its disapproval of the Virgin's nudity. Renaissance artists portrayed the Virgin in domestic settings or naturalistic landscapes.

The virginity of Mary is a core doctrine of the Church. She conceived without carnal knowledge, and was herself conceived in the same way. At the Annunciation, the angel said: "As a virgin thou shalt conceive, as a virgin thou shalt bring forth, as a virgin thou shalt nourish."[7] Thus, Mary was endowed with perpetual virginity, and may be shown protected in a symbolic walled garden, the *hortus conclusus*. In the early 17th century, Pope Paul V proclaimed a new type of *Immaculata* derived from Revelation: "There appeared a great wonder in heaven; a woman clothed with the sun, and the moon under her feet, and upon her head a crown of twelve stars."[8] This became a highly popular devotional image, especially with the Jesuits.

The Virgin was believed to have important powers of intercession, which partly accounts for the popu-

VIRTUES

The three Theological Virtues are faith (*fides*), hope (*spes*) and love (*caritas*, traditionally translated as charity).[1] The four Cardinal Virtues, so called because they are the "hinges" (Latin *cardines*) on which the Theological Virtues hang, are justice (*iustitia*), prudence (*prudentia*), temperance (*temperantia*) and Fortitude (*fortitudo*). There were also minor virtues, such as hospitality, humility and innocence. The Latin nouns are all feminine, hence all these virtues were personified as women.

Faith may be resolute and majestic, personified by a woman with a book, heart, cross, chalice or lighted candle. She is often shown standing at a font or with her foot on a cube.

Faith, after a 16th-century engraving by Lucas van Leyden.

Hope may be shown with an anchor or with a ship on her head (voyaging hopefully). She may carry a basket of flowers (promise of fruit) or stretch out to a crown. A crow can appear as her symbol, its cry suggesting to the Romans the word "tomorrow" (Latin *cras*).

Love The greatest of the Pauline virtues, is represented as a young woman. She may hold clothes for the naked, food for the hungry, or a flame, candle or flaming heart. She may suckle infants or, less often, appear as a pelican feeding its young – with its own blood, according to legend. Love may hold a cornucopia or bowl of fruit, emphasizing her bounty and kindness. Other symbols include the phoenix and the hen.

Justice may hold the sword of power and scales of judgment. In the later 16th century, she was shown blindfold to symbolize her impartiality and incorruptibility. She may also be seen giving alms to the righteous and punishing the wicked. Other symbols are a feather, the number four, a globe, a lion, a sceptre and a thunderbolt.

Prudence may hold a book of wisdom, or a serpent;[2] she may have more than one head to signify that she learns from the past and also has foresight, or she may hold up a mirror (self-knowledge) to reflect truth. Other symbols are an anchor, compasses, deer and elephants.

Temperance can be seen with a pitcher with which to dilute her wine, or a bridle and a bit to enforce restraint. The pitcher may appear with a torch (quenching lust). Other common attributes are a clock, a sheathed sword or amethyst.

Fortitude may be shown with a column (a reference to the biblical Samson, who brought down the columns of the temple of his Philistine captors). She may also be warlike, with helmet and shield and often accompanying a lion. Other symbols are a camellia, a carp and a club. She may also be represented by the Apocryphal heroine Judith or by Hercules (in Greek myth, Herakles).

larity of her image and for the number of churches dedicated to her. She may be present with John the Baptist in the Last Judgment, and in private commissions the donors may be presented to her by saints. She was also painted in thanksgiving for deliverance from plague or after a military victory. The **Virgin of Mercy** may open her cloak, under which the chosen or faithful can shelter.

The *Mater Dolorosa*, or **Virgin Mourning**, shows her weeping alone or over the dead body of Christ. The **Pietà**, in which Christ's body lies in her lap, developed out of the Lamentation over Christ's body, and is prefigured in images of the Virgin and Child, where the Christ Child lies in his mother's lap. The **Seven Sorrows of the Virgin** were: Simeon's prophecy of Christ's mission and suffering;[9] the Flight into Egypt; the Loss of the Holy Child in the Temple; the Meeting on the Road to Calvary; the Crucifixion; the Deposition; and the Entombment.

The symbolism of the Virgin Mary as an ideal of motherhood is unique in its nature and range, and in certain respects the Christ Child is her chief attribute. Her other attributes include the crescent moon (borrowed from the Egyptian mother goddess Isis); the dove of the Holy Ghost; the unicorn; the lily or iris; crystal or windows (which remain unbroken as light passes through, symbolizing the virgin conception); a lamp; blue, red, violet or grey clothing; the Tree of Life; a flowering branch (Tree of Jesse); a bridge or ladder; and seven swords (Seven Sorrows).

Virginia

According to legend,[1] Virginia was the daughter of a centurion. A Roman magistrate, Appius Flaudius, made her a slave so that he could possess her. Her father plunged a knife into her breast to save her honour, as depicted by Guillon Lethière in *Death of Virginia*. In the consequent uprising the magistrates were overthrown.

Virginity

A symbol of spirituality and purity, especially as a chosen state. Vows of virginity by women symbolized their renunciation of worldly desires and dedication to the service of a divinity. In Rome, the virginity of the six maidens who guarded the sacred fire of Vesta guaranteed the purity of the fire itself. Virgins of the sun god in Peru similarly ensured flawless attention to his needs. In both traditions, the penalty for transgression was severe.

Virgin birth added an additional dimension of the supernatural to this symbolism of purity. It suggested a return to the original void in which creation was not an everyday, but an extraordinary event. Hence the number of gods, heroes or sages reputedly sired by gods and born from human virgins, including the Roman twins Romulus and Remus who were abandoned to wolves after their mother was embarrassingly impregnated by the war-god Mars. Great virgin goddesses who preceded the Virgin Mary included Ishtar, the Babylonian and Assyrian personification of the planet Venus. Like other virgin goddesses, including the Greek Athene and Artemis (Minerva and Diana to the Romans), Ishtar was also a warrior goddess, suggesting that virginity was sometimes closely linked with forthright freedom of action.

Virtues *see panel opposite*

Virginia:
[1] *Livy, The History of Rome III:xliv–xlviii*

Virginity: *see individual names*

Virtues and Vices, The Battle of the

The battle between the Virtues and Vices may be illustrated by personifications of pairs of opposites, sometimes set against one another in niches:[1] Faith against Idolatry; Hope against Despair; Charity against Avarice or Envy; Humility against Pride; Justice against Injustice; Chastity against Lust; Patience against Anger; Temperance against Gluttony or Anger; Fortitude against Inconstancy; and Prudence against Folly. From the Renaissance, the deities of antiquity may take on the role of the Virtues and Vices: Minerva (in Greek myth, Athene), Apollo, Diana (Artemis) and Mercury (Hermes) fight for the Virtues; Venus (Aphrodite) and Cupid (Eros) for the Vices. An example is Perugino's *Battle Between Love and Chastity*. The Virtues are often armed and are usually the victors.

Vishnu

A god of the *trimurti*, the Hindu divine triad of Brahma, Vishnu and Shiva. Vishnu is the preserver of the cosmos that emanates from Brahma and is reabsorbed by Shiva before emanating again from Brahma. In

Vishnu, from a 19th-century painting.

Hindu cosmology, between emanations Vishnu rests in the cosmic waters on the back of the snake Ananta ("The Infinite"). He is the world's protector: whenever it comes under threat, Vishnu appears in one of a number of avatars or incarnations in order to save it. Two of these incarnations, Rama and Krishna, are important deities in their own right.

In early myth, Vishnu is praised for measuring and pervading the universe in three strides, confirming it as a place for both gods and humans to dwell. He is identified with the cosmic pillar, the axis of the universe which supports the heavens and connects them to the earth. Vishnu's consort is Lakshmi or Shri, the beautiful goddess of good fortune. She is said to have arisen from the Churning of the Ocean, over which Vishnu presided.

VISHNU, THE AVATARS OF
See panel, opposite right

Vishvamitra *see* Seven Sages, The

Void

A Buddhist and mystic symbol of escape from the round of existence, conceived as the total absence of ego or desire – a state of selfless spiritual revelation and limitless compassion.

Volcano

Destructive anger or creative force. In Hawaii the volcano is a symbol of the destroying mother, personified by the goddess Pele, who lived in the great active crater Kilauea. A female goddess tends the fires of the underworld in Maori myth, and it is from her that the trickster Maui steals fire for humans. In some versions, the

VISHNU, THE AVATARS OF

Vishnu manifested himself in various human and animal avatars or incarnations to save the world from evil. The number of avatars was eventually set at ten, although their identities may vary. The usual sequence is as follows:

Name	Form	Relevance
Matsya	Fish	Saved the first man, Manu, from the world deluge
Kurma	Tortoise	Supported Mt. Mandara during the Churning of the Ocean
Varaha	Boar	Raised the earth from the ocean on its tusks
Narasimha	Man-lion	Killed the demon Hiranyakashipu
Vamana	Dwarf	Vanquished the demon Bali
Parashurama	Human	Killed the hundred-armed demon Arjuna
Rama	Human	Killed the demon king Ravana
Krishna	Human	Killed the demon king Kamsa
Buddha	Human	Misled the sinful to ensure their punishment
Kalkin	Human	The avatar to come: a messianic figure

VISHNU, THE AVATARS OF: *see* Churning of the Ocean, The; Krishna; Rama; *and individual names*

Greek Prometheus steals fire from the divine smith Hephaistos, whose forge is beneath a volcano. In Zoroastrian myth, Ahriman, the spirit of evil, is trapped in the crater of Mt Demavend, near Tehran – a seminal association of evil with everlasting fire. More generally, volcanic activity is linked with passion.

Volsung

A warrior of Scandinavian myth, the son of Rerir and great-grandson of the god Odin. Volsung was the father of the warrior Sigmund and grandfather of Sigurd.

Vulture

Now a metaphor for opportunistic greed, but in ancient Egypt a protective symbol. Nekhbet, the great vulture goddess of Upper Egypt, was the guardian of the pharaoh, whose queen wore a vulture headdress. That vultures fiercely guarded their young led to the legend that all vultures were female. In ancient Iran, vultures were purifiers, speeding the processes of bodily disintegration and rebirth. Bodies are fed to them in Tibet as a final act of compassion. Vultures are tutelary spirits in some Indian myths. In Rome, they were sacred to Mars and thought to have prophetic powers. They were also associated with old age and were therefore ridden by Saturn.

Vulva

Female generative power – in Western iconography most directly represented by the lozenge. The gate, passage and birth symbolism of the vulva is spiritualized in Christian art as the mandorla. In Tantric Buddhist art, the *yoni* is an important motif, depicted as two adjoining arcs symbolizing the gateway to spiritual rebirth. In Hinduism, the *yoni* can appear as a ring or rings at the base of the lingam dedicated to Shiva as creator.

Volsung: *see* Sigmund; Sigurd

Vulture: *see* Birds

Vulva: *see* Apple; Lingam; Lozenge; Mandorla; Peach; Pomegranate; Well

Wakan Tanka

"Great Mystery", the supreme divinity of the Lakota (Sioux) people. Wakan Tanka is conceived of as a remote creator who governs the universe through various aspects of his being. These aspects are all addressed as "Father", while the transcendent Wakan Tanka is "Grandfather". Wakan Tanka presides over important sacred pipe rituals of the Lakota.

According to the Lakota creation myth, the first four gods, known as the Superior Gods, were Inyan (Rock), Maka (Earth), Skan (Sky) and Wi (Sun). These deities grew lonely and created other aspects of Wakan Tanka. The first of these were the Associated Gods, consisting of Moon, Wind, Falling Star and Thunderbird. Next came the Kindred Gods: Two-Legged (humans and their relatives, bears), Buffalo, Four-Winds and Whirlwind. Finally, the God-Like, more abstract beings related to the soul and sacred power: Nagi (Shade of the Dead), Nagila (Shade-Like), Niya (Breath of Life) and Sicun (Spirit Power).

Wall

Beyond its obvious protective function, a wall is a symbol of separation. A walled garden (*hortus conclusus*) is a symbol of virginity, specifically of the Virgin Mary. The Western Wall in Jerusalem, a relic of the ancient Temple, is hallowed by Jews as a symbol of the aspiration for a renewed Israel.

Walnut

Symbolizing fertility (the seed within) and wisdom or prophecy (hidden knowledge), walnuts were traditional food at the December solstice and fertility emblems at Roman weddings.

Wand

An emblem of supernatural powers and magical transformation, associated with sorcerors and magical beings.

Wandjina

An ancestral spirit of the Dreamtime, in the Aboriginal mythology of Australia's Kimberley region. Each clan is said to possess a *wandjina*, linked with an animal, as its protective ancestor.

War

Classical literature recounts many epic tales of war, which may arise from wounded pride or personal affront, the most famous being the Trojan War. A war may be conducted in the cause of freedom, as illustrated by Delacroix's *Liberty Leading the People*, or of missionary zeal, as in depictions of the Crusades.

Images of war have often been commissioned for public halls as political propaganda to incite or sustain national pride. Uccello's tapestry-like *Rout of San Romano* resembles a jousting tournament, giving war a decorative quality. Other artists have illustrated the futility and horror of war. Dürer's engraving *Knight, Death and the Devil* of 1513 shows a warrior riding forth oblivious to his grim companions. Rubens' *Allegory of Peace and War* illustrates the benefits of peace. In his *Consequences of War*, War, led by Disaster, tramples the civilized arts. Goya's etchings *Disasters of War* depict the savagery of war; his *Colossus* likens an invading army to a giant trampling the earth. Picasso's huge monochrome *Guernica* commemorates the destruction in 1937 of the Basque town of Guernica by Nazi bombers acting for General Franco.

Washing

An important purification rite; pools for ritual ablution are known from ancient Egyptian and Indus Valley temples. In Islam, it is the custom to wash the face, hands and feet before worship five times daily. In Buddhist initiation ceremonies, novice monks ritually wash away their past lives. By washing his hands after his trial of Christ, Pilate sought to absolve himself of guilt for the Crucifixion.

Wasp

Usually associated with a vitriolic personality, the wasp in some African traditions symbolizes evolution and control over other forms of life. In Mali, the mason wasp was the emblem of a shamanistic élite.

Watatsumi-no-kami

The Japanese god of the sea, ruler of the oceans and numerous lesser deities. His daughter Toyotama-hime married Hiko-hoho-demi ("Fireshade"). They were the grandparents of Jimmu-tenno, first emperor of Japan.

Water

An ancient and universal symbol of purity, fertility and the source of life. In many cosmologies, life arose from primordial waters, a symbol of formless potentiality. In a general sense, water is an emblem of all fluid-

Water symbolism: women bathing in a fountain in the Garden of Youth, after a 15th-century Italian painting.

ity in the material world and of dissolution, mingling, cohesion, birth and regeneration. The *Rig Veda* praises water as the bringer of all things. Dew, spring water and rain in particular may be credited with sacred and curative properties as gifts of the earth or sky.

Reverence for water as a purifier is reflected in religious ablution rituals. Christian baptism combines the purification, dissolution and fertility aspects of water symbolism: washing away sin, effacing an old life, giving birth to a new one. Water can be a metaphor for spiritual nourishment and salvation, as when Christ tells the woman of Samaria: "Those who drink of the water that I will give them, will never be thirsty."[1] Springs flowing from the Tree of Life in paradise are symbols of salvation. Myths of sinful societies destroyed by a flood illustrate water's cleansing symbolism. Water was once thought literally to reject evil, hence ducking in water to discover if someone was a witch – a person who floated was presumed guilty.

Water is also equated with wisdom, as in the Daoist image of water always finding its way around obstacles. Restless water is a Buddhist symbol of the impermanence of all things; still water symbolizes meditative insight. In psychoanalysis it represents the depths of the unconscious.

Waters often divide the worlds of the living and the dead, of the natural and the supernatural. Lake and spring divinities, traditionally prophetic or healing, were often propitiated with gifts – the origin of throwing coins in fountains and making wishes.

Water Lily *see* **Lotus**

Watermelon

In southeast Asia the watermelon is a symbol of fecundity because of its number of seeds – hence the Vietnamese custom of giving watermelon seeds to a bride and groom.

Wawilak Sisters, The

Two ancestral heroines of the Dreamtime, according to the Aboriginal mythology of the Yolngu people of Arnhem Land. The Wawilak (or Wagilag) journeyed across the primordial

The Wawilak sisters inside the serpent Yurlunggur, from a bark painting.

landscape, shaping the environment and naming creatures and plants. The younger sister was pregnant and later bore a boy, and the elder carried a baby boy in a cradle. The elder sister unwittingly allowed her menstrual blood to fall into a pool, angering the serpent Yurlunggur, who lived there. The serpent caused a great storm and flood. The sisters sang songs to appease him, but Yurlunggur swallowed the women and their sons, then reared up into the sky as a rainbow.

The deluge receded. Yurlunggur returned to earth at a spot that became the first initiation ground of the Yolngu and regurgitated the sisters and their sons. Two men came along and learned the sisters' songs, then carried out the first Yolngu rites of passage, initiating the boys into adulthood.

Weapons

Ambiguous symbols of aggressive or defensive power, oppressive or liberating. Many weapons are linked with truth, aspiration or other virtues, and in myth and legend magical weapons are given to heroes. Weapons are often ceremonial emblems of authority or justice. Collectively, weapons usually symbolize warfare, and are shown being broken or burned in allegories of peace. A favourite Renaissance theme was the triumph of love over war, as in Botticelli's *Mars and Venus* (1483) where Cupids (the attendants of the goddess Venus) play with the lance of the sleeping war god.

Weaving

An ancient symbol of cosmic creation, conceived as a continuing process in which events are woven in an ever-changing pattern on a changeless warp. In Japanese myth, the sun-goddess Amaterasu controls this process in a heavenly Weaving Hall. The cosmic symbolism of weaving goes back at least to the Babylonian goddess Ishtar. Counterparts were Neith in Egypt, with her sacred spider, and Athene in Greece. Individual destinies are woven into the pattern as long as the thread is not cut by one of the Fates – the Moirai in Greece, Parcae in Rome, Norns in Scandinavia. Weaving represents cohesion, in Chinese thought the constant interplay of Yang warp and Yin weft. In Buddhism, the process symbolizes the weaving of an illusory reality.

Web

The web shares much of the creative symbolism of weaving and of the loom as an image of the structure of cosmic and individual destiny. The fragile web is a Buddhist emblem of *maya* (the world of illusion).

Wedding *see* Marriage

Week

An artificial division of time, probably based on the fourfold division of the 29-day lunar cycle and the mystical significance of the number seven. A further influence was the astrological system of "seven planets", each of which gave its name to a day of the week – the moon, Mars, Mercury, Jupiter, Venus, Saturn and the sun.

Well

A symbol of salvation, life, knowledge, truth, purity. In most traditions, but especially Judaism and Islam, wells had sacred significance as sources of life. The imagery is specific in the story of God revealing a well to Hagar and her son Ishmael[1]. Water rising from the earth symbolized feminine bounty. In China and elsewhere the well was linked directly with the womb and vagina. Psychologically it is an image of a path to the depths of the unconscious. Wishing wells or wells of knowledge, memory, truth or youth draw may be a source of magical powers including, in Celtic myth, the power of restoring life.

West *see* **CARDINAL POINTS, THE**

Whale

An image of the colossal in nature, but also an ancient womb symbol of regeneration, most clearly expressed in the biblical story of the prophet Jonah who was swallowed and regurgitated by a "great fish". In the gospels, Christ draws a parallel between Jonah's experience and his own impending death and resurrection. The whale is often linked with Leviathan, the biblical sea monster. Medieval images portrayed a whale's mouth as the gate of hell.

The whale is linked with the idea of initiation in Africa and Polynesia. In southeast Asia there are myths of spiritual heroes delivered by a whale. The great whale in Herman Melville's novel *Moby Dick* (1851) can be interpreted as a symbol of destructive sexual repression.

Wheat, Wheatsheaf *see* Corn

Wheel

One of the supreme symbols of cosmic momentum – the force that drives the planets and stars – and of ceaseless change and repetition. It is a symbol of fate, time, destiny and the Zodiac. The Egyptians linked the revolving potter's wheel with the creation of humankind. The development *c*.2000BCE of spoked

wheels made the wheel motif conclusively solar, the spokes suggesting the sun's rays. Gods specifically linked with the wheel are usually solar or all-powerful – Shamash and Baal in the Near East; Zeus, Apollo and sometimes Dionysos in Greece; Vishnu-Surya in India. In the biblical visions of the prophet Ezekiel, wheels appear as symbols of God's omnipotence.

A motif of a cross within a circle (a wheel cross) predates the invention of the wheel and also appears in pre-columbian America, where wheels arrived only with the Spanish. This ideogram appears to be a symbol of totality and the divisions of space. The original purpose of prehistoric Native American "medicine wheels", rocks laid out in the form of great spoked wheels, is unknown; some seem to be aligned to celestial events.

The advent of chariots made the wheel a major symbol not only of the sun but of power and dominion generally in Egypt and Asia. The symbolism of the rotating wheel dominates much of the iconography of Buddhism. The Wheel of Existence carries humanity through life, death and rebirth, from one incarnation to another in a ceaseless cycle as long as it clings to illusion. Only the Wheel of Dharma (the Buddha's teaching) can end the cycle.

Wheel symbolism significantly influenced the choice of the lotus and rose as the dominant symbolic flowers of East and West. In Indic thought, the *chakras* or energy centres of the body are shown as rotating lotuses. The rose windows of Christian cathedrals are wheel symbols of spiritual evolution.

Whip, Flail, Scourge

A symbol of power and authority. In Egypt, the flail was part of the

The Buddhist wheel of the Dharma, from a depiction of c.700CE.

pharaoh's regalia, an emblem of ruler-ship, judgment and also fertility (as an attribute of the ithyphallic god, Min). The same symbolism, including sexu-al, attaches to the whip. The Roman Lupercalia festival featured priests running about striking women with thongs to drive out sterility. Christ symbolized his authority by using a whip to chase money-changers from the Temple. The whip or scourge is also an instrument of Christ's Passion. Whipping was a popular medieval means of driving the Devil out of witches, and of mortifying penitents. Kings were symbolically chastised by using a "whipping boy" as a stand-in.

Whirlwind

A manifestation of divine power among Native American peoples of the Plains and in the Near East. In the Bible, God speaks to Job from a whirlwind. Hindu iconography por-trays storm gods, notably Rudra, with braided hair expressing the spiral energy of the tornado. The whirlwind plucks objects into the air and so reverses the symbolism of the whirlpool; it is associated with ascent and powers of flight, including the flights of witches and demons.

White

A symbol of purity, truth, innocence and the sacred or divine. Although it has some negative connotations – fear, cowardice, surrender, icy coldness, blankness and the pallor of death – white usually represents the positive in the black–white antithesis found in most symbol systems.

White is almost universally the colour of initiation – the word "candi-date" derives from the Latin for "shin-ing white". White is the colour of Christian baptism, confirmation and marriage. The white dove symbolizes peace and the Holy Spirit, the white lily (an attribute of the Virgin) and white bridal dress denote chastity. As the colour of spirituality and sanctity, truth and revelation, white was worn by priests in the pagan as well as the Christian world. The pallor of a corpse and the whiteness of bones doubtless account for the fact that deities of the dead, ghosts, vampires and other grim spirits are white or white-faced. This may be the origin of the wearing of white for mourning in China, Rome and, for centuries, much of Europe. White mourning may also symbolize the deceased's initiation into a new existence.

White Buffalo Woman

A mysterious and beautiful woman of the Buffalo people, according to Lakota myth. She brought the Lakota the sacred pipe central to their ritual.

Whore

In the Book of Revelation, the "great whore" or "harlot" is Babylon: "The great whore that sitteth upon many waters."[1] Babylon in turn is a symbol of Rome, which was persecuting Christians at the time Revelation was written. The hatred of Babylon was based on the sixty-year exile of the Jews in Babylon that followed the destruction of Jerusalem by the Baby-lonians in 597BCE.

Widjingara

The first human to die, according to the Worora people of Australia's west-ern Kimberleys. Windjingara was killed by *wandjina*s who, contrary to marriage rules, had wanted to steal a woman betrothed to someone else.

Whirlwind: *see* Spiral; Wind; Witchcraft

White: *see* AFTERWORLDS; Alchemy; Baptism; Black; DEATH; Dove; Egg; Initiation; Island; Knight; Lily; Marriage; Mercury; Sacrifice

White Buffalo Woman: *see* Wakan Tanka

Whore: *see* Mother
[1] *Revelation 17:1*

Widjingara: *see* Djunggun; Wandjina

Wind: *see* Aeolus; Air;
Breath, Breathing; Flora;
Whirlwind
[1] Virgil, *Aeneid I:50–65*
[2] Ovid, *Met VI:675–721*

Widjingara later became the native cat (*Dasyurus*), a nocturnal marsupial that scavenges on corpses.

Willow

In Jewish tradition a tree of lamentation. The willows by the rivers of Babylon where the Jews mourned for Zion (Psalm 137) may not have been the weeping willow, but in legend this species has mourned ever since. It is a Buddhist emblem of humility and compassion, linked with the bodhisattva Avalokiteshvara.

In the East, the willow is a symbol of the springtime of love, feminine grace and the sorrow of parting. It is one of the most celebrated motifs in Chinese art and decoration. It was a Daoist metaphor for patience, resilience and immortality. In Tibetan tradition, it is the Tree of Life. Analgesics extracted from willow bark may account for its association with health, easy childbirth and other medical and magical benefits in both East and West.

Wind

A symbol of the animating spirit that can be felt and heard but who remains invisible. The Bible begins with the Spirit of God moving over the face of the deep; the Hebrew word for "spirit" also means "wind". The Indo-Iranian wind-god Vayu is cosmic breath. The Aztec wind-god Ehecatl (an aspect of Quetzalcoatl) puffs the sun and moon into motion.

The winds also appear as divine messengers and as the forces controlling the cardinal directions. In Greek myth there were four winds, ruled by Aeolus, who kept them in a dark cavern and tempered their fury.[1] The east wind came from Arabia and Persia, where the morning sun rose; the

balmy west wind, Zephyr, blew from shores warmed by the setting sun; the south wind brought rain and clouds; the north wind (old, bearded Boreas), whipped up storms of snow and hail.

Boreas fell in love with Oreithyia, daughter of Erechtheus of Athens, and for a long time wooed her in vain. At first he tried persuasion, but when this failed he swept her to his home in an icy blast.[2] In Homer's *Odyssey*, to ensure the hero Odysseus has a calm voyage, Aeolus gives him all the ill winds in a bag. But a crewman opens it, with disastrous consequences.

Throughout the world demons were thought to ride violent winds, bringing evil and illness. Wind is associated with rumour, a symbolism perhaps derived from hunting and "getting wind of" a scent. Its importance in pollination also made it a sexual symbol in China. Wind is also a powerful symbol of change, inconstancy, bragging and the ephemeral – its dominant meanings in recent times.

In art, winds may be depicted as winged heads, with their cheeks puffed out from blowing, or as winged

The gods of the four winds, from an illustration to Virgil's Aeneid.

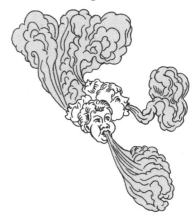

personifications. The cold winds may be shown, like Boreas, as old men with shaggy beards and hoary locks, the warm winds as youths.

Wine

A symbol of vital force, joy, spiritual blessing, healing, salvation, truth and transformation. The juice of the grape held the mysterious power to change itself into something more potent – and to change those who drank it. This, and the blood colour of red wine, is the basis of its sacramental symbolism. Made in the Near East at least 5,000 years ago, wine was widely regarded as a divine blessing, proof of the vigour of nature and the beneficial spirit animating it. In Jewish ritual, wine commemorates God's blessing on his people. Islam reserves this blessing only for those who have reached paradise.

Elsewhere in the Mediterranean world, wine was linked with fertility and life after death (the significance of libations poured on the earth). In the cult of the Greek god Dionysos (in Roman myth, Bacchus) wine was a symbol of ecstatic union with the god himself, and in mystic rites it was equated with his sacrificial blood. Christianity gave this symbolism new force: "Those who eat my flesh and drink my blood abide in me, and I in them."[1] Wine representing Christ's redeeming blood is drunk at the sacrament of Eucharist; in Catholicism, the wine is believed literally to be transformed into Christ's blood; in other denominations it is more symbolic. Hence wine is a symbol of new life in Christ, of resurrection and the kingdom of heaven.[2] But blood streaming from pressed grapes symbolizes God's wrath on humankind.[3]

A subsidiary symbolism of wine is that it produces truth, either by "opening the heart to reason", in a rabbinical phrase, or by loosening the tongues of liars and hypocrites. The Bible takes a fairly tolerant view of wine-drinking as a folly. Noah is shamed rather than condemned for it.

Wings

Symbols of speed, ascent, sublimation, aspiration, supremacy, liberty, intelligence, inspiration. Wings are emblems of the divine, often linked with solar deities; the Egyptian sun god was often depicted as a winged solar disc. In Christian art the Holy Ghost is represented as a dove. Winged flight is commonly seen as a divine gift, but mortals who seek to fly too close to the gods are doomed to plummet to earth like Bellerophon or Icarus.

Winged creatures in art can be frightening or angelic. Scaly or bat wings are commonly linked with evil and Satan. Fairies are more delicately winged, like butterflies, but may also be mischievous. The artistic convention of giving angels wings appeared in about the 6th century CE, based on Greco-Roman and Near Eastern images of winged deities such as the Greek messenger-god Hermes (Mercury to the Romans), whose winged sandals and helmet were also worn by the hero Perseus. Also winged were the sleep-god Hypnos (Somnus) and his son Morpheus; the goddess Nemesis; and the monstrous Harpies, Sirens and Theban Sphinx. The personifications of Fame, History, Peace, Fortune and sometimes Father Time may also have wings. Winged snakes or dragons combine earth and sky symbolism.

Winter *see* **SEASONS**

Wine: *see* Blood; Dionysos; Grail; Transformation; Vine
[1] *John 6:56*
[2] *Matthew 26:29; Mark 14:25; Luke 22:18*
[3] *Revelation 14:20*

Wings: *see* Angels; Bat; Birds; Butterfly; Devils; Disc; Dragon; Fan; Feathers; Snake; Sun; VIRTUES

Wisakedjak

The trickster figure of the Cree people of North America, also known by the anglicized form "Whiskey Jack". In Cree myth, the supreme being Gitchi Manitou asked Wisakedjak to teach animals and people to live in harmony, but instead he sowed discord. Gitchi Manitou angrily sent a great flood which only Wisakedjak and a few animals survived. The world and its inhabitants were created anew, but Wisakedjak kept few of his powers.

WISDOM *see panel, right.*

Witch of Endor

In the Bible,[1] King Saul of the Israelites expelled "those that had familiar spirits" (witches) from the land. But later he feared defeat by the Philistines and sought to consult a witch. His servants recommended the witch of Endor and, in disguise, he went to her at night. By her magic she summoned up the prophet Samuel from the dead, who confirmed that Saul had offended God and would be defeated. Salvator Rosa illustrated the scene in *The Spirit of Samuel Called up Before Saul by the Witch of Endor*.

Witchcraft

In Europe, witchcraft was a legacy of pre-Christian period and the practice of consulting mediums and wise men and women for healing, divination and many other matters was widely popular – indeed it never truly died out. However, from the 13th to 18th centuries witchcraft came under the active suspicion of the Church and in 1484 the Pope instructed the Inquisition to root it out as heresy and an activity of the Devil. At the height of witch-hunting hysteria, in the 16th

WISDOM

Divine wisdom appears personified in the Hebrew Bible as a female figure and later as Sophia (Greek, "wisdom"). In medieval paintings, Wisdom also holds a book but often has a snake at her feet. Prudence, an aspect of wisdom, shares many of the same symbols, especially the snake. Water, especially a spring, was often linked with wisdom (as in the "fount of wisdom"). From the Renaissance, wisdom was personified in Western art by the goddess Minerva (Athene) who holds a book and olive branch, and is accompanied by her sacred owl. Another notable ancient deity of wisdom is the Egyptian god Thoth, later identified by the Greek with Hermes and credited with the authorship of a great book of mystic and magical wisdom.

Wisdom was linked with the colours gold and blue; the number seven; the triangle; other symbols include birds generally; a bee; a cap, dragon, fool (by inversion), lotus, griffin, hazel, heart, peacock, scroll, Greek sphinx, sword, tongue, unicorn and walnut. Precious metals and jewels were important symbols, especially gold and silver, chrysolite, jade, diamonds, pearls and zircon.

and 17th centuries, old women in particular became scapegoats for all manner of human misfortune such as crop failure, madness or illness. Ironically, perhaps, the worst excesses were committed by Protestants; contrary to popular belief, the Inquisition had relatively rigorous standards of justice.

In the ancient world, witches were most closely associated with necromancy, calling up the dead; a classic example is the witch of Endor in the Bible. Horace described Roman necromancy involving the slaughter of a black lamb. Traditional witchcraft symbols include nocturnal animals such as black cats and owls; toads, wolves or foxes, and snakes.

Wodan

The ancient Germanic forerunner of the Scandinavian Odin. Wodan brought good fortune in battle but finally sentenced his followers to defeat and death. Like Mercury, with whom the Romans identified him, Wodan was a guide in the underworld. He also came to be associated with the sky, symbolized by the eagle. Wodan was linked with runes and divination, and was the inspiration of poets and heroes. Kings revered him as their divine ancestor. His wife was the goddess Frea. The god was known to the Anglo-Saxons as Woden and gave his name to Wednesday.

Wolf

Wolves symbolize ferocity, cunning, rapacity, cruelty and evil – but also courage, victory, nourishing care. In many societies, the wolf in myth, folklore and fairy tale is a famous predator. Stories of witches turning into wolves and men into werewolves symbolized fears of darkness and demonic possession and violence. Christian symbolism of the Good Shepherd (Christ) and his sheep (the faithful) naturally made the predatory wolf a symbol of Satan and heresy. Paintings of St Francis of Assisi with a wolf refer to the story that he tamed one.

Chinese tradition also associated the wolf with rapacity and lechery. In Norse myth, the giant wolf Fenrir is a chaos symbol, swallowing the sun at the end of the world. In Celtic myth, too, the wolf is a sun-swallower.

Elsewhere, the wolf may be a triumphal symbol and an emblem of warriors. It was sacred to Apollo in Greece and to Odin in Norse myth. Sacred to the Roman war-god Mars, it was an omen of victory if sighted before battle. The positive image it had for Romans derives from the legend of the she-wolf suckling Romulus and Remus, the legendary founders of Rome. This image of fierce maternal care that reappears in the folklore of India and may account for the many stories of wolves as ancestors – of Genghis Khan for one.

In Native North America the wolf was a dancer symbol, associated like the dog with ghosts and the guidance of spirits in the afterlife. In Shoshoni myth, the wolf was a creator figure. In early times, Wolf and Coyote were the most important people, but Coyote always tried to defy Wolf. One day they discussed death. Wolf said that when people died – for no one had died yet on earth – they could be brought back to life by shooting an arrow under them. But Coyote argued that if that happened every time someone died there would soon be no room on earth. So Wolf decided that Coyote's son would be the first to die.

After his son's death, the grieving Coyote soon came to Wolf and asked for him to be revived as Wolf had suggested. However, Wolf reminded Coyote of his own remark that when people die, they should remain dead. It has been that way ever since.

Wodan: *see* Frea; Mercury; Odin

Wolf: *see* Coyote; CREATION; CULTURE HERO; DEATH, THE ORIGIN OF; Devils; Dog; Fenrir; Romulus; Sheep; Witchcraft; Mboom

Woman

Woman is the receptor, carrier, animator, protector and nourisher of life. Symbolism derived from this fact dominates the depiction of women in art, mythology and religion in all ancient traditions and is reflected in the emblems most often associated with them. These include womb symbols such as the cave, well or fountain; containers such as the vase, pitcher, cup, urn, sheath, basket, boat and boat-shaped lunar crescent; hollows such as the furrow or valley; fecundity symbols such as trees and fruits; and specifically sexual images such as the shell, lozenge or inverted triangle. The earth itself is frequently portrayed as a woman and mother.

The traditional qualities most often associated with women are intuition, emotion, the unconscious, love and purity; but also (which no doubt reflects a largely masculine view) inconstancy and passivity. But women's power and strength is reflected in many formidable goddesses, from Athene and Artemis to Kali and Chalchiuhtlicue.

Women are strongly linked with magic, divination and prophecy. The monthly menstrual cycle leads to women being identified strongly with the moon, which in most cultures is female or associated with a female deity. In Western art, women personify the majority of the vices and virtues, because these terms are grammatically feminine in Latin.

Womb *see* Woman

Wood

Protection – a symbolism based on ancient belief in benign tree spirits and on universal traditions in which the tree is an expression of maternal nourishment and the life force. The superstition of touching wood comes from the supposed magical powers of ash, hawthorn, hazel, oak and willow. In Indian tradition, wood is the primal substance shaping all things – Brahman.

In China wood is one of the Five Elements (with fire, earth, metal and water), linked with spring and the east.

Woodpecker

A symbol of protection in most traditions, probably from its habit of embedding itself in "mothering" tree trunks. Like some other noisy birds the woodpecker was also credited with prophetic powers.

In Roman myth a woodpecker carried food to the twins Romulus and Remus, the legendary founders of Rome. In ancient India and in some Native American traditions, its drumming was said to warn of storms or avert thunderbolts. For others it was a call to battle.

Woot

An ancestral culture hero in the mythology of the Kuba people of the Congo, central Africa. In one Kuba creation myth, the god Mboom had nine children called Woot, and each assisted in creating the world. The first six formed the landscape and the seventh Woot, the Sculptor, created the first people from wooden balls. Death first came to the world when the eighth Woot killed the ninth Woot in a quarrel.

Another account describes how Mboom vomited human beings, including Woot. All the humans and animals lived harmoniously in one village and spoke the same language.

But Woot was expelled for having sex with his sister Mweel, who bore a son. Woot then cursed the land, which grew dark and barren. Eventually the villagers persuaded Woot to lift his curse. He went into exile with his followers, shaping the landscape as he went and creating more animals, plants and tribes, each with its own tongue. Woot became the ancestor of the Kuba kings and nation.

Word

In Jewish and Christian tradition the Word (Greek *logos*) is God's creative utterance, the agent of creation. In the Bible, God's first creative act is to say "'Let there be light'; and there was light"[1]. The gospel of John, consciously echoing the start of Genesis, begins: "In the beginning was the Word, and the Word was with God, and the Word was God." Here, the eternal and pre-existent Christ is identified as the Logos or Word, the creative expression of the divine.

In Indic traditions (such as Hinduism and Buddhism), it is said that the sacred syllable *Om* was the primordial sound that brought the manifest world into being.

Works and Days, The

A poetic work by Hesiod (*c.*700BCE), an agricultural treatise and a major source of Greek myths. In the first part Hesiod addresses his brother Perses on the benefits of a just life, citing many myths.

Worm

A symbol of dissolution and mortality, used in some paintings of grubs on flowers or fruit. More unexpectedly, in some mythologies, such as Ireland, worms may be ancestral emblems,

taking up the symbolism of larval metamorphosis.

Wreath, Garland

In life, a symbol of superiority or sanctity; in death, of eternity or immortality. Woven of flowers or leaves and worn on the head, wreaths are living crowns, suggesting both victory and vitality. In both Classical and Judeo-Christian traditions, wreaths were originally royal or sacred attributes, often believed to have protective powers. Initiates or followers identified themselves with a particular god by wearing wreaths made from his sacred plant or flower. Sacrifices were garlanded as a means of consecration. Victors at the ancient Olympic Games wore wreaths honouring Zeus (the Olympian olive or Nemean parsley), Poseidon (the Isthmian pine) and Apollo (the Pythian laurel).

Bridal wreaths of blossom suggest new beginnings, joy and fertility. Funeral wreaths of flowers acknowledge mortality but their circular form has the symbolism of the circle (completion, continuity, eternity).

Wren

In Welsh tradition, the little king of the birds, and in Ireland a bird associated with prophetic powers. A versatile songbird, the wren is an emblem of happiness for Native Americans.

Wurulu-Wurulu

Trickster beings in the Australian Aboriginal mythology of the western Kimberleys. Similarly disruptive to the Ngandjala-Ngandjala, the Wurulu-Wurulu steal honey from bees' nests with bottle-brush flowers (*banksia*) tied to sticks. If a nest is found empty, Wurulu-Wurulu have been there first.

Word: *see Om (Aum)*
[1] *Genesis 1:3*

Works and Days, The: see Theogony, The

Worm: *see* VANITY

Wreath, Garland: *see* Circle; Crown; FLOWERS; Laurel; Olive; Pine, Pine cone; Ring; Sacrifice; VICTORY

Wren: *see* Birds

Wurulu-Wurulu: *see* Argula; *Mimi*; Namorodo; Ngandjala-Ngandjala; TRICKSTER; Unguramu

Xiwang Mu, based on a porcelain figurine.

Xbalanque and Hunahpu

The Hero Twins of Mayan myth, whose story is told in the *Popul Vuh*, the sacred book of the Quiche Maya. The twins' playing of the Mayan ball game so annoyed the gods of Xibalba, the underworld, that they challenged the boys to a game.

The twins entered Xibalba and passed safely through many perils until Hunahpu was decapitated by a bat. The game was about to begin, so his brother persuaded a turtle to act as his head. When the gods became distracted, Xbalanque replaced the turtle with a real head.

The twins then impressed the gods by cutting themselves up and reassembling themselves. The gods asked that this be done to them and the boys happily obliged – but left them dismembered. This was the twins' final victory. The twins re-emerged from the underworld as the sun and moon.

This myth reflected a Mayan belief that after death a ruler should endeavour to outwit the underworld gods and then be reborn in the heavens.

Xi He

The queen of heaven, in early Chinese mythology. Xi He was the wife of Di Jun, the lord of heaven, and mother of the Ten Suns. Every day Xi He escorted one of the suns around the sky from their home in the Fu Sang tree, a giant mulberry that grew beyond the eastern horizon. This continued every day for many years until the suns rebelled against their parents and appeared in the sky all at once. Yi the Archer saved earth from the burning heat by shooting all but one of the suns from the sky.

Xibalba

"Place of Terror", the Mayan underworld. Xibalba was said to consist of nine levels. It contained numerous "houses" in which the dead faced a range of perils, for example the House of Knives, House of Fire, House of Jaguars and House of Bats. The underworld was entered through caves or ponds and lakes. The Hero Twins, Xbalanque and Hunaphu, overcame many of the perils of Xibalba when they journeyed to see the gods of the underworld.

Xilonen

An Aztec goddess of corn (maize). Xilonen was the protector of the young ears of corn and was associated with the maize deities Centeotl and Chicomecoatl.

Xipe Totec

"Flayed Lord", an Aztec god (of pre-Aztec origin) presiding over plants and springtime fecundity. During his festival, sacrificial victims were flayed and their skins worn by his devotees. The skin would rot and fall away, revealing the living man, symbolizing a new plant emerging from a husk. In the Aztec creation myth, Xipe Totec was also identified with the aspect of the god Tezcatlipoca who ruled the first of the five "Suns" or world eras, thereby launching a cosmic sequence in which the destruction of each world was followed by its recreation.

Xiwang Mu

"The Queen-Mother of the West", a powerful tyrant goddess who was said to live on the sacred Mount Kunlun, the legendary abode of the celestial immortals, far to the west of the Chinese heartland. She was the wife of the Emperor of the East and originally a fearful deity. In later Chinese tradition Xi Wang Mu became the queen of heaven, wife of the Jade Emperor, and in this equally powerful but less forbidding role she was known as Wang Mu Niang Niang.

In both early and later Chinese traditions Xi Wang Mu was the keeper of the elixir of immortality. In her gardens grew the trees which bore the peaches of eternal life. They ripened once every six thousand years and were then eaten by the gods and goddesses in order to replenish their immortality.

Xochipilli and Xochiquetzal

The male and female Aztec deities of flowers. Xochipilli ("Flower Prince") was a summer deity who also presided over dancing, games, feasting and painting. However, he also possessed a more sinister side as the god who sent boils, piles and sexually transmitted diseases to those who had illicit intercourse during periods of fast. His counterpart Xochiquetzal ("Flower Quetzal") presided over pregnancy, childbirth and other aspects of female fecundity. She was the patron of women's crafts and was also venerated by the skilled artisans who served the wealthy élite.

The goddess Xochiquetzal, from the Codex Borbonicus, *a 16th-century Aztec manuscript.*

Yam

The Canaanite god of the sea. Yam, like his Babylonian counterpart Tiamat, embodied the forces of chaos and disorder, and was envisaged as a monstrous creature. Yam challenged the storm god Baal for sovereignty on earth. Baal killed Yam, scattering his remains, demonstrating that he, the lord of storms, controlled the divine waters that fell as fertilizing rain.

Yama

The Hindu and Buddhist god of the dead and ruler of hell. In Vedic myth, Yama was the first man, the eldest son of Vivasvat, the sun. (In later myth the first man was said to be Manu). Vivasvat appointed Yama king of the dead. In Tibetan Buddhism, death is the perpetuator of the cycle of birth, death and rebirth, hence Yama is depicted clutching the Wheel of Existence.

In Chinese myth, a Yama (Chinese Yan) is a ruler of hell and judge of the dead. The chief Yama, Yanluo, oversees ten law courts. In nine of these, the dead are judged and sentenced. Yanluo heads the first court and a Yama heads each of the others. Sinners are sent to one of eighteen punishment regions. In the tenth court, they receive new bodies before being reborn.

Yama, the Chinese ruler of hell, from a 14th-century CE painting.

Yamato-takeru

"The Brave One of the Yamato region", the greatest hero of Japanese mythology. The son of the legendary emperor Keiko, he first revealed his ferocity when he killed his elder brother for showing disrespect for their father. Keiko was impressed and sent his young son to kill two of his enemies, a pair of fearsome brothers. The prince accomplished the task.

The young hero then subdued the land of Izumo and killed its chief, Izumo-takeru. Next, he journeyed far to defeat the Emishi or Eastern Barbarians. A chieftain tried to kill Yamato-takeru by luring him into entering a grassy plain and then setting fire to it. Yamato-takeru's sword, found by the god Susano in the tail of a dragon, magically cut down the blazing grass and from that time became known as Kusanagi ("Grass-Mower").

On his return journey, the hero killed a deer that was really a god, and later declared that he would kill a boar that was also a deity. The gods made mortally ill, and Yamato-takeru travelled to the Plain of Nobo to die. On his death he turned into a white bird and flew off toward Yamato.

Yantra *see* Mandala

Yao

A mythical early ruler of China renowned for his humility and modest way of life. During his reign, Yi the Archer came to earth to tackle the ten suns that appeared in the sky. With Yu and Shun, Yao was revered as one of the Sage Rulers of Antiquity.

Yarikh

The Canaanite god of the moon. One myth recounts the arrangements for Yarikh's marriage to Nikkal, the moon goddess, and the subsequent birth of his son.

Year

A completed cycle of the seasons. Hence the traditional significance of the Western and Eastern New Year as a celebration of the approach of spring, renewal and regeneration.

Yei

A group of Navajo creator deities invoked during curing ceremonies by masked impersonators. The chief of the Yei is known as Talking God.

Yellow

The symbolism of yellow varies considerably according to its hue. Warm yellows share the symbolism of gold. In China both were emblems of royalty, merit and the centre. Yellow was the colour of youth, virginity, happiness and fertility. But in the Chinese theatre, yellow make-up was the code for treachery. This symbolism is widespread and explains why Jews (the supposed betrayers of Christ) had to wear yellow in medieval Europe and yellow badges under Nazism.

Links between yellow skin and fear or disease account for yellow denoting cowardice and quarantine. A yellow cross marked out plague houses. Yellow is also the colour of dying leaves and yellow-green of putrid flesh. This may account for its link with death and the afterlife.

Yellow has high symbolic value in Buddhist countries through its link with the saffron robes of monks. This colour, previously worn by criminals, was chosen by the Buddha as a symbol of humility and separation from materialist society.

Yamato-takeru: *see* Kusanada-hime; Susano

Yao: *see* Yi the Archer; Yu

Yarikh: *see* Nikkal; SUN, MOON AND STARS

Yellow: *see* DEATH; COLOURS; Gold; Sun

The emperor Yao, from a painting of the Song Dynasty.

Yew

A tree of immortality, which often seen in English graveyards, and associated with strength, resilience and magical powers (Druid wands as well as bows were made of it). In superstition, yew was lucky to touch but unlucky to bring inside the house (its leaves and seeds are poisonous).

Yggdrasil

The World Ash, a great tree which links the upper, middle and lower regions of the cosmos, in Norse cosmology. The name means "Horse of Ygg", another name for the god Odin, who is said to have hanged himself from the tree in an act of self-sacrifice that enabled him to acquire the power of the magical runes used in divination. The tree's roots lie in the underworld above a spring that is a fount of wisdom. Dew was said to be moisture that fell from its branches high above Midgard (earth), the middle region of the cosmos.

Yi the Archer

A divine hero of Chinese myth. In the beginning there were ten suns, the sons of the rulers of heaven. Each day one of them would appear in the sky, but one day, in the time of the wise emperor Yao, they disobeyed their parents and appeared all at once. At first the people on earth were delighted, but the heat soon withered their crops and calamity threatened.

Di Jun, the lord of heaven, sent one of his mightiest aides, the archer Yi, to tackle the problem. He intended Yi to order nine of the suns home, but he became so angry when he saw the suffering they had caused that he shot all but one of them dead with his bow.

Yi was acclaimed a hero by the peo-

Yi the Archer, from an early 20th-century painting.

ple but Di Jun angrily banished him with his wife Chang E to live as mortals on earth. Chang E was upset at losing her immortality and acquired some elixir of immortality from Xiwang Mu, the Queen-Mother of the West. Half the elixir was meant for Yi, but Chang E took it all in the hope of returning to heaven. Instead she went to the moon. Yi realized what had happened and became reconciled to his mortality. In some accounts he was later forgiven by Di Jun and went back to heaven.

Yin and Yang

In Chinese belief, the two opposing but interacting and mutually dependent forces of creation. Yin (which originally meant "Darkness") and Yang (originally "Light") came to be seen as cosmic forces that interacted to produce all the phenomena in the universe. Yin and Yang may be seen in contrasting pairs such as female and male, life and death, good and evil, and so on.

This unity in duality is symbolized in China by the circular emblem known as the *taiji* (*tai-chi*): a circle equally divided into a dark, female half and bright, male half, each with a small dot of the opposite colour. This simple image is one of balanced dynamism, symbolizing the interdependence of contrary forces and principles in the cosmos. The Yin-Yang symbol implies that each divided half contains the seed of the other.

Creative tension, alternation and fusion between Yin and Yang generates change and motion, evolution and involution. Yin, which precedes Yang, is female, damp, dark, passive, soft, pliable and intuitive, and is associated with the earth, valleys, trees

An octogram with the Yin-Yang symbol at its centre.

and flowers and lunar animals and birds. Yang is masculine, dry, bright, active, hard, inflexible, and rational, and is associated with the sky, mountains and solar animals and birds.

Yinlugen Bud

According to the Chewong people of Malaya, a tree-spirit who taught humans to share food after hunting and how to bear and raise children.

Ymir

In Norse myth, an androgynous cosmic giant of fire and ice who arose from Ginnungagap, the abyss of chaos, at the beginning of creation. In one account, Ymir spawned the first man and woman and then three creator gods called the Sons of Bor. The three gods slew Ymir and formed the earth from his body, the ocean from his blood and the sky from his skull.

Yoke

Mainly a symbol of oppression and submission. Yoke-shaped structures were used by the Romans to humiliate defeated armies, which had to pass under them. Another meaning is "union", "joining together". This is the literal meaning of Sanskrit *yoga* ("yoke"), used of a range of physical and mental disciplines aimed at union with the divine.

Yoni *see* Vulva

Yu the Great

A mythical emperor of China, traditionally said to have ruled between 2205 and 2197BCE. In the days of the ruler Shun there was a great flood. Shun appointed Yu to tackle the deluge, so he laboured for thirteen years to build canals which drained the floodwaters into the sea. Shun rewarded him by abdicating in his favour. Yu founded the mythical first imperial dynasty, the Xia.

Yule Log

The Celtic and Germanic centrepiece of a twelve-day midwinter festival which influenced Christmas and New Year customs. The ritual burning of a sacred oak log symbolized the dying of sunlight at the December solstice and heralded its rebirth.

Yurlunggur

A great serpent, in the origin myth of the Yolngu Aboriginal people of Arnhem Land. Yurlunggur is believed to be manifested in the rainbow.

Yurupary

"Manioc Stick Anaconda", a culture hero of the Barasana people of Colombia. Yurupary stole fire for humans from the underworld. He used it to kill his brother Macaw, but Yurupary also burned to death and his bones became the charred logs of the first manioc garden.

Ymir: *see* CREATION; HUMANITY, THE ORIGIN OF

Yu the Great: *see* FLOOD MYTHS; Shun; Yao

Yule Log: *see* Christmas tree; Oak; Solstice

Yurlunggur: *see* Wawilak Sisters, The

Yurupary: *see* CULTURE HERO

The mythical emperor Yu, from a painting of the Song dynasty.

Zagreus *see* **Dionysos**.

Zaleucus, The Judgment of

Zaleucus (7th century BCE), the magistrate of a Greek colony in Italy, was required to pass judgment on his own son, who was accused of adultery. His son was found guilty and faced the prescribed penalty of losing both eyes. The people were compassionate and intervened, but rather than defy the law, Zaleucus insisted that both he and his son each lose an eye.[1] He is portrayed in art as an example of justice.

Zano, Saint

Little is known of Bishop Zano of Verona (died *c*.372CE) save that he was a wise and zealous preacher. A fish hanging from his crozier is probably a symbol of Christ, though a local tradition claims that Zano enjoyed fishing.

Zenobius, Saint

Zenobius was bishop of Florence (died *c*.390CE), his native city. He is depicted in Florentine art with the fleur-de-lys, the city's emblem, decorating his cope,

as in Domenico Veneziano's *St Lucy Altarpiece*. A panel of the predella in the Fitzwilliam Museum, Cambridge, England, shows Zenobius miraculously restoring a dead child to life.

Zero

The void, mystery, nothingness, death – but also eternity, the absolute or essence of reality, totality, the cosmic egg or womb, potentiality, the generative interval. Pythagoras saw zero (a sign known from Babylonia, but developed mathematically in Arabia and India) as containing all things.

Zeus

The king of the Greek gods and ruler of the skies. Zeus was the youngest son of the Titans Kronos and Rhea and the brother of Demeter, Hades, Hera, Hestia and Poseidon. Kronos feared that his offspring would overthrow him, so he devoured each of them as Rhea bore them. But when the last-born, Zeus, appeared, Rhea tricked Kronos by giving him a swaddled rock to eat. Rhea placed Zeus into the care

ZEUS, THE CONSORTS OF

The following are the most notable of Zeus' sexual partners and offspring.

ZEUS, THE CONSORTS
OF: *see individual names*

Name	Status	Offspring
Wives:		
1 Metis	Oceanid	Athene
2 Themis	Titan	The three Fates
		The four Seasons
		Dike ("Justice")
		Eunomia ("Order")
		Eirene ("Peace")
3 Hera	Olympian; sister of Zeus	Ares
		Hephaistos
		Eileithyia
		Hebe
Other consorts:		
Alkmene	Queen of Sparta	Herakles
Antiope	Princess of Thebes	Amphion and Zetheus
Danaë	Princess of Argos	Perseus
Demeter	Olympian; sister of Zeus	Persephone
Europa	Princess of Phoenicia	Minos, Rhadamanthys, Sarpedon
Eurynome	Oceanid	The three Graces
Ganymede	Prince of Troy	
Io	Princess of Argos	Epaphos
Leda	Princess of Sparta	Castor and Polydeuces
		Clytemnestra
		Helen of Troy
Leto	Titan	Apollo and Artemis
Maia	Pleiad	Hermes
Mnemosyne	Titan	The nine Muses
Semele	Princess of Thebes	Dionysos

of Gaia in a cave on Mount Ida, Crete, where the goat-nymph Amalthea nurtured him on milk and honey.

Later, Zeus caused Kronos to regurgitate his siblings and together they overthrew first their father. Zeus and his brothers drew lots to determine their particular domains: Zeus gained the heavens, Poseidon the seas and Hades the underworld.[1] Zeus chose Olympus, the world's highest mountain (to the Greeks) as the home of the new ruling deities, who were hence known as the Olympians.

Zeus was the supreme lawgiver, the highest authority in all matters human and divine. He underwrote the power of rulers and upheld the social order. He punished transgressors but was benevolent toward the virtuous. His chief weapons were thunderbolts.

Zeus had three wives in succession, Metis, Themis and his sister Hera. The "Sacred Marriage" of Zeus and Hera symbolized the importance of wedlock in Greek society. Even so, Zeus had many extramarital consorts and offspring (*see panel on previous page*).

The Roman god Jupiter, or Jove (Latin: Iuppiter, Iovis), was early on identified with Zeus. Like Zeus, he was probably a sky and weather god in origin (Jupiter means "Sky Father"). He was central to Roman religion, the protector of the state and its rulers and the upholder of honour and justice. His greatest temple, founded *c*.500BCE and dedicated to Iuppiter Optimus Maximus ("Best and Greatest Jupiter"), stood on Rome's Capitoline Hill. Most myths about Jupiter are adapted from those of Zeus.

In art, Zeus or Jupiter is a majestic figure: mature but athletic with long curly beard and hair, often enthroned and holding a sceptre or thunderbolt. His emblem, an eagle, may be nearby.

This image is based on a bronze statue of c.*450BCE that almost certainly depicts Zeus wielding a thunderbolt.*

Zhang Guo

The sixth of the Eight Immortals of Daoist myth. He was said to have lived at the time of the empress Wu (ruled 690CE–705CE) and was famed for his magical skills. He possessed a mule that could walk for thousands of miles and be folded up when not in use. Zhang Guo bestowed babies on couples and his portrait would often be hung in the marital bedroom.

Zhu Rong

According to early Chinese myth, Zhu Rong was the benevolent ruler of the universe and god of fire. He is said to have defeated the malevolent water god Gong Gong in a battle for control of the cosmos.

Ziggurat

An ancient Mesopotamian stepped temple built of brick and forming a symbolic sacred mountain. Ziggurats probably inspired the biblical Tower of Babel (Babylon), a symbol of human pride and folly. According to one theory, the great Babylonian ziggurat had seven levels, each representing a heavenly body (sun, moon and the five planets then known).

Zigzag

An ancient sign, based on lightning, of power, heat, fertility, battle and death. It was the attribute of storm gods. The letter S in the Norse runic alphabet was the zigzag lightning-flash Sigrune ("Victory rune"). Two Sigrunes were the emblem of the Nazi SS.

Ziusudra

A king who, Sumerian myth, was the sole survivor of a great flood sent by the gods in an attempt to destroy humanity. The full story of Ziusudra

– the earliest known account of the Mesopotamian flood myth – is not extant, but it apparently begins with the gods An and Enlil deciding to destroy humanity, which had angered them. However, the wise god Enki forewarned Ziusudra, who built a great vessel and was able to ride out the floodwaters.

After seven days of darkness and deluge, the waters receded and the sun god Utu reappeared. Ziusudra left his vessel to make an offering of thanks to the gods. This appeased An and Enlil, who repopulated the earth and granted Ziusudra eternal life.

Zodiac

The zodiac is one of the oldest and most persistent of all symbol systems. The sun, moon and planets appear to us to move against the background stars in a very narrow band of sky, because they all orbit on or close to the ecliptic, the apparent path of the sun around the earth. The significant stars in this band, which extends 6° on either side of the ecliptic, are divided into the twelve constellations of the "zodiac", a term that comes from the Greek *zoidiakos kuklos* ("circle of creatures" – Libra, the scales, is the only inanimate zodiacal image).

In astrology, the band of the zodiac is divided into twelve equal 30° segments, or "houses", each "ruled" by the sun, moon or a planet, and each having a name and "sigil" or symbol. In the course of the year, the sun passes through each house, entering Aries (the ram) on the spring equinox in the Northern Hemisphere (March 21) and followed by Taurus (the bull); Gemini (the twins); Cancer (the crab); Leo (the lion); Virgo (the virgin); Libra (the scorpion); Sagittarius (the archer); Capricorn (the goat-fish); Aquarius (the water carrier); and Pisces (the fishes).

Over thousands of years, the actual zodiac constellations have shifted relative to the earth and now no longer correspond to their astrological houses; for example, the point where the sun enters the house of Aries is now in the constellation Pisces. Indian astrology maintains a fixed zodiac pegged to the actual constellations, but the Western and Islamic tradition moves its zodiac with the spring equinox point.

The zodiac symbolizes a persisting belief that celestial bodies influence human life. The aspect of the heavens, such as the position of a planet in a sign of the zodiac, was held to be mirrored in one's character and physical and mental wellbeing. Astrology was particularly popular from the 14th to 16th centuries, when it was still held that the universe was centred on the earth, and offered a rich symbol system for artists. The zodiac signs were used to illustrate the twelve months of the year and their corresponding agricultural labours. The banker Agostino Chigi even had a ceiling painted with his own astrological chart by Peruzzi (Villa Farnesina, Rome).

Zu

The Babylonian storm god, usually depicted as a great bird. According to the Akkadian version of a Sumerian myth, Zu stole the Tablet of Destiny (divine decrees that bestowed supreme power on their possessor) from the god Enlil. The tablet was wrestled back by the champion of the gods, Marduk (Lugulbanda in Sumerian accounts). Zu was then apparently brought before the god Ea (Enki to the Sumerians) for punishment.

Zodiac: see Arrow; Bull; Crab; Goat; Fish; Lion; Moon; Pitcher; PLANETS; THE; Ram; Scales; Scorpion; SEASONS, THE; Star; Sun; Twelve; Twins; Virginity; Water; Wheel

Zu: see Anu (1); Ea; Enlil; Marduk

Acknowledgments

The general editor should like to thank all those at Duncan Baird Publishers who were involved in the production of this book, and Duncan himself for asking me to edit it. The book owes much to Jane Tresidder and to the London Library.

The publishers wish to acknowledge the original contributions of Roy Willis, Sarah Carr-Gomm and Jack Tresidder, the authors, respectively, of *Dictionary of World Myth, The Dictionary of Symbols in Western Art* and *Dictionary of Symbols.*

The publishers also wish to thank the following contributors for assistance with material:

Professor John Baines (Egypt)
Dr Mary Beard (Rome)
Dr Martin Boord (Tibet)
Dr John Brockington (India)
Dr John Chinnery (China)
Dr Guy Cooper (North America)
Dr Hilda Ellis Davidson (Northern Europe)
Dr Simon Goldhill (Greece)
Professor Robert Layton (Australia)
Professor C. Scott Littleton (Japan)
Dr John MacInnes (Celtic World)

Dr Geraldine Pinch (Egypt)
Professor the Reverend Canon J.R. Porter (Middle East)
Dr David Riches (Arctic regions)
Dr Nicholas J. Saunders (Central and South America)
Dr Ing-Britt Trankell (Southeast Asia)
Dr Piers Vitebsky (Arctic regions)
Dr James Weiner (Oceania)
Dr Faith Wigzell (Eastern and Central Europe)
Dr Roy Willis (Africa and Southeast Asia)

Bibliography

General

Campbell, Joseph. *The Masks of God.* Penguin: Harmondsworth, 1982. *The Inner Reaches of Outer Space.* Harper and Row: New York, 1988. *The Way of the Animal Powers: Historical Atlas of World Mythology.* Vol. 1. Times: London, 1983.
Dundes, Alan. (ed.) *The Sacred Narrative: readings in the theory of myth.* University of California Press: Berkeley, 1984.
Eliade, Mircea. *Cosmos and History: the Myth of the Eternal Return.* Harper and Row: New York, 1959, rep. 1985.
Kramer, Samuel N., *Mythologies of the Ancient World.* Doubleday: New York, 1961.
Lévi-Strauss, Claude. *Myth and Meaning.* Routledge: London, 1978.
Maranda, Pierre. *Mythology: selected readings.* Penguin: Harmondsworth, 1972.
Propp, Vladimir. *Morphology of the Folktale.* University of Texas Press: Austin, 1968.

Africa

Davidson, Basil. *Old Africa Rediscovered.* Gollancz: London, 1959.
Finnegan, Ruth. *Oral Literature in Africa.* Clarendon Press: Oxford, 1970, rep. 1976.

Mbiti, John S. *African Religions and Philosophy.* Heinemann: London, 1969.
Willis, Roy. *There Was A Certain Man: spoken art of the Fipa.* Clarendon Press: Oxford, 1978.

Arctic Regions

Damar, D. *Handbook of North American Indians: Arctic.* Smithsonian Institution: Washington, DC, 1984.
Ray, Dorothy Jean. *Eskimo Masks: Art and Ceremony.* University of Washington Press: Seattle, 1967.
Weyer, Edward. *The Eskimos.* Yale University Press: New Haven, 1932.

Australia

Layton, R. *Uluru: an Aboriginal history of Ayers Rock.* Aboriginal Studies Press: Canberra, 1986.
O'Brien, M.. *The Legend of the Seven Sisters.* Aboriginal Studies Press: Canberra, 1990.
Warlukurlangu Artists. *Kuruwarri: Yuendumu Doors.* Aboriginal Studies Press: Canberra, 1987.
Western Region Aboriginal Land Council. *The story of the falling star.* Aboriginal Studies Press: Canberra, 1989.

Celtic Regions

Green, Miranda J. *Dictionary of Celtic Myth and Legend.* Thames and Hudson: London, 1992.

Loomis, R.S. (ed.) *Arthurian Literature in the Middle Ages. A Collective History.* Oxford University Press: Oxford, 1959.
MacCana, Proinsias. *Celtic Mythology.* Hamlyn: London, 1975.
McCone, Kim. *Pagan Past and Christian Present in Early Irish Literature.* Maynooth Monographs 3, 1990; reprinted 1991.

Central America

Carrasco, David. *Ancient Mesoamerican Religions.* Holt, Rinehart and Winston: New York, 1990.
Coe, Michael D. *The Maya.* Thames and Hudson: London, 1987.
Fagan, Brian. *Kingdoms of Jade, Kingdoms of Gold.* Thames and Hudson: London, 1991.
Townsend, Richard. *The Aztecs.* Thames and Hudson: London, 1992.

China

Chang, K.C. *Art, Myth and Ritual.* Harvard University Press, Cambridge, Mass./London, 1983.
Christie, A.H. *Chinese Mythology.* Hamlyn: London, 1968.
Werner, E.T.C. *Myths and Legends of China.* Harrap: London, 1922.

Egypt

Faulkner, R.O. (edited by C. Andrews.) *The Ancient Egyptian Book of the Dead.* British Museum: London, 1985.

Hart, G. *Egyptian Myths*. British Museum: London, 1990.
Lurker, M. *The Gods and Symbols of Ancient Egypt*. Thames and Hudson: London, 1980.
Quirke, S. *Ancient Egyptian Religion*. British Museum: London, 1992.
Shafer, B. (ed.) *Religion in Ancient Egypt: gods, myths and personal practice*. Routledge: London, 1991.
Thomas, A.P. *Egyptian Gods and Myths*. Shire, 1986.

Germanic regions
Davidson, H.R.Ellis. *Pagan Scandinavia*. Hamlyn: London, 1984.
Owen, G.R. *Rites and Religions of the Anglo-Saxons*. David and Charles: Newton Abbot, 1981.
Todd, M. *The Early Germans*. Blackwell: Oxford, 1992.

Greece
Carpenter, T.H. *Art and Myth in Ancient Greece*. Thames and Hudson, London, 1991.
Easterling, P.E. and Muir, J.V. (eds.) *Greek Religion and Society*. Cambridge University Press, 1985
Kerenyi, C. *The Heroes of the Greeks* Thames and Hudson: London, 1974.
Morford, Mark. and Lenardon, Robert. *Classical Mythology*. Longman: New York, 1991.
Vernant, J-P. *Myth and Society in Ancient Greece*. (Trans. by Janet Lloyd.) Zone Books: New York, 1990.

India
Dimmitt, Cornelia. and van Buitenen, J.A.B. *Classical Hindu Mythology: A Reader in the Sanskrit* Puranas. Temple University Press: Philadelphia, 1978.
Ions, Veronica. *Indian Mythology*. Hamlyn: London, 1967.
Kinsley, David. *Hindu Goddesses: Visions of the Divine Feminine in the Hindu Religious Tradition*. University of California Press: Berkeley, 1986.
Kuiper, F.B.J. *Ancient Indian Cosmogony*. Vikas Publications: New Delhi, 1983.
Mahabharata. (Trans. and ed. by J.A.B. van Buitenen.) Vols 1–3. University of Chicago Press: Chicago, 1973–78.
O'Flaherty, Wendy Doniger (trans.) *Hindu Myths, A Sourcebook*. Penguin: Harmondsworth, 1975.

Japan
Aston, W.G. (trans.) *Nihongi* [*Nihonshoki*]. Charles E.Tuttle Co.: Tokyo, 1972.
Philippi, Donald L. (trans.) *Kojiki*. University of Tokyo Press,1968.

Middle East
Dalley, S. *Myths from Mesopotamia: Creation, The Flood, Gilgamesh and Others*. Oxford University Press: Oxford/New York, 1989.
Gray, J. *Near Eastern Mythology*. Hamlyn: London, 1969.
Hinnells, J.R. *Persian Mythology*. Hamlyn: London, 1973.
Kramer, S.N. *Sumerian Mythology*. (rev edn.) Harper: New York, 1961.
Ringgren, H. *Religions of the Ancient Near East*. S.P.C.K., London/ Westminster Press: Philadelphia, 1973.

North America
Burland, C.A. and Wood, M. *North American Indian Mythology*. Newnes: London, 1985.
Erdoes R. and Ortiz, A. (eds.), *American Indian Myths and Legends*. Pantheon: New York, 1988.
Mariott A. and Rachlin, C.K. *American Indian Mythology*. Mentor: New York, 1968.
Plains Indian Mythology. Thomas Crowell: New York, 1975.
Radin, P. *The Trickster*. Philosophical Library: New York, 1956)
Turner, F.W., III. (ed.) *Portable North American Indian Reader*. Penguin: Harmondsworth, 1977.
Walker, J.R. *Lakota Myth*. University of Nebraska: Lincoln, 1983.

Oceania
Grey, Sir George. *Polynesian Mythology*. Whitcombe and Tombs: London and Christchurch, 1965.
Lawrence, P. *Road Belong Cargo*. Manchester University Press: Manchester, 1964.
Malinowski, B. *Magic, Science and Religion*. Anchor Books, 1954.

Rome
Dowden, K. *Religion and the Romans*. Bristol Classical Press: London, 1992.
Gransden, K.W. *Virgil, the Aeneid*. Cambridge University Press: Cambridge, 1990.

Perowne, S. *Roman Mythology*. Newnes: Twickenham, 1983.
Scullard, H.H. *Festivals and Ceremonies of the Roman Republic*. Thames and Hudson: London, 1981.

Slav regions
Ivanits, Linda J. *Russian Folk Belief*. M.E. Sharpe Inc.: Armonk, New York/London, 1989.
Jakobson, Roman. "Slavic Mythology" in *Funk and Wagnalls Standard Dictionary of Folklore, Mythology and Legend*. Vol. II, pp.1025–28.
Leach, M. and Fried, J. (eds.) Funk and Wagnalls: New York, 1949–50.
Warner, Elizabeth. *Heroes, Monsters and Other Worlds from Russian Mythology*. Peter Lowe: London, 1985.

South America
Bray, Warwick. *The Gold of El Dorado*. Times: London, 1978.
British Museum. *The Hidden Peoples of the Amazon*. British Museum Publications: London, 1985.
Fagan, Brian. *Kingdoms of Jade, Kingdoms of Gold*. Thames and Hudson: London, 1991.
Moseley, Michael E. *The Incas and Their Ancestors*. Thames and Hudson: London, 1992.
Saunders, Nicholas J. *People of the Jaguar*. Souvenir Press: London, 1989.

Southeast Asia
Davis, R.B. *Muang Metaphysics. A Study of Northern Thai Myth and Ritual*. Pandora: Bangkok, 1984.
Izikowitz, K.-G. *Fastening the Soul. Some Religious Traits among the Lamet*. Göteborgs Högskolas Arsskrift, 47, 1941.

Tibet and Mongolia
Norbu, Namkhai. *The Necklace of Gzi, a Cultural History of Tibet*. Information Office of H.H. Dalai Lama: Dharamsala, 1981.
Peacock, J. *The Tibetan Way of Life, Death and Rebirth*. Duncan Baird Publishers: London, 2003.
Tucci, Giuseppe. *The Religions of Tibet*. Routledge: London, 1980.
Yeshe De Project. *Ancient Tibet*. Dharma Publishing: Berkeley, 1986.

Index of Themes

Key:
Apollo *standard entry in dictionary*
Hares and rabbits *feature entry in dictionary*
*Cross-references below refer to this index only,
not the main dictionary*

Index of Supplementary Words

Index of Supplementary Words

Index of Supplementary Words

Index of Supplementary Words

Index of Supplementary Words